PRIVATEERS OF THE REVOLUTION

War on the New Jersey Coast, 1775–1783

A Map of the country round Philadelphia including part of New Jersey, New York, Staten Island, &
Long Island, from *The Gentleman's Magazine* [London, 1776]. Courtesy Geography and Map
Division, Library of Congress.

PRIVATEERS OF THE REVOLUTION

War on the New Jersey Coast, 1775–1783

Donald Grady Shomette

4880 Lower Valley Road • Atglen, PA 19310

Published by Schiffer Publishing, Ltd.
4880 Lower Valley Road
Atglen, PA 19310
Phone: (610) 593-1777; Fax: (610) 593-2002
E-mail: Info@schifferbooks.com
Web: www.schifferbooks.com

For our complete selection of fine books on this and related subjects, please visit our website at www.schifferbooks.com. You may also write for a free catalog.

Schiffer Publishing's titles are available at special discounts for bulk purchases for sales promotions or premiums. Special editions, including personalized covers, corporate imprints, and excerpts, can be created in large quantities for special needs. For more information, contact the publisher.

We are always looking for people to write books on new and related subjects. If you have an idea for a book, please contact us at proposals@schifferbooks.com.

Come, brave boys, and fill your glasses,
You have humbled one proud foe:
No brave action this surpasses;
Fame shall tell the nations so.
Thus be Britain's woes completed,
Thus abridged her cruel reign,
Till she, ever thus defeated,
Yields the sceptre of the main.

—PHILIP FRENEAU

Contents

Appendices

Acknowledgments

In the late spring of 1974, as newly appointed director of a small non-profit research organization called Nautical Archaeological Associates, Inc. (NAA), I had the distinct privilege of leading a very modest underwater investigation of Revolutionary War-era shipwreck sites in the tea-colored waters of the Mullica River, New Jersey. It was during the research for that project and the actual field investigations that followed that my interest in the forgotten history of privateering on the New Jersey coast was born. My attention was first drawn to these sites by my good friend and colleague Kenneth Hollingshead, then serving with the National Oceanic and Atmospheric Administration, and as a board member of NAA. Without Ken's push to examine the once-important privateering hamlet of Chestnut Neck and the waters it affronts, as well as his significant participation in the fieldwork, this book would never have been given birth.

I am also indebted to the other participants in that groundbreaking work on the Mullica. These include: NAA members Eldon Volkmer, Larry Pugh, Nicholas Freda, my brother Dale E. Shomette; Gordon Watts and Leslie Bright of the North Carolina Department of Archives and History; and Dr. Lorraine E. Williams of the New Jersey State Museum.

For reading and providing superb advice, dissection, and welcomed critiques of this work during the course of the several decades of its evolution, I want to offer my heartfelt appreciation to my longtime friend, colleague, and mentor, historian Dr. Fred W. Hopkins, Jr., without whose influence and support I would have many years ago ceased writing. He provided a much needed critical review of the text without which this work would not have reached fruition. I would like to also recognize Fred Leiner, a scholar of American privateering, for his extensive review, analysis, and valuable comments regarding the history and legal ramifications of the famed but extremely complex Olmstead-*Active* prize case.

As a former staff member of the Library of Congress, I have long been aware of the pitfalls of research into which one can fall in the great and small archives and libraries of the world. Without the aid of their librarians and staff members, too numerous to mention herein, this work would have suffered greatly. I have indeed benefited from their assistance over the many years of researching for this study, especially from the staffs of the National Archive and Record Service, the Naval Heritage Command in Washington, DC, the Public Record Office in London, and at my old home for more than two decades, the Library of Congress. There I received wonderful support from, among the many, Virginia S. Wood, a most gifted librarian, researcher, and historian who guided me through much of the local and regional history of coastal New Jersey. I would particularly like to thank David N. McKnight, Director and Curator of The Rare Book and Manuscripts Collection at the Kislak Center for Special Collections, Rare Books and Manuscripts, University of Pennsylvania Libraries, and his staff for their assistance regarding the remarkable *Tagebuch des Capt. Wiederholdt*. I must also recognize my very dear friend and colleague, the late Jennifer Rutland, former head of the Poetry and Literature Center at the Library of Congress, for reading and editing much of the manuscript in the very early years of its incubation period.

And finally, I would like to thank my lovely wife Carol Ann Shomette for all of her love and critical support over the lifetime it has taken to see this project through.

Introduction

"... had there been no privateers ..."

Spring 1808. As he had done many times over the last quarter century, the old man walked slowly along the rim of Wallabout Bay, a short distance from his farm at the edge of the growing town of Brooklyn, New York. Now and then he stopped to pick up the human bones eroding from the sandy shore or lying on the beach: a skull here, a femur there, some already bleached and brittle by many years of exposure to the sun. Occasionally he would encounter evidence of an entire skeleton peeking out from what had been one of numerous mass graves dug along the sandy bank. Gently he placed the remains in a bag that he carried for the purpose, as he had done so many times before. Now and then, perhaps remembering, he would turn and gaze wistfully out from the shoreline to another set of bones. Those, however, were the relics of a once-great Royal Navy warship converted in her seniority to a hulking penitentiary of death, now abandoned and rotting away, slowly sinking into the fetid black muds of the little embayment on the East River. He may have summoned up memories of the privateersman half a lifetime ago, during the great War for American Independence, and of the tales of their captures and brutal imprisonment aboard that same hulk, the prison ship *Jersey*, now putrefying in the developing marshland of the ever shrinking Wallabout. He may have recalled the cruel, horrible days and nights they had spent in her squalid hold, a thousand mariners at a time, all prisoners of war, thirsting, moaning, puking, and suffering, with as many as ten a day dying from disease, starvation, and unending brutality. Some had escaped, but they were few in number, and most had perished. Now he carried with reverence what was left of their fragile remains, for they had once been his brothers in arms.

He was not alone, for he had been joined on this and other bone walks by fellow members of the Tammany Society, a three-year-old New York social and political organization, who were also there to collect the seemingly endless and neglected remnants of the unknown mariners who would one day be memorialized as the "Prison Ship Martyrs." The bones were, in fact, all that remained of countless seafaring heroes and scallywags, captains courageous and quasi-pirates, adventurers and sea-dogs, indeed Everyman that had fought in a revolution upon the great waters for both profit and country, in a war that altered the course of world history.

Now, he and his mates headed home after filling at least twenty hogsheads with the bones of the dead, mostly privateersmen who had three decades earlier exhaled their last mortal breath aboard *Jersey* and others like her. There they would deposit their recoveries for burial in a sepulcher of remembrance. It would someday become a tomb of patriotic commemoration to the tens of thousands of American privateersmen who, in pursuit of freedom as well as riches, had paid the ultimate price in the painful birthing of the United States of America.

. . .

The story of *Jersey* and the many thousands of prison ship martyrs who expired within her dark, pestilential bowels, was once an iconic piece of American history: it is little remembered today. So, too, was the often-swashbuckling trade that the majority of her unfortunate inmates had practiced, namely privateering—that is, governmentally sanctioned commerce raiding for profit by private ships of war—during the many long years of the American Revolution.

Unfortunately, the tale of American privateering in that great conflict is today little known and often deeply mired in romantic myth and misinformation. It has frequently been maligned as legalized piracy, a charge sometimes historically not far from the truth, although during the Revolution privateers were regulated by law and specific operational procedures issued by the Continental Congress. Although not without flaws, the rule of law and adherence to the "privateering instructions" were generally upheld throughout the war. Murder, torture, rape, and theft of personal property, the practice of true pirates, were alien to most American privateersmen. Legal adjudication and the sale of captured ships and their cargoes by officials of the state were mandatory, albeit with the profits thereof going to the owners and investors in the privateers' voyage, and to the participants themselves.

The story of privateering during the American War for Independence has, for the most part, been a chronicle largely constrained, in the few reliable histories that have actually been written, by regional and cultural biases. These have come to focus upon the leading role of New England's countless privately owned warships and the mercantile establishments, speculators, and profiteers who pumped the monetary lifeblood into the unique wartime industry that supported them. The many hundreds of privateers of Massachusetts alone, bearing either Continental or state commissions, have been deemed, in the eyes of most scholars and the public alike, as the preeminent sea rovers of their age. Their bold, profitable, and often sagacious cruises ranged from the West Indies to the coasts of Nova Scotia and even into European waters, inflicting enormous damage on enemy commerce on the high seas and major distress on his economy ashore. Their stories have been oft told by the great New England Brahmans of American history, whose works on privateering in general have come to be the accepted truths. Sadly, owing to the early and overwhelming dominance of the Eastern academic establishment, little or no address has been awarded to the considerable but lesser known privateering initiatives of the states of the Middle Atlantic and the deep South, or of their opposites, the Loyalist and British privateers of New York, Canada, the West Indies, and Great Britain.

At the same time, the contributions by privately armed men of war have been assailed by many notable scholars, who deprecated their services for contributing little to the actual war effort on either side but profits for those involved. Privateers have long been criticized by many, and correctly so, for successfully seducing seamen away from regular sea service, and for siphoning off ships, arms, war materiel, money, and energy from national and individual state naval programs. Indeed, as one member of the Continental Congress of 1778 so aptly noted: "The privateers have much distressed the trade of our Enemies, but had there been no privateers is it not probable there would have been a much larger number of Public Ships than has been fitted out, which might have distressed the Enemy nearly as much & furnished these States with necessaries on much better terms than they have been supplied by Privateers?"[1]

Yet such views may be somewhat conflicted. In a war in which the Continental government and eleven of the thirteen states had their own navies, as well as thousands of operative privateers, all under separate commands and governments, wherein all men were deemed equals, it is not surprising that confusion and competition for resources prevailed, especially where profit was involved.

The American Revolution was by any standard a truly maritime war that governed the overall land strategies of the British, French, and Spanish. Yet, unlike America's powerful allies with great navies of their own, the Continental and state naval establishments of the United States had to be constructed from scratch, all largely manned by skilled but militarily untrained mariners. It is therefore not surprising that American naval forces were seldom able to conduct serious offensive operations of any truly strategic merit. For the Americans, to control the seas against a numerically far superior, better-trained, better-armed Royal Navy, which enjoyed a tradition of victory, was simply an impossibility, and was recognized as such by all sides. Thus, the Continental Navy, the state navies, and, most importantly, the privateers had little alternative but to address the readiest means of damaging the enemy at sea in the only way possible, that is, by preying upon his commerce and interdicting his supply lines to his forces on the American mainland. This, with infrequent convoy duty, formed the chief occupation of the entirety of America's sea force, both public and private. Yet, it was one that John Adams, a major proponent of privateers as well as a national navy, declared was a short, easy, and infallible method of humbling the foe, to weary him and make the war economically painful enough to force the British public to cry out for an end. Adams's views, though not universal among his peers, were popular enough for Congress to undertake, at the same moment in time, the establishment of a national navy, as well as to authorize privateering as a means to wage war against the mightiest maritime power on earth.

It has been stated by no less than the great naval historian Alfred Thayer Mahan in his seminal work, *The Influence of Sea Power Upon History, 1660–1783*, that the commerce war waged by the Americans was of importance, but only secondary to gaining full control of the sea itself. Indeed, Mahan deemed harassment of the enemy's commercial base as an important factor, but declared it was delusional and futile to consider it as the most direct means to winning the war. "Especially," he wrote in 1890, "is it misleading when the nation against whom it is to be directed possesses, as Great Britain did . . . the two requisites of a strong sea power,—a wide-spread healthy commerce and a powerful navy."[2]

The injury inflicted upon British commerce, though very substantial, some have argued echoing Mahan, was not enough to render their national war effort inoperative. Moreover, the inability of privateers to operate in concert offensively or defensively with regular naval forces, or in squadrons of their own, proved ineffective, one example being the famous 1779 Penobscot Expedition debacle in which an entire American fleet, including privateers, was forced to self destruct. Conversely, in later years it has also been suggested that, in light of the impact of the submarine warfare of World Wars I and II, the destruction of a maritime nation's sea commerce can indeed be an effective means of bringing an opponent to heel.

Such was the American attitude, right or wrong, during the Revolution. Yet, there can be no question of the impact of at least 1,738 American Continental commissions being issued to vessels bearing nearly 15,803 guns and manned by over 60,245 seamen—as well as up to 1,000 more privateers sailing under individual state commissions in New England,

and an unknown number in several other states. The innumerable captures of enemy supply ships, transports, and troops on the high seas indeed proved of inestimable military significance. The British fear of American privateers interdicting soldiers and supplies bound with reinforcements for General John Burgoyne's army in Canada, for example, caused repeated delays in convoy departures, which substantially slowed his invasion of New York in 1776. At the same time, privateer captures of British gold resulted in much needed financial assistance for General Benedict Arnold to build a war fleet on Lake Champlain to further dispute Burgoyne's movements. Though Arnold was defeated in the ensuing naval battle, the invasion was stalled until 1777, a delay ultimately resulting in the devastating British surrender at Saratoga. It was that defeat that significantly contributed to the establishment of the American alliance with France.

That privateers were unable to provide adequate support of regular naval forces is usually only addressed in broad terms by critics of the industry, but never in regard to faulty organization of forces to which they were attached or inadequate management. In one of the great American naval disasters of the war, the poor leadership of Commodore Dudley Saltonstall during the Penobscot Expedition, in regard to both the regular naval forces and the dozen privateers engaged, need only be employed again as an example. That privateers could effectively operate in small squadrons of their own kind, the wolf packs of their day, was in fact successfully demonstrated time after time against enemy commerce at sea and in raids ashore.

Privateers repeatedly slowed and sometimes halted the flow of British trade, strategic war materials and troops while capturing thousands of enemy vessels and millions of dollars in prizes and cargo. In 1778, the privateer menace was so great that they even managed to oblige the British high command in New York to order an embargo on all shipping from the city lest they suffer further losses. Every necessity required to support both the British and their Hessian mercenaries had to be brought to America via the sea, at first by single merchant vessels chartered for the purpose by His Majesty's government. By the fall of 1775, the dramatic number of losses of chartered vessels obliged the British thereafter to dispatch troops and supplies under escort of strong men-of-war, an expensive and difficult necessity that lasted to the close of hostilities. Warships that might have been employed in offensive operations or enforcing the blockade of rebel ports were thus diverted from such missions. Privateers forced British insurance rates to rise to astronomical levels. Guns, munitions, uniforms, food, and countless other items necessary for the war effort, as well as both luxury and essential domestic goods captured by American privateers, flowed into American markets providing a form of prosperity as never before seen under British rule, though it was quickly countered by runaway inflation. Thus, the deployment of privately owned warships, fielded not at public expense but by private entrepreneurs and speculators, provided a most public wartime service, albeit one wedded to peculiar capitalistic attractions. A young man who enlisted in the Continental Army had a very good chance of dying from either disease or battle, with little to show for his service upon returning home. One who enlisted aboard a privateer, with a chance of becoming wealthy overnight from prize money acquired by capturing enemy ships and their cargoes, was also doing his patriotic duty by still supporting the Revolution. It was a temptation that drew tens of thousands of men, mariners and landsmen, young and old alike, to sign up for a privateering cruise at seaports along the entire Atlantic coast.

With the British capture of New York City in the summer of 1776, the complexion of the infant privateer war changed dramatically from one that was New England-centric to a much wider conflict that would range along the entirety of the Atlantic seaboard of North America, as well as in the rich hunting grounds of the West Indies and elsewhere. By 1777, American privateers, sailing under "letters of marque and reprisal" issued by the Continental Congress to the states for dispersal to private parties and to agents overseas, were operating not only out of American ports, but from French islands of the West Indies and French ports on the mainland of Europe. Soon afterwards, as the sea war escalated, English and Loyalist privateers were authorized by the British Admiralty to sail from Great Britain, Canada, the West Indies, and eventually even the captured outports on the American mainland, most notably the port of New York, against American and allied shipping. The Americans responded. In 1779, as the war shifted ever further southward, no fewer than 207 Continental commissions were issued for privateering cruises, 125 of them from Pennsylvania alone. By 1781, 560 Continental commissions were issued, of which 155, or thirty-six per cent, went to Pennsylvania vessels.

With the Cape May Channel, New Jersey, providing egress to the Delaware River and the Port of Philadelphia, seat of the Continental Congress and the second largest privateering entrepôt in the United States, being less than 120 miles south of the entrance to New York Bay, the Atlantic frontier lying between was bound to be of significant importance. The first to recognize the utility of the barrier islands and sounds running along New Jersey's Atlantic coast were the privateer syndicate owners of Philadelphia. They recognized that the shifting shoals and intricate inlets such as Cranberry, Brigantine, Little Egg Harbor, and Great Egg Harbor, which required knowledgeable local pilots to shepherd vessels through them, offered to their fleet of small, private men-of-war both refuge and support facilities. Hotbeds of smuggling before the war, they were places where provisions and munitions could be supplied, prizes brought in, and their cargoes off-loaded for sale at public vendues. Most inlets were too shallow to permit access by the great, deep-draft British men-of-war and, at least in the beginning, there was a paucity of small enemy warships of shallow enough draft that could safely enter. In addition, when New York City and Staten Island were occupied in the summer of 1776 by British and German mercenary forces, the New Jersey coastal outposts from which countless American privateering expeditions would be launched were within easy range of the major choke point through which British convoys needed to pass. Guarding the entrance to New York Bay, the dangerous waters of Sandy Hook, into which the vast majority of seaborne supplies and reinforcements from Europe had to enter, became a rich hunting ground that sometimes rivaled the West Indies. Indeed, rare was the convoy, either arriving or departing, that was not menaced or assailed. Many Pennsylvania and New Jersey owners of privateers, such as Blair McClenachan, Robert Morris, and Charles Pettit, made fortunes from the boldness of swift, fast ships such as *Chance*, *Fair America*, and *Holker*, legends in their own time, commanded by such daring skippers as Stevens, Decatur, and Keane, who struck with deadly efficiency time and again.

As the war progressed, the French alliance ignited a dramatic escalation in the number of active American privateers and a stunning increase in British losses. Between 1778 and 1780 the number of Continental commissions to privately armed men-of-war jumped from 128 to 298. By 1781, the number would rise to 560. By the spring of 1778, Lord George

Germain, the British Secretary of State for the American Colonies, was forced to call for a change in strategy on both land and sea. No longer was the destruction of General George Washington's elusive rag-tag army the prime objective. The military occupation of key ports along the Atlantic seaboard, the blockading of major commercial estuary systems, the capture or destruction of the American merchant marine, and the neutralization of such forward privateering bases such as Chestnut Neck at Little Egg Harbor and Toms River on the New Jersey coast, would become the order of the day. About the same time, permission was granted for British and Loyalist firms and individuals to secure commissions to conduct privateering operations against the Americans and their allies, a privilege hitherto generally opposed by the British Admiralty. As a result, the privateer war on the New Jersey coast intensified as never before. By late 1778, with the activation of the Board of Loyalist Associators in New York under former New Jersey Governor William Franklin, son of Benjamin Franklin, an ongoing and frequently brutal seaborne mêlée erupted between generally non-commissioned American partisans operating from small, lightly armed whaleboats, and Loyalist "Refugees" doing the same. Kidnapping, murder, and a near-civil-war stasis ensued on the New Jersey coast, serving little strategic purpose for either side, but deepening the hatred between royalists and rebels that would never mend. The cruel execution of a soldier and one-time privateersman named Joshua Huddy in mid-1782 even threatened to derail the long-awaited peace negotiations.

Yet, even as talks of an end to the war and possible American independence were underway in Europe, the darker side of privateering, one that offered neither profit nor freedom, was asserting itself in ways that horrified the American public, but for which little could be done. On board the foul prison ship *Jersey* and many of her sisters at New York, which had been employed almost since the beginning of the war to house maritime prisoners of war, hundreds of captured American privateersmen, navy sailors, and other mariners were dying each month. General Washington implied it was an intentional campaign of neglect and starvation meant to eviscerate America's ability to man its navies, privateers, and trading ships and to destroy its very capacity for seafaring by annihilating its maritime manpower. Indeed, few who were incarcerated aboard the "hell ships" would live long enough to survive the war, and as many as 11,500 were reported to have died before peace was achieved.

This is the story of privateering during the Revolutionary War, but not the usual one. Indeed, it was not my intent to address the entirety of that unique industry during the conflict, which would unquestionably require many volumes. It is, instead, a narrative of the long-ignored hostilities on the New Jersey coast, a then-barren, lightly populated, and altogether wild shore backed by miles of desolate pine barrens, salt marshes, meandering tea-colored streams, and isolated hamlets. Before the war it was the haunt of rowdies, smugglers, and highwaymen, as well as a few iron-mongers, fishermen, and farmers struggling to eke out a living as best they could. When war came, it was replete with British recruiters, rebel coast-watchers, and a struggle at sea that married the fight for independence with the quest for riches in an industry and manner of warfare that has long been ignored by history. The ways of the privateer and the whaleboat warrior—this is their memorable story. I hope to have done them justice.

—DONALD GRADY SHOMETTE

PART ONE

RESOLVED

"That, the inhabitants of these colonies be permitted to fit out armed vessels to cruise on the enemies of these United Colonies."

I

A Justifiable Piracy

"For the use of the Continent."

When His Majesty's imposing 64-gun ship-of-the-line *Asia* dropped anchor in seven fathoms of water in the East River at 9:30 a.m., May 26, 1775, an otherwise bright Friday morning in New York City, the political loyalties of the colony of New York, as well as its most important port, were never more divided.[1] Slightly more than a month after the Battles of Lexington and Concord ignited the flames of independence, New York City was in turmoil. As recently as May 1, some citizens of the city had chosen a Committee of One Hundred "to stand or fall with the liberty of the continent," while many others, loyal to the British Crown, watched in fearful silence. Events inimical to royal authority and control in both the New York colony and New England had been escalating almost daily since then. Representatives from every colony except Georgia had convened the Second Continental Congress in Philadelphia on May 10, the same day that Fort Ticonderoga, controlling the strategic waterway between Montreal and New York, was captured by a pair of squabbling militant firebrands, Benedict Arnold and Ethan Allen, and a back-country rag-tag band calling themselves the Green Mountain Boys. Two days later Crown Point, ten miles north of Ticonderoga, also capitulated. On May 13, the Continental Congress, acting upon the request of insurgent interests in the city and colony of New York, appointed commissioners to determine military posts and the number of troops needed to man them in the colony. They quickly resolved that New York defenses, manned by 3,000 men, be established at Kings Bridge in the Hudson Highlands and on Lake George. On May 18, the British fort of St. Johns on the Richelieu River, south of Montreal, was captured by Arnold and Allen. On the day before *Asia*'s arrival at New York, the only good news for Loyalists was that the Boston garrison under General Thomas Gage had been reinforced by troops under Generals John Burgoyne, Henry Clinton, and William Howe.[2]

Asia's commander, Captain George Vandeput, was not intimidated by the swiftly changing scene. When informing New York Lieutenant Governor Cadwallader Colden of his arrival, he stated emphatically: "you may depend upon my Endeavours, on your application, to give every such aid as may be Necessary towards supporting the legal Authority of Government, and ensure the safety of His Majesty's faithful Subjects in the Province of New York."[3]

With her big guns commanding the city, *Asia*'s very presence readily re-established a sense of royal control. It induced something of a temporary but forceful truce between the Crown's supporters, the rebel faction, and those who simply preferred neutrality while the seemingly more significant events were being played out in New England. As hostilities continued to escalate and spread, however, the counterfeit tranquility was not bound to last. Revolution was coming and would soon envelop the entire Atlantic seaboard, from the fog-shrouded Gulf of St. Lawrence to the sweltering Sea Isles of the Georgia coast. And one of the great crucibles of conflict, though generally ignored by history, was destined to focus on just 150 miles of the largely uninhabited coast lying between New York Bay and Delaware Bay, the outlets of two of the great estuary systems of North America and the very portals to the two power centers of war, Philadelphia and New York.

• • •

It was on the rainy afternoon of August 23, 1775, that King George III issued his formal proclamation declaring thirteen of England's North American colonies to be in a state of rebellion and sedition and directing the absolute suppression of all resistance. Three days later and half a world away, unaware of the momentous action just taken by the Crown, the Rhode Island General Assembly was initiating measures that would contribute to the ultimate failure of the King's objective. Already incensed that the British ministry, "lost to every sentiment of justice, liberty and humanity," was continuing to send troops and ships of war to America "to destroy trade, plunder and burn its towns, and murder its people," the Assembly passed a remarkable set of resolutions. Among the most significant objectives of the action that came to be known as the Resolves of the Rhode Island General Assembly was that an American fleet should be built as rapidly as possible. The Assembly deemed such an undertaking to be absolutely essential "to the preservation of the lives, liberty and property of the good people of these colonies." To forward its resolves the Assembly instructed the colony's delegates to the Continental Congress "to use their whole influence at the ensuing congress for building at the Continental expense a fleet of sufficient force for the protection of these colonies." On October 3, the delegation formally laid its instructions before Congress, which thereupon resolved to address the issue two days later.[4]

In the meantime, disconcerting intelligence arrived in Philadelphia that, along with the introduction of the Rhode Island scheme, would influence the very course of American history. Two unescorted brigs "of no force" had sailed from England for Quebec on August 11, laden with arms, powder, and other stores, and would soon be arriving on the St. Lawrence River. On October 5, the idea of fielding ships to intercept the two vessels was introduced in Congress and its practicality was hotly debated. A vociferous minority declared such a scheme as "the most wild, visionary, mad project that ever had been imagined." For the Continental government to engage in naval warfare against the mightiest maritime power on earth, they said, was like "an infant, taking a mad bull by his horns." Some opponents vigorously warned that "it would ruin the character, and corrupt the morals of our seamen. It would make them selfish, piratical, mercenary, bent wholly upon plunder."[5]

"The opposition," wrote John Adams of Massachusetts, a leading proponent of the measure, "was very loud and vehement. Some of my own colleagues appeared greatly alarmed at it, and Mr. Edward Rutledge [of South Carolina] never displayed so much eloquence as against it. He never appeared to me to discover so much information and sagacity, which convinced me that he had been instructed out-of-doors by some of the most knowing merchants and statesmen in Philadelphia."[6]

In truth, the mariners of the American colonies were devoid of their own naval traditions, having been, often as not, little more than an annex to that of the British Navy during previous conflicts. There was, moreover, a well-deserved concern for the general lack of military discipline, the dearth of native infrastructure, and the poverty of the country when compared to the motherland. Such hardships, together with the overwhelming naval superiority and superb military organization of the foe, seriously limited the field of endeavor. Nevertheless, it was quite clear that the patriotic cause, to be successful, would require the organization and deployment of armed men afloat. Led by Adams, the advocates supporting some form of naval measures answered the "formidable arguments and this terrible rhetoric . . . by the best reasons we could allege, and the great advantages of distressing the enemy, supplying ourselves, and beginning a system of maritime armed naval operations . . . in colors as glowing and animated." The vote was carried, and a committee comprised of John Langdon of New Hampshire, Silas Deane of Connecticut, and John Adams was appointed to prepare a plan for intercepting the two vessels.[7]

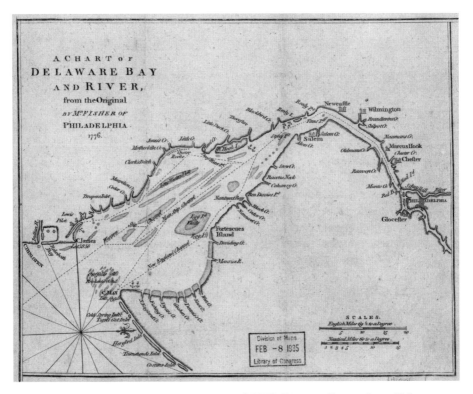

Joshua Fisher, *A Chart of Delaware Bay and River* [1779]. Courtesy Geography and Map Division, Library of Congress.

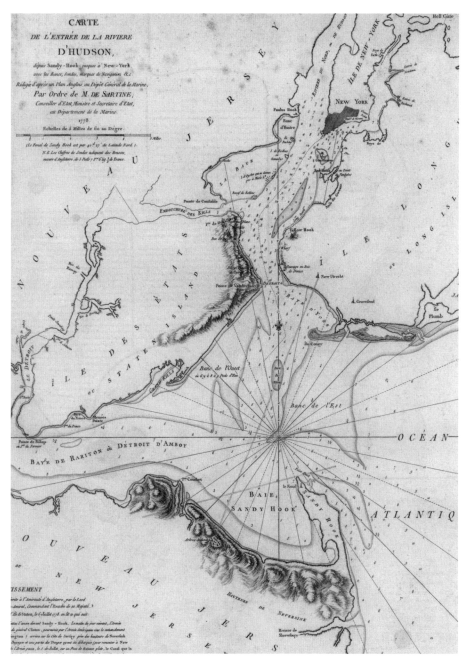

A 1778 French map showing New York Bay and environs. *Carte de l'entrée de la rivière d'Hudson, dépuis Sandy-Hook jusques à New-York avec les bancs, sondes, marques de navigation &c.* Dépôt Des Cartes Et Plans De La Marine, France. Courtesy of the Geography and Map Division, Library of Congress.

John Adams, 1784. From *The Boston* magazine, John Norman, engraver. Courtesy of the Rare Book and Special Collections Division, Library of Congress.

Silas Deane, ca. 1783. After drawing by Pierre Eugène Du Simitière. Reproduction from *The European magazine, and London review*, October 1783. Courtesy Library of Congress.

Submitted soon afterwards, the committee plan called for a letter to be sent to General George Washington at Cambridge, commander-in-chief of all American forces then besieging the British Army in Boston, to apply to Massachusetts for two armed vessels to interdict the two brigs and secure them "for the use of the Continent." Moreover, the warships were to seize any other transports used by the British army or navy in America. The governors of Rhode Island and Connecticut were also asked to send out vessels as soon as possible for his use. All were to be "on the continental risque and pay, during their being so employed." For the first time, Congressional authority was being extended to field ships of war, albeit ones borrowed from individual colonies.[8]

Despite the forward motion, the very idea of Congress fielding its own naval force, as proposed by Rhode Island, was immediately met by heated opposition and attempts at parliamentary obfuscation. The issue was again set aside until October 7, when it was scheduled for further debate. When discussion resumed, Samuel Chase of Maryland, who opposed the scheme because of the expense that would be incurred, declared: "It is the maddest idea in the world to think of building an American fleet. We should mortgage the whole continent." He preferred to focus upon mounting a defense of the enemy's next most likely target, New York, and allocate the very limited financial resources available to fortifying the Hudson River, although he reluctantly agreed not to oppose the deployment of two swift vessels for intelligence gathering. Stephen Hopkins of Rhode Island, who may have introduced the Rhode Island plan on October 3, declared that he would not be opposed to putting off the debate, provided there be assurance that the instructions would be addressed soon. Robert Treat Paine of Massachusetts, during an apparent moment of vocal disorder among the delegates, seconded what he erroneously believed to have been a motion by Chase to table the issue altogether, obliging the Marylander to remind him that he had never made such a motion.[9]

Finally, John Rutledge of South Carolina moved that a committee be appointed to prepare a formal plan and provide an estimate of the cost of actually building and fielding an American fleet. John Joachim Zubly of Georgia seconded the motion, but the issue continued to meet resistance. "I am against the extensiveness of the Rhode Island plan," declared Christopher Gadsden of South Carolina, "but it is absolutely necessary that some plan of defense by sea should be adopted." His colleague Rutledge confessed that he wanted to hear all the arguments, both for and against, before he drew his own conclusions. "I want to know how many ships are to be built and what they will cost." Samuel Adams of Massachusetts reinforced Rutledge's concern by stating the obvious, that the committee would be unable to make an estimate of cost until it knew precisely how many ships were to be built in the first place. Zubly moved that, since Rhode Island had taken the lead in proposing a maritime force, delegates from that province be appointed to prepare a plan. With a motion already on the table, John Adams immediately pointed out that Zubly's motion was out of order and should be put off for a week. Another motion was made to appoint a committee to address the whole subject, which elicited more "light skirmishing" between Zubly, Rutledge, Gadsden, and others.[10]

"It is like the man that was appointed to tell the dream and the interpretation of it," scoffed Silas Deane as his fellow delegates quarreled. "The expense is to be estimated, without knowing what fleet there shall be, or whether any at all." Still the opposition to both the plan and the appointment of a committee to evaluate its feasibility raged on.[11]

In a peak of frustration, Rutledge declared that it was the minority's desire to demean the Rhode Island plan and the establishment of a committee to assess it. "The design," he said, "is to throw it into ridicule. It should be considered out of respect to the colony of R[hode] Island who desired it." Nevertheless, the motion to appoint a committee was deferred.[12]

The proponents for a navy would not be stilled. On October 9, when Elbridge Gerry of Massachusetts presented a report on the expenses of the army at Cambridge and other military issues, he reminded the assembly of the significance of the efforts by his own province to send out not only state-armed warships but privateers as well. He noted, in quite strong terms, the necessity of such measures and vigorously lobbied the great Massachusetts firebrand himself, Samuel Adams, that Congress must also "fit out a heavy ship or two, and increase them as circumstances shall admit, the colonies large privateers, and individual small ones, [and] surely we may soon expect to see the coast clear of cutters."[13]

Congress did just that. On October 13, the assembly finally ordered two vessels to be prepared to intercept enemy ships carrying military stores and provisions to British forces, and took the momentous step of appointing a Marine Committee to administer the action. The first seeds of a truly Continental Navy had been planted. Deane, Langdon, and Gadsden were appointed a committee to prepare an estimate of expenses and to contract with proper persons deemed suitable to undertake the work.[14]

Three days later, the first chairman of the committee, Silas Deane of Connecticut, formally submitted a prepared proposal for fitting out a Continental Navy, which was read the following day. The justification for the action was clear. Yet, it was obvious, even to many advocates for a navy, that a Continental fleet could never hope to equal in either numbers or firepower the mighty Royal Navy, with its approximately 270 warships, including 131 ships-of-the-line, each carrying sixty or more guns, and manned by 28,000 seamen. Although barely more than a hundred were in active service, forty-three would be on the American Station by March 1776. It was a substantial force to reckon with. Nor could the Congress hope to pay for a large Continental force. Deane and others firmly believed that to adequately contest the enemy on the high seas and injure him where it most hurt, namely in his overseas commerce, it would be necessary to also authorize the fielding of private vessels of war, which could be accomplished at private expense with little economic burden to the public. Privateers had played a significant role against France in the last war and had made wealthy men out of quite a number of merchants and mariners alike. It was a fact not likely to be forgotten this time around. Deane, however, was well aware of the dangers of unleashing privateers without adequate administration and controls by both Congress and colony governments; without these, outright piracy and chaos might easily flourish. Thus, as a preamble to the proposal, he carefully addressed the current situation and its relevance to privateering.[15]

There were, he estimated, at least 10,000 seamen in the northern colonies who had been thrown out of work by the recent hostilities. Neither seamen and shipowners nor mechanics and riggers, who were dependent upon the maritime industry, could "possibly rest easy in their destitute, distress'd situation," with their ships rotting at anchor and their families starving. The prospects for many of them to turn to privateering, Deane asserted, with or without benefit of commissions, were predictable:

> They will not revolt from the cause but reprisal being justifiable as well by the laws of nature as of nations, they will pursue the only method in their power for indemnifying themselves, and reprisals will be made. This will at best be but a justifiable piracy & subject to no law or rule, the consequences may be very pernicious. The first fortunate adventurer will set many more on pushing their fortunes. . . . Should private adventurers take up the m[atter], every one will soon make his own law & in a few years, no law will govern, the mischief will grow rapidly & our own property will not be safe. Such adventurers are already entered upon, witness several captures made by the provincials without order or direction. This calls upon us to take up & regulate at the first setting out. It will afterwards be out of our power. Our coasts will swarm with roving adventurers, who if they forbear plundering of us or our immediate friends, may thro necessity invade the property of the subjects of those with whom we wish to stand well, & bring accumulated mischief on these colonies.[16]

The chairman's prescient warnings did not go unheard.

John Adams was equally cognizant of the dangers inherent in unregulated privateering, but considered it as a viable balance to the fielding of a small regular naval force. Although the war itself was still largely confined to New England, he worried about its possible expansion.

Indeed, on October 18, the Royalist Governor of New York, William Tryon, had been forced to take refuge aboard HMS *Halifax*, in New York Harbor, or face the wrath of an ugly mob. Twelve days later he took up residency on the *Dutchess of Gordon*, moored in the harbor, along with the colony's Attorney General, John Tabor, and other officials. With *Asia*'s guns and those of other ships that were arriving and departing, the great warship continued to dominate the harbor and a substantial component of the population still remained disinclined to violent conduct. Though Adams was unaware of the events in New York, it was not without some insight that he wrote to James Warren on the day after Tryon's expulsion: "Should we be driven to a war at all points . . . a public fleet as well as privateers might make prey enough of the trade of our enemies to make it worth while."[17]

Congress voted on October 30 to authorize two additional vessels, "for the protection and defense of the United Colonies," and formed a Naval Committee of seven, including John Langdon of New Hampshire, John Adams of Massachusetts, Stephen Hopkins of Rhode Island, Silas Deane of Connecticut, Richard Henry Lee of Virginia, Joseph Hewes of North Carolina, and Christopher Gadsden of South Carolina, to attend to the management of naval affairs.[18] By doing so it was fully committing itself to a policy of creating and maintaining a regular navy, one of the most important military initiatives in American history. The Rubicon of commitment had been crossed. Implementation of one of the boldest concepts of the Revolution was something else.

• • •

Early in the revolt, it had become clear that some Continental naval capacity would soon be required to patrol American waters, not only in New England where the seat of war then lay, but also along the mid-Atlantic seaboard between New York and the Chesapeake Bay, to which it would soon spread. Indeed, it was to become a strategic necessity. Recruitment of Loyalists amidst a divided population, especially in New York, to provide reinforcements for the British Army besieged in Boston, could only be effectively achieved or hindered by sea. On the very day that Silas Deane was submitting a proposal for fitting out a Continental Navy, October 16, one particular event, a shipwreck, served to illustrate that fact.

The vessel was the 293-ton *Rebecca and Francis*, owned in London by one James Mather and commanded by a New Hampshire mariner named Hastings. The ship had been sent to America as a transport in the spring of 1775 to bring reinforcements to General Thomas Gage's besieged garrison at Boston. On June 16, one day after George Washington was named Commander-in-Chief of the Continental Army, *Rebecca and Francis* arrived from Cork, Ireland, laden with troops belonging to the 40th Regiment of Foot.[19]

By mid-summer 1775, as the siege of Boston intensified, Gage grew increasingly desperate for more reinforcements with each day's passage. On July 18, he ordered Captain Duncan Campbell and a certain Lieutenant James Smith Sims to proceed to New York aboard the diminutive ship recently arrived from Cork as fast as possible on a special recruiting mission. Upon arrival, they were to receive on board "such men as may be inclined to serve his Majesty." Campbell was also directed to attend to the arrival of ships expected from Scotland, to prevent any of the emigrants aboard them from joining the rebels, and "to procure as many men out of them as you possibly can . . . and to give every encouragement to all the Scotch and other nations that will join you." The commander of *Asia*, Captain George Vandeput, was to provide all possible assistance in his power. Though Campbell and Sims were authorized to remain as long as necessary, they were to return to Boston as soon as possible, "bringing as many volunteers with you as you can procure."[20]

Campbell had once served as a regular British Army officer before the outbreak of hostilities, but had been retired for some time and was living comfortably on half-pay with his wife and children on the banks of the Hudson when called back to service. Working as a surveyor in Dutchess County, New York, he had been happily settled there for some years amidst a largely Tory population until the rebellion first erupted in Massachusetts. Promised a company command, he was soon engaged in recruiting fellow citizens still loyal to the Crown. On July 20, he sailed from Boston to New York on *Rebecca and Francis,* as ordered. Within a short time the ship had come to anchor off the city and was soon shuttling recruits from Dutchess County from shore to ship. By early September, *Rebecca and Francis* had returned to Boston with sixty-seven new volunteers recommended by New York Governor William Tryon (although some would later claim to having been pressed). All were Loyalists bound to join Gage's army. Also in the company were a number of women and children, and a handful of "well known enemies to American Liberty" who had taken the opportunity to flee to the protection of the British in Boston. The latter included Jonathan Simpson, a merchant, and Samuel Waterhouse, "addressers of Gage and [Thomas] Hutchinson," the royal governor of Massachusetts, a certain Mr. Sheaf, George O'Sullivan, a "famous or rather infamous" Loyalist despised by the rebels, and Dr. Benjamin Loring, late of Philadelphia, who had recently served as house surgeon to one of the "ministerial hospitals there."[21]

The mission was deemed successful enough that Hastings, Campbell, and Sims, two sergeants, Hugh Morrison and William Forster, and twenty-one privates belonging to Lt. Colonel Allan Maclean's Royal Highland Regiment of Emigrants, were quickly dispatched back to New York to conduct more recruiting. They departed from Boston Harbor on October 5 in company with a 20-gun ship and a transport bound for Halifax with troops. This time, the mission would not end as successfully as before.[22]

Entering or departing from New York Harbor was sometimes a difficult thing for shipping, especially with frequently unpredictable winds and sour weather that could keep vessels at sea or stuck in port for days, weeks, or even a month or more. It was also not uncommon for ships beating about, awaiting a favorable breeze and decent sea conditions, to face just the opposite. Indeed, many were the sad souls driven ashore on the coasts of New Jersey or Long Island as they arrived or departed New York Bay and were suddenly confronted with turbulent conditions. And there were, of course, the not infrequent pilot errors.

So it was with the unfortunate *Rebecca and Francis*. Whether it was sea conditions or pilot error that caused her to end up well south of Sandy Hook and the entrance to

New York Bay is unknown. What is known is that at 3 a.m., on the extremely hazy morning of Monday, October 16, the ship was accidentally run hard aground and stranded with her head ashore on Brigantine Beach, a half mile south of Little Egg Harbor, New Jersey. It was later reported in the Philadelphia newspapers that she had been beached "with seventeen seamen," a Capt. Duncan Campble [*sic*], a Lieut. Sims, a recruiting serjeant [*sic*], and fifteen or twenty ragamuffin fellows, that had ran from New York and [en]listed" in the British Army. Only much later was it reported that thirteen women had also been on board. Fortunately, no lives were lost.[23]

Being well aware that they were quite probably in hostile territory, Campbell and his men quickly set about disposing of several of the ship's cannon, sixty firelocks, bayonets, cartouche boxes, two and a half barrels of powder — all that was aboard — as well as some soldiers' clothing, to prevent these things from falling into rebel hands should they be captured. Neither Hastings and Campbell, nor Sims and their men were disposed to tarry and await a rescue. Almost as soon as the sailors had reached the shore, they crossed to the mainland and "took to the woods," leaving the ship on a careen "with the sand nearly up to her quarter deck." Almost as soon as they made shore, Campbell reportedly "offered a large sum in half johanneses to any man there, to put them on board a man-of-war, which they apprehended not to be far distant." The request was refused. Nevertheless, both officers, who disguised themselves as fishermen, and a few others were finally able to secure a small boat and set off for Amboy, New Jersey, or New York City, where they hoped to find HMS *Asia*. It was later alleged that the captain carried £1,500 in cash with him, which may have been to pay enlistment bounties. Soon they were coasting northward along the barrier island shores of New Jersey.[24]

News of the Loyalist stranding spread quickly throughout the countryside and was immediatly relayed to Philadelphia; where it was delivered on the afternoon of October 17 by a resident living some twenty-five miles distant from the wrecksite. A few days later, New York also learned of the event from an incoming North Carolina schooner that, in passing, had sighted the hulk lying ashore on her beam ends. The schooner's captain, one John Bates, reported that on the same evening as sighting the wreck, "a Boat came out of Cranberry Inlet [opposite Toms River], with some People in her, three of whom appeared like Gentlemen, and said they had been a Gunning, but their Ammunition being out, they would be glad of a Passage to New-York." Bates graciously took the men aboard, but soon encountered headwinds that forced him to take shelter in the inlet.[25]

The following morning, as the schooner lay to, Bates's passengers transferred to a sloop just then preparing to sail from the inlet for New York. Then, less than an hour before the sloop was to depart, a party of armed men from Egg Harbor, consisting of a Captain Lovermen, a Lieutenant Cook, and six militiamen from the adjacent county appeared. They were sent, they said, by the Pennsylvania Committee of Safety, in a "tedious pursuit of one day and two nights," to arrest the men from *Rebecca and Francis*. After securing the strangers aboard the sloop as prisoners, Lovermen informed Bates who they were. Though his own men were worn out with fatigue, the militia captain noted proudly that he had already captured the rest of the ship's crew. Now, they had the whole lot.[26]

On Saturday, October 21, Captain Hastings and three of his crew were brought to Philadelphia under a guard commanded by Major Richard Westcot of Egg Harbor (of whom more later). By October 24, Campbell, Sims, and the rest of their soldiers had also been brought up and interrogated by the Pennsylvania Committee of Safety. General Gage's written instructions to Campbell, which had been discovered upon the captain's person, were also read by the committee. On the following day the transcripts of the examination and Gage's instructions were read by Congress and ordered published. Copies were soon in the hands of the New York Convention.[27]

Captain Hastings and his crew (several of whom claimed they had been pressed into service), after being examined by the Committee of Safety, were quickly ordered released. Campbell and Sims were to be confined as "close prisoners" in the Philadelphia city jail, but kept apart from their own men, who were also to be confined, as "they have acted, and intended further to act, a part inimical to the Liberties of America."[28]

The true loyalties of those who had been recruited by Campbell or crewed under Captain Hastings, mostly being simple farmers or laborers whose allegiance to either side of the conflict in its earliest stages, in many cases, were not easily assessed. A case in point was Daniel Calligher, who had been among the soldiers taken. After two months of incarceration, he appealed to Captain Nicholas Biddle of the Continental Navy for release from confinement to take up service aboard an American warship.

Last August Travelling Towards New York from this Town [Philadelphia], Looking for Work and finding none, hearing of the King's Proclamation to go to Boston and there have full Employment I went on Board A Transport where Afterwards I was forced to Remain as A Soldier though Quite Contrary to the proclamation, (as it Said therein) that any Person who wanted Susteanance, to Go Immediately on Board one of his Majesties Ships, Go to Boston and there have full employment, [(]without being an Enemy to America) this I agreed to No Worke at that Season being to be found, here and there detained before Now as I always loved the freedom of America and will Cheerfully Conquer or Die in its Cause if you Take me out of prison where I am Confined for being providentially Cast on Egg Harbour. I Shall Serve you As Long as Necessity requires.[29]

By mid-January 1776, Congress recommended to the Pennsylvania Committee of Safety that "there appear no material Reasons for detaining them [the soldiers] in Prison that they may be discharged, as the Expence of maintaining them runs high." About the same time, Campbell submitted a petition to Congress to be released on parole, a request that "was not attended to." Finally, in mid-March Congress approved of his release specifically to attend to his ailing wife. He was later permitted "to reside with his wife and family in the city of Burlington, in the western division of New Jersey."[30]

As for the unfortunate *Rebecca and Francis*, by October 23 the ship had reportedly gone to pieces, although it was thought the guns might be saved. That all had not been lost, however, is certain, for on November 23 the Pennsylvania Committee of Safety, "understanding that a Quantity of Sail Cloth taken out of the wreck of the *Rebecca & Frances*, and Sails and other materials belonging to her are to be sold on Tuesday next [November 28] at Absecon Beach," directed its agent, Captain James Moulder, to attend the sale and purchase for the colony's use the sail cloth, sails, cable, rigging, and other materials "if they can be got at low prices, taking into Consideration the Expences of bringing them here."[31]

The "dangerous practices," as John Hancock, President of Congress, called the recruitment operation that Campbell had been undertaking in New York, were but a hint of future problems to be faced by the Continental government. It quickly ordered the New York Provincial Congress to investigate and secure all possible accomplices engaged in like acts. The need for coastal patrol, especially on the raw, isolated New Jersey coastline, had been underscored. For the first time in the war the Continental government recognized the vulnerability of these naked, windswept shores to enemy incursions.[32]

The next time would prove even more instructive—and pivotal.

• • •

The forming of a regular naval establishment from scratch was a task fraught with countless hurdles, not the least of which was the laying down of rules and regulations, and the establishment of competent tribunals to "determine the propriety of captures" that would inevitably be made. Acting in response to a November 8, 1775, letter from General Washington requesting guidance in regards to vessels already captured by American forces, Congress appointed a committee to consider the question. The Marine Corps was established two days later. On November 25, the committee submitted its recommendations regarding captured enemy vessels, which Congress resolved to act upon. It was, indeed, a most historic occasion. John Adams, the committee secretary, would later write triumphantly of the event in his autobiography: "I have been particular in transcribing the Proceedings of this day 25 of November 1775, because they contain the true origin and formation of the American Navy."[33]

The draft recommendations were comprehensive. All vessels of war employed in "the present and unjust war against the United Colonies" that should fall into American hands were to be seized and forfeited. All transports in the same service, having on board any troops, arms, munitions, clothing, provisions, or military and naval stores of any kind were likewise to be liable to seizure and forfeiture. Although the committeemen were focused upon vessels engaged by the Continental government, the umbrella covered private armed vessels as well. Thus it was also included that no "master or commander of any vessel shall be entitled to cruise for, or make prize of any vessel or cargo before he shall have obtained a commission from the Congress," or from agents appointed for that purpose in one or more of the colonies. The organized and just processing of prize cases was also of paramount importance. It was thus recommended to the legislatures of the colonies that they should, as soon as possible, "erect courts of Justice, or give jurisdiction to the courts now in being for the purpose of determining concerning the captures to be made … and to provide that all trials in such case be had by a jury under such qualifications, as to the respective legislatures shall deem expedient." All prosecutions, of course, were to be conducted in the aforesaid court in the colony in which the capture was made. If a prize was taken on the open sea, the case was to be tried in such colony as the captor found convenient, "provided that nothing contained in this resolution shall be construed so as to enable the captor to remove the prize from any colony competent to determine concerning the seizure, after he shall have carried the vessel so seized within any harbor of the same."[34]

One of the most important proposals of all pertained to appeals. The committee resolved and made quite specific recommendations regarding procesural limitations: "That in all cases an appeal shall be allowed to the Congress, or such person or persons as they shall appoint for the trial of appeals, provided the appeal be demanded within five days after definitive sentence, and such appeal be lodged with the secretary of Congress within forty days afterwards, and provided the party appealing shall give security to prosecute the said appeal effort, and in the case of the death of the secretary during the recess of Congress, then the said appeal to be lodged in Congress within 20 days after the meeting thereof."[35]

The committee was specific in stating that any captures made by a vessel or vessels fitted out at private expense by a private person or persons were to be for the use of the owner of the said vessel or vessels. However, when vessels employed in a capture were fitted out at the expense of any one of the United Colonies, one third was to be for the use of the captors, and the remaining two-thirds to the use of the said colony. When a vessel was fitted out at the Continental charge, one third belonged to the captors and two thirds to the use of the United Colonies. If the captured vessel was a vessel of war, then the captors would be entitled to one half of the value, and the remainder belonged to the colony or the Continental Congress, after the necessary charges for condemnation proceedings had been deducted. And finally, recommendations were made to the appropriate distribution of prize shares for Continental Navy vessels for the officers and crews.[36]

Although the specifics regarding the distribution of proceeds realized by the condemnation and sale of prizes by private, state, and Continental vessels would ultimately be changed dramatically, a plan had at last been set in motion. The recommendations, largely framed by Adams and heavily based on British regulations, provided not only a template for the adoption of the official "Rules and Regulations of the Navy of the United Colonies," which were formally approved by Congress on November 28, but the basics, if not the specifics, for handling prize captures by private armed vessels.[37]

The deed had finally been done and, by the end of November, the Naval Committee had purchased four vessels to be converted into warships, the ships *Alfred* and *Columbus*, and brigs *Cabot* and *Andrew Doria*. More would soon be authorized.

Though forward motion was being made at the Continental level, eleven colonies of the still loose federation, with distinct sentiments of independency reigning supreme, moved to protect their own particular interests by forming their own state navies; Delaware and New Jersey did not. At first, the state navies, which provided the second significant American naval component of the war, were under the administration of the individual state committees of safety, and later under the boards and naval committees of state legislatures. The largest of these was Virginia, with seventy-two vessels of all classes. The smallest belonged to Georgia, which would eventually field only a handful of galleys and a single schooner.[38]

Deane recognized that while a regular naval establishment was being built from the ground up, which could take months if not years, it would also be necessary to authorize privately armed vessels to take up the slack. Thus was formed the third and, it might be argued, the most important class of vessel to be engaged during the Revolution. It was, he felt, an inevitable action, but one that would have to be regulated from the start. There were, of course, advantages to having both a regular navy and privateers. Whereas a Continental Navy or state navies would have to be paid for and supported from the public weal and would, of necessity, be limited in size, privateers would be supported by private entrepreneurship as a for-profit undertaking and add no weight to the public debt. Indeed, Deane and fellow delegates John Adams and Benjamin Franklin had, all along, championed not only the forwarding of a regular naval force, but also the adoption of privateering as a short, easy, inexpensive, and effectual means of humbling British commerce. That all three classes of vessels, and the men who sailed them, would eventually overlap and sometimes complement each other in their particular missions, however, was inevitable. Competition for men and resources was not yet a consideration.

By the close of the Revolution in 1783, privateers would occasionally be engaged in squadrons or on expeditions in concert with both Continental and state navies. In a number of instances, vessels that had been purpose built or purchased for Continental service ended their careers in state navies, or as privateers under syndicate ownerships. A few state navy vessels, along with their officers and crews, would even be released from state service from time to time to go privateering to improve a state's finances. Not infrequently, some officers who began as privateersmen would transfer their service to Continental and state navies, and vice versa. Some officers and men engaged in the naval service who found themselves unemployed ashore, perhaps because they lacked a ship or billet or because their ships were in for long-term repairs, would frequently sign on as privateersmen during their down time, especially towards the close of the war. Thus, the mixture of Continental and state naval vessels, their officers and men, operating in concert with privateers towards a common military goal, though sporadic, was not exceptional.

The concept and practicality of employing privately owned vessels to wage war against an enemy upon the high seas, of course, was not new. Indeed, its antecedents extended back to the days of King Edward I and had been employed by the major and minor powers of Europe ever since. The tradition of privateering in the colonies was substantial. From the very onset of the colonial period in America, English and colonial letters of marque vessels and privateers had canvassed the oceans in quest of Spanish, French, Dutch, and Portuguese prizes during the numerous wars that had blighted the Western Hemisphere. Substantial fleets had been manned and fielded by provincials for the great 1690 expedition under William Phips against Quebec. William Pepperrell's successful assault on the great fortress of Louisburg, Nova Scotia, in 1745, had also been supported by colonial privateers.

As late as the French and Indian War, the English American colonies had engaged in privateering with substantial success, providing a profitable field for American entrepreneurship and enterprise. As a hatchery for many young seamen, it would prove of inestimable service two decades later. Literally hundreds of colonial privateers, manned by thousands of American seamen and licensed by the Crown, had ventured forth from waterways and inlets all along the eastern seaboard in search of lucrative prizes. Yet the term privateer was (and is) often misused and usually misunderstood. Even during the

Revolution, the nomenclature was frequently applied to Continental and state warships, most commonly the smaller ones, even by individuals with some knowledge of maritime affairs, and was often misapplied even in official correspondence. It is thus necessary to provide some parameters as to what a privateer was.

The issuance by a national government of a "letter of marque and reprisal," an official warrant, commission, or license, authorized a designated agent to search, seize, or destroy the assets and property belonging to a national government or party that had committed some offense under the accepted laws of nations against the citizens of the issuing nation. The commission usually granted the right for private parties operating under the commission to raid and capture enemy merchant shipping, warships, or property of an enemy nation at war. Quite literally, the formal statement of the warrant authorized the agent to pass beyond the borders of the nation ("marque" meaning frontier or boundary), where he might engage in searching for, capturing, or destroying the assets, resources, or personnel of the adversarial party. Technically, the measure might not always be against a nation but a foreign party, and might, on certain occasions, be considered a retaliatory procedure short of a full declaration of war, intended to vindicate the action to other sovereign nations in the context of undeclared hostilities ("reprisal"). Legally and politically, however, it was often a delicate undertaking and always one fraught with unexpected consequences. Without the formal assurance of such warrants, commissions, or proof thereof being present, the agents could indeed be, and sometimes were, considered pirates under the commonly accepted laws of nations. As with the issuance of a warrant for domestic search, seizure, arrest, or death, the commission necessarily had to contain a certain degree of specificity to guarantee that the designated agent would not exceed his authority and the intent of the issuing agency or government. In reality, the line between piracy, which was the seizure of the property of others without a license, in both war and peace, and privateering, with a license, was razor thin and sometimes crossed.

When a privateer commission was issued by a body or political entity in revolt against its own sovereign or government, as it was by the Cromwellians during the English Civil War, by the Americans during the American Revolution, and by the Confederacy during the American Civil War, the legality of the commission was usually not recognized by the established government. Often, vessels carrying letters of marque issued by revolutionary governments were simply addressed as pirates by the national state against which the rebellion was mounted. Although Continental letters of marque and privateer commissions issued during the Revolution were taken somewhat more seriously by the enemy than those autonomously granted by states, such as Massachusetts and Rhode Island, the British never formally acknowledged the commissions of any American private men-of-war as lawful. Though outright executions were almost never carried out (albeit frequently threatened), privateersmen were officially considered by the Crown as nothing less than pirates and were regularly treated with extreme severity.

Prior to the Revolution, vessels operating under letters of marque were usually armed merchantmen primarily engaged in commercial enterprise but authorized to make prizes whenever possible during a voyage. During the war they were generally referred to as privateers, but, strictly speaking, the term privateer as it was used during the conflict, was most normally applied to privately owned and armed vessels specifically fitted out for warlike uses and carrying no commercial cargo. To further blur the edges of definition, it should be noted that armed vessels of all kinds, even Continental Navy warships, sometimes served as cargo carriers under certain circumstances. Moreover, both Continental and state government vessels were from time to time fitted out and deployed as privateers, separate from regular navy authority. Such actions often created serious interpretive problems for American Admiralty and Appeals courts when it came to prize cases and libel issues.

• • •

By late fall, the pressure on the Continental Congress to authorize the commissioning of privateers was growing. On November 27, Simeon Deane, of Wethersfield, Connecticut, wrote his brother Silas, that he was solicited "by a number of gentlemen to ask, thro' your influence whether the Congress will grant commission to private adventurers to fit out a privateer or privateers to take British property on this coast, or in the West Indies." He pointed out that should privateering be adopted to operate in the latter, "you are sensible that the first opportunity may be very advantageous, and as well disposed of in this Colony as anywhere, especially as the persons now applying are your good friends and would prosecute the affair immediately."[39]

Deane and other advocates who supported a truly Continental Navy were not only optimistic but also aggressive in regards to the positive aspects of authorizing the deployment of privateers as well. Congress was thus gradually spurred to begin consideration of its role in the forwarding of not only a regular navy but also the establishment of guidelines for the issuance of letters of marque and privateer commissions, albeit not before some preliminary investigations were carried out. Not surprisingly, John Adams was assigned the task of assessing the ability of Massachusetts to produce the manpower needed to provide service in his represented area, "either as marines, or on board of armed vessels, in the pay of the continent, or in the pay of the province, or on board of privateers, fitted out by private adventurers." His selection for the task was undoubtedly because his own province had also been among the first to field armed vessels against the British, and he was already one of the most vocal advocates for a navy. Like most of his colleagues, he was cognizant that the British were well aware of the danger posed by Yankee mariners. As one member of the House of Lords had already declared, America was nothing less than "a great nursery where seamen are raised, trained, and maintained in time of peace to serve their country in time of war," although their country was no longer Great Britain! Adams was instructed to seek out the names of experienced mariners belonging to seaports in Massachusetts who were qualified as officers and commanders for armed vessels, where they lived, and other pertinent data. Moreover, he was to inventory what available craft were suitable for armed service, what their specifications were, and where the best places were to build new ships and manning privateers. On November 5, he asked James Warren and Elbridge Gerry for help.

"I want to know," he queried, "what is become of the whalemen, codfishers, and other seamen belonging to our province and what number of them you imagine will be enlisted into the service of the continent, or of the province, or of private adventurers, in case a taste for privateering and maritime warfare shall prevail. Whether you think that two or three battalions of marines could be easily inlisted in our province."[40]

That a taste for privateering was indeed developing fast throughout New England, and soon along the entire Atlantic seaboard, was not surprising. Since November 1, 1775, when the General Court of Massachusetts passed "An Act, for the Encouraging the Fixing out of Armed Vessells, to defend the Sea Coasts of America, and for Erecting a Court to Try and Condemn all Vessells that shall be found infesting the same," the province's government had been commissioning privateers without the blessing of the Continental Congress. Although as many as 767 individual Continental commissions would be issued to Massachusetts vessels, nearly a thousand would be authorized by the state without congressional approval. The port of Salem, alone, would field 158 privateers, which would account for 458 captures.[41]

By early December, the first privateers from Connecticut had been placed in service, again without approval by Congress, and sometimes even without commissions from their own provincial government. Ironically, one of the first petitions from a privately armed vessel for condemnation of a prize under the authority of Congress soon came in when Captain Simeon Sellick, who commanded a small Connecticut sloop that, without benefit of a commission, had taken, at Turtle Bay, New York, a vessel laden with King's stores valued at £1,500. Owing to the spirit of rebellion that was prevailing, Congress conveniently overlooked what would otherwise have been legally termed piracy. Some undoubtedly recalled the prescient words of Silas Deane regarding the dangers of unrestricted privateering. Nevertheless, Sellick was awarded "£100 like money as a reward for his expences, trouble and risk," in return for which he gave up his prize "for the Continental use."[42]

Congress finally began to move as the new year dawned and popular pressure continued to increase in a number of the colonies to formally authorize privateering. In early January, Samuel Ward, a Rhode Island delegate, noted: "The fitting out of privateers, a treaty &c many of us have in contemplation & as soon as we can prepare others shall carry into execution."[43] Many provinces were already in the process of starting to outfit their own regular naval forces. By mid-month it was being reported that an agent from the south, Captain Robert Cochran, had arrived in Philadelphia to recruit 500 seamen for the infant South Carolina Navy, and was offering terms so lucrative that it endangered Congress's own efforts to forward the scheme for establishing and manning a Continental Navy. It was, unfortunately, but a foretaste of the competition that was to come for able-bodied seamen by Continental and state governments, as well as privateering interests.[44]

Before further action could be taken, however, the escalation of the war in general and, more specifically, the dramatic capture of a British ship in New Jersey waters would provide the tipping point for formal Congressional approval of privateering as an acceptable means of warfare. The vessel in question bore the unlikely name *Blue Mountain Valley*; its seizure would prove to be the first of many made on the Jersey coast in a dramatic act that some considered nothing less than outright piracy.

II

Blue Mountain Valley

"And so God send the good ship to her desired port of safety."

On September 26, 1775, British Admiralty Secretary Philip Stephens forwarded to Vice Admiral Samuel Graves, Commander of the American Station at Boston, via HMS *Centurion*, a list of "the several ships and vessels taken up to carry stores, provisions and live stock to North America for the use of His Majesty's fleet and forces in those parts." Stephens instructed the admiral to station some small ships under his command to meet and escort them safely into port. Among the scores of vessels to be brought in was the provision ship *Blue Mountain Valley*.[1]

About the middle of October, *Blue Mountain Valley* prepared to sail from the Downs to the westward of Cape Clear in company with thirty-six other transports laden with stores and provisions. The manifest of the ship, dated at London, September 30, 1775, read as follows:

> Shipped by the Grace of God in good order & well conditioned by Mure, Son & Atkinson, by order of the Right Honorable the Lords Commissioners of his Majesty's Treasury, in & upon the good ship called the *Blue Mountain Valley*, whereof is master, under God for this present voyage, John H. Dempster and now riding at anchor in the River Thomas [Thames], and by Gods Grace bound to Boston—One hundred & seven & a quarter cauldron of coals, one hundred butts of porter branded CALVERT, one hundred & twelve & a half quarter of beans, fifty tons, twelve hundred weight of potatoes, ten casks of sour krout, eighty hogs, thirty-six puncheons for water—which are to be delivered in the like good order & condition (the danger of the seas, mortality of the [blank space] and consummation of their provender only excepted) under the Commander in Chief of His Majesty's Forces in America which he shall direct, free of freight. In witness whereof the master or purser of the said ship hath affirmed to four bills of lading all of this teno[r] & date one of which being accomplished the other three are to stand void. And so God send the good ship to her desired port of safety. Amen.[2]

The lading, shipped by order of the government and at its risk, was for the use of the King's beleaguered troops in Boston "or any other port in America where the said Troops might be stationed." The ship also carried a letter for the Commander in Chief of His Majesty's troops in America. Many of the transports in the convoy were scheduled to turn off for the West Indies, including one that carried two troops of light horse destined to winter in those quarters. But Captain Dempster's vessel, being "a sharp built ship" that "would make as good weather on a winter coast as any," steadfastly maintained her course for America. There would be, unfortunately for all concerned, no armed escort to protect her or the other transports in the fleet while en route, for the Royal Navy, having been caught unprepared for the growing rebellion, was already stretched dangerously thin.[3]

The voyage, unhappily for those engaged, quickly evolved into a most horrendous one. Almost as soon as the fleet had left the Downs, it was assailed by a "dreadful gale of wind" that drove many ships ashore on the coasts of England and Ireland. For *Blue Mountain Valley*, which had emerged battered but intact, the remainder of the passage would be equally harrowing, with sour weather dogging her all the way across the Atlantic.[4]

Arriving on the coast of North America about January 1 or 2, 1776, with his vessel in a leaking condition, Dempster reckoned his position to be a little to the northward of Boston, but as he was unable to strike soundings his true position was uncertain at best. The blustery winds were now blowing off the continent and prevented his every effort to approach the coast for three weeks. In one of the severe gales, the upper gudgeon iron of the ship's rudder assemblage broke and the middle one worked loose. Dempster reluctantly judged it best to stand to the southward in hopes of making landfall in a more moderate climate. Having suffered consistently dirty weather, loss of sails, and a very long passage, his ship was definitely in a dangerous state and he feared that her rudder must be unhung before he could proceed much further. Moreover, though he had sailed with an adequate forty puncheons of drinking water, supplies were now running dangerously low, not because of consumption, but because of the containers that carried the ship's supply. The water casks, which had been provided by the government, had all been new and unseasoned, and leaked profusely. The crew, which was on an average allowance of two quarts per day, would eventually be reduced to three pints. Of the eighty hogs that had been aboard when they left the Downs, all intended for the army, only ten remained alive. No doubt thanks to the weather, the greater part of the stock had died even before they had cleared the English Channel, and "the chief part of the remainder before they struck soundings on the coast of America."[5]

Finally, on January 18, *Blue Mountain Valley* came within sight of land near Egg Harbor, New Jersey, and promptly stood in a northerly direction along the coast for Sandy Hook in hopes of meeting one of His Majesty's men-of-war that was supposedly awaiting her. The following day they were again driven from the land by yet another violent gale. The weather moderated on the 20th and near evening land was again sighted. The captain's instructions, however, had explicitly forbidden him to enter either Boston "or any other port or harbor in America 'till he had spoken with some of His Majesty's ships, proper orders having been sent out for that purpose," and he had seen none. Indeed, he could not be certain such orders had even arrived. Needless to say, he was deeply concerned about the ship's safety, which was indeed "very precarious on this side of the water, in these times."[6]

Dempster was forced to make a tactical decision. When the Sandy Hook Lighthouse was spotted on the morning of January 21, he immediately ordered three guns fired to summon a pilot, having resolved to send the ship's chief mate, Joseph Woolcombe, into New York. Woolcombe was "to go on board of the ships of war in port" in order to "get some intelligence or directions from them how . . . [he] was to proceed with the . . . ship, and [determine] whether he could be furnished with a pilot or convoy." There was, of course, the very distinct chance that rebels had taken over the city, yet the ship's situation was uncertain at best and required immediate relief. There seemed little alternative.[7]

About 1 p.m., a local pilot named William Dobbs, accompanied by four men, Robert Hogg, George Stewart, a man named Lewis, and another named Carr, all belonging to the Port of New York, boarded the ship from a skiff. Dobbs asked the captain if he had signaled for a pilot, to which he was answered in the negative. For all the skipper knew, they could have been spies sent from the rebels! He politely informed Dobbs that he only wanted to put a man ashore, and a price was soon agreed upon. The pilot then asked inquisitively "from whence the said ship came and whence she was bound?" Dempster answered in a cursory manner that she was from London and bound northward, but intentionally avoided mentioning any port by name. The pilot was then casually queried if there were any men-of-war at New York, and replied that there were only two. It was just the answer Dempster wanted. Indeed, he and the chief had already agreed upon a plan of action before the pilot stepped aboard. In the event the mate did not return within twenty-four hours, the captain was to conclude that he had been taken prisoner by the rebels, in which case the ship would immediately put to sea. A few minutes later, Woolcombe and the New Yorkers were en route to the city.[8]

Woolcombe carried with him several letters from the captain, some of which were ostensibly intended for home via the next ship out while others were for delivery to persons in the city. The letters included: one addressed to the skipper's brother George Dempster, Esq., of Oxford Street, London, a Member of the House of Commons and a friend to America; one from John Townsend of London to his brother in New York, Robert Hunter, Esq., of Coleman Street, London; and one to Richard Cardin, Esq., of Bucklersbury, London, detailing the long passage and current situation. Woolcombe had also penned a letter to his own father to inform him of the recent difficult voyage. The captain, "to be fully satisfied of the propriety of going into New York," apparently assumed that the danger inherent in sending the mate ashore was justified, especially since he had been three weeks on the American coast without seeing or speaking with a single one of the King's ships. Indeed, given the unknown status of the spreading rebellion, the captain appeared "greatly amazed at not seeing any of the men-of-war."[9]

As Woolcombe and Dobbs approached New York City, the mate asked the pilot if it would be possible to put him aboard HMS *Asia*, then anchored in Gravesend Bay. Dobbs revealed his true colors and replied with indignation that he wouldn't do it for £100, exclaiming: "Do you think I'll betray my country?" The skiff arrived at the city docks about 6 p.m., and landed at White Hall Slip. Shivering from the cold, Dobbs asked the mate to go into a public house with him to get some punch and warm up. It was a suggestion to which Woolcombe, equally chilled from the haul across the harbor, readily agreed. The public house, however, proved to be a veritable lair of rebels. Upon entering the tavern, both the mate and pilot, whose loyalties were as yet unknown to those within, were seized and searched by a number of armed men belonging to the city guard, and instantly stripped of the letters. Both men were taken to a barracks and confined.[10]

Dobbs was almost immediately hauled before the New York Committee of Safety and examined. The committeemen listened intently as the pilot informed them that he had learned that *Blue Mountain Valley* was a transport from England, laden with porter and coal for the British Army, and Woolcombe was her mate. The ship, the rebel committeemen were told, had been thirteen weeks out from England, and was in a very distressed condition waiting for direction and assistance from the Royal Navy in New York. Dobbs vehemently denied, however, that he had "promised to put Woolcombe on board of one of the ships of war, but only promised to bring him to the city; [and] that Woolcombe did not mention anything about the going on board of the ships of war, or either of them, until he was near the city, and that he, the said William Dobbs, refused to put him on board."[11]

The New York Committee of Safety, satisfied with Dobbs's story and assured of his allegiance, released him, and then deliberated throughout the afternoon and evening on the importance of *Blue Mountain Valley* and what to do about her. New York had sent seven delegates to the Continental Congress, but many still harbored hopes of mending the rift with the Mother Country, though the governor had already been forced to flee for his safety. The city of New York itself was still heavily Loyalist in its sympathies and almost entirely defenseless. To make the committee's situation even more ticklish, *Asia* and *Phoenix*, two great British warships, now lay in the harbor, and could open fire at the slightest provocation with disastrous consequences. Yet the committeemen could not pass up the opportunity to prevent an important supply ship from reaching His Majesty's forces in Boston. Given the local situation, however, it was decided that outright action would have to be carried out by proxy.

At 8 p.m., the committee prepared a report outlining the situation to William Alexander, Lord Stirling, Colonel of the 1st New Jersey Regiment of the Continental Army, the only rebel military unit close enough to the city to be of help. Fearing the possibility of spies and thus for their own safety, they requested that the source of the information be kept secret and that the report be destroyed after he had read it. The committeemen were convinced that the seemingly innocent letters found on Woolcombe were "directed to certain persons under fictitious directions," and were actually intended to be conveyed by him to one of the men-of-war. They were also certain that if the transport received relief, that she would undoubtedly proceed to Boston "laden with all kinds of stores for the [British] army." It was almost certain that, if the enemy warships were to learn of the presence of the transport, they would, "doubtless, send down their boats" to her assistance and defense. Apparently relying upon some information gleaned from Dobbs's interrogation, *Blue Mountain Valley* was described as "a ship of between three and four hundred tons, a galley-built ship, without a head, has yellow sides, blue quarter-boards with the trophies of war painted on the quarter-boards; has six three-pounders [*sic*, four-pounders] on the quarterdeck. She has, it is thought a quantity of ammunition on board. She has about twenty hands, and is hovering off and on, without the [Sandy] Hook, and will not leave that station till she receives intelligence from shore." She was also described as being "100 feet from stem to stern above." Perhaps the most interesting thing about her was that the committeemen considered her capable "of making a ship of war of 20 six pounders and 10 three pounders." Fortunately, she was but weakly armed and actually had on board only four half barrels of powder "with shot in proportion." Her complement of sixteen men, two officers, and two boys, the committee believed, could be easily overcome.[12]

The committeemen begged Lord Stirling and New Jersey to take action: "It would greatly serve the public cause could she be seized. There are the most evident reasons why we, in New-York, ought not, in point of prudence, do it. We have two [Royal Navy] ships-of-war lying here, and our exports, as yet, happily uninterrupted by them. This discovery cannot be kept long a secret and we deem it our duty to submit this case to your immediate attention."[13]

The following day, Woolcombe himself was brought before the committee, consisting of six or seven men, and cross-examined. Committeemen John Morin Scott and Alexander McDougall took the lead in the investigation. Although the two officials grilled the prisoner for hours about the ship and her lading, the subject of their questioning remained resolutely mute. The hapless mate was rigorously interrogated again on January 23. It was only then that the committeemen finally learned that the ship had sailed from the Downs with twenty-five or twenty-six other transports, and had been—and still might be—lying off Sandy Hook. The interrogators also learned that after Woolcombe was to have delivered the letters to one of the men-of-war, he was to have been picked up by the transport, which was to have stood close to shore precisely twenty-four hours after he left her. Having extracted all of the information they could, and not wishing to exacerbate the wrath of the Royal Navy commanders then in New York Harbor, the committeemen, perhaps unwisely, ordered the prisoner's release along with the letters found upon him, and issued a permit allowing him to board either of His Majesty's ships without further molestation. If the Royal Navy had hitherto been unaware of the transport's presence, they soon would be well informed.[14]

In the meantime, Lord Stirling, upon receiving the plea from the New York Committee, moved with celerity. Indeed, upon being handed the committee's express, he set off immediately from Elizabethtown the next morning. With a party of thirty men of his regiment, "supposed in order to take the vessel," he proceeded by way of Perth Amboy on a "secret enterprise" that was revealed to no one. Urgency was imperative, however, for that evening another express arrived in Elizabethtown, New Jersey, with a second letter for Stirling, or in his absence the chairman of the town's Committee of Safety. As the former had already departed, the chairman of the Elizabethtown Committee, Robert Ogden, opened it and learned to his consternation "that an armed vessel with a detachment of marines & seamen was sent off from New York that day from the ships of war in New York to the transport ship." With Stirling already on his way and entirely unaware of the enemy's rescue effort, action was deemed of the utmost importance. The new intelligence was quite accurate, for Captain Hyde Parker, Jr., commander of HMS *Phoenix*, then at New York, upon finally receiving the report of the incoming ship lying off the Hook, had already dispatched a detail of fifteen men and a lieutenant in a pilot boat to assist. Unfortunately for *Blue Mountain Valley*, when the British party reached Sandy Hook, the ship had already departed for the rendezvous with Woolcombe, albeit only shortly before, and the reinforcement returned to report that there were no vessels in sight.[15]

Unaware that the enemy pilot boat had already turned back, Ogden convened a meeting of the Elizabethtown Committee at 6 p.m. and concluded that Stirling, now en route to seize the transport, was unaware of the enemy reinforcements sent to its aid. The Committee therefore resolved to dispatch a detachment of a hundred volunteers and three or four boats to assist him. The move to send an additional force, however, may not have been entirely founded upon altruistic or patriotic motives. An express rider was sent ahead notifying Stirling of the Committee's action, but more specifically "to remind" him that the volunteers should receive a share of the prize "according to the regulations that were or should be made by the Continental Congress."[16]

The volunteers were quickly furnished with three boats, ammunition, provisions, and about 110 stand of arms (80 for the townsmen who enlisted in the expedition and 30 for Stirling's New Jersey Continentals). Between midnight and 1 a.m., January 23, Ogden's small boat armada was ready to sail but, obstructed by tide and ice, could proceed no further than the New York Narrows. They thus set out with a fair wind by way of Perth Amboy, and about 2 a.m. fell in with Stirling's expedition, now enlarged to forty men strong, which had just impressed into service a local pilot boat shallop named *York* belonging to one Michael Kearney. Many of the newcomers were gentlemen from Elizabethtown who "voluntarily came on this service under the command of Col. [Elias] Dayton & Co. [Edward] Thomas." The volunteers, by now cold and tired, were already beginning to lose heart. Hoping to retain as many as possible, and expecting the transport to be richly laden, Stirling promised a bonus of £100 sterling to the first man who boarded her.[17]

The volunteers stayed and the expedition pressed on. At sunrise, from the masthead of one of the boats, a lookout spied a ship at sea about six leagues southeast of Sandy Hook, and the little flotilla immediately stood for her. At 10 a.m. the *ad hoc* adventurers boarded *Blue Mountain Valley* and took her without opposition. They were soon dismayed to find the ship laden with little more than coal, porter, and sauerkraut. Lord Stirling, in particular, was disappointed, having expected a vessel filled to the railings with valuable arms and ammunition. But a prize was a prize and she was now his responsibility. By the following day, he had brought her to anchor off Amboy, with the intention of carrying her into the sound between Staten Island and the mainland.[18]

Dempster later recounted his own version of the capture, albeit with some inflated figures, as follows:

> . . . they fitted out four vessels, with about 60 men each, in all upwards of 200 men, an overmatch as you may easily believe for a ship with four small guns, and sixteen hands in all, after being 13 weeks at sea, and hardly able to keep the ship from sinking. When the vessels made their appearance, I took them for vessels from the men-of-war, the officer commanded the party being dressed in the uniform of a Lieutenant of the Navy, and I did not then know my mate was taken prisoner. They boarded the ship in every part, and carried her about ten or twelve miles up a river [from] where two of the King's ships lay, to a place called Elizabeth-Town, making a prize of the ship and cargo and myself a prisoner on parole.[19]

Miraculously, Stirling's expedition had not encountered the British force sent out from New York to bring in *Blue Mountain Valley*. Ogden preferred to consider it the

An east prospect of the City of Philadelphia as viewed from the New Jersey shore of the Delaware River (detail), heart of the Pennsylvania privateering industry that flourished along the mid-Atlantic seaboard during the American Revolution. Published by Thomas Jeffreys, near Charing Cross, London, 1768. Courtesy Prints and Photographs Division, Library of Congress.

"great good fortune" of those who had returned to the city "not having discovered the ship to the great disappointment of our people."[20]

News of the capture spread north and south immediately, the scope of action and value of the prize increasing with every mile and at every telling. Within hours, Philadelphia was abuzz with titillating news of the taking of a rich enemy ship on the high seas, in freezing weather, by landlubbers in small boats carrying little more than sidearms. Intelligence was also immediately forwarded to Vice Admiral Molyneux Shuldham, who received "the disagreeable news that the ship *Blue Mountain Valley* loaded with coals, porter, &ca was seized off Sandy hook by William Alexander commonly called Lord Sterling he having arm'd two sloops from Elizabeth Town for that purpose."[21]

As word of the capture continued to radiate, Stirling personally saw to the ship itself. The day after the capture he had brought her into the sound near Blazing Star, where he promptly ran her aground. By lightening, however, he was able to have her refloated again by the morning of January 26 and brought up to Elizabethtown Point. He then ordered her sails unbent and cargo offloaded, and brought into the town "for the use of the Continental Congress." The ship was now placed under the charge of Captain William Rogers, who had been recommended to the colonel by the New York Committee of Safety, and assigned a guard from a detachment of the New Jersey regiment. Rogers was instructed to see that Dempster's private property, and that of his officers and men, "be preserved and secured until such further order as aforesaid." A manifest and bill of lading was forwarded to Congress. Stirling recognized Captain Dempster's brother George as a "valuable friend of North America in the House of Commons . . . a sensible genteel man, all of whose property, about £100. Sterling is on board," and requested that the property in question be restored to him. He also requested that the trifles belonging to the mate and men be returned, "for they behaved extremely well, and were very useful to us in working the ship; and the sailors are now assisting the soldiers in unlading her." Congress consented to his wishes on January 31. As for his own efforts, and those of the men who aided him, Congress loudly applauded Stirling for his "alertness, activity and good conduct . . . and the forwardness and spirit of the men, and others, from Elizabeth town, who voluntarily assisted him in taking the ship *Blue Mountain Valley*." Having been made aware of the nature of the cargo, Congress ordered that all lading that was perishable be immediately disposed of by sale.[22]

Stirling was apparently impressed with the prize, if not her cargo, and echoing the New York Committee's comments on her strengths proposed that she be converted into a man-of-war. On January 28, he wrote the committee: "the ship is about 100 feet long on the main deck, and will commodiously carry 20 six & 10 three pounders."[23] The committee, in its current situation of course, with the Royal Navy breathing down its neck, could do little if anything about outfitting and arming a man-of-war.

By February 2, the cargo of *Blue Mountain Valley*, with the exception of the coal, had been unloaded and brought up to Elizabethtown. Stirling patiently waited a week for a directive from Congress regarding what should be done about the prize, but was rapidly growing restive about the delay. In the meantime, Captain Dempster actively lobbied for his return to England, while several of his crew expressed their willingness to work their ways home or through the West Indies. Congress soon ordered the captain's release—but did little about the ship.[24]

The behavior of Captain Dempster, much less the capture of his ship, was not well received in British government circles. Governor William Tryon of New York, in exile now aboard the ship *Duchess of Gordon*, then lying off the city, informed Lord Dartmouth that the captain's actions carried "the appearance of carelessness, if no more." Tryon wasn't the only one disturbed by the affair. Captain Hyde Parker, Jr., commander of HMS *Phoenix*, one of the warships anchored off Gravesend, ordered the pilot boat *York*, which had been impressed into service by Stirling, confiscated "on the pretence of her having been employed on that service." Although the owner, Michael Kearney, protested vigorously that his boat had been "seized upon" by Stirling, Parker was unimpressed and "thought it proper to seize upon her" himself, leaving it to Vice Admiral Shuldham to determine "how far they can justify such an act of piracy." As a final touch, he chose to employ *York* as the very vehicle to carry the bad news to the admiral, and with predictable results.[25]

The word piracy had finally appeared in regards to a ship capture. It was a word that would soon be used to address all American actions on the high seas, and especially in regards to that ancient mode of warfare that had been employed by all European powers since Medieval times—namely privateering.

III

The Privateering Resolves

"The sea will swarm with men-of-war & some privateers before long."

Blue Mountain Valley remained in the care of the Elizabethtown Committee of Safety throughout the early days of February 1776. Her lading of porter and beans was safely stored ashore, but the potatoes, which were mostly rotted, and the coal, were still aboard. Dempster and his crew, as yet unaware that Congress had ordered their release—undoubtedly out of respect for the captain's brother, a Member of Parliament sympathetic to the American cause, as much as a consequence of the crew's good behavior—were held as prisoners "at large" and were free to roam at will. Yet, Ogden was concerned about the security of the vessel and the coal aboard, which was "in great demand for making arms." He feared that an armed force dispatched at night from New York, only fourteen miles away, might try to destroy the ship.[1]

Ogden wrote to John Hancock on February 10, prodding Congress to consider the danger to the ship and its cargo, and to decide in what manner it might be disposed of. Perhaps a little too eager for the monetary benefits of the expedition, he was particularly solicitous that the prize money be distributed quickly among the captors in a correct and fair manner, even before the prize itself was placed up for auction, and provided a list of those who had taken part in the action. He also enclosed a bill for the wages of his men and requested that address be given as to the status of Dempster's adventure, or share in the voyage, which amounted to £120, and what should be done about it.[2]

The formal manner of libeling and condemning the prize and cargo, handling any possible appeal by the owner, and distributing any profits derived from the sale of the vessel and its lading had already been set by Congress on November 25, 1775. Yet it was clear that the actual specialized judicial mechanism for addressing such captures, namely Admiralty Courts, were lacking in almost every colony in which the rebellion had taken hold, including New Jersey. The pressure on Congress, as exhibited by the *Blue Mountain Valley* affair, to do something, anything, for such events—already being replicated in New England—were most certainly going to continue up and down the eastern seaboard. Congress was, in fact, quite cognizant of the consequences of inadequate handling of prize cases in the absence of a formal Court of Admiralty, as it was of the need to specifically secure this particular ship and its lading. Until now, with many still believing an agreement might yet be worked out with the Mother Country, Congress and most of the colonies had addressed such issues haphazardly, on a case for case basis. The establishment of Admiralty Courts, some felt, would make rapprochement impossible. The *Blue Mountain Valley* affair, however, would help tip the scales towards concerted action, albeit not without some fits and starts.

On Tuesday, February 20, Samuel Chase of Maryland was appointed by Congress to draw up a form, which was soon revised by Richard Smith of New Jersey, for the disposal of the prize and cargo lying at Elizabethtown, "no judge of the Admiralty being yet appointed in New Jersey." The move served as a spur, for the matter concerning the institution of Courts of Admiralty was finally brought forward and formally debated for the first time. But "the necessity of taking the whole government from the King's substitutes [colonial Vice Admiralty Courts] was descanted upon and postponed." The issue of the actual security of the ship was again set aside, but could not be long ignored. On February 25, Lord Stirling requested Congress, through New Jersey delegate William Livingston, to provide on behalf of Michael Kearney restitution for the confiscation of his boat by the British.[3] Two days later the convention finally resolved to have all the prize cargo landed and secured in some safe place to await further orders of Congress. On March 19, Congress finally passed another resolution that the value of the "passage boat" *York* be made good to the boat's owner.[4]

Viewing the apparent tepid Congressional action regarding *Blue Mountain Valley*, New Jersey only feebly attempted to tackle the issues at hand. On February 29, when the talks resumed, the New Jersey Provincial Congress resolved only to defer the thorny issue of the establishment of a Court of Admiralty until the next day. Thus, the debate was again postponed. The body met at New Brunswick on March 2 and resolved that all transport vessels having on board troops, arms, munitions, clothing, provisions, or any other military stores for the British Army or Navy, or those carrying any goods, wares, or merchandise for their use that "now are, or hereafter shall be within any of the United Colonies," would be liable to seizure and confiscation. Applying the resolution retroactively, it ordered that *Blue Mountain Valley* "shall be and is hereby confiscated to the use of the captors, pursuant to the general directions for distribution, resolved on by the said honorable Continental Congress."[5]

The New Jersey Provincial Congress, lacking a formalized protocol in such matters, resolved that the ship be disposed of by two agents, one of whom was to be appointed by Lord Stirling, and the other by the Elizabethtown Committee of Safety. All necessary charges and expenses arising from guarding and securing the prize, and supporting her seamen while in captivity, were to be deducted from the proceeds of the sale. The amount produced by the sale of ship and cargo, after expenses, was to be divided among all of the captors, including the militia sent out by the Elizabethtown Committee and the Continental Army soldiers who had participated in the expedition. All of the goods, wares, and merchandise found aboard that belonged to Captain Dempster, the mate, and seamen were to be permitted to go any place "they may think proper (his Majesty's fleet or army only excepted)." And finally, it was recommended that the captors "make some gratuity to each of the seamen on board, to enable them to travel to some other parts in pursuit of business."[6]

The sale of *Blue Mountain Valley*, with all of her tackle, apparel, and cargo "consisting of a quantity of excellent New Castle coal, and a quantity of London porter, beans, peas, bread, flour, beef, pork, cannon, powder, and a number of articles to[o] tedious to mention" was advertised in the *New York Gazette* on Monday, March 18, the same day the public vendue was held in Elizabethtown.[7]

It had been a laborious process to get this far, but the corner had finally been turned. News of the bold capture, which had in fact been carried out without opposition, by landsmen in small boats, in the immediate vicinity of powerful British warships, and without loss, had continued to spread. Along the Delaware, particularly in Philadelphia, appetites already aroused by the successes of "Washington's Navy" and the private armed vessels in New England throughout the fall and winter of 1775–1776, had been keenly whetted by the *Blue Mountain Valley* affair closer to home. Then, on February 26, no fewer than fifteen prizes taken by the New Englanders were advertised to be tried at Ipswich, Massachusetts, and a dozen more at Plymouth on March 25.[8] By the time the titillating news arrived in Philadelphia, pressure on Congress to formally authorize the issuance of letters of marque and to embrace the establishment of state-promised Courts of Admiralty had already been growing by the hour. Now Congress appeared ready to act.

• • •

Despite the ultimate fate of *Blue Mountain Valley,* the ship's initial capture, combined with the earlier successes of the daring New Englanders on the high seas, did much to incite Pennsylvanians, particularly in Philadelphia, to aggressively press Congress to approve the fitting out of privateers in every province. On February 13, 1776, delegate Samuel Chase of Maryland notified the assembly that the following day he would move that Congress "recommend to all the colonies to fit out privateers." Though his move came to naught for unknown reasons, the public outcry for action was becoming incessant, particularly among the merchant community. Little more than a week later, the delegates were informed "that a petition to the Congress, is signing fast by the inhabitants of this city [Philadelphia], for leave to fit out privateers, and make reprisals on all British vessels, to indemnify them for the losses they have sustained by the depredations of British men of war. Indeed it seems hard very hard that Britain is seizing all American vessels and that Americans are not permitted to return the compliment." The petition was formally presented on March 1 by a large delegation of Philadelphians requesting that Congress take action and grant leave for privateers and letters of marque from all of the colonies to seize ships of Great Britain, Ireland, and other British dominions.[9]

The issue of Congressional authorization of privateering was finally racing towards a head. Even Robert Morris, who, as the new chairman of both the Secret Committee of Correspondence and the Marine Committee that managed most of the commercial, maritime, and naval affairs of Congress, personally opposed privateering (at least at first), predicted that on both sides ". . . the sea will swarm with men-of-war & some privateers before long." Indeed, he noted with concern, Loyalists on the West Indian island of Antigua were already pressing the Crown for commissions to fit out their own vessels against the Americans.[10]

On March 13, the issue returned to the floor, and from noon to 4 p.m. Congress vigorously debated the merits of the petitions for allowing privateers to cruise against the British. Samuel Chase was armed and ready, and offered a set of propositions governing the measure. George Wythe of Virginia suggested a preamble to the Chase proposal. The move proved popular among many, but not all, of the delegates. Although their motives are uncertain, Thomas Willing of Pennsylvania and Thomas Johnson of Maryland were vehemently opposed. John Jay of New York was a strong supporter of the issuance of letters of marque, but questioned privateering on its moral merits. The debate resumed on Saturday, March 16. Jay offered his own set of propositions that went nowhere. Benjamin Franklin warned that without a formal declaration of war preceding any resolution on privateering, American privateers would be simply construed by the British as pirates. Again the issue was unresolved and debate was ordered to continue the following Monday.[11]

When the new week began, the hotly contested privateering issue was finally determined "after an able debate" on March 18, and several resolutions were adopted. The first of these gave leave to commission privateers and letters of marque to cruise against British property, but the vote was not unanimous. New Hampshire, Massachusetts, Rhode Island, Connecticut, New York, Virginia, and North Carolina had voted for adoption while, surprisingly, Pennsylvania and Maryland, provinces with substantial maritime interests that would benefit from the actions, were opposed. The reasons for their objections are only speculative. Ireland had been expunged from the target list, as were other British dominions, which struck Samuel Chase of Maryland and Richard Smith of New York as absurd. "Why make war upon only part of the King's subjects," Smith wrote, "especially since the Irish Parliament had declared itself wholly against the Americans and had only recently approved the King's request to transfer 4,000 British troops stationed in Ireland to American soil." If such was his reason for objection, it was not because of the resolution in principle, but owing to its lack of inclusiveness. The remainder of the colonies, New Jersey, Delaware, South Carolina, and Georgia, were deemed not sufficiently represented in Congress to vote.[12]

The following day, the resolutions concerning privateering were embodied in a report of the committee of the whole and finally agreed to. Wythe and two others were directed by the committee to prepare a formal Preamble justifying the proposed Act, although some restrictions had yet to be resolved. On March 22, Wythe presented a draft of the Preamble to Congress and, with Richard Henry Lee of Virginia, moved for an even more stunning amendment to the resolution itself wherein the King of England rather than the Ministry "was made the author of our miseries." Here, for the first time, was a formal attempt to lay blame for the current hostilities and the grievances that led to them at the foot of the British monarchy itself, and not simply Parliament, as was hitherto the case. It was a symbolic gesture at first, but one destined to gain ground in the months ahead.

The chief supporters of the amendment were Wythe, Lee, Chase, Jonathan Dickson Serjeant of New Jersey, and Benjamin Harrison of Virginia. Jay, Johnson, and James Wilson of Pennsylvania vigorously opposed the amendment on the supposition that such a statement would effectually sever the monarchy from the colonies forever. There could be no chance of a negotiated settlement, no going back, or returning to the protective fold of the Mother Country if it were adopted, and some were not prepared to make the final leap to independence just yet. The alternative was certain to be a long and bloody fight. The debate was heated and lasted four hours, until Maryland interposed its veto and put the issue to rest until the following day. The rising tide of opinion, however, could not long be restrained.

Finally, on March 23, Congress passed several resolutions authorizing privateering and formally entered them into the journals of Congress. Though the issue of laying blame upon the monarchy was put aside, the momentous privateering resolves would one day be widely regarded as a milestone on the road to American independence, preceding by less than three weeks the equally significant decision of April 6 to open American ports for the first time to direct foreign trade.[13] As for the resolutions, although no one cared to make note of it, they followed the long accepted guidelines for privateering set down by the enemy himself!

Both the Preamble and the final Resolutions were comprehensive in scope.

Whereas the petitions of the United Colonies to the King, for the redress of great and manifest grievances, have not only been rejected, but treated with scorn and contempt, and the opposition to designs evidently formed to reduce them to state of servile subjection, and their necessary defense against hostile forces actually employed to subdue them, declared rebellion; And whereas an unjust war hath been commenced against them, which the commanders of the British fleets and armies have prosecuted, and still continue to prosecute, with their utmost vigor, and in a cruel manner; wasting, spoiling, and destroying the country, burning houses and defenseless towns, and exposing the helpless inhabitants to every misery, from the inclemency of the winter; and not only urging savages to invade the country, but instigating the negroes to murder their masters; And whereas the Parliament of Great Britain hath lately passed an Act, affirming these colonies to be in open rebellion, forbidding all trade and commerce with the inhabitants thereof, until they shall accept pardons, and submit to despotic rule, declaring their property, wherever found upon the water, liable to seizure and confiscation; and enacting, that what has been done there by virtue of the royal authority, were just and lawful acts, and shall be so deemed; from all which it is manifest, that the iniquitous scheme, concerted to deprive them of the liberty they have a right to by the law of nature and the English constitution, will be pertinaciously pursued. It being therefore necessary to provide for their defense and security, and justifiable to make reprisals upon their enemies, and otherwise to annoy them, according to the laws and usages of Nations, the Congress, trusting that such of their friends in Great Britain (of whom it is confessed there are many entitled to applause and gratitude for their patriotism and benevolence, and in whose favor a discrimination of property cannot be made) as shall suffer by captures, will impute it to the authors of our common calamities, Do Declare and Resolve, as followeth, to wit:

Resolved, That, the inhabitants of these colonies be permitted to fit out armed vessels to cruise on the enemies of these United Colonies.

Resolved, That all ships and other vessels, their tackle, apparel, and furniture, and all goods, wares, and merchandises, belonging to any inhabitants of Great Britain, taken on the high seas, or between high and low water mark, by any armed vessel, fitted out by and private person or persons, and to whom commissions shall be granted, and being libeled and prosecuted in any court erected for the trial of maritime affairs, in any of these colonies, shall be deemed and adjudged to be lawful prize; and after deducting and paying the wages of the seamen and mariners on board such captures, as are merchant ships and vessels, shall be entitled to, according to the terms of their contracts, until the time of the adjudication, shall be condemned to and for the use of the owner or owners, and the officers, marines, and mariners of such armed vessel, according to the rules and proportions as they shall agree on: Provided always, that this resolution shall not extend to any vessel bringing settlers arms, ammunition or warlike stores to and for the use of these colonies, or any of the inhabitants thereof, who are friends of the American cause, or to such warlike stores, or to the effects of the settlers.

Resolved, That all ships or vessels, with their tackle, apparel, and furniture, goods, wares, and merchandises, belonging to any inhabitants of Great Britain, as aforesaid, which shall be taken by any of the vessels of war of these United States, shall be deemed forfeited, and divided, after deducting and paying the wages of seamen and mariners, as aforesaid, in such manner and proportions as the assembly or convention of such colony shall direct.

Resolved, That all vessels, with their tackle, apparel, and furniture, and cargoes, belonging to the inhabitants of Great Britain, as aforesaid, and all vessels which may be employed in carrying supplies to the ministerial armies, which shall happen to be taken near the shores of any of these colonies, by the people of the country, or detachment from the army, shall be deemed lawful prizes, and the court of admiralty within the said colony is required, on condemnation thereof, to adjudge that all charges and expenses which may attend the capture and trial, be first paid out of the monies arising from the sales of the prizes, and the remainder equally divided among all those, who shall have been actually engaged and employed in taking the said prize. Provided, that where any detachments of the army shall have been employed as aforesaid, their part of the prize money shall be distributed among them in proportion to the pay of the officers and soldiers so employed.

Ordered, That the foregoing resolution be published.[14]

The privateering resolves were printed in the *Pennsylvania Gazette* on March 27, 1776, and heartily endorsed. John Adams for once crowed perhaps the loudest with delight. "The continental vessels, the provincial vessels, and letters of marque and privateers will be let loose upon British trade."[15]

• • •

Although the hard part of debating and passing resolutions to authorize privateering had been completed, there was still the fundamental business of the issuance of commissions. Congress resolved on April 3 that blank commissions for private ships of war and letters of marque and reprisal, signed by the President of Congress, were to be sent to the general assemblies, conventions, and councils or committees of safety in each of the United Colonies, "to be by them filled up and delivered to the persons intending to fit out such private ships of war, for making captures of British vessels and cargoes, who shall apply for the same." Blank bonds were sent along with the commissions and were to be posted by the owners to guarantee that captains of vessels would follow instructions provided by Congress to the letter or forfeit the amount of the bond. The signed bonds were to be returned to Congress. Each applicant for a commission was to produce in writing, on a form provided for the purpose, the name and tonnage of his vessel, the number of her guns and the weight of metal they fired, the names and residences of the owners, the names of the commander and other officers, the number of crewmen, and the quantity of provisions and warlike stores shipped. The document was to be delivered to the Secretary of Congress or the Clerk of the House of Representatives, convention, council, or committee of safety of the colony in which the vessel was to be commissioned. Before a commission could be granted, the commander would be required to deliver a bond, with sufficient sureties "in the penalty of five thousand dollars, if the vessel be of one hundred tons or under, or ten thousand dollars, if of a greater burthen," payable to the President of Congress, and to be held in trust for the use of the United Colonies. (In 1780, bond requirements would be raised to $20,000 for all vessels regardless of size.) Specific instructions were to be issued with each commission, and the holder would be held responsible to make reparations for all damages sustained "by any misconduct or unwarrantable proceedings of himself, or the officers or crew" of the vessel.

The Congressional instructions that were to be issued to every commander were standardized. Some articles were included for quite practical purposes. One third of every privateer's company was to be landsmen. This requirement was undoubtedly included to prevent drawing away all of the available experienced seamen from Continental and state navy service, as those services offered lower wages, tighter discipline, and far smaller shares of prize money, and were generally less inviting. The commander was authorized to attack by force of arms, subdue, and capture any vessel belonging to the inhabitants of Great Britain encountered on the high seas, or between the high water and low water mark of the shore, with the exception of vessels bringing persons intending to settle and reside in the United Colonies.

Also to go unmolested were vessels bringing arms, ammunition, and other warlike stores to the colonies for the use of the inhabitants who were considered friends to the American cause. All such vessels, however, might be subjected to "a peaceable search" and must provide satisfactory information on the ship's lading and destination. Any vessels carrying soldiers, arms, gunpowder, ammunition, provisions, or other goods considered contraband to any British forces, land or sea, were to be considered legitimate targets. All prizes and their ladings were to be taken to some convenient port of the United Colonies to permit proper proceedings before courts that were to be appointed "to hear and determine causes civil and maritime." The commander or one of his principal subordinates was also instructed to "bring or send the master and pilot; and one or more principal person or persons of the company of every ship or vessel" to a judge or judges of the aforesaid court as soon as possible after the capture, to be examined under oath regarding the "interest or property of the ship" and her ladings. All passes, sea briefs, charter parties, bills of lading, cockets, letters, and other documents and writings found on board were to be delivered to the judge proving the affidavit of the commander was produced "without fraud, addition, subduction or embezzlement." Every ship and cargo was to be preserved as taken until the court properly authorized a sentence and the capture was adjudged a lawful prize. "No selling, spoiling, wasting, or diminishing the same, or breaking bulk" was to be permitted until the court's judgment was made.

If any commander, officer, or crewman should "in cold blood, kill or maim, or by torture or otherwise, cruelly, inhumanly, and contrary to common usage, and the practice of civilized nations in war" any person aboard a prize, the offender was to be severely punished. At convenient opportunities, commanders were to send to Congress written accounts of captures made, including the number of captives, copies of the commander's journal, and any intelligence that may be discovered concerning the enemy's designs, or the destination, motions, and operations of his fleets or armies. No prisoners were to be ransomed, but were to be disposed of in a manner that Congress or the individual colony government should direct. All commanders were to observe the instructions given by Congress. Failure to adhere to instructions would result in the forfeiture of the commission, and the commander was to be held liable "to an action for breach of the condition" of his bond, and responsible to any party "grieved for damages sustained by such malversation."[16]

• • •

While Congress was fervently debating the pros and cons and then voting on the adoption of privateering as an acceptable mode of warfare against the Mother Country, British anger over the seizure and sale of *Blue Mountain Valley* was finally about to be vented. On the night of March 26, eight days after the sale of the ship's cargo, and only hours before the Congressional resolutions on privateering were published, the Royal Navy would have its revenge.

At 10 p.m., a cutting-out expedition was quietly launched from HMS *Phoenix* and *Asia*, then moored in Gravesend Bay and off Bedloe's Island (modern Liberty Island). The official objective of the well-armed and well-manned small boat operation was to rescue another rebel prize called *Lady Gage*. The ship had been impounded while at anchor nearby earlier in the season and had been recently taken to a wharf at Elizabethtown, from which it was expected she would sail for Philadelphia to be fitted out as a man-of-war. The cutting out party was directed to tow her to safety, and then proceed to board and destroy *Blue Mountain Valley*. With Hyde Parker personally directing the expedition, two boats under the command of a lieutenant were dispatched to cut out *Lady Gage* or, if that proved impossible, to set her afire.

At the same time, the lieutenant was to send a boat to Elizabethtown Point, where *Blue Mountain Valley* lay, "and if the officer found her unguarded, he was to board her and set the ship on fire." Both orders were executed with "punctuality and without loss."[17]

Lady Gage, "a fine new ship, and a remarkably fast sailing one," was taken without opposition, cut from her moorings, and towed to Gravesend Bay. The raiders then turned their attentions to the ill-fated transport. "The men-of-war's men set fire to the ship *Blue Mountain Valley*," according to William Livingston, but the blaze "was happily extinguished." That the British had, in fact, achieved their goal, however, is suggested by the total disappearance of the ship *Blue Mountain Valley* from the historic record thereafter. Now it was the Americans' turn to be angered and bluster about revenge. "If they appear on such another frolic," wrote Livingston to Robert Treat Paine the following day, "I believe the town's men here will make them repent it."[18]

• • •

Captain John Hamilton Dempster secured passage to Europe at his earliest opportunity aboard the ship *Catherine*, Captain Moore, bound for Newry, Ireland, where he arrived on May 5, 1776. "And happy was I," he wrote, "to get away." Most of his men made it to New York "where all was in confusion," as many Loyalists prepared to desert the city. The ship's carpenter offered himself to a vessel bound for Belfast.[19] By then, however, the *Blue Mountain Valley* affair was already but a forgotten footnote of recent history. Yet, it had been instrumental in spurring the American Revolution into an entirely new phase. Privateering had been legitimized, at least in the eyes of Americans. Now, the remote coastal inlets and hamlets along New Jersey's Atlantic frontier were about to become a centerpiece of warfare on the mid-Atlantic seaboard, with an intensity unlike any ever experienced before in the region.

–IV–

First Patrol

"To pay the pirates for their usage."

Early on in the war, both the British and Americans understood that the sparsely populated New Jersey coast from Cape May to Sandy Hook, and the myriad complex of remote inlets, sounds, and rivers between, would prove of significant importance to the eventual course of the expanding conflict. Yet, few anticipated that its primary role would be in the growth of American privateering on the mid-Atlantic seaboard.

The New York Committee of Safety was, perhaps, the first to recognize the strategic value of these inlets and waters, albeit only as they related to the security and supply of New York City and Long Island. They were particularly concerned about the safety of Egg Harbor, New Jersey, "as a place of debarkation for certain necessities." The "necessities" from that place were both strategically and commercially significant. Iron, for the manufacture of armaments as well as for domestic goods, was produced at several iron works, such as at Batsto on the Mullica River. Lumber, from the surrounding "Pine Barrens" was an important product needed to fire the furnaces of the iron works. It was also deemed absolutely necessary for the British sugar and rum trade with the West Indies. Indeed, the importance of an embargo on lumber shipped from Egg Harbor to British trading firms was noted in a communication from an America trader on St. Eustatia in April: "Lumber is £40 per M. and in making sugar hogsheads every second stave is made out of boards brought from Egg Harbour, and they [the British] will not have hogsheads for rum nor molasses; and the Congress would do right to forbid any lumber being shipped from any part of the Continent."[1]

Fearful that the British might easily seal up or destroy the little ports from which such important raw materials as iron and lumber flowed, the committee recommended to the New York delegates to the Continental Congress on January 22, 1776, the same day as the capture of *Blue Mountain Valley*, that a small redoubt be constructed at Egg Harbor with barracks for two hundred men and garrisoned by a proper captain's guard. The fort, they believed, should be situated so as to command the entrance to the harbor and be provided with cisterns to take rain water for drinking. Timber, particularly cedar, was plentiful and would answer the needs for all necessary woodwork. To complete the defense, the committee suggested that a row galley mounting a 6-pounder in her stem should be provided to patrol not just at Little Egg Harbor, but all of the New Jersey inlets.[2]

The New York Committee of Safety acted properly by submitting their request (albeit veiled as a suggestion) to the Continental Congress. Technically, though not in fact, the ardent Loyalist Governor William Franklin, illegitimate son of Benjamin Franklin, though placed under house arrest by New Jersey militiamen in January 1776, still administered the government of New Jersey. Thus, the interference in the affairs or upon the territory of New Jersey, which contained a substantial Loyalist population, especially along the coastal sounds, was still a touchy problem even though the war was raging in other quarters and would most certainly spread. The questions of payment, maintenance, and whose troops would form the garrison was thus tactfully deferred to the honorable delegates to the Continental Congress. After all, reasoned some, why should New York, the next most likely target of British military strategists and already bereft of every military article, including grapeshot for the few cannon in the province, pay for and man a fort in New Jersey?

In April 1776, General Washington, fresh from his recent victory at Boston, arrived at New York to commence preparations for the expected enemy offensive against the city and the Hudson Valley. One of his first initiatives was to begin fitting out another fleet, similar to but even smaller than his little "navy" employed in Massachusetts, to begin patrolling neighboring waters. Aided by the New York Committee of Safety, he ordered the sloop *General Mifflin* and the schooner *General Schuyler* be readied for service, which was no small order given the paucity of supplies. Within a short time, a number of other vessels, either entirely or partially under his or the Committee's control, were operating in New York and contiguous New Jersey waters.

Not until May, however, soon after the formal resolutions of Congress concerning privateering were enacted, did one of Washington's senior officers, General Israel Putnam from his headquarters in New York, begin to take up the slack in preparedness for the Atlantic frontier of New Jersey and New York. He began by suggesting to the commander in chief a specific plan for the protection of the coast, the interdiction of supplies bound for the Royal Navy, and the protection of American supply and munitions ships. The scheme called for the dispersal and stationing along the coast of a number of armed sloops, schooners, and whaleboats that had been procured or requisitioned by New York but manned by the Continental Army. The armed sloop *General Mifflin* and four whaleboats would patrol between Barren Island and Hog Island Inlet, near Rockaway, Long Island. The armed schooner *General Schuyler* and two whaleboats would patrol Fire Island Inlet. The sloop *Hester* and a number of whaleboats under the command of Lieutenant Benjamin Tupper would be assigned to protect the western shore of New York Bay from Amboy to Sandy Hook. The schooner *General Putnam*, a lightly armed vessel, carrying only a dozen swivel guns and manned by thirty seamen under the command of Captain Thomas Creiger, was selected "to proceed down to Shroseury [Shrewsbury] Inlet, Shirk [Shark] River, and Cranberry Inlet even down to Egg Harbor on the western shore near 140 miles range from Sandy Hook" to protect the southwestern approaches to Long Island. Putnam believed that the inlets on the Jersey coast would offer protection to the schooner in case she should be overmatched and would serve as good points from which to sally out to surprise supply ships bound for the Royal Navy blockaders off New York.[3]

Putnam's plan was farsighted for with the British buildup for the impending invasion of New York, and the blockades of New York Bay and the mouth of the Delaware already a reality, remote places such as Little Egg Harbor, with its overland route to Philadelphia, had become doubly important. Indeed, the precarious viability of the Delaware as a safe avenue of entry was already becoming a moot point. Well aware of the strategic importance of the Delaware, Pennsylvania had begun to build and field a small navy of its own, which

Israel Putnam, by Esnauts and Rapilly. Courtesy Prints and Photographs Division, Library of Congress.

was, together with a contingent of the infant Continental Navy and a system of forts and batteries along the river approach to Philadelphia, expected to protect the principal avenue to one of America's greatest seaports and seat of the rebel government. Yet the constant British blockade of Delaware Bay between Capes May and Henlopen, which controlled the main channel approaches to the river's entrance, had already extracted a dreadful toll on rebel shipping. Skirmishing and open combat were inevitable.[4]

In two successive days of fighting on May 8 and 9, a force of thirteen Pennsylvania Navy row galleys challenged and ultimately drove off two powerful British men-of-war, HMS *Roebuck* and *Liverpool*, from the mouth of Christiana Creek, near Wilmington, Delaware. Yet, the vulnerability of the Delaware itself was painfully evident to all. Although the mightiest navy on the planet had been bloodied, it was only a matter of time before it returned in force to extract revenge.[5]

General William Howe arrived off Sandy Hook on June 25, 1776, with the small vanguard of an army destined to grow to massive proportions. Seven days later he would land unopposed on Staten Island with 9,300 troops. By August 12, thirty-two thousand men would be encamped there, forming the largest single military body to be assembled at one location in America during the Revolution. On August 22, he disembarked 15,000 troops on Long Island and five days later defeated Washington's 10,000-man army at the Battle of Brooklyn. The seizure of New York on September 15, following the paralyzing American defeats during the Long Island Campaign, would usher in a seven-year occupation of the city and, much to the discomfort of American patriots everywhere, witness its rapid conversion to the most important British naval base on the American seaboard.[6]

Once British control of the city established an environment to which refugee Loyalists could return, those whose loyalties were uncertain could now come out and openly declare for the Crown. Eventually, it was also to become the primary base for Loyalist privateering on the continent, although not nearly as quickly as many had hoped. The road to securing official approval for such endeavors was, indeed, anything but easy and was directly hindered by the Prohibitory Act of 1775. The Act, which had been passed, in concert with King George III's proclamation of August 23, 1775, to subdue the rebellion by decree authorizing a blockade of all rebel territory, also prohibited all manner of trade and commerce in each of the thirteen colonies. The objective was, of course, to destroy the rebel economy, making it impossible to continue the insurgency. Any ships found trading would be considered, in effect, enemies to the Crown and forfeited to His Majesty. For the Loyalists in New York City, concentrated on an island of fealty situated in a colony divided in its allegiances, the situation was frustrating: New York was technically considered by the government to be in a state of rebellion, which meant that they could conduct neither open trade, as their colony fell under the strictures of the Act, nor privateering, which had yet to be authorized by Parliament despite initiatives to that end by William Tryon, New York's governor in exile.[7]

With the Crown's embargo on all exports in effect and only naval stores, provisions and certain commodities required by the navy, army, and civilian populace permitted to be imported under special government license, trading restrictions quickly began to prove debilitating to those who were sacrificing all for their monarch. It was more than discomfort that caused a degree of chafing between the Navy command and New York's civilian officialdom, including those who served in the Chamber of Commerce, the Superintendent of Pilots and Captains of the Port of New York, and later the Board of Loyalist Refugees. Though Vice Admiral Lord Viscount Richard Howe and his brother Major General Sir William Howe had been allowed unrestricted power to suspend the Prohibitory Act for any section of the colony that they deemed to be in a state of peace with the Mother Country, and with a mighty army and navy to back them up, the two siblings never bothered to do so. Indeed, with the admiral serving as naval commander-in-chief in a metropolis deemed a military district, with powers superceding even Governor Tryon's (as civil government had been suspended), and with the authority to establish his own trade restrictions if necessary, relax those extant if he saw fit or necessary, and even authorize privateering if he thought it might be advantageous to the war effort, he proved completely indolent except in cases beneficial to his own interests.[8]

Thus, it was not surprising that New Jersey's Atlantic frontier would prove of merit to the privateering war, as would its value in myriad other ways. Captain Creiger, who eventually took up a semi-permanent station there in that pivotal summer of 1776, was informed, as were other naval officers as well were informed of the value of its countless recesses as sanctuaries and places from which covert operations might be launched.

In their instructions to Continental Navy commanders and vessels chartered by the Secret Committee of Correspondence, the Marine Committee of the Continental Congress soon began to regularly recommend both Cape May and Little Egg Harbor as places to send prizes into or in which they could seek safety from either inclement weather or enemy forces of superior size. On May 22, the sloop *Montgomery*, Captain William Rogers commanding and belonging to the short-lived New York Navy, became the first American warship to pay a visit to Little Egg Harbor, although only to take on wood and water.[9] John Barry, captain of the Continental Navy brig *Lexington*, was the first known Continental naval officer to take advantage of the haven at Egg Harbor, proceeding there in early July 1776 to heave down his ship preparatory to a long cruise.

Before long, the Navy had begun sending prizes and prisoners in as well. On July 13, when Captain Lambert Wickes, commander of the Continental brig *Reprisal*, captured the Liverpool schooner *Peter*, captained by John Muckelno, en route from St. Vincents with rum, sugar, coffee, cocoa, and cotton, he decided to send her into "either of the Egg Harbors, if she can get in there, if not into any other port on the coast."[10] Captain John Paul Jones, on a cruise out of Boston in the Continental sloop *Providence*, arrived a bit later in the month with the schooner *First Attempt* under convoy. His selection of Little Egg Harbor, into which he slipped on the night of July 29, as a place of refuge was not one of choice but necessity. "I should not have put in here," he informed John Hancock, President of Congress from a safe anchorage in the harbor, "had not the wind been directly contrary with an appearance of bad weather and none of us well acquainted on this dangerous coast." Nevertheless, Captain Jones had sanctuary when he needed it.[11]

In early August, Captain Barry would send one of his first prizes into Egg Harbor. Soon afterwards, a vessel sent to the West Indies on the account of Congress to procure military hardware, put into the harbor laden with 600 stand of arms and 10 tons of powder.[12]

In the meantime, Congress finally took some action of its own for the defense of the harbor. On June 24, more than five months after the submission of the proposal for a fort and naval defense, the Congressional committee appointed to consider which harbors in North America were important enough to require fortifications resolved "that the Marine Committee be empowered and instructed to build, man, and equip two large row galleys for the defense of Little Egg Harbor, so called in the colony of New Jersey." No mention was made, however, about the construction of the earlier proposed fort.[13]

• • •

Throughout the summer of 1776, it was *General Putnam*'s duty to remain stationed at the treacherous entrance of Little Egg Harbor. Captain Creiger was specifically charged with the mission of protecting the inlet, as well as the vessels and important facilities within, including the strategically important iron works on the Mullica, at Batsto, from enemy intruders. The task would not be easy given the enormous increase in the number of British cruisers at Sandy Hook and the troop buildup for the Long Island Campaign. On July 5, while on patrol nine miles south of the bar at Little Egg Harbor Inlet, Creiger saw two sails to the northward. The wind being light, he ordered *Putnam* under oars to proceed toward the vessels to investigate. Finally, a breeze from the south came to his

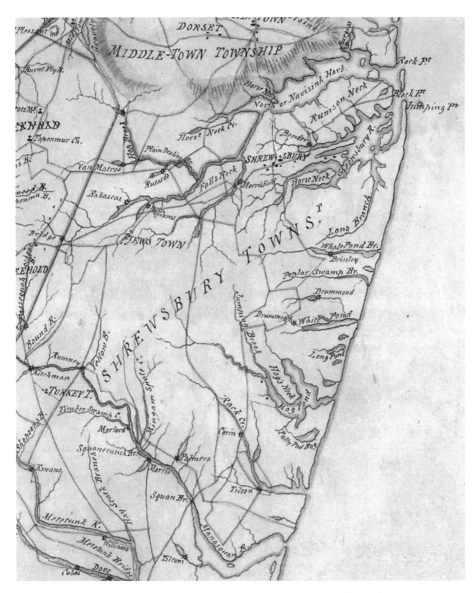

The New Jersey coast from Navesink Harbor to Manasquan, ca. 1769. Detail from *Three maps* [i.e. map on 3 sheets] *of northern New Jersey, with reference to the boundary between New York and New Jersey.* Courtesy Geography and Map Division, Library of Congress.

aid and he commenced an eleven-hour chase of what he believed to be enemy merchantmen. When the Americans finally overhauled one of their intended prey, however, they were in for an unwelcome surprise: the ship proved to be a man-of-war, incorrectly assumed to be a British privateer of twenty guns. The lightly armed *Putnam* was a poor match for the cruiser and, after taking a broadside at practically point blank range, was forced to run aground on the Jersey coast near the tip of Manasquan Inlet.

When fifty of the enemy seamen attempted to board the beached schooner, however, they were handled "so roughly that they were obliged to make a scandalous retreat." Even so, *Putnam* remained in place, out of reach but not out of range of the deeper draft warship, and suffered under a punishing long-range fire for five hours before the foe retired at dusk to the open sea. Upon inspection, the Americans counted seventeen holes in the schooner's mainsail and her hull had been injured from hits in several more places. Moreover, while she remained stranded, heavy surf was continually breaking over her, causing additional damage and structural weakness. Undaunted, Creiger managed to refloat his ship on the tide, limp into a nearby inlet, make repairs, and return to his station.[14]

Expecting a British supply fleet bound for New York, Creiger maintained a close watch on the waters off the south Jersey coast, hoping "to pay the pirates for their usage." Time and again the diligent officer was frustrated from achieving his revenge. "There appeared six sail one day, and seven sail the other day," he wrote in disgust, "but they are all large ships under strong convoys, so there was no doing anything with them." And to make matters worse, well-armed British frigates—against which he was certainly no match—continually prowled the coast and blockaded the Delaware, obliging many vessels with shallow enough draft to seek sanctuary amidst the shoally inlets on the Jersey coast.[15]

Creiger was finally awarded one more opportunity when he sighted a British frigate and her tender off Little Egg Harbor on August 20. The tender, a sloop, was armed with ten guns but considered fair game when the Americans discovered that she was more than a mile and a half from the frigate: it was just enough distance to allow her to be picked off before the man-of-war could respond. Yet, try as he might, Creiger could not wean the servant from the master or induce her to take up the gauntlet. *Putnam* reluctantly was obliged to give up the chase.[16]

The little New York schooner's career was destined to be short and would end on a most unhappy note. Conditions aboard the vessel, which was small and low in the water, had never been comfortable. Moreover, hard duty on the unprotected coast had taken a serious toll on both crew and ship. By the beginning of September provisions were all but expended despite Captain Creiger's repeated requests for supplies, all of which were ignored by the New York Convention. Then, on September 21, the Convention, which was then convened on the Hudson River at Fishkill, received a letter from Thomas Quigley, the ship's mate, dated September 4 at Cranberry Inlet, bearing a petition from sundry officers and marines aboard. From the context of the petition, it became immediately apparent that a mutiny had occurred. Another letter soon arrived from the skipper himself, who had quit the ship and returned home, recommending that owing to the vessel's poor condition it should no longer remain in service. He was promptly summoned to report in person, but owing to the absence of certain members of the assembly, the Convention was not convened and once again the captain returned to his home at Kings Bridge where he wrote out a full report to defend his actions.[17]

Thomas Creiger presented the sad state of affairs to the New York Convention on September 26. The epistle was instructive, at best, regarding the difficulties of protecting the coast, and disconcerting about the inability of the New York assembly to address the needs of men so employed.

> Gentlemen, I must, in the first place, acquaint you that my provisions being expended, having not more on board than will support the company about fifteen days; in the next place, my vessel being very small and low in the water, my greatest ordnance being twelve swivel-guns, the shrouds very old and not trustworthy, my best bower cable being very poor, the vessel very weak and leaky, which weakness proceeded from her lying on a bar and heavy surf breaking over her when I was run on shore by a man-of-war, the people much exposed when under sail, or even in hard rains the water pouring into their cabins, which prevents them of lying into their beds, (diligent search has been made in order to stop the leaks, but all to no purpose,) daily complaints being made by my people in regard to the vessel's condition, and the season of the year advancing towards cold and stormy weather; this, gentlemen, is certainly the condition of the vessel.[18]

His crew, Creiger complained, had neither shoes nor stockings, and the majority of them had not even a second shirt for their backs to face the chill of early autumn. No money had been advanced to them nor had they any but that which they had brought in their own private purses. Although he had applied for fresh meat, none had been provided. Worse, there was no rum, "which has occasioned much disturbance on board." Indeed, when they insisted they be provided a half pint per day, the same allowance as provided aboard Continental Navy vessels, they had become surly. "A riot was made just before I left the vessel in regard to their allowance of rum," he wrote, "in which affair I was obliged to make use of my authority amongst some of the principal ringleaders, upon which some of them have undertaken to complain of my conduct to your Honours by letter."

Creiger was incensed by the complaints against him, issued by the likes of a common boatswain, carpenter, or gunner, "men who sacrifice everything that is dear to them for a single can of grog; men whom I have picked up and put in office on purpose to have the vessel manned, and as the vessel is but very small I was glad to pick up any trash." He took some consolation in the fact that none of his principal officers, Lieutenant Thomas Quigley, Second Lieutenant David Walker, Master Eliakim Little, and Mate Cornelius French, were among the complainants for they were "men of good families and characters, hearty in the cause of liberty."

Creiger recommended that the vessel be laid up as unfit for any further service during the present season, for to keep her longer in commission, he felt, "will only be a great expense, without the gleam of any profit or service . . . on that part of the coast, where the vessel is, [and] only be picking the publick's pocket, as nothing is to be met with there but frigates, sloops-of-war, and large tenders, which we are not able to engage." Though he personally wished to continue to serve in the present cause he did not wish to do so as commander of *General Putnam*, and recommended the accounts of the vessel be settled and her crew paid off, all matters that he chose to leave to the Convention.[19]

The Convention appointed a committee to assess the situation and make recommendations. Nearly two weeks later, on October 7, the committee recommended that the officers and crew of the feisty little schooner *General Putnam* be paid off, and the vessel, together with her arms, cannon, ammunition, boats, tackle, rigging, and furniture, be immediately sold. The assembly so resolved and an agent was immediately appointed for the purpose.[20]

For nearly a month, coastal New Jersey would have neither state nor Continental patrols or guards.

• • •

Though many Continental and various state navy warships were to call at Little Egg Harbor during the ensuing years of the American Revolution, General Putnam was the only known vessel of war to have actually engaged in protecting the harbor, though several were assigned the task. Indeed, as early as July 17, 1776, events were already underway that would lead to the eventual abandonment of the plan to position two row galleys at the harbor for its defense. The massive enemy buildup at Staten Island, both in troops and warships, had frightened the Continental government sufficiently enough to warrant a recommendation to the New Jersey Convention "to cause all stock on the seacoast, which they shall apprehend to be in danger of falling into the hands of the enemy, to be immediately removed, and driven back into the country to a safe place."[21]

It was obvious that protection was required at more important locations. On July 30, for instance, General Hugh Mercer, writing from Perth Amboy, where a substantial community of Loyalists resided, and justifiably feeling that region to be in peril, requested that row galleys be built on the Raritan River to give Continental forces control of the sound and to prevent the approach of enemy vessels. The idea was echoed again as valid in a plan placed before the New Jersey delegates to the Continental Congress on August 3.[22] Amidst the chaos and confusion of war, and submissions of competing plans relative to countering enemy threats to the Jersey coast, however, the row galley protection for Little Egg Harbor was all but forgotten. Well before the final departure of *General Putnam* in September, the sanctuary was beginning to shift for itself. As early as late spring 1776, it had already begun to assume an identity that the enemy would come to curse as "a nest of rebel freebooters." It was also one that many Americans would come to equate with wartime opportunity. For some, its remote recesses would serve as a launching platform for the achievement of incredible wealth and even fame, and for others little more than a place to die.

–V–

Chance and *Congress*

"Thousands of schemes for privateering are afloat
in American imaginations."

The first vessels to receive their commissions as privateers under the Continental resolutions and instructions were two tiny sloops named, appropriately enough, *Chance* and *Congress*. Both were former New York pilot boats owned by a new syndicate formed especially for the purpose and registered under the name of Joseph Dean and Philip Moore and Company of Philadelphia. The two little vessels were destined to help incite a frenzy for privateering that was out of all proportion to their actual size and success. It was to be a mania that, once set in motion, would influence the very course of the American Revolution and would forever link the two vessels with the meteoric rise of Little Egg Harbor and, later, other such enclaves on the New Jersey coast as some of the premier privateering centers on the mid-Atlantic seaboard.[1]

Chance was a diminutive vessel, only forty-five tons burthen, lightly armed with four carriage guns and manned by forty-five seamen under the command of Captain John Adams, a native of the hamlet of Chestnut Neck, on the waters of New Jersey's Mullica River. She, like her sister and many other privateers that would follow in her wake, was fated to serve under a number of different skippers and in the employ of several owners during her substantial career. Her consort *Congress* was a vessel of 50 tons, slightly better armed with six carriage guns and manned by a crew of equal numbers under the command of Captain George McAroy of Philadelphia.[2] Both sloops would employ Little Egg Harbor as their initial port of re-entry from their first cruise and, eventually, like countless privateers that followed, as a regular forward base of operations thereafter.

Chance and *Congress* received formal letters of marque as private vessels of war from Pennsylvania on April 11, 1776. In so doing, they were thereby authorized "to fit out and set forth . . . in a warlike manner, and by and with the said sloop[s], and the crew[s] thereof, by force of arms, to attack, seize, and take the ships and other vessels belonging to the inhabitants of Great Britain, or any of them, with their tackle, apparel, furniture, and loading, on the high seas, or between high water and low water, to bring the same into some convenient ports in the colonies, in order that the courts, which are or shall be appointed to hear and determine causes, civil and maritime, may proceed in due form to condemn the said captures, if they be judged lawful prizes." The formal Continental commissions were granted after security bonds of $5,000 were submitted for each. There being a shortage of gunpowder in the colony, Philip Moore, on behalf of the owners, requested that he be allowed to purchase 400 pounds of powder from Congress, which was agreed to on the same day the privateering resolutions were passed.[3]

Captains Adams and McAroy were undoubtedly anxious to get to sea. Finally, after making last minute preparations, *Congress*, designated as lead ship in a small van consisting of *Chance* and two outward bound merchant schooners, was provided with a pilot on April 15 to take the vessels down the Delaware to Cape May. Seven days later, the cockleshell warships reached Delaware Bay with their two charges close behind. Unfortunately, a 44-gun British blockader, HMS *Roebuck*, Captain Andrew Snape Hamond commanding, which had only recently taken station, was on the alert and spotted the little convoy attempting to escape into the open ocean via the Cape May Channel. Hamond took up immediate pursuit and after a chase of a dozen leagues managed to overtake the two fat merchantmen, but lost the swifter and far more dangerous privateers. He later wrote that he "had the mortification to learn from my prize that the sloops were New York pilot boats, very fast sailers, that had been fitted at Philadelphia as privateers." He vowed that *Roebuck* would be there waiting and ready if and when the rebel cruisers returned.[4]

The two diminutive sea raiders headed directly for the rich hunting grounds of the West Indies. Despite the risk of capture by British cruisers, which was even greater there than off the American mainland, the opportunity for gain was exceptional. Moreover, as American privateers began to follow in the path of *Chance* and *Congress* and cruise with increasing regularity in these same waters, friendly French islands such as Martinique would provide the added advantage of serving as convenient havens for many harassed or disabled commissioned rovers, as well as a few operating with only state commissions.[5]

Working in almost synchronized tandem, *Chance* and *Congress* literally frolicked in the West Indies. Cruising at the mouth of the Bahamas Channel, they easily scooped up three heavily laden merchantmen bound from Jamaica to London. These captures, *Reynolds*, Captain Heylock Rusden, *Lady Juliana*, Captain Christopher Stephenson, and *Juno*, Captain Samuel Marson, proved to be extraordinarily valuable prizes. Their combined manifests indicated that they were carrying at the time of their capture 1,052 hogsheads of sugar, 246 bags of pimentos, 396 bags of ginger, 568 hides, twenty-five tons of cocoa, forty-one tons of fustic (a yellow dye wood), 260 puncheon (21,840 gallons) of rum, seventy pipes (8,820 gallons) of Madeira wine, a cask of turtle shells, and several live turtles (this last item intended for Lord North). Of equal importance, however, were the 22,420 Spanish dollars in specie and 187 pounds of silver plate also found aboard. The prizes were wisely sent into Cape Ann, Martha's Vineyard, and Dartmouth, Massachusetts, since neither Adams nor McAroy wished to chance losing them to British blockaders still patrolling the Delaware. Soon afterwards, on April 30, *Congress* took the schooner *Thistle*, Charles Roberts commanding, laden with flour, lumber, and 200 gold Spanish "half Joes," from Pensacola, Florida, and sent her into remote Sinepuxent Inlet, on the Atlantic barrier coast of Maryland. Rather than run the gauntlet into the Delaware, *Chance* and *Congress* chose, as many after them would, to first put into Little Egg Harbor. There, the specie and silver, which had been transferred from aboard the prizes, were taken out, divided equally between the two privateers, and then shipped overland to Philadelphia. With the treasure safely underway by land, the happy pair of sloops made a successful run for the city, easily evading the great, lumbering man-of-war *Liverpool*, and reached home safely on June 5.[6]

It was thus that the little privateers *Chance* and *Congress* became the first privately armed ships of war bearing Continental commissions to employ the sanctuary of that tiny, isolated port on the New Jersey coast, which was soon to gain fame as one of the most important privateering centers on the Atlantic seaboard. They and innumerable others that repeatedly mimicked their successes would sally from there again and again at the expense of English merchants and the British Empire.

• • •

The voyage of *Chance* and *Congress* did much to stir up further interest and excitement in the art of privateering. Indeed, at Philadelphia they were the talk of the town for weeks. Their first voyage had been an impressive and profitable success and all concerned parties were undoubtedly overjoyed. It was soon being reported in the press that each owner or shareholder had received at least £5,000 for his share of the investment return and that even the common seaman's share was as much as £500.[7]

The capture of the four rich merchantmen proved an excellent example of what a simple but enterprising sailor or a savvy investor stood to gain with a little daring, a proper ship, and a capable commander and crew. Moreover, as some entrepreneurs quickly realized, the hunting season of war was just beginning and game was plentiful. Because British commerce was wholly dependent upon the sea, and every component of the King's armed forces in America was almost entirely reliant upon supplies and reinforcements sent from Europe by ship, the pickings promised to be inordinately rich indeed. "Now," noted one New England politician after news of the success had spread, "is the time to pick up homeward bound West Indiamen," before winter and the Royal Navy could put a crimp in such easy pickings. Indeed, the opportunistic atmosphere for engaging in privateering was almost intoxicating, even among the richest members of Congress. "Pray inform me," wrote Congressman Elbridge Gerry of Massachusetts to a colleague back in Boston, "whether we cannot fix out a privateer or two & send for some woolens & linens on the coast of England? Two fishing schooners with eight guns each & forty men would bring us three or four rich Londoners in three or four months time, and I think we want spirit if the same is not attempted." Many businessmen and mariners followed that advice.[8]

Robert Morris, who was initially one of the few delegates to Congress who was less than supportive of privateering, was nevertheless sanguine regarding its potentials. He wrote in a letter to Silas Deane, one of the most zealous adherents for the action: "I fancy many more West Indian Men will be taken this summer & probably Great Britain may have cause to repent the prohibitory act, especially as they have more property to loose than we have."[9]

The owners of the privateers *Chance* and *Congress* were elated with their success. Their good will towards Congress, which had granted the commissions and provided the powder, and for the American cause in general, was in considerable evidence. Although no record of any negotiations between the cash-strapped assembly and the ship owners have been found, it is recorded that "Congress having great occasion for hard money, made application to the owners, & they very generously furnish'd it, which Congress look'd upon as of essential service." On June 12, the Deane and Moore partnership formally offered to exchange $22,000 in hard Spanish-milled dollars that were acceptable almost anywhere for Continental paper dollars that would soon be unacceptable everywhere.

The following day, John Hancock graciously received the generous offer on behalf of Congress. The silver specie, in three large boxes, along with $187,000 in Continental paper money, was shipped to General Philip Schuyler in New York on June 17 to help support the faltering Canadian Campaign.[10]

Now privateering fever swept across the colonies, and it was perhaps as virulent in the Port of Philadelphia as any place in America, including New England. "The affair of taking the sugar ships," noted one observer, "has so animated the people here that they are fitting out 5 or 6 privateers more here." Delegate John Adams gushed with pride for his countrymen. "Our privateers have the most skill or the most bravery, or the best fortune, of any in America," he bragged. Now, one James Deane (not to be confused with Joseph Dean), possibly a silent shareholder in one of the successful privateers fitted out under a Continental commission, bought out a controlling interest in at least one of the sloops, *Congress*. He acquired a new partner in the person of one Major Jonathan Bayard, partner in the shipping firm of Bayard, Jackson and Company and a contractor with the Continental Congress. Deane and Bayard received a new commission for their vessel from the Pennsylvania Committee of Safety on June 17, 1776. It would be the second of many such ventures for both Deane and *Congress*, which was quickly readied for another voyage and sent out to the Jersey coast for final refit.[11]

Sailing alone under the command of a new skipper, John Craig, *Congress* put to sea from her forward base at Little Egg Harbor. By the end of the month, she had already captured another extremely rich prize, the brigantine *Richmond*, taken while en route from London to Halifax via the West Indian island of Nevis with a cargo of rum, sugar, molasses and more gold—£20,000 worth. News reached Philadelphia on the evening of August 1 that a prize crew had taken the capture into Egg Harbor and one can well imagine the excitement as details began to filter out of the little Jersey hamlets on the Mullica. The prize crew on *Richmond*, it was said, had hid the gold in its casks to prevent discovery. Immediately after the capture, it was reported in breathless anticipation, *Congress* had taken off in pursuit of a big three-decker. When Thomas Jefferson informed a colleague that because of the capture of the valuable West Indiaman "the spirit of privateering is gaining ground fast," he was expressing what was already becoming obvious to everyone. Game was plentiful, for an island nation such as Great Britain was entirely dependent on the sea, and her forces in the American colonies were totally reliant upon seaborne supply. The floodgates of freelance commerce raiding were now opened from the Deep South to New England.

Soon after *Richmond* was brought in, another prize, a brig captured by the 12-gun Pennsylvania privateer brigantine *Hancock*, Wingate Newman commanding, and commissioned on June 15, arrived at Egg Harbor. Word soon circulated that Newman had also taken a large 500 to 600-ton, 3-decked, 14-gun ship named *Reward*, laden with rum, 1,100 hogsheads of sugar, and twelve bales of cotton, as well as several brass and iron cannon, and sent her into Boston. Interestingly there were also found aboard "a number of Turtle directed to Lord North, with his name cut in the shell, the best of which, Capt. Wingate Newman, Master of the Privateer, is determined to send to the Hon. John Hancock." On August 15, James Warren of Massachusetts wrote to Samuel Adams, making an observation that could well have applied to the entire country: "The spirit of privateering prevails here greatly. The success of those that have before engaged in that business has been sufficient to make a whole country privateering mad. Many kinds of West India goods that we used to be told we would suffer for want of, are now plentier and cheaper than I have known them for many years."[12]

With news like that who could wonder at the difficulty the infant Continental and state navies began to have in recruiting seamen and arming their naval vessels? The competition for able seamen, as well as guns, munitions, and ships, was intense. Men were flocking in droves to sign up on privateers. In every state issuing letters of marque, recruitment for regular army and navy service, as well as acquisition of guns and powder for ships of both Continental and state navies, was soon being stymied. By early August, it was reported in New England that Massachusetts seaports "are drain[e]d very much by those agoing a privateering." James Warren informed John Adams from Boston: "We have nothing going forward here but fixing out privateers, and condemnation and sale of prizes sent in by them, so many that I am quite lost in my estimate of them." In the meantime, the Continental frigates *Raleigh*, *Boston*, and *Hancock* lay at Boston and at Newport unable to put to sea for want of both guns and men. "This delay disgusts the officers, and occasions them to repent entering the [Continental] service."[13]

The recruitment problem only intensified as privateering increased. In Maryland, Governor Thomas Johnson complained that he was doing his utmost to fit out even a single Maryland Navy vessel with sixty hands, "but the privateers and the high wages given by the merchants, make it most difficult to get men of any sort." By fall, it was reported in Boston, almost every vessel from twenty tons to 400 tons was being fitted out as a privateer, despite a paucity of available armaments, as the "spirit for privateering is got to the highest pitch of enthusiasm." Even small carriage guns were being sold for the incredibly high price of $400 per ton. Yet the successes of the New Englanders, like those of the Pennsylvanians, were dazzling. "We have nothing here except captures from the British trade, which are likely to increase," Benjamin Franklin was informed from a correspondent in Boston. "Our own navigation is almost wholly turn'd into privateering, so that their cruisers can take little or nothing from us but empty hulls, while their ships come fast to us richly laden'd."[14]

With privateer owners offering large sums in advance to recruit seamen against their share in prize money, wages from one and a half to double that of Continental seamen, and twice the overall prize rate offered by the Continental Navy, it was no wonder that Commodore Esek Hopkins, the senior commander in the Navy, repeatedly lamented the difficulties of recruitment. By the end of September, as he was attempting at Philadelphia to fit out and man the first true Continental Navy fleet to sail from American shores, he informed Congress that "there are so many privateers a fitting out which give more encouragement as to shares it makes it difficult to man the Continental vessels."[15]

At Newport, Rhode Island, Captain John Paul Jones complained to Robert Morris that as quickly as he recruited seamen, they were enticed away as soon as they received their month's pay in advance. Some, he suggested, were even encouraged to desert to privateers by the very contractors charged with building America's warships, many of which were also outfitting privateers. "It is," he lamented bitterly, "to the last degree distressing to contemplate the state and establishment of our Navy. —The common class of mankind are actuated by no nobler principle than that of self interest—this and this only determin[e]s all adventurers in privateers; the owners as well as those whom they employ. And while this is the case unless the private emolument of individuals in our Navy is made superior to that of the privateers it can never become respectable—it never will become formidable—And without a respectable Navy—Alas America! . . . If our Enemies, with the best established and most formidable [*sic*] Navy in the Universe, have found it expedient to assign all Prizes to the Captors—how much more is such policy essential to our infant Fleet."[16]

Congress, though slow to move, was not immune to complaints of the Navy regarding the causes of manpower deficiencies. Acting upon a report of the Marine Committee, on October 30 it authorized an increase of the shares of the "commanders, officers, seamen, and marines in the continental navy" to one half of the value of merchantmen, transports and store ships taken as prizes. They were also to receive the whole value of ships of war as well as enemy privateers. When the improved incentives failed to boost recruitment, on March 29, 1777, Congress resorted to offering bounties. The Marine Committee was duly authorized to advance to every able seaman that entered service "any sum, not exceeding forty dollars, and to every ordinary seaman or landsman, any sum, not exceeding twenty dollars; to be deducted from their future prize money."[17]

Despite the manpower problem that the onset of privateering induced for the Continental and state navies, armies, and militias, many delegates to Congress were nevertheless captivated by the stunning success of *Chance* and *Congress* and the others that were duplicating their adventures, from New England to the West Indies.

William Hooper, in a message to Joseph Hewes, was almost giddy as he wrote of the New England privateering triumphs at sea. "Privateering is attended with amazing success in New England," he wrote. "Not a day passes without a fresh acquisition. They took a Vessell not long ago with 1600 pieces of woolen on board. The Soldiers may bless God for that. Also an armed vessell of 16 Guns—& the Privateer which took the latter was left in pursuit of a three decker with Sugars mounting 20 Guns & by a private letter we are informed that the last was taken and on her way into Newbury port."[18]

Most now believed that only a combination of privateers and regular naval warships would best serve the war effort. For many, however, it was the financial rewards that counted, and few opposed the melding of patriotism with profit. Richard Henry Lee of Virginia, for one, was simply in awe of the fortunes that were quickly being made by others. John Adams informed his wife Abigail: "Prizes are taken in no small numbers. A gentleman told me a few days ago that he had summed up the sugar, which has been taken [by Pennsylvania privateers], and it amounted to 2000 Hdds [hogsheads] since which two other ships have been taken and carried into Maryland. Thousands of schemes for privateering are afloat in American imaginations. Some are for taking the Hull ships, with woolens for Amsterdam and Rotterdam—some are for the tin ships—some for the Irish linen ships—some for the Hudson Bay ships—and many for the West India sugar ships. Out of the speculations," he correctly predicted, "many fruitless and some profitable projects will grow."[19]

The first blushes of success, however, had not enraptured everyone in Congress. "Those who have engaged in privateering are making large fortunes in a most rapid

Robert Morris. Courtesy Prints and Photographs Division, Library of Congress.

manner," wrote Robert Morris of Pennsylvania on September 12. "I have not meddled in their business which I confess does not square with my principles for I have long had extensive connections and dealings with many worthy men in England & cou[l]d not consent to take any part of their property because the government have seized mine, which is the case in several instances." Yet, not even he could long resist the allure. In less than three months, Morris, who had been sworn in to Congress on November 4, 1775, and soon dominated both the Marine Committee and the powerful Secret Committee of Correspondence, would himself succumb to the game to become one of the foremost speculators in privateering in America. At first, safely sheltered behind a mantle of secrecy, then through the firm of Willing, Morris & Co., and finally in collusion with a wide array of business associates, he would time and again channel not only his fortunes but those of the government for his personal gain—some of which would never be repaid—and profit substantially, most notably in privateering adventures and speculation in prize commodities.[20]

• • •

The capture of *Richmond* by *Congress* was a significant milestone in the early history of Revolutionary privateering, and even more so for Little Egg Harbor. It was the first of many privateer prizes to actually be brought in there over the years to come, and by one of the first ships to receive a commission under the Continental instructions. Rich prizes such as *Richmond* were soon to be sent into Little Egg Harbor, and later other coastal New Jersey inlets, on a frequent and then almost dizzying basis. Only two weeks later, in fact, on August 23, while still on station at the inlet, *General Putnam* assisted in bringing over the bar, albeit with a substantial effort, the heavily laden prize *Black River*, taken by a Maryland privateer called *Enterprize*, Captain James Campbell commanding. This prize was a 300-ton merchantman carrying a cargo of molasses, captured while en route from the West Indian sugar island of Dominica to Bristol, England, and was the first vessel taken by a privateer from a state other than Pennsylvania to enter the inlet.[21] Within a short time other prizes, taken by New Jersey men from the coastal settlements themselves, would soon be sent in on a regular basis.

The devastating effects of the American privateering onslaught were immediate and far-reaching, and nothing was more disconcerting to the Crown than Britain's own statistics on the captures by privately armed warships. Lloyd's of London would later estimate that during the first two years of war American privateers captured five times as many British ships as taken by the Royal Navy. Although the richest American hunting grounds were still in the West Indies, North American coastal waters, from Georgia to the St. Lawrence (and especially the approaches to New York), and even European seas were becoming increasingly dangerous for British shipping.[22]

It was the utility of such New Jersey havens as Little Egg Harbor, Toms River, and Mays Landing, not only for privateers and their prizes but also for the Continental Navy captures and their prisoners-of-war, that quickly became apparent to all. Merchantmen, too, were also beginning to employ Egg Harbor as a safe alternative to Philadelphia. Less than a week after the arrival of *Richmond*, it was reported in New York that a heavily laden sloop carrying £4,000 worth of indigo, twelve or thirteen days out of Charleston, had put in there to offload.[23]

The natives of Little Egg Harbor and the other coastal settlements knew a good thing when they saw it. They were not about to let the fortunes derived from privateering in prize ships and cargos go by default to the big Philadelphia syndicates. Their very geographic locations, protected by shallow bars, shoally waters, and narrow waterways made these miniature ports eminently suitable not only for receiving prizes but also for serving as safe havens for privateers from other ports, and even for fitting out rovers of their own. Indeed, a month before *Black River* was so laboriously assisted over the bar at Little Egg Harbor Inlet, it was noted in the *Memorandum Book* of the Pennsylvania Committee of Safety that privateers were now actually being fitted out *at* Egg Harbor. And what was more, many seamen from the infant Pennsylvania Navy, deserting in droves, had to be brought back bodily from the New Jersey coastal ports, particularly Egg Harbor, where they had gone to enlist aboard privateers. And so it began.[24]

–VI–

Citizen Warships

"Men of war you must take care to avoid."

The privateers that operated out of Little Egg Harbor, though bearing commissions from many states, were to become as numerous and varied as any on the Atlantic coast of North America. Many, particularly during the early days of the war, were hastily converted from merchant vessels, pilot boats, and fishermen, some of which had been brought in as prizes. Later in the war many others were purpose-built specifically for the business of sea raiding. In the beginning, small but swift vessels were the order of the day, constructed not for battle, which was avoided at all costs, but for speed and maneuverability. Sloops, schooners, and brigantines were common, and the fast Bermuda sloop, sometimes referred to as the West Indian or Jamaica sloop, was much sought after.[1]

The Bermuda sloop was a vessel usually about sixty-five feet in keel length, having a straight, rising floor, well-rounded bilge, and somewhat upright topsides, giving it a rather heart-shaped midsection in some extremes. The stem was usually well-rounded in profile and the hull drew much more water aft than forward. The freeboard to the main deck was low, but to offset this many vessels usually had high bulwarks pierced for carriage guns and a high, short quarterdeck or stern cabin with its roof strongly vaulted athwartships. The main deck of this vessel type was heavily crowned, or arched. The mast raked a good deal and usually quite gracefully. As for sails, these diminutive craft carried at least two or more headsails, a large gaff mainsail fitted with a boom, a square course, topsail, and topgallant sail, all of which gave the vessel a quite elegant profile. The Bermuda sloop, however, created a problem in manning, particularly when based in a small port such as Chestnut Neck, just seventy-seven and a half nautical miles south of New York, where available manpower was marginal at best (the Pennsylvania Navy deserters notwithstanding), for the rig in such a large-hulled vessel required big crews. Thus, the more easily manned schooner rig was often applied.[2]

One of the most popular and perhaps fleetest of vessels to be employed in the privateering business during the early days of the war was the almost pocket-sized pilot boat schooners such as *Chance* and *Congress*. This craft type had a small boat hull with a moderate rise in the floor, rather marked bilges, and flaring topsides. Most drew substantially more water aft than forward. As with most such vessels engaged in privateering, the stem profile was usually rounded and unadorned by a knee or by moldings and carvings, which reduced unnecessary weight. They were often flush-decked and low-sided, having no bulwarks but rather a mere plank-on-edge, or log rail. Their two masts were long and gracefully raked, unsupported by standing rigging, as was the short bowsprit. The typical pilot-boat schooner set a large jib, a loose-footed and altogether overlapping gaff-foresail, a boomed gaff-mainsail, and a large main-topmast staysail between its masts. The accommodations were usually very limited and often quite primitive since its cruising range was not wide. Before the war this vessel type was common and quite numerous about the Virginia Capes and was often referred to as the "Virginia pilot boat." Other colonial ports, particularly at New York and in the Delaware River and Bay, readily adopted both the model and rig. During the period of the Revolution, the pilot-boat schooner was rarely over fifty-five feet in length, thirty-five to forty-five feet being the average, but, with speed considered the most essential requirement for a privateer, the pilot-boat was one of the most sought after for that service in the early days of the war.[3]

Another seagoing schooner of note, often employed out of Egg Harbor by the privateer syndicates of Pennsylvania, New Jersey, Maryland, and Virginia, was also the first developed on the Chesapeake. This vessel drew much water aft, and the main deck was but a little above the waterline. It had a strongly rising floor, well-rounded bilge, and some tumblehome in the topside amidships, giving it a characteristic heart-shaped midsection not unlike the Bermuda sloop. These vessels usually had a rounded stem profile, sometimes with a small gammon-knee head and were rarely adorned with moldings and carvings. They had high main-deck bulwarks pierced for carriage guns, and many built before 1780 had high, short quarterdecks. They were relatively sharp-ended and, like the small pilot-boats, were built to sail very fast; they carried a large spread of sail in the square-topsail schooner rig of the period, consisting of two or more headsails, fore and main sails, main-topmast staysail, fore course, square topsail, topgallant and, occasionally, square main topsails with light sails in addition. This class of vessel was extremely popular during the Revolution and could be armed with as many as fourteen carriage guns on an eighty-foot deck. Many brigs and brigantines were constructed along the lines of this vessel type during the war, if not before, and a number are likely to have been employed by the privateers of Egg Harbor and Toms River. Some records indicate that a number of such schooners and brigs were, in fact, brought in as prizes and of these, several were converted to privateers. These small, sleek craft types bearing streamlined profiles had already seen considerable service not only in legitimate commerce, but also, before the war, as smugglers and in illegal trading operations. Not surprisingly, they were destined to take a heavy toll on enemy shipping.[4]

One of the most common, but diminutive vessel types employed along the New Jersey coast and venturing out of such ports as Egg Harbor, New Brunswick, and Amboy, was the whaleboat, a narrow, double-ended vessel, rarely exceeding twenty feet in length and usually sprit-rigged if rigged at all. Eight- to ten-ton sloop-rigged craft, occasionally as large as thirty-six feet in length, were also fielded, the virtue of these vessels being that they could be easily launched from shore and, when the wind failed, could be propelled by oarsmen. As readily deployed from beach or inlet as from a harbor environment, they were usually lightly armed with swivel guns, blunderbusses, or a small cannon mounted in the bow, and sometimes carried only small arms. Most whaleboats were rowed with eight or more oars and usually open, but for long voyages were occasionally decked. Crews ranged in number from less than a dozen to as many as thirty, and were usually armed with pistols, muskets, blunderbusses, cutlasses and/or swords. The virtue of these vessels was that they required only a modest amount of capital, and were sometimes sent out by enterprising citizens who, unlike the larger syndicates or well-heeled entrepreneurs, could afford to pool only a small amount of their resources. If one was lost, a replacement could be readily built and fielded in a matter of weeks. Able to suddenly appear out of remote inlets and shallow sounds to pounce upon unsuspecting prey, they were known to some, first in New England and later along the mid-Atlantic coast, as "Spider Catchers." For the masters of British and Loyalist merchantmen, transports, and supply ships, the patriot whaleboats, launches, and occasionally barges, soon became synonymous with the many hazards of sailing along the New Jersey coast or on the Delaware. As the war progressed, these small boat privateers increased in number, and many began to cooperate quite effectively in flotillas of three to five vessels or more, occasionally pouncing on much larger ships in successfully coordinated attacks. Such vessels were also frequently seen on the waters of the Chesapeake, Long Island Sound, and Vineyard and Nantucket Sounds off New England, but proved most successful of all on the New Jersey coast and in New York Bay.[5] By late 1778, with the activation of the Board of Loyalist Associators in New York, the whaleboat became the vessel of choice for partisan refugee amphibious and paramilitary operations on both sides, but greatly enhanced the larger Tory privateer war.

When the British began to react to American privateering successes early in the war by placing more armament aboard their cargo ships, sending Royal Navy convoy escorts with them to and from America, and, by 1778, weeding out through capture the slowest and most inefficient American privateering craft, shipyards engaged in building privateers adapted. American shipowners and builders began looking ahead to the day when enemy merchantmen would be even better protected, risks would be greater, and cruises ever further afield would be necessary to make a profit. They soon began to reconsider vessel design, speed, and handling. How well did certain vessels sail close to the wind, a trait which determined their ability to snatch a prize from an escorted convoy and escape quickly? Much thought was given to the appropriate application of fore-and-aft rigs vs. square rigs, as they measured up against the design, speed, and fighting qualities of their adversaries. Increasingly, address had to be made to achieve a better balance between the escalating size of privateer crews and the space allocated aboard to house them, as well as a vessel's capacity to carry greater armament, shot, and stores.[6]

The sharp lines of the swift Chesapeake and New England vessel types were enlarged in craft that began to be built to carry more armament specifically for privateering. Few if any of these sharp hulls were constructed exceeding 120 feet in length, and most were small enough that under an ample spread of canvas they could usually out-sail the fastest enemy cruiser of like or even greater size. Efforts to reduce overall weight, however, influenced a ship's armament. Cannon that lined either side of the deck were usually light, small-bore pieces that necessitated less "tumble home" to bring weight to the center of the hull. Moreover, with lighter guns, recoil was diminished and required less reinforcing timber. Cannon and reinforced timbering were usually kept free of the bow and stern to do away with the need for heavier, rounded ends and added displacement. As cruises were often of short duration, this new breed of privateer required fewer provisions and storage space. Prize goods taken aboard after a capture usually consisted of only the smaller and most valuable items, while the remainder was sent to a safe, friendly port aboard the prize itself under the care of a prize crew.[7]

Armament to provide the thunderous voice of the citizen warships varied. At the beginning of the war, vessels entering the privateering business were lightly armed and provisioned. Their goal, of course, was to quickly capture merchantmen, transports, and supply ships, and not to engage enemy warships. Any damage received in a broadside-to-broadside fight could send a privateer limping into the nearest port before a cruise had barely begun, make her an easy target for the next British warship that happened along, or even worse, lead to her capture and a financial loss for her owners. One such vessel, quite typical for her calling, sailed with only four small carriage guns, all smoothbore 2-pounders (a cannon was identified by the approximate weight of its shot), six swivel guns, and "a suitable quantity of muskets, blunderbusses, cutlasses, pistols, powder, ball and other military stores." For provisions she carried ten barrels of beef, a hundredweight of bread, some flour, rice, beans, and potatoes. A crew of twenty-five officers and men manned her. Her provisioning was considered, at the time, quite sufficient for a short cruise against enemy merchantmen that were usually lightly armed and sailing without escort.

By 1781, when the greatest number of privateers of the entire war were granted commissions, some vessels carried as many as twenty-four guns (the average was about fifteen) and crews of 150 men or more. The principal reason for such outsized complements was the need not only to handle sails and rigging, man the guns, and supply sharpshooters or marines, but to provide enough men to board an enemy ship, crews to man prize vessels, and guards to watch over captured prisoners and prevent recaptures by the original crew. The early days of easy picking, when diminutive vessels of about fifty tons, such as *Chance* and *Congress*, which sailed with fifty men or less, had quickly passed (although small vessels would never go entirely out of usage). Yet, the paucity of foundries in America, most of which had little knowledge of artillery production owing to earlier manufacturing and trade restrictions of the British, the wait for an adequate or balanced array of cannon by the Continental and state navies often put privateering interests at the back of the line. Captured guns and those purchased from foreign sources did much to alleviate the shortage, but throughout the war both ordnance and powder were always more in demand than could be adequately supplied. Indeed, it was not uncommon for some vessels to sail with antiquated weapons of dubious reliability. Such was the case when the brazen little New Jersey whaleboat *Skunk* rowed out of Egg Harbor (sans commission) under the command of Captain John Golden in the summer of 1779 on a remarkable career that would result in no less than nineteen prizes. When she put to sea she did so with just a dozen crewmen and a pair of ancient, rusting guns of questionable utility that were more dangerous to her own men than the enemy![8]

The relationships between owners, masters, crewmen and their ship were frequently as ephemeral as the winds, and usually governed by little more than a mutual desire for profit. Yet, their objectives were always the same—capture as many prizes in the shortest time and safest manner feasible, always taking care not to expose their own ship to danger unless absolutely unavoidable, and make as much money as possible.

To do so required excellent leadership, intelligence, experience, considerable acumen, seamanship, risk, and, most of all, a plan. Typical of the sailing instructions given to a privateer commander at the beginning of a voyage were those provided by the primary owners of the cutter *Revenge*, a Continental Navy warship that had been sold out of service to John M. Nesbitt & Co. and Andrew and Hugh Hodge of Philadelphia, two firms that would be responsible for launching at least twenty-one privateering cruises in eighteen vessels which they owned outright or in which they had shares. The orders were given to the ship's commander, Captain Gustavus Conyngham, a naval officer famous for his daring and success, who was on official leave to go privateering in his late command. It was not an unusual move for Conyngham, who was allowed to take the cutter out as a privateer under a Continental commission authorized on May 2, 1777. Indeed, a number of Continental naval officers such a Thomas Truxtun, Silas Talbot, Joshua Barney, and others, would do so when such opportunities arose.

"Sir," wrote the owners. "The cutter *Revenge* being now completely fitted and almost manned, you will proceed with her to sea, as expeditiously as in your power; to fully complete your manning, you had best stop off at Salem or Cohenzy [*sic* Conhansy, NJ], where we believe you may meet with a number of good men ready to enter, at Cape May it is likewise possible some may enter with you, and it is not improbable but if you are known off Egg Harbor some may go off to you from thence; indeed you must endeavor to get off men from every part of the coast to keep up your complement, and if you are lucky enough to take a prize or two soon after your going out they will crowd to you."

The cruise was to be at the risk of and on the account of the owners, they pointed out, so Conyngham's main objective was "to look after good rich merchantmen rather than privateers, not that we would have you to avoid these when they come in your way, many of them will sell for a good deal of money here, but it is not so much your business to look out for them, or to engage those of such a force as to risk by your engagement a damage to your vessel that may oblige you to return into port and break up your cruise."

The owners suggested that they believed it prudent "to stretch pretty well off until your landsmen are recovered of their sea-sickness and we get the crew in good order and well acquainted with working the vessel, guns, &c."

Conyngham was instructed to take a station that he judged best to intercept merchantmen bound into New York, "many of whom may now be looked for from the West Indies as well as from Europe." When he had his men "in order," that is, adequately trained and ready to take a station in the shipping lanes close to shore, he was to take care to avoid the enemy men-of-war, most of which were more powerful than *Revenge*. They reminded him that it was not his business nor in the interests of the owners to engage vessels fitted for war of superior or even equal force "as by this means your cruise may be knocked up." To avoid such contact, he was advised to alter his station from time to time, "for fear the enemy should get intelligence of you," which could only be had "by some vessel to whom you gave chase escaping you, or on the return of prisoners to New York who may be landed from your prizes."

It was his business, however, "to see and attack all merchantmen with resolution let their force appear what it will, for many of those though large and show a great number of guns are but indifferently manned, and their seamen not having the same view of gain, will not fight so obstinately as those on board cruising vessels."

The owners believed that few of the merchantmen bound for New York expected to meet an American cruiser on the New Jersey coast and suggested that Conyngham at first deceive them by pretending to be a New York privateer or man-of-war's tender. To do so, "you may amuse them until you find a convenient opportunity to board or attack them, but your judgment and prudence will direct you the conduct necessary to pursue on this and every other occasion."

All large prizes taken were to be sent to Philadelphia, but for safety's sake were to be escorted by *Revenge* as far as the shelter of the Delaware Capes. Smaller prizes, of little value, could be sent into Egg Harbor "as you can have your men immediately off again, and your prize master must take care of her until an express can come over to us which you are to direct him to hire and send over to us." If the Delaware Bay should at any time be so guarded so as to prevent getting prizes in there, he was instructed to send them into Egg Harbor as well, and if too large for that harbor, they were to be sent into the Chesapeake Bay, to Boston or some other port in New England, and if deemed very valuable *Revenge* was to accompany them all the way in to those places as required.

It was probable, the owners noted, that a number of captured seamen might well be enlisted as crewmen aboard *Revenge*. However, Conyngham was advised not to trust either Englishmen or Scotsmen, "but the Irish we believe in general would as soon fight for us as for the English." With the additional men, he might even make one of the enemy's little fast sailing vessels a useful tender to his own ship.

"Keep up a supply of powder, shot, provisions, rum, or any necessary you may want out of your prizes," the owners instructed, "and if you should want anything from us, put a letter on shore at Egg Harbor or Cape May, and we can lodge what you want at either of these places."

And finally, in closing a most comprehensive set of instructions, the owners acknowledged that "many things may occur that we cannot particularly direct you in, and in such cases you must act as you judge best and most conducive to our interest; having with you officers, strict discipline as possible and good usage of your crew we would recommend, you gaining their opinion and esteem will be of singular use, a general benefit to the cruise, and an ease to yourself."[9]

Unfortunately for Captain Conyngham, *Revenge* was soon afterward captured by HMS *Galatea* and sent into New York. Already famous for his earlier exploits against the British and thoroughly despised by them, he was accused of piracy on the premise that on an earlier voyage he had sailed without a proper commission, which was untrue. Nevertheless, he was sent to England in chains and incarcerated in Mill Prison at Plymouth to await trial and probable execution. Fortunately, the redoubtable captain managed a stunning mass escape with about thirty other privateersmen and naval men, and eventually found his way to safety in Holland.[10]

• • •

From early on, the war at sea had gone amazingly well for the American privateers as well as the infant Continental Navy, which, combined, had already outstripped the enemy in overall captures. Between March 10 and December 31, 1776, American privateers had taken over 342 prizes (of which forty-nine had been recaptured, eighteen released, and five burned at sea, and the remaining 279 brought into port). The Continental Navy had made sixty captures, bringing the total of American captures to 402 vessels. By contrast the Royal Navy had made only 140 captures, (of which twenty-six had been recaptured). It had been a significant factor in inflicting economic loss to British commerce. The interception of troops and military stores had hastened the evacuation of Boston and helped check British advances southward from Canada.[11]

Many privateers infested the coastal waters of New Jersey: they came from all over the new nation. Some came to use the harbors as homeports while others appeared seeking only temporary sanctuary from weather or enemy warships. Some employed the facilities at Chestnut Neck or The Forks, Mays Landing or Toms River to refurbish, careen, or repair. Others came simply to sell their prizes. Many merchantmen, unwilling to hazard a run through the occasionally strong cordon of enemy blockaders that frequently patrolled the Delaware Capes, or who were entirely barred by the British occupation of the Delaware River and Bay in late 1777 through mid-1778, employed the harbors as terminal points for embarking or disembarking produce and merchandise. Unhappily, few privateersmen concerned themselves with the documentation of their exploits. It was profit that counted, and it was largely in the recording of their profits and losses that their fame was inscribed. And soon, a handful of venturesome men, scallywags, and sailors of fortune would come to dominate the maritime events on New Jersey's shores and influence the course of history.

–VII–

Coast Watchers

"It is more praiseworthy in an officer to loose his vessel in a bold enterprise than to loose a good prize by too timid a conduct."

By the end of October 1776, unlike the heady, burgeoning American privateer war at sea, the Continental Army had been plagued by defeat after defeat, beginning with the Battle of Brooklyn. All but crushed in that horrendous engagement, Washington and his bloodied survivors had escaped to Manhattan, only to be repeatedly assaulted and driven ever farther north. After the defeat at the Battle of White Plains on October 28, American forces had little alternative but to relinquish the island of Manhattan, with the exception of the stronghold of Fort Washington, and retire into northeast New Jersey. New York City was now securely in British hands and almost overnight had become the core of all major Royal Navy activities on the mid-Atlantic coast. The Revolution itself was in serious jeopardy of collapsing. The Marine Committee of Congress was not unaware of the ramifications of the events in New York and New Jersey, and resolved to keep a close watch on enemy naval movements, taking up where Captain Creiger had left off. To do so they would have to put ships as close as possible to New York City, the main British base in the United States: that meant somewhere on the north coast of New Jersey, dangerously close to Sandy Hook, and directly in harm's way.

On November 1, 1776, the Marine Committee ordered Captain Elisha Warner, skipper of a fast, pocket-sized Continental sloop called *Fly*, to proceed to the coast of Shrewsbury, New Jersey, less than ten miles south of Sandy Hook, and to take station along the shore there in such a position as to enable him "to see every vessel that goes in or out" of New York Bay. The committee correctly believed that most of the vessels entering the estuary "must be transports, store ships and provision vessels arriving or expected to arrive at that place for supplying our enemies with provisions and other stores." It was *Fly*'s job to intercept as many as she could.[1]

Warner was instructed to secure a good coasting pilot and, if pursued by a vessel of force, to run close inshore, via Cranberry Inlet, into Toms River, or any other convenient inlet along the Jersey coast. He was also directed to "keep an especial look out for all vessels inward or outward bound and whenever you discover any give chase, make prizes of as many as possible, and as fast as you take 'em send them for this port [Philadelphia], unless you hear men-of-war take station at our [Delaware] Capes, and in that case send them into Toms River, Egg Harbor or any other safe place, and as fast as your people arrive here we will send them or others over land to Toms River or Shrewsbury from whence you can take them on board again, therefore you must keep this station and pursue this business as long as possible unless we send you other orders."[2]

The Continental Navy schooner *Wasp*, commanded by Lieutenant John Baldwin, was ordered to accompany *Fly*. Both Warner and Baldwin were instructed to "act in concert, consult the best stations and best method of cruising, and be sure to pursue your objective." The Marine Committee, well aware of the dangerous assignment it was handing out, added that it was "more praiseworthy in an officer to loose his vessel in a bold enterprise, than to loose a good prize by too timid a conduct." The committee warned the two officers that they were not to let any frigates get between them and the land, since the deep draft warships could not pursue them in the nearshore waters, but could easily take them on the high seas. It was also believed by the planners in Philadelphia that the enemy suffered from a dearth of tenders of sufficient force and speed capable of taking *Fly* or *Wasp* in either a race or a head-to-head contest. Moreover, the local country people could be counted upon to help drive them off if they attempted to follow inshore.[3]

To order a ship to sea was one thing. To get her adequately manned in these times was another, for capable seamen were now to be had at a premium. Not only were they sought after by both the Continental and Pennsylvania navies, but also by the various syndicates and commercial houses fielding privateers. Thus, both Warner and Baldwin were obliged to employ any means possible to man their ships. It was a mission the two officers pursued with unrestrained vigor, including raiding sister services. On November 4, the Pennsylvania Committee of Safety was informed by Commodore Thomas Seymour of the Pennsylvania Navy that the two Continental officers "had received and detained diverse men belonging to the armed boats of this state, and declared their intentions of receiving and detaining as many more of the said men as they shall be able to obtain." The Committee of Safety instructed Seymour to request the Continental Marine Committee to order the return of the seamen, though in vain.[4]

The Marine Committee had more important concerns—and getting both *Fly* and *Wasp* into the field was imperative. The enemy was reportedly on the move, and in massive numbers. By now the Royal Navy had at least eighty-three ships and vessels of war on the American Station, including two ships-of-the-line, ten 50-gun men-of-war, and seventy-one frigates, sloops-of-war, and smaller craft, with the greatest portion now anchored at or near New York.[5]

Having received critical intelligence concerning enemy troop activities, on November 11 the committee issued additional instructions to Warner. The British at New York, they informed, were about to embark 15,000 troops on board transports bound for an unknown destination. "The station assigned you makes it probable that we may best discover their destination by your means for it will be impossible this fleet of transports can get out of Sandy Hook without your seeing them." He was instructed to take up such a station with *Fly* to prevent even the slightest possibility of the transports passing unseen. *Wasp* was to act in direct concert with *Fly*, and Warner was ordered to confer with Baldwin on "what is best to be done," and to "give him orders accordingly." When the enemy fleet moved, the two officers were to watch their motions and to send a boat ashore with a letter to inform the committee "the moment they get out to sea and shape their course." If the fleet should sail southward, "either the *Fly* or *Wasp* which ever sails fastest must precede the fleet—keeping in shore ahead of them." If it was discovered that they were bound for the Delaware Capes, *Fly* was to run into some convenient inlet on the New Jersey coast and send an officer or "some proper person" overland to Philadelphia with an account of their motions. The dullest sailer of the two vessels was to follow the fleet, watch its motions, and send information about its probable destination by express as soon as its objective was known for certain. Should the fleet make for the Chesapeake, Warner was instructed to put into some Atlantic inlet on the Eastern Shore peninsula of Maryland and Virginia and immediately send word to the Councils of Safety in both those states. If they should make for North Carolina or Georgia, or go north instead of south, a similar course of action was directed.[6]

The mission given to *Wasp* and *Fly* was deemed to be among the most critical to be assigned any Continental Navy vessels to that date. "In short we think you may by a spirited execution of these orders prevent them from coming by surprise on any part of this continent, and be assured you cannot recommend yourself more effectually to our friendship. If you could find an opportunity of attacking and taking one of the fleet on their coming out it might be the means of giving us ample intelligence."[7]

Although records of the actual proceedings of the two little warships are unknown, they apparently pursued their objective with vigor. *Fly* almost certainly engaged in combat at some point, as suggested by orders from the Marine Committee issued to her captain on November 29, just two and a half weeks after receiving orders, mentioning both injured crewmen and the disabled condition of the sloop. "We have sent Doctor Smith," read the orders, "to take charge of the wounded men belonging to *Fly*, and since the vessel is no longer in condition for prosecuting the cruise you are to return with her into this port [Philadelphia] as quickly as you can bringing with you the wounded men, and the surgeon now sent to take care of them."[8]

As it turned out, the massive troop movements had not been destined for an offensive on the Delaware, the Chesapeake, or the Deep South as feared, but against the last Continental stronghold on upper Manhattan Island. The transport fleet never peeked beyond Sandy Hook. Instead, on November 16, General Howe stormed Fort Washington, the last rebel stronghold on the island, overlooking the Hudson, by both land and sea. Four days later Fort Lee, New Jersey, on the opposite side of the river on the Hudson Palisades, was also taken by a brilliantly orchestrated amphibious assault. The last of Washington's forces, those few that had eluded capture, were forced into abject retreat through New Jersey, then across the Delaware and into Pennsylvania.

For the first time, the Royal Navy, which had sporadically blockaded the Delaware, and now controlled New York and the lower Hudson, began to focus some of its attentions upon the Jersey coast. On December 7, Captain Andrew Snape Hamond, then at New York, instructed the commanders of HMS *Camilla*, *Pearl*, *Perseus*, and *Falcon* "to proceed along the coast to the southward . . . looking into Egg Harbor in [*sic* on] your way." It was the first such instructions of the war, but would not be the last.[9] Indeed, within a few weeks the Marine Committee would learn of British intentions for the entire American coast. From a recently paroled mariner named Robert Bevan, who had earlier been taken captive while entering the Delaware, committee chairman Robert Morris was informed "that he heard Capt. Hammond & other officers say they are now determined to put a total stop to our trade. Six frigates were sent out to cruise of[f] Georgia & Carolina, six of[f] the Capes of Virginia, & six of[f] our capes. They have fixed signals & stations so as to keep a complete line along the coast and are determined to keep these stations throughout the winter if possible."[10]

That the enemy was conscientious in his efforts to close off not only major entry points, but also the remote and shallow but well-used inlets of the New Jersey coast, was emphasized on December 18 when *Wasp*, having retaken a French schooner recently captured by the enemy while trying to slip into the Delaware, tried to bring her into Egg Harbor. Since the departure of *Fly*, Lieutenant Baldwin had been employing the harbor as a base for taking on provisions and stores and had already sent in a number of captures. This time, however, he was almost taken by surprise when a fleet of fifteen sail hove in sight, two of which were line-of-battle ships. One or two frigates and an armed brig immediately took up pursuit, and would have taken him had he not relinquished the prize and darted into the inlet.[11]

The following day in Philadelphia, Thomas Paine published a work entitled *The Crisis*, with its opening tract destined for immortality: "These are the times that try men's souls." And indeed, they were.

On January 1, 1777, Lieutenant Baldwin received instructions from the Marine Committee to heave his schooner down, prepare for a three-month voyage, and settle his accounts at Egg Harbor. *Fly* would soon depart never to see the little port again.[12]

· · ·

As the months of the New York City occupation in 1776 turned from fall into winter, Royal Navy prizes began to cluster along the waterfront and in the East River in ever increasing numbers. Yet shortages of all manner of goods, as well as the destruction of a major component of the city by fire in late September, began to be acutely felt by the civilian population. Many of the Loyalist citizenry, chiefly in the merchant class, cut off from trade by their own government's Prohibitory Act, desired a change in the state of affairs and were eager to engage the rebels at their own game, particularly as it related to privateering, but British bureaucracy and the Howe brothers kept getting in the way.[12]

One of the principal barriers to both trade and Loyalist privateering was that the city lacked an official Vice Admiralty Court that could legally condemn cargoes and get them into commercial circulation. In theory, a prize that had not been legally condemned, had not broken bulk, and had not been sent into a port prescribed by the Prohibitory Act, was simply in a state of limbo. Nevertheless, the Royal Navy continued to send prizes into the most convenient harbor available for safe keeping, New York, with the resultant effect that some of their cargoes often literally rotted at dockside as the ships themselves, untended, also began to leak and deteriorate. Some goods, however, began to filter into the local economy as a handful of merchants managed to secure, usually through extra-legal means, exportable cargoes such as tobacco. Unhappily, owing to the rules and regulations of the Prohibitory Act, they usually found it impossible to ship.[13]

Governor Tryon, who, as early as January 1776, had commented on New York's potential use as a privateer base, readily recognized the city's plight. In December of that year he had begun considering establishing a Court of Admiralty on his own, without leave of the home government and, on January 9, 1777, had gone so far as to declare he would open it the following week (though the actual authority for doing so fell within the jurisdiction of the Board of Admiralty, albeit with the approval of Parliament), only to postpone it a few days later. Nevertheless, he had even gone so far as to consider two prominent New York Loyalists, Robert Bayard for the post of Judge and David Mathews as Registrar, though one critic declared Bayard "a person of very inferior abilities, and totally ignorant as to all matters of the law." Though the court did not open as he had wished, Tryon nevertheless continued to champion its establishment. In London, Lord George Germain, though siding with many senior officers in the Royal Navy that a court was desirable, noted that while the Port of New York remained under the restrictions of the Prohibitory Act, a Vice Admiralty Court there would continue to lack proper authority to condemn prizes.[14]

The British homeland and His Majesty's loyal colonies in the West Indies, of course, did not have the same restrictions. They had, however, suffered grievously, from the very outset of the war, from the devastating incursions of American privateers fitted out in both American mainland and neutral French ports. Though West Indian merchants had requested protection, little help had been forthcoming, and some began to take matters into their own hands. Indeed, as early as April 1776, though lacking commissions and contrary to both British and international law, some began to back privateers of their own operating out of Jamaica, Antigua, Tortola, and elsewhere. Not until rebel privateers began to invade European waters did Parliament, prompted by the hue and cry of merchants and shippers alike, feel obliged to take action. In January 1777, a bill was introduced into the House of Commons, passed on February 6, and then forwarded to the House of Lords where, under the title "Act for enabling the Lords of the Admiralty to grant Commissions . . . ," it was approved and then awaited the Royal assent.[15]

The substance of the act, essentially an appendix to the Prohibitory Act, was published for the first time on March 11 in the London *Public Advertiser*, and within four days it was reported that applications for commissions for letters of marque and reprisal to combat American privateers, indeed against "all ships belonging to those American colonies which are now in actual rebellion against the Mother-country," were being submitted to the Lords of the Admiralty. Finally, on March 27, 1777, with Parliament's passage of the bill, King George III issued official instructions to "Commanders of private Ships and Vessels employed in Trade, or retained in our Service . . . enabling our Commissioners for executing the Office of Lord High Admiral of Great Britain, to grant commissions for the seizing of all Ships and Vessels, Goods, Wares and Merchandizes, Chattels and Effects whatsoever, belonging to the Inhabitants of the Colonies now in Rebellion," as well as all British and Irish ships trading with those colonies. Included in the instructions was a comprehensive list of sixteen articles. On April 10, the *London Chronicle* reported that the first four ships "that have been fitted up as Letters of Marque against the Provincials, came out of dock, and began to take their guns on board, in order to sail." Unfortunately for Loyalists in New York and elsewhere, the bill only applied to privateers operating out of England.[16]

By May, the first British vessels bearing commissions as letters of marque began to appear in West Indian waters. Many islander privateers were also operating, although illegally and without commissions or official sanction, often violating the sovereignty of neutral nations by the seizure of their vessels. It was a fact that caused considerable dissension between Secretary Germain, a supporter of the privateering initiative, and First Lord of the Admiralty John Montagu, the Earl of Sandwich, who opposed it. Indeed, not until January 10, 1778, would the issue in the West Indies be resolved by the granting to West Indian governors the authority to commission letters of marque. The authorization, however, did not extend to New York.[17]

Eventually, not only the seas off Great Britain, but the waters of the West Indies and the United States would be churning with British and, eventually, Loyalist privateers, the latter venturing forth from island maritime centers such as Bermuda, Barbados, Grenada, Dominica, Jamaica, and the Bahamas, as well as Great Britain itself. In New York, however, which suffered perhaps more severely from the rebel privateers than any loyal enclave on the North American continent, the path would be delayed, much to the chagrin of city merchants who were still yearning to fight back.

By the end of March 1777, conditions regarding prizes taken by His Majesty's ships that were being sent into New York and the shipment of prize goods had become so troublesome that even Admiral Howe, now burdened with the management of many scores of cargo-laden captures tied up at wharves or lying at anchor in clusters off the city, complained to the Admiralty. He informed Secretary Philip Stephens that "as no Court of Admiralty for trying the Legality of the seizures can yet be held at New York, And the King's Service does not admit of Men to be spared for the removal of those Captures to any Port in His Majesty's Allegiance, great Waste of the Cargoes by Theft and Decay in all the Vessels detained, is likely to ensue, to the Prejudice of the Claimants in whose favor the decision of the Property may be heretofore determined."[18] A course correction, however, regarding both the creation of a New York Vice Admiralty Court and the authorization of both British and Loyalist privateering was already in the works.

Within two weeks of the Crown's consent to British privateering, Admiralty Secretary Stephens wrote to inform Admiral Howe regarding the Vice Admiralty Court problem. "I have their Lordships permission to acquaint you," he wrote, "that a Bill is now preparing and will be presented to Parliament for authorizing the Board of Admiralty to institute such a Court." Word arrived in New York City regarding the Admiralty's newly granted power to approve letters of marque, but the news would not be published in the press until June 2.[19] Howe, concerned that the fielding of privateers would seriously impact the manpower pool needed by the Navy, as it had with the rebels and their paltry naval forces, did nothing.

By mid-summer British letters of marque vessels began appearing at New York, undoubtedly much to the chagrin of New Yorkers who were not permitted to enter the game themselves. Indeed, between July and December no fewer than ten privateers, *Sarah Goulburn, Sir William Erskine, Brilliant, Blenheim, General Howe, Britannia, Ellis, George,* and *Patty,* as well as an unidentified ship commanded by Daniel Squirer, arrived at New York, and two more, *Fanny* and *Marlborough,* put in at British-occupied Newport, Rhode Island. Several were accompanied by or had already sent in prizes before them, which was still illegal under the Prohibitory Act.[20]

Not until the first week in September would word reach the Port of New York of "An Act to authorize the carrying of the Captures therein mentioned into any Part of his Majesty's Dominions in North America" (dubbed the "Prize Act") and be published in the city newspapers, legalizing that which was already being done.[21] The act permitted prizes to be sent into ports, such as New York, that were occupied by British forces but located in rebellious colonies. Now prize goods could also be legally exported, although the Prohibitory Act remained the main set of regulations administering procedure. A license was required to enter a port with a prize and to ship captured goods. Yet, for reasons unknown, the Howe brothers refused to permit the export of prize goods, until belatedly approving a warrant in October officially authorizing the existence of the Vice-Admiralty Court itself.[22]

On September 16, the Vice Admiralty Court of New York was officially deemed operational with Robert Bayard presiding as Judge. Bayard's first case was heard the following day, a libel involving the 130-ton, 10-gun, Virginia Navy brig *Raleigh*, which had been taken in April 1776 off the Virginia Capes. A week later, a ruling was made and the prize was condemned.[23]

Slowly, but surely, the backlog of libels and eventual condemnations were processed. Indeed, it is of some note that Bayard, despite his critics, would administer his post satisfactorily. Nevertheless, with General Howe's refusal to grant licenses to export prize commodities, only one permit had been issued by the beginning of January 1778. Unrest among the merchant community now became surly and Howe slowly began to loosen restrictions, that is, until June 21, 1778. On that date, he instituted an embargo on all exports from New York, limiting licenses to only those vessels sailing with stores and provisions destined for the army and navy.[24]

And while the King's commanders at New York continued to dither, the privateer war against them continued to take its toll.

General William Howe, by John Goldbar, engraver. Reproduction from *History of the war with America, France, Spain, and Holland* by John Andrews, 1785–86. Courtesy Rare Book and Special Collections Division, Library of Congress.

Admiral Richard Howe. Reproduction from *History of the war with America, France, Spain, and Holland* by John Andrews, 1785–86. Courtesy Rare Book and Special Collections Division, Library of Congress.

–VIII–

Courts and Ports

"An Anchor and Thirteen Stars"

From the very earliest days of British administration in the American colonies, the adjudication of maritime affairs by the colonial Vice Admiralty Courts provided an indisputable constant of law and justice that continued until the onset of the Revolution. It was thus not surprising that the example set by English admiralty law would eventually serve as a model for the establishment of judicial processes involved in American maritime and naval affairs, especially as they related to the legal intricacies of privateering. Yet, at the outbreak of the Revolution, power and control over maritime matters pertaining to the fitting out of privately armed vessels and adjudication of prizes were in complete chaos with overlapping and sometimes conflicting authorities being asserted by the Continental Congress, provincial governments, and even local officials. Fortunately, in its Resolves of November 25, 1775, and March 23, 1776, and in its subsequent instructions of April 3, 1776, regarding the institution of privateering and the condemnation of prizes, Congress managed to bring some order into the situation.

Among the instructions to all masters of privateers, formulated by the Marine Committee, were orders that prizes were always to be brought into convenient ports of the United Colonies and "that proceedings may thereupon be had, in due form, before the courts, which are or shall be there appointed to hear and determine causes civil and maritime." After any capture, the Congress ordered, the master and pilot and one or more principal persons of the ship's company were to be taken to the judge or judges of the aforementioned court "to be examined upon oath, and make answer to the interrogatories which may be propounded, touching the interest or property of the ship or vessel, and her lading; and, at the same time . . . deliver, or cause to be delivered, to the judge or judges, all passes, seabriefs, charter-parties, bills of lading, cockets, letters, and other documents and writings found on board, proving the said papers, by the affidavit of yourself [the ship's master], or of some other person present at the capture, to be produced as they were received, without fraud, addition, subtraction or embezzlement."

The form, intent, and prerequisite of evidence on which various courts of admiralty could base decisions was thus established and held up as a model for all states to imitate.[1]

The first two years of the war were, in general, an incredible boom time for American privateering. Yet, though Lloyd's of London estimated that rebel privateers had taken more than five times as many British ships during that period than vessels that had been captured by the English, the American system for actually handling and processing prizes, at least in some states such as New Jersey, had yet even to be set in place.

Until the early spring of 1777 the majority of the known prizes and cargoes brought into Little Egg Harbor were libeled in Pennsylvania rather than under the laws of New Jersey. Indeed, as late as the end of March prizes still lying at Egg Harbor would continue to be sold at public vendues usually held at the Coffee House in Philadelphia.[2] The Pennsylvania Provincial Assembly, having appointed a committee to consider the recent acts of Congress, had already resolved on its own on March 26, 1776, just three days after the Continental privateering resolutions had been enacted, to erect a Court of Admiralty at Philadelphia which would be "constantly held" for the purpose of trying the justice of any capture of vessels made under the resolves of the Continental Congress. Although the intention of the Pennsylvania action was to address only vessels brought into Philadelphia, the move would in practice serve to contend with vessels carried into New Jersey ports as well until the latter state was able to enact its own resolutions on the matter. The judge commissioned to hold court was to have the power to issue warrants to the marshal of the city and county of Philadelphia. The marshal was to be appointed by the Committee of Safety and was empowered to summon a jury from Philadelphia County to appear before the judge at such time and place as the court should appoint.[3]

The Assembly further resolved that any person or persons who might bring into the colony and file a libel against any vessel or vessels "that have been offending or employed by the enemy, contrary to the Resolves of the Honorable Continental Congress," such persons were required to provide a full account, in writing, of the time and manner of the capture. This task was usually the job of the prize master and was carried out on the behalf of the owner and ship. In the report, it was required that the captor provide a description, "to the best of his knowledge," of the employment the captured vessel had been in when taken. All papers found aboard the vessel were to be handed over to the judge as evidence.

The process for action was clearly defined. When a bill was submitted to the court by a captor, the judge was to cause a notification to be made announcing the date and time set for the trial in at least two public newspapers printed in Philadelphia. The judge was to have the marshal summon a jury of a dozen "good and lawful men" who were to be sworn in, attend the hearing, and return with a "true verdict." If the jury deemed that the evidence indicated that the vessel had been armed or employed by the enemy or otherwise justified capture, the judge was empowered to condemn the ship, its cargo, and appurtenances, which were then to be sold at public vendue. If the court held that the prize was not enemy property, it was to be released to the captain and crew. Although such releases were uncommon, it was rare, even with such a verdict being rendered, that the collection of damages incurred as a result of the capture, the consequent delay in the voyage, and loss or spoilage of cargo was ever carried out. The trial was to be paid for out of the money the vessel and cargo produced by their sale at auction and was to be delivered to the Treasurer of Pennsylvania. If the vessel was ordered released, the libellant was required to pay for court costs. Any monies exceeding the cost of condemnation were to be "delivered to the captors, their agents or attorneys, for the use and benefit of such captors and others concerned therein." If two or more commissioned vessels made a joint capture at the same time, the moneys resulting from the sale were to be divided in proportion to their men. Proceeds were usually divided with one half going to the owners, which was further sub-divided according to each investor's interest. The other half went to the officers and crew, with shares distributed in accordance with articles signed at the commencement of the cruise.[4]

The trial and condemnation process was usually *pro forma*. At the trial, the owner of the vessel in question, or any other concerned persons acting in his behalf, would be allowed to show cause why the vessel, cargo, and appurtenances should not be condemned. In the case of recaptures of vessels taken by the enemy, the process was the same, and the original owners' claims were no longer valid as the vessel was considered to have passed into the ownership of the enemy and was therefore an enemy property, even if a British court had not condemned it. All appeals were to be handled by Congress or persons appointed by Congress for further hearings and trial provided the appeal request was demanded within five days after the Pennsylvania Court of Admiralty had made a definitive sentence. Appeals were to be lodged with the Secretary of Congress within forty days after the trial provided the party appealing rendered security to prosecute the action. In the case of the death of the Secretary of Congress or during a Congressional recess, the appeal was to be lodged with Congress within twenty days after the meeting thereof.

The judge of the court was to appoint an able clerk to keep a record of all court proceedings. All depositions of witnesses were to be taken before the judge and filed in the clerk's office. These were to be admitted as evidence in the event of the death or absence of said witnesses. Depositions were to be taken *ex parte* on notice being given to the adverse party as the judge directed and appointed. And finally, the judge, jurors, marshal, and clerk were to be paid out of the public treasury.[5]

On April 5, 1776, two days after Congress produced its "Instructions" for privateers, the Pennsylvania Assembly appointed one George Ross of Lancaster County to the Judgeship of the Philadelphia Court of Admiralty. Ross was a well-respected attorney, ardent patriot, and less than three months later would be a Signer of the Declaration of Independence. On April 10, the Committee of Safety named Matthew Clarkson as marshal to the court.[6]

The process was not without its flaws, principal among them being that many involved in the court could be considered to have serious conflicts of interest. Clarkson, for example, besides serving as marshal to the court, would become owner or shareholder in no fewer than five Pennsylvania privateers, including: the brig *Marbois* [September 1780], sloop *Cornelia* [October 1780], brigantine *Navarro* [July 1781], sloop *Sally* [August 1781], and schooner *Mayflower* [January 1782]. Despite such transgressions, which were in fact little more than a mirror of some delegates to the Continental Congress itself, the machinery for Pennsylvania had been quickly and efficiently set in place to address what would immediately become a major wartime industry—the adjudication, condemnation, and sale of privateer prizes and their cargoes.[7]

As in all previous wars, the Court of Admiralty of one combatant was often biased against the merchant marine and navies of the enemy, especially when it came to libels against prizes: during the Revolution, it was occasionally against vessels belonging to other states and even allied nations. It was not unusual that prizes and their cargoes were placed up for auction well before their cases were even brought to trial on the supposition that the evidence against them was so overwhelming that there could be no doubt about the outcome. The Marine Committee of Congress was from time to time prone to act on a presumption of guilt before a verdict had been rendered, as were the various state Admiralty Courts. Late in 1776, for instance, when the Continental Navy schooner *Wasp* brought into Egg Harbor a prize schooner laden with Indian corn and oats that had been bound for the Loyalist-dominated low counties of New York, the warship's commander, John Baldwin, had sent the master and five prisoners to Philadelphia. All of the prisoners had recently been aboard HMS *Falcon,* where they had rendered an oath of allegiance to the King, signing papers to that extent. When the prize was taken, the papers were found and sent to Philadelphia with the captives. Upon being apprised of the situation, Robert Morris forwarded the papers to the Pennsylvania Committee of Safety. Since there was no Judge of the Admiralty in New Jersey and Judge Ross was away in Lancaster, Morris wrote John Hancock, the President of Congress, that he had decided to send wagons to Egg Harbor to fetch the corn and oats "to feed the Continental [Army] horses in the city" before the case could be heard in court. As for the schooner itself, he wrote, "I am of the opinion it would be best to sell her without waiting for condemnation as the proofs of her guilt are clear & incontestable and she lies in too much danger to wait patiently for the usual forms. However Congress or the Marine Committee will please to give a positive order what must be done in this respect." With Morris as chairman of the Marine Committee, the decision, of course was self-evident.[8]

Morris was, in fact, merely following what had apparently already become accepted practice in nearly every state. When the evidence against them appeared overwhelming, prizes and their cargoes were often being sold well before the courts legally condemned them. The probability that such practice would lead to even greater abuses of the system and, in turn, to an ever-growing caseload of appeals to Congress itself would soon become a reality.

· · ·

For New Jersey, the almost instantaneous establishment of a Court of Admiralty in Philadelphia had set an example, but the moment for erecting its own system was simply not quite right. That was partly due to the fact that New Jersey, in a painful state of flux and divided loyalties, initially lacked adequate executive and legislative will to undertake the task. Until the late spring of 1776, the government had been technically under the administration of a Loyalist, Governor William Franklin, bastard son of one of the Revolution's foremost champions, Benjamin Franklin. Not until July 15 was Governor Franklin formally declared an enemy, placed under arrest by order of Congress, and sent to Connecticut a month later to be imprisoned in the hellhole of the Simsbury mines. Other factors also contributed to the inordinate influence of Philadelphia over the prize issue. Among these was that ships holding Pennsylvania commissions quite frequently sent prizes into New Jersey coastal ports because of the sporadic blockading of the Delaware: there was simply nowhere else close to home that was convenient to seek shelter. Yet, after unloading at remote Jersey coastal sites such as Little Egg Harbor, the prizes were often sent into the Delaware and, at least in the early years, eventually to Philadelphia where they usually ended up in the hands of Pennsylvania buyers.

The delicate problem that had been all but avoided by New Jersey legislators was partially cleared up on October 5, 1776, by the passage of an act authorizing the new governor, William Livingston, and his council to establish "by ordinance or commission, a Court of Admiralty; and also such and so many Custom Houses, with their necessary officers, to be commissioned by the Governor or Commander in Chief for the time being, as to the said Commander in Chief and Council shall appear expedient and necessary." The act was to remain in force for one year, "and from thence to the end of the next session of General Assembly, and no longer."[9] Unfortunately, the new law had certain drawbacks, not the least of which was that, unlike in Pennsylvania, the mechanism for actually designating the location for convening a court appears not to have been clearly outlined.

One of the first tests for the act came in early 1777 with the capture of the brigantine *Defiance* by Colonel Richard Somers and a militia detachment at Great Egg Harbor. Machinery for the implementation of the act had still not been set up, owing to "the inconveniency of holding a Court of Admiralty," a direct result of the earlier British occupation of key sectors of the state. Washington had driven the British from the capital, but British and Loyalist forces still remained posted in New Brunswick and Perth Amboy. A special act of legislation, dated February 28, 1777, thus had to be created to legally dispose of the brig. Somers and his men, the court claimed, had acted as "Sea Coast Guards at Great Egg Harbor" and therefore the authority of disposal of the prize rested with the state. A notice posted by Marshal Isaac Kay dated March 1 was published in the *Pennsylvania Evening Post* to formally inform the public that the vessel, together with her tackle, apparel, and furniture, then lying in the mouth of Tuckahoe River near Great Egg Harbor Inlet, and her cargo of molasses, sugar, coffee, coca, salt, cotton, and sundry whaling gear would be sold at public vendue at the house of John Somers at Great Egg Harbor on March 12. In truth, the move was an attempt to finally bring regulation to chaos, since hitherto many privateers and wreckers had been operating along the New Jersey coast without commission, disposing of the prizes as they saw fit, albeit illegally by state laws. Now, remoteness of situation could no longer be given as an excuse.[10]

Under pressure from the Continental Congress to institute more definitive measures, the New Jersey legislature finally passed a new and comprehensive acts, the first on October 8, 1778, and the next on December 5, 1778, directing the procedure for the appointment of customs house officers and re-establishing a new Court of Admiralty. Provision was made as to the mode of practice and free-bill was prescribed. Officers of the court were to be defined as judge, register, marshal, proctors, and advocates.[11]

Further legislation regarding the jurisdiction of the New Jersey Court of Admiralty was passed on December 18, 1781, and provided, among other things, for a seal "with a device of an anchor and thirteen stars on the face of it, and a legend round the border with these words 'Admiralty Seal of New Jersey.'" This act was later revised on November 29, 1782, and remained in force until repealed by legislation on June 3, 1799.[12]

During the course of the Revolution, Courts of Admiralty were convened regularly at numerous locations in New Jersey: at Trenton, first at the home of Ranssalear Williams, and then in August 1778 at the Court House; at Haddonfield; at the home of Gilbert Barton, innholder, in Allentown; at Mount Holly at the homes of Zachariah Rossclin, James Endall, and Isaac Wood; then, beginning in September 1779, at Burlington Court House. William Livingston, Jr., and Joseph Bloomfield would serve as registers, while Isaac Kay, John Stokes, and Joseph Potts would, at various times, hold the office of marshal. Public vendues of prizes and their cargoes would be held as the situation required at no less than fourteen locations throughout the state, including: Samuel Cooper's Ferry on the Delaware; Freehold; Greenwich; Salem; Mays Landing; Toms River; Chestnut Neck; at Richard Westcoat's inn and later Henry Thorn's at The Forks on the Mullica; Manasquan; at the home of Garret Schanck in Middletown; and in New Brunswick, Elizabethtown, and Absecon Bridge.[13]

• • •

With the establishment of a New Jersey Court of Admiralty, several locations—most notably Little Egg Harbor, Mays Landing, and Toms River—saw almost constant visitation by court marshals Stokes and Potts. Both Chestnut Neck and The Forks had become important centers for the outfitting, provisioning, sale, and trade of American privateers from many states, but in particular those bearing Pennsylvania commissions. Both sites were located miles up the muddy Mullica River, whose serpentine curves, constantly shifting mudflats, and sometimes extraordinarily swift current were as much a deterrent to enemy attack as the bars and polders of the inlet itself.

For the most part, the two settlements seemed to enjoy a rather symbiotic relationship, one most certainly dictated by nature and overland connections to the Delaware ports. Chestnut Neck, nearest to the sea, appears to have been an outfitting and terminus point for the deeper draft vessels. In the later years of the war, The Forks, closer to Philadelphia and Trenton, enjoyed the privilege of dominating the sale of prize vessels, as well as cargoes and products brought in by blockade runners, and played a predominant role in the regional timber export trade. From time to time, each settlement seems to have encroached upon the role of the other but the relationship was apparently amicable. Between the two there was a near monopoly of privateering-based activities in the area. Other settlements on the coast, most notably Mays Landing, approximately fifteen miles up the Great Egg Harbor River, supported privateering to some degree but never to the extent of Chestnut Neck and The Forks. Until at least 1778, mastery of this regional monopoly seems to have been orchestrated by a number of Philadelphia groups. After that time, control and sales of the Egg Harbor privateers and their prizes fell largely into the hands of local speculators with Philadelphia connections such as Joseph Ball, Richard Westcoat, and the Leaming syndicate of Cape May and Philadelphia.

At the beginning of 1777, Chestnut Neck could hardly be considered a town. It was, in fact, more on the order of a hamlet nestled on the marshy shores of the Mullica approximately five miles upstream from the river outlet into Great Bay, also known as Flat Bay. The hamlet consisted of barely a dozen dwellings, an inn belonging to one George Payne, several storehouses for prize cargoes, and a landing belonging to John Adams, the first commander of *Chance*. It was said that one Daniel Mathis also maintained a tavern nearby. The taverns, like those elsewhere on the coast, served as places where business transactions, prize sales, and socializing were conducted among those who had come to buy and sell. The dozen families residing at Chestnut Neck all bore solid British names, such as Smith, Davis, Bowen, Mathis, Johnson, and Higby, and most were involved directly or indirectly in maritime activities.[14] Their dwellings, though simple, were adequate. Micajah Smith, a farmer-cum-boatbuilder-turned privateersman, possessed a "plantation" consisting of "a large dwelling-house, barn, stables, and cow houses" with "three or four valuable fishing places" adjoining or within his property.[15] Smith had received his land as a grant from King George III and apparently also constructed boats on nearby Nacote Creek prior to the Revolution.[16]

Thus ensconced on lands occasionally referred to by later historians as "Smuggler's Woods" because of the illegal pre-war proclivities of the natives, it is likely that many, if not all, of the residents of Chestnut Neck had become involved in some aspect of privateering and the transporting of prize cargoes—and on occasion large numbers of prisoners of war—overland to the Delaware. When Philadelphia fell to the British on September 26, 1777, and the American-held forts along the Delaware succumbed in late November, the overland route was altered to Burlington, Dunks Ferry (modern Beverly), and other more secure destinations, from whence some prize cargoes found their way to Washington's army shivering at Valley Forge.[17]

But what of the port of Chestnut Neck itself? Situated on the fingertip of Chestnut Neck Ridge, a narrow, slightly elevated strip of land projecting from the west into the wetlands of the lower Pine Barrens just a few miles from the entrance to the lower Mullica River on Great Bay, which was itself five or six miles from Little Egg Harbor Inlet, its remoteness made it an enviable base for privateers. The river that flows adjacent to the site, in modern times, is frequently thirty to forty feet in depth in spots but perforated by numerous shoal areas that still require a substantial knowledge of the bottom terrain if a sizeable vessel is to traverse it safely. The shoreline, within the last half-century, has receded and partially silted up at various points, but etched away at others. Indeed, in about 1800, the inlet opening itself migrated as a result of a severe storm. There still exists a deep drop-off near the old town site, adjacent to a modern marina and not far from the pier facilities, a geological relic of the period of the Revolution that has remained constant. Thus, it is probably safe to assume that, during the maritime heyday of Chestnut Neck, ships could safely anchor in the river or tie up at water's edge at John Adams' Landing or adjacent to Payne's Tavern with a great deal of security.[18]

The Forks, unlike Chestnut Neck, was considerably more developed and provided much of the non-war-related material necessary for survival. From the *Pennsylvania Packet* an advertisement placed by Elijah Clark, one of the largest landowners in the region and a principal player in the privateering game, boasted that his holdings there included:

A sawmill and grist-mill, both remarkable for going fast and supplied with a never-failing stream of water, the mills within one mile and a quarter of a landing, to which vessels of seventy or eighty tons burthen can come, skows carrying seventy or eighty thousand board feet of boards go loaded from the mill; there is sufficient quantity of pine and cedar timber fit for rails near the river side, which may be easily exported to those parts of the country where they will sell to great advantage; there is also on the premises, a dwelling house that will accommodate a large family, a barn, stables, and out-houses, also a number of houses for workmen and tradesmen, a smiths shop, wet and dry goods stores and indeed every building necessary and convenient for carrying on business and trade extensively, for which the situation of the place is exceedingly well calculated both by nature and improvement.

And, of course, the nearby Batsto Furnace was already producing large quantities of cannonballs for the Pennsylvania Council of Safety.[19]

Throughout the spring of 1777, the Little Egg Harbor ports seemed to have served as a preliminary staging area, primarily for the Philadelphia privateers, yet remained remote and seemingly sheltered from attack, despite the ever-increasing number of enemy cruisers operating along the Jersey coast. The myth of total security, however, was soon to be shattered.

Egg Harbor

"Nothing had given such Surprize thro Europe as the Success of our privateering Business."

By February 1777, the diplomatic news regarding support in Europe for the American revolutionaries was anything but encouraging. Franklin and Deane, the American delegation to the Court of King Louis XVI, struggling to secure not only French monetary assistance but also recognition of the United States as a nation and a full military alliance, could report little forward motion. On April 17, Roger Sherman, a delegate to Congress from Connecticut, informed Jonathan Trumbull, Sr., that from the last reports received from Franklin and Deane, no treaty had yet been concluded, although they held out the "probability" that both France and Spain would eventually enter the war. But nothing was certain. Even worse was word that the enemy intended "to bend their force against New England and Extirpate them & enslave the Inhabitants of the Southern States."[1]

The most encouraging news was the impact the American privateering offensive, though disjointed and without overall direction, was having on British commerce. The depredations had become so enormous that merchants in Britain had laid before Lord Sandwich a memorial stating that captures made by privateers had cost their West Indian trade more than £1,800,000 sterling in losses and driven insurance rates up to a phenomenal 28 percent. "Britain begins to totter," wrote one observer, "her Trade is cut off, & her Merchants become Bankrupt. Several considerable [West Indian] Houses have failed, which have drawn many others into the Ruin. We learn from St. Eustatia that two of the American Privateers have taken nine transports & two Guineamen, part of which arrived safe at Martinique."[2]

Oliver Wolcott, another Connecticut delegate, issued a cautionary note: "Nothing had given such Surprize thro Europe as the Success of our privateering Business." However, he was disturbed regarding the enemy's countermeasures. A bill to grant letters of marque and reprisal to British vessels, which had been hitherto opposed by the British Admiralty, was already passing in Parliament, and the Royal Navy's "Press for Seamen continued Very violent tho' not equally productive as it had been, which together with the great Preparations in France and Spain with the sure Protection which our Ships received in their Ports, forbid every Expectation that Peace would continue long between those Powers."[3]

Indeed, despite the constant string of actual defeats suffered on the North American continent, many in Congress took heart in the positive effects the news of American privateering successes was having in the courts of Europe. Regarding recent intelligence from London, John Adams, in a letter to James Warren, wrote that "so many Bankruptcies were never known. Two W[est] I[ndies] Houses have failed for one Million two hundred Thousand Pounds. 'Stand firm,' says our Friends in England, 'and nothing can hurt you.'

Benjamin Franklin, by Claude Louis Desrais, artist, Pierre Adrian Le Beau, engraver. Courtesy Prints and Photographs Division, Library of Congress.

The British ministry are very angry with France for the assistance she gives Us and threaten to declare War." Moreover, a quarrel between the British and Spanish over the Musqueto Shores of Central America threatened to erupt at any minute into a military confrontation.[4]

Not unexpectedly, Congress moved to press on with the effort to induce both Bourbon powers in Europe, France and Spain, to join against England. To do so, it was deemed necessary to divide the two delegates to France between the Court of Louis XVI and the Spanish. Franklin would remain in Paris and Deane would be dispatched to Seville. Moreover, efforts to establish commercial treaties with other European powers were also being initiated. Of equal importance was the expansion of privateering operations based on foreign soils, most notably those of French shores, both in Europe and the West Indies. On May 4, Charles Carroll of Carrollton of Maryland was able to report, undoubtedly with some joy: "The French in Martinico have applied to Congress for commissions to cruize agt. the English trade. Several commissions have been granted already. I think these steps must inevitably draw on a war between France & England."[5]

The positive sentiments towards the success of American privateering efforts, and the bloody escalation of the war on both sides were, by the spring of the year, enough to convince many closet supporters of privateering to go public, including Robert Morris, who had most publicly condemned such activities while privately supporting them. Morris, who had secretly engaged in the burgeoning practice, in concert with the American agent in Martinique, William Bingham, wrote to his partner on April 25: "My Scruples about Privateering are all done away. I have seen such Rapine, Plunder & Destruction denounced against & executed on the Americans that I join you in thinking it a Duty to oppose and distress so Merciless an Ennemy in every Shape we can. Therefore it matters not who knows my Concern with [Captain John] Ord as I am now ready to encrease the Number of my Engagements in that Way." The success of Morris's investment in the fielding of the privateer *Rattlesnake*, Captain Ord, from Martinique with an entirely French crew, and her profitable and highly publicized capture of nine transports and two Guineamen, most certainly must have played a role in his decision as well.[6]

Another significant and positive aspect of the war was a distinctive increase in direct foreign commerce with European trading syndicates that had never existed before the onset of hostilities. Though at the outset quite limited in scope, the prospects seemed hopeful. In early May, a number of merchant ships from the continent, though repeatedly chased by British blockaders guarding both the Delaware and Chesapeake bays, managed to successfully elude their pursuers and reach their destinations. "Thus," wrote John Adams to his wife Abigail, "you see We can and will have Trade, in spight of them. . . . And this Trade will probably increase fast. It requires Time for The Stream of Commerce to alter its Channell. Time is necessary, for our Merchants and foreign Merchants to think, plan, and correspond with each other. Time is also necessary for our Masters of Vessells and Mariners to become familiar with the Coasts, Ports and Harbours of foreign Countries — and a longer Time still is needfull for French, Spanish, and Dutch Masters and Mariners to learn our Coasts, and Harbours."[7]

It soon became even more apparent that the tiny New Jersey port of Egg Harbor, and even some adjacent sites such as Toms River, although remote and isolated, would be among the more important destinations that both American and foreign captains would become intimately familiar with. In mid-May intelligence was received in Philadelphia of the arrival at Egg Harbor of a vessel from France with a cargo of clothes and between 3,000 and 4,000 stand of arms. Moreover, the vessel carried English newspapers published as late as the end of February, as well as significant intelligence from the American Commissioners in France, written in March, and from Arthur Lee in Spain.[8]

That both commercial and privateering operations in and around Egg Harbor and the adjacent coast would not go without contest was also a given. In mid-April, when a Connecticut privateer called *Lyon*, commanded by one Timothy Shaler (Shayler or Shealor) captured a pair of enemy store ships off Sandy Hook, bound from Cork for New York, the difficulties of conducting privateering operations in the region would be illustrated.[9] On April 19, while sailing southward along the Jersey shore and adjacent to Long Beach, the three vessels encountered HMS *Mermaid*, a 6th rate, 28-gun man-of-war, Captain James Hawker commanding, against which the little 10-gun privateer stood little chance. Within short order, one of Shaler's two prizes, *Experiment*, laden with coals, was retaken. The second prize, named *Hazard*, laden with oats, was run on the beach and destroyed at the same time. *Lyon*, which found herself unable to escape, was also driven ashore and hopelessly stranded.[10]

Nevertheless, the importance of such forward New Jersey coastal inlets as Egg Harbor, as places from which privateers could operate and as secure safe havens when necessary and into which they might send prizes despite the hazards, was not lost on a number of enterprising entrepreneurs. Primary among them were three men, Richard Westcoat, Colonel John Cox, and Joseph Ball, whose quiet role in the business end of privateering would come to epitomize the less glamorous but no less important component of the industry itself.

Born in 1733, the son of Daniel and Deborah Westcoat (or Westcott), Richard Westcoat had been half-owner of the important Batsto Iron Works as early as 1766, which he later sold. With the outbreak of the war, he became an early volunteer and was noted as a dashing officer in the cause of liberty. Seriously wounded during the Battle of Trenton, he had been obliged to convalesce at his home near Egg Harbor, but retained his rank as major in the Third Battalion, Gloucester County Militia, then commanded by his neighbor, Colonel Elijah Clark, master of Pleasant Mills plantation. Upon Clark's resignation in 1777, Westcoat assumed command, a position that would prove important to the military defenses of the Little Egg Harbor basin. In concert with Cox and Clarke, he provided significant leadership in organizing and facilitating the running of the frequent British blockades of the region and, during the winter of 1777–78, in the smuggling of supplies overland to Valley Forge, as well as the commercial and privateering activities at Egg Harbor.[11]

Before the war, Colonel John Cox had been a Philadelphia merchant and trader, endowed with a most entrepreneurial spirit. In 1770, he had, in company with one Charles Thomson, purchased the Batsto Iron Works from its then owners, Reuben Haines, Joseph Burr, John Cooper, and the Walter Franklin family. Three years later he secured sole ownership by purchasing the shares of his partner Thomson.[12] The Batsto Iron Works, under Cox's ownership, would soon become of enormous significance to the commerce of the region. In June 1775, an advertisement in the *Pennsylvania Gazette* is unquestionably indicative of the importance of the works It read:

MANUFACTURED AT BATSTO FURNACE, in West New-Jersey and to be sold either at the works or by the subscriber, in Philadelphia, a great variety of iron pots, kettles, Dutch ovens and oval fish kettles, either with or without covers, skillets of different sizes, being much lighter, neater and superior in quality to any imported from Great Britain, Potash, and other large kettles, from 30 to 125 gallons, sugar mill gudgeons, neatly rounded, and polished at the ends; grating-bars of different lengths, grist-mill rounds; weights of all sizes, from 7 to 56 lb.; Fuller plates; open and close stoves, of different sizes; rag-wheel irons for saw-mills; pestles and mortars, sash weights, and forge hammers of the best quality. Also Batsto Pig-Iron as usual, the quality of which is too well known to need any recommendation.

JOHN COX[13]

By the fall of 1776, Batsto iron was in such demand that continuing labor shortages threatened to impugn production. In November, Cox was obliged to advertise in Philadelphia for woodcutters. The voracious furnaces at the iron works required a constant supply of wood to continue production, and Cox promised "sober industrious men may make wages, by cutting some wood at two shillings and six pence per cord." There was also a need to hire shallops to haul the iron on the perilous route between Egg Harbor and Philadelphia.[14] As the war began to focus more sharply on New Jersey, labor problems increased as the state's manpower began to be dissipated by military call-ups. The problem, however, was partially rectified on June 5, 1777, when the New Jersey legislature exempted ironworkers, including those from Batsto and Mount Holly, which Cox also owned, from compulsory state military service. He was then authorized to set up a company of fifty men and two lieutenants, with himself as captain, which were to be exempt from military duty except in case of outright invasion.[15]

Prior to the onset of war, Cox had served as a member of the Philadelphia Committee of Correspondence and Council of Safety. When a regiment called the Philadelphia Associators was organized, John Cox was chosen as major of the Second Battalion, and later elected lieutenant colonel. As hostilities erupted and quickly engulfed New Jersey, it seemed ordained that Batsto would soon become an important arsenal for the Continental Army. Indeed, well before the Declaration of Independence, Cox had contracted with the Pennsylvania Council of Safety to provide large quantities of cannon balls. Such issues as conflict of interest were ignored for the production of war supplies was paramount, and it mattered little where they came from—as long as they were to be had.[16]

It had originally been intended that deliveries would be made by water, via the Mullica, the Atlantic, and then the Delaware, but with a strong blockade of the latter in effect, the plan had to be altered. Thus, on May 20, 1776, the Pennsylvania Council of Safety resolved to dispatch five or six wagons to Batsto to bring off "with all possible expedition the Shot he made for account of this Committee." Two days later, Cox informed the Committee that six wagons had been loaded and were ready to begin the trek to Cooper's Ferry where they would arrive the following evening. Three more had already been dispatched. Cox was to receive £2,481.55 in payment. And more significantly, the feasibility of overland transport of heavy military goods and supplies from the Mullica to the Delaware was proven. The lesson learned would not be lost on those who, in the near future, would be engaged in merchandising prize cargoes brought in to Little Egg Harbor.[17]

Yet, in the summer of 1777, it was the operations of the critically important Batsto and Mount Holly iron works that were first and foremost on Cox's management agenda. The New Jersey General Assembly was well aware of the importance of both works to the war effort and, in session, resolved: "Whereas it is highly expedient that the Army and Navy of the United States of America should be furnished as speedily as possible with a Quantity of Canon, Cannon-Shot, Camp Kettles and other Implements . . . , which the Furnace at Batsto and the Forge and Rolling Mill at Mount Holly are well adapted to supply, . . ." and began to increase orders. The plants also produced large salt-water evaporation pans that were needed for the production of salt for the army.[18]

Both plants continued on, albeit always desperately short of skilled workers undoubtedly owing the military manpower drain caused by the war, the remoteness of the site, and the sheer, back-breaking labor involved. In late June, in an effort to ramp up production, Cox advertised in the *Pennsylvania Evening Post:*

> Wanted at Batsto and Mount Holly iron works a number of labourers, colliers, nailors, and two or three experienced forgemen to whom constant employ and best wages will be given—four shillings per cord will be paid for cutting pine and maple wood. For further information apply to Colonel Cox's counting house on Arch street, Philadelphia, to Mr. Joseph Ball, manager at Batsto, or to the subscriber at Mount Holly. RICHARD PRICE N.B. The workmen at these works are by law of this State exempt from military duty.[19]

Cox's first engagement in the business of privateering began in August 1776 as co-owner with one John Chaloner of Philadelphia of the 12-gun Pennsylvania brigantine *General Mifflin*, commanded by Captain John Hamilton, late of the Pennsylvania Navy. It had not been a profitable venture, though while sailing in company with another Pennsylvania privateer, the *Rattlesnake*, Captain David McCulloch commanding, *Mifflin* had captured a rich English merchantmen from which "prize effects" valued at £3,000 had been taken. Unfortunately for all concerned, Hamilton's ship was run ashore on the bar off Sinepuxent, Maryland during a blinding snowstorm in March 1777 "by ignorance of the pilot" and totally lost along with nineteen of her crew.[20]

The third and perhaps most important member of the group, Joseph Ball, was a clean shaven, cherubic-faced Presbyterian whose dimpled chin, dull brown eyes, and receding forehead belied a most dynamic core. He had, before the war, served as Cox's agent in Philadelphia; following the latter's acquisition of Batsto, the business relationship between the two men grew considerably. Upon the opening of hostilities, when the manager of the iron works, one William Richards, left Batsto for military service, Ball assumed his job. His move to Batsto was not without its benefits, for there he met one Sara Lee, to whom he was soon betrothed. On the Mullica River, his proximity to and growing personal and business relationships with Cox, Clark, and Westcoat would serve him well in the years to come. As manager of Batsto, where he would spend more and more of his time, he was credited with being directly responsible for its heavy munitions production and efficient operations under what can be called severe wartime conditions. Moreover, while at Batsto he would lay the foundations of administrative experience for a subsequent career as a major American financier and corporation executive.[21] But it was in the promulgation of privateering on the New Jersey coast that he would most excel at. And it was in privateers that his fortunes, and those who were associated with him, would be founded.

• • •

As the winter of 1776–77 slowly dissipated and the war escalated, British warships along the mid-Atlantic seaboard started to increase in almost incremental numbers. Reports began to come in with unnerving regularity, noting that this American blockade-runner or that privateer had been captured, driven ashore, or sunk by the enemy. The strict blockade of the Delaware was unquestionably proving costly to patriot shipping. On March 12, 1777, for example, HMS *Daphne* and a Royal Navy tender chased ashore, at Cape May, Captain Thomas Rawling's Philadelphia register ship *Sally*, bound for the Delaware from Nantz, France. Rawlings and his men made their escape, but when the tide came on the ship was refloated and hauled off as a prize by the enemy tender. Owing to the paucity of cannon in the state, the Philadelphia papers lamented the fact that *Sally* had not carried a single gun to defend herself against mere boats or small tenders, "else in all probability her cargo at least might have been saved, which would have been very acceptable to the public." It was publicly stated that the ship was not as valuable as some had imagined because she carried only a cargo of lead of "which we have lately received great supplies, so that we can provide every red or blue coated plunderer with a full pound of it, if an ounce should not prove sufficient to make him honest." The facts regarding the loss, however, were otherwise. In truth, the ship had carried a cargo "of immense consequence to the Continent," primarily gunpowder and other military supplies from France, which had secretly been contracted for by the firm of Willing, Morris and Company (Robert Morris, Chairman of the Marine Committee, being a full partner therein) on the account of the Secret Committee of Correspondence (Robert Morris also being the Chairman thereof).[22]

Only nine days after the loss of *Sally*, a pilot boat sloop serving as a tender to HMS *Phoenix*, brought into Gravesend Bay, New York, a prize captured in Cranberry Inlet, opposite Toms River, during a swift cutting-out raid. The prize, a sloop named *Wanton*, belonging to Samuel Burling and commanded by John Mount, was taken while in ballast and sent to Halifax. To some it appeared that the British were finally beginning to focus attention upon the Jersey coast and, with little to stop them, their successes seemed relentless. Indeed, by the onset of June, one Hessian officer noted, "The English ships have been so active that this harbor [New York] is full of prizes. The Delaware is almost entirely blocked. Every ship that the fleet can dispense with has been made ready to cruise."[23]

Not all the news for the rebel patriots was as bad as on the Jersey coast, where British and Hessian forces, by the onset of June, began to mass for a major expedition whose objective could only be guessed at. On June 20, Charles Carroll of Carrollton, a Marylander and the only Catholic delegate to Congress, informed his father of major privateering successes against the enemy:

We this day have accounts from Boston from a gentleman of undoubted reputation, that two transports from England with Hessians on board are likely taken by one of our privateers, one of which with 82 prisoners is arrived at Por[t]smouth & the other hourly expected. The Hessians shewed the greatest joy, when our men boarded them, & offered their services as guards over their own officers. They sailed with 600, which is all the reinforcements to be expected from them, & as there were 3 of our Privateers together & the transports were but 6 days from land I expect a good account of the remainder. A ship from England to Quebec is also brought in, she had 4000 blanketts & a valuable cargo of other woolens on board.[24]

• • •

As Generals Washington and Howe were commencing their spring maneuvers and counter-maneuvers, and a great deal of naval activity was being reported in and about British-held New York, an unidentified brig hove to off Little Egg Harbor Inlet on June 10 and made a signal for a pilot to attend her. Joseph Sooy (Sowey), accompanied by his brother and two boys, was soon on his way to lend assistance. A native of Chestnut Neck, Sooy was considered to be one of the best pilots in the area, but was unaware of the vessel's identity. Unfortunately for him, the ship proved to be HM Brig *Stanley*, Richard Whitworth commanding, serving temporarily as a tender to HM Sloop-of-War *Haerlem*. The pilot and his crew were immediately captured. Almost as soon as Sooy was aboard, *Stanley* raised anchor and proceeded to the mouth of Great Egg Harbor Inlet before word of the capture could spread. There, another signal was raised and the local pilot, a Mr. Golden, and his own small crew set out in a longboat to assist. But "on approaching near enough to finding she was a vessel of force, he immediately put about and pushed for shore, the enemy's boats pursuing, with only two men showing themselves." When about a hundred yards from the shore Golden perceived a number of armed men, hitherto concealed, rise up in the pursuit boat and commence firing. With musket balls peppering the waters all around them, the Americans made it to shore by the narrowest of margins and took immediate flight.[25]

Although Golden had escaped, the capture of Joseph Sooy portended serious danger for Chestnut Neck. Unbeknownst to the Americans, British intelligence regarding the increasing usage of Egg Harbor, almost certainly through Loyalist informants, had provided Captain Andrew Snape Hamond, senior Royal Navy commander in the region, with critical data. Thus, he ordered a cutting out operation of patriot vessels believed to be in the river. In a June 10, 1777 directive issued to Lieutenant Richard Knight, commander of *Haerlem*, he wrote:

> And whereas I have received intelligence that several of the Enemies Vessels are lately arrived at Egg Harbour, You are therefore in your way to endeavour to look into that place and if it shall appear to you to be practicable to cut them out or destroy them. You are to take the Hotham and Stanley Tenders under your command (who are directed to accompany you thither for that purpose) and use your best endeavours against the enemies Vessels; which Service being performed, You are then to give Orders to the Hotham Tender to join the Preston at New York, and Send the Roebucks Tender back to me with an Account of your proceedings; making the best of your way afterwards with the Sloop under your command to join the Admiral without further loss of time.[26]

Both Colonel John Cox, now owner of the Batsto Furnace, and Lt. Colonel Elijah Clark, of the Third Battalion, Gloucester County Militia, who had much to lose if the enemy attacked, feared "that he will be made use of by the enemy to bring in their tenders and pilot them up the bay and river." With the enemy having a knowledgeable pilot, which they had hitherto lacked, Cox's and Clark's worst fears were soon realized. Two days later *Haerlem*, *Stanley*, a small schooner of eight guns called *Delaware*, and an armed pilotboat of six guns were piloted over the bar at Little Egg Harbor to conduct a classic cutting-out operation. The tiny squadron immediately proceeded up the Mullica to Chestnut Neck. There the British found riding at anchor two brigantines, *Ann*, commanded by a Captain Bradley, and *Nancy*, commanded by a Captain Montgomery, one being a letter of marque and the other a merchantman laden with tar and lumber. Both were taken, apparently without resistance, along with a considerable quantity of stock. And there was absolutely nothing that anyone could do about it.[27]

In desperation, Colonel Cox fired off a letter to his influential Philadelphia business associate, Charles Pettit, informing him of the raiders who, in his opinion, were likely to remain at Chestnut Neck to intercept a number of ships hourly expected to return from the sea. Fortunately for the vessels that Cox was worried about, Lieutenant Knight declined to tarry so far inland, in enemy territory, on such a narrow waterway; he returned to New York on June 15 with the vessels taken at Egg Harbor and three others, the schooner *Apollo*, William Forsyth, sloop *Industry*, and another as prizes in company.[28]

The raid had clearly illustrated just how vulnerable Little Egg Harbor was from assault by sea, now that the enemy knew his way in. Fortunately, Knight had arrived when only two vessels were in port. A few days earlier or later and the story would have been vastly different. The losses could have been far worse. Colonel Cox, above all, stood to lose perhaps the most if his holdings at Batsto were to be destroyed in a subsequent raid. Disturbed, he promptly notified Pettit, a speculator in privateers like himself, that he fully intended to do something about it. He had already established some defense works on a long narrow island in the middle of the river near The Forks but Chestnut Neck, further down, stood entirely undefended.[29]

"I shall go down to Chestnut Neck tomorrow," he wrote, "with a number of men in order to erect a small fortification of 8 or 10 guns to protect [*sic*, prohibit] them [the British] if possible from penetrating the country." A man of his word, Cox, aided by Richard Westcot, who was then in charge of government stores at The Forks (where he also operated a tavern), proceeded to build a fortification at their own expense at the Fox Burrows, commanding the approach to Little Egg Harbor. Colonel Elijah Clark ordered down a guard of twenty men and promised to "order down as many more to assist in doing the necessary work." A description of the works a year after construction indicated that they consisted of a battery with six embrasures erected on a level with the water and situated so as to rake the channel of the river. A second battery was erected on a "commanding eminence" or highland with a platform of guns "en barbette." Although powder and provisions were in short supply, Cox was able to arm the forts with cannon salvaged from the 95-ton Connecticut privateer *Lyon*, lately commanded by Captain Timothy Shaler. The vessel, as earlier noted, had been driven ashore in mid-April by HMS *Mermaid* on nearby Long Beach, and apparently dumped her guns to get off, but was captured nevertheless. As she had been armed with eight double-fortified 4-pounders and two double-fortified 6-pounders complete with carriages, gunner's implements, swivel guns, powder, ball and all the artillerist's necessaries, it is likely the elevated battery was armed with the extra four guns.[30]

Later, on September 20, 1777, Cox's local business associates, Elijah Clark and Richard Westcot, would present a bill of particulars for the construction of the fort in a memorial to the General Assembly of New Jersey, then convened at Haddonfield. In the memorial the two men claimed "they had erected, at their own expense, a small fort, at the Fox Burrows, near the Port of Little Egg Harbor, and had purchased a number of cannon for the defense of the said port, relying on the public for payment of the expense." The memorialists were duly refunded £430, 1 shilling, and 3 pence for their efforts.[26]

Despite a seeming error in payment, the whole affair was undoubtedly correct and above board. The remains of *Lyon* and her armament had been placed up for auction at George Payne's Tavern at Chestnut Neck on July 9, 1777, and, in all likelihood, Clark and Westcoat, who was at that moment still a major in the Gloucester Country Militia stationed there, purchased her. The weapons and materials were donated to the cause and at the same time insured the safety of property further upriver—property in which all three men had a vested interest![31]

Yet, the men operating on the brown tannin-colored waters of the Mullica River, Westcoat, Cox and Ball, assisted from time to time by Elijah Clark, would provide a most unique combination of talents critical to the patriot cause —and at the same time to their own pocketbooks. They would organize the repeated running of the British blockade, the military defense of the Little Egg Harbor basin, the transport of significantly important supplies overland to Washington's army at Valley Forge, and, finally, the fielding and support of countless privateers and the sale of their prizes.

Nonetheless, British cruisers continued to take their toll of privateers and blockade-runners alike. Just ten days after the auction at Payne's Tavern, a rebel schooner from Barnegat, bound for the West Indies, was chased and captured by HMS *Solebay*, a 6th-rate, 28-gun man-of-war, Captain Thomas Symonds commanding.[32]

· · ·

The recent cutting-out operation against vessels at Chestnut Neck and the increasing numbers of captures of American shipping in general, had hit a nerve. Yet, it was but a sting compared to the massive operation launched by General Howe on July 23 as he departed Staten Island with 15,000 troops bound for Philadelphia. To everyone's surprise, the enormous armada sailing southward along the New Jersey coast did not turn into the Delaware as had been expected, but proceeded on towards the Virginia Capes. In a maneuver intended to confuse the Americans, it was Howe's plan to ascend the Chesapeake to the Head of Elk, at its northern extremity, march overland through Maryland, Delaware, and Pennsylvania and take the capital city of America from the rear. Although all eyes remained focused on the enemy juggernaut, the fallout from the expedition as it passed very slowly down the mid-Atlantic seaboard only served to reinforce the growing awareness of the vulnerability of the Jersey shores.

About 1 p.m. on the very day the fleet sailed, an alarm was raised at Great Egg Harbor when cannon fire was heard along the shore, four miles to the southward of the inlet. Fifteen militiamen had been at work, possibly at the local salt works, and immediately mustered and marched towards the sound of firing. They soon discovered that a squadron of enemy warships, having been in chase of a small schooner twenty-two days out of Martinique, had driven her ashore. The ships in question proved to be an unidentified warship, reportedly a frigate of thirty-two guns, and the tenders *Stanley* and *Delaware*. The frigate had come to anchor three-quarters of a mile from the beach, but the two tenders and a trio of barges came in much closer to the shore. All had commenced a steady firing on the stranded schooner and the men who had come to assist her. It had already become a scene all too common on the Jersey shore, and would be repeated many times over in the years to come. For four or five hours the bombardment continued without much effect as the militiamen and the schooner's crewmen worked furiously to unload her of a valuable cargo of molasses, sugar, limes, and dry goods. Then, at high water, the ship bilged even as much of the remaining cargo thrown overboard was being driven ashore by the waves and secured by the men on the beach. Fortunately, no lives were lost.[33]

Another warship arrived on the scene about 7 p.m. and anchored further up the beach, causing some anxiety among the party working the wreck site. From "the preparations we discovered them making [we] expected they would land in the night." Expecting a land attack, the beach party thus turned its attention to constructing a "tolerably good breastwork from the rum casks and sand" and vigorously prepared to prevent the enemy from destroying the salvaged cargo. It was not the defensive preparations that stymied the expected assault, however, but a strong wind that began blowing from the northwest, which forced the assailants to stand to sea.[34]

Three days later, on Saturday morning, July 26, 1777, at least seventy sail of enemy ships, all part of Howe's great armada, were spotted beating off Little Egg Harbor with a southerly wind behind them. It seemed strange to General Washington that if the enemy's destination was the Delaware his progress was so slow. "From this event," the commander-in-chief informed Israel Putnam, "there seems to be little room to doubt that the destination is into Delaware Bay and against the City of Philadelphia. . . ."[35] He was only half right.

The van of General Howe's army and the fleet entered the Chesapeake bound for the head of the bay on August 15. Unwilling to hazard the intricate maze of forts, obstructions, and naval defenses the rebels had erected on the Delaware, Howe began his march on Philadelphia via the open back door. On August 25, he debarked his troops at the north end of the bay at Head of Elk (modern Elkton), Maryland. Despite Washington's valiant efforts to stall his approach on September 3 near Cooch's Bridge, Delaware, and on September 11 at Brandywine Creek, Pennsylvania, barely twenty-five miles from the city, the enemy proved unstoppable. At Washington's urging, Congress abandoned Philadelphia on the 18th and retired to York, Pennsylvania. Three days later, twenty miles north of the city, in a surprise attack at Paoli Tavern, the British fell upon an American division under General Anthony Wayne, inflicting yet another agonizing defeat. On September 26, Philadelphia, the capital and largest city in the United States, was finally occupied. Two months later, after a determined defense by patriot forces on land and water against overwhelming odds, the lower Delaware was entirely closed down, and with it the Philadelphia privateers. Despite the loss, the small force of Continental cruisers, state navy warships, and the sixty-nine privateers bearing Continental commissions had captured an estimated 464 enemy vessels during the year, of which seventy-two had been recaptured; the Royal Navy, with about eighty vessels on the North American Station made about as many in return. But somehow, the war on the Jersey coast would continue.[36]

At the same time, the seeds for another kind of maritime conflict, one fought largely in the courts rather than on the high seas, had already been planted more than 1,500 miles to the south, in the West Indies. The first of its many battles would begin off Egg Harbor. The course and climax of the subsequent contests in Philadelphia would influence not only the Revolution but also the maturing matrix of American admiralty law. It would, indeed, ultimately result in nothing less than one of the first verifications of the supremacy of the Constitution of the United States in the highest court of the new nation.

–X–

O You Damned Rebel

"You have no commission and I intend to make a prize of your vessel."

As he emerged from the grimy jail in which he had only recently been incarcerated at Montego Bay, Jamaica, 29-year-old Gideon Olmsted had not relished much of the last seven months of his life. Indeed, his mariner's tale had been one of misfortune and woe ever since he had sailed from Hartford, Connecticut, on that cold mid-December day in 1777 as captain of the first vessel he could call his own. It had been an auspicious occasion when, for £189, he had purchased the ship, a 75-ton schooner called *Seaflower*, at Westerly, Rhode Island, in partnership with his brother Aaron and a friend named Abraham Miller. He had just mustered out of the army in April, and had returned to the life of a mariner, a vocation in which he had previously been engaged since the age of twenty, but always for someone else.

After bringing *Seaflower* to Hartford to take on a load of horses, tobacco, bricks, barrel hoops and onions destined for Port Louis, Guadeloupe, Olmsted began his first voyage as master and commander of his own ship. He had signed on six good men: Israel Dening, mate, and John Buckland, John Hodge, Eliphalet Forbes, Israel Fox, and Hezekiah Burnham, seamen. The only noteworthy event of the voyage was a brief and cordial meeting with an American privateer, after which he arrived safely at Port Louis on January 15, 1778, and quickly sold his cargo. Taking on another lading for home, however, mostly molasses, coffee, tea, and salt, took more than a month.[1]

Though war raged elsewhere, it must have seemed at the time but a distant specter—that is until April 7, when he encountered a pair of ships bound from British-occupied Philadelphia for the Bay of Honduras. One of the vessels proved to be a 20-gun British privateer called *Weir*, Captain Samuel Williams commanding. With *Seaflower* mounting only two pair of swivel guns for defense, Olmsted had little choice but to capitulate without firing a shot.[2] It was then that the New England mariner's ordeal had begun, one that would come to occupy more than thirty years of his life and influence the very course of American judicial history.

• • •

Captain Williams treated his prisoners well, and on April 21 sent Olmsted, Forbes, Fox, Buckland, and Burnham ashore near St. Ann's Bay, Jamaica in a boat, but retained Dening and Hodge as it would be necessary for them to testify when he libeled the schooner as a prize. The boat set the Americans ashore about sundown at a private estate called Boge, six miles from St. Ann's, and from there they set out on foot for the bay, where they arrived weary and sore. At a tavern, Olmsted later recorded, "We got a bowl of grog and got into a room by ourselves and drank General Washington's health and hoped that it would be our turn next and lay down upon the floor and went to sleep." After nearly two weeks of waiting at St. Ann's Bay, Olmsted and his men managed to secure passage on a vessel belonging to one John Oray bound for French-held Cape St. Nicholas Mole, Santo Domingo, where they hoped to find a vessel sailing for America. Unfortunately, Dame Fortune vanished again ten days out of St. Ann's and within sight of their destination, about May 16, when they were spotted by a Royal Navy tender belonging to HMS *Niger*, 32-guns, which had been patrolling there since early in the year. Believing Oray's boat to be an American rebel, the tender promptly took her as a prize. Having five American mariners on board did not help her captain's pleas of innocence.[3]

"She carried us back into Kingston," wrote Olmsted. "After we got in they set us at liberty. We went ashore but had no money nor credit, as we thought. But luckily I found one M. Robert Crose who was an American who was very kind to prisoners and told me that I and my people might live at his house until we could get a chance to go to the Mole."[4]

After ten days, accompanied by Crose, and with Olmsted, Forbes, Fox, and Burnham agreeing to work as seamen, the stranded adventureres were finally able to board a sloop bound for the cape, while Buckland found passage on a French schooner. Soon afterwards, Burnham became mortally ill, possibly from an infectious boil on his foot that had debilitated him since late April. On June 15, the sloop was obliged to turn into Port Morant, on the southern tip of Jamaica, to repair a leak. There Olmsted and his men carried their suffering shipmate ashore where he died the next day. On the day following the funeral, Buckland, who had come in aboard an English cruiser that had just captured the French vessel on which he had sailed, rejoined the three seamen.[5]

Somehow the quartet of Americans managed to find passage again, this time aboard a French sloop bound for Port-au-Prince where, rumor had it, a French brig lay about to sail for America. Their information, however, was only partially correct. On June 29, upon arrival at Port-au-Prince, they met a Frenchman named Proshon, owner and commander of the 16-gun privateer brig *Polly*, which sailed under an American letter of marque. Proshon immediately offered Olmsted eight shares in a privateering cruise to the northward, probably as mate, and promised that the first port he would be stopping at was in America—if he was unable to take any prizes off Jamaica. Olmsted was undoubtedly delighted and agreed to go, as did Buckland, who signed on as prize master and was to draw three shares. Fox, too, shipped aboard, but Forbes thought better of it and parted company.[6]

Unfortunately for all concerned, the cruise of *Polly* was to be short-lived. About 2 p.m., July 8, 1778, she fell in with the 280-ton, 16-gun Royal Navy sloop-of-war *Ostrich*, Captain Peter Rainier commanding, off the east end of Jamaica. The engagement that ensued can only be described as a classic sea fight.

"Before we came up with one another we were under French colors," Olmsted later recorded of the battle. "She fired a shot athwart us. We hauled down our French colors. We came alongside one another. The ship hailed and told us to bring to or he would fire into us. We hoisted our Continental colors at our main top gallant head and fired a broadside into her, which she immediately returned."[7]

The fight then became general, with broadsides exchanged on both sides. Splinters and large hunks of wood flew through the air as volleys of ball and small shot smashed into the sides of the combatants, piercing, shredding, and crushing human bone and flesh. As the two warships sliced through the rough water, Captain Rainier managed to run his ship's bowsprit over *Polly*'s quarterdeck, thereby locking the two vessels together for boarding. Within minutes, all of the French and Americans on the quarterdeck, with the exception of seven stout fighters, Olmsted and Buckland among them, had abandoned their post. Those resolute defenders who stayed, however, were determined to hold or die. Armed with spears and tomahawks, the British, seeing the mass desertion, attempted to climb across their bowsprit and rush the deck. But they had failed to bring small arms or pistols. The defenders, having their own guns loaded, and a supply of extras on the deck, were able to check the fierce onslaught. Among them, Buckland had taken a blunderbuss and, though wounded in one leg, resisted with undaunted spirit. As he fought, a fire flask fell so close that his good leg was severely burned, but still he battled like a man possessed. The assault was finally repelled by "the dexterity of Mr. Proshon, the French captain, [who] jumped down upon the main deck and drove up the men."[8]

For what must have seemed an eternity, the two warships remained grappled, and the bloody action continued unabated. Both sides fought with small arms, blunderbusses, hand grenades, fire flasks, spears, and tomahawks. From time to time cohorns, small mortars mounted in the tops, lobbed grenades with devastating results upon the enemy contestants aboard *Ostrich*. Then, after half an hour, the two ships separated and fell off a short distance to resume the battle, albeit still at point blank range, with cannon and small arms. At the outset, Buckland, with three other Americans aboard, had managed one of *Polly*'s guns, but he had been badly wounded and was removed from his station. Within a short time, however, he had returned to his gun to bravely continue the fight. Olmsted would later commend his friend by noting: "That gun was fought the best aboard." For the next two exhausting hours, the bloody contest continued without respite until at last *Ostrich* hauled down her colors in surrender and the firing stopped. *Polly*'s crew gave three cheers and tried to hoist out her boats to take command of their prize. Only then did the full, grim devastation wrought by battle become immediately clear. Both vessels had been battered into virtual hulks, their rigging was shredded to pieces, but worse, all of their small boats had been shattered so badly that none could float. *Polly* had won a Pyrrhic victory at best and, as it turned out, a temporary one at that.[9]

Captain Proshon had little time to consider his situation, for before his men were able to repair a boat and board *Ostrich*, an 8-gun brig-sloop, HMS *Lowestoff's Prize*, Lieutenant Hibbs commanding, appeared on the scene with her brilliant colors flapping from her taffrail. *Ostrich* immediately took heart, and with her new ally, resumed the engagement anew. *Lowestoff's Prize*, carrying only small guns, however, did not dare to come alongside the better-armed privateer, which had been able to get off a broadside on her at her first appearance. The brig-sloop wisely chose to play off *Polly*'s stern and bow, raking her as opportunity allowed. In the meantime, with the two principal contestants still within pistol range of each other, the engagement had soon resumed its previous level of ferocity.

Olmsted had maintained his fully exposed position at the wheel on the quarterdeck, steering the ship for a full five glasses, two and a half hours, of the battle. Three men had already been killed at the helm before he had taken it, and ball and shot continued to fly all about him attempting to claim the fourth helmsman. At one moment he had narrowly missed being hit directly by a cannonball although the force of the wind, as it passed by, had caused one arm and his thigh to swell, but he quickly regained his composure. In the midst of the fight, Captain Proshon came up from the main deck, where he had been encouraging his men, and joined Olmstead, who was by then standing alone, and expressed his delight that he was unhurt. Then, in an instant, the course of action changed.[10]

As *Polly*'s brave commander was at "the height of his glory" surveying the battle from the quarterdeck of his ship, a cannonball struck off the top of his head, splaying gore all around. Within minutes, word of the captain's death had circulated about the main deck and immediately promulgated panic. Those who had been fighting with demonic fury only moments before began to scream "Haul down the colors." Before the act itself could be undertaken, however, half of the crew had opened the hatches and climbed below deck as a sign of surrender. To add insult to injury, no sooner had the colors come down than Lieutenant Hibbs brought *Lowestoff's Prize* alongside "nigher than he had been at the time of engagement," then his men issued three cheers and unleashed a final broadside into the already surrendered and defeated privateer.[11]

The battle had lasted for three and a half hours, with the principal contestants never more than pistol shot distance from each other. Olmsted later reported that *Polly*, which had begun the fight with 100 officers, men, and boys, had suffered better than half of those aboard killed or wounded. *Ostrich* had lost all of her officers killed or mortally wounded and more than half of her 120 crewmen. Incredibly, it was *Lowestoff's Prize* that claimed the victory, though she had been content to do little more than waltz about the two main contenders, vulture-like, until both had all but succumbed to exhaustion.[12]

When Lieutenant Hibbs boarded his new prize he called for her captain. Olmsted, now *Polly*'s only surviving senior officer, informed him that he was dead. Where was the lieutenant? Also dead. What about the second lieutenant? Mortally wounded. "What officer are you, you damned rascal?" demanded Hibbs. Olmsted lied, answering that he was merely a passenger. The attempt at deception was obviously transparent, and the lieutenant ordered him to produce the ship's papers or he would run him through. "Where's the captain's sword," he asked. Somewhere on the deck, Olmsted answered bluntly. The Englishman was livid with the curt replies. "He seemed to be in such an agony and still threatening to put us all to death," said Olmsted later. "I could not tell what he wanted."[13]

Polly's surgeon, clerk, some of the wounded, and a few of the uninjured were transferred to *Lowestoff's Prize*. The remainder of the prisoners were ordered into *Polly*'s hold. Fortunately for Olmsted, whose arm and leg had swelled up considerably from the near miss, the prize master allowed him to lie upon the deck along with a number of other wounded. His shipmate and friend, the brave Buckland, had been among those carried aboard the Englishman to have his wounds dressed.[14]

For the third time in as many months, Gideon Olmsted found himself an English prisoner. But this time his personal hell was about to take on a new dimension, prompted, no doubt, by Hibbs's examination of *Polly*'s papers. "I stayed aboard very quiet until the next day," Olmsted later reported in his memoirs. "Lieut. Hibbs, the Capt. of the brig, came aboard, called me up to him and told me that I was a damned villain and said, 'Did not you say that you was nothing but a passenger aboard?' and drew out his sword and, said he, 'I will run you through, God damn you.'"

Olmsted asked whether he was going to kill him, a helpless prisoner totally within the officer's power, in cold blood.

"Damn you," retorted the lieutenant. "One cross look or if you speak a word I will run you through."

Olmsted stood there for some moments, neither speaking nor looking at his tormentor. Suddenly, without provocation or warning Hibbs struck him in the jaw with his fist, drawing a torrent of blood. He then ordered the prisoner to get into his boat for he intended on taking him on board the brig for a proper flogging. Dutifully, the American began to take up some clothes that he had tied up in a handkerchief but stopped when Hibbs told him that if he carried anything aboard he would be put to death.

Upon boarding the man-of-war with his prisoner, Hibbs shouted an order to his quartermaster: "Tie that damned villain up and give him 39 [lashes] and put it on well or I put it on to you." The quartermaster dutifully procured a cord with which to do the officer's bidding.

Staring at his prisoner with utter contempt, Hibbs challenged him: "O you d[amned] rebel, what have you to say for yourself?"

"I told him that I [had already] told him that I was his prisoner and could say nothing else," Olmsted recalled.

Relenting slightly, the officer rescinded the flogging order but directed the quartermaster in a different torture. "Tie him up forward with his hands behind him. And draw his hands up taut to that ringbolt," which was about two feet from the deck. The fixture was too high for the prisoner to sit and too low to permit standing without experiencing extreme agony. For two hours Olmsted was made to suffer continuous pain which he described as worse than having a tooth drawn.

While the American struggled to maintain his senses, a schooner was spotted standing towards the warship. The British immediately took her to be a rebel privateer. Hibbs briskly queried the prisoner if he would fight if he were untied.

"I told him I would not," said Olmsted later. "Then he told me I should be shot. I told him if he had any feelings for a man in distress he would run me through the heart to put me out of my misery for that was all I desired of him. Then the schooner came up with us. She proved to be one of their cruisers. Then I lamented my hard fortune that [the] same ball that killed Capt. Proshon did not miss him and kill me."

Olmsted remained chained to the eyebolt for several more hours before he was released by the quartermaster and brought aft to face Hibbs again. By then, his arms were so strained that he was unable to even raise them to pull off his hat. When he approached the officer, he was immediately reprimanded.

"You damned villain, how dare you come before me with your hat on?"

The American made a second attempt to remove his hat, and with a great deal of difficulty and pain finally got it off.

"O you damned rebel, what have you got to say for yourself?"

Again Olmsted repeated his earlier comment. "I told him I could say nothing."

"Put that damned scoundrel into the hold and don't let him see daylight," Hibbs ordered.

Olmsted was thrown into the hold, already occupied by a score of French prisoners, "and as hot a place as ever I was in." When the hatches were laid over all but about a foot of the length of the hatchway, the tropical air became stultifying.[15]

The following day, *Lowestoff's Prize* arrived at Montego Bay. Olmsted was locked in one hundred-pound irons and consigned to the sweltering hold for several more days. Finally, after being transferred to a dungeon in the town fort, he was stripped of his clothes and two gold half Johannes, "half Joes," in Spanish hard money and $80 in paper money. With nothing but a shirt and trousers, a pair of old shoes, and an ancient tattered hat, he was eventually set at liberty. Anything, he now considered, was better than a British prison cell.[16]

It was then that he began his real odyssey!

• • •

Fortunately, not everyone at Montego Bay was hostile. Indeed, there were even a few friendly Americans in residence, albeit most were still loyal to the Crown. Olmsted soon made acquaintance with one of these, a Mr. Johnson, who befriended, clothed, and offered him shelter until midsummer.[17] But the New Englander was eager to get home anyway he could. Buckland was still crippled by his wounds, but Fox had somehow managed to secure passage for the injured shipmate and himself on board a sloop called *Independence*, bound for Rhode Island, then largely under British occupation. The parting was undoubtedly difficult. Olmsted gave both men some money that had been provided to him by another generous soul named Hambottom, and secured a guarantee from Johnson to provide his two friends with anything they wanted, which Olmsted himself promised to reimburse.[18]

On August 1, Olmsted finally managed to secure work as a hand aboard the sloop *Active*, Captain John Underwood master, bound for New York, the main British base of operations against the rebellion in America. He found on board a number of others who, like himself, had been down on their luck. Among these new shipmates were two English seamen and three Americans, Artemas White, Aquila Ramsdell, and David Clark, who had been taken prisoner by the British warship *Royal George*.[19] All had been placed aboard *Active* to work their way to New York where, upon arrival, Olmstead later wrote, they would most likely be impressed into the Royal Navy. Counting three gentlemen passengers and two Negroes, Captain Underwood, Mate James Taylor, and the hired hands, there were in all thirteen men aboard besides themselves. Olmsted immediately befriended his fellow Americans. They at once began to conspire together to mutiny. Few could have guessed that they would soon make history off the coast of Egg Harbor, New Jersey, fifteen hundred miles away, and certainly in a manner that none could have imagined.[20]

• • •

Laden with a cargo of rum, sugar, and supplies for the British fleet and army at New York, *Active* joined a London-bound convoy on August 11 under the protection of HMS *Glasgow*, a 20-gun ship, and two sloops-of-war. For nearly three weeks she remained with the fleet until it reached 34° north latitude, and then bore off for New York with two sloops in company. One of the sloops was from Jamaica, while the second was none other than Olmsted's own *Seaflower*, which had only joined the convoy that same day, as she had been unable to get water and provisions enough to carry her to London.[21]

The trio of sloops pressed on together until the morning of September 4, when *Active* lost sight of her consorts during a squall. That same evening, the Eastern Shore of Virginia came into view. Soon afterwards, she spoke Captain Sibble's notorious 16-gun privateer *Tryon*, just out of New York, which relayed some stunning news. The British had abandoned Philadelphia and the American response was immediately being felt upon the high seas. The privateer warned Captain Underwood that if he didn't keep well off the coast he was likely to be taken by American cruisers that were now swarming like hornets about the Virginia Capes. The message was heeded and *Active* was steered in a northeasterly course until out of harm's way.[22]

Aside from a brief sighting of the two erstwhile consorts, who were sailing dangerously close to the rebel-infested shore, the next day or two passed without incident. Unknown to Captain Underwood, however, his four American crewmen, White, Ramsdell, Clark, and Olmsted, had entered into a secret cabal to seize the ship at the first opportunity, their resolution having been strengthened by news of the enemy abandonment of the Delaware. On September 5, to prepare the way, one of the conspirators managed to secure what he believed to be the only supply of lead musket and pistol shot aboard. Unfortunately, he had managed to overlook a supply sequestered in the captain's cabin, an oversight that would soon result in trouble. The opportunity the four men wished for, however, came much earlier than anticipated.[23]

On Sunday, September 6, about 2 p.m., in latitude 38° 10' north, off Assateague Island, Maryland, *Active* spoke another Loyalist warship. This time the cruiser was Captain Bridger Goodrich's privateer *Hammond*, just out of New York. The news related to Captain Underwood was unsettling. Goodrich reiterate the same information that the previous privateer had relayed regarding the British abandonment of Philadelphia and the Delaware River, but also reported that American cruisers had become "very numerous within shore all along from Egg Harbor to New York and if we kept any further in we should be taken, and if we saw any sail it would most certainly be a rebel privateer for there was an embargo upon all British cruisers in New York, and he [Goodrich] should not get out if he had not been in favor with the Admiral [Gambier] by giving him intelligence of the French fleet." He advised Underwood that he should "hold in with the land until he got in the latitude of 40 and to make some part of Long Island." The privateersman offered to Underwood the loan of two swivels until he got to New York.[24]

Underwood replied that *Active* already carried two carriage guns and a pair of swivels, which was about all his small crew could handle.[25]

The news from New York was equally disconcerting. The Royal Navy, it seemed, more hard up for seamen than ever, was indiscriminately pressing into service every mariner that came into port. Olmsted asked the privateer's crewmen whether the navy was pressing Americans into service as well, and was told that "it made no odds what countrymen they was for they pressed all."[26]

As soon as the two vessels parted company, an obviously nervous Captain Underwood ordered the crew "to fixing our guns in order to keep off the small crafts." The reluctant demeanor of the Americans aboard did not go unobserved. An English sailor named George Roberts sternly warned them that if attacked and the "Yankees don't fight, they would turn guns upon them." For Olmsted and his colleagues, the prospect of forcible impressment in an English man-of-war to fight their own countrymen, or being fired upon for not fighting, was more than they could take. Although outnumbered by the crew and passengers by three to one, the conspirators decided the mutiny would have to be carried out that same night.[27]

Two of the Americans, Olmsted and Ramsdell, and an English seaman named Robert Robson, who was loyal to the captain, had the watch upon deck from 8 p.m. to midnight. Underwood was below in his cabin. At 11 p.m., Ramsdell quietly summoned Ward and Clark, the other two conspirators, on deck, and with Olmsted as ringleader hurriedly finalized the details of their plot to seize the ship and carry her into Egg Harbor as a prize of war. The plan was simple. The captain, mate, and passengers would be confined to their cabin, locked in before they even knew what was happening. Robert Robson and George Roberts would be kept on deck as prisoners and made to help sail the ship.[28]

Before midnight, Clark went below to avoid any suspicion. In the meantime, the conspirators quietly gathered every tool available with which to defend themselves, including three axes and a crowbar. They summoned a Negro who was asleep in the forward hold, fastened down the scuttle over his egress, and ordered him to stay forward, remain quiet, and he would not be hurt.[29]

At the appointed time, Olmsted called the watch as usual. Clark and Roberts came up. As soon as they were on deck, the conspirators hauled up the ladder and secured the companionway by heaving heavy cable and other encumbrances across it. The captain and his crew and passengers were now confined below with no way out, and Olmsted set a direct course for the privateering enclave of Egg Harbor. "As soon as Robson and Roberts saw what we were about," recalled Olmsted, instead of fighting they begged the Americans not to hurt them. They were told they would be safe if they remained passive. "We told Robson to take the helm and steer. We had coiled so much of the cable before they [the crew and passengers] found it out they could not get out though they made several attempts. We secured them down and jibed the boom and steered NW with a pleasant breeze."[30]

Without warning, a pistol shot flashed from the tiny cabin window at the stern, which was too small to pass through but large enough for a man's head or gun to stick out. Olmsted was struck in the thigh, but fortunately the projectile failed to puncture the flesh. The mutineers were momentarily perplexed, having thought that they had secured all of the available bullets the day before. After counting their assets, they discovered they had but six cartridges of powder for the two deck cannon, eight or ten for the swivel guns, and a hornful of powder for sidearms (which they had unfortunately not been able to secure), as well as a supply of cannonballs on deck.[31]

"We pointed the guns aft," Olmsted later recalled,

> and told them if they fired out again we would fire into the cabin. They fired once or twice but did not hurt anybody. We thought it a pity to kill them though we could do it several times as they put their heads out of the cabin windows to try to shoot us. They told us that if we would let them come up they would use us well and would set us ashore on Long Island. I told them that I had been deceived by the British party and would not trust none of them. There was not much done after that that night.[32]

At daylight the following morning, the crewmen, who could clearly observe the mutineers topside between the cables that had been lashed across the companionway, again began an intermittent fire upon them from this new quarter. Clark was wounded in the thigh, and Olmsted was again grazed. The mutineers, who possessed the real firepower, lost their patience and angrily responded with two 4-pounders fired directly though the bulkhead and into the cabin, and then quickly covered the holes with canvas from the foresail. The firing from the cabin temporarily ceased, but Underwood was not finished. The captain, enraged over the attempt to take his vessel from him, began to entertain the audacious, even insane, idea of blowing up the quarterdeck with gunpowder. Fortunately for all, by the prudence, pleas, and persuasions of the passengers, he refrained from doing so until a scheme of a less hazardous nature might be put into play. Within a short time Underwood and his crew had managed to wedge the rudderpost from below deck, effectively disabling the vessel by preventing the mutineers from steering her.[33]

Olmsted and his companions scoffed at the effort, and boasted to their captives that they could steer the ship without a rudder, and were not in the least worried about British cruisers, for as they neared Egg Harbor they were well out of enemy territory. Moreover, though their captives had a stock of victuals, water, sidearms, and ammunition to continue their resistance from below, there were also plenty of provisions to sustain Olmsted and his men as well—half a dozen sheep and goats, two coops of chickens, a barrel of corn, a cask of rum, and twenty gallons of water.[34]

Underwood's men persisted. Soon they had succeeded in cutting a hole out of the companionway so that they could better see out. The rebels responded by placing the muzzle of a swivel gun loaded with musket balls into the hole and threatened to open fire if the crew cut any more holes or did anything more to hurt them. Then they quickly set to regaining steering control by knocking away some planks on the stern to gain access to the wedges. While thus engaged, one of them noted that "there seemed to be some movement" in the cabin which then caused one of the more nervous mutineers to fire the swivel. Though no one inside was hit, the smoke from the blast was suffocating, driving all of the captives to put their heads out the window to breath, all the while beseeching the mutineers whether they meant to kill them or not. With the crew thus exposed and brought low, Olmsted noted, "we could easily put them to death if we had a mind to . . . We told them we would not hurt them if they would be peaceable below," and then returned to knocking away the planks at the stern. A truce was finally agreed upon after some negotiations, managed on behalf of the crew by Robert Jackson and James Holmes.[35]

In his account of the events of that fateful day in his life, Gideon Olmsted did not gloat, although he might well have. Jackson and Holmes, he reported matter-of-factly, "told us that if we would be easy a few moments they would try to prevail with Capt. Underwood to unwedge the rudder. We left off knocking away the stern. They unwedged the rudder." In return the mutineers promised that when they were close enough to Egg Harbor to disembark, they would take the ship's boat and leave *Active* in the possession of the skipper and his crew. Whether or not that was their true intention will never be known, as subsequent events would deem otherwise.

By then it was about noon, Monday, September 7.

We had a pleasant breeze at the southward in 35 fathoms of water off Egg Harbor by our soundance [*sic*, soundings]. We kept her NW. They asked us if we would cook them a fowl. We told them that we had cooked some mutton that day and they might have some of that. They told us that they would be obliged to us for some of that. We gave them a leg of mutton over the stern into the cabin windows. They did not make any disturbance in the cabin. At sundown we was in 23 fathom of water. We had a pleasant breeze all night.

The next day, however, would prove anything but pleasant.[36]

• • •

At sunrise on September 8, Olmsted and his men discovered that *Active* was in only thirteen fathoms of water and not far from land, which was observed to the northwest. Egg Harbor and their own country were finally within reach. About this time, they spotted a sail to the northwest, squarely between themselves and their destination. To reduce their profile on the horizon they quickly hauled down their canvas, all the while watching the stranger's motions. It was impossible to tell which way she was headed. The four mutineers decided that if she proved to be British and they were obliged to put further out to sea to avoid her—and the gibbet—they had only enough water for six days. They decided, while their ship lay at rest, to expand their consumable liquids by burning the alcohol out of the rum supplies, and then let it stand in the cool air. When they were done, the liquid was "as weak as grog."[37]

For some time they watched nervously as the stranger stood out by the wind until she was west of *Active*. Olmsted soon made her out to be a brig. Whether or not the stranger had seen the sloop is uncertain, but when the skittish mutineers finally decided it was time to run to the north and began to pile on all sail, they were immediately chased. Olmsted recalled the events that then transpired with matter-of-fact simplicity: "As soon as we made sail the brig hove about and stood athwart us," he wrote. "She looked ahead of us. By then we thought she was a British cruiser as she seemed to try to cut us off from the land."

Active was now within only three tantalizing leagues of her destination, but the Americans had little choice but to run. The stranger, wearing British colors, fired a gun. The shot fell astern of the fleeing sloop but had the desired effect. Olmsted ordered the square sail hauled down and his vessel hove to. Within a short time the brig had run alongside and hailed, asking where the merchantman was from and where bound. From Jamaica for Egg Harbor, the American replied. With that, undoubtedly much to Olmsted's relief, the brig suddenly hauled down the Union Jack and raised Continental colors.

"What sloop are you," the brig asked.

"We told them," Olmsted recorded, that "she was a prize taken from Capt. John Underwood and his seamen."

Olmsted asked for the stranger to identify herself. He was informed she was the *Convention*, Thomas Houston commander, belonging to the state of Pennsylvania. The vessel was, in fact, a Pennsylvania Navy warship, built in 1776, and one of the few in the fleet to escape destruction after the British capture of Philadelphia in 1777. The warship was armed with a deadly battery of 12-pounders and at least two 4-pounders, and had formally been dispatched to go a privateering on behalf of the cash-strapped state; *Active* had little choice but to follow orders.[38]

Houston, a highly regarded and well-connected officer in the Pennsylvania Navy, hoisted out his boat and sent his lieutenant aboard to inspect *Active's* papers. Olmsted informed the officer that both the papers and the prisoners were confined in the cabin, "and we did not intend to let them out before we got into port." The New Englander was apparently well aware that if the captain and crew were released upon the deck, that the mutineers might well be considered by the courts as having technically returned control of the ship over to them again and could not legally claim *Active* as a prize. The lieutenant informed his commander of the situation, and ordered Olmsted to board the brig to be questioned by Houston face to face. "I told the Capt. We did not want any assistance," but was obliged to board anyway.

With his first concern focusing upon the possible presence of enemy ships or merchantmen in the area, Houston first questioned Olmsted on any recent sightings. Had he seen any other vessels lately? The New Englander responded that the last vessel he had seen was a privateer brig out of New York the previous Sunday, which had reported that no more privately armed ships were permitted to sail from that place because of the danger of American privateers. He had not seen any other vessels off these shores.

I told him [Houston] there was two sloops that left the fleet when we did but they parted with us three or four days before and they were somewhere near the capes. As they had not heard of the British troops leaving Philadelphia they intended to keep very nigh. He asked whether they were both from Jamaica. I told him one was; the other was a sloop that was taken from me and a good cargo of molasses and dry goods and had been carried to the Bay of Honduras but was then bound to New York. He asked whether they had any guns aboard. I told him they had none except the sloop that was taken from me. She had four swivels.[39]

Perhaps fully expecting Captain Houston to take off after the two sloops as soon as possible, Olmsted asked where he was bound.

"I am going to carry you to Philadelphia," replied captain.

Indignantly, the New Englander retorted: "We can carry ourselves either to Philadelphia or to Egg Harbor."

"You have no commission and I intend to make a prize of your vessel."

Possibly stunned by the announcement, yet somehow managing to maintain his decorum, the New Englander responded sarcastically. "I think the State of Pennsylvania will not thank you for bringing in vessels that were acoming in themselves."

"I will do as I please," said Houston, who immediately took the sloop as his prize. There was absolutely nothing Olmsted or his shipmates could do, as they watched the Pennsylvanian and his men break into the cabin and take Underwood and the former crew of *Active* as prisoners.[40]

A Solemn Mockery

"Principles so destructive of the union."

Not surprisingly, *Active* and *Convention* made their first stop at Little Egg Harbor, possibly to secure information regarding blockaders that might be patrolling the Delaware Capes and river. Soon afterwards they entered the Delaware and ran a short distance upriver before coming to. Much to the mutineers' chagrin, Captain Houston treated the British prisoners almost as old friends and termed them "gentlemen." White, Ramsdell, and Clark, having also been transferred to *Convention*, looked to Olmstead for direction. What was he going to do? "I told them I did not know," the Hartford native later wrote. "I asked what the Capt. of the brig [Houston] told them. They said all the Capt. said was he told his people to carry them pirates aboard of the brig."[1]

It may have enraged Olmsted, who had been handled so callously by the enemy, when he observed Underwood and his crew being permitted to return to the comfort of their sloop, albeit as prisoners, while he and his comrades, who had taken the prize at enormous risk to their own lives, were not even permitted to board and retrieve their clothes. To be called pirates only added further insult to the injury. But for the moment there was no recourse, and the four men were kept aboard the brig for the night. "We was obliged," Olmsted remembered bitterly, "to lie in the hold among a passel [of] people that was very lousy."[2]

The passage up the Delaware was without incident, except for the extremely cold and stormy weather, which afforded Olmsted considerable discomfort, having only a shirt and pair of pants to wear. He and his mates were at a loss to understand Houston's actions, as they were confined aboard his ship like common criminals, while Underwood and his crew were allowed every liberty, including being permitted to go ashore in their finest clothes. Olmsted was not only cold and irate over his treatment, but to add to his misery, he had become infested with lice in *Convention*'s hold. When he asked one of the privateer's officers what Houston intended to do with him and his mates, the officer replied "that he heard him say he was going to carry us out to sea," to be set ashore at Egg Harbor. Olmsted responded, perhaps nonchalantly, that it would be all right with him, but he would rather go up to Philadelphia aboard *Active*. That evening, Houston informed Olmstead that he could board the sloop but must say nothing to Underwood, who had sworn he would shoot his former captors as the architects of his own current misfortune.[3]

On September 11, before reaching port, Houston boarded the prize and stripped her of all the cabin furniture, several barrels of beef, a barrel of rum, a chest of medicines, and half a barrel of powder, thereby illegally breaking bulk before it could be included in the inventory required for the libel and condemnation process. He then instructed the prize master to prohibit anyone aboard from going ashore except Underwood and his men, undoubtedly intending to prevent any of the mutineers from filing a libel before

Houston's prize master could. Nevertheless, the following day, when a boat put off for Chester, Olmsted somehow managed to go with it despite Houston's orders to the contrary. From Chester he set out on foot for Philadelphia, and reached the city limits a little before dark and well ahead of *Active*.[4]

Upon his arrival, Olmsted immediately paid a visit to Major General Benedict Arnold, the Continental Army commander of Philadelphia, and a fellow native of Hartford, Connecticut. The general proved to be a sympathetic listener as the seaman related the tale of his capture of *Active*, its subsequent seizure by the Pennsylvania state-owned privateer, and his own ill usage by Captain Houston. Olmstead informed the general that he had neither money nor friends in Philadelphia with which to secure it. Arnold consoled his fellow countryman and told him "we should not lose our right for the want of money and if it was as I told the story, by the laws of the Congress the prize belonged to us." Moreover, the general promised to back him in his quest.[5]

On Sunday morning, September 13, *Active* finally arrived off Philadelphia and anchored in the stream. Olmsted resolved to reboard her, see his shipmates, relate to them his meeting with Arnold, and then disembark with them. Again they were restrained from going ashore until the following day. As soon as they landed at the wharf, however, they proceeded into the city intending to formally libel the sloop under their names in the Philadelphia Court of Admiralty. By the time they finally had the paperwork in order, however, Houston had already filed his own libel on behalf of *Convention*. To further complicate matters, a new player named James Josiah had also interposed. Josiah had been commander of a Pennsylvania privateer called *Le Gérard* (named after the new French minister to the United States) that had been cruising in concert with Houston and, having been within sight of the capture, also claimed a share of the prize. Unwilling to let the issue go unchallenged, Olmsted and his shipmates proceed to interpose their own counter claim for the ship and cargo as their exclusive prize.[6]

Nearly six weeks passed before a jury was summoned. On October 31, the jury was convened before Judge George Ross of the Court of Admiralty for the Port of Philadelphia. Ross was considered a man of impeccable reputation, but a Pennsylvanian through and through. Houston, commander of a Pennsylvania Navy warship on a special privateering cruise sent out by the Pennsylvania Navy Board specifically for the financial benefit of the state, and Josiah, also a Pennsylvanian with a Pennsylvania privateer commission and Pennsylvania crew, requested that the sloop *Active* and her cargo of 130 hogsheads of rum, and the smaller quantities of coffee, cocoa, beef, limes, and pimentos be adjudged to their ships, their officers and men, and the state as their lawful prize. Olmsted and his three shipmates sued for the prize on the grounds that it was they that were first in subduing and overcoming the sloop. The question presented before the court, however, was whether or not the four mutineers had *completely* subdued Underwood and his men and entirely ended hostilities before *Convention* and *Le Gérard* appeared on the scene. On October 4, after the facts had been presented, the jury reached a verdict. The dozen Pennsylvanians declared that the New Englander and his men had not, in fact, achieved full control of *Active* when she was taken by the Pennsylvania warship and so presented its conclusion accordingly. The decision was against Olmsted and his shipmates.[7] Nevertheless, one quarter of the prize money resulting from the sale of the ship was to be awarded to Olmsted and his fellow claimants, but three quarters of the proceeds would to be awarded to the state of Pennsylvania as the owners of *Convention*, and to the owners of *Le Gérard*, John D. Mercier and Joseph Fisher & Company.[8]

Though his Yankee dander was up, Olmstead was without friends, influence, or money. In a virtually foreign land, he had little choice but to turn to his distinguished fellow countryman from Connecticut, Benedict Arnold, for the promised financial support needed to appeal the verdict. The general, who was at the time facing a court case of his own that had been pressed by his political enemies and rivals, admired Olmsted's exploits. He believed that he and his men had been ill-treated, and again proved quite sympathetic. Being a risk-taker who had, himself, recently engaged as a one-sixth owner in a 10-gun, 30-man Connecticut privateer called *General McDougall*, he knew something of how the game was played.[9]

Along with a Philadelphia merchant named Stephen Collins, Arnold soon provided Olmsted with the financial backing and political clout necessary to bring his case before the Committee of Appeals of the Continental Congress. Gideon Olmsted was about to begin a legal battle as difficult and dangerous as any uprising at sea. The canny general's support did not come cheap. The cost of providing surety on the appeal would be a one-half interest in the proceeds of *Active* and her cargo. Yet, Olmstead was resolved to see it through whatever the outcome. As the agreement might well be construed in some circles as influence peddling by Arnold, the two men attempted to maintain secrecy regarding the alliance, but for naught. On November 12, a letter from an anonymous writer, who later proved to be Timothy Matlack, Secretary of the Pennsylvania Council and one of Arnold's bitterest political enemies, appeared in the *Pennsylvania Packet* hinting at the agreement. "It is whispered," read the article, "that some gentleman of high rank, now in this city, have introduced a new species of champerty, by interesting themselves in the claim. . . . If this be so, there is no doubt but that the conflict is in itself void, and the seamen are not bound to fulfil it."[10]

Although the article did not charge either Arnold or Collins by name, the general was incensed and dispatched an aide to the paper to find out who had written the piece. He was enraged when refused the information. Five days later, he wrote a letter to the *Packet* defending his reputation. He explained, in a candid manner, that some of his countrymen and neighbors from Connecticut were in the city and in distress, and he had taken an interest in their plight to prevent them from being cheated, and excused himself from further comment by noting that any public discussion might jeopardize their cause.[11]

Despite the shadowy allegations in the press against him, Arnold's influence helped accelerate Olmsted's case. Gouverneur Morris, a delegate to Congress from New York, was soon secured as the appellant's legal counsel. On November 28, 1778, just a little over three weeks after the ruling by Judge Ross, Congress formally referred the case to the standing Committee on Appeals, which had been established to exercise appellate jurisdiction in prize cases. The committee consisted of William Henry Drayton of South Carolina, William Ellery of Rhode Island, Oliver Ellsworth of Connecticut, and John Henry of Maryland, a balance of two Yankees and two Southerners. On December 12, the committee convened in the State House in Philadelphia for a full hearing of the contesting parties.[12] Three days later, on December 15, much to the delight of Olmsted and his partners in the suit, the committee announced its judgment. The verdict was clear and precise.

Left: Gideon Olmstead in his later years. Courtesy of the Prints and Photographs Division, Library of Congress.

Center: Benedict Arnold. Courtesy of the Prints and Photographs Division, Library of Congress.

Right: Gouveneur Morris, after drawing by Pierre Eugène Du Simitière. Reproduction from *Portraits of generals, ministers, magistrates, members of Congress, and others, who have rendered themselves illustrious in the revolution of the United States of North America,* R. Wilkinson, pub., 1783.

The committee decreed that the judgment and sentence of the Court of Admiralty "be in all parts revoked, reversed and annulled." It further decreed that the sloop *Active* "with her tackle, apparel and furniture and the goods, wares and merchandizes laden and found on board her at the time of her capture as mentioned in the claim and answer of Gideon Olmsted, Artimus White, Aquilla Rumsdale [*sic*] and David Clark" be condemned as a lawful prize on behalf of the appellants. Furthermore, it was also decreed that the process issued out of the Court of Admiralty to the marshal of the court to sell *Active* and her cargo at public vendue at the highest price possible, be paid to the appellants after deducting the costs of the trial and expenses incurred in the sale of the vessel and her cargo. He was also to pay $280 to the appellants "for their costs & charges by them expended in sustaining and supporting their said appeal."[13]

Olmsted's victory seemed assured. The Committee on Appeals had not only reversed the sentence of the Philadelphia court, but also instructed Judge Ross to order its decree to be executed and the money paid to the appellants. Matthew Clarkson, the marshal for the city and county of Philadelphia, who was himself engaged in the great game of privateering on the side and the source of the leak on Arnold, was ordered to sell *Active* and her cargo, pay the costs incurred, and turn the remainder over to the appellants. Olmsted's joy, however, was to be only momentary.[14]

Although no one could have foreseen it, the *Active* case had brought to the forefront a troublesome legal question regarding the viability of several of the November 25, 1775, Congressional resolutions by calling for a standing Committee of Appeals to exercise appellate jurisdiction in prize cases. One of the resolutions stated: "That it be and is hereby recommended to the several legislatures in the United Colonies, as soon as possible, to erect courts of justice, or give jurisdiction to the courts now in being for the purpose of determining concerning the captures to be made as aforesaid, and to provide that all trials in such case be had by a jury under such qualifications, as to the respective legislatures shall seem expedient." A subsequent resolution granted that "in all cases an appeal shall be allowed to the Congress, or such person or persons as they shall appoint for the trial of appeals, provided the appeal be demanded within five days after definitive sentence … and provided the party appealing shall give security to prosecute the said appeal."[15]

The legal question presented was whether the resolutions of Congress allowed a court on appeal a *de novo* review of facts, or was appellate review limited to questions of law. Pennsylvania believed it was the latter. When the state passed an act on September 9, 1778, that finally established a Pennsylvania State Court of Admiralty to replace the Philadelphia court, presided over by a judge appointed to a term of three years by the Supreme Executive Council of the state, it explicitly provided for jury trial and declared that a jury finding "shall establish the facts without re-examination or appeal." Thus, a legal conundrum of significant proportions, pitting state against Congress, had been born, lending major ammunition to Pennsylvania's aggressive response to the appeals process itself.[16]

Ten days after the ruling against Houston, the Pennsylvania Council sought a reconsideration of the verdict on the grounds that the state had outfitted, manned, and fielded *Convention* as a state privateer and commissioned another called *Le Gérard*. On December 28, Judge Ross, citing the new state law passed on September 9, though recognizing the authority of the appeals commissioners, defiantly refused to execute the decree of Congress or change the verdict in his own ruling. It had been Pennsylvania's position all along that the state had authority by statute to change the practice common to English admiralty law by granting trial by jury. Thus, the resolutions of Congress authorizing appeals should be seen as contemplating only review of questions of law. Pennsylvania regarded facts found by a jury under this interpretation as sacrosanct. On December 28, Ross ordered the marshal of Pennsylvania to ignore the instructions of the Committee on Appeals and to sell *Active* and her cargo and pay the net proceeds into the Pennsylvania court pending disposition of the case. Olmsted was almost certainly stunned, and noted in his journal: "All the reason he gave was that the Congress had no right to try a case that had [been settled by the Court of Admiralty of Philadelphia]." The cargo, but not yet the sloop, was sold immediately for £47,981 2s 5d Pennsylvania currency, of which £11,496 9s 6d was to be Pennsylvania's share as owner of *Convention*.[17]

Olmsted refused to surrender and moved to prohibit the sale of *Active* by the marshal. On the same day as Ross's latest ruling, the Committee on Appeals entertained a motion by the appellants that the marshal again be instructed to execute the directives of the Court of Appeals. The committee adjourned after agreeing to reconvene to consider the motion at 5 p.m., Monday, January 4, 1779. No one, least of all Olmsted, could have imagined that in promulgating this action he was embarking upon a torturous legal journey that would become the focus of perhaps the earliest and most significant efforts in American history to resolve the issue of states' rights, establish federal supremacy, and define some of the salient parameters of American appellate law.

During the weekend before the Court of Appeals was to reconvene, Olmsted and Arnold learned that Judge Ross had decreed that the money resulting from the sale of the prize and its cargo was to be paid into his court at 9 a.m. on January 4, eight hours before their own appeal was to be heard. Arnold had already guessed the course that the Pennsylvanian's hurried directive would take. "I am informed from good authority," he noted in a postscript to the Committee on Appeals on the eve of the requested action, "that a member of the Assembly has applied to get the money paid into his [Ross's] hands, and if he should succeed in this it will probably be paid into the Treasury [of Pennsylvania], and the claimants will have the whole State to contend with in their own government." In a hasty effort to counter the Pennsylvania action, Olmsted and the general beseeched the Appeals Court to reconvene at 8 a.m. instead of 5 p.m. to consider issuing an injunction prohibiting payment of the proceed to the Pennsylvania Admiralty Court and requiring the money be released instead to the appellants. The Appeals Court duly authorized an injunction, albeit one which directed the marshal to retain the funds in his hands until ordered to do otherwise. Loyalty to the state, in this case, trumped allegiance to Congress. Although the injunction was formally served upon him before he paid the money into the Pennsylvania court, the state-designated marshal, who was beyond the jurisdiction of the Court of Appeals, nevertheless proceeded to turn it over to Judge Ross, who provided a written receipt for it. As soon as the money had been turned over to the Pennsylvania court, Judge Ross deposited it with the Treasurer of Pennsylvania, David Rittenhouse. Rittenhouse provided a security bond to indemnify Ross in the event that he, by due process of law, according to the decree of the Court of Appeals in the case of the sloop *Active*, was somehow compelled to pay the same. The Treasurer received £11,496 in U.S. loan certificates, as the state's split of the prize taken by *Convention*, which was to be shared with her crew.[18]

The lines of combat had been clearly drawn. The Committee on Appeals, authorized by the Congressional Appeals Resolves of 1775 regarding prizes, had issued a decree and writ on appeal, which Pennsylvania blatantly refused to obey. For two weeks the Appeals Committee, "unwilling to enter upon any proceedings for contempt, lest consequences might ensue ... dangerous to the public peace of the United States," declined to hear any more appeals from the appellants until "the authority of this court be so settled as to give full efficacy to their decrees and process." Thus, on January 19, it passed the dilemma to Congress itself and filed a report and formal protest, requesting that its lines of authority be confirmed. Two days later, Congress appointed a special committee chaired by Thomas Burke of North Carolina, and comprised of William Floyd of New York, Samuel Holten of Massachusetts, William Paca of Maryland, and Jesse Root of Connecticut, to render the precise parameters of congressional authority on prize appeals.[19]

Then began a sometimes-heated series of exchanges and accusations between Burke and other members of Congress and the President of the Pennsylvania Council, Joseph Reed. On January 25, Reed wrote to the President of Congress, John Jay, regarding the reversal in the *Active* case and seeking "some arguments or documents ... be offered to them on behalf of the State before their report is concluded on." The following day, Pennsylvania formally complained to Congress that General Arnold had illegally "purchased" a half interest in the lawsuit regarding Olmsted's claim to the prize sloop *Active* to personally profit from the prosecution.[20]

Although the *Active* case had placed the Congress and Pennsylvania at loggerheads, a much broader concern began to color the actions of the Continental government. Congress was loath to possibly jeopardize the war effort by alienating Pennsylvania, which was then the principal supplier of provisions for the Continental Army, and several other states that held similar views regarding appeals. Indeed, by now, cases regarding like appeals were pending for both Massachusetts and New Hampshire, which had their own laws for judging maritime captures, and whose own courts were now refusing to allow appeals to the Congressional Committee on Appeals, except in cases of prizes taken by Continental Navy vessels.[21]

The special committee's preliminary report was read on February 2. The document staunchly maintained the right of Congress to review determinations of fact as well as law in appeals from state prize court actions, and unequivocally declared the supremacy of Congress in all questions of war and peace, including the legality of captures on the high seas. Pennsylvania Delegate Daniel Roberdeau, who was among the many members of Congress known to have dabbled in privateering, quietly kept Reed apprised of Congress's actions. He even suggested that, if necessary, he could stall its efforts regarding the appeals issue if his own state so desired. On February 13, he informed Reed: "Congress have now under consideration the report of the Committee of Appeals. On this important subject the delegates of this State would be glad of your advice, which I am desired to ask of their behalf. . . . P.S. We can put off the business in right of the State if advised."[22]

Congress spent the entire day of March 3, 1779, in rancorous debates on the report of the Committee on Appeals. The delegates differed on practically every issue placed before them. The lines of contention regarding state's rights vs. Congressional supremacy were clearly drawn. "The State of Pennsylvania," noted John Fell of New Jersey, "being of opinion the Court of Appeals, established by Congress, had no authority over Courts of Admiralty where the jury were judges of facts, Congress say they have a right of sovereignty in all Admiralty affairs whatsoever in the last resort."[23]

Three days later, Congress formally reasserted supremacy and its right to reexamine questions of both fact and law in prize law appeals, regardless of contrary state laws. Reed was incensed and, while unable to alter congressional resolve, wrote a critical letter to the Board of War. Although the letter is no longer extant, from the context of events it would appear that he may have touched upon Pennsylvania's irreplaceable support to the war effort, and the negative influence the decision by Congress might have upon it. In effect, Pennsylvania was threatening to hold the war effort hostage over the issue of its own court supremacy. The results of the threat, which of course was never formally stated as such, were immediate. Congress began to temporize, obfuscate, and vacillate.

In the meantime, additional appeals cases similar to the *Active* suit began to arise, further taxing Congress's resolution in such matters, especially as they regarded the two strategic states bordering the Delaware. Not long after the onset of the *Active* libels in Pennsylvania, the New Jersey Admiralty Court ruled in the case of *Stevens v Henderson*. This case involved the claims of a mariner named John Henderson and his associates, who had overcome the master and crew of the British schooner *John and Sally*, commanded by Captain Rufus Gardner, which carried a rich cargo of Jamaica spirits and Muscavado sugar. Henderson and his mates claimed the schooner and cargo as their prize. But before they could reach Egg Harbor or any other Jersey port, they were captured by the famed Pennsylvania privateer *Chance*, now commanded by Captain David Stevens. Stevens libeled the prize and her cargo at Trenton on August 27, but the court awarded both to Henderson, who had filed a counter claim. Stevens thereupon appealed the case to Congress. Congress received the case on October 23, 1778, and referred it to the Committee on Appeals. Because of its similarity to the now notorious *Active* controversy, the *John and Sally* case was delayed while Congress temporized over the determination of the limits of the committee's jurisdiction in prize cases. The standstill prompted Henderson to petition Congress no less than three times in 1779, for an expeditious review of the case. On March 6, when Congress finally defined the authority of the Committee on Appeals, the Committee resumed its review of the case. For committeeman William Henry Drayton, the issue was simple. "The court," he wrote, "declared that Congress having determined that their jurisdiction on appeal extended to a control as well over the verdicts of the juries as over the decrees of judges in courts established for the decision of captures on the high seas, & thereupon having no doubt that their authority could be effectually supported, we're not ready to proceed in the dispatch of causes." The President of Congress, having formally made the declaration, allowed the appeal from New Jersey to be heard. On March 11, the New Jersey court's findings were upheld and Stevens's appeal was denied.[24] Olmsted may have again taken heart, but again not for long.

In the meantime, the Pennsylvanians continued their offensive. Gouverneur Morris, who had served briefly as Olmsted's attorney, found himself the subject of slanderous tales. Ironically, he was among those in Congress who were less than supportive of the supremacy of Congress over state's rights issues—at least as they pertained to admiralty decisions and appeals cases. Yet, he and General Arnold were both accused of having purchased a share of *Active*, and of suborning witnesses. Most notable of those who had been bribed, some said, was Robert Jackson, one of those locked in the cabin of *Active* during the mutiny, and one of Houston's main witnesses.

Joseph Reed challenged Morris on the charges. Morris defended himself in an open letter to the President of Pennsylvania, but published in the local press and intended for the eyes of the public at large as well.

"I undertook the suit," he wrote on April 9, 1779, "because it appeared to me just, and because, the captors being represented as poor, I did not believe there were many of the [legal] profession who would do as I did undertake to serve them for nothing." He noted that General Arnold had also offered to be their security to him, and that if they were successful in recovering the money they could pay him. If not, the loss of the suit would be their only loss and there would be no charge for his services. He then addressed the charge of suborning Jackson, "a sick gentleman from Jamaica" who had taken some offense "at something I said which carried to his mind the idea that I thought he might be influenced by the gift of what he had on board the vessel to give false testimony against the captors." Morris declared Jackson's charges against him both weak and futile.

> This he mentioned to you. I took the first opportunity after you had told me of it, to convince Mr. Jackson of his mistake, which was done in such manner that he appeared to be perfectly satisfied. The fact was this. Genl. Arnold sent for Mr. Jackson to enquire into the nature of the case. I was present when he came, and in the course of the conversation I put some questions to him. After that was over,

then, as a gentleman who felt for and wished to relieve the distresses which (from the mutability of human affairs) he might in his turn be afflicted with, I enquired into his health and circumstances; and as he had open letters to New York, I asked for those which were directed to my former friends there, or were written by any such in Jamaica, intending if it were necessary to aid his negotiations for money in this city. He had not his letters with him but assured me that on these subjects he was perfectly at ease. I then as an American expressed my hopes that he had not been plundered or ill treated by my countrymen, and my confidence that, notwithstanding the apparent ingratitude of their conduct, at which he seemed much enraged, they would not take from him his wearing apparel, and such other things as had been customary to leave in the possession of persons in his situation. How he came to misinterpret what I said I cannot conceive, but the fact stands as I have stated it, and no one who knows me, nor indeed any other but a very base and wicked one will believe me capable of the infamy of suborning a witness.[25]

After Morris's most public defense, the accusations were never brought up again.

• • •

As the weeks rolled by, Gideon Olmsted and his shipmates waited patiently for Congress to enforce its decision, while that "deliberate" body chose to put off the day of reckoning. It was proposed, as a palliative measure perhaps, and in order to support the honor of Congress in the affair, that the Treasurer of the United States be authorized to pay the appellants a sum equal to the product of the sloop *Active* and her cargo, which was to be charged to the state of Pennsylvania, though no one knew when or if Congress itself would ever agree to such a measure.[26]

Finally, the appellants submitted another memorial requesting compensation for the *Active* in accordance with the decision of the Court of Appeals or, failing that, a specific statement from Congress admitting that nothing was to be expected. On April 24, 1779, their letter was read and hotly debated. The memorial once again placed Congress on the horns of a dilemma: if it paid the claimants their due, it would have to come from the Treasury of the United States, which was usually empty, and would require a substantial effort to secure recompense from Pennsylvania, which would only further antagonize an already irate but key component of the war effort; if a statement was issued that nothing was to be expected, it would effectively destroy the validity of any future appeals cases and undermine the sovereignty and supremacy of Congress. A precedent would have been established that might never be reversed. It was not without reason that Congressman John Fell entered into his diary: "That sloop gives a great deal of trouble." Thus, Congress again deferred debate, this time until September 15.[27]

The *Active* case, though postponed for nearly half a year, could not deflect the onslaught of other cases that continued to besiege the Committee on Appeals. A number of these were directly relevant to Olmsted's claims, and were therefore put on hold as well. One of the more salient controversies involved the seizure by Massachusetts privateers of the Spanish ships *Valenciano*, Captain Joachim de Luca, and *Santander y los Santos Martires* [*Holy Martyrs*], Captain Joseph de Llano. The issue, dealing with the capture of neutral foreign national merchantmen by American privateers, was laid before Congress on April 24, 1779, and referred to the Committee on Appeals, but being one with diplomatic sensitivities and international ramifications, was again intentionally left unattended. The problem was that the ships belonged to a sovereign power that was likely to recognize the United States as a nation and join the war effort as an ally.

Unfortunately, Massachusetts, like Pennsylvania, did not recognize the supremacy of the Appeals Court on certain issues. With the Massachusetts appeals proceedings, after much delay, finally scheduled to begin in June, the acting agent for Spain, Juan de Miralles, was prompted to put his government's full weight behind the two Spanish appellants, and sent a memorial on their behalf to Congress, which along with his own and a supporting memorial from France, were received in succession on May 18 and 19, 1779.[28]

Not surprisingly, already embroiled in the controversy with Pennsylvania, Congress was reluctant to be drawn into a similar conflict with Massachusetts. Again the matter was referred to another special committee, this time consisting of Thomas Burke, James Duane, and James Lovell, rather than the Committee on Appeals. On May 20, Burke's committee presented a set of compromise recommendations that Congress adopted two days later. In truth, the recommendations did little to address the core problem. Congress again sidestepped the issue by reaffirming its pronouncements of March 6 "relative to the control of Congress by appeal in the last resort over all jurisdictions for deciding the legality of captures on the high seas," and merely requested "the several states ... take effectual measures for conforming" to the previous resolve. With both the French and Spanish governments closely watching America's every move in this regard (as their own merchantmen had from time to time been seized), the committee attempted to spell out Congress's absolute authority for safeguarding the laws of nations while simultaneously avoiding "*arbitrary* interpositions in [State] judicial proceedings." In recognition of the fact that Massachusetts might well reject Congress's authority and right to hear an appeal in this case, Congress soothed its French ally and soon-to-be ally Spain, vowing it would in any event "cause reparation to be made" to the two foreign appellants. It was a signal designed to both save face and to expand international good will—without upsetting Massachusetts.[29]

In a letter of May 24, 1779, to the new French Minister to the United States, Comte Conrad Alexandre Gérard, John Jay sought to quell any international disputations that such matters as the *Valenciano* and *Santander* cases in Massachusetts might cause. He wrote:

> I am directed to assure you that as soon as the matter shall in due course come before them they [the Committee on Appeals] will attend very particularly to the cases of the vessels stated in the note from Don Juan Miralles to have been sailing under the flag of his Catholic Majesty & captured by armed vessels under the flag of the United States and that they will cause the law of nations to be most strictly observed—That if it shall be found after due trial, that the owners of the captured vessels have suffered damage from the misapprehension or violation of the rights of war & neutrality, Congress will cause reparation to be made in such manner as to do ample justice & vindicate the honor of the Spanish flag.[30]

The following day Congress passed several more resolves declarative of its powers respecting maritime cases, occasioned by the "difficulties" incurred by the *Active* case, and by the recent disallowance of appeals in Massachusetts, and instructed President Jay to transmit them to the states. Still, the problem persisted, and reappeared in a New Hampshire prize case, in which the Committee on Appeals simply revised its admiralty laws to conform to the congressional resolutions of November 25, 1775, and March 6, 1779. Although the committee asserted Congress's jurisdiction in the case, it clearly wished to circumvent yet another confrontation between Continental and state authority the likes of which still simmered in the unresolved case of *Active*.[31]

• • •

In late September 1779, a year after the *Active* capture, Olmsted's most recent memorial was finally taken up. Again Congress appointed another committee, Jesse Root, William Paca of Maryland, and Henry Laurens of South Carolina, "relative to carrying into execution the decree of the court of appeals concerning the sloop *Active*." This time, the prognostications regarding the case and a possible settlement between Congress and Pennsylvania appeared good. The Pennsylvania Assembly announced its willingness to confer with the Committee. The good news was relayed on October 1 to Jesse Root, the new chairman of the Committee on Appeals. Only the day before, the Pennsylvania Assembly had appointed Joseph Gardner, John Smilie, and Thomas Smith to meet with Root and his fellow committeemen. Unhappily, the gesture of good will was destined to go nowhere, as the Pennsylvania assemblymen had been "strictly instructed that they observe the former Resolutions of the House on this subject as the rule of their conduct." The standoff continued.[32]

Olmsted and his colleagues refused to be thwarted in their campaign, and on October 13 submitted yet another memorial. Congress again vacillated. It was by now evident that neither a resolution to the impasse nor satisfaction for Olmsted and his fellow appellants would likely be forthcoming in the immediate future if at all. In a summing up, New Jersey delegate William Churchill Houston wrote on November 12:

> Much law-ammunition has been spent on the occasion, and the difference is not yet adjusted. Certain it is that the Resolutions of Congress of 1775, on Admiralty jurisdiction, say, the facts shall be established by a jury. Lawyers say there is this distinction between trials by jury and trials by witnesses, that in the former case the facts find are not re-examined, in the latter they are. Our law [in New Jersey] for erecting a Court of Admiralty allows an appeal in all cases whatsoever, but it must be acknowledged that an appeal on matter of fact from the verdict of a jury has not a good sound. And yet juries are too often worse qualified to decided in maritime causes than any other.[33]

Olmsted could no longer afford to continue a fight that appeared hopeless under the current political impasse and legal obfuscation by Congress. He resolved to return to doing what he had acquired a taste for—privateering. Returning to his home in Connecticut, he began to seek a command. On March 22, 1780, he took charge of the 12-gun Hartford sloop *Hawk* and a crew of sixty. Six months later, on September 16, he sailed bearing another Connecticut letter of marque as commander of the 16-gun Hartford privateer *Raven*, with a crew of forty, owned by himself, his brother Aaron, and former associate Abraham Miller. Again, in April 1782, he put to sea as skipper of the 16-gun, hundred-man Connecticut brigantine *General Green*.[34] Despite the constant flurry of activity and sea adventures that encompassed his life during these last years of the war, Gideon Olmsted never gave up his hopes for prize money in the *Active* case.

• • •

The years following the peace passed quickly. Like many ex-privateersmen, Olmsted resumed his old vocation as a merchant ship captain to support himself and his family. Finding no support from Congress, he began a new campaign of petitioning the Pennsylvania Assembly that would continue until he was fifty-nine years old. By then, his old shipmates and partners in the first appeals had either died or lost interest, but Olmsted remained resolute, for America was evolving. A new Constitution of the United States was ratified in 1789, a Supreme Court was established to address the new law of the land, and Judge Ross died the following year. It was a new day and a new order.

With his old nemesis now gone, Olmsted filed a suit in assumpsit (a legal action to enforce or recover damages for breach of contract) in the Court of Common Pleas of Lancaster County, Pennsylvania, against Ross's executors for money "had and received." A judgment of £2,248 4s 7¼d was awarded by default, albeit the defendants received no notice of the suit until after the final judgment. Undoubtedly taken by surprise, the executors promptly sued the former Treasurer of Pennsylvania, David Rittenhouse, on his bond. As it turned out, Rittenhouse himself had kept the U.S. loan certificates paid to him pending his release by the state for giving a bond of indemnity to protect Ross should he have been compelled to pay the certificate's amount to Olmsted. Within short order, the case worked its way up to the Pennsylvania Supreme Court. However, Thomas McKean, now Chief Justice of Pennsylvania, tried but failed to recuse himself because he had briefly sat as President of the Continental Court of Appeals in 1778 when Olmsted's case was being heard. Though being constrained to express an opinion, he nevertheless concluded and declared that the re-examination of facts found by a jury was repugnant to "the genius and spirit of the common law" and that "the decree of the committee of appeals was contrary to the provisions of the act of Congress and the General Assembly, extrajudicial, erroneous and void." His fellow Justices, Edward Shippen (father-in-law of Benedict Arnold) and Jasper Yeates, did not concur on this point, but agreed with him in ruling that the Lancaster County Court of Common Pleas, a court of common law, had no legal jurisdiction over what was deemed an admiralty case, and Rittenhouse would not be held libel on his bond.[35]

Olmsted had again been beaten, but remained unbowed. His fight, however, was no longer unique in many respects. In New Hampshire, a case regarding the prize ship *Lusanne* had followed a similar torturous path with suits, appeals, and counter-suits that were not settled until they had been heard by the U.S. Supreme Court. In 1795, in the *Lusanne* case, known as *Penhallow v. Doane*, the Supreme Court had denied New Hampshire's jurisdiction and stated that decrees of admiralty courts established by the Continental Congress could be enforced in federal courts under the Constitution. The ruling gave Olmsted new hope.

Then, on June 27, 1796, Rittenhouse died. For the next six years, Olmsted marshaled his resources and will for another attempt to collect the full compensation due him. Not until May 27, 1802, however, was he able to bring suit in the U.S. District Court for Pennsylvania against Rittenhouse's daughters, Esther Waters and Elizabeth Serjeant, the executrices of the late Treasurer's estate, seeking enforcement of the original 1778 Court of Appeals decree. The estate, of course, included the U.S. loan certificates handed over to their father by Judge Ross from the proceeds of the sale of the sloop *Active*.[36]

U.S. District Court Judge Richard Peters decided in favor of Olmsted on January 4, 1803. For the old privateersman the judgment was undoubtedly sweet, but for Peters, the case could not have come at a worse time. Partisan politics and fears of impeachment had become the order of the day, at the local, state, and national levels, in a highly inflamed political environment for the new nation that pitted republicanism against federalism. Much to Peters's dismay, it had more than once been proposed that the ardent republican-minded Pennsylvania legislature should try to impeach the judge as a federalist judiciary. Pennsylvania refused to concur with the U.S. District Court's ruling.[37]

By now, Chief Justice McKean had become Governor McKean of Pennsylvania and was no longer willing or able to recuse himself from the issue. Advocates for the Commonwealth looked to him to provide a further roadblock to Olmsted. He did not disappoint them. The Pennsylvania Assembly, with McKean's influential prompting, interposed itself between a national court ruling and state residents Waters and Serjeant by passing an act on April 2, 1803, that expressly forbid the execution of Judge Peters's decree and asserting the State's interest in the money. The Attorney General of Pennsylvania and the Governor himself were instructed by the legislature to protect the two heiresses from Federal process servers. The Assembly justified the move by advancing the Eleventh Amendment regarding suits "in law or equity" as a bar to suit against Pennsylvania.[38]

Republican newspapers such as the *Aurora* lauded the assembly's resolve and cautioned that "if the Federal Courts, under the insidious cover of legal forms and technical decisions, can legislate for the separate States, or set aside their legislative acts, or bring State independency under the control of jurisdiction, the spirit of the Union is destroyed and the liberties of the people will be brought to the footstool of aristocracy."[39]

The danger of hostilities, even open insurrection, was palpable in the streets of Philadelphia. Undoubtedly hoping to avoid inciting armed conflict between the state and federal government on his opinion alone, and perhaps fearing possible reprisals and even impeachment proceedings should he force the issue and uphold his earlier ruling, Judge Peters declined to act further. Had he done so and tried to enforce his decision, the act might well have been interpreted as a move by the "Federal judiciary" against a "Republican legislature," resulting in civil conflict. In so doing, however, he had also knowingly cleared the way for consideration by the highest court in the land, the United States Supreme Court.[40]

Olmsted recognized the enormous political significance that the case had assumed. He had continually found it difficult to retain lawyers in his earlier attempts, owing to political conflicts, and he was well aware of why Congress had been dilatory during his repeated efforts to secure compensation during the war. He was not ignorant of the partisan battles now raging in Pennsylvania, indeed across America, which were defining the young nation's politics and policies. His case had, by now, become more than an issue of money and compensation. It had become a personal matter of principle and justice, which he would pursue for as long as it took, and regardless of the cost.[41] Thus, on May 18, 1807, just as Judge Peters had hoped, Olmsted's latest legal counsel sought a rule to show cause why the district court's decree should not be carried into execution. The counsel for the two female defendants simply pointed to the act of April 2, 1803, asserting the state's interest in the money, and citing the Eleventh Amendment as a bar to the suit. And again, as anticipated, the State refused to act.[42]

This time Olmsted pressed ahead taking his case all the way to the Supreme Court. On March 5, 1808, he sought a mandamus (a writ issued by a superior court ordering a lower court to perform a specified duty) against Judge Peters to secure and execute his 1803 decree. On February 20, 1809, Chief Justice John Marshall rendered the tribunal's decision, granting the writ of peremptory mandamus, and directed that the decree in favor of Olmsted be complied with, and that the two executrices, Waters and Serjeant, deliver the prize money to the claimant.

"If the legislatures of the several states may, at will, annul the judgments of the courts of the United States and destroy rights acquired under those judgments," Chief Justice John Marshall wrote, "the constitution itself becomes a solemn mockery, and the nation is deprived of the means of enforcing its laws by the instrumentality of its own tribunals. So fatal a result must be deprecated by all; and the people of Pennsylvania, not less than the citizens of every other state, must feel a deep interest in resisting principles so destructive of the union, and in averting consequences so fatal to themselves."[43]

After more than thirty years of expensive and frustrating legal efforts, Gideon Olmsted, mariner, privateersman, and citizen, had won a landmark decision in the highest court of the land, in a legal odyssey that had severely tested the bounds of national power and jurisprudence. On March 24, 1809, Judge Peters issued an execution order pursuant to the Supreme Court's mandate. Enforcement, however, was another matter.

As before, Pennsylvania physically refused to acquiesce and, as feared, resorted to military force. Anticipating that a United States marshal would attempt to serve the execution process issued by Judge Peters, Pennsylvania Governor Simon Snyder, in accordance with the act passed by the Pennsylvania legislature, ordered General Michael Bright of the Pennsylvania State Militia to protect Elizabeth Serjeant and Esther Waters against the Federal agent's attention. The threat of armed conflict in Philadelphia was overwhelming as militiamen surrounded the Rittenhouse home, quickly dubbed "Fort Rittenhouse," at the corner of Arch and Seventh Street.[44]

When the marshal discovered that massed militia guarded the residence of the ladies, he notified the militiamen that in three weeks he would return with an armed posse. The warning echoed hollow. For five weeks, between March and April 1809, the standoff continued. It was fortunately resolved not by gunfire and the spilling of blood but by stealth. While bored militiamen milled about, the resourceful Federal marshal managed to elude troopers who had, during the preceding weeks, lost their vigilant edge, and climbed over a back fence, entered the Rittenhouse estate from the rear, and served the writ upon the two surprised ladies. Chief Justice William Tilghman of the Pennsylvania Supreme Court, after hearing an application for habeas corpus, chose to remand both Serjeant and Waters to the custody of the marshal.[45] Upon payment by the governor of money made available under an ambiguously worded act of April 4, 1809, appropriating $18,000 for use in connection with the Olmsted matter, the two women were released.[46]

Governor Snyder was not quite finished. On April 6, he wrote to President James Madison urging that the federal government desist from enforcement of the court's decision. A week later, Madison replied in no uncertain terms that "the Executive of the United States is not only unauthorized to prevent the execution of a decree sanctioned by the Supreme Court of the United States but is expressly enjoined, by statute, to carry into effect any such decree where opposition may be made to it."

Despite Bright's having operated at the direction of the governor of Pennsylvania, a federal grand jury indicted both the general and his officers on charges of obstruction of justice. The trial was convened before U.S. Supreme Court Justice Bushrod Washington, nephew of George Washington. A special verdict issued by the jury found Bright to have resisted federal authorities, though having done so under the constituted authority of the Commonwealth of Pennsylvania. The jury left it to the court to decide whether such actions, under the unique circumstances, constituted a crime. Despite an argument by the defense that the general and his officers acted according to orders, Justice Washington entered a judgment of conviction. General Bright was fined $300 and a term of three months imprisonment. Each of the lesser officers was fined $50 and one month in jail. Seeking to nip potential future discord in the bud, President Madison pardoned all of the defendants, and considered it a veritable blessing that "The affair of Olmsted has passed off without the threatened collision of force."[47]

. . .

Gideon Olmsted was sixty-one years old when he was accorded his rightful due. His rewards, monetarily, however, were anything but grand and would not actually be paid until he was eighty-four years of age. Indeed, had he accepted the one-fourth offer made in 1778, he would likely have been economically better off, for in the end he received $35,718.47. Though, for its day, the amount was considered enormous, the unending court battles and legal expenses, totaling $22,873.44, had eaten up two-thirds of his award. And as usual, it was the lawyers who were the big winners.[48] In a larger sense, however, Olmstead's crusade and persistence had paid off, for the legacy of his fight was enduring. On June 26, 1888, in an address before the Yale Law School, Supreme Court Justice Stanley Matthews stated: "This [the *Active* case] appears to have been the first case in which the supremacy of the Constitution was enforced by judicial tribunals against the assertion of State authority."[49]

Olmsted left Philadelphia for Connecticut in 1810 where he lived for the remainder of his life, except for a brief return to his favorite profession—privateering—during the War of 1812. He was finally laid to rest in 1845, at the age of ninety-six. The legacy resulting from his privateering adventures and incredibly tenacious pursuit of his legal and financial rights had finally been enshrined in American law.[50]

PART TWO

DEPREDATIONS
UPON THE TRADE

"Accept our terms without delay,
And make your fortunes while you may."

–XII–

Riches Beyond Expectations

"To be Sold at Public Vendue."

The summer of 1778 was to usher in a banner year for the privateers of Little Egg Harbor, indeed for those of all the privateering centers on the Atlantic seaboard. With a pending national alliance with France, the prospects for a successful campaigning season on both land and sea seemed at hand, even though the British jails and prison ships at New York, Halifax and elsewhere were already overcrowded to bursting capacity with seamen, primarily privateersmen. There seemed no end to those still willing to hazard the game. The entire nation, from New England to the Deep South, it appeared to many, had gone privateering crazy, frequently with serious unintended consequences. William Whipple, a member of Congress from New Hampshire, expressed the ongoing complaint of many in the regular naval services, that privateering continued to cause a drain on men needed for public ships, as well as inflicting a downgrade in public morals. Writing in July from his beloved Portsmouth, to fellow congressman Dr. Josiah Bartlett, he bemoaned the virus of privateering as if it were the plague. "No kind of business," he wrote, "can so effectually introduce luxury, extravagance and every kind of dissipation that tend to the distraction of the morals of people. Those who are actually engaged in it soon lose every idea of right and wrong and, for want of an opportunity of gratifying their insatiable avarice with the property of the enemies of their country, will, without the least compunction, seize that of her friends." The proclivity of some privateersmen to conduct their actions without moral conscience allowed them to "operate with more violence in this country, in its present unsettled state, than in any country where all the powers of government can be vigorously exercised. . . . Besides all this, you may depend no public ship will ever be manned while there is a privateer fitting out."[1]

Nevertheless, for Lord George Sackville Germain, the British Secretary of State for American Colonies, the portents for an end to the revolution in America had all but evaporated, even as Washington's little army, though repeatedly bloodied, poorly supplied, and often starving, remained a force in being, and as other rebel armies seemed to materialize from the earth itself. The humiliating defeat of Lieutenant General John Burgoyne's entire army of invasion at Saratoga, by one such force under General Horatio Gates in October 1777, had all but wrecked British strategy in the north. But also of significance, the drain on British commerce caused by American privateers was becoming unbearable. Lloyd's of London estimated that American warships and privateers had captured 331 British vessels during the year, of which number only fifty-two had been retaken. To avoid losses, some merchants had even resorted to the practice of shipping their goods in neutral bottoms, and sometimes even in French ships.[2] New and immediate measures had to be taken as the British government braced for potential combat with the French, a military foe far greater on land and sea than any it had encountered anytime during the early days of the American rebellion. Thus, on March 8, Germain issued secret instructions to Major General Sir Henry Clinton, who had replaced Major General Sir William Howe as commander-in-chief of all British, German, and Loyalist forces in America, to reset the focus from the destruction of Washington's little army, which had remained a threat to New York, to subduing the ports of the north, from which the bulk of Continental and state naval vessels and privateers sailed. "If you shall find it impracticable to bring Mr. Washington to a general & decisive Action early in the Campaign," he wrote, "you will relinquish the Idea of carrying on offensive Operations within Land & as soon as the Season will permit, embark such a Body of Troops as can be spared from the Defence of the ports you may think necessary to maintain, on Board of Transports under the conduct of a proper Number of the King's Ships, with orders to attack the ports on the Coast from New York to Nova Scotia."

Sir Henry Clinton. Detail from engraving in *The history of America, from its discovery by Columbus to the conclusion of the late war*, by William Russell. [London, 1778], Courtesy Prints and Photographs Division, Library of Congress.

In addition, the general was ordered to destroy, whenever possible, all ships, warehouses, wharves, trade commodities, shipyards, naval stores, and property deemed necessary to incapacitate the Americans "from raising a Marine or continuing their Depredations upon the Trade of this Kingdom." He was first to attack with two armaments both Connecticut and New Hampshire, and then unite against Boston.[3]

Although it was impossible for all of the components of the directive to be immediately addressed, and the need was great to consolidate forces by evacuating the British Army from Philadelphia to New York, it was clear that privateering, particularly from the New England and mid-Atlantic states, was having a telling effect upon British commerce and would have to be stopped. Germain thus believed that this new course of action would be required to give some backbone to the Prohibitory Act, which had hitherto only served to restrain and damage both British and Loyalist trade rather than injure the rebels. Severely impairing the rebels at sea would, in turn, serve to establish a relatively secure environment for British oceanic commerce. Once the coastal ports of New England had been dealt with, the same attention could then be delivered to the mid-Atlantic and then southern shores.[4]

On March 13, Great Britain received the unwelcome—but not unexpected— news that France and the rebels had signed a treaty of commerce and friendship on February 6 and established a formal alliance that all but insured French entry into the war. The conflict, it seemed, was now no longer simply confined to putting down an internal revolt, but to fighting an international campaign on a worldwide basis, from the far reaches of India to the Americas. Moreover, an enormous increase in American privateering was likely to ensue, from not only the United States but from mainland Europe and French and Spanish holdings in the West Indies. It now required the British to institute again a comprehensive retrenchment for prosecuting the fight, to rethink Germain's proposed strategy, and to extensively increase the range and magnitude of operations. The key elements, of course, protecting commerce on the high seas and Britain's widespread colonial possessions, conducting the naval war against both the Americans and French, and attacking, closing off or destroying rebel ports great and small, would require a far greater number of ships and men than even the Seven Years War. Despite disputes over whether to concentrate the ships of the Royal Navy in North America, extend them to the far reaches of the British Empire, or retain them in a defensive mode in home waters, Germain's aggressive policy in behalf of the former was finally accepted.[5]

The war at sea, especially against American privateering, was about to escalate precipitously. Before the end of the year, not only the privateers of New England, but those of the New Jersey coastal ports as well would draw the scathing attention of the British high command. Little Egg Harbor would briefly become the center of the firestorm. Indeed, over the next few months, the notoriety of the little Mullica River ports of Chestnut Neck and The Forks were destined to increase a hundredfold, at first as places where every type of merchandise could be obtained at auction prices, and then as a major hub of escalating privateering activity. This particular regional rise in fame was due to three events: the British evacuation of Philadelphia and abandonment of the Delaware; the involvement, for the first time, of Joseph Ball, manager of the Batsto Iron Works, with speculation in and outfitting of privateers; and the retirement of Richard Westcoat from active military service. None of it had been easy.

By January 1778, British naval strength had increased substantially. There were approximately 274 warships of all classes ready for service, with ninety-two already on the American Station, thirteen at Newfoundland, and forty-one in the West Indies. By the end of the year, the effective total would grow to 317, with a major component assigned to defensive convoy protection, because of an increase in American privateering, rather than aggressive naval action.[6] From the very outset of British control of the Delaware and occupation of Philadelphia, communication with and transportation to and from the New Jersey coast had suffered commensurately. During the nearly nine months between

September 26, 1777, when the British arrived, and June 18, 1778, when they left, wagon trains from The Forks had been forced to take a detour route via Burlington for the crossing of the Delaware at Dunk's Ferry (present Riverton). Now, with the enemy's departure from the region, a return to the old overland passage to the Delaware River was practically guaranteed. Then, on July 6, the arrival at the Delaware Capes of a French fleet under Vice Admiral Jean-Baptiste, Comte d'Estaing, with 4,000 French troops and a newly appointed French minister to the United States, Conrad Gérard, heralded a new era of opportunity for privateering as well as a powerful new ally for America. In September, a regular overland, two-day stagecoach trip was opened by one Samuel Marryott and ran from Peter Well's Landing at Great Egg Harbor via The Forks to Samuel Cooper's Ferry on the Delaware, opposite Philadelphia.[7] A return to overland transport of prize cargoes was again deemed plausible—and far less dangerous than by sea.

Then, there was Joseph Ball, a Philadelphia Quaker by origin, who was in his late twenties at the outbreak of the Revolution. Ball had, noted one wag, "the face of a cherub and a mind as sharp as a steel trap," and was destined to become one of the richest men in America. In later life he would acquire substantial holdings in Pennsylvania, Maryland, Delaware, and the District of Columbia and, of course, New Jersey—all largely founded upon the profits of his involvement in privateering and eventual ownership of the Batsto Iron Works.[8]

Because his residence was located only a mile or so from The Forks and several hours' horseback ride from Chestnut Neck, where literally scores of prize vessels were sold at public vendues during the war, Joseph Ball had a unique advantage over other men who were obliged to travel great distances simply to attend such events. Indeed, he had ample opportunity to inspect, first hand, the prize ships and their cargoes as soon as they were brought in, well before the announcements of their captures had been published. In the summer of 1778, before the first of many large-scale vendues were even announced, he was already well armed with privy information at auction time, some of which was provided by the very skippers of privateers that had captured the vessels being sold. He already knew which vessels were sound, speedy craft, which had the best sailing abilities, and which were candidates for early retirement. If, as one historian has suggested, the weather turned sour on auction day and the roads leading to The Forks and Chestnut Neck became quagmires, many prospective bidders would simply not show up and Ball would acquire a privateer, a prize vessel, or even a blockade runner at a bargain price. Moreover, through his connections on the Delaware, he might sell shares in the latest acquisitions, which he could then afford to refit, arm, and send off as newly minted privateers.[9]

Ball enjoyed a particularly advantageous position at Batsto, one that would allow him to benefit from his excellent contacts with the right people in the various ports on the Delaware. With such connections he was able to raise money or sell shares in privateers with ease, albeit usually behind the scene, and with someone else listed as owner. He was equally adept at divesting himself of prize cargoes at a healthy dividend. There was no lacking business associates either, although a cabal of five men seem to have allied themselves at one time or another in many of the privateering concerns based at Egg Harbor. These men were: Charles Pettit, Assistant Quartermaster General of the

Continental Army; Colonel Elijah Clark; Major Richard Westcoat; Major General Nathaniel Green of the Continental Army; and, of course, Colonel Joseph Ball.[10]

Ball's attentions did not turn to matters of speculation overnight. He needed an incentive. Between September 1777 and the summer of 1778, there were few public vendues of prizes and their cargoes held at Chestnut Neck or The Forks. Prior to the British capture of Philadelphia some vendues had been held there, but Pennsylvania privateering activities had been severely retarded during the occupation. Few Pennsylvania commissions were granted, and those that had been were frequently sent as blank commissions to vessels operating out of French ports in the West Indies and often manned entirely with French crews, albeit under American officers and under Pennsylvania authorization. From mid-1777 until June 18, 1778, the Delaware might as well have been the Thames River in England, and the New Jersey coastline from Cape May to Sandy Hook was largely cut off from overland commercial traffic. The few industries that operated in the region, primarily salt, timber, and iron production, existed in a frequent state of peril. Outside of a handful of derelict and private vessels, there was a paucity of bottoms to be sold as most prizes were being diverted to safer ports in New England or in the South. With the strategic anchorages at both ends of the state in enemy hands, the privateer base of Little Egg Harbor temporarily wilted. Indeed, it had been a bad year for privateering in general as only seventy-three Continental commissions, mostly from New England states, for vessels carrying a total of 730 guns, are known to have been granted and bonded (although the actual total may be somewhat higher). It was barely half of the previous year's muster.[11]

A third reason for the upsurge in the sale of prizes and cargoes on the Mullica was the application of full-time attention to the commerce by Richard Westcoat, master of The Forks. On September 20, 1777, Westcoat received a commission as major in Colonel Richard Somer's Third Regiment, Gloucester County Militia, taking rank retroactively from 1775. He had already seen action in a skirmish at Mount Holly on December 23, 1776, and had been seriously wounded three days later at the Battle of Trenton. He had recovered enough from his wounds to serve at Little Egg Harbor, where he assisted in the construction of Fort Fox Burrows, from June 1777 until March 31, 1778, when he resigned his commission, presumably to focus on operations at The Forks.[12]

It is interesting to note that soon after Westcoat's exit from military service the sales of prize ships, cargoes, and ex-privateers increased dramatically at The Forks and Chestnut Neck. It was on Westcoat's estate at the former that auctions began to be held, sometimes on a round-the-clock basis, from June 1778 onward. Both Ball and Westcoat were frequently mentioned in advertisements for public vendues held at Little Egg Harbor's two foremost settlements and both men seemed to have managed much of the trade thereafter.

Westcoat, like his neighbor Colonel John Cox, who was by then heavily invested in the iron business and salt mining, played a most profitable double role by serving as a commissioner for Gloucester County to procure and collect clothing for the New Jersey regiments of the Continental Army. It was undoubtedly no coincidence that he had been appointed at a time when many of the prize cargoes sold at auction at The Forks and Chestnut Neck consisted of clothing and, on occasion, military uniforms and accoutrements.

It is, thus, not surprising that he prospered considerably acting as a middleman. In 1779, the apex of the privateering years at Little Egg Harbor, he was able to purchase, in association with one Edward Black, the Pleasant Mills plantation of Elijah Clark. In November 1781, soon after the Franco-American victory over Cornwallis at Yorktown, he settled his accounts with Gloucester County and New Jersey at the same time, coincidentally, that the vendue sales at Little Egg Harbor were all but discontinued, though the war would officially go on, especially at sea, for another two years. During his reign, however, fully 56 percent of all sales undertaken in the Little Egg Harbor region were held at The Forks, and the master of The Forks profited commensurably.[13]

• • •

Although men like Westcoat, Cox, and Ball would play host to some of the most successful and audacious privateers of the age (and not a few scallywags as well), the vessels that actually roamed the New Jersey coast in search of prey and employed its remote, shoally inlets and sounds as places of refuge and refit, belonged to many states. From the notices of admiralty proceedings and extant vendue records, it would appear that the majority of privateers that most frequently operated in these dangerous waters were officially commissioned by neighboring Pennsylvania. During the Revolution, no fewer than 521 known letters of marque and privateer commissions were issued by that state to vessels mounting at least 4,386 guns, and manned by more than 17,941 crewmen, second only to Massachusetts in total number of ships, men, and guns fielded. By comparison, New Jersey officially commissioned only a handful of privateers, while most of its owners and syndicates, such as Thomas Leaming and Son of Cape May, preferred to operate from the more commodious and protected environs of Philadelphia under easily acquired Pennsylvania commissions. From the bond data that has survived, a total of at least 291 known individuals were listed as owners or part owners in Pennsylvania privateering ventures, although countless silent partners most certainly also participated. A review of these commissions reveals that one commission was issued without an owner's name listed, several more noted the State of Pennsylvania as owner, and another indicated the United States as owner. The fielding of this veritable armada of small and large private men-of-war required a known total of $7,055,000—but possibly as much as $7,250,000 or more—in bond money to be posted, in amounts ranging from $5,000 to $20,000 per vessel, based upon tonnage. As often as not, the owner and skipper were among those who put up the bond. Usually, bonders not mentioned as owners or officers of the vessel were, nevertheless, shareholders in the venture.[14]

A Scottish immigrant and entrepreneur named Blair McClenachan, who was both a patriot and one of the most adept venture capitalists of his day to engage in privateering, was considered to be one of the most successful and relentlessly aggressive investors of all. He first became interested in the game in mid-June 1776, soon after his departure from military service and just as the frenzy for privateering in Philadelphia was hitting its peak. He had paid his dues to the cause of liberty early on, having volunteered at the very outset of the Revolution as a simple private in the Continental Army, during which time he participated in both the Battle of Trenton and the Battle of Princeton. That his devotion to American independence was rewarded, however, is attested to by the fact that by the end of the war he had become one of the richest men in Pennsylvania, all from the fruits of privateering on a truly monumental scale. He possessed a talent for investing in the fastest ships and employing the most capable commanders, and for successfully networking among the powerhouses of politics, policy, and money. It was a genius that rapidly earned him a fortune, the sobriquet of "Midas" of the Revolution, and a seat in Congress after the war.

McClenachan was, first and foremost, a shrewd businessman who knew how and with whom to bargain, barter, or belittle. During the course of the war he would own outright or in part no fewer than fifty-five Pennsylvania commissioned vessels, more than ten and a half percent of all of letters of marque issued in that state, and was unquestionably a silent partner in numerous others. He frequently invested in privateers from other states, most notably Maryland, and allied himself in ventures with powerful politicians such as Robert Morris. Gifts to such notables as George Washington often helped smooth the waters when necessary. Several of his most famous privateers of record, such as *Holker* and *Fair American*, would earn him millions of dollars in prize money, and many hundreds of thousands of dollars more for their officers and crews. These fortunates dubbed him "The Millionaire Maker." As such, his advice on naval matters and personnel was even sought out by the government of Pennsylvania. In his primary pursuit, namely privateering on an industrial scale, he was not alone. Along with four other men, operating alone or in company with each other or with other syndicates, 173 privateering cruises, or thirty-three percent of the known total ventures operating under Pennsylvania commissions, would be launched. The other members of this influential Philadelphia party included: Joseph Carson, who fielded forty-six vessels; Mathew Irwin, who owned or had shares in twenty-six ventures; his brother Thomas Irwin, who participated as owner in twenty of these; and Robert Morris of the Continental Congress, who owned or had shares of twenty-six cruises out of Pennsylvania and several out of other states, most notably Maryland, and from the French West Indies island of Martinique. It was noted by the Marquis de Chastellux, a French nobleman visiting America in 1780, that:

> it will scarcely be believed that amid the disasters of America, Mr. Morris, the inhabitant of a town barely freed from the hands of the English, should possess a fortune of eight million *livres* [between £300,000 and 400,000 sterling]. It is, however, in this most critical times that great fortunes are acquired and increased. The fortunate return of several ships, the still more successful cruises of his privateers, have increased his riches beyond his expectations, if not beyond his wishes. He is, in fact, so accustomed to the success of his privateers, that when he is observed on a Sunday to be more serious than usual, the conclusion is, that no prize has arrived during the preceding week.

Yet, the financial leaders of these adventures could not have profited without the almost incestuous network of syndicates and individuals who dared chance their livelihoods and wealth with them in what can only be described as risky investments.[15]

Not all named individuals listed as owners of Pennsylvania-commissioned vessels were Pennsylvanians, and not all Pennsylvania commissions were issued to Americans or even in the United States. Commissions of convenience were occasionally issued to individuals and syndicates of other states, such as New Jersey, Maryland, and even Massachusetts. Blockades of the Chesapeake and Delaware, or intense naval activity in New England waters, sometimes where heavy enemy cruiser patrols or ongoing land-sea operations made sailing hazardous if not suicidal, also made it more convenient for privateering interests in those areas to go elsewhere for formal commissions. Thomas Leaming and his son, Thomas, Jr., of Salem, New Jersey, had engaged in no fewer than seventeen ventures, but usually gave Philadelphia as their residence for bonding purposes.

Between 1779 and 1781, the noted Maryland merchants Samuel and Robert Purviance and Richard Curson secured no less than five Pennsylvania commissions for their ships. Nathan Nichols of Massachusetts, owner of the privateer *Fly*, was typical of those from his region who went to Pennsylvania when the circumstances demanded it. Not surprisingly, Pennsylvanians also went to other states for commissions, usually when the Delaware was closed or Pennsylvania commissions were in short supply. Moreover, some states, such as Maryland and Virginia, which lacked adequate maritime infrastructures such as enjoyed by Pennsylvania, frequently imported talented commanders, seamen, and investors from Philadelphia to field privateers from their own states.[16]

Given the enormous profits that might be made in speculation, the issuance of letters of marque by agents of both the Continental government and Pennsylvania to foreigners, often in absentia, was not uncommon. Commissions of convenience, for example, were issued to a Spaniard named Juan Joseph de Arbulu, who commanded his own brig *Amigos del Pays* and to Arnott Cormerais, a Frenchman who was part owner and skipper of the sloop *Sarah*. Indeed, when Robert Morris finally decided to enter the game, he secretly sent blank commissions to William Bingham, the Continental agent at Martinique in the West Indies, along with a recommendation that a captain named George Ord be awarded a command. Under Morris-Bingham ownership and Ord's command, the privateer brig *Retaliation* sailed from the island manned by an entirely French crew but bearing a Pennsylvania commission well before France entered the war. The complicity of the French in the affair drew the wrath of the British government and helped promote hostilities between the two European powers, but failed to curb the practice Morris had set in motion. Soon European privateers were being fielded in the American cause from friendly European ports as well, most notably France, thanks to the diplomatic endeavors of the American commissioners and agents there.[17]

Within a year of its implementation, the business of American privateering had grown to such proportions that the ownership of larger privateers was frequently split into eight, ten, sixteen, and even thirty-two or more shares. Often selling and trading in shares was carried out in a way not unlike the trading of stocks today. It was not only the moneyed men, but the Everymen of seaport communities—farmers, shop keepers, attorneys, physicians, and common laborers caught up by the prospects of instant wealth—who gambled in privateering ventures, sometimes purchasing shares as collateral and selling futures, occasionally hedging bets by taking chances on several ventures at a time. It was not uncommon for a privateer to be registered under an individual's name, a partnership, syndicate, or company of convenience formed for the purpose but owned by numerous partners who were the only ones who knew who the actual investors were. On occasion, some officially listed shareholders were little more than prominent fronts for leading politicians or citizens of stature, who sought to avoid being associated directly or indirectly with what the public might consider as speculation or profiteering—which was often the case. Moreover, ships were bought and sold at a dizzying rate: a vessel might be owned by one company when she sailed, but return to a whole new set of owners upon the completion of her cruise, and then sold again before putting back to sea. Typical of the last was the four-gun schooner *General Livingston*, built at Cohansey, New Jersey, and variously owned by the Elmers of Salem, the Sinnicksons of Cumberland County, and lastly by a consortium headed up by Joseph Carson and Mathew Irwin & Company of Philadelphia.[18]

If the ownership of privateers and of shares in a given cruise seems incredibly crowded, with seemingly endless variables, the job of commanding such vessels was equally uncertain. It was not unusual for the captain who began a cruise under one owner to return and find himself out of a job because ownership of the vessel had changed hands while he was at sea. The kings of privateering repeatedly employed the most successful commanders. Out of a total of 332 known skippers commanding Pennsylvania letters of marque vessels, fifty, or fifteen percent of the total, accounted for 193 cruises, or thirty-seven percent of all known privateering expeditions fielded from the state. Four commanders, John Burrows, George Curwin, John Stillwell, and Nicholas Vallance, accounted for no less than six cruises apiece, and six more, John Craig, Stephen Decatur, Henry Hawkins, James Montgomery, Matthew Strong, and Samuel Young, each commanded at least five cruises. It was, of course, not uncommon for a skipper to also be an investor in a vessel that he or a colleague might command on any given expedition, and some were rewarded with overnight wealth, as was the case of *Chance* and *Congress*. Men who had sole or part ownership of the vessels they commanded captained no fewer than thirty-two ventures, more than six percent of the whole.[19]

Securing a crew for a privateer was, by this time, becoming almost as difficult as it was for the Continental and state navies, as increased captures by Royal Navy warships and a growing force of Loyalist privateers had begun to severely impact the manpower pool of able-bodied American seamen. Indeed, by mid-1779, American privateer recruiters were increasingly obliged to rely upon untrained landsmen as more and more skilled mariners fell prey to British and Loyalist cruisers and were consigned to prison ships from which barely one out of ten would survive the war. The procedures for enlistment, however, never varied. Every man who signed aboard a privateer was obliged to sign (or if illiterate, place his X mark) upon a document called the Articles of Agreement. These articles clearly defined the ship's discipline, each man's duties, workstations, and precisely what each individual's shares of proceeds were to be from lawful captures sold at vendues. Despite the growth of the enemy's naval presence, the lure of privateering was as powerful as ever. The temptation is, perhaps, best exemplified by one Andrew Sherburne, a New England teenager whose eldest brother, Thomas, had just returned from a successful voyage aboard Captain Daniel McNeill's Massachusetts privateer *General Mifflin*, which had captured thirteen prizes in a single cruise. "On my brothers return," he wrote,

I became more eager to try my fortune at sea. My father, though a high Whig, disapproved the practice of privateering. Merchant vessels, at this period, which ran safe, made great gains, seamen's wages were consequently high. Through my father's influence Thomas was induced to enter the merchants' service. Though not yet fourteen years of age, like other boys, I imagined myself a man. I had intimated to my sister that if my father would not consent that I should go to sea, I would run away and go on board a privateer. My mind became so infatuated with the subject that I talked of it in my sleep, and was overheard by my mother. She communicated what she had heard to my father. My parents were apprehensive that I might wander off and go on board some vessel without their consent. At this period it was not an uncommon thing for lads to come out of the country, step on board a privateer, make a cruise and return home, their friends remaining in entire ignorance of their fate until they heard it from themselves. Others would pick up their clothes, take a c[h]eese and a loaf of bread and steer off for the army. There was a disposition in commanders of privateers and recruiting officers to engage this spirit of enterprise in young men and boys.[20]

· · ·

On the Jersey coast, it might be said that there were three major wartime industries. The first, of course, was privateering; the second was salt production; and the third was iron. It was the first two that drew the most hostile attentions of British military planners, but it was salt produced on the coast, in facilities at Manasquan, Shark River, Toms River, Barnegat, and other places, that was perhaps the most strategically important of commodities, for without it the very survival of the Revolution itself might be in jeopardy.

Salt was a strategic necessity, employed in salting fish and meat for long-term preservation. Without salt there could be no fishing industry and no storage or transshipment meats (except for some smoked items). Moreover, salt, being a basic necessity of life, was imperative for the continued health of the nation, without which the war effort could easily founder. From the very beginning of hostilities, General Washington was well aware of the importance of salt, hitherto a largely imported commodity from the West Indies, and the coastal works that would be needed to produce it. "Every attempt must be made to save it," he warned. Congress, too, was aware of its worth, and as early as December 1775 recommended to the various assemblies and conventions that they promote salt making in their respective provinces. By the spring of 1776, Congress was apprised of a growing scarcity of salt in several regions, and circulated an article on the manufacture of that most important of commodities. A bounty was offered to salt importers. In August of that year, North Carolina warned Congress: "Should Britain spread her immense Navy along our coasts our supplies [of salt] from abroad are at an end; upon ourselves must we rely, and should we fall short in our attempts, the consequences are too alarming to predict & must be obvious to every one."[21]

By October, John Adams reported that in Pennsylvania salt was growing very scarce, "and what we shall do for want of it, I know not." At the end of the year Congress was informed that the production of pork by New Jersey, a major supplier of that necessary commodity, would cease, owing to a lack of salt. By February 1777, salt was selling in

Philadelphia for sixty shillings a bushel, four times the previous year's price, and a month later it was reported that there was no more than 1,200 bushels of salt stored in the entire city.[22] New Jersey quickly began consideration of erecting a state-managed facility, but backed away when private operations burgeoned along the coast. With the intensifying British blockade and consequent disruption of seaborne commerce, however, salt had become a most precious commodity, especially in dense urban centers such as the Port of Philadelphia, with no saltwater frontage of its own. Pennsylvania had already begun erecting salt works at Toms River, but faced difficulties in keeping an adequate number of men, all from New Jersey, employed, owing to militia call-ups in the host state, and appealed to the Continental Congress for assistance.

In an effort to correct the problem, Congress passed a resolution on April 8, 1777, recommending "to the Governor and Council of Safety of New Jersey not to call into the field such part of their militia, not exceeding forty, as are necessarily employed in the salt works now erecting in their State by the Governor of Pennsylvania; provided it be not inconsistent with the laws of the State." Governor Livingston and the New Jersey Council of Safety responded that the recommendation was inconsistent with the militia law of the state. However, if Pennsylvania were willing to carry on the work with Pennsylvanians, they offered that "care shall be taken to have them exempted as above, though they will also be liable to be called into the field by the said act as it now stands, as becoming, by their residence here, subjects of this State to that purpose."[23]

In June 1777, Congress finally appointed a committee to develop ways and means to supply the new nation with this most basic necessity. The committee recommended that each state offer financial incentives to both producers and importers. New Jersey responded by declaring that each salt work erected in the state might exempt up to ten employees from military service. With the British at New York having the ability to descend upon unprotected coastal works at any time, however, the danger to those engaged in the industry was obvious. The problem was compounded by the British occupation of Philadelphia in September 1777. Washington's army was successfully cut off from its coastal supply of salt, and many Americans were obliged to produce their own from seawater as best they could.[24] With the retreat of the British Army to New York, however, salt works again began to expand in number and size on the New Jersey coast. One of the largest was at Manasquan Inlet.

Unfortunately, the ability to adequately protect the industry was left to the state militias of New Jersey and (at Toms River) Pennsylvania, which were far from reliable and rarely a match for British regulars.

With the onset of spring 1778, even as the enemy was preparing to abandon Philadelphia, the Jersey coast was again menaced by the threat of British and Loyalist attacks. Enemy privateers were finally being commissioned in New York and in the West Indies, although the number of armed rebel vessels was beginning to escalate as well, thanks to the opening of French ports to American commerce raiders. Yet the danger on the mid-Atlantic frontier was visceral.

On a bright Sunday morning, April 5, the worst fears of the salt producers in northern New Jersey were realized when a force of British regulars 150 strong belonging to the 35th and 71st Regiments, commanded by Captains Robertson and Porterfield, arrived off Sandy Hook under convoy of the armed sloop *George* to pick up a reinforcement of forty Royal Marines and a Loyalist unit belonging to the New Jersey Volunteers. From there they had sailed under the protection of HMS *Fowey* and arrived at their destination, Manasquan Inlet, at 8 a.m. the same morning. The landing of 135 men made two hours later on the south side of the inlet was so unexpected that no defense was attempted. The raiders' objective was simply to destroy a massive rebel salt works complex there as quickly and efficiently as possible.[25]

Although surprise appears to have been total, that such actions were at least anticipated is probable.

The Manasquan complex, at the head of Barnegat Bay, was extensive, with no less than a hundred houses. In each house, the invaders discovered between six and ten large copper pans and kettles for the purpose of boiling salt from seawater. One of the houses, said to be the property of Congress, was estimated to be worth at least £6,000. With deftly destructive precision borne of years of practice, the troopers fell upon the salt works and systematically demolished it building-by-building, kettle-by-kettle, and bed-by-bed. Immense quantities of salt, beef, salted and dried hams, sides of bacon, flour, corn, and hay were systematically put to the torch and destroyed. A Boston sloop partially laden with flour was taken off as a prize. Finally, at 3 p.m., the raiders re-embarked without the slightest molestation.[26]

The following day a small reconnaissance party, piloted by a noted Tory named Thomas Oakesom, landed at Shark River. With the wind coming out of the east causing dangerously high surf, and the sudden appearance on the scene of fifteen rebel horsemen, however, the raiders judiciously re-embarked, having destroyed only two small salt works at that place. It was reported in the *New Jersey Gazette* that the arrival of the cavalry "occasioned them to retreat with great precipitation, indeed they jumped in their flat-bottomed boats in such confusion that they sunk one or two of them." Whatever the truth may have been regarding the boats, by April 7, without losing a man, the raiders had returned to their cantonments in New York, having inflicted a serious blow against the rebel's ability to provision themselves. The only consolation that the rebels could enjoy, perhaps, was that some of the works were owned, in part, by suspected Loyalists, "much to their dissatisfaction and to the gratification of the Americans."[27]

The raid served as a major warning to all rebel coastal facilities, but did little to obstruct privateers from operating out of those same shores. Unfortunately, the warning apparently went unheeded by most. Little Egg Harbor, in fact, began to experience a resumption of business dealings in prize cargoes as early as May 1778, as if nothing had happened. On June 20, just two days after the British occupation of Philadelphia ended, a major prize cargo auction was held at Richard Westcoat's inn at The Forks.[28] The first of many massive sales of actual prizes ever to be held on the Mullica was scheduled for July 28 and 29, again at Westcoat's tavern, and was duly trumpeted in the pages of the Philadelphia press. It was to be a mammoth disposal of ships and cargoes calculated to draw a huge crowd from the urban centers on the Delaware, and bidding was expected to be high.

There was a wide selection of vessels to choose from and all were advertised. A total of nine bottoms were placed up for auction under the direction of Marshal John Stokes and included: the brigantines *Industry*, *Carolina Packet*, and *Prince Frederick*, the sloops

Dispatch (or *Despatch*), *Canester*, *Speedwell*, *Jenny*, and *Polly's Adventure* (also advertised as *Molly's Adventure*), and the schooner *Bachelor*. Of the nine, Joseph Ball, manager and now owner of the Batsto Iron Works, and an associate named Nicholas Nichols would fully own or acquire shares in at least three: the 150-ton *Industry*, the 50-ton *Speedwell*, and the 30-ton *Polly's Adventure*.[29]

Though the sale or purchase of a prize ship or privateer may have been a financial risk, the physical danger, of course, lay in obtaining that prize. In 1778, Ball is known to have had shares in several privateering vessels as a silent partner. Two of these were representative of the risk an investor took in engaging in the game: one turned a healthy profit, and the other a distinct loss. The first was the Pennsylvania schooner *St. John*, a sturdy vessel of ten guns manned by a crew of forty-five seamen under an ex-Pennsylvania Navy galley commander named John Rice (who had put up the $10,000 bond Pennsylvania currency), and operated under the publicly registered ownership of two of Ball's Philadelphia connections, Joseph Carson and Michael Dawson & Company. The second vessel was the Pennsylvania sloop *Susannah*, also of ten guns and forty-five men, commanded by a tough fighter named Hugh Stocker, owned by Joseph Carson and Joseph McCullough, and commissioned on July 31.[30]

St. John was perhaps typical of the majority of privateers employed during the American Revolution in that almost nothing but the barest essentials are known about her. She received her commission from Pennsylvania on July 4, 1778, and, after a successful voyage, a few lines in a newspaper article. About all that can be found concerning this little ship is that she, in company with an unidentified New England privateer, managed to recapture a brig and a sloop that had been taken earlier by the British. The captures were made by the Americans about the end of July or the first of August, after which the prizes were brought into port, ostensibly Little Egg Harbor, and sold.[31]

Several vessels Ball sent out during the Revolution proved to be an investor's nightmare. When *Susannah* sailed out of Great Bay soon after her commissioning, she was hell-bent on taking as many prizes as possible. On August 29, unfortunately, she managed to fall in with two ships under the convoy of the Royal Navy tender *Emerald*. The tender was a sloop of ten guns and enjoyed a reputation as a successful and pugnacious combatant. *Susannah's* feisty skipper, Hugh Stocker, ignored caution and boldly sought to cut out the two tempting prizes before the enemy could respond, but failed. *Emerald* and *Susannah* were soon embroiled in a slugging match during which the two convoy vessels managed to escape. Though she had suffered the loss of her captain and several crewmen dead or wounded, through superior seamanship the British tender, which had placed herself in harm's way and saved the convoy, was able to cut off combat and also escaped. *Susannah* suffered only one dead and several wounded, but her return to Egg Harbor was gloomy. It was true that she had faced down an enemy of equal strength in combat and enhanced her commander's reputation as a fighter, but she had been forced to return home empty handed, and in need of extensive and expensive repair, which was anything but welcomed by investors. The expedition had proved a net financial failure for Ball and his colleagues.[32]

The diminutive Little Egg Harbor privateer *Glory of America*, Captain William Williams commanding, was even less lucky. On August 20, she encountered the sixteen-gun New York Loyalist letter of marque brig *Tryon*, Captain George Sibbles, and was sunk in bloody combat. The crew, fortunately, was rescued and transferred to HMS *Maidstone*. All were transported to New York where they were, no doubt, incarcerated aboard one of the rotting prison death ships lying off the Battery or in the East River.[33]

An American privateer engages a British merchantman. Extract from the memoirs of Ebenezer Fox, published with notes by C. Fox in 1847 as *The Adventures of Ebenezer Fox in the Revolutionary War*, by Ebenezer Fox.

Despite such losses, it was, in fact, the beginning of an extremely bullish time for the Egg Harbor sea raiders. Wolf packs of privateers began to infest the New Jersey coast, operating in pairs, trios, and even larger numbers with stunning success. The situation soon became so hazardous for British vessels, including their own privateers that had only recently been authorized by the Admiralty to operate out of New York, that a temporary embargo had to be placed by the Admiralty prohibiting any and all cruisers and merchant vessels from sailing from the city alone. Still, incoming ships from England, absolutely necessary to keep the city and the troops cantoned therein supplied, continued to sail at peril. Now even convoys sailing with powerful, armed escorts were at risk. In August, when a British supply fleet of fourteen vessels arrived at New York from London after a seven-week voyage, they reported the loss of the brigantine *Recovery* on August 20. The vessel was carried into Egg Harbor, almost as if it were an everyday occurrence. No fewer than a half dozen Pennsylvania privateers that had been operating in two groups of three each had accosted the ship. With two rival packs, one of which operated out of Egg Harbor, claiming the vessel and her valuable general cargo of dry goods, china and queen's ware, beef, porter, pork, bar iron, and cordage as a prize, the battle would eventually end up in a bitter court fight over ownership. It was, however, small consolation for the British ship owners, their insurers, the captured crewmen, or the British Army and citizens in New York in need of the provisions and goods.[34]

Ship after ship fell easy prey and Egg Harbor was, from time to time, choked with prizes. The overflow extended over to Mays Landing on the Great Egg Harbor River, where several richly laden captures such as *Lark*, *Lucy*, and *Hannah* had to be taken. Notice after notice appeared in the Philadelphia and Trenton newspapers beginning with the word "To be Sold at Public Vendue . . ." at Chestnut Neck or The Forks.[35] Each advertisement usually included the name of the ship or ships to be sold and a long list of both mundane and exotic cargoes, often enumerated in detail, such as rum, tobacco, oranges, lemons, limes, pineapples, sugar, coffee, beef, indigo, mahogany, silks, satins, carpenter's tools, and so on. The lists, in some cases, were practically endless. Anything and everything could be had for the right price.

Large multiple prize vendues became the order of the day. Typical was the sale held at Chestnut Neck on September 8, 1778. Placed up for auction were four vessels including a French dogger of 100 tons called *Rising Sun*, a 110-ton brig called *Governor Henry*, a 130-ton brig called *Nancy*, and a 75-ton tobacco sloop called *William*. Their cargoes of salt and tobacco were not exotic but, given the inflated market prices then prevailing, would prove quite lucrative. Marshal John Stokes dutifully gave notice of the auction, which was published in the *New Jersey Gazette*, and on the prescribed date the sale commenced. Prospective buyers were furnished with an inventory of each vessel and its cargo on the appointed day. The terms were cash on delivery when a ship was sold. Neat, clean, quick and profitable.[36]

• • •

That privateering was rendering a valuable service to the American war effort was apparent. Yet, by the summer of 1778, the system was still subject to abuses and continued to be detrimental to both the Continental and state naval services. William Whipple, writing to Josiah Bartlett on July 12 from Portsmouth, New Hampshire, expressed just such concerns and reiterated his uneasiness at the morality of the practice.

> I agree with you that the privateers have much distressed the trade of our Enemies, but had there been no privateers is it not probable there would have been a much larger number of Public Ships than has been fitted out, which might have distressed the Enemy nearly as much & furnished these States with necessaries on much better terms than they have been supplied by Privateers? . . . No kind of Business can so effectually introduce Luxury, Extravagance and every kind of Dissipation, that tend to the destruction of the morals of people. Those who are actually engaged in it soon lose every Idea of right & wrong, & for want of an opportunity of gratifying their insatiable avarice with the property of the Enemies of their Country, will wit out the least compunction seize that of her Friends. . . . There is at this time 5 Privateers fitting out here, which I suppose will take 400 men. These must be by far the greater part Countrymen, for the Seamen are chiefly gone,

& most of them in Halifax Gaol. Besides all this, you may depend no public ship will ever be manned while there is a privateer fitting out. The reason is plain: Those people who have the most influence with Seamen think it their interest to discourage the Public service, because by that they promote their own interest, viz., Privateering.[37]

Privateering was a venturesome, risky game, and the dismal failures were often countered by spectacular successes that more than compensated for losses. Such was the case of the redoubtable sloop *Chance*. During the late summer, *Chance* again put to sea, this time under the command of Captain David Stevens, a native son of Egg Harbor who, the record suggests, on occasion disposed of his scruples as deemed necessary for profit. The sloop, though nominally under the ownership of Joseph Carson & Company of Philadelphia, was heavily invested in by Joseph Ball, Charles Pettit, and John Cox, who had put up £4,216 sterling combined to outfit her. It is unclear whether or not the veteran privateer put to sea alone or in company with another vessel, although the latter is likely. What is certain, however, is that she would operate in concert with the three-gun Pennsylvania schooner *Fly*, owned by Peter January and John Paine & Company of Philadelphia, and commanded by Captain Micajah Smith, also of Egg Harbor. Together the two little privateers would effect several major captures that would eventually help to foment British outrage and draw further armed attacks upon the Jersey shores.[38]

Chance and *Fly* were to be lavishly rewarded for their singularly important voyage, for somewhere off the New Jersey coast the two privateers, while apparently operating in concert with three others as a wolf pack, fell in with elements of the Irish Sea Fleet en route to New York. The adventurers deftly cut out at least two fat merchantmen that were quite probably wallowing far behind the bulk of the convoy. The triumphant raiders, making good their escape, returned to Chestnut Neck and, for Stevens at least, certain notoriety. The convoy, it was later reported at New York, had been under the protection of HMS *Sibyl*, Captain Parrot commanding, and had sailed from Cork on May 27 with the victuallers *Hero, Baltimore, Achilles, King George, Mary, Fairlee,* and others. On August 31, The *New York Gazette and Weekly Mercury*, a Tory newspaper, reported somewhat erroneously of their safe appearance, noting only that the "above mentioned ships were attacked off Egg Harbor the day before arrival by 5 privateers, but beat them off with much ease, and would have taken them all, had they [the privateers] not made use of their oars with uncommon [speed]." No mention was made of the two unnamed vessels that were taken.[39]

News of the captures, however, was not long in getting out. On September 2, the *New Jersey Gazette* commented: "We hear several prizes were taken last week, and brought into Egg Harbor; among which is a vessel from London, with goods to the amount of 20,000 pounds sterling."[40]

The prizes were richly laden indeed. The larger of the two, a magnificent London merchantman called *Venus*, was a veritable floating shopping center. Her immense cargo was scheduled to be sold on Monday, September 14, by way of public vendue at both The Forks and Chestnut Neck, where she had been moored. Notice was posted that "The vendue [was] to begin at ten o'clock in the forenoon, and continue from day to day until the whole is sold." It was well worth the journey to Little Egg Harbor for the speculators and buyers. This "very valuable cargo of the ship *Venus*," it was advertised, consisted of "fine and coarse broadcloths, fine and coarse linens, calicoes, chintzes, lawn and cambricks, silks and satins, silk and thread stockings, men's and women's shoes, a great variety of medicines and books, hardware, beef, pork, butter, cheese and porter, in short, the greatest variety of all kinds of merchandise, too tedious to be inserted."[41]

And even as one of the richest of prizes to be brought into Little Egg Harbor was being auctioned off, the parade of captures continued: a schooner bound from Jamaica for New York with a cargo of rum; a schooner from Nantz taken by the British, recaptured by privateers, and sent in; a brigantine taken en route from London to New York; a sloop laden with tobacco; and on and on and on.[42]

The circus was not to be allowed to proceed completely undisturbed, for the increased assault on the British supply lines had finally struck a nerve in New York. Neither the embargo nor the Royal Navy, it seemed, could blunt the American privateering depredations at sea. A growing concern that the Royal Navy could not afford to remain on the defensive against the rebel rovers for much longer had begun to take root at the highest levels of command. In the meantime, however, pinprick cutting out operations to keep the rebels off balance would have to do.

On September 18, only four days after the auction of the *Venus* and her cargo was held, two warships, HMS *Delaware* and HM Brig *Halifax*, accompanied by two armed tenders, a brig and ship, came to anchor close off the bar at Cranberry Inlet, opposite Toms River. The little squadron was being shepherded by a former smuggler-turned-Loyalist spy named William Dillon who had lived on what was then called Dillon's Island, now Island Heights. The four vessels lay at anchor off the bar throughout the night, but the following morning, between 7 and 8 a.m., seven armed boats, with twenty or thirty men in each, departed into the inlet on a cutting out expedition.[43]

Their targets included the 200-ton ship *Washington*, formerly the Bristolman *Love and Unity*, and two sloops reported by Dillon to be lying near the bar, most with their crews still aboard. The former had been taken as a prize by the local militia after her crew had overcome their skipper, one Captain Grover, and "designedly" run the ship ashore near Toms River, laden with several thousand bottles of London porter, a large quantity of beer and ale, red and white port wine, eighty hogsheads of loaf sugar, salt, flour, cheese, queensware and delftware. Captain Benjamin Pratt, commander of the Connecticut privateer sloop *Princess Mary*, claimed the ship at a Court of Admiralty hearing held at Trenton on August 28. Three days later *Love and Unity* was placed up for auction along with another recent prize, the schooner *Indian Delaware*, and sold by Marshal John Stokes at Toms River, while the balance of the cargo was soon afterwards disposed of separately two days later at Manasquan. The ship was then purchased by a Philadelphia consortium of privateer speculators headed by Thomas Irwin, George Kennedy, and William McCullough & Company, and placed under the command of Captain Thomas Fletcher. Outfitted with eight guns and a crew of thirty men, and commissioned on September 9, she was taken into adjacent Cranberry Inlet and anchored near several sloops to make final preparations for her first privateering cruise.[44]

When the enemy raiders, two armed British ships and two brigs, arrived unexpectedly and came close to the bar of the inlet where they lay all night on September 18, pandemonium at Cranberry Inlet reigned supreme. The following morning, between 7 and 8 o'clock, the invaders dispatched seven armed boats to retake *Washington*. Captain Fletcher, his mate, boatswain, and three sailors, the *New Jersey Gazette* later reported, managed to make their escape to the mainland in a boat belonging to one of the nearby sloops. "Soon after they got ashore, a certain Robert M'Mullen (who some time since was condemned with Robert Dillon to be hanged for burglary in Monmouth, and both having been reprieved, the former entered himself aboard of this ship) took the boat and made off to the enemy, huzzaing as he went. Dillon, who also joined them some time before, was supposed to pilot the British vessels into the inlet." *Washington* and one sloop were promptly captured and burned. Another sloop was carried off as a prize along with ninety-six barrels of flour. Four years later another Dillon would lead the British, this time to Toms River, where they would capture the Toms River blockhouse and burn much of the town.[45]

Despite the dramatic increase in the privateering population in coastal waters, the vulnerability of the New Jersey coast was again made self-evident. Yet, it was Egg Harbor itself, the very heart and soul of rebel privateering on the Jersey shore, that perhaps most irked the British naval high command in New York. It was likely that, even as General Clinton was taking charge of the British Army in New York City with orders to strike against American ports in concert with the Royal Navy, the navy began to focus more intently upon privateers. Vice Admiral James Gambier arrived at New York in the late summer of 1778 to replace Admiral Howe in command of the North American Station. He brought with him a new resolution to exterminate the growing rebel privateering menace, which was already proving more costly than the Continental and all the state navies combined. His first objective, as Germain's directives to Clinton had clearly outlined, was against New England, from which the numerically largest body of privateers was based. Then he would turn his attentions upon Egg Harbor, the second largest "nest of rebel freebooters" in America.

Under Gambier's personal instructions, a large British fleet of upwards of forty-five sail, led by HMS *Carysfort*, under Captain Robert Fanshawe, carrying 4,000 troops under General Charles "No Flint" Grey, set sail on September 4 from New York bound for Buzzard's Bay, Massachusetts, to assail rebel privateers and commercial shipping in the bay and at Martha's Vineyard. Upon arrival in the bay on September 5, the fleet pressed northward up the Acushnet River, landing about 6 p.m. in the evening on the west bank of the stream at Clark's Point. Throughout the night and into the following morning, New Bedford suffered in a conflagration of destruction as shipping, large magazines, mills, homes, churches, and storehouses were set ablaze, the flames of which could be seen at Newport, Rhode Island, some twenty miles away.[46]

As the destruction of New Bedford was underway on the opposite side of the river at the village of Fairhaven, the 38-man artillery garrison of a diminutive earthen fort, mounting eleven guns, and commanded by an elderly and reluctant colonel, opened on the fleet; the fire was returned only briefly. Then, just as quickly as they had opened fire, the garrison spiked their ordnance, and abandoned the works, albeit leaving their flag flying. By noon, September 6, after completing the destruction of New Bedford, General Grey had marched his troops around the head of the Acushnet, where they burned the principal part of the houses. From there they moved to the eastern shore of the river and then "doubled back to Fairhaven" where a local 150-man militia force under Major Israel Fearing was convening for the defense of the town. After setting fire to mills and houses at the town landing, demolishing the abandoned earthworks, and destroying the fort's iron guns and a large stores of ammunition, the British proceeded toward the village itself. There they were met by a staccato of heavy fire from Fearing's militiamen. The skirmish was short, with the loss totaling four killed and sixteen captured on the American side, and one killed, four wounded and sixteen of General Grey's troops missing.[47]

His work of destruction at New Bedford and Fairhaven completed, General Grey and his troops retired to their boats. The devastation at New Bedford had been nearly total. One count reported that eleven houses, twenty-one shops, a ropewalk, along with goods and naval stores of all kinds, and no fewer than thirty-four ships had been lost at New Bedford alone. Overall, at both towns, seventy vessels, many of them prizes taken by privateers, as well as a handful of privateers and smaller craft had been destroyed. Magazines, wharves, storehouses, warehouses, vessels being built on stocks, all of the buildings at McPhearson's wharf, and the mills and dwellings at Fairhaven had gone up in smoke. The fort and its artillery had been reduced to a state of uselessness. Several estimates at the amount of property destroyed ranged from £20,000 to £100,000, with one as high as £323,266, mostly from losses in ships and goods. But it was the destruction of the shipping that hurt the most, for as one German officer later commented: "Loss of ships is felt more by the rebels than any other loss. They must finally become docile, for a burned child shuns the fire."[48]

Following the devastation of New Bedford and Fairhaven, General Grey tarried only long enough to send his aide, Captain John Andre, back to New York to request that additional transports be sent to carry off the livestock for the British Army's larders in New York, which he expected to take from his next target, the island of Martha's Vineyard. Though his original intent had been to assail Nantucket Island as well, with the fleet slowed by surly winds, the general chose to focus his entire attention upon Holmes Hole (present day Vineyard Haven) on the Vineyard, a little over twenty miles distance from the Acushnet.[49]

Upon his arrival aboard *Carysfort* on September 10, Grey was met by a delegation of three of the local citizens who had been dispatched to query his purpose in coming. The general's demands were given without delay: he wanted no less than 300 oxen and 10,000 sheep, as well as all of the local militia's arms and all public funds immediately delivered up from the defenseless inhabitants. If the demands were not met, he threatened to land his troops and take them by force. Given the record of his destruction on the Acushnet, it was clear he meant business. It had been a tall order, but within two days, the islanders had rounded up and delivered to the fleet 130 oxen and 6,000 sheep. Angry at the speed with which the deliveries were being made, the general ordered a contingent of troops to hasten the roundup and to burn any vessels found in the area. By September 14, the required number of sheep, the militia arms, and £950 in tax money intended for the Continental Congress had been delivered. The following day the expeditionaries set sail, and arrived at New York City on September 17.[50]

The surprise had been total and, with the Americans able to muster less than a few hundred defenders, who proved ineffective, the end result for the rebels had been ruinous. The success of the expedition was savored by the British and offered a grim portent of what may lay in store for the Americans at Egg Harbor and indeed all of the coastal enclaves. "What a proof of the Bedford enterprise," wrote William Knox, Lord Germain's under secretary, not long after the attack,

> of the propriety of the orders so repeatedly given for attacking the rebel sea ports, and what a reflection it is upon Lord Howe's character that Gambier, in his short absence, has done more to subdue the Rebellion than his lordship during the whole of his command. It was always clear in speculation that the Militia would never stay with Washington or quit their homes, if the coast was kept in alarm, but the experiment having now been made, the effect is reduced to a certainty. Surely somebody will ask Lord Howe why he has never attempted anything of this kind.[51]

And Gambier was not finished yet.

Despite the substantial success of the expedition north, it was the capture of the two ships of the convoy from Cork by privateers operating from that most remote privateering center of Chestnut Neck, less than a hundred miles south of New York City, that had tripped the scales for the next foray by the Royal Navy and made the British high command "decide upon the destruction of this harbor."[52]

–XIII–

Skulking Banditti

"I am the more surprised at their taking them so much by surprise."

The planning for the expedition against the American privateering base at Little Egg Harbor was well concealed. Much of the preparation was, in fact, hidden amidst the not-so-secret organization for a major foray to the West Indies. General Washington's spies, however, had been quite active. In a letter to the Comte d'Estaing, dated September 19, 1778, he carefully noted the motions of the enemy and a plethora of intelligence concerning the British fleet in New York and the recent arrival there of a considerable flotilla of transports. He also noted somewhat disdainfully that the force that had just destroyed New Bedford "has been employed in collecting cattle and sheep at Martha's Vineyard and other places in the sound," but said nothing of the privateer losses.[1] Unknown to the general, even as he wrote, several warships that had participated in that very expedition were en route to New York to take on supplies and troops for an equally formidable raid, this time against the privateers of the New Jersey coast.

Among the vessels threading their way from New England to New York were six ships already slated for the attack on Egg Harbor (one of which would be removed before the expedition was launched). Newest and brightest of the lot was His Majesty's 16-gun sloop-of-war *Zebra*, a 306-ton, 125-man warship commanded by Captain Henry Colins. *Zebra* had been selected as flagship of the attack squadron possibly because of her shallower-than-normal draft. The largest and probably oddest-looking of the set was the 16-gun schooner-rigged row-galley *Vigilant*. This vessel, manned by 150 seamen and marines under the command of Lieutenant John Christian, bore the distinction of having once been the largest transport to enter American waters in the opening days of the war. She had originally been a square-rigged ship of 863 tons burthen called *Empress of Russia* (sometimes referred to as *Grand Dutchess of Russia*). In 1777, she had been specially converted to an armed hermaphrodite-rigged row-galley at New York to participate in the campaign against the Delaware River forts. Also included in the armada were three other smaller row-galleys, including *Cornwallis*, Lieutenant Johnson, *Dependence*, Lieutenant Robertson, and *Comet*. All were vessels of sixteen guns and each was manned by a crew of forty men. Among those included in the squadron ranks was the armed sloop *Greenwich*, a small vessel manned by a crew of fifty and commanded by a Lieutenant Spry. *Greenwich* had most recently served as a dispatch vessel during the New Bedford raid and was, no doubt, expected to provide much the same service during the Egg Harbor operation.[2]

At New York, several last minute additions were made to reinforce the squadron. HM Sloop-of-War *Nautilus*, a three-year-old vessel of sixteen guns and 125 seamen and marines, had only days before been relieved of active blockade duty in Whitestone

Bay and sailed to Staten Island to rendezvous with the squadron. Captain John Belcher, her commander, was relatively new to his ship, having assumed charge as recently as May. Both *Nautilus* and her crew, however, were no strangers to New Jersey waters, having conducted extensive blockade duty in the Delaware over the recent months.[3]

Two New York Loyalist privateers, *Grandby* and *Experiment*, had also been induced to join the expedition, possibly as transports, but no doubt lured by promises of rich rebel booty expected to be found at Little Egg Harbor. *Grandby* was a small sloop of fifty tons, ten guns, and forty crewmen under the command of Andrew Saw and fresh in from a most profitable cruise off Cape Henlopen. *Experiment*, a schooner of one hundred tons, sixty men, and fourteen guns, was skippered by Alexander McPherson and owned by Neil Jameison of New York. This vessel had spent the summer, under the command of Captain David Squires, cruising the lucrative but hazardous coast of North Carolina where she had taken seven prizes on her own, including a French ship of twenty guns. All of these had been sent into New York and earned a tidy fortune for her owner and shareholders.[4]

In addition to the warships of the flotilla, two tenders belonging to *Experiment* and *Nautilus* were also assigned to the operation, as were a number of flatboats. Apparently at the last minute, *Comet* was withdrawn from the squadron for reasons unknown.[5]

In planning the Egg Harbor expedition, the British high command wished to leave no stone unturned and attempted to avail themselves of every possible opportunity. Ever since September 1776, when the city of New York was partially destroyed by a major fire, stores and provisions, naval supplies and timber stocks had been acquired with considerable difficulty and dispensed with great economy. Food shortages were an ever-present problem that was relieved only by transports sent from Europe and occasional foraging expeditions into the rebel-infested countryside. The devastating raid on the New England port of New Bedford in early September, of course, was partially undertaken as a forage-in-force. Another "provisioning" raid, reasoned the British, might be mounted not only to secure needed goods but also to double as a diversion to draw American relief forces away from the Egg Harbor expedition.[6]

Making the most of this unhappy necessity, General Henry Clinton ordered Major General Charles Cornwallis to forage with some 5,000 men on the west side of the Hudson River and General Wilhelm Knyphausen with 3,000 Hessians into Winchester County to do the same on the east. Upon first learning of the enemy's motions, Washington feared a thrust against the Hudson River Highlands or possibly against allied French naval forces fitting out at Boston. Clinton, however, was using Cornwallis's "move into Jersey . . . partly to favor an expedition sent to Egg Harbor."[7]

Washington would not be moved. The diversion by Cornwallis failed to unseat the Continental Army; only small bodies of troops were sent out to check and annoy the enemy. Unfortunately, one of these forces, Lieutenant George Baylor's Third Continental Light Dragoons, was cut off at Old Tappan in Rockland County, New York, and thirty-six men were savagely massacred in their sleep and another thirty-six captured. Washington still refused to budge from his position in upper New Jersey. By then, a substantial British naval force was already in motion.[8]

• • •

On Tuesday, September 29, the Royal Navy ships-of-war under the command of Captain Henry Colins and the contingent of private armed vessels slated to participate in the advance against the south Jersey coast rendezvoused off Staten Island. The following morning regular army and militia units under the overall command of Captain Patrick Ferguson began to embark. Ferguson, a noted marksman, inventor of a repeating rifle, and partisan leader, was on detached service from the 70th Regiment of Foot and had been given the honor of leading the land forces in the coming assault. His command consisted of 300 British regulars, tried and true, belonging to the celebrated 5th Regiment of Foot, and one hundred Loyalist rangers belonging to the Third Battalion of New Jersey Volunteers. Both units were veteran fighters, the 5th having suffered through the bloody victory at Bunker Hill and in the New York and Philadelphia campaigns; and the Volunteers, better known as Skinner's Greens after the organizer, Brigadier General Cortlandt Skinner, former Attorney General of New Jersey, and their green uniforms, having engaged in countless partisan battles and raids. Skinner's Greens, in fact, had earned for themselves an unenviable reputation for no-quarter fighting that was to haunt them throughout the Revolution. They were destined to reinforce that bloody reputation at Little Egg Harbor.[9]

Provisions for the expedition and the more than 1,000 men engaged were in short supply and some of the ships, *Grandby*, *Greenwich*, *Dependence*, and *Cornwallis* in particular, were very ill-provided with bread, rum, and other necessaries. Moreover, several of the ships were also in serious need of refitting, careening, and general repairs. Nevertheless, it was decided to embark against Egg Harbor immediately, for the agenda of war was unrelenting. Speed was imperative if the Americans were to be caught napping as they had been at New Bedford, and the longer the task force remained at Staten Island the greater the chances of the Americans learning of the expedition's true objective. Colins decided to set sail on the tide.[10]

Unfortunately, it was already too late to conceal such secrets. Spies were everywhere. Late in the evening of September 29, Governor William Livingston of New Jersey was roused from his bed to receive an urgent message from Brigadier General William Maxwell of the Continental Army informing him of the impending British move against Egg Harbor. Forgetting the lateness of the hour—3 a.m.—Livingston "called a Council, and took measures to defeat the enterprise."[11]

• • •

On the morning of September 30, 1778, the British attack force, under Captain Henry Colins, weighed anchor and slowly proceeded, ship by ship, over the bar at Sandy Hook. The wind was strong and out of the north. By noontime the squadron was passing the Sandy Hook Lighthouse and by evening had formed into a formidable looking flotilla. Unfortunately for Colins, the wind shifted to the south as his task force was running adjacent to Neversink and the weather rapidly began to deteriorate. Trouble was just beginning and the forward motion of the squadron all but came to a halt for the next several days.[12]

On October 2, the weather turned even worse and one of the transports became disabled. *Nautilus* obligingly took the stricken vessel under tow. The following afternoon, the hawser between the two ships broke and the transport found herself suddenly separated and adrift from her guardian. Such incidents soon became frustratingly common. Forced to constantly tack against a strong south wind, between October 2 and 3, the fleet was able to gain only three or four leagues. By the 4th the squadron had become seriously distended, exposing the weaker or more isolated vessels to possible attack by rebel privateers.[13]

On the morning of October 4, *Nautilus* sighted a sail to the westward making for *Zebra*, at the time some miles distant and still adjacent to Neversink. The unidentified vessel in question soon proved to be HM Brig *Halifax*, a vessel of six guns and eight swivels, commanded by Lieutenant William Quarme. The lieutenant, as it turned out, "being on a cruise on this station, and thinking his vessel might prove useful," soon joined the expedition.[14]

The fleet was still scattered after *Halifax* joined and it was necessary to regroup before further hazards were encountered. A signal was raised for the squadron to come under the stern of *Zebra*. The order was repeated again in the evening—only moments before the galley *Dependence* raised her own signal, but one of distress.[15]

Galleys, shallow draft craft that could be sailed and rowed, having been created for employment in riverine environments rather than for the open sea, were not perhaps the most seaworthy vessels in the Royal Navy. Yet, they were extremely useful in the sounds, rivers, and lakes of America and found continual employment throughout the war on both sides. So, once again *Nautilus* came to the rescue, taking the damaged ship in tow. Late in the evening the wind diminished, shifted, and at last permitted the fleet to proceed unimpeded.[16]

The squadron finally dropped anchor off the bar of Little Egg Harbor on the afternoon of Monday, October 5. A voyage that normally consumed a day or so in good weather had taken the British five. Adding to their undoubted frustration was still another unfavorable shift in the wind after the ships had dropped hook, effectively prohibiting entry into the inlet with the tide. Still, Colins was determined to compensate for the loss of time already incurred. The element of surprise might still be had, he believed, if further delay could be avoided or even partially circumvented. Acting with resolution, he ordered the more maneuverable and shallow draft vessels, *Halifax*, *Cornwallis*, *Dependence*, *Nautilus's* tender, and one of the armed sloops over the bar and into the harbor as soon as the next tide permitted. The heavier draft vessels would simply have to be lightened and brought over during a more favorable wind. Two officers and a detachment of soldiers, possibly more, were also sent over in *Nautilus's* tender and in other vessels. It was imperative that the harbor and river be sealed off as soon as possible to prohibit the last minute escape of any rebel privateers that might be there.[17]

Frustration was heaped upon frustration as the weather steadfastly refused to comply with British plans. A good stiff wind continued to blow out of the northwest for the rest of the day and well into the next.[18] Attempts by the remainder of the squadron to cross the bar were obviously impossible in the face of such natural opposition. There was little else Colins could do but to proceed with lightening his vessels for the crossing, sit tight, and hope his arrival had yet to be discovered.

The Americans at the Chestnut Neck privateering base were, of course, already well aware of his approach and had everything to gain by the British delay. An urgent message to Philadelphia was sent by express announcing the foe's impending arrival. "The enemy," it read, "have made their appearance, and are coming in. There are to the number of twenty sail—two frigates, several barges, sloops and schooner, and three row-galleys with latine sails. Several sail of vessel are here, and nothing to protect them. All possible assistance is expected from you."[19]

Samuel Cooper, part owner of a salt works near Chestnut Neck, wrote from Philadelphia to his partner John Little, who was managing the works, to warn him in the event that he was still unaware of the oncoming furies. "I have just learned that there is an expedition going on towards Egg Harbor and I understand you have a quantity of salt there. I hope you will think as I do and remove it as soon as possible, for depend on it the works will be destroyed and there should be no time lost." Then he added, as if to reinforce the importance of saving whatever was possible: "Salt sells for eight pounds in town."[20]

There was much to protect at Chestnut Neck, but defensive measures were generally ignored in lieu of evacuation. The fort at Fox Burrows was suddenly and mysteriously found to be devoid of cannon. The ordnance that were to have been placed in the works by Cox, Westcot, and Clark, if indeed they had provided them at all, were gone; they may well have been stripped by visiting privateersmen who seemed to be eternally scavenging for guns, provisions, and naval gear for their vessels. There were, undoubtedly, a number of swivel guns mounted aboard the ships at anchor in the Mullica that were of too deep a draft to be hauled further upriver, but they would be useless against the more than 110 cannon of the British warships should they cross the bar. Many other vessels of "considerable" size, upwards of fifteen to twenty sail with a "considerable quantity of European and West Indies goods," lay unmanned and defenseless in the river. Several privateers were also trapped, but, for the most part, were able to evacuate upstream. The great *Venus* of London, the capture of which may have tripped off the attack in the first place, ironically, lay swinging gently at anchor, empty of cargo but still too deep in the water to be taken upriver to safety. Another rich prize, the schooner *Fame*, captured only a few days before by Yelverton Taylor in the little four-gun Pennsylvania privateer sloop *Comet*, was also there, her cargo of sugar, coffee, molasses, pimentos, and "excellent Jamaica spirits" having been scheduled to go on auction Wednesday at Payne's Tavern.[21]

Although the evacuation was hurried, there had been enough warning to permit many prizes to be moved upstream, as well as an enormous amount of prize cargo, which was then hauled overland to safety. Some reports indicated "most of the valuable goods, & part of the vessels were removed to The Forks thirty miles above, and were saved." Other accounts indicated that *all* of the stores, public and private, were removed at the first alarm. George Payne, for example, had managed to carry off all of his stock and household furniture well before the enemy arrival. Ten vessels, mostly prizes too large to ascend to the upriver sanctuary of The Forks, had to be dismantled, scuttled, or sunk to prevent recapture. Undoubtedly the scuttling of most, if not all, had been undertaken in hopes that they could be refloated after the British departed. Many of these vessels were relieved of their naval apparel, furniture, and rigging in the event that the ships were totally destroyed by the enemy. At least something, reasoned the ever-speculating men of Egg Harbor, could be saved for auction at a later date, even if the British wiped out the empty shell of a hamlet.[22]

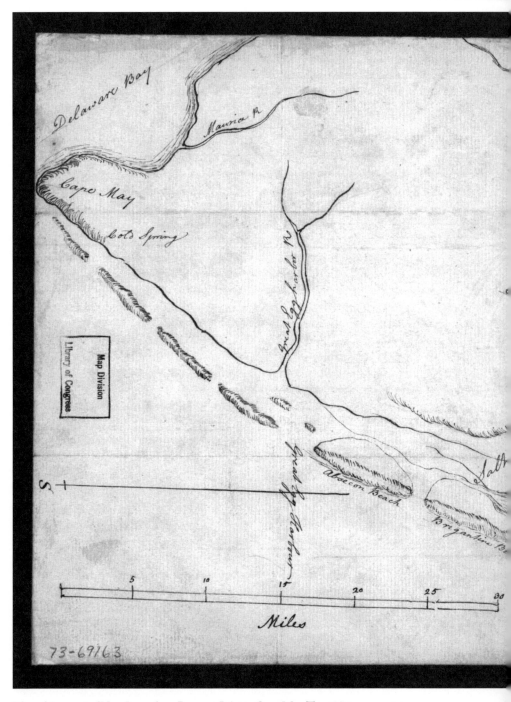

Map of the coast of New Jersey from Barnegat Inlet to Cape May. This 1770 manuscript map detailing the Little Egg Harbor region, prior to hostilities, shows the location of Osborns Island (A), Egg Harbor Meeting House (B), the Fox Burrows Harbor, later site of a battery (anchor sign); The Forks (D); Batsto Furnace, Forge and Landing (E, F, F); and Chestnut Ridge Landing (G), later site of the privateering base. Courtesy Geographic and Map Division, Library of Congress.

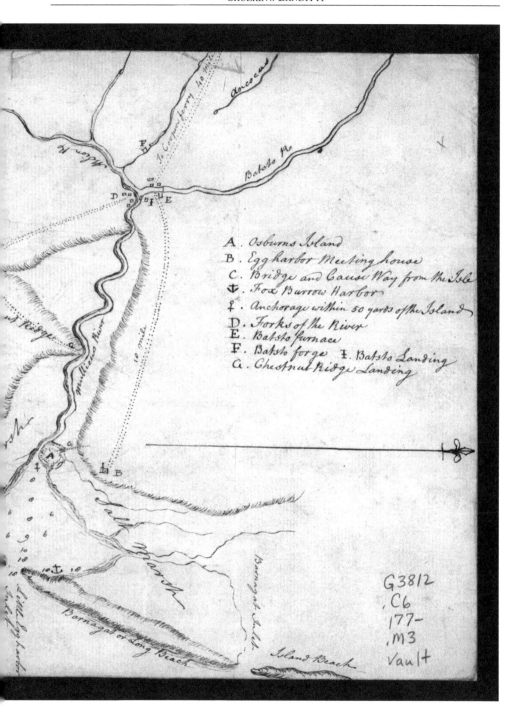

A. Osburns Island
B. Egg harbor Meeting house
C. Bridge and Cause Way from the Isle
⚓. Fox Burrow Harbor
⚓. Anchorage within 50 yards of the Island
D. Forks of the River
E. Batsto furnace
F. Batsto forge   ⚓ Batsto Landing
G. Chestnut Ridge Landing

G3812
.C6
177-
.M3
Vault

. . .

At 7 a.m. on Tuesday, another British transport and two armed sloops loaded with troops were able to pass over the bar despite a prevailing northwest wind. Colins was already aboard one of the ships in the harbor, having left orders for *Zebra*, *Vigilant*, and *Nautilus* to join those vessels already inside the inlet as soon as the wind and tide permitted.[23]

It was then that Colins learned "by some information we received that intelligence of our intentions had reached the rebels several days preceding our arrival" and four privateers, three carrying six or eight guns apiece, and an armed pilot boat, had already escaped. Both he and Ferguson, believing that preparations for a very warm reception must have been underway for several days, felt it was imperative that prompt action be taken. Thus, as Ferguson later explained, it was "determined to allow no further time, but to push up with our galleys and small craft, with what soldiers could be crowded into them, without waiting for the coming in of the ships."[24]

Accordingly, the galleys and armed sloops, having already been lightened to lessen their drafts for the ascent up the muddy Mullica, were loaded with as many soldiers and marines as possible. The remaining troops were ordered into flatboats and brought along for the express purpose of being employed in the assault.[25]

At daybreak, October 6, the British landing force, personally led by Colins and Ferguson, shoved off for Chestnut Neck. The route across the bay and then up the winding Mullica was extremely difficult to traverse, even in times of peace, owing to the frequently shoally, unchartered nature of the waters and the lack of knowledgeable pilots. With a rebel surprise attack from either or both sides of the river anywhere along the route being a distinct possibility, delays were doubly vexing. When the sloops *Grandby* and *Greenwich* ran aground off Osborns Island and could advance no further, Colins briefly halted the ascent, and then left the two privateers to fend for themselves. The expedition could not afford to await the sloops' recovery and proceeded on without them. By late afternoon, the flotilla had reached the extensive salt marshes a few miles below Chestnut Neck. Landing in this extremely spongy region, where a man could easily sink to his chest in mud, was found to be impossible. It was thus deemed necessary to go ashore directly or immediately above the rebel works protecting the approach to Chestnut Neck itself. Either way Colins feared the landing was likely to be hotly contested.[26]

Advancing with *Cornwallis* and *Dependence* in the van, both Colins and Ferguson apparently preferred to close with the rebel works head on. The Americans who had remained behind to defend the position "ranged themselves in numbers" in the breastworks to meet the onslaught. As the British moved up adjacent to the works, firing broke out. Which side opened the engagement is unknown, but it was probably the King's men with their powerful artillery clearing the way for the landing parties. The guns of the Royal Navy were all that was necessary to effectually stifle the pitiful American resistance that was attempted. Like well-oiled clockwork, Ferguson's soldiers waded ashore under covering fire from the gunboats and within minutes drove the "skulking banditti" from their works and into the woods.[27]

The composition of Ferguson's opposition is unknown for certain although it was probably composed of Cox's Batsto Militia, the Gloucester County Militia, and a mélange of privateersmen and townsfolk. Whatever the force was, it was never a serious match for professional soldiers and Royal Navy artillery, and the defenders were brushed off without loss. Had there been artillery to rake the narrow channel as had been intended, the brief engagement might have ended differently. As it was, British casualties consisted of only one soldier of the 5th Regiment being wounded in the leg. Ferguson later reported rather proudly "we have neither lost a man by the enemy nor deserting since we set out."[28]

Relieved of their opposition for the time being, upon reaching the town itself, the British and Loyalist invaders set to work in an orgy of destruction. Since all of the vessels left behind at Chestnut Neck had been dismantled, scuttled, or completely sunk, Colins ordered that whatever remained above water be destroyed and burned. It had been his hope, with a keen eye on prize money, that at least some of the ships might have been recovered intact. Yet, he was later to report, "notwithstanding my solicitude and wishes to recover the property of the King's subjects, to get them down here [Little Egg Harbor Inlet]; I therefore ordered them to be fired and destroyed: The storehouses and settlements here, which seemed so particularly adapted to the convenience of this nest of freebooters, I was also of opinion with the commanding officer of the troops, should be destroyed, which was accordingly done, also the battery . . . and the works on the hill."[29]

The seamen were allocated the task of destroying the shipping and the soldiers the job of obliterating the village and its defences. The invaders were thus employed in their mission of destruction throughout the evening and well into the next day until noon. The journal of *Nautilus*, which had in company with *Zebra* and *Vigilant* finally passed over the bar at 6:30 p.m. on October 6, reported that the blaze of the burning could be seen from Little Egg Harbor Inlet, at least a good ten miles away. Only a single residence escaped total destruction, and that belonged to Micajah Smith, one of the very men responsible for the capture of *Venus* and the resultant British reaction.[30]

By the morning of October 7, as the annihilation of Chestnut Neck, its warehouses, and shipping neared completion, Ferguson and Colins were faced with an important decision: should they attempt to penetrate further upriver towards The Forks and Batsto or retire to the safety of their fleet in Little Egg Harbor? Colins later explained the reasons for his choice in a report to Admiral Gambier: "Had the weather admitted of our arriving more opportunely, we had it in view, to attempt penetrating to the Forks, where the rebels have some small privateers, and a few other inconsiderable trading vessels, but as the country had long been alarmed, the natural difficulties attending the bringing the galleys and armed vessels unprovided with pilots, up so shoal and narrow a channel through a commanding country would have been so much increased by the efforts of a prepared enemy, that we could not entertain much hopes of success." More importantly, the two commanding officers had just received intelligence that a strong American force of Continental and militia troops properly provided with artillery were collecting at The Forks to meet them.[31]

• • •

Why did the Americans wait until the British were within the gates of Little Egg Harbor before reacting? It is a question that apparently has been been asked only once, and then just four days after the destruction of Chestnut Neck. Major General William Alexander, Lord Stirling, in a letter to Washington dated October 11, 1778, commented: "I am the more surprised at their taking them so much by surprise, as notice of this expedition was at least aforenight ago sent to Governor Livingston. . . ."[32]

Livingston had, in fact, been notified of the impending attack on the night of September 29 by General Maxwell and had promptly summoned a council meeting at 3 a.m. As soon as Stirling heard of the raid, he immediately placed his own troops, then stationed at Princeton and Frenchtown, at the disposal of New Jersey. It was not until October 3, however, that Major General Benedict Arnold, military commander of Philadelphia, was notified of the coming attack. Without hesitation he ordered Colonel Thomas Procter's Pennsylvania State Regiment of Artillery and an additional hundred militiamen to march the following day to the threatened area. At 3 p.m., Monday, October 5, the Continental Congress itself entered the fray and resolved to order Count Casimir Pulaski's newly formed Legion of Horse and Foot to proceed "to assist in the defense of Little Egg Harbor against the attack now made by the enemy at that port." Having arrived at Trenton from Philadelphia only the day before, Pulaski received the order to mobilize late Monday evening and, to his credit, embarked on the march the next morning "with all his troops, in high spirits and with alacrity." On October 8, two days after Chestnut Neck had been attacked, an indigenous reinforcement of some 300 New Jersey militiamen under Colonel Samuel Furman also began a movement southward in support of Pulaski.[33]

Although the American military reacted vigorously and without delay upon receiving their orders, it was already too late. Why nearly half a week was permitted to pass between the receipt of Maxwell's intelligence and the initiation of troop mobilization remains a mystery. Neither Livingston nor Stirling, who had placed his troops at the governor's disposal, had ignored the seriousness of the report. Arnold moved as soon as he heard the news. But why had it taken so long for Arnold or Congress to be notified?

The answer may lie in the transactions of Livingston's council meeting on the night of September 29, which can only be approached as pure conjecture. It is possible that the governor and his advisors wished to adopt a wait-and-see attitude as to the probable destination of the British attack force. After all, the enemy had often planted false information or conducted elaborate feints in the field, such as Howe's end run to the Chesapeake in 1777, to throw American forces off guard. The five-day delay in the British timetable caused by the unfavorable winds may have also induced American officials to consider Maxwell's intelligence as inaccurate or perhaps falsely planted to achieve such ends. As it was, the only benefit derived from the information was to provide early notice of a possible attack on Chestnut Neck to allow time for evacuation.

The distance from Cooper's Ferry opposite Philadelphia, via Burlington, to The Forks was computed on contemporary maps to be fifty-seven miles, and from Trenton to Bordentown, forty-one miles, the first being at least three days' hard march, and the second two days'.[34] Nevertheless, considering that stage coach trips from The Forks to Cooper's Ferry, in good weather and over dry roads, approached two days in length, both Colonel Procter's Pennsylvania Artillery and Count Pulaski's Legion of Horse and Foot made fairly good time in reaching their endangered destination.

Procter's unit had been established in October 1775 as a Pennsylvania artillery company that, by the following year, consisted of two companies officered by one major, one captain, and two lieutenants. The unit was enlarged in 1778 and transferred to the Continental Army as the Pennsylvania State Regiment of Artillery. A veteran of numerous engagements, such as Germantown and Brandywine, the unit had suffered considerable losses and was seriously under-strength at the time of its movement towards Chestnut Neck.[35]

Pulaski's Legion was a more recent creation of the Continental Congress and was made up of numerous veterans and a contingent of enemy deserters. A 30-year-old Polish nobleman and cavalry officer, Count Casimir Pulaski, who had fled his homeland in 1772 with the defeat of his father's Confederation of Bar and the First Partition of Poland, led the unit. On September 15, 1777, he had been given the post of "Commander of the Horse" by the Continental Congress and received his American baptism by fire at a skirmish at Cooper's Ferry and in the Battle of Germantown soon afterwards. Two days later and only a few weeks before receiving marching orders for Little Egg Harbor, Pulaski had suggested to the Continental Congress that he be permitted to command an independent body of mounted troops. The request was granted and Pulaski's Legion came into being. The Legion's first encounter with the enemy, in response to the attack on Egg Harbor, unfortunately, would prove anything but illustrious.[36]

–XIV–

No Quarter Be Given

*"Your expedition to Egg Harbor will be felt at a distance
like an attack upon a hen-roost."*

Captain Henry Colins must have felt a little disturbed on the morning of October 7 as all
of his potential prizes went up in smoke, and even more so in knowing that anchored just
a few miles upriver were still vessels aplenty for the taking. Yet his intelligence sources,
whatever they may have been, seemed explicit: "the rebels had collected all their strength
to that point, consisting of Procter's Artillery, and some regular force from Philadelphia,
in addition to a large body of militia, provided with cannon." Specifically, Ferguson pointed
out, the rebel force consisted of a detachment of foot, five field pieces, and a body of light
horse. It was "therefore determined to return without loss of time and endeavor to employ
our force with effect elsewhere."[1]

At noon the British withdrawal from Chestnut Neck commenced. Unhappily for
Colins, as his flotilla proceeded downriver towards Great Bay, both *Grandby* and *Greenwich*
were found to be still hard aground despite the assistance of seamen dispatched from
Nautilus some hours earlier. Coming to anchor abreast of the two stranded vessels, Colins
ordered everything possible taken off to lighten them. The work of unloading was to go on
all night before the vessels were finally refloated.[2]

During the delay, and "notwithstanding the very great diligence and activity of Captain
Colins and the gentlemen of the navy," Ferguson took the opportunity to wreak further
havoc upon the property of the Little Egg Harbor rebels. Under cover of several gunboats,
his troops made two descents on the north side of the river, penetrating several miles into
the countryside. These raids, as Samuel Cooper predicted, resulted in the destruction of
three salt works, the razing to the ground of "stores and settlements of a chairman of the
committee [of Safety], a captain of militia, and one or two of their virulent rebels, who had
shares in the prizes brought in here, who had all been remarkably active in fomenting the
rebellion, oppressing the people and forcing them, against their inclination and better
judgment, to assist in their crimes."[3]

Ferguson was cognizant that a number of Loyalists also inhabited the area and assured
his superiors that "no manner of insult or injury had been offered to the peaceable inhabitants,
nor even to such, as without taking a lead, having been made, from the tyranny and influence
of their rulers, to forget their allegiance."[4]

There is a local tradition that recalls that the British were, in fact, welcomed with a
feast by one Tory farmer. Having earlier concluded that the nearby salt works on Osborns
Island would eventually attract His Majesty's troops, he had set a generous table—officers
only, no doubt, being invited—and was left completely unharmed.[5]

Captain Colins succeeded in refloating the two stranded vessels by the morning of
October 8 and ordered the flotilla to once more get underway. Frustration, however, mounted

as *Greenwich* ran aground again. This time Colins continued onward with *Cornwallis*, *Experiment*, *Grandby*, the flatboats, and other small vessels, leaving only the galley *Dependence* behind to attend to the stricken ship. By 4 p.m., he had rejoined *Zebra*, *Nautilus*, and *Vigilant* and was already beginning to consider his next move.[6]

The breeze had been blowing steadily out of the southwest, fresh and clear, throughout the day and there was every reason to believe such luck would hold. "I shall take the most early opportunity of the wind," Colins wrote Admiral Gambier the next day while awaiting *Dependence* and *Greenwich*, "to leave this place (and if the weather proves favorable as to admit of it) we have it in view to employ ourselves on our return to New York on looking into Barnegat and Cranbury [*sic*] Inlets, and to destroy or bring off any vessels that may happen to be there, and demolish the salt works, which are very considerable on the shores of these recesses."[7]

Colins was going to make the best of the wind, but the Americans were aware of such necessities and were fearful that the British might also descend upon Great Egg Harbor as they had upon Little Egg Harbor. Others, such as Lord Stirling, feared their next target would be Elizabethtown and not along the coast, and correspondingly placed his troops in the best position to guard that post and the northern end of New Jersey.[8]

While the Americans were desperately attempting to guess the next British move, Captain Colins sat comfortably in his cabin aboard *Zebra* writing out a full report of the expedition thus far to Admiral Gambier. To his credit, the captain was, and could afford to be, lavish with praise. "I think it my particular duty to inform you," he wrote, "the officers and seamen I have had the honor to command on this service have manifested their best endeavors in their duty; I should also think myself wanting, if I omitted to acquaint you, that Captain Ferguson the commanding officer of the detachment of the Army, as well as every officer and man under his command, have shewn the utmost zeal and forwardness to co-operate in every thing for the advancement and benefit of His Majesty's service."[9]

Just before Colins returned to the anchorage, a rebel brig, "very old and unfit," was brought in as a prize and stripped of her sails and rigging. The captain did not wish to bring the prize around to New York—he would have enough trouble with his own fleet—but was happy to learn the vessel was carrying a valuable cargo of lumber that was worthy of being saved. The New York dockyard was woefully in need of every supply and particularly lumber. Thus Colins gleefully added a P.S. to his report: "I have ordered her cargo to be put on board the transports knowing how serviceable such a supply will prove to the dock yard."[10]

By now the longboats from *Nautilus* and other vessels of the squadron were already busily engaged in unloading the brig of her cargo. Soon *Experiment* and *Dependence* were sighted coming down the river, and everything seemed to be falling into place for a strike further up the Jersey coast. Colins ordered *Halifax* to return to New York with the dispatches and patiently awaited the lumber brig's off-loading to be completed, a resupply of the several ship larders to be made, and the re-embarkation of troops from the two tardy warships.[11]

On Saturday, October 10, Colins received a letter from Admiral Gambier with some explicit instructions. Both the admiral and General Clinton were concerned about the safety of the expedition now that all British forces, namely those belonging to Cornwallis, had been removed from New Jersey, leaving Colins and Ferguson as lightning rods for an

American attack. It was because of this danger that the expeditionary force was ordered to return to New York immediately. Barnegat would have to wait another day. [12]

Once again, however, the weather conspired to frustrate the orders of the British high command. On Sunday the wind shifted drastically. The change in direction was followed by a severe storm. And once again the Royal Navy was forced to batten down the hatches. [13]

• • •

The British had provided the American forces then pressing forward to the coast with the need to make some critical decisions. Where did the raiders intend on striking next and how much longer would they tarry in Little Egg Harbor? Upon the departure of the enemy from Chestnut Neck, it had been erroneously reported in Philadelphia that Procter, Pulaski, and the New Jersey militia were redirecting their march towards Great Egg Harbor "at which place it was expected the enemy would attempt to land." The report was little more than rumor; Pulaski, though he undoubtedly intended to put himself within rescue distance of that place, had no intention of letting the British out of his sight once he arrived on the coast. Procter remained poised in the neighborhood ready to march at a moment's notice toward Great Egg Harbor, yet close enough to support Pulaski as needed. The Pennsylvania militia, though dwindled to only half of their original number by desertion—as was often the case on forced marches—were within sixteen miles of Little Egg Harbor by Thursday, October 8, and Sam Forman's unit was finally, belatedly beginning its march toward the endangered shores. [14]

By the evening of October 8, Pulaski's Legion had reached the little Quaker settlement then known as Middle of the Shore (modern Tuckerton), marched down the Island Road until they reached the farm of James Willets, where they established headquarters. From Willets's farm, Pulaski enjoyed an excellent view from the salt marshes, a veritable panorama of the harbor and the masting of the enemy fleet riding triumphantly at anchor therein. A few hundred yards to the west of the farm, the Count stationed the 1st Troop of Horse, the artillery, and a portion of his infantry. Farther south, about two tenths of a mile down the Island Road in the direction of Great Bay, in the untenanted house of Jeremiah Ridgeway, a Quaker, he stationed an advance picket of forty-five to fifty troopers under the command of Lieutenant Colonel the Baron de Bosen, second in command of the Legion. Thus ensconced, the Americans set to watching the British in Little Egg Harbor—but apparently not too intently. [15]

• • •

Captain Colins was having a devil of a time with the weather. On October 11, the wind had shifted from the southwest to the southeast and then to the northeast, locking him ever so tightly in the harbor. The storm that had accompanied the shift had been severe, whipping up waves high enough to broach *Nautilus*. At 2 a.m., Captain Belcher was forced to strike his yards and topmasts and, at noon, the topgallants to prevent them from being carried away. The storm continued to rage well into the following day, but fortunately for the British eventually began to diminish without causing serious damage. [16]

The subsiding gale brought with it more than clear weather for the invaders. About 3 p.m. a small boat came abreast of *Nautilus* and disgorged a rebel officer and five men. The officer proved to be Acting Sub-Lieutenant Carl Wilhelm Joseph Juliat (also noted as Franz Karl Joseph Juliat), an 18-year-old German who had deserted from Hessian forces at Rhode Island in early August. He had subsequently made his way to Pennsylvania and on September 2, with special permission from Congress, joined the unit being formed by Pulaski just three days before the Legion marched for Egg Harbor. Sometime earlier, he had been involved with a pair of lieutenants named Fuhrer and Kleinschmidt, both deserters, in a scheme to raise a corps of volunteers for the American service from German deserters. Baron de Bosen, who despised the young officer for being a renegade, had apparently treated Juliat with some severity during the march. Some later claimed that the youth determined to revenge himself against his tormentor and left camp with several other men under the pretense of going fishing. When he and the men did not return after the storm, it was presumed that the fishing party had drowned.[17]

Juliat's hatred of de Bosen must have run deep, for he faced certain retribution for desertion if, upon retuning to the British, his identity was discovered. He thus informed Ferguson that he was a Frenchman by the name of Bromville and had held a captaincy in the Legion of Pulaski. It was with a certain degree of cleverness that he sought to stir up the British against the Americans stationed at Middle of the Shore. "He and the deserters," Ferguson later reported, "informed us that Mr. Pulaski has, in public orders, lately directed no quarter be given."[18] This provocative information, whether true or not, was to Ferguson nothing less than a veritable challenge.

Whatever the young German's reasons were for returning to the service of his former employers, he and the unimproved weather conditions conspired to provide Ferguson with, as the captain himself put it, "an opportunity of performing a gallant and meritorious piece of service" for the king. Juliat proceeded to inform Ferguson of "some very satisfactory intelligence of the Legion of Pulaski," which had been posted, he said, approximately ten miles from the fleet, at a small Quaker farm on the Island Road, with three companies of foot, three troops of horse, a detachment of artillery and one brass field piece.[19]

Juliat must have paid particular attention to informing his superiors of de Bosen's forward position as well as of the general lay of the land. The information, combined with the alleged and challenging "no quarter" edict by Pulaski, tantalized Ferguson. He soon developed a plan to employ an idle day in an attempt that would be made with safety and all probability of success upon the Legion and prevailed upon Colins to enter into the design. It was, therefore, "with particular satisfaction, that the detachment marched against a man capable of issuing an order so unworthy of a gentleman and a soldier."[20]

Accordingly, at 11 p.m., October 14, 250 soldiers and marines embarked aboard a flatboat and gunboats of the squadron. Under the protection of *Vigilant* they proceeded towards Osborns Island (also known as Mincock or Faulkinburgh's Island) ten miles away. Five hours later the assault force, personally led by Captain Ferguson and accompanied by Juliat as a guide, landed unopposed.[21]

The little tract upon which the British first set foot belonged to one Richard Osborn, Jr. Upon landing, Ferguson immediately dispatched a party of soldiers to secure Osborn, his dwelling and everyone happening to be inside or on the premises. Both the proprietor and his 29-year-old son Thomas were instantly apprehended. The latter was threatened with a drawn sword unless he consented to guide the army across the salt marshes to Baron de Bosen's exposed rebel picket.[22]

After marching a mile, the British came to a narrow defile and bridge over what was locally referred to as "The Ditch," now know as Big Creek. Amazingly, the bridge, a natural selection for a defensive post, was neither fortified nor guarded. Quietly, the troopers moved on, leaving a party of fifty men to secure the position and loosen the planks on the bridge for easy removal in case of pursuit.[23] In complete silence, the raiders pressed ahead. A mile. Another half mile. Then battle.

The British exploded with unrestrained fury upon the drowsy rebel pickets, forcing them to retreat with loss. Surprise was complete. The fight that ensued was largely one of bayonets and cold steel waged by the masters of that specific art of warfare. During the initial confusion of the first alarm, Thomas Osborn somehow managed to slip away from his captors and conceal himself in a low meadow from which he observed the entire bloody fight.[24]

As soon as the pickets had been overpowered, Ferguson's 200-man force made a made rush for the three houses in which the baron's infantry was cantoned. The Americans inside, suddenly awakened by the shouts of the British, frantically attempted to defend themselves. De Bosen, with sword and pistol in hand, heroically tried to lead his men in a desperate charge against the surrounding enemy. Almost instantly the double-deserter Juliat pointed him out while shouting, "this is the Colonel—kill him." De Bosen, said to be a remarkably stout man capable of fighting like a lion, was immediately attacked by overwhelming numbers, pierced by several bayonets at one time, and fell dead where he stood.[25]

The fight turned quickly against the still groggy Continentals who were outnumbered four or five to one. Lieutenant de la Borderie, de Bosen's subaltern, was soon down and wounded. The remaining defenders, though crying for quarter, were cut down time and again, their blood spilling freely into the marsh grasses. Ferguson later explained away what many were to consider a barbaric massacre. "It being a night attack, little quarter could, of course, be given, so that there were only five prisoners."[26]

The raiders now had the opportunity to destroy part of the American baggage and equipment as well as the cantonments, but Ferguson claimed "the houses belonged to some inoffensive Quakers, who, I am afraid, may have sufficiently suffered already in the confusion of the night's scramble." In truth, there was little time to consider anything but retreat. Procter was within two miles with his corps of artillery which included a pair of brass 12-pounders and a single 3-pounder; Pulaski's cavalry had been alerted and were already hastening towards de Bosen's defeated picket, and "the militia of the country" were also somewhere in the neighborhood. Thus, Ferguson reported, "I thought it hazardous, with two hundred men, without artillery or support, to attempt anything farther, particularly after Admiral Gambier's letter."[27]

As often is the case, two versions of what occurred next, exist. "The enemy," Pulaski later reported to Congress, "fled in great disorder, and left behind them a great quantity of arms, accoutrements, hats, blades, &c." It was believed that some twenty of the raiders were cut off and forced into the woods seeking refuge. Unable to flush them out, Pulaski believed they had sought and found sanctuary among the local Tories.[28]

Obliged to chase the retreating British force along the narrow road through the salt marshes below Ridgeway's farm, the cavalry's mobility and progress were extremely hindered.

Pulaksi later reported:

> We took some prisoners and should have taken many more, had it not been for
> a swamp, through which our horses could scarcely walk. Notwithstanding this,
> we still advanced in hopes to come up with them, but they had taken up the planks
> of a bridge for fear of being overtaken, which accordingly saved them; however,
> my light infantry, and particularly the company of riflemen, got over the remains
> of the plank and fired some vollies on their rear. The fire began again on both
> sides. We had the advantage, and made them run again, although they were more
> in number.

Fearful that he would not be able to come to the aid of the riflemen in their exposed
forward position if the enemy made a counterattack, Pulaski recalled his infantry though
it had suffered no casualties whatsoever during the chase. In contrast to Pulaski's account,
however, Ferguson reported that the American pursuit was not vigorous at all but was
undertaken "with great modesty" and allowed his own forces to return and re-embark in
complete security. By 10 a.m., October 15, the British were boarding the warships in the
harbor and undoubtedly congratulating themselves on having carried out a completely
successful raid.[29]

Pulaski returned to the Ridgeway farm, the initial scene of battle, to tend the wounded
and bury the dead. En route from the marshes he encountered Thomas Osborn, who had
just come out of hiding after observing the British retreat. The frightened farmer
unsuccessfully attempted to explain his story to the Count, who spoke little or no English.
Unfortunately, the excitement of the preceding events and the general circumstances of
Osborn's situation were so pitched that no one believed him. The soldiers, understandably
angry over the brutal deaths of their comrades, fastened the helpless man to a tree and
began to flog him mercilessly. The farmer was saved from almost certain death only
through the intervention of several officers, after which both he and his father were sent
as prisoners to Trenton where they were roughly incarcerated. Both men remained in jail
until October 30, at which time a court examined them, cleared them of all charges of
complicity, and released them.[30]

The raid had been a clear-cut British victory. Ferguson reported only two men of
the 5th Regiment and one of the New Jersey Volunteers missing, apparently captured
during the retreat. Two soldiers of the 5th had apparently been wounded and Ensign
John Camp of the Volunteers injured by a stab in the thigh. If twenty-five men had been
cut off, as Pulaski claimed, they were apparently able to escape and return to the fleet
rather quickly. Many years later, one American participant of the engagement, Captain
Paul Bentalou, would claim in his memoirs that only a few British stragglers were taken
during the retreat but exceeded in number the loss of the Americans during the engagement,
which seems highly unlikely. Patriot casualties were, in fact, considerable for the forces
engaged. Pulaski later estimated the dead, wounded and missing at twenty-five to thirty
men. Ferguson claimed the rebel toll was fifty, and Loyalist newspapers reported sixty
American casualties, including a lieutenant colonel, two captains, an adjutant, and three
or four other officers.[31]

• • •

Back aboard their warships and transports the victorious invaders settled into their cramped quarters once again. The wind was still unfavorable, now blowing directly out of the east, keeping the squadron a virtual prisoner in Little Egg Harbor. Soon after the return of the troops, an unidentified sloop was sighted and a pinnace from *Nautilus* and several armed boats were sent in pursuit. The sloop was brought in the next morning and, reported Colins, proved to be an American privateer, "one of the piratical crew that infests these inlets." The rebel seamen, however, had managed to escape in their boats before the ship was overtaken by the British. The prize itself was an extremely small vessel that mounted only six swivels and a single 2-pounder, typical of the many diminutive privateers that had successfully operated with impunity from the New Jersey inlets for the last two years.[32]

Despite such occasional excitements, conditions aboard the crowded, stranded fleet must have been extremely uncomfortable. Soon after Ferguson's return, Colins noted ominously in a report to Admiral Gambier that there was now a serious shortage of provisions throughout the squadron. "You will perceive," he wrote, "by the weekly accounts which I have the honor to transmit you that the provisions of the fleet here grow scanty, particularly the articles of rum and bread, the transports are also in the same state, owing to one of them joining us without any, the *Grandby*, *Greenwich*, and galleys came also ill provided; If therefore we should be so unlucky as to be detained here seven or eight days longer by the winds, which you may judge of by the weather with you, I think it will be a prudent precaution to send a small vessel to us." But food was only part of the problem. "Water also is very scarce with us, as we have not been able with all our industry to procure enough for our daily expense and that which we get is exceedingly bad."[33]

Even when it was learned that water was available and the transports were sent to obtain a supply from a remote section of the harbor, conditions did not improve. Provisions had to be rationed and divided among the fleet. Tensions mounted. A marine was punished for drunkenness. The wind continued to frustrate all but a few attempts at escape. During a relative lull in the breeze on October 18, one of the private armed sloops managed to pass over the bar and sail away. Time was occupied in rafting the lumber supply taken from the prize brig to the various transports with enough room to accommodate such cargo. At 11 p.m., October 19, another vessel, this time a tender, managed to slip over the bar.[34]

The lull continued throughout the night. On the morning of October 20, the sky was clear and the air breezy—but this time the breeze blew favorably from the northwest. Colins made his move. At 6 a.m., preparations were made to get underway, and within two hours the fleet was under sail. The way over the bar was treacherously shoally. At 9:30 a.m., *Nautilus* began to pass over, but not without first striking the hard sandy bottom several times. Captain Belcher, anticipating the danger, ordered all sails up to force the ship across. One false breeze or shift in the wind and he would run aground. Soon, the ship was again floating free in its natural element. Colins followed suit but was not as fortunate.[35]

Within minutes, HM Sloop-of-War *Zebra* was hard aground on Little Egg Harbor Bar. Captain Belcher, observing Colins's predicament, immediately brought his ship to rest with his best bower anchor planted in eight fathoms of water and quickly dispatched boats and an officer to lend assistance. Captain Colins struggled to free his ship throughout the day and the following night, using every means possible—lightening the vessel by removing guns and heavy gear, kedging, and towing—but all efforts were in vain. *Cornwallis* and *Dependence*, light, maneuverable vessels that could be powered by oars when necessary, were sent to assist, as were the transports and the remaining New York privateer. Nothing, including the tide, could budge the big warship. The flagship was deemed to be hopelessly stranded and would have to be abandoned. Finally, at 9 a.m., October 21, *Zebra* was put to the torch to prevent possible rebel capture.[36]

An hour after the flagship of the Egg Harbor expedition was set ablaze, the squadron sailed for New York led by the new flagship, HMS *Vigilant*. At 1 a.m., October 22, in the pitch darkness of night, the magazine of *Zebra* blew up. The departing British fleet could hear the monstrous explosion from ten leagues away. Soon after the blast reverberated across the miles of salt marshes, Count Casimir Pulaski reached Philadelphia and notified the city that the danger had abated. The enemy had departed. The attack on the American privateering stronghold of Little Egg Harbor was now history.[37]

• • •

On the evening of October 22, Captain Henry Colins's squadron approached Sandy Hook Lighthouse, and by the following day had come to anchor in the East River. At 2 p.m., Ferguson's troops were sent ashore at Staten Island to return to their camps. *Nautilus* proceeded into the North (Hudson) River and came to anchor three hours later, after finding Admiral Gambier and several ships of the Royal Navy there.[38] The following morning she returned to the East River, came to off King's Wharf, and unbent her sails.

A signal was raised from HMS *Monmouth* on Saturday, October 24, for the convening of a Court Martial to address the circumstances concerning the loss of *Zebra*, and to determine responsibility for it, if any, and declare any penalty that should be imposed: it was a standard naval procedure following the destruction or loss, from any cause, of any of His Majesty's ships. The outcome of the inquiry seemed obvious.[39] Loyalist sentiments were in need of a boost and the expedition against Egg Harbor could only be construed as a victory and the loss of *Zebra* as unavoidable. Ten American ships or prizes had been destroyed, a rebel privateer and merchantman taken, a privateering center and its defenses devastated, several salt works obliterated, and a strong rebel force of regulars and cavalry defeated. The cost had been only several wounded and one British sloop-of-war—and that had been accidental.

Captain James Murray, a British officer, echoed Loyalist sentiments privately in a letter to his sister. "I must not forget to tell you," he wrote, "that Pate Ferguson is returned from a successful expedition against Egg Harbor which did him credit; the particulars you will see in the newspapers. We have been a little employed of late in burning and destroying and we are in hopes that the fashion may take root, which perhaps might prove as speedy a means to finishing the rebellion as what has been hitherto adopted."[40]

Admiral Gambier, in an official dispatch to Admiralty Secretary Philip Stephens, which included Captain Colins's report of the expedition, stated his belief that the move "sensibly annoyed the rebels," and only regretted "the season approaching that will be repugnant to such proper measures of exertion."[41]

Colins was not to suffer for the destruction of *Zebra*, a loss sustained by an unavoidable accident during the course of duty and under specific orders. Five months later, on March 5, 1779, he was promoted to the permanent rank of Post Captain.[42]

Captain Ferguson also received his share of credit for the affair and was raised several notches in the esteem of Sir Henry Clinton. A year later, on October 26, 1779, he was appointed a Major in the 71st Regiment of Foot and achieved a marked degree of fame and notoriety as the leader of partisan forces during the British campaigns in the southern states. Almost two years to the day from the destruction of Chestnut Neck, Ferguson was defeated and killed at the Battle of Kings Mountain, South Carolina, which was later considered by Clinton as the beginning of the end of British military supremacy in America.[43]

As for the Americans, after Little Egg Harbor there was precious little to do but lick their wounds and pick up the pieces. Washington wrote Arnold concerning the loss on October 23: "I am sorry at the destruction of property at Egg Harbor; but in attending to the general object of war, we must at times submit to such losses, or depend on the exertions of the military for their protection."[44]

Pulaski and his Legion were not to suffer many recriminations for their part in the defeat, and the Count went on to obtain a certain degree of fame—like his opposite, Ferguson—in the deep south. While leading a brave but futile charge on October 9, 1779, during the Savannah Campaign, he was mortally wounded and died a few days later aboard the Continental brig *Wasp*.[45]

As for the young deserter-traitor Juliat, he was handed over to Hessian officials at New York and placed under arrest for desertion. General von Knyphausen, believing that the man had been captured by American forces instead of his having been a deserter, released him with orders to rejoin his regiment at Newport, Rhode Island. Upon arrival, however, he was again arrested, this time by Major General Carl Ernst Johann von Bose. Charges against Juliat included: indebtedness to fellow officers, enlisted men, and citizens of Newport; collaborating with the enemy; and other miscellaneous offenses. He was eventually dishonorably discharged and returned home in January 1781 aboard the transport *Minerva*.[46]

The immediate effects of the attack upon the communities of Little Egg Harbor were varied. Several patriots reconsidered their positions, at least property-wise. Elijah Clark attempted to sell his plantation, mills, and holdings at The Forks. Micajah Smith, having been fortunate enough to be spared total destruction, placed his holdings at Chestnut Neck up for sale soon afterwards. Thomas Heston, owner of the salt works on Osborns Island, put his works on the auction block in the spring.[47] Yet, the true objective of the British attack—the destruction of the Little Egg Harbor privateers—as the next few years would show, proved to have been but a temporary expedient.

Three days before the *New Jersey Gazette* noted Pulaski's return from Egg Harbor, the philosopher-firebrand Thomas Paine caustically appraised the net result of the British incursion: "Your expedition to Egg Harbor will be felt from a distance like an attack upon a hen-roost and expose you in Europe with a sort of childish phrensey."[48]

The American privateer war on the New Jersey coast had experienced a setback. Within mere weeks, however, the seas would again swarm with the relentless sea raiders almost as if nothing had happened.

XV

Sixteen Strong

"If only a single frigate had been sent along as convoy everything would have been saved."

Even as the British fleet felt its way though the painfully shallow maw of Little Egg Harbor on October 20, 1778, the privateers and speculators they had sought so ardently to put out of business were already beginning to pick up the pieces and start all over again. The Forks had emerged unscathed, as had the privateers that sought and found refuge there and on the open sea. It was all that was necessary.

A great deal had been saved from the ruin, and the firm of Ludwig Kuhn and Company, owners of the prize brigantine *Industry*, acquired just before the raid, was the first to advertise the sale of salvaged goods at a public vendue. The auction was to be held at Richard Westcoat's on November 6 and the advertisement ran in the Pennsylvania newspapers on the very day *Zebra* ran aground on Little Egg Harbor Bar. Thirteen sails, twenty-six coils of running rigging, "and sundry other articles too tedious to mention" were offered up, all apparently rescued just prior to or immediately following the British assault.[1]

On Tuesday, December 15, another public vendue was held, this time at Samuel Cooper's Ferry on the Delaware. The sale included the prize schooner *Good Intent*, recently taken by Yelverton Taylor in Thomas Leaming's spunky little four-gun sloop *Comet*, along with an enormous range of goods removed to safety from *Venus* before the British attack. Two weeks later, on New Year's Eve, the privateer *Friends* (even though she had yet to be tried), captured by Captain David Stevens, and his famed sloop *Chance*, in which he had taken *Venus*, were put up for auction at Colonel Westcoat's at The Forks.[2] Settling up on the profits from *Venus* herself, the cargo of which, it would seem, had been saved in its entirety, was not completed until the early spring of 1779. On March 20, Captain Stevens, attempting to finally close the book on the affair, penned an announcement to be published in the *Pennsylvania Packet* a week later. "Notice is hereby given," he wrote, "to all the seamen and landsmen that were on board the armed sloop *Chance* when she captured the ship *Venus* and made a prize of her, that they meet the subscriber at Colonel Richard Westcott's at The Forks on Little Egg Harbor, then and that to receive their respective dividends of the prize money; and likewise all those that purchased shares from said sailors are requested to meet at the same place, on Thursday the second day of April next."[3]

Even the destruction of Chestnut Neck could not make a dent in the activities of the Egg Harbor privateers. True, ten prize ships had been destroyed and two others, including a small privateer, had been captured, but the ships lost were primarily prizes to begin with and did not constitute a serious loss to the body of privateering itself. The storage and service facilities of the town were totally ruined but accommodations could be found elsewhere until the damage was repaired. Thus, vessels that would have normally been sent into that port were diverted to nearby Mays Landing or up to The Forks and sold. Undoubtedly, the larger privateers may have even employed Mays Landing as a refitting or careening center until Chestnut Neck was again in operation.

As early as November 1778, vendues were being scheduled at Mays Landing, on the Great Egg Harbor River, to handle the overflow, and on the 11th the first major auction was held there after the British raid of October. Five vessels of various sizes and cargoes were placed up for sale. These vessels were: the brig *Recovery*, a large, heavily laden ship taken while en route from London; the schooner *Caroline and Hannah*; and the sloops *George*, *Lark*, and *Commerce*.[4]

The British were almost immediately made aware that the rovers had not been quieted. On Monday, November 2, less than two weeks after the British departure, the *New York Gazette and Weekly Mercury* reported on the resumption of activity by the Egg Harbor privateers. "Friday last," read the bulletin, "Capt. Wedham arrived here from Providence. Last Sunday week he was chased by a schooner privateer, from Egg Harbor, as far to the eastward as Martha's Vineyard." It was to be a rude message indicating that the nest of rebel privateers may have been hit, but the swarm was still intact.[5] Indeed, British maritime activity all along the shores of New Jersey and neighboring New York in general would become even more dangerous and American privateers more audacious than before.

The increase in American privateers being brought into New Jersey ports was clearly evidenced by an upsurge in libels. On January 12, 1779, at the first New Jersey Court of Admiralty convened in the new year, no fewer than seven prizes were libeled at the home of Gilbert Barton in Allentown. The vessels included the schooners *Good Intent*, *Fame*, *Fortune*, *Rambler*, and *Friends*, and the sloops *Charming Polly* and *Thomas Cromwell*. A surge of new libels at subsequent courts would follow.[6]

The Admiralty Courts of both Pennsylvania and New Jersey were often called upon to address libels regarding wreck recoveries, which seldom made more than a paragraph in the newspapers. But when an enemy ship of importance was lost, that was something else. In December 1778, when it was learned at Trenton and New York that a richly laden, armed British vessel bound from Halifax to New York City had been driven ashore near Barnegat, both sides reacted as might be expected. The crew, sixty in number, had immediately surrendered themselves to New Jersey militiamen and were carried to Bordentown as prisoners of war. More than £5,000 worth of goods was salvaged from the wreck, and would eventually be libeled in the court.[7]

The privateers were again proving themselves to be real troublemakers. One of the first such vessels to initiate action against the British after the October raid was the trim Pennsylvania sloop *Hornet*, under the command of the doughty Captain David Stevens of Philadelphia. Soon after the attack on Chestnut Neck, when Joseph Ball had decided to divest himself of *Chance* and invest in the fortunes of a newer vessel, Steven had assumed command and Colonel Cox had put up part of the $10,000 bond money and almost certainly owned a substantial share in the cruise.[8] The 70-ton *Hornet* proved to be an excellent choice. Though commissioned to carry eighteen guns, she was armed on her first voyage with only eight 4-pounders and six swivel guns, and manned by a crew of fifty. Stevens immediately teamed up with Captain Benjamin Pratt and his seven-gun East Haddam, Connecticut, sloop *Princess Mary*, which was also now operating out of

Egg Harbor.[9] In late November, the pair recaptured a British prize sloop lately taken by the Loyalist privateer *Harlequin* of New York.[10] Soon afterwards, Stevens fell in with another New York privateer named *Two Friends*, Captain James Conn, mounting six carriage guns and a dozen swivels and manned by a crew of twenty-two. This vessel was taken, apparently without a fight, sent into the Mullica, and sold on New Year's Eve 1778, along with the veteran *Chance*, at Richard Westcoat's.[11] For the privateersmen, it was a welcomed omen for the new year to come, but not everyone was delighted, especially in Massachusetts, which had borne the heavy strike by the British in the September attacks in Buzzards Bay, Martha's Vineyard, New Bedford, Fair Haven, and Holmes's Hole. Moreover, the Continental Navy at Boston and elsewhere still suffered from the privateering "fever" that seemed ever present.

On December 17, 1778, William Vernon, of the Navy Board at Boston, vented his frustration to John Adams. Continental ships then in port, he complained, could readily be sent out "if it was possible to get Men, wch [*sic*] we shall never be able to accomplish, unless some method be taken to prevent desertion, and a stopping of Private Ships Sailing until our ships are Mann'd." He deplored "the infamous practice of seducing our Men to leave the ships and taking them off at a out-port," and with other base methods that made it impossible for a squadron, or even a single vessel to put to sea.

Vernon saw only one possible solution: an embargo upon all privateers and commercial vessels should be placed throughout the United States until the Continental Navy was completely manned. "You can scarcely form an Idea," he wrote, "of the Increase and groath of the extravagance of the people in their demands for Labour and every Article for Sale &c.; dissipation has no bounds at present; when or where it will stop, or if a reform will take place, I dare not predict." It was, unhappily for Vernon, a futile wish at best.[12]

Privateering along the New Jersey coast and on the approaches to the British stronghold of New York City was beginning to have a serious impact by the end of 1778. For the British, the interdiction of supplies to New York, combined with the viciously cold winter of 1778–79, soon brought incredible hardships to the inhabitants, as well as to the soldiers and seamen cantoned therein. The military journal of one normally stoic Hessian officer, General Carl Leopold Baurmeister, suggested just how bad it had become.

> The storms have been terrible, and also the subsequent cold spell and the deep snow. All of this was as strange to us as it was unpleasant. Some twenty transports and smaller vessels were entirely destroyed by the ice which the ebb tide brought down the North [Hudson] River into the harbor. As a result, the officers of the 16th Regiment of Dragoons, who were to sail to England, lost the greater part of their equipage; but even more lamentable is the loss of seventy-two sailors, of whom there has been a great shortage anyhow.
>
> How cold it was can be appreciated from the fact that wild geese and ducks froze to death by the Thousands on the shores of Long Island and Staten Island. They were most greedily eaten by the soldiers and the inhabitants, for the provisions had become very low. There was no more flour, and the small amount of good oatmeal mixed with the spoiled did not make wholesome biscuits for the soldiers.[13]

Conditions were no different on the Jersey coast. During one of the bitter snowstorms in March, the prize sloop *Success*, laden with a valuable cargo of rum, molasses, coffee, and cocoa, which had been taken by the British privateer brig *Diligence*, was driven ashore on the north beach at Barnegat while en route to New York. The prize master and three hands were promptly captured, quite probably by the Toms River militia, and sent to Princeton. The prize was later advertised for sale where she lay, on Island Beach, with the auction being conducted at the home of Daniel Griggs at Toms River. Yet the privateers continued their work, despite the weather. Indeed, as early as February 8, 1779, the first batch of prizes taken in the New Year, the sloop *Fancy* (also reported as *Fanny*), taken by Major John Cook, and the schooner *Hope*, taken by one John Chadwick, together with their cargoes of pitch, tar, and salt, were being advertised for sale on March 1 at Toms River by Marshal Joseph Potts.[14]

By the spring of 1779, the British were lamenting more than ever the incursions on English commerce and the punishing interdiction of inward and outward bound transports, victuallers, and military cargo ships by the privateers of Egg Harbor and the other coastal enclaves, and with good reason. On May 3, General Baurmeister noted in his journal that a large force under the command of General Edward Mathews of the Guards Regiment, including four flank companies under the command of Colonel John Watson, the 42nd Regiment of Foot, Lord Rawdon's Irish Volunteers, the Hessian Prinz Carl Regiment, and a six-piece train of light artillery, had embarked aboard a number of ships, taking with them a month's worth of provisions. "It is supposed," he stated, "that they are to go to Egg Harbor, for the rebels have sixteen strong new privateers and a frigate there, and four weeks ago unfortunately captured six three- and four-masted ships on their way to Georgia and took them into Boston."[15]

These captures were obviously quite annoying to the British and especially to the Hessians since among the prizes was a royal provision ship carrying Colonel Johann Christoph von Kohler, Lieutenant Wilhelm Studenroth, and Ensign Henrich Pauli, together with their men en route to join von Trumbach's Regiment in the South. The insurance company that covered the voyage was obliged to stand the loss of £80,000 sterling, since the ships had also been loaded with English goods and wines. "If only a single frigate had been sent along as convoy," lamented the distraught Hessian, "everything would have been saved." As it was, only two ships from the entire convoy escaped.[16] Fortunately for Egg Harbor, General Mathews was destined to plague Virginia and not the New Jersey coast.

Chestnut Neck was again a viable privateering community by the end of July 1779. It had apparently been re-outfitted with the necessary storage and repair infrastructure, and with accommodations for the visitors and buyers attending the newly scheduled vendues. On July 27, the snow *Friendship*, with a cargo of staves, rice, boards, molasses, tobacco, tar, fustic, and several slaves, was auctioned off. Two weeks later five ships and their cargoes were sold at a single auction.[17] The destruction wrought by the British capture of Chestnut Neck had been all but erased in little more than nine months.

• • •

One of the highlights in the Revolutionary War privateering history on the New Jersey coast occurred in October 1779, when a waterlogged prize brig loaded with hundreds of exhausted Hessian soldiers came to anchor off Chestnut Neck. The account of the brig's dramatic but sad odyssey actually began at New York weeks before, in early September, when the German von Knyphausen and von Lossberg regiments received orders to prepare for embarkation, along with all their baggage and those sick who could withstand a sea voyage. Their destination was rumored to be Quebec or Halifax, although no one among them knew for certain, for it was a military secret kept from even the convoy shipmasters.

It had already been a most harrowing campaign for the battle-weary Hessians, for most of them had been among the 918 captured in the humiliating defeat at the Battle of Trenton on December 26, 1776, where they had suffered the loss of 105 of their comrades.[18] The prisoners had been exchanged only a few days later and, owing to reductions, battle losses, sickness, and desertions, were soon afterwards formed into a combined battalion. Now, however, as they prepared to board the transport in New York Harbor, one of six scheduled to carry several regiments, they were allowed to act independently again. On the evening of September 8, the transport brig *Triton* and her five sisters, escorted by HMS *Renown*, departed New York without fanfare, apparently bearing only orders to join a larger convoy forming off Sandy Hook where they would be issued sailing instructions.

The British transport ship *Triton*. Pen and ink sketch by Hauptmannes Andreas Wiederholdt, included in *Tagabuch des Capt. Wiederholdt Vom 7 October 1776 Bis 7 December 1780*. Courtesy University of Pennsylvania Library.

On board *Triton*, the Hessian passengers included a sick lieutenant colonel of the Leib Regiment named Carl Philip Heymill, two captains, a lieutenant, an ensign, a surgeon, and nearly two companies of jager infantry belonging to the von Lossberg Regiment. One of the infantry officers, Hauptmannes Andreas Wiederholdt, who had been sick for nearly a month, nevertheless maintained a most descriptive diary of the ensuing events. He noted that the brig was armed for defense with six small cannon and a pair of swivel guns, but was manned by a crew of only seven men. Moreover, with more than 214 troopers aboard as passengers she was both overcrowded and quite uncomfortable. That was soon to be the least of his complaints.[19]

On September 9, almost immediately after departure, the brig ran head on into a violent gale. The little flotilla of six vessels was quickly scattered, despite the efforts of the convoy guardship *Renown*, which was doubly troublesome for the shipmasters that had not been informed of their destination. Captain Jonathan Cooper, master of *Triton*, having no idea as to his final objective, had little choice but to put back for Sandy Hook on the morning of the 10th. Within a short time an unidentified vessel was sighted. *Triton* immediately prepared for battle in the event the stranger was one of the many rebel privateers infesting these waters. Thirty-six soldiers were ordered to take charge of the brig's six small guns, six men to a gun, which were promptly cleaned and loaded. The stranger, however, proved to be a friendly transport with elements of the British 48th Regiment embarked on board. Throughout the next day the two ships kept company, and on the following morning fell in with the assembling convoy. The fleet consisted of no less than twenty-three transports and commercial sloops left to the care of two small warships of twenty and fourteen guns. Two green sailors were transferred to *Triton* to help flesh out her crew.

Everyone aboard breathed a sigh of relief soon after *Triton* joined the convoy, and for the next two days everything went well. Unfortunately, on September 13, the weather had already begun to degenerate and continued stormy through the 14th with ever increasing winds. By the evening of the 15th, a veritable hurricane had arrived in full force. Amidst the pitch-blackness of night and the howling tempest, the fleet was scattered indiscriminately for miles about the ocean. About 9 p.m., like many other vessels, *Triton* suffered several crippling injuries when her mainmast broke off below the main yard. As terrified seamen and soldiers alike struggled to clear the wreckage away, the foremast snapped just above the deck and disappeared into the sea. Then, as Captain Cooper attempted to nail up a darklight in the cabin, assisted by Captain Wiederholdt, the sea suddenly burst in, throwing them head over heels.

At the mercy of the tempest, the brig was assailed by mountainous waves with deadly force. One cannon after another began to break away from its fastenings, their heavy carriages caroming them about the deck, smashing everything in their paths. Four of the ship's guns burst clear through the bulwarks into the sea. One of them carried with it the great iron cauldron in which all of the passengers and crew cooked their meals. A fifth gun crushed the fastenings of the hatch and loosened them, then was catapulted off its own carriage like a projectile through a hatchway onto the deck below. Landing on a large chest belonging to Captain Wiederholdt, which contained an assortment of wines and spirits, mustard, vinegar, and other goods hard to come by, the gun utterly destroyed it and the contents. Its fall, however, had been broken, and the ship's hull had miraculously escaped damage.

The sixth gun continued to run about the afterdeck just over the cabin, demolishing everything in its path, including the ship's wheel. No one dared attempt to bring the rampaging behemoth to heel for fear of being crushed to death. No one could even work the pumps for fear of being struck. Four of the ship's company refused to struggle any longer and retired to their bunks in utter fear; the remainder of the crew rebuffed every effort to bring the piece to rest. Many of the Hessians, too, with their sick commander unable to instill any sense of order, lay about weeping, praying, or just sighing at what they were certain was to be their last hours on earth.

Captain Wiederholdt alone refused to give up and repeatedly entreated his troops to bring the rampaging gun to a halt and get back to working the pumps. He pleaded, reminding them that God had brought them into this great danger and, if they did their part, would carry them out of it by bringing on better weather or sending a ship to their aid. Some of the soldiers, he later wrote, were too "stunned or stupid with fright" to work, and others professed that they were too sick (which, given the sea conditions, was not unlikely). The captain persisted, reminding the men that he himself had been suffering from a fever for a month, but, like them, had no choice but to do something for the common safety. Unless they worked together, they would all die together. He tried cajolery. There were men, no doubt, that were stronger than himself, he said, who had enough affection for him that, in this darkest of hours, they might still follow his lead and do as he instructed. He promised them that he would stay with them on the storm-tossed deck, working side by side with them and sharing their fate if they would just all pull together to save their own lives. Still, the Hessians, who had many times bravely marched into harm's way in fierce battles ashore, cowered in utter fear.

In sheer despair, Wiederholdt cried out: "Is there no under-officer who is in health and has ambition and a Hessian heart, who will follow and help me?" A sergeant and two corporals slowly started up. Then others stepped forward. Soon fifteen or twenty men had stepped into the breech. "Well, then, come along!" said the officer. "Let us first try to pitch the cannon into the sea." After several failed and quite dangerous attempts, in which one soldier had his arm broken in two places and Wiederholdt's little finger was crushed, the gun was finally subdued and pushed over the side.

The victory over the gun inspired new hope among the Hessians and soon they were again laboring at the ship's injured pumps in four-man relays. The work was exhausting, and each relay team, all of whom had to be tied or cling to the stump of the mainmast so as not to be carried away, would pump furiously for six to eight minutes at a time, and then be relieved. When the pump broke about 3 or 4 a.m. and could not be repaired in the stormy dark, they fell to bailing for their lives. The work was dangerous in the extreme, with thunderous black waves repeatedly washing across the deck. One soldier was carried overboard in the darkness, but at the last instant managed to grasp a line and hold on for dear life. Though shrieking for help, the darkness and sounds of the tempest masked his precise location. "Where are you?" shouted Wiederholdt. "Hanging on to the ship," answered the terrified soldier; "I can't hold on much longer. Help me quickly, or I shall fall into the sea and drown." Desperately, his comrades searched about, but in vain. Suddenly, miraculously, a wave washed him back aboard. Despite the dangers, the Hessians never ceased bailing and kept at it without letup until morning when enough light came on to allow repairs to be made to the pump.

Wreck of the transport ship *Triton*. Pen and ink sketch by Hauptmannes Andreas Wiederholdt, included in *Tagabuch des Capt. Wiederholdt Vom 7 October 1776 Bis 7 December 1780.* Courtesy University of Pennsylvania Library.

While the soldiers labored throughout the night, Wiederholdt had become suspicious of *Triton*'s master and some of his men who he had observed moving about the ship's boats with a lantern. Believing they intended to launch one of them, leaving the ship without a crew, and the Germans to their fate, he asked the captain what he was doing. "Oh, nothing. I am only seeing if they [the boats] are fast enough," came the reply. Unconvinced, the Hessian asked for the lantern, and on receiving it, promptly handed it to one of his men. Then, taking the master by the arm, he escorted him down to the cabin and placed him under arrest. A guard was stationed at the door. When the morning came, however, it was discovered that no one, English or German, would be leaving the ship for the boats had been injured beyond repair and had to be cast into the sea. Captain Cooper was released.

By midday of September 16, the storm began to subside, and the following day the skies were clear enough for a noon observation, which showed 37°19' north latitude. To everyone's undoubted dismay the brig had been driven as far south as the Virginia Capes, but precisely how far from land was anyone's guess.

Triton was a perfect mess, and everyone was put to work clearing away the wreckage of the masts and shattered bulwarks. A close inspection of the hull found it sound and without major leaks. Cooper's men jury-rigged a mast on the stump of the mainmast, and the next day another where the foremast had been. Now the soldiers had time to dry their clothes and knapsacks on deck, for everything on board was soaked in salt water and slime from the bilge. On Sunday the 19th, everyone, soldiers and sailors alike, gave thanks for their deliverance from the tempest. Together, the soldiers and crew sang a common hymn, but in their own national tongue. The 10th Psalm was read in German. Undoubtedly of particular inspiration were lines 23 through 30:

They that go down to the sea in ships, that do business in great waters;

These see the works of the Lord, and his wonders in the deep.

For he commendeth, and raiseth the stormy wind, which lifteth up the waves thereof.

They mount up to the heaven, they go down again to the depths: their soul is melted because of trouble.

They reel to and fro, and stagger like a drunken man, and are at their wit's end.

Then they cry unto the Lord in their trouble, and he bringeth them out of their distress.

He maketh the storm a calm, so that the waves are still.

Then they are glad because they be quiet; so he bringeth them unto their desired haven.

The hardened sailors, who were no less thankful for their salvation than their passengers, showed considerable reverence and, much to the astonishment of the Hessians, also prayed.

Under the jury-rigged sails, and aided by moderate weather, the barely manageable hulk of *Triton* pressed slowly northward, once more toward the privateer-infested seas of the Jersey coast. With the crippled transport now lacking even a single big gun to fire for its own protection and all but helpless, Wiederholdt agonized over the ship's defense in the event of attack. If a privateer should appear, he considered, why not conceal his men, decoy a boatload of rebels on board, and seize them as prisoners? The enemy would then be unwilling to fire into the brig for fear of injuring their own men. Moreover, he dare not board under force of arms owing to the superior numbers of the Hessians. It was a scheme born of desperation, but one that fortunately would not be tested when the first rebel privateers finally appeared.

The passage north, well off the Eastern Shore coast of Virginia, Maryland, and Delaware, went by without incident. Finally, on Saturday, September 25, the Delaware Capes were sighted. Now knowing exactly where he was, Captain Cooper again turned seaward to avoid the enemy "freebooters." Everyone took heart, for with a fair wind they might actually make Sandy Hook and safety in two days. Sunday, at daybreak, the weather was again fine, but the silhouette of two sails soon marred the horizon. Perhaps wishfully thinking the vessels might be ships sent from New York to patrol outside the harbor or to assist vessels damaged in the recent storm, Wiederholdt sprang into the cabin and reported the sightings to the convalescing lieutenant colonel and the other officers. All, including the incapacitated colonel, dressed and hurried topside. As the two vessels bore down on the transport, it was soon discerned that one was a sloop and the other a schooner. "But oh! How were our hopes betrayed!" exclaimed Wiederholdt to his diary, "for when they came near and hoisted their flags of thirteen stripes, our joy was turned into sorrow."

The schooner, which carried fourteen guns, proved to be Captain Yelverton Taylor's Pennsylvania privateer *Mars*, owned by Thomas Leaming of Cape May and Joseph Fisher of Cape Henlopen and Philadelphia. The sloop was the 10-gun Philadelphia vessel *Comet*, which had been sold by Thomas Leaming since last commanded by Taylor, and was now owned by Thomas Pryor and Robert Bridges and commanded by Captain Stephen Decatur, Sr., of Cape May.[20] The two privateers had come alongside *Triton* by 8 a.m., and ordered her master to lower one sail and bind the helm to starboard. Then, each of the rebel vessels sent aboard an officer and five men as the prize had been jointly captured. The Americans were no doubt stunned to discover they had taken a ship bearing 214 bone weary jagers. Cooper and several of his men were transferred to *Mars*, but Colonel Heymill excused himself on account of his illness. A line was run to the prize, which was then taken under tow by the schooner, and a course set for Egg Harbor.

For Captain Taylor of *Mars*, a brief return to the security of the snug New Jersey coastal sanctuary would be welcomed. Only days before he had fought and captured a British privateer called *Active* (not to be confused with Olmsted's *Active*) in a knock-down-drag-out engagement replete with boarding and bloody hand-to-hand fighting. It had been a difficult cruise and his men were undoubtedly still licking their wounds and exhausted when they happened upon *Triton*. It was thus with some dismay then, that while turning towards Egg Harbor with his latest prize under tow, that Taylor discovered himself being pursued by a powerful British frigate. He managed to summon up one last bit of seamanship to elude the enemy by adroitly ducking into Barnegat Inlet with *Triton* still in tow. It was a hazardous entry point for anyone unfamiliar with the channel or in a hurry, but both vessels miraculously managed to escape almost certain capture. Yet, the crisis was far from over.[21]

Upon the enemy's departure, Taylor released *Triton* to the care of the prize crew, cautiously exited the inlet with his own ship, and turned his bow southward toward the entrance of Little Egg Harbor. Although the record is unclear as to precisely what happened next (the Philadelphia papers claimed the privateer was struck, presumably by a flaw in the wind, when she turned to windward), what is certain is that somehow *Mars* was carried among the breakers barely two gunshots distance, or about 600 yards, from *Triton*'s anchorage, and capsized.[22]

The disaster was not as bad as it could have been and the incident elicited only a few words in the Pennsylvania and New York press. The loss of a privateer schooner and but a single man out of a crew of sixty was, indeed, barely newsworthy in September 1779 as far more important events were unfolding elsewhere. Spain was joining America as an ally in its war against the British, and an enemy assault on Savannah, Georgia, was about to begin by land and sea. What did make the news, however, was the arrival of several hundred enemy prisoners of war at Little Egg Harbor on September 29 aboard a horribly injured transport, on the verge of sinking, and now manned by only six prize crewmen. Few people but a handful of investors, who would have to bear the expense, would pay much attention to the announcement that *Mars* "will be got up again" to fight another day.[23]

The American privateer schooner *Mars* and sloop *Comet*. Note the flags, each containing thirteen stripes, sans stars, with *Mars* flying her ensign of seven red stripes and six white, while *Comet* displays five red, four blue, and four white stripes. *Comet's* lines and rake of mast suggest a Bermuda sloop configuration. Pen and ink sketch by Hauptmannes Andreas Wiederholdt, included in *Tagabuch des Capt. Wiederholdt Vom 7 October 1776 Bis 7 December 1780*. Courtesy University of Pennsylvania Library.

Abbildung

des Schooner Mars, welches ein Amerikanischer Privateer, Capit. Taylor commandirte, 14 sechspfündige Canonen führte und in Compagnie mit der Schloop Comet, die im Sturm verunglückten, und mit hessischen truppen besetzte Schiffe Triton & Molly wegnahmen, und denselben Tag noch untergieng.

Abbildung

der Schloop Comet, welches ein Amerikanischer Privateer, Capit. Decator commandirte, 10 sechspfünd: Canonen führte, und in Compag: des Schooner Mars die im Sturm verunglückten, und mit hessischen truppen besetzten Schiffe Triton & Molly wegnahmen.

H. Winterholt.

• • •

Of the six transports in which the men of the Lossberg and Knyphausen regiments had set sail from New York, only one returned.

The transport *Badger*, carrying part of the Lossberg regiment, was disabled by the loss of her fore and mainmast in the storm. Hounded for two days by a wolfish pair of American privateers, the ship was resolutely defended by the German soldiers aboard who, when fired upon, refused to be boarded and resisted with small arms. On October 9, however, a 12-gun privateer aggressively attacked her and would not be denied. Having no cannon, the transport was forced to surrender. A lieutenant, three ensigns, and twenty men were taken on board the privateer, together with the equipment of the remaining Hessians. A Hessian captain, who was sick, a surgeon, and most of the enlisted men were left aboard. On October 10, the British frigate *Solebay* appeared on the scene, retook *Badger*, and subsequently brought her safely to New York.

The unfortunate transport called *Polly* (referred to in some reports as *Molly*), carrying Major Johann Friederich von Stein and the Guards (Leib Company) of the von Knyphausen Regiment, had also been on the verge of sinking. Like *Triton*, she too fell into the hands of privateers somewhere off the Delaware and was taken to Trenton and from there to Philadelphia.

Another transport was captured by the 16-gun privateer *Pickering*, out of Salem, Massachusetts, along with a Hessian major, captain, lieutenant, ensign, judge advocate, and 150 non-commissioned officers and privates of the Knyphausen Regiment.

A fifth transport, *Adamant*, the largest and newest in the convoy, carrying Major Ludwig August von Hanstein, and the Leib and Lossberg companies belonging to Colonel Friedrich Wilhelm Freherr von Lossberg's Regiment, was lost at sea with all hands. The fate of the sixth vessel was unknown and she was also assumed lost.[24]

Additional sufferings and losses to the convoy ships carrying both British and German troops had also been devastating. The *King George* transport, upon which Colonel Johann August von Loos and his men had been traveling, had been forced to land at New York along with HMS *Renown*. "Their condition was deplorable, as was that of many of the British 44th Regiment, which had embarked aboard the frigate *Craford* and the transport *Favorite*, which had been without food for thirteen days."

The prisoners taken in *Triton* were sent from Little Egg Harbor to Philadelphia where they arrived on or about October 6. Ten days later Marshal Joseph Potts published a notice in the *Pennsylvania Packet* announcing the sale of the brig at Chestnut Neck on October 21 along with a "quantity of blanket drillings, clothes, plush, baize, linens, complete suits of regimentals, flannel and linen drawers, small arms, and other articles." The prize sloop *Hope*, taken by Decatur in *Comet* and Captain Rufus Gardner (not to be confused with the British skipper of the same name) in the 12-gun Pennsylvania schooner *Enterprize*, along with a cargo of forty hogsheads of rum and a quantity of tar were also to be sold.[25]

• • •

Storms, such as the one that beset *Triton* and her convoy, claimed countless victims and most certainly had a serious effect upon the British war effort that has seldom been taken into consideration by modern historians. On March 22, 1779, for example, during a blinding snowstorm, the transport *Mermaid*, belonging to Whitehaven, England, was driven ashore at Egg Harbor while en route from Halifax to New York. Nearly a hundred persons perished and the remainder, "by the exertions of the inhabitants on shore, were saved." Later reports claimed that out of 170 persons aboard, only twenty had been rescued. As news continued to trickle in, the toll of lost ships and men climbed even higher. Two other vessels, it was said, including a Boston sloop from the West Indies, which had lately been captured by the British, had been driven ashore at Egg Harbor along with *Mermaid*. On December 28, 1779, a severe nor'easter smashed into the middle-Atlantic coast wrecking wharves and shipping. The Loyalist privateer *Britannia*, which lay near Sandy Hook, dragged anchor and was driven ashore amidst a large field of ice. Fatigued by the fight to save their ship from destruction, her crew was soon afterwards made prisoners by the rebels. In January 1780, another storm was equally destructive to both sides, and provided coastal wreckers with a veritable salvor's bonanza. When the blow was over, initial reports reaching Trenton indicated that a British first-rate man-of-war and two other large ships had been cast away to the southward of Egg Harbor and a number of hands had taken to a boat endeavoring to escape. They were then, the report said, pursued, captured, and brought back to the harbor as prisoners of war. *The New York Journal and General Advertiser* reported on January 31, 1780, that nearly forty American vessels had also been driven ashore "on different parts of the coast from Egg Harbor, as far southward as the Eastern shore of Maryland and Virginia."[26]

Such tragedies as losses at sea from dirty weather, however, were to be expected on both sides. After all, it was in the nature of seafaring and those were the chances that one took. Everyone suffered, including the privateersmen. More than one such cockleshell warship was to venture out of Egg Harbor in search of rich prizes only to end up a total wreck upon some lonely stretch of beach. For a first-time investor, it was often viewed as part of the risk and forgotten—until the vessel in question was injured or lost. One such case was that of a Pennsylvania speculator and an ill-fated privateer called *Minerva*.

The unfortunate odyssey began when a Philadelphia entrepreneur named Stephen Girard, an occasional smuggler adept at forging customs declarations, bribery, and other nefarious activities, learned that a schooner called *Minerva*, in need of reconditioning and overhauling, was for sale at Chestnut Neck. Bitten by the privateering bug, he promptly set about to gain control of her at the least possible cost. He personally supervised the refitting and rearming of his new property and, by the fall of 1778, the vessel was a quite proper privateer. She was well-armed with twelve carriage guns, 1,065 shot, four blunderbusses, thirty cutlasses, nineteen muskets with 852 cartridges, two pistols, sixty-five hand grenades, and eighteen boarding pikes, as well twenty-five handcuffs for anticipated prisoners. For dire emergency situations she was supplied with a case of amputating equipment. After a bond of $10,000 was posted on October 29, a commission was duly granted.

Not long after *Minerva* put to sea under the command of Captain Arthur Helme, she encountered a violent storm that drove her from her intended course and opened her caulking. When the weather had cleared, Captain Helme found himself off the Cape Fear River, North Carolina. A derelict Virginia pilot boat called *Barbary*, laden with tobacco and a number of dead men, was sighted and taken. This decrepit prize was manned with a prize crew and sent to Chestnut Neck. Unfortunately for the leaking privateer, the capture of the derelict proved to be the pinnacle of its short career.

Soon after *Barbary*'s departure, as *Minerva* headed north, yet another gale struck the unfortunate privateer, shredded her sails, and reopened her seams. Helme was now obliged to dump eight of the ship's guns overboard in order to reach the nearest harbor of convenience, which proved to be an isolated hamlet at Chincoteague Inlet, on the Eastern Shore of Virginia. From there he notified the ship's owner of the perilous situation. Girard reluctantly dispatched a thousand dollars to begin necessary repairs. By then, however, another problem had arisen: the crew had disappeared, taking with them the ship's valuable rigging.

Minerva was to remain frozen in for the remainder of the winter and was never to see Chestnut Neck again. After Helme was finally able to patch up the hull, he left Chincoteague in the spring of 1779 bound for Philadelphia. Unfortunately, he again managed to wreck his ship, this time for good. *Minerva* was declared a total loss although Girard managed to recover his investment from the sale of the prize cargo taken from *Barbary*, which was eventually taken into service as a cargo ship.[27]

As Girard discovered, like so many before and after him, privateering was not for the faint of heart or the shallow pocketbook.

XVI

The Cruise on Clover

"Our concerns in navigation at Egg-harbour are yet in the clouds."

Ambition and opportunity alone often go hand in hand, but when stimulated by the promise of substantial monetary gain, sometimes produce success beyond all expectations. So it was with investing in privateers during the American Revolution. But, as with any speculative ventures, ambition, opportunity and money were frequently not enough without the support of Dame Fortune—and influential connections, as Joseph Ball expereinced following the resurrection of privateer operations out of Egg Harbor in 1779.

Ball was just thirty-two years of age when, for £55,000, he purchased the Batsto Iron Works in early 1779 from its most recent owner, Thomas Mayberry, who had acquired it from Colonel Cox. A few months later, on April 2, he added to his holdings by purchasing Richard Westcoat's expansive Pleasant Mills plantation, including his dwelling, grist and saw mills, and myriad other structures.[1] Not surprisingly, it was around the young capitalist's newly acquired empire, situated on the twisting, muddy Mullica River, squarely in the heart of the remote Jersey Pine Barrens, that an even more convoluted association of Philadelphia-based privateering interests then began to take shape.

On October 4, 1779, barely six months after Ball acquired Batsto, Colonel Cox again reinvested in his former holding by purchasing a one-twelfth interest in the iron works. Other prominent moneymen of Pennsylvania and New Jersey were soon to also procure interests in the operation. All were also deeply engaged in speculating in the privateering industry, either secretly or publicly. One of the most prominent was Charles Pettit, a Trenton attorney of substantial influence and connections, an expert accountant, and a man destined to become an American financial giant.[2] Prior to the war, Pettit had served as Secretary to William Franklin, New Jersey's last provincial governor, but, unlike the governor, he saw his interests linked to loyalty to the Revolution rather than the Crown. As a youth he had been a boyhood friend of one of General Washington's key officers, General Nathaniel Greene, under whom he would later serve as Assistant Quarter Master General of the Continental Army. Always seen wearing his powdered wig, knee britches, silk stockings and shoes festooned with silver buckles, Pettit was once described as the archetypal "old school gentleman" of the Revolutionary age.[3] Whatever the impression his public appearance may have conveyed to others, his intelligence, worldly wisdom, and business acumen were substantial. He was, for instance, careful not to publicly take full title to his share of the Batsto enterprise, which provided the Continental Army with munitions, until he had been relieved of his quartermaster duties. It was a trait he had perhaps acquired early on in the war, having been a silent shareholder in numerous privateers operating out of Egg Harbor as late as 1778.[4]

Left: General Nathaniel Greene (detail), Quartermaster General of the Continental Army, and silent partner in the Little Egg Harbor privateering organization of Cox, Ball, Pettit and Greene. Reproduction from *History of the war with America, France, Spain, and Holland* by John Andrews, 1785-86. Courtesy Rare Book and Special Collections Division, Library of Congress.

Right: Colonel John Cox, a former Philadelphia merchant and trader, owner of the Batsto Iron Works, and one of the key managers of the Little Egg Harbor privateer operations. Reproduction of miniature in *Salons Colonial and Republican* by Anne Hollingshworth Wharton, 1900.

Another of those who re-entered the fray, as noted, was Colonel Cox, who had been appointed Assistant Quarter Master General in 1778, along with Pettit, in an indirect arrangement with General Greene (whose own acceptance of the Quarter Master post rested upon their acceptance), with a pledge that he would divest himself of any interest in the Batsto works. In the Quartermaster's Office, Cox was placed in charge of purchasing and examining supplies and was deemed by Congress "the best qualified for that Purpose of any other man." Pettit handled all auditing and was charged with the management of all funds coming from the treasurer. Green, who was allowed to receive a one percent commission on all payments, would place orders and see to delivery. However, it was perhaps significant that the general took care to divide his commission in thirds between himself, Cox, and Pettit to avoid any public outcry of profiteering and maintain a public face of disinterest that he desperately sought to encourage.[5]

It was undoubtedly through Ball's connection with Cox, that Pettit and Greene, as well as four other key investors from Philadelphia, John Bayard, Mathew Irwin, Thomas Irwin, and "Midas" himself, Blair McClenachan, all major players in the game of privateering, soon acquired an interest in Batsto. Pettit and Cox took another one-sixth share each, along with General Greene who entered the business in March as a silent shareholder. The general claimed that he had purchased his interest to supply pig iron for his own Covert Forge. On October 4, the same day Ball sold a one-twelfth interest in the Batsto iron works to Cox, he also sold a two-twelfth interest to each of the four Philadelphia privateering investors.[6]

That the seven men were intimately and intricately linked through the Batsto connection is without question. It is almost without doubt that their financial manipulations, certainly as they related to privateering and prize sales, extended well beyond that. Yet, owing to the secrecy with which they and others like them conducted their affairs, much is left to speculation. By the time Blair McClenachan acquired his share in the Batsto works, he had already backed no fewer than nineteen Pennsylvania commissioned privateering cruises with fourteen individual vessels, as full or partial owner of the vessels engaged or as a principal shareholder. Bayard had financed at least five voyages, while the Irwins had supported thirteen more between them, either jointly or independently. All four men were undoubtedly also silent shareholders in many others. All had prospered in their enterprises, as well as through their social and business connections. McClenachan, at least one historian has surmised, was, indeed, intimately linked to Charles Pettit and quite probably to General Nathaniel Greene himself.[7]

Though there were many successful, and even more unsuccessful, adventurers willing to chance it all on privateering on the New Jersey coast, none were more representative of the breed than the triumvirate formed by Greene, Pettit, and Cox, three men of position, importance, and connections to men such as McClenachan, Bayard, and the Irwins. But it was with the Irwins that Pettit, undesignated leader of the triumvirate, seems to have formed a special association.

Although their collaborations were often covert and their names were shielded from the public, perhaps for reasons considered less than ethical, it would appear from fragmentary letters and records that the Batsto triumvirate began to jointly engage in maritime matters shortly after their appointments as quartermasters. Pettit and Greene most likely undertook their first adventure together when the former was induced in May 1779 to invest £12,000 with the latter in a quarter interest in the recovery of two burnt "frigates." The objective was to utilize one wreck to fully repair the other and get it back into service. Unfortunately, the project languished and a year later both hulks were still "laid up by their unwieldiness and the timidity of some of the owners and the negligence of some of the others." Not until the spring of 1781 would the new ship built from the wrecks of the two hulks be completed and named *Congress*, and the two men would be able to retrieve part of their investments. But by then, however, they had moved on to more lucrative fields.[8]

In the fall of 1779, the New Jersey coast witnessed a rebirth of American privateering activity, but also a substantial increase in Loyalist privateering. Both Greene and Pettit, from the comfort of Philadelphia, joined the fray by investing not only in the iron works at Batsto but in private ships of war. Most of these operated from the Jersey ports, and, on at least one occasion, from Boston as well.[9]

On January 1, 1780, the 12-gun schooner *Hunter*, a Pennsylvania-commissioned vessel with a crew of sixty, owned by James Vanuxem and Lardner Clark of Philadelphia and commanded by Captain John Douglass, set out upon a cruise. It was to be the first privateering venture of the year out of the city. The triumvirate secured a one-sixteenth share in the expedition, with John Cox and Captain Douglass posting the $10,000 bond required.[10]

The engagement of both *Hunter* and her commander for a cruise out of the Delaware may have come with certain baggage that the investors apparently ignored. Douglass, it appears, was a brave, aggressive officer, but with certain faults. His capacity to command was proven as early as February 1779, when the feisty schooner, then mounting only ten guns was operating out of Egg Harbor. On February 10, *Hunter* engaged the superior 16-gun New York brig *Bellona* in a horrific ninety-minute engagement. After suffering extensive damage, the schooner was obliged to break off combat, albeit leaving the brig a perfect wreck and unable to follow.[11] It was a costly engagement for investors, but one that no doubt earned the captain much praise for standing up to a far more heavily armed vessel.

Nevertheless, *Hunter* was quickly repaired and fitted out for another cruise under Douglass's command. On April 20, she brought in a prize schooner from St. Kitts with 135 hogsheads of rum, which Pettit informed Greene, "will about clear the Privateer and will put the rest of the cruise on clover."[12] Soon afterwards, however, Douglass ignored the Congressional privateering instructions when he encountered and captured two Spanish ships, the *Santander y los Santos Martires* [*Holy Martyrs*], and the *San Francisco de Paula*, alias *Valenciano*, (both mentioned earlier) and sent them into Massachusetts. The problem was that Spain, an ally long supportive of the war against Great Britain, had opened its ports to American shipping and trade, and would, if events continued unimpeded, enter the war on the side of the United States. The capture of the two ships by an American privateer threatened to explode into a diplomatic crisis that placed the hard-won alliance with France and the growing friendship with Spain, a potential ally, in jeopardy.[13]

Word apparently had yet to reach Philadelphia when Pettit wrote glumly of yet another capture, obtained at great cost, and reported to Greene on April 30. The prize in question was a Jamaicaman, but in the fight to take her *Hunter*

came off with a Flea in her Ear after an engagement with a ship from Liverpool. She is returned to port and the Captain thinks the Vessel not fit for the purpose. The owners have therefore concluded to sell her; and this moment they consulted me about buying a new Brig for Captain Douglas which will mount 16 guns. To effect this will cost near 80,000 pounds of which the sale of the *Hunter* will produce between 50 and 60 thousand. I have a good opinion of the Captain, of the proposed Brig and of the scheme save that they ask about 20,000 pounds more for the Brig than she cost; but at the present depreciation I do not know whether she could be built for less. She was launched about 3 weeks since and will soon be ready. I gave Mr. [Lardner] Clark the acting owner my opinion against giving so great an advance but told him that as our share was small I would not stand in the way of the rest. . . . I believe I told you I had relinquished the one-fourth I had taken in a new Brig with Mr. B. [Blair] McClenachan. She carried too little cargo in proportion to the value of the vessel to make any Profit.[14]

Whatever concerns Pettit may have had regarding the triumvirate's investments in *Hunter*, he undoubtedly was soon to learn of the far more unfortunate consequences of Douglass's capture of the two Spanish ships that had been sent into Massachusetts. The seizure of vessels of a neutral but friendly state by an American privateer served not only to damage the developing relationship between the United States and Spain, but also undermined the already weakened rapport between Congress and Massachusetts.

When an appeal was filed with the Superior Court of Judicature at Concord by one Pedro Blanco, representing the injured parties, and then the Superior Court of the State, he was rebuffed on the grounds that no papers could be found regarding the affair.[15] Soon afterwards, on May 19, Don Juan de Miralles, the unofficial agent for the Spanish government, with the support of Conrad Alexandre Gerard de Reyneval, the French Minister Plenipotentiary of France, took up the cudgel and sent a memorial to Congress seeking Congressional interposition in the Massachusetts Admiralty case regarding the captures. The memorial was laid before Congress on April 24, and referred to the Committee of Appeals, which at the time was also struggling over the *Active* case brought before them by Gideon Olmstead. On May 18, memorials from Captains de Luca and de Llano were also received, and then another from Conrad Alexandre Gerard.[16]

The matter, which, like the *Active* case, involved the issue of Continental supremacy over state admiralty judgments in appeals, quickly became a most serious headache for Congress, which was loath to be drawn into a clash with Massachusetts when it was already engaged in the ongoing Olmstead case with Pennsylvania. Unlike the *Active* standoff, however, the Spanish and French memorials were not forwarded to the Committee on Appeals for action, but to a committee of three, consisting of Thomas Burke of North Carolina, James Duane of New York, and James Lovell of Massachusetts, to present compromise recommendations. On May 22, Congress adopted the proposals and, in turn, moved to "prepare a system of regulation for marine jurisdiction." The Continental government was cognizant that Massachusetts was likely to reject its right to hear an appeal in this case. Thus, in a gesture calculated both to save face and court goodwill with Spain and France, five days later Gerard was given a strong reassurance by John Jay, Secretary of Congress. Jay informed him: "That if it shall be found after due trial, that the owners of the captured Vessels have suffered damage from the Misapprehension or violation of the rights of war & Neutrality, Congress will cause Reparation to be made in such manner as to do ample justice & vindicate the honor of the Spanish flag."[17]

Captain Douglass, who caused the political firestorm, did not escape the condemnation of Congress. On the recommendation of the Marine Committee, as a result of the solicitations of Gerard and Miralles, a resolution and judgment were issued against him on August 12, 1779, for the illegal capture of the two Spanish vessels. Douglass, however, had already "absconded out of the State of Pennsylvania" to elude punishment.[18]

Whatever punishment Congress may have intended for Douglass, it went unserved, and was apparently ignored by authorities, for, by 1781, the captain was again in command of a five-gun Pennsylvania privateer brigantine called *Minerva*, owned by Thomas Irwin and John Earle of Philadelphia (not to be confused with Captain Helme's ill-fated vessel of the same name).[19]

...

The great risk in privateering investment was, perhaps, best illustrated by the case of one of the first and largest vessels in which the triumvirate speculated, barely a year after the British attack on Chestnut Neck. The vessel in question was the 20-gun Pennsylvania ship *Revolution*, manned by a crew of sixty and commanded by Captain John McNachtane of Philadelphia. Greene and Pettit apparently had learned of her in late November. That the capabilities of McNachtane as a commander were known to them is probable, however, as he had last commanded the privateer *Lady Gates* in September 1778, a vessel owned by Thomas and Mathew Irwin. Although *Revolution*'s commission listed only Samuel Morris, Jr., and Company of Philadelphia as owners, both Pettit and Greene silently opted to become shareholders in the venture, in what may have been the first of the triumvirate's major "Egg Harbour concerns." The acquisition of shares were, as historian Arthur D. Pierce notes, mostly through Joseph Ball, and neither of the two investors may even have known much if anything about the ship, as Cox was the go-between and appears to have carried out actual transactions, as he would frequently do at Egg Harbor, on behalf of the group.[20]

That there was some disharmony in the process, at least from the perspective of Pettit and presumably Greene, was evidenced in several communications between the two men regarding a number of privateer ventures, such as *Revolution,* in which they were silent shareholders, all launched about the same time in late 1779 and early 1780. Pettit informed Greene on January 5, 1780: "I have never yet been able to get either an account or a shilling of money from our last year's concerns at Eggharbour. My name does not appear in the business and therefore I am the more easily put off; and our good friend [Cox] who represents these concerns has wealth in so many ways that he does not feel the delay."[21]

Pettit, however, was an expert at working the systems. On December 31, 1779, despite a coating of ice over much of the Delaware, *Revolution* had successfully put out from Philadelphia, passed Reedy Island, and was preparing to press into the open Atlantic, though most other vessels remained frozen in harbor. Pettit was elated with the ship, noting she "sails like the wind and [is] bound to Dominque [Dominica]." In a twist not uncommon in such behind the scenes speculations, he quickly disposed of his one-sixteenth share in the voyage "at a clear advance" of £7,000 for a substantial profit as soon as she had reportedly cleared the Delaware, and then reinvested in the same vessel for a one-sixteenth share for less than half that at an advantageous moment.[22]

The bargain investment, however, soon came back to haunt him when *Revolution* was forced ashore on the southern New Jersey shores of the Delaware and was unable to escape into the ocean as first reported. Not surprisingly, he was upset at having purchased shares in the venture "on the presumption that the Ship was at Sea," and had presumed "from her fast sailing I don't know but I could have sold out at double first cost or near it, but unfortunately she was caught in the lee . . . and is now on shore near Cohansie [Cohansey] Creek. The Guns and Rigging I hear are got on shore and there is hopes of saving the Cargo and Hull, in which case the savings will be worth near first cost. We have an adventure of six or seven Hhds. [hogsheads] of tobacco on board besides our share of the Cargo and Ship."[23]

He was doubly concerned about how his silent partner on the Mullica, Colonel Cox, was handling things, such as the acquisition and disposal of prize cargoes. "That business [at Egg Harbor] has vexed me," he informed Greene, "and I have spoken more fretfully to our Friend Col. Cox than I ever did on any other occasion to induce him to procure a Settlement, as he stands between us and the People who have the management of those affairs."[24]

Revolution would eventually be refloated and repaired, after her cargo of tobacco was landed and sold, but at the inordinate expense of £100,000. By the late spring of 1780, she was again ready for sea and this time dispatched to Martinique on a trading voyage, during which she took at least one lucrative prize. Yet, this cruise also ended poorly for the triumvirate when, on her return in June, she was chased by HMS *Galatea* and barely managed to escape. Unfortunately, she ran aground on the Virginia coast soon afterwards (where local inhabitants plundered her of most of her cargo of wine), and was obliged to land her lading of rum, molasses, and coffee at Metompkin Inlet, on the Eastern Shore coast of the state.[25]

In less-than-adequate shape to continue operations, it was deemed necessary to refit *Revolution* in Virginia for her next voyage, this time to the Dutch island of St. Eustatia. Pettit was again animated over the performance of the big letter of marque that had hitherto caused him so much concern. "The ship sails remarkably well," he later wrote, "she was chased divers times going out, among others by a copper-bottomed frigate noted for swiftness who chased her into Martinique but did not gain on her."[26] Yet, even this good fortune was eventually to abandon the ship, although, it appears, not before Pettit, Greene, and their colleagues had divested themselves of further involvement in the career of the big letter of marque. In August 1780, she was again delayed in Virginia after having taken just one prize.

"Would you choose to sell out as she now is," Pettit queried Greene, "or carry your concern through the voyage? She . . . would now sell for 60,000 pounds or near it for an eighth. . . . [S]he stands the owners near 40,000 pounds an eighth as money was at the time of advancing it for disbursements at her departure in April last. Her prize will net the owners about 100,000 pounds. Her voyage, without that, would hardly clear its way."[27]

Pettit decided for the three investors that it was now time to dispose of their shares in *Revolution*, and perhaps wisely so. In April 1781, when she again sailed under Captain McNachtane, this time armed with twenty-six guns, she was under the ownership of Pettit's Philadelphia colleagues, Mathew and Thomas Irwin, and captured at least two small prizes, the 20-ton sloop *Cornwallis*, Jeremiah Bassett, and the brig *Malton*, Captain Hall. Both were sent into the Delaware. Then, sometime before August 11, her career was brought to an abrupt end when she fell in with the New York privateer *Triumph* and was taken and sent as a prize into the city.[28]

Another speculation Pettit entered into for the triumvirate about the late spring of 1780 was a one-fourth share in the 12-gun brigantine *Duke of Leinster*. Once again he quickly became disenchanted with the venture. "I got rather unwarily concerned in it," he later informed Greene, "and have repented it ever since, and have been trying to get quit of it. I sold one-eighth the beginning of June [1780] at first cost and took a ninth of the [brig] *Morning Star* at 20,000 pounds in part pay. I have been constantly on the

Charles Pettit's letter documenting the share value of the Little Egg Harbor letter of marque *Revolution* following a profitable voyage. Donald Shomette Private Collection, Dunkirk, Maryland.

watch to get rid of the rest and believe I shall sell it at 10 pct. advance to be paid in Loan Certificates. . . . I do this to get rid of a foolish bargain — the only one I have found cause to blame myself for making." Pettit managed to divest the triumvirate of *Leinster* in return for loan certificates and the share in the ten-gun *Morning Star*, but was unable to exchange the certificates for real money. Finally commissioned on January 20, 1781, *Duke of Leinster* was owned by John Barclay and Company of Philadelphia.[29]

Morning Star, owned by Andrew Hodge and Company of Philadelphia, and commanded by Captain James Johnston, proved as great a disappointment as *Leinster*. Pettit bemoaned this investment as well. "I took the one-ninth at 20,000 pounds (while she was at sea) expecting, and so did the owners, that on safe arrival it would be worth 40,000 pounds. On looking into her affairs I found little chance of profit and some risk of loss. I therefore sold by the hump without either, being determined to be rid of such a concern."[30]

Despite such misadventures, Pettit did not limit his privateering and trading to Pennsylvania interests only, nor was he above relying solely upon recommendations of others to engage in speculation in ventures by vessels unknown to him. One such tip involved the 8-gun Pennsylvania brigantine *Lady Gates*, Captain George Stewart (the same formerly commanded by McNachtane), and not only owned but also bonded for $10,000 by the Irwins of Philadelphia on December 18, 1779. Soon after receiving her commission, *Lady Gates* put in at Boston. In the meantime, Pettit was approached by one Colonel Hay who informed him that his assistant, a Major Hale, was intending to refit the vessel at Boston with an additional eight guns, and offered him the opportunity to acquire a one-eighth share in the cruise. Pettit at first demurred, noting that he could not engage without Greene's approval, which was, however, soon secured, although the share was reduced to one-sixteenth.[31]

By July 1780, when Pettit finally managed to assess the success or failure of this particular investment, he was so dismayed that he resolved never to reinvest in the "old and crazy" brigantine again. Though the vessel was sold at public vendue for £37,000 after being unloaded, he reported that the management and operations of Lady Gates had been so poorly conducted that "I would rather have given away our part than invested money in a fresh outfit." Colonel Cox, who appears to have had some role in the whole affair, was strongly directed to give the manager of the business "an overhaul as he was the offensive owner."[32]

About the same time as the triumvirate was engaged as shareholders in the Revolution and Lady Gates ventures, Pettit and Greene also became involved in several others, including the former New York sloop Hetty and the Pennsylvania brigantine Duke of Leinster. On January 17, 1780, Pettit informed Greene that they had just acquired a one-eighth interest in the letter of marque called Hetty. This vessel, a fine, large Bermuda sloop, had been left in the Harlem River, New York, in 1776, then taken and fitted out by the enemy as a tender or privateer. She had been recaptured in 1779 and brought into Philadelphia as a prize. Sold to Mathew and Thomas Irwin and Company, she was lengthened, rigged as a brig, and armed with sixteen guns. Manned by a crew of fifty, she was commanded by Captain Thomas Houston [also noted as Houghton], the former skipper of the state of Pennsylvania's privateer Convention, which had caused Gideon Olmstead so much grief. As the Delaware was frozen over, Pettit reported that the ship would be ready for sea "as soon as the Ice permits." However, some delay was apparently incurred, and Houston was not awarded the commission until March 28. Thanks, no doubt, to the ice, his ship would not put to sea until April. Though probably of little consolation to Pettit and Houston, the enemy was equally hamstrung by the winter ice, which had covered the Hudson in January, and was reportedly eleven feet thick. The sound between Staten Island and the New Jersey mainland was a solid sheet of glassy white. Nothing was moving on either side.[33]

The trading voyage of the letter of marque Hetty proved a near disaster when she was spotted and pursued by a British warship, sprung her masts, and was forced into the Dutch West Indies island entrepôt of St. Marten, where her lading brought a dreadful price. Upon her return to America, after a most miserable and unproductive cruise, what was at first mild dissension among her owners erupted into blistering quarrels. Never one to ignore an opportunity, Pettit quietly negotiated a deal with one of the owners while the rest were arguing, and sold him the one-eighth share he and Greene owned at the rate of £180,000 for the whole, approximately half the sum amount, just before Hetty was "struck off at Vendue."[34]

Despite the ups and downs of speculating in privateer cruises and letter of marque trading voyages, the Pettit-Cox-Greene triumvirate continued to engage in the business, often with only very minor shares throughout 1780. One such minor venture was "three-fourths of one-eighteenth, or one twenty-fourth" share in the 6-gun schooner *Buckskin*, John Perryman master, owned by none other than Robert Morris and a partner named Peter Whiteside. Another was in a £600 investment in a ship called *Alliance*, Captain Smith. Neither proved profitable.[35]

By midsummer, the triumvirate had begun to fall apart. Pettit, who attempted to wax philosophically regarding the ups and downs of the last few years of speculation, informed Greene on August 27: "Our concerns in navigation at Egg-harbour are yet in the clouds as to my view of them, tho' I have some accounts respecting them. They were at first not as profitable as we had expected, and there are some losses to reduce those that afforded profit I have all along comforted myself with this reflection, that is if I rec'd nothing from them, they began from nothing, having advanced no money originally for them."[36]

Within nine months the informal organization that had supported so many expeditions was all but dead. Pettit noted on May 27, 1781, that Colonel Cox now confined himself entirely to the cultivation of his farm at Bloomsbury, New Jersey, "which is in a flourishing way." General Greene was commanding the Continental Army in the South. Pettit alone continued to engage in the great game with a new set of allies, such as Francis Gurney, Clement and Charles Biddle, and others, even as the war was approaching a pivotal turning point on the grassy fields surrounding a small Virginia seaport called Yorktown, several hundred miles to the south of the Jersey coast.

On September 29, 1781, Charles Pettit's last known speculation in a privateering venture, the cruise of the little 7-gun Pennsylvania brigantine *Active*, Charles Biddle commanding, began. It's subsequent successes or failures and ultimate fate are unreported.[37] Less than a month later, on October 19, 1781, General Sir Charles Cornwallis would surrender his entire army to the combined Franco-American armies under Generals George Washington and the Comte Jean Baptiste de Rochambeau on the outskirts Yorktown, as the British military fifes and drums played a tune called "The World Turned Upside Down."

To many, it seemed, the American War for Independence was almost over. But for the combatants ensconced in New York, New Jersey and Pennsylvania, it was business as usual, though becoming uglier than ever.

XVII

Strike, You Damned Rebels

"They gave three cheers and said they would never leave her."

Fortune may favor the bold privateer, but at sea a fast, well-armed and manned sailing vessel and a canny, sagacious commander often tilted the odds even more. So it was with one of the swiftest and most famous privateers of the Revolution to blaze a profitable and, for the British, devastating path along the Jersey coast and elsewhere on the Atlantic frontier. The vessel in question was the Pennsylvania brig *Fair American*, owned by Blair McClenachan, and commanded by Stephen Decatur, Sr., of Cape May and Philadelphia. When McClenachan and Charles Miller & Co. purchased *Fair American*, they acquired one of the fleetest vessels afloat, purpose-built for her mission. They also increased their chances for success tenfold by securing one of the most successful privateersmen on the Atlantic coast as their commander.[1]

Born in 1751, the son of a French Protestant émigré to Rhode Island, Stephen Decatur had been a merchant captain before the war. Shortly before the birth of his son, Stephen Decatur, Jr., in 1779, he had decided to go a privateering like many in the maritime trade. Though Stephen, Jr., was destined to leave his own blazing historic marker in the pages of American history as a U.S. Navy commander during the Barbary Wars and War of 1812, Stephen, Sr., would pave the way as a captain of several incredibly successful privateers, most notably the galley *Retaliation*, the sloop *Comet*, the 150-ton brig *Fair American*, and finally in the ship *Royal Louis*.[2]

Fair American was first commissioned for a four-month cruise and bonded for $10,000 at Philadelphia on April 20, 1780. Armed with sixteen guns, and manned by an oversized crew of 130 seamen and marines (to accommodate the many prizes expected to be taken), she was unable to slip down the Delaware until the end of May. During the next three months, however, Decatur would more than make up for lost time. Indeed, his successes would become almost legendary. Soon after leaving Philadelphia, in company of the Massachusetts privateer *Jack*, Nathan Brown, and the Pennsylvania privateer *Argo*, Stephen Snell, *Fair American* captured her first prize, the sloop *Swallow*, a 70-ton vessel bound from Madeira for New York laden with wine and 30,000 ropes of onions, pork, beef, bread, powder, and ball. The sloop was taken without incident as she was armed with only four 3-pounders and an equal number of swivels. After escorting the capture into the Delaware, Decatur was soon back on the Atlantic cruising in company with *Argo* along the Jersey coast and then in the rich and dangerous hunting grounds off Sandy Hook and New York Bay, where they began to hammer the enemy's trade and supply vessels. Almost immediately, he fell in with a large ship carrying 400 tons of dry goods and fruit bound for the city. As before, in what would become almost a ritual, the captured vessel, with a small prize crew aboard, was escorted as far as Cape May to prevent recapture and then sent alone to Philadelphia. Off New York again, having parted company with

Argo but rejoined by *Jack*, *Fair American* soon took a schooner laden with china and, as before, accompanied her to Cape May before sending her upriver.[3]

After the delivery of their captives at Philadelphia, each of the prize crews would secure passage back down to Cape May where they rejoined the privateer. The downriver trip, usually in a small, unarmed vessel, could be hazardous. Owing to the recent and increasingly frequent infestation of the lower Delaware by small groups of Loyalist whaleboat partisan raiders that had, by late 1779, begun to plague the region, the threat of attacks had accelerated to dangerous levels by the spring of 1780.[4]

Predatory raids and counter-raids by both patriots and Loyalists were, of course, nothing new along the Jersey coastline, especially in the Raritan region where concentrations of the Crown's supporters were especially strong. But the greatest threat most recently began to emerge from New York. In April 1780, General Sir Henry Clinton, urged by Lord George Germain to utilize the King's faithful subjects within British lines to annoy the seacoasts of provinces in revolt and to distress rebel trade, authorized the establishment of a Board of Directors of the Associated Loyalists, under William Franklin. The board's mission was to preside over Loyalist interests, coordinate their social and political activities, and raise funds (through lotteries), which, assisted by the British, also helped provide money, arms, and small sailing craft for paramilitary operations. The access to watercraft (mostly whaleboats, usually thirty-five feet or so in length, as well as other small vessels) operating out of shallow rivers, inlets, and marshlands on the coast, provided the Associated Loyalists, or "refugees" as they soon became known, with the means of conducting amphibious operations in remote coastal areas from the shores of Long Island to the Delaware Capes. The news of the danger was first reported at New London, Connecticut, and quickly spread. "The British government of New-York have issued proclamations," one such report said, "offering the refugees there to supply them with armed boats, provisions, and warlike stores, all at free cost, to go and plunder on the rebel shores (as they call them) and to cruise in the rivers, to distress the persons who live near the water. This is a late resolution at New-York. It is said near 100 boats are collected at Hunting-bay, and that many people are moving their effects from the towns on the sound." By the time *Fair American* sailed, refugees, in a spate of unbridled guerilla warfare, had already begun to turn the New Jersey shores into a scene of "waste and havoc."[5]

For *Fair American*'s prize crews, in their voyages up and down the Delaware, the hazard had increased with each trip, and occasionally turned nasty. On one such occasion, twenty prize crewmen returning to Cape May embarked at Philadelphia aboard a small schooner, unarmed except for a single short four-pounder brass gun acquired in the city and intended for the quarterdeck of *Fair American*. Because the piece was to be used primarily to contest any boarding at close quarters, no round shot had been sent, only empty cartridges which were to be filled with musket balls once aboard ship. When an enemy refugee boat was observed approaching between the New Jersey and Delaware shores, the prize crewmen rushed to lash the gun to the bitts as best they could with a rope, as there was neither gun mount nor carriage aboard. A charge was placed, but lacking a ball or a canister of grapeshot, a bag of old nails, hooks, and thimbles was jammed in, filling the piece to the muzzle. As the Loyalist turned to come alongside, the privateersmen let fly with their one and only shot. The enemy boat, which was less than eight or ten yards distance, was brutally raked fore and aft. "It came on them, unexpected, like thunder," recalled one of the prize crewmen. "The shrieks and moans were terrible. She pulled 26 or 28 oars. Laying for a minute in that situation, and the few that remained unhurt saw our deck full of men, expecting we were well armed, we saw about 4 or 5 got out their oars and pulled away from the Jarsey [*sic*] shore. The gun carried away the lashing and fell over the opposite side of the deck, however it was not wanted more. The following day the schooner arrived at Cape May, where Mrs. Decatur resided with her infant son when her husband was at sea." Soon the privateer returned with another prize, and picked up the men.[6]

It was quite clear that infestation of the coast by refugee vessels had become a serious problem. One incident illustrates the point even better. While patrolling off the entrance to New York Bay on May 28 at about 6 a.m., *Fair American* spied two small sails standing in for Sandy Hook. The Americans took up pursuit immediately, and quickly began to overtake their prey, when

> . . . at 8 o'clock the smallest sail bore away, and we stood after a small river schooner which we took, she proved to be a prize loaded with Indian corn, taken by a whale boat of 34 feet long, open decked, called the Lewistown Revenge, commanded by __ Hall, mounting one blunderbuss in her bow, one swivel in her head, and fifteen muskets, with 13 men; we then gave her chace, and took her about 10 o'clock: He has a proper commission and has been on our coast since the 13th of March, during which time he has taken 28 prizes; loaded with different produce for the Philadelphia market, and is the boat that has so much annoyed the trade of our bay and river this spring. We send her up with the Captain and people; and her prize this tide.[7]

A few days later, *Fair American* put out again, this time sailing on a southerly course. As she was approaching Charleston, South Carolina, on a fine, moonlit night, her lookout spied a large sail to the leeward. "We bore up and run down so close till we could perceive her ports," recalled crewman Jacob Nagle. "She proved a 44-gun ship. We hauled our wind, and she made sail after us, but we were soon out of sight of her, and shortly after fell in with an English brig laden with merchandise. Sent her to Philadelphia."[8]

Fair American was not clear of enemy warships, however, and on the following day had the misfortune to fall in with two massive Royal Navy ships-of-the-line, each carrying seventy-four guns. Suddenly, a dead calm draped itself across the sea before *Fair American* could flee. Decatur crowded on all the sail he had in a desperate attempt to escape, but without a breath of wind there seemed to be no hope. Then, unexpectedly—and much to the horror of her crew—the privateer began to drift directly towards the enemy. "We then perceived why we neared them so fast," Nagel later wrote in his memoirs. "The line of battle ships, knowing there was a strong current, let go a ketch [*sic*, kedge] anchor, and riding by it, we not observing the current, was drifting down upon them, and if a breeze had not sprung up would have been under their guns in 15 minutes. We left them and run north to cruise off New York."[9]

Decatur's run of good luck seemed endless despite numerous close calls. Captures continued to be made and sent towards the Delaware River and the Pennsylvania and

Jersey ports with uncanny frequency. When *Fair American* finally turned northward again, now accompanied by no less than three prizes—a large ship laden with dry goods and West Indian fruit, a brig laden with rum, and a sloop also carrying the same spirituous beverage—she soon faced yet another encounter with an enemy warship. As the privateer and her gaggle of prizes neared port, she sighted a British frigate that gave chase. As the warship approached this time, the American welcomed her not with heels but a round of cannon fire. As Decatur had hoped, the frigate's skipper proved all too eager to capture the more lightly armed rebel and took up hot pursuit. *Fair American*, however, being a far faster vessel, hove to until the enemy came nearer, fired another round at her, and made all sail. The procedure was repeated several times as the rebel cruiser methodically drew the frigate ever further away from the prizes. By this maneuver, the two headmost prizes were able to escape. Unfortunately, finally realizing that he had been tricked and finding he would come up entirely empty handed if he kept chasing the faster privateer, the enemy commander altered course and made directly for the sloop. This vessel, which was well astern of the other two prizes, was soon recaptured.[10] But two saves out of three wasn't bad!

Soon after putting about again for Cape May, Decatur fell in with another incredibly successful McClenachan-owned 16-gun privateer brig named *Holker*, Captain Roger Keane commanding. *Holker* was already one of the most famous privateers of the Revolution, having earned a massive fortune for everyone involved with her. When she joined *Fair American*, she was fresh from her most recent capture, a 16-gun ship with seventy-two hands, laden with 400 hogsheads of spirits, 100 barrels of cotton, some coffee, and other items, which had just been sent into the Delaware. Now, with this party of sea raiders operating together, the stage was set for a bit of high theater. After capturing their first prize together off Sandy Hook on August 2, the 100-ton brig *Gloucester*, William Stokes, bound from Madeira to New York with wine, and then escorting their prize to the Delaware Capes, they were joined by another sea raider, the 12-gun Pennsylvania brig *Enterprize*. Commanded by Captain Peter Day, *Enterprize* was owned by Thomas Leaming of Cape May and John Murray of Philadelphia. The three commanders decided forthwith to sail together as a squadron.[11]

On August 7, the deadly trio fell in with the King's mail ship *Mercury Packet*, bound from Falmouth, England, for New York. Decatur may not have reckoned for an easy conquest for the ship, commanded by Captain Joseph Dillon and mounting sixteen 6-pounders and four big 18-pounders, was far more heavily armed than his own. He nevertheless resolved to make the attempt, no doubt encouraged by the backup that might be provided by the other privateers sailing somewhere close by. Well aware that sheer aggressiveness often served to intimidate a crew that had little to lose but their lives in a fight, he decided to run alongside the enemy and engage.[12]

As *Fair American* pulled up parallel to her quarry, Decatur ordered a broadside unleashed and was immediately answered in kind. It took only a second broadside, however, to evince surrender. Captain Dillon, unwilling to take on not just one but three American warships, ordered his colors struck, albeit not before the mail was tossed into the sea. Seaman Nagle took apparent delight in Dillon's excuse for the surrender. "We could hear the screeches of women on board," he said. "When boarding we found seven ladies on board going to New York to their husbands that were officers in the British Army. Capt[ain] Decatur permitted them to remain in their own cabins and took good care they should not be molested, and when brought to Philadelphia, he got permission from Congress to send them to New York to their husbands. The English capt[ain] said he would not have struck if it had not been for the ladies being on board."[13]

For the rest of the month, the trio of privateers (with *Enterprize* being replaced by the privateer *General Greene* about mid-month) literally frolicked off Sandy Hook, taking prize after prize after prize in a riot of conquest. The schooner *Nancy* succumbed on August 7, followed by the schooner *Arbuthnot* on the following day, then in quick succession came the schooners *Poplar*, *Gage*, *Lewis*, the British privateer *Queen Charlotte*, the ship *Lady Margaret*, the sloop *Dispatch*, and several unidentifieds. Two of the prizes were recaptures of British prizes, and one of the unidentifieds was retaken by British prisoners on board while en route up the Delaware. The majority of prizes were libeled and sold at public vendue in Philadelphia.[14]

During the latter part of the long cruise, Decatur began to make a practice of escorting most of his prizes in, at least as far as Cape May Channel, leaving little to chance for an enemy recapture. Returning through the increasingly refugee-infested, shoal-filled waters of the Delaware, however, was now about as hazardous as any action at sea. On one occasion, while coming in with a captured brig abreast of her, presumably through the Cape May Channel favored by most privateersmen, Decatur discovered that the prize drew far more water than his own ship and did his best to give the prize more room to maneuver. Unfortunately, in so doing his own ship became stranded on a shoal. There was at the time a heavy, rolling surf, which caught the privateersmen by surprise and suddenly hove their ship on her side. Fortunately, Decatur had ordered the guns well secured; had they given way, as aboard the hard-luck *Triton*, they might well have stove open her bulwarks. All hands were ordered to the weather side, and all sails were set in a desperate effort to drive her over the reef of sand. Suddenly, a heavy swell followed by frothy surf hurled the ship across and again into her own element. As she was light, there was little damage. "We filled her sails and got into the channel and run up to the prize at the anchoring ground."[15]

Shoally waters and enemy cruisers were not the only dangers encountered in privateering. On August 31, as *Fair American*, *General Greene*, and *Holker* were returning to Philadelphia to replenish their water, provisions, and stores, and to pick up prize crews, they spied a pair of Continental Navy ships in the river. The two warships proved to be the frigates *Trumbull*, Captain James Nicholson, and *Deane*, Captain Samuel Nicholson, both preparing to sail, but desperately in need of men. The incoming privateers were stopped off Reedy Island by boats sent out from the frigates and then boarded by press gangs. Against the protests of the commanders of all three privateers, the ships were stripped of men, twenty-one from *Fair American*, nineteen or twenty from *Holker*, and an equal number from *General Greene*.[16]

With his crew reduced in number, from deployments to bring prizes in and now by impressments by the Continental Navy, to such an extent as to be crippled, there seemed little choice for Decatur but to inform the brig's owners and appeal for assistance. On September 2, Charles Miller, one the ship's principals, submitted a petition to

Congress seeking the return of the impressed seamen. "That the Privateer Fair American" he wrote,

> having fitted out here on three Months Cruize Against the enemies of the United States from the 25th July last, that said privateer having within the said time been very fortunate in taking Prizes which she was obliged to man in order to send them into Port, and by which reason the said Privateer became at last so scarce of hands as to Oblige her to return up the River in Order to take her Men, Provisions &c again on board.
>
> That before said Privateer could get her men & Provisions on board the frigates *Trumbull* & *Deane* sent their Boats along side and took out Twenty one Men which if said men cannot be got again it will break up the Cruize to the great detriment of the Owners, your Petitioners therefore pray that an Order may be Issued for the delivery of said men, that the said Privateer may be enabled to pursue her Cruize. . . . That said frigates have likewise been on board the Privateer Brig *Holker* which is exactly under the same circumstances with the *Fair American* and took nineteen or twenty out of her, she being likewise detained for want of said men, and pray that an Order may be Issued for the delivery of said men.[17]

With the fame of *Fair American*, *Holker*, and even *Enterprize* already becoming etched in the public psyche, it would appear Congress was not prone to delay on referring the petition to the Board of Admiralty with directions to take action. Thus, on the same day as they received the petition, the Board instructed Captain Nicholson to release the men and return them to the two privateers. At the same time, they advised Miller of their actions by letter, enclosing a copy of the orders to Nicholson, with the caveat that the privateer owner was to personally deliver it to the captain or have one of the privateer officers do it. As the two frigates were probably already underway, it seemed clear that the move was designed to frustrate the return of the seamen. If such was the case, it apparently had little impact, for by the third week in September *Fair American* was again ready to sail. *Holker* followed a week later, with specific orders, probably from owner Blair McClenachan, who also was part owner of *Fair American*, for the two ships to cruise together between New York and Charlestown, South Carolina.[18]

• • •

About October 1, not long after setting sail again, Decatur took the brigantine *Fame*, Moses Griffin, his first prize of the new cruise. Joined soon afterwards by *Holker*, the two privateers then took the brig *Rodney*, Captain Wignall, on October 7. Ironically, on the following day they captured another brig, also called *Rodney*, William Ribbons, bound from Plymouth, England, to Charlestown, with brandy, wine, and cordage. Soon afterwards, the Scottish thirty-four-man brig *Richard*, William Robinson, carrying a pair of 9-pounders and eight 16-pounders, bound from Glasgow for Charlestown, also succumbed, having proved no match for the faster, more heavily-armed Americans. All four vessels were sent to New Jersey or Pennsylvania ports. On October 14, off Charleston Bar, the

Pennsylvania sea raiders met a more than worthy opponent in the Scottish brig *Richmond*. Decatur had already learned of *Richmond*'s presence from *Richard* and was ready for another haul. The brig's skipper was unaware of *Holker*'s presence in the area (for she was some distance beyond the horizon). Captain Robinson, believing his consort, the well-armed and manned *Richmond*, could easily take *Fair American* in a fair single ship-to-ship fight, loudly boasted of her nearby proximity and dared the Americans to fight her.[19]

It was 10 p.m. when *Fair American* finally sighted *Richmond*. The Scotsman was commanded by Captain George Jameson, a toe-to-toe fighter, and manned by a crew of seventy-five. With his two-decker mounting sixteen guns, two 9-pounders, eight 6-pounders, and six 4-pounder cohorns, Jameson held a slight advantage in weight of metal in a single-ship combat and a distinct superiority in elevation. It is uncertain if Decatur knew just where his own consort was, but perhaps cognizant that the sound of gunfire would be heard at some distance, he determined to take on *Richmond* regardless of the disparity between his own and the enemy's force. "She being a lofty ship and the sea running high for our low vessel," Nagle later recorded, "she had the advantage of us." The Scotsman kept on her course with steering sails both low and aloft on both sides, having the wind right aft. Yet, *Fair American* had the advantage of speed and superior maneuverability, which Decatur knew how to use. Evening was settling in, so without any delay, he proceeded to run around the enemy under two topsails to deliver a stinging pair of broadsides, which killed one and wounded three before darkness forced a halt to the action. He knew that if the quarry didn't escape during the darkness, the contest could be resumed in the morning. He refused to allow Jameson the chance, and closely shadowed his ship throughout the evening.[20]

That night, *Fair American*'s crew received a meal of bread, cheese, and grog and lay at their quarters, prepared to fight at a moment's notice. At dawn, Decatur asked his company if they were still willing to engage an enemy of superior firepower. "They gave three cheers and said they would never leave her." Soon afterwards, they spoke *Holker*, which had just come up. The two privateers immediately agreed to cooperate and quickly ran up on both sides of the slower, more heavily laden enemy. Though now outgunned, outmanned, and outsailed, the brave Scotsman refused to surrender. Once resumed, the engagement became as hot as any Decatur had ever experienced. By 10 a.m., *Fair American*'s foremast and mainmast had each been hit in two places, and her rigging had been severely shredded. *Holker*, too, had suffered, but with only one man killed and another wounded, she required only superficial mending. Still, this was no ordinary challenge, for the Scotsman's officers and crew had proved not only brave and resolute but superb marksmen as well.[21]

After an hour and a half of close action, the two privateers were obliged to haul off and patch their wounds. Decatur ordered the masts fished and the rigging repaired, as did the commander of *Holker*. *Richmond* continued on under full sail, persistently struggling to put as much distance between herself and her assailants as possible, but in vain. By early afternoon, the privateers, having rushed their repairs, were once again off in full pursuit and closing fast upon the chase. Within just a short time they had again caught up with their prey and, like a pair of wolves circling for the kill, resumed the action. It wasn't until 1 p.m. that *Fair American* was finally able to run along the starboard side of the Scotsman, with *Holker* dogging her quarter.

Nagle tersely described the action that followed: "Though she was under full sail, low and aloft, we shot ahead under our two topsails, jib, and mainsail, and bore up across her bows and raked her fore and aft. The enemy shooting a head we gave her a broad side on the starboard side. The enemy continuing her course, we fell under her stern and raked her with several broad sides. At length she struck her colors." The final encounter had lasted forty-five minutes. The prize was immediately boarded. The brave captain, chief mate, and second mate had been killed in the fight, leaving only the boatswain to carry on. Yet, all on board had exhibited unvarnished valor. One passenger, a British officer, had stood fully exposed on the quarterdeck throughout the battle firing a musket, though he could have easily claimed sanctuary below. Captain Keane reported only one man killed aboard *Holker*.[22]

The Americans were undoubtedly stunned but delighted when boarding crews from both privateers first set foot aboard their prize. They quickly discovered that the ship alone was valued at £175,000 sterling, and carried not only a chest of silver plate, and two boxes of gold watches, but also a hold filled with a profusion of dry goods. And there was wine, wine, and more wine, "wine between decks, and all the boats full of wine, the quarter deck stowed with hampers of cheese, and between every gun in the waist, pipes of wine."[23]

Despite the temptation to celebrate their victory, the privateersmen were all business. Decatur dispatched ten of his best men to make repairs to *Richmond*. With his own vessel short of water and provisions, it was his intention to transfer whatever was aboard the prize to resupply his own larder and water casks, but nature dictated otherwise. An old enemy appeared, one that was far more powerful than a fleet of line-of-battle ships. Before the transfer could be undertaken, a fierce gale sprang up and forced the two privateersmen to lie to, their great prize being higher out of the water than themselves. Decatur and the commander of *Holker* decided to set *Richmond* and her prize crew before the wind on their own, and make for the Delaware Capes.[24]

The tempest continued for several days, tossing about the light privateers with frightful disdain. The two ships soon became separated. Aboard *Fair American*, Decatur ordered the topmasts struck, and a number of guns and empty water casks to be filled with seawater and moved to the hold to lower the ship's center of gravity to prevent capsizing. With ninety-seven prisoners aboard, including seven ship captains taken from recent captures, provisions were nearly used up, there being nothing left but "2 or 3 bags of bread dust," a quart of water, and a half pint of flour per man. The flour, unfortunately, was useless as no fresh water could be spared to mix it into cakes. By the time the gale had finally ceased and a new course was set for the Delaware Capes, the water situation had become critical and the weary crew was becoming surly.[25]

Possibly as a punishment for violation of his rationing orders (the record is quiet on the subject), the inventive Decatur ordered that a gun barrel be placed at the top the foremast. For each man to receive his ration of water, he would be required to climb to the foretop, retrieve the barrel and bring it down to the scuttle butt on the quarterdeck, suck his ration through the touchhole, and then return it before he could have another. The creative but severe rationing method was quickly abandoned, however, as many of the crewmen were so weak—some near death—that they could not suck at all, much less ascend the ratlines to reach the foretop. Decatur ordered rations cut to a pint per man.[26]

As the ship pressed north, she encountered yet another horrific gale, just as she had begun to skirt the coast of Cape Hatteras, North Carolina. The storm continued without letup for several days, driving the privateer amidst the famously perilous, ship-killing shoals. Continuous soundings were taken, day and night. Nagle was convinced that "if we had not been so light and drew so little water, we must have perished." Fortunately, the gale finally ended and a light breeze sprang up from the southward, pushing the badly bruised privateer northward toward the Delaware. Then, just as she came abreast of the treacherous Hen and Chicken Shoals and everyone rejoiced at the sighting of Cape Henlopen Lighthouse, a freak northwest wind suddenly laid her on her beam-ends. Water instantly began to pour through the main hatchways. Decatur coolly ordered the mast cut away to help right her. It was an order more easily given then carried out. In desperation, the enfeebled crewmen hacked at the mast for their lives. Before they were half way through, the sails gave way on their own and were shredded into pieces. Miraculously the privateer righted herself. By now the gale had increased even more, driving the ship ever closer to the deadly shoals, upon which countless unfortunates had come to grief over the previous century. All four main anchors as well as a kedge anchor were let go, and the topmasts were struck to help stabilize her. Suddenly and mercifully the winds shifted, now driving the privateer seaward.[27]

A View of Lighthouse at Cape Henlopen, Taken at Sea, August 1780. The light announced to mariners their proximity to the ship-killing shoals, such as the Hen and Chickens, which laced the southern entrance to Delaware Bay. Not all evaded them, as evidenced by the remains of a shipwreck in the illustration. Reproduction from *The Columbian Magazine, or Monthly Miscellany,* February 1788. Courtesy Rare Book and Special Collections Division, Library of Congress.

For the next three days, the tempest continued, pushing the hapless cruiser this way and that off the Delaware and New Jersey coasts. Soon, every drop of fresh water aboard had been expended, with the crews subsisting primarily off rainwater. Finally, the skies cleared and *Fair American*, propelled by a southerly zephyr, again made for the Delaware. Decatur put in at Cape May to obtain fresh water, revivify his half-dead men, and briefly visit his wife and infant son. Then it was on to Philadelphia, but even the short trip up the river, unfortunately, would be fraught with hazards.[28]

With a fair wind and a lovely moonlit night to assist her, the battered privateer, from all outward appearances, looked to be little more than "a distressed merchantman." Her topgallant had been struck, and her ports were down. All of her guns had been housed fore and aft, and in the evening moon's glow she appeared to be a perfectly helpless and nearly derelict. Suddenly a refugee "pickarooning" boat from New York, quite probably the 30-ton *Restoration*, was observed standing directly for her. The enemy vessel, it was later learned, "had done much mischief to the small craft" in Delaware Bay and had herself been bound upriver for Marcus Hook intending to cut out a flour-laden brig, when she encountered the American privateer. When within hailing distance, obviously mistaking Decatur's bedraggled brig for a defenseless merchantman, the stranger shouted: "Strike, you damned rebels," and fired a swivel gun to accentuate the order.

Luckily, all of Decatur's hands were on deck. "Aye," he shouted with a loud voice, and then ordered two guns to be cast loose. The Loyalist, hearing the orders, instantly realized that he wasn't dealing with a mere freight hauler and began to shear off towards the shore and into the night. The privateer pursued. Almost simultaneously, the two vessels ran aground. Decatur nevertheless ordered one of his guns unlimbered and brought to bear on the enemy. Suddenly, out of the blackness another vessel, a sloop, suddenly appeared coming down beside the privateer. Decatur ordered a 6-pound shot fired at her, which quickly brought her alongside in submission. The sloop, laden with dry goods from Philadelphia, proved to be a prize recently taken by the Loyalist.[29]

Twenty men and a 6-pounder were quickly transferred to the recaptured prize. Once the gun was aboard, the sloop immediately set off under oars to engage the stranded schooner. Then she too ran aground. At that precise moment, Decatur opened up with two of his own on his erstwhile assailant, and after several well-placed shots, heard a cry for quarter coming from the dark silhouette of the enemy ship. The Philadelphia sloop, which by then had managed to get off the shoal, soon came alongside the foe, boarded, and took her. It was then that the prize crew discovered that the Loyalist had captured and placed the sloop owner's own son in irons below deck. Tragically, one of the shots from *Fair American* had killed him, and another had taken the leg off one of the refugee crew. All in the darkness of a Delaware night.[30]

At Marcus Hook, many of the privateersmen went ashore to make their way up to Philadelphia on foot to avoid Continental Navy press gangs that were said to be roaming about the waterfront in boats and afoot. The seamen, no doubt, were eager to get home, though the voyage had been inordinately successful. During the two cruises of *Fair American* under Decatur's command, they had taken no less than twenty prizes. Upon reaching the city, however, they were dismayed to learn that the total had been somewhat reduced. A British cruiser had retaken one prize, laden with silk. But the worst news concerned the hard-fought *Richmond*. Her own hands had managed to overcome the prize crew, apparently with the assistance of at least one or two turncoats among the Americans, and recaptured their ship. "The chief of the men being English," Nagle later wrote, "they hoisted the jolly boat out, though full of shot holes, and put the two prize masters into her with some water, bread, and salt beef and set them adrift and made for Charles Town. Having a fair wind, they got in. The owners that she was consign'd to seized the ship and gave them [the original crew] five guineas each for bringing her into port." Two of the former *Fair American* men who had been instrumental in the recapture were eventually to fall into American hands and were tried in the Admiralty Court at Philadelphia on April 23, 1781. One of the men, Nicholas Coleman, was acquitted. The other, Thomas Wilkinson, was convicted and sentenced to death by hanging near the city.[31]

As the news of the incredible triumphs and travails of the privateer *Fair American* began to circulate, even more stunning news from Boston arrived in Trenton in the form of a letter dated August 8. The letter detailed the odyssey of a British convoy fleet of thirty-seven ships en route from Great Britain to Quebec that had met with "some interruption on their passage off the Western Islands." Before departing England the shipmasters had been assured that all rebel privateers operating in New England waters had been destroyed in a recent campaign on the Penobscot River in Maine, and "the risk was nothing." The insurance underwriters had received but a ten percent premium. Then, while the convoy was en route, a French ship-of-the-line fell in with them and captured twelve vessels, all of which were reportedly sent to the West Indies as prizes. Soon after the shattered remnants of the convoy reached North American waters, a wolf pack of New England privateers from Salem, Newburyport, Boston, and Cape Ann captured eighteen more, four of which were provision ships, and the rest bearing miscellaneous cargoes. The remaining seven vessels, laden with military ordnance, managed to reach the St. Lawrence River but were believed to have fallen in with a 30-gun Connecticut ship called *Deane*, and two others. It was declared to be the "richest and most capital stroke made on the British trade this war." And the New Englanders had carried it out.[32]

The successes of the friendly New England rivals mattered little to Decatur, who was soon off in command of yet another ship, the 22-gun *Royal Louis*. The *Fair American*, after time for refit, set sail on yet another adventure under the short-lived command of one Joseph Jackways, who had taken over on December 9, 1780, but would die at sea. On May 22, 1781, *Fair American* would sail yet again, this time under the command of Captain Phineas Eldridge of Philadelphia, who, with such a perfect and swift vessel under his direction, was enormously successful. On one such expedition in the fall of 1781, he took at least six prizes, four of which belonged to an inward convoy of ninety vessels headed for New York and Charleston. The prizes sent into Philadelphia, it was reported, "will prove very valuable, as their cargoes consist of a variety of articles, such as cheese, butter, porter, beer, flour, ironmongery, dry goods, &c." One of the captures belonging to the convoy, a London ship of twelve guns, "the loss of which will be greatly felt by the enemy," was sent into Egg Harbor. Before all was said and done, *Fair American*, under Eldridge's command, had, by herself or in concert at various times with *Holker* and Gideon Olmstead's Connecticut privateer *Raven*, taken ten prizes. Then, on January 2, 1782, during a sortie from Delaware Bay, her good fortune evaporated when she fell in with and was taken by HMS *Garland*, Captain Charles Chamberlayne.[33]

It seemed an inglorious end for the terror of the seas, so remarkable for the depredations she had committed on the British trade over the previous two years, always escaping the enemy by her swift sailing capabilities and worthy commanders and crews. She was escorted with some pomp into New York, where her capture was regaled in the New York press. Tried and condemned in the New York Admiralty Court, she was readily snapped up by British and Loyalist investors, refitted, and sent to sea once again to leave another distinctive mark on history. But this time as a Loyalist privateer.

–XVIII–

Whaleboats and Refugees

"The freebooters on our side have been extraordinarily lucky."

The town of Toms River was a small, nondescript hamlet, ensconced on the banks of a river, from which its name was derived, that drained into Barnegat Bay and opposite Cranberry Inlet. Had the Revolution not interceded, this relatively remote settlement, in a district strongly divided in loyalties, might have passed peacefully and entirely unnoticed in the history books. Before the war, its diminutive population, like other inhabitants along the sparsely occupied New Jersey coastal area, had derived their livelihoods from oystering, fishing, milling, hauling lumber, and occasional smuggling. With the onset of war, it was to become an important center for salt production and privateering. The dwellings were simple. A bridge crossing the river joined the town with buildings owned by several townsmen, both Whigs and Tories, engaged in salt production. A warehouse stood nearby, used for salt storage from the myriad salt works erected at various locals in the region, both major and minor, as well as for provisions for workers engaged in production and transportation of the commodity. Such major operations as the Pennsylvania state salt works at Toms River, the Union Salt Works at Squam, another at Shark River, and a fourth at Newlin's factory on Barnegat Bay were indeed dependent upon both adequate land and water shipment capabilities. And Toms River was the hub of it all.[1] As a consequence, from the very beginning of the war, the tempo of life and industry there had accelerated noticeably. As one historian of coastal New Jersey noted:

> Toms River, for such a small village, was evidently quite a busy, lively place, between the militia, the Refugees and the arrival and departure of privateers and their prizes; the arrival of boats and teams with salt from the several works along the bay; the departure of teams for West Jersey with salt, oysters, fish, etc., and their return with merchandise; the visits of business men from different parts of the State to purchase captured vessels or their cargoes, and the rafts or scows from the sawmills with lumber for vessels to carry to places in the State when they could run with safety.[2]

Cranberry Inlet, nearly opposite Toms River, which had opened up about 1740, was now deemed by some as possibly one of the best inlets on the New Jersey coast, second only to Little Egg Harbor, for the use of privateers as a safe base of operations and as a reception center for prizes. From there, lookouts could monitor the coastal shipping lanes, and especially the arrivals and departures of vessels at New York, permitting interdiction of fat enemy supply ships bound in and troop ships bound out. The town's location made it equally valuable as a hub for salt production and distribution. The Pennsylvania state-owned salt works, erected by Thomas Savadge under a contract authorized on June 24, 1776 by the Pennsylvania Council of Safety, had cost £400 to build, but wasn't the only such site nearby. Savadge loaded

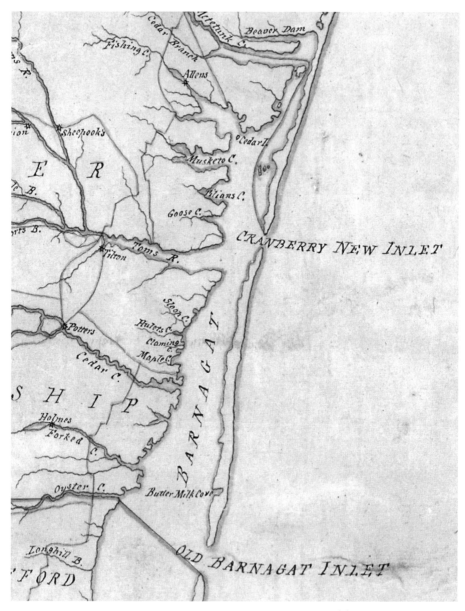

Cranberry Inlet, opened during a storm in 1740, no longer exists, but during the Revolution provided egress to the salt works at the town of Toms River, and a forward base for both American privateers and whaleboat warriors. The New Jersey coast between Old Barnegat Inlet, Toms River, and Cranberry Inlet ca. 1769, detail from *Three maps* [i.e. map on 3 sheets] *of northern New Jersey, with reference to the boundary between New York and New Jersey.* [1769?]. Courtesy Geography and Map Division, Library of Congress.

his product at Coates' Point, at the juncture of Barnegat Bay and Toms River, some 600 yards from the river and nearly half a mile from the bay. Other establishments in the area included one founded some distance north of the point, and another at Goodluck Point on the south side of the river. Salt produced at these works was transported by boat to the town, where it was stored until it could be transported overland by wagon to various destination points.[3]

That Toms River would draw enemy attentions, particularly those of Loyalist refugees expelled from the region, is not surprising. The town itself was usually weakly defended by twelve- and four-month militiamen from the county, whose duties also included checking contraband trade between Tory sympathizers and the British and Loyalists at New York, and to assist privateers and prizes brought into the inlet. Self-defense, however, was not enough, especially when the perceived or actual threat of attack seemed imminent. On November 2, 1776, an officer and twenty-five soldiers from Pennsylvania and a pair of howitzers were dispatched to occupy the works and storehouse to protect its property. It would not be the last time.[4]

Little attention was given by the British to the remote little hamlet in the months following the occupation of New York and solidification of the enemy's control of Manhattan Island and New York Bay. Indeed, not until 1777 would the first enemy depredations begin. They would remain a threat ever after. The first alarm came on January 27, 1777, as a small enemy sloop entered Cranberry Inlet. Another sloop, belonging to James Randolph and others, was promptly boarded "Chiefly by Tories . . . and the rest of them little better," with the intent of cutting her out of the inlet along with a prize schooner that lay nearby. Unable, for reasons unknown, to get the sloop underway, they were in the process of plundering the vessel when a party of militiamen arrived obliging the raiders to retire. On Monday, February 3, the raiders returned again, invested and occupied Randolph's home, then carried off the prize schooner's sails and rigging, which had been stored therein for safekeeping; they then fitted out the schooner and prepared her to sail. The following morning, as the raiders were getting underway, they ran aground near the Pennsylvania-owned salt works, opposite the town, where a small body of militiamen were ensconced; they promptly abandoned the prize. Unwilling to leave empty handed, they again descended upon Randolph's sloop, anchored near Good Luck Point, where another band of militiamen timidly watched them strip the vessel of sails and rigging and anything else they could carry, and then put out to sea unchallenged.[5]

Distressed by the vulnerability of the Toms River property, on February 5, the Pennsylvania Council of Safety dispatched a company of infantry and two cannon to protect the Pennsylvania salt works. Barracks were ordered to be erected, as well as an ammunition storage magazine for the men engaged under Savadge's direction. The Pennsylvania government requested that the New Jersey legislature permit their deferment from active militia duty as the work they were engaged in was of great importance to the war effort. Still, Thomas Savadge, belatedly reporting on the raid to the Pennsylvania Council of Safety on February 10, expressed his opinion that if the surrounding country were to be defended it would have to be by Continental troops or militia from another state, implying that the local militia was useless. He also recommended that one or two row galleys should be sent to protect Cranberry Inlet as well as those others on the coast. "I am in expectation of another Vissett from them," he concluded, "being informed that Colonel [John] Morris is preparing a strong party [of New Jersey Volunteers] to Come by land, & at the Same time two Tenders or a Galley are to come into the inlett. If this be true, the [salt] Works are gone and every thing else they please; for the people here Will Chiefly take part With them as soon as there Appears a Sufficient number to repel the few Militia that there is any dependence on."[6]

Robert Morris, Chairman of the Maritime Committee of Congress, was also informed of the threat and recommended that Captain John Rice and his Pennsylvania Navy row galley *Convention* be dispatched "not only to save the Salt Works untill a proper Land force can be appointed but wou'd also, probably be very usefull in retaking some of the Prizes the Men-of-war send along shoar for New York." Moreover, in case of an attack planned against Philadelphia, the vessel could be useful in intelligence gathering and could, if necessary, retire into the Delaware to assist in defense.[7]

The Pennsylvania Council of Safety, prompted by Savadge's and Morris's concerns, ordered the Pennsylvania Navy schooner *Delaware*, instead of *Convention*, to be fitted out and dispatched with all expedition to the Pennsylvania salt works, and "there to remain for the defence thereof, until further order from this Board." It would appear that neither *Convention* nor *Delaware* were actually dispatched to Toms River but relegated to cruising between Cape May and Egg Harbor and escorting incoming merchantmen to safety on the Delaware. In any event, British forces were soon occupied elsewhere, and by July 1777 would be engaged in a major move against Philadelphia via the Chesapeake.[8]

In early 1777, Toms River, like Little Egg Harbor a few months earlier, began to welcome prize vessels sent in by patriot privateers from other states. One of the first was the schooner *Popes Head*, which had been captured by the privateer *Sally and Joseph*, William Rhodes, owned by John Innes Clarke and Joseph Nightingale, of Providence, Rhode Island, which was apparently employing the town as a base, and James Randolph as prize master.[9]

That loyalties of the town's inhabitants, like those of a significant portion of coastal New Jersey, were divided at the beginning of the war was not surprising. A few Loyalists had left early on to support the Crown, while others simply remained silent as in many other towns and hamlets in the region, hoping for an early resolution to the conflict, but generating distrust and suspicion between neighbors and former friends. Toms River was no exception. In late July 1777, as General Howe's 15,000 troops were departing from Staten Island aboard 260 ships for operations against a unknown target, no one on the American side had a clue as to their destination. Assuming there might be raids in the wake of the great armada, wherever it might be going, Pennsylvania dispatched another company under Captain John Nice to Toms River to protect its salt works. The British, of course, had a much grander target, Philadelphia.

Then the marauders began to arrive. On November 5, raiders destroyed the salt works at Shrewsbury. On Christmas Day, 1777, when Colonel John Morris, commander of a unit of the New Jersey Royal Volunteers, or Royalists as they called themselves, arrived at Toms River hell-bent on a demonstration of destroying the salt works and other facilities, he discovered many buildings with the letter "R" painted upon them. The painting had been carried out by one John Lawrence, on the orders of General Cortlandt Skinner, former Attorney General of New Jersey and organizer of the New Jersey Volunteers Regiment. It was inferred that some of the quiet supporters of the King had signed a pledge to refuse aid to the rebels and to remain steadfast with the Crown. As one historian later wrote: "The partnership business in some of the salt works above Toms River, which had their depot in the village, seems at times to have perplexed armed parties of both sides, as some owners were known active patriots, and others sympathized with the British." The salt warehouses remained. But the reprieve was only temporary, for on April 15, 1778, a British raiding party of 135 men, mostly royalists under a Captain Robertson, arrived and destroyed the salt works. The hamlet of Toms River, however, remained, and the salt works were soon rebuilt.[10]

Despite the temporary loss of the salt works, the utility of the town's location, as at Chestnut Neck on the Mullica, continued to attract privateering interests, albeit not in the same numbers. A month after the destruction of the salt works, rebel small boat operations emanating from Cranberry Inlet began sending prizes into Toms River. In May, three Connecticut galleys arrived at Cranberry Inlet with several captured vessels. And by August 10, no fewer than eight privateers were reported by the notorious Virginia Loyalist privateersman Bridger Goodrich as operating out of the hamlet. Goodrich, in command of a New York-based privateer named *Hammond*, was able to capture three of the eight, two of which were small New England schooners named *May Flower* and *Sally*, manned by forty-three men and armed with five carriage guns and ten swivels. The third was a 25-man Jerseyman commanded by Captain Joshua Studson (or Stutson), a resident of Toms River, armed with six carriage guns and ten swivels.[11]

As 1778 wore on, the proximity of Toms River to New York proved to be both a blessing and a curse. Naval encounters in and near Cranberry Inlet were no longer infrequent, and small boat guerilla plundering raids along the coast by both sides were becoming common and increasingly vicious. Often promulgated on the pretext of previous outrages committed against Loyalists by the rebels, sometimes with cause, outright murders or revenge killings were frequently committed by whaleboat raiders based at Sandy Hook and Long Island. Some notorious but successful partisan raiders, such as Captain "Bloody" John Bacon, Richard Lippincott and others, earned a short-lived notoriety, but did little to influence the course of the conflict, which in many ways was turning into a form of civil war in New Jersey.[12]

The Americans operating from Jersey shores were not without their own brand of whaleboat raiders. One of the most prominent was Captain William Marriner, a native of New Brunswick, New Jersey, and former tavern keeper in New York City, who first gained notoriety in the summer of 1778 by a daring revenge raid to secure British and Loyalist men of rank suitable for prisoner exchange. The dramatic foray on June 11, which set out from Matawan Creek, on the southwestern shores of Raritan Bay, did not go unreported in the patriot press.

> Wm. Marriner a volunteer with eleven men and Lieut. John Schenck of our militia went last Saturday evening from Middletown Point to Long Island in order to take a few prisoners from Flatbush, and returned with Major Moncrieff and Mr. Theophilus Bache [President of the New York Chamber of Commerce] (the worshipful Mayor [of New York] and Tormentor-General, David Mathews, Esq., who has inflicted on our prisoners the most unheard of cruelties and who was the principal object of the expedition being unfortunately in the city,) with four slaves and brought them to Princeton to be delivered to his Excellency the Governor.

Mr. Marriner with his party left Middletown Point on Saturday evening and returned at six o' clock the next morning having traveled by land and water above fifty miles and behaved with the greatest bravery and prudence.[13]

Such inland raids for Marriner (sometimes reported as Marun) became common, for both profit and practical purposes. On November 3, 1778, he conducted an incredibly daring foray from the Jersey shore with seven volunteers from Lord Stirling's forces, and landed in the heart of enemy territory at New Utrecht on Long Island. In a lightening raid the little band captured and carried off Simon and Jacques Cortelyu, "two famous tories in the enemy's line," as well as $5,000 in specie and other property. The prisoners, though soon paroled on their own recognizance at New Brunswick, were held for exchange for two citizens of New Jersey detained by the British.[14]

When not engaged in raiding inland, Marriner kept busy harassing enemy shipping with whaleboat crews, making the most of every favorable circumstance. When a fleet of small enemy vessels, having sought protection from the weather, lay anchored in a cluster in a cove behind Sandy Hook, he led a small flotilla of whaleboats across the bay, boarded and took three sloops and an armed schooner. Unfortunately adverse winds and tide pushed the sloops ashore. Unable to free them, Marriner stripped the three stranded prizes of cargo and appurtenances and set them ablaze. After nimbly escaping with the remaining prize schooner in hand, which was laden with a valuable cargo, his men received $1,000 dollars each in prize money for one night's work.[15]

• • •

The complexion of the privateer war on the middle Atlantic seaboard began to change, at first slowly, and then with resounding speed owing to many factors, not the least of which was the belated but critically important authorization by the Crown for Loyalist privateers to be fielded from New York and other British colonial bases. No longer were the American privateers operating on the Jersey coast obliged to dodge just the leviathans of the Royal Navy. They now had to deal with scores of enemy privateers, which transformed the matrix of the conflict. The very observant Hessian General Baurmeister, who kept tabs not only on events ashore, also dutifully reported to his superiors in Europe regarding the maritime scene, often relating to the new seaborne initiatives stemming from Loyalists. At the end of February 1779, he gleefully wrote:

The freebooters [Loyalist privateers] on our side have been extraordinarily lucky. Between the 1st of January and the 4th of February they have brought forty-six prizes into this harbor alone, and between the 16th of December and the 28th of January, twenty-two into the Bermudas. The warship Le Lion, forty guns, with a cargo of fourteen hundred hogsheads of tobacco surrendered to the frigate Maidstone, twenty-eight guns, after a three-hour engagement. The cargoes of most of the prizes are also of great value. On these prizes, moreover, we found some letters from Virginia which complain bitterly that almost all their ships fall prey to the British, that trade is completely paralyzed and that the plantations are desolate.

On the prizes taken in the Delaware were some letters from Deane to Mr.

Franklin in Paris, in which there are more specific complaints about the evil consequences of paper money, the resultant hopeless feeling among the Continental troops, the increasing discord among the members of Congress as well as among the highest generals of the army, the shortage of grain, flour, and salt, and the impossibility of erecting magazines . . .

The homeless loyalists who are still here are fitting out forty vessels to cruise under cover of six armed British ships and land anywhere between Rhode Island and Portsmouth and between here and Egg Harbor. They will keep all their booty without exception, which has greatly encouraged them, for all of them had been well-to-do, but have lost everything and are fortunate to be still alive.[16]

For the Americans the difficulties caused by the rise of Loyalist privateering was compounded by many other factors, including shortages of grain, the disastrous loss of crops in the South caused by excessive rains and weevils, a want of animal husbandmen and farmers owing to military call-ups, and the general demands of war itself. But mostly, it was the enemy privateers that made shipping "difficult if not impracticable," as several delegates to Congress reported on March 1, "being well informed, that upwards of one hundred private Cruisers (exclusive of large ships, Frigates, & Sloops of War belonging to the British Government) are now infesting the Coast, & make the Navigation more hazardous than it has heretofore been."[17]

As early as April 1779, it was reported that no fewer than sixty-two New York privateers were blockading Chesapeake Bay, and another thirty-two were patrolling off the Delaware Capes. Within a month, it was reported at New York that the merchants of Boston and Baltimore had given up insurance and were calling in their shipping. The Chesapeake had been sealed off and the Delaware was rarely open. For the British, control, at least partially, of both great estuary systems was proving rewarding indeed. Between April 8 and May 1, no fewer than forty-nine prizes, vessels that had attempted to break the privateer blockade, had been sent into New York by Loyalist ships, eleven into British-occupied Rhode Island, and sixteen into Bermuda. Five more had been brought into New York by refugee whaleboats operating under the newly formed Board of Associated Loyalists, which added some £22,000 sterling to their treasury. These prizes were being refitted as private armed ships for the protection of Loyalist trade and to escort their privateers a certain distance in departing and arriving in port.[18]

Though New York privateers and the whaleboat raiders of the Associated Loyalists appeared to be numerically in the ascendancy, their rise was not without difficulties, especially from their opposites. In June, from his perch in New York City, General Baurmeister lamented in one of his reports home:

If only their sea force [the rebels], instead of constantly increasing, were on the decline, too. . . . Of the one hundred and twenty-one New York privateers reported in April, to which some twenty have since been added, sixty-one have been captured. They have three strong frigates and five armed ships in addition to thirty-one privateers cruising between Sandy Hook and the Delaware and Chesapeake Bay. New London maintains nineteen privateers, one frigate, and six armed ships, while two frigates, nine armed ships, and twenty-two privateers are running out of Boston. These last are cruising along the Halifax route and capturing many ships.[19]

Three month later, he was still complaining, especially regarding the Loyalists, some of whom were proving to be less that trustworthy. "Since it has become known that Spain has entered the war," he wrote, "more New York privateers have been fitted out. However, greater care is being taken that only good loyalists receive permission to do this, for among the first, some forty went over to the rebels and did us considerable damage."[20]

By 1780, the refugee whaleboat raiders had become more sagacious than ever. In late February, a spirited party of fourteen refugees set off in a whaleboat, presumably from their base at Sandy Hook, bound for Egg Harbor. Upon arrival, they posed as patriot Jerseymen sent to scout out information regarding some British transports that had reportedly just sailed from New York. Hearing that potential prey were in the offing, a trio of rebel privateers then in Egg Harbor, accompanied by a pilot boat, hurriedly scurried out and headed up the coast eager for prizes. As soon as the privateers, the only armed craft in the region, were out of sight, the whaleboat sailed into the Delaware and ran into the seclusion of the Maurice River, in which they hid, awaiting any unwary vessel that happened by. The wait was short and their first victim proved to be a ship manned by a crew of nine, laden with Indian corn and flour. After releasing the crew on parole, they proceeded up the Delaware and captured nine more ships with the same cargoes, discharging each of the crewmen on parole. Lacking enough men to carry the prizes off, they were forced to burn eight of them. Soon afterwards, they captured three more small vessels also laden with food and engaged five of their crewmen to join them. With a total of five prizes, manned by only nineteen men, they set off for New York. Offsetting winds, however, obliged them to sail too close to Cape May, and one of the three smaller vessels was recaptured. However, on February 21, the remaining craft were able to find shelter in a local harbor to ride out the dirty weather before proceeding home. It was expected that in exchange for the fifty-six sailors that they had paroled, a like number of British seamen prisoners would be sent in from Elizabethtown.[21]

With such daring raids, the Delaware was growing more dangerous for American commerce every day, and the New Jersey coastal ports, such as Toms River and Little Egg Harbor, were becoming as important as ever, especially as launching places for their own small boat operations. In the spring of 1780, Captain Marriner launched another raid, this time on Loyalist shipping. On the night of April 18, in a single whaleboat manned by only nine men, he dropped down the Raritan River from New Brunswick and crossed the bay to Sandy Hook. Just inside the Hook, protecting the cove into which he had conducted his earlier raid, lay HMS *Volcano*, and nearby, under the protection of her guns, lay the brig *Black Snake*, formerly a Rhode Island privateer that had been taken by HMS *Galatea*. A prize crew of twenty, under Captain Cornelius French, manned the brig. Marriner approached her under muffled oars, quietly and without alarm, counting upon surprise to compensate for the disparity in numbers. In a rush, the Jerseymen were aboard, overwhelming and disarming the sleepy prize crew of twice their own number in a matter of seconds, and then locking them in the forecastle before a shot could be fired. Within a few seconds more, Marriner cut the brig's anchor cable. Slowly and silently she began to drift off into the darkness, even as the *Volcano* wistfully slept on.[22]

Soon afterwards, on April 20, Marriner fell in with and, after a "sharp resistance," captured the brig *Morning Star*, armed with six swivels and manned by a crew of thirty-three. The enemy lost three killed and five wounded during the action. Marriner carried his prizes into Little Egg Harbor, where both were promptly sold.[23]

Black Snake was purchased by a consortium of men from Monmouth County with principal shares owned by two ardent Whigs, James Randolph of Toms River and Captain Joshua Huddy, a resident of Colt's Neck, about five miles from the town of Freehold. Randolph and Huddy readily secured a privateer commission from Pennsylvania on August 18, 1780, armed the boat with a single gun, and manned her with a crew of fourteen, with Huddy in command, to go on a cruise, presumably out of Toms River. The cruise, apparently was less than successful, and *Black Snake* disappears from the record. As for Huddy, he resumed his command as a captain in the New Jersey militia and within a short time would play a key roll in a dramatic event that threatened to influence the very outcome of the American Revolution. But more on Huddy later.[24]

In the meantime, Marriner and other raiders like him continued to cause serious consternations amidst the enemy high command in New York. Though British operations under Major Generals William Philips in Virginia and Charles Cornwallis had been quite successful in the deep South, they were constantly in need of reinforcements. Major General Henry Clinton, in New York City, was disappointed in providing the needed assistance, in part owing to the whaleboat raids, chiefly against Long Island, mounted from both New Jersey and Connecticut. Hessian Major General Carl Leopold Baurmeister lamented their impact upon Clinton's plans. "We shall know within a short time what General Clinton expects to do. . . . The fleet . . . is ready to sail. Battery pieces have been put on board, and thirty transports are ready to take on troops," he wrote on April 26, just eight days after Marriner's most recent foray. "However, we [the Hessians] cannot spare many troops, for small vessels are constantly coming to the Long Island shore, where they burn things, make surprise raids, and never return without carrying out their designs. Some rowboats even came out of the Raritan to below New Utrecht, captured the Brunswick Major von Maybaum [von Meibom] and his nephew, Lieutenant von Maybaum, in their quarters, and took them to Amboy."[25]

• • •

One of the most famous of the of the American whaleboat warriors was Captain Adam Hyler, a 45-year-old emigrant from Baden, Germany, who may have once been impressed into the British Navy, where he learned the ways of the sea. By 1780, Hyler had become a respected citizen of the town of New Brunswick, New Jersey, from which he operated a small fleet of trading sloops before the war, running between the town and New York. Like Marriner, Hyler's career as a whaleboat privateer was brief, but it was even more spectacular. Like many small boat raiders on both sides he chose to conduct his attack not on the open Atlantic but in protected bays, inlets, and coves, often within range of enemy fortifications or major ships of war, and usually against superior numbers, but always by surprise, from aboard his lightly armed sloop-rigged whaleboat *Revenge*.

Hyler first appears on the scene, albeit with little note, leading a party of whaleboatmen out of New Brunswick in a daring expedition down the Raritan and along the Staten

Island coast to capture an enemy merchant sloop called *Susannah* in November 1780. Then, on February 20, 1781, a pair of whaleboats, possibly Hyler accompanied by one Captain Dickie, emerged from the Raritan, captured two prizes and retired with them back into the river.[26]

That Hyler engaged in other forays during the spring and early summer is probable, but they went unreported. Not until the hot mid-summer of 1781, as events hundreds of miles away in Virginia were slowly beginning to move towards a climax on the banks of the York River, did he achieve a measure of fame on the American side and notoriety on the British and Loyalist side in New York.

The first of a truly daring sequence of adventures was to take Captain Adam Hyler on a plundering and prisoner-hunting raid into the very heart of enemy territory: Long Island, New York. To reach his destination it was necessary to sail from New Brunswick down the meandering, shoal-cluttered Raritan to the river's outlet near the village of Amboy, and then hug the eastern Staten Island shoreline (occupied by two regiments of Skinner's Greens, and the British 57th Regiment of Foot) into Raritan Bay. From there he had to cross New York Bay to reach the western shoulder of Long Island. It is unknown precisely where Hyler intended to put ashore, but it may have been near the hamlet of Utrecht, a noted Loyalist village that was also an occasional billet for Hessian troops. The unquestionably hazardous voyage through the middle of heavily patrolled enemy waters, undoubtedly at night, can only be imagined. The account of his march inland and the result of his expedition were reported in the press with only a very few words: Hyler and his men "marched three miles and a half into the country, and made Captain Jeronimus Lott, a Lieutenant-Colonel of Militia, and one John Hankins, a Captain of a vessel, prisoners, and brought them safe to New Brunswick."[27]

Precisely two months later, on Friday, October 5, word reached Hyler at New Brunswick that a cluster of no less than five British vessels was lying nestled in a protected anchorage in a cove within Sandy Hook. Hyler immediately rounded up his crewmen, mobilized *Revenge* and a pair of armed whaleboats, and set out on a seemingly impossible mission. At Amboy, he waited for dark, and then set out on a long, eastward course toward the enemy anchorage more than fifteen or sixteen miles away.[28]

Upon arriving in the inky darkness near the tip of the Hook, the Americans discovered a Royal Navy warship looming large, but resting quietly at anchor. A quarter-mile beyond, under the Sandy Point Lighthouse, a squat log fort with a battery of a dozen swivel guns manned by Loyalists backed up the naval defenses. Less than a quarter of a mile from the warship the five sleeping vessels Hyler had come for lay snuggly anchored. Three of the craft were merchantmen, but two were gunboats, probably privateers, one mounting four 6-pounders, two to a side, and the other a 3-pounder and six swivel guns. Either of the gunboats was more than a match in firepower for the little American flotilla.[29]

Hyler counted on total surprise and the enemy's confidence that they were safely anchored under the protective cover of the great warship. Moving slowly forward under muffled oars, he launched a silent reconnaissance in the dark and discovered the merchantmen seemingly deserted, their crew having gone ashore for the night. Aboard the privateers, though manned, it appeared that the watch was but poorly kept, as it was aboard the great man-of-war. For the raiders the scene could not have been more promising.

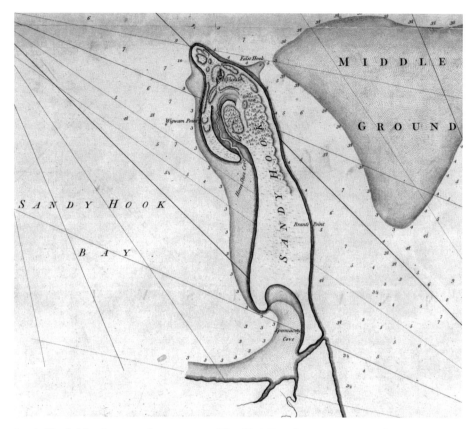

Sandy Hook, New Jersey, at the entrance to New York Bay, showing position of lighthouse and the coves used by the British as protected anchorages, frequently visited by Captain Adam Hyler and his whaleboat warriors. Detail from *A chart of the bar of Sandy Hook the entrance of Hudson's River in the Province of New Jersey; survey'd in 1782, by ieutt. Hills, of the 23d. Regt. and private draftsman to His Excellency the Commander in Chief.* London, Wm. Faden, 1784. Courtesy Geographic and Map Division, Library of Congress.

Noiselessly, and with barely a ripple on the water, the three whaleboats closed with their prey. *Revenge* would board the stronger of the two privateers, with the second whaleboat to take the other and the third to take the three merchantmen. The Americans came alongside their targets without being discovered, cast their grapnels, and then swarmed aboard. The surprise was absolute. Before any resistance could be mounted, most of the enemy seamen found themselves prisoners below deck. Only a handful of men aboard one of the privateers managed to flee aft, launch the longboat, and escape. Aboard the merchantmen only one sleeping watchman was discovered, and on another was found a mother and her four children. The action had taken less than fifteen minutes, without the loss of a man.[30]

Hyler was well aware that the men that had escaped would soon sound the alarm and the guns of the great warship and probably the fort would shortly be thundering.

The refugees had, in fact, made directly for the defense works, which immediately opened a stuttering fire in the direction of the captured vessels, even as Hyler and his men worked quickly to relieve their prizes of guns and fuses, a cask of powder, sails, cordage, cargo, and prisoners. On one vessel bound in for New York were found 250 bushels of wheat and a quantity of cheese belonging to Captain Richard Lippincott, the notorious Loyalist raider from Long Island.[31]

The range for the fort's little swivel guns, which were intended to stave off an attack on the lighthouse and the nearby Loyalist camp rather than conduct a long-range bombardment, was too short to allow them to even find their mark in the darkness. The noise quickly aroused the great warship from its slumber nearby, which also took to firing blindly in the night. For the whaleboat warriors it was clearly time to leave, but owing to now contrary winds and tide, Hyler determined it would be impossible to escape with all the prizes. Four of the five vessels were quickly put to the torch. The exception was the ship carrying the mother and her four children, which was left behind. Then, under oars alone, the raiders disappeared into the darkness bound for home as the waters behind them were peppered by the blind cannonade from the man-of-war.[32]

The raid, which resulted in the destruction of four enemy ships without a single man lost or wounded, instantly made Hyler and his men local heroes. Then, to add insult to the enemy's injury, just eight days later, on October 13, he dared to return to Sandy Hook with *Revenge* and the two whaleboats, and silently cut out an enemy sloop and two schooners directly under the guns of the fort. One of the schooners was a Virginia pilot boat, armed with a single 4-pounder. As on the previous raid, it was discovered that all but two crewmen, both aboard the pilot boat, were ashore. As before, the three prizes were captured by stealth, daring, and surprise, again without loss. Unfortunately, after successfully bringing them off, they found the sloop to be a very dull sailer. After the discovery of a British galley lying off the coast of Staten Island, it was decided to burn the prize three miles from the fort rather than risk recapture. One of the schooners was run aground by accident in the dark, stripped and abandoned rather than burned, undoubtedly to avoid drawing attention to their presence in the area. The pilot boat schooner was safely brought into port.[33]

Captain Hyler had not finished with Sandy Hook, where a substantial cantonment for armed Loyalists had been established, and from which numerous raids against rebel towns, farms, shipping, and militia bases had been launched. Just nine days after his last raid, Hyler once again set forth in *Revenge*, this time unaccompanied by other whaleboats, to conduct a plundering expedition against the "refugee town" itself. The moment proved opportune as the Loyalist units billeted on the Hook were off on their own plundering foray into Monmouth County. Moreover, the bulk of the Royal Navy shipping at New York City had temporarily departed from their anchorage near the city to keep an eye on a French fleet off the coast. That which remained was occupied with protecting the sixty-one sail of English provision and merchant shipping that had just come in, leaving the gateway to the bay and the waters within Sandy Hook entirely unguarded. After landing unopposed three-quarters of a mile from the Sandy Hook Lighthouse, Hyler was soon making off with not only plunder, but also half a dozen "noted villains," among whom was the captain of the guard and men assigned to protect the lighthouse.[34]

Hyler's string of successes grew even longer on the night of Saturday, November 9–10, when he again ventured with *Revenge* and a small party of men into the New York Narrows. This time he fell upon the British cargo ship *Father's Desire*, laden with rum and pork, easily capturing her and her fourteen-man crew, again without loss. While bringing his prize off with the intention of sailing her into the Raritan, however, *Revenge* was unfortunately run aground on a shoal, by which time the enemy had been alerted and was approaching in force. Once again, Hyler was obliged to set fire to his prize and escape, albeit not before he had removed part of the cargo. Several days later, twenty hogsheads of rum and thirty barrels of pork were advertised for sale at public vendue in New Brunswick.[35]

As his reputation for daring spread, more men and more boats began to join Hyler's little flotilla. On December 15, 1781, while in command of as many as eight sturdy whaleboats, manned by nearly a hundred men hungry for prizes and revenge for refugee attacks on the Jersey coast, he again set off. Once more his destination was the New York Narrows. There he fell in with and captured two refugee sloops commanded by a notorious Tory known as Shore Stephens, who had been on an expedition to trade with Loyalists at Shrewsbury. The prizes, laden with dry goods, sugar, rum, and, most importantly, £600 in specie, were carried back to New Brunswick without incident.[36]

By onset of 1782, after nearly five months of embarrassments caused by the audacious whaleboat privateersman from New Brunswick, the British command in New York finally resolved to conduct a retaliatory raid specifically intended to capture "the celebrated partisan" Hyler or, at the very least, destroy his boats. On Wednesday, January 9, an expedition under the command of one Captain Beckwith, composed of elements of the 40th and 42nd Regiments of Foot as well as a strong force of refugees, 200 men in all, set off in six boats bound for Hyler's base on the Raritan.[37]

The landing at New Brunswick at 5 a.m., just before daylight the following morning, was successfully made before major opposition could be raised. For the next two hours, the invaders burned and plundered in a well-planned and executed manner. Though Hyler escaped capture, his whaleboat flotilla did not. It was quickly located and destroyed or carried off, but not before the Monmouth Militia appeared on the scene. The fight was short, with several refugees believed to have been killed, four of which were verified, and several others reportedly carried off. None of the militiamen were killed although five were wounded and six more taken as prisoners.[38]

Adam Hyler escaped to fight another day, his reputation as a daring whaleboat privateersman having already been sealed. That he had been wise enough before the attack to disburse at least some of his eight-boat fleet to various other locations on the New Jersey coast is altogether possible, for his raiding operations continued. At least one of his boats had been lodged at Toms River. Its fate and that of the town's patriot defenders were soon tested, even as one of the most celebrated privateering actions of the war was beginning to unfold on the Delaware.

By the Rule of Contrary

"Success to Hyder Ali."

Owing to the depredations of the myriad refugee whaleboat raiders, the situation on the Delaware and all along the New Jersey coast was growing ever more desperate by the day. With the Continental Board of Admiralty having expired "of sheer inanition" in mid-1781, and all naval affairs, as well as national monetary issues, being relegated solely to Robert Morris as Superintendent of Finance and Agent of Marine, it was clear that relief would not be coming from the Continental Congress anytime soon. Pennsylvania and New Jersey would have to look out for their own. By late February 1782, the Philadelphia merchant community and even many of the privateer syndicates, in desperation, were obliged to seek assistance, if not outright rescue, from their own legislature. It was soon moved that "the state of Pennsylvania…determined to fit out, at its own expense, a number of armed vessels, the operation of which were to be confined within the thoroughfare to their capital," meaning the Delaware River. New Jersey would have to look out for itself.[1]

At the beginning of March, upon learning that a resolution would soon be submitted in the Pennsylvania legislature to provide for the acquisition of a private warship, a consortium of Philadelphia merchants, Thomas Fitzsimons, William Allibone, Francis Gurney, a business partner with Steven Decatur, Sr., and undoubtedly others, anticipating approval but unwilling to await the formalities, secured a loan from the newly founded Bank of North America to purchase and arm a vessel on behalf of the State even before a commission was guaranteed.[2] The most immediately obtainable ship, a dilapidated privateer brig named after a Muslim ruler, Hy'der Ally, who had rebelled against British rule in India and nearly succeeded, belonged to three Philadelphia men, John Wright Stanly, John Wilcocks, and Nicholas Low, who had themselves armed the ship with a dozen old guns and a crew of forty, and secured their own Continental letter of marque commission in late November 1781. The acquisition of the brig by Fitzsimons, *et al*, came none too soon, for *Hyder Ally*, as she was commonly referred to, had taken on a cargo of flour just before her purchase, with the intent of dropping down the Delaware and hoping to run the blockade to get to sea on her own. She was immediately ordered back to refit.[3]

Upon her return to the Philadelphia waterfront, *Hyder Ally* met her new commander, a handsome young man of only twenty-two years of age. A Maryland-born mariner of enormous merit and intelligence, he was already a battle-tested veteran. His name was Lieutenant Joshua Barney of the Continental Navy, and his reputation had, since the very onset of the war, been meteoric. Though formally recommended to the command by Daniel Smith, secretary of the new commission that was formed by the State of Pennsylvania to address the acquisition of an "armament" of vessels to protect commerce on the Delaware, Barney almost certainly could tip his hat to the influence of his good friend Robert Morris, now the Superintendent of Finance and Agent of Marine for the Continental Congress.[4]

Born July 6, 1759, in Baltimore, then but a scattering of houses on the Patapsco River, Barney had gone to sea at the tender age of eleven under a Chesapeake Bay pilot, and, in January 1772 apprenticed aboard a Liverpool trader. At the age of fifteen, while on a voyage to Nice, then belonging to the Kingdom of Sardinia, he had assumed command of the ship *Sidney* upon the sudden death of the captain, his sister's husband, and completed a most successful voyage. By the end of his 16th year he had made several adventurous voyages to Europe and had participated in a major, albeit failed, Spanish attack against the Dey of Algiers. Soon after his return to Baltimore, the Revolution began in earnest, and Barney enlisted as master's mate on one of the first vessels of the infant Continental Navy, the tiny sloop *Hornet*, upon which he had the honor to raise for the first time the American flag over an American warship. Later, aboard the schooner *Wasp*, he participated in the first American fleet operation of the war, Commodore Esek Hopkins's descent upon New Providence Island. In early 1777, as lieutenant of the Continental frigate *Virginia*, which was abandoned by her less-than-able captain, Barney found himself in command and facing a superior foe to which he was obliged by a rebellious crew to surrender. In the process, he became the youngest commander of a frigate in the Continental Navy. Soon exchanged, he then found himself serving aboard the *Andrew Doria* and played a prominent role in the defense of the Delaware. His gallantry in combat and capacity for command had long since distinguished him to many leaders of the Revolution, including General Washington, Benjamin Franklin, John Hancock, Samuel Adams, and especially Robert Morris. In 1779, he was captured and sent as a prisoner of war to the hell-hole of Mill Prison in England, from which he escaped to Amsterdam by a clever ruse. Eventually making his way home to America, he arrived in Philadelphia only five days before being offered command of *Hyder Ally*.[5]

Some might ask why a Continental Navy officer would accept command of a privateer. The answer, quite simply, was that there were hardly any billets open in the Navy owing to the loss of so many ships. Barney, with the prospect of an independent command all his own, even that of a quasi–letter of marque for the State of Pennsylvania, was both flattered and agreeable. It was, of course, not uncommon for Continental Navy officers to accept a post in a state navy or as a privateer officer while they awaited another assignment in the regular navy.[6]

On March 25, Barney boarded his new command for the first time, and immediately set about selecting officers and crew and refitting the vessel. Despite his youth, finding officers and crewmen to serve under him had never been difficult for Barney. His fame and desperate mission had already garnered some public attention, but his recruiting campaign was unquestionably assisted by the publication in broadside form of a poem by the unofficial poet of the Revolution, Philip Freneau, entitled "Barney's Invitation."

Captain Joshua Barney, ca. 1788.
Photographic reproduction of portrait by
Charles Wilson Peale. Courtesy Prints and
Photographs Division, Library of Congress.

Come all ye lads that know no fear,
To wealth and honor we will steer
In the Hyder-Ally *Privateer*
Commanded by bold Barney.

She's new and true and tight and sound
Well rigged aloft and all well found—
Come and be with laurel crown'd—
Away and leave your lasses!

Accept our terms without delay,
And make your fortunes while you may—
Such offers are not every day
In the power of the jolly sailor.

Success and fame attend the brave.
But death the coward and the slave—
Who fears to plough the Atlantic wave
To seek out bold invaders?

Come then and take a cruising bout—
Our ship sails well, there is no doubt;
She has been tried both in and out,
And answers expectation.

Let no proud foes that Britain bore
Distress our trade, insult our shore—
Teach them to know their reign is o'er,
Bold Philadelphia sails!

We'll teach them how to sail so near,
Or venture on the Delaware,
When we in warlike trim appear,
And cruise without Henlopen.

Who cannot wounds and battle dare,
Shall never clasp the blooming fair;
The brave alone their charms shall share
The brave and their protectors!

With hand and heart united all
Prepared to conquer or to fall,
Attend, my lads! To honor's call—
Embark in our Hyder-Ally!

From an Eastern prince she takes her name,
Who, smite with freedom's sacred flame,
Usurping Britons brought to shame,
His country's wrongs avenging.

See, on her stern the waving stars—
Inur'd to blood, inur'd to wars
Come, enter quick, my jolly tars
To scourge these haughty Britons.

Here's grog enough—then drink a bout!
I know your hearts are firm and stout;
American blood will ne'er give out,
And often we have proved it.

Though stormy oceans round us roll
We'll keep a firm undaunted bowl,
Befriended by the cheering bowl.
Sworn foes to melancholy:

While timorous landsmen lurk on shore,
'Tis ours to go where cannons roar—
On a coasting cruise we'll go once more
Despisers of all danger:

And fortune still that crowns the brave
Shall guard us o'er the gloomy wave—
A fearful heart betrays the knave,
Success to Hyder Ali.[7]

• • •

Within a week, recruitment of a hundred crewmen, including Barney's brother-in-law Joseph Bedford, and approximately ten marines had been completed. Justus Starr, a Philadelphian, seven years older than Barney and just five feet three inches tall, with light brown hair and a brown complexion, had served as first lieutenant on *Hyder Ally* under her previous commander, Henry Hawkins, and would continue on in the same rank under Barney. For his second lieutenant he took on Luke Merriman, a resolute and clever fighter after his own mold. His small band of marines, Bucks County smoothbore riflemen all and commanded by a lieutenant named Scull, "had never been on board a ship" in their lives, but were the kind of crack marksmen he might need. They were all immediately set to work refitting the ship, and in the evening drilled in gunnery by the light of battle lanterns.[8]

Upgrading the vessel, which was a clumsy and dull sailer at best, was a challenge. First, her cargo of flour, recently taken aboard by her former owners, had to be unloaded. Her bulwarks had to be pierced for more gunports, and her decks needed reinforcement to sustain the weight of the additional ordnance, upgraded from twelve to sixteen deck guns, all 6-pounders. Her interior had to be altered to accommodate the newly recruited crew. Rigging had to be renewed and her canvas unbent. Nets had to be strung along her sides to prevent boarding. And finally, ammunition and stores of all kinds had to be brought aboard and stowed before she could be considered in fighting condition. Barney and his men worked miracles. Within thirteen days of his assuming command, the brig was made ready for duty.[9]

On April 2, Allibone and Barney posted the required $20,000 bond, and Barney was immediately granted a letter of marque commission by the "Admiralty of the United States in Congress" as master of *Hyder Ally*, recorded as a ship of one hundred tons burthen and manned by a crew of one hundred (suggesting the marines had yet to be officially taken on).[10] Five days later, on Sunday, April 7, in the early mist of dawn, and barely eighteen days after Barney's return from Europe, *Hyder Ally* cast off with a gaggle of seven other vessels in company. The young captain's instructions were plain and simple: "to convoy a fleet of merchantmen to the [Delaware] capes, but on no account proceed to sea; it being the intention of the state simply to protect its own people, within its own waters, and chiefly from the annoyance of the 'refugee boats.'"[11]

The voyage down the Delaware proceeded without incident until, near the end of the day, with the hitherto favorable breeze failing, the convoy was obliged to come to and anchor under Cape May to await a fair wind to take them to sea. Here, they were soon joined by yet another merchantman, which had apparently been tardy in departing Philadelphia with the convoy. Then, as evening began to fall, Barney observed two ships standing northward from the direction of Cape Henlopen. Upping anchor and making sail in the dark of night, amidst the dangerous shoals of the Delaware Capes, was not an option. Besides, there was even a possibility the vessels were not hostile.[12]

With the dawn of April 8, it became immediately clear to Barney that the convoy had indeed been spotted and that the two vessels in question were anything but friendly. They were, in fact, a pair of enemy cruisers. The largest of the two proved to be HMS *Quebec*, a 32-gun frigate commanded by Captain Christopher Mason, and the other was the notorious *General Monk*, an infamous, fast sailing, 20-gun sloop-of-war, "coppered to the bends" (formerly Silas Talbot's Rhode Island privateer *General Washington* which had surrendered to the Royal Navy's 74-gun behemoth *Culloden*). Under the command of a most capable officer, Captain Josias Rodgers, she had captured over sixty American vessels in just a single year's service in the Royal Navy.[13]

For the British, who had also observed the Americans on the evening of the 7th, although they could not distinguish their total number, the prospects before them—eight ships that unquestionably belonged to the enemy, huddled at anchor in the roads—was too tantalizing to resist. They had been sailing north the previous evening when they sighted the American convoy, and pressed just beyond the entrance to the Cape May Channel before dropping anchor at dusk to block the rebel's only possible escape route to sea. Captain Mason was fully prepared to intercept any vessel that ventured forth, even as he planned for the coming morning.[14]

· · ·

About daylight, April 8, as the two British warships prepared to get underway, Captain Rodgers, who had just received orders "to enter Cape May road, to reconnoitre the enemy, and to attack them, or not, as he found expedient," was delighted to observe a trio of British privateers coming in and raised a signal for them to join him. "This he conceived to be a very fortunate incident," his biographer would later note, "for with the assistance of these privateers, he did not doubt, but he should be able to capture, or destroy, the whole of the enemy's squadron."[15]

It was about this time, when only one of the privateers, the 16-gun brig *Fair American* (the same famed vessel taken a little over three months earlier by HMS *Garland*) responded, that things began to go poorly for His Majesty's men-of-war. Rodgers waited in vain for the two recalcitrant privateers to join him. Perhaps they feared impressment of their seamen by His Majesty's ship, or perhaps the chance for easy pickings divided five ways was not to their liking. Nevertheless, Rodgers quickly communicated his design to *Fair American* and "received every promise of support." Whatever the cause, in the end *General Monk* was obliged to weigh anchor and get underway without them.[16]

Barney, prepared for the worst, had already dispatched a pilot belonging to the convoy to go ashore the evening before and watch for the foe. The pilot soon returned with word "that there were several vessels belonging to the enemy, coming round the cape" and advised the convoy to get underway. At 10 a.m., Barney perceived three oncoming warships to be part of the larger force (apparently having also learned of the two privateers that refused to come in), and reacted instantly. Without hesitation he "made signals to his convoy to get under way immediately and return up the Bay" with all speed and keep as close to shore as possible, where the deeper draft enemy warships could not follow. An hour later, even as the convoy "weighed anchor, crouded all the sail they could, and stood up the river, to avoid falling into the enemy's hands," he was able to make out that the oncoming squadron consisted of a frigate, a ship rated as a sloop-of-war, and an armed brig. The British, too, were closely observing the actions of their intended prey, which "manifestly appeared undetermined what to do."[17]

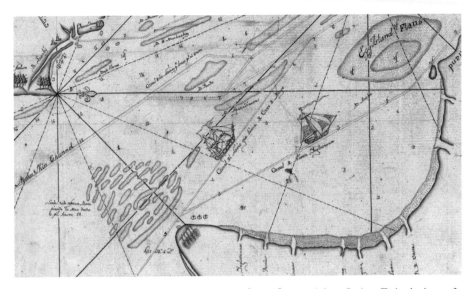

Delaware Bay. This detail from a manuscript map, [177-?], copied from Joshua Fisher's chart of Delaware Bay and River, defines the shipping channels, shoals, and soundings employed by both British and American vessels during the Revolution. Courtesy Geography and Map Division, Library of Congress.

At noon, hoping to seize upon the confusion that appeared to have taken hold amidst the convoy, *General Monk* and *Fair American* came into Cape May Road. In the meantime, Captain Mason had assigned himself the mission of proceeding higher up to prevent the Americans from escaping upriver, but found the Cape May Channel lacking enough water for his ship to swim in and was obliged to laboriously sail westward around the Overfalls and to proceed up the Henlopen Channel to enfilade the retreating convoy.[18]

Despite the confusion of the moment, with instructions to flee as fast as possible, the captains of the convoy had followed orders, albeit in a most hurried fashion, with but a single exception. The 12-gun Pennsylvania letter of marque ship *General Greene*, Captain Haskal Freeman, manned by a crew of forty-five, was no stranger to encounters at sea. She had been in service under various owners and commanders since December 1779, but this was Freeman's first such command and he seemed, at least initially, eager to prove himself.[19] Indeed, as he "very gallantly determined to abide the issue—he hailed Captain Barney . . . and made known his intention, in case of an engagement, 'to stick by him!'" Unfortunately, almost as soon as action commenced, he apparently became panic-stricken. In a desperate attempt to get to sea, *General Greene* was run aground on the shores of Cape May. Her hitherto bold commander and crew, with their capture now almost a foregone conclusion, managed to jump ashore from the jib boom and made their escape.[20]

Now, it was clear to all that the only opposition would be from the dull, clumsy little American brig *Hyder Ally*, commanded by a captain barely twenty-two years of age, manned by a volunteer crew of unknown capacity and a small body of frontier "marines," who had never set foot upon a ship in their lives, much less fought a battle at sea.

• • •

While *General Monk* was briefly occupied with taking the stranded *General Greene*, *Fair American* made straight for two ships of the convoy that were attempting to enter the safety of the Morris River, paying little more heed than loosing a single broadside as she passed *Hyder Ally*, to which Barney made no reply "determining to reserve his strength" for the second enemy ship, now coming up rapidly. Haste, on both sides, was to prove costly, as one of the pursued ships, the 12-gun brig *Charming Sally*, in the pandemonium of flight, grounded on the east side of the Overfalls, about the same time as *Fair American* ran hard aground on Egg Island Flats, leaving *General Monk* to continue the pursuit alone.[21]

As *General Monk* moved swiftly up the channel, passing *Charming Sally* on her port, she "wantonly and infamously" fired a volley of small arms into the stranded vessel, wounding the chief mate and pilot. Within a short time she had dropped a boat with thirteen or fourteen men, who took possession of the prize. Their control was short-lived. After about an hour of captivity, *Sally*'s crew rose up and retook the ship, secured their former captors, and managed to refloat her. Hoping to maneuver the brig into deeper water and save her, however, they proceeded but a half mile when they unfortunately ran aground again on the flats. Seeing at least one other vessel in the distance coming up (presumably *Quebec*) and a battle about to get underway between *Hyder Ally* and *General Monk*, they thought it "advisable" to make their escape to shore in both the *Monk*'s boat and their own, which was quickly affected.[22]

In the meantime, Barney maintained his position astern of his convoy in Cape May Channel, "watching the motions of the enemy with all the eagerness and anxiety natural to so important a trust." The only hope for the remaining convoy's flight to safety, he knew, was to throw his ship into harm's way and fight a delaying action. It was clear that, although the enemy privateer's grounding had evened the odds slightly, it had not dampened the ardor of the foe who was now steering straight for Barney.[23]

Though resolute in his mission, Barney could easily see the odds were against him. The oncoming ship was both trim and larger than his own dull sailer, and capable of outmaneuvering her at every measure. Moreover, the enemy was pierced with a dozen ports per side, through which a battery of 9-pounder carronades poked their ugly black noses, capable of throwing double the weight in metal of his own eighteen guns, four long 9-pounders and twelve 6-pounders. Moreover, the enemy ship was manned by a seasoned crew of 136, with literally scores of captures to their credit, compared to his own untested, green crew that had just come aboard. It was, Barney knew, absolutely imperative that the action be swift and decisive, for soon he must also encounter a far more powerful foe that was standing up on the opposite side of the Delaware to cut him off. Not long after the engagement that was about to ensue, Barney would recall thinking that as the sleek warship approached "she would blow us to atoms, but we were determined she should gain her victory dearly."[24]

Having no knowledge of the smaller ship's strength, and concerned that his short-ranged carronades might be a handicap in the event his foe had long guns, Captain Rodgers determined to close quickly upon her quarter and press the attack by boarding. He undoubtedly took heart when he observed the American cut her boat adrift and appeared to be doing everything to escape, firing two bow chasers in desperation at a distance of a hundred yards. As he approached to within pistol range without firing he discovered the American "so full of men, and so well provided with defenses against boarding, that he was obliged to alter his plan, and trust the event, however unwillingly, to a carronade."[25]

Barney surmised that the brazen, close approach was probably due to the enemy's "impression that her unequal foe would not venture to make battle." Indeed, they may have even begun to congratulate themselves on another easy capture as they maneuvered ever closer to their prey without firing a shot from their main battery. If such was the case, they were sadly mistaken, for at that moment *Hyder Ally*'s gunports were raised and a well-directed broadside blasted, at pistol shot range, into the oncoming man-of-war "which spoke her determination in a language not to be misunderstood."[26]

At this critical juncture, Barney employed a clever *ruse de guerre* designed to deceive and confuse: "he gave orders to the man at the helm to interpret the next command he should give him aloud *a revers*, or in his own words to the seamen, 'by the rule of *contrary*.'" Then, at the proper instant, as *General Monk* was closing on his starboard quarter, Barney shouted loudly to the helmsman: "Hard a-port your helm! Do you want him to run aboard us?" Hearing clearly his foe's orders, Rodgers ordered his own helmsman to turn to port to keep abreast of the enemy and prevent being raked by him. At that moment, on cue, *Hyder Ally* put her helm to starboard instead of port, bringing her directly across *General Monk*'s bow. Much to Barney's delight and Rodgers's surprise, the two vessels were suddenly afoul of each other, the American jib boom firmly entangled in the Englishman's forerigging, placing *Hyder Ally* in a raking position against which the *General Monk* could offer little response. Then, even as the American crewmen lashed the two warships together, making it impossible to separate the antagonists apart, the second crashing broadside flashed immediately from *Hyder Ally*'s starboard battery, sweeping all before it amidst splinters, bone, and flesh. Then came another and another. Additional 6-pounders from the port battery were turned around and brought to bear by means of their breech tackle, with even greater devastating consequences for the foe.[27]

> The rapidity, well directed aim, and vigorous effect, with which she [*Hyder Ally*] fired into the entangled ship, are almost inconceivable — more than *twenty broadsides* were fired in *twenty-six* minutes, and scarcely a shot missed its effects; entering in at the starboard bow, and making their way out through the larboard quarter, the grape, cannister, and round shot, all did their duty![28]

Though the two ships were bound together, it was apparently not so tight as to prevent some of *General Monk* guns from coming to bear on the American ship. Years later, Rodgers's biographer suggested that the two warships were actually battling it out broadside to broadside. He claimed that the captain's fears regarding the use of his guns, all carronades (some of which were reportedly re-bored 6-pounders to make them 9-pounders), had grown very "heated, by which they became quite unmanageable,

By the Rule of Contrary: Hyder Ally vs. General Monk, April 8, 1782. *Painting courtesy of Peter Rindlisbacher, 2014.*

and many of them overset, by which several of the men were much bruised. We with great concern soon found our short guns (carronades) to become totally unmanageable and that two-thirds of the shot we fired did not strike the hull of our antagonist." Luke Mathewman, a participant in the battle, would later write that they "fought with the muzzles of the guns almost rubbing together." However, Mary Barney, using Joshua's own unpublished handwritten memoirs as her source, noted quite succinctly that *Hyder Ally* remained lashed to the bow of *General Monk* throughout the duration of the engagement. The situation, however, did not entirely discount the British from being able to employ several of their sternmost port guns fired at an acute angle on the American's starboard stern.[29]

As broadside after broadside raked *General Monk*, plowing down men, dismounting cannon, and slicing braces and rigging to ribbons, her sharpshooters went about their own business with deadly precision. In order that he might better observe and direct the action, Barney had placed himself atop the binnacle, fully exposed on the quarterdeck. When a musket ball passed through his hat, just grazing the crown of his head, and another tore off the skirt of his coat, he summoned Mr. Scull, the commander of his Bucks County "marines," and instructed him to direct his riflemen's fire into the enemy's fighting top from which he had just been so much annoyed. The order was immediately obeyed, and within minutes every man in the enemy's tops had been brought down.

A few minutes later, one of the riflemen, less acquainted with the rules of naval subordination than he was with the rifle he employed with such skill, called from one of *Hyder Ally*'s fighting tops to Barney: "Captain!" shouted the rifleman. "Do you see that fellow with the *white hat*?" Then the rifleman's musket spoke, and Barney immediately saw the man in the hat "make a spring at least three feet from the deck, and fall to rise no more."

"Captain!" said the marksmen, undoubtedly with a smile across his face, "that's the third fellow I've made hop."[30]

The smoothbores were sweeping the enemy's decks clean. After the fight, it was discovered that all of the British seamen killed by small arms fire had been shot in the head or breast, which Barney attributed to the coolness of the backcountry riflemen, and their true and deadly aim. Indeed, one of the backwoodsmen had often attracted the captain's attention during the contest by inquiring of him several times, "who made the musket he was using?" As might be expected, owing to the heat of battle, "he was treated roughly for his intrusion—but being asked why he made this strange inquiry, particularly at this moment in time, he replied "with the greatest sang froid," while he was loading his piece, "because it was the best smooth bore he ever shot with in his life!"[31]

Still, Barney remained ensconced atop the binnacle directing the fight until he observed one of his officers, holding the cook's axe in his hand, "in the very act of raising it to cleave the head of one of his own men, who had deserted his gun and skulked behind the mainmast." At that instant, a round shot splintered the binnacle under Barney's feet. The officer, supposing his captain to be wounded, threw down the axe and ran to his assistance, only to discover him recovering his footing and, luckily, unhurt. The officer immediately picked up his axe and returned to dispatch the deserter, but found him now "fighting as bold and fearlessly as the bravest of the crew!"[32]

And still the cannons roared — at least those belonging to *Hyder Ally*. After a little over fifteen minutes of battle, the British guns had been silenced, but the flash of their muskets continued unabated. In desperation, Rodgers attempted a maneuver to extricate his ship from the death grip of *Hyder Ally*'s forerigging. Barney immediately countered by dispatching some of his own men into *General Monk*'s rigging to cut whatever lines they could and prevent the sails from filling. Soon British sails were flapping helplessly in the breeze, making the ship totally unmanageable.[33]

Captain Rodgers's situation was becoming hopeless, as his losses mounted and with no prospect of relief from the still grounded *Fair American* or from the frigate *Quebec*, which was too far away to render assistance. Several bowposts had been "knocked into one," the "rigging so much shot as to render it impossible to haul off." Moreover, the first lieutenant, master, purser, surgeon, boatswain, and chief gunner had all been killed or wounded and the shattered deck was covered with dead and injured seamen and marines. Then, even as Captain Rodgers was considering "the mortifying necessity of striking his majesty's colours to the *Hyder Ally*," a shot crushed into his foot and helped decide the issue. Unable to stand and observing the Americans about to board, his braces and running rigging so cut that he no longer had power over his ship, there was no alternative but to order the colors hauled down in surrender.[34]

The American victory was complete.

After barely twenty-six minutes of "vigorously rapid and short" battle, possibly one of the briefest and most decisive on record, and twenty-two broadsides from *Hyder Ally*, twenty of *Monk's* men lay dead and thirty-three wounded out of a crew of 136. *Hyder Ally's* casualties amounted to four killed and eleven wounded. Among the American casualties was Barney's brother-in-law, who had been stationed in the maintop and, while behaving with great gallantry, was severely wounded in the groin, the effects from which he would never recover. Surprisingly, he had not felt the wound until he descended to the deck after the action was over, at which point he collapsed from loss of blood and was carried below.[35]

Without bothering to inquire what vessel she was, Barney immediately dispatched his first lieutenant, Justus Starr, and thirty-five men to take possession of *General Monk*. Captain Rodgers, his bloody foot wrapped in a shirt, and in an understandably sour temper while in Starr's presence, immediately ordered one of his attendants to fetch his personal fowling piece from his cabin. When the attendant returned, bearing "a very splendid silver-mounted fusil," he handed it to his captain, who in a rage immediately pitched it overboard, saying: "This shall never become the property of any d___d rebel."[36]

With *Quebec* now approaching the main channel barely two or three miles away, Barney had to act fast. Rodgers had not only lost his ship, but fortuitously for the Americans, he had also failed to destroy his signal book. It was an oversight that his captor quickly took advantage of. Immediately after the action, Barney ordered the British flag to be raised again aboard *General Monk* and the American flag hauled down on his own ship to further confuse the enemy into believing that the fight had resulted in a British victory. The frigate almost straight away came to anchor. The ruse worked.[37]

Though Barney may have considered an attack on the stranded and helpless *Fair American*, the thought passed quickly. He knew it would not be long before *Quebec* finally realized what had happened. Having suffered little damage to his own ship aloft, as soon as he was able to separate her from the prize and Lieutenant Starr managed to get *General Monk* underway, the two former combatants prepared to set sail upriver. It was not, undoubtedly, an easy task for Starr as the prize he now commanded was a gory one, with dead and wounded lying about in profusion, decks slippery with their blood and gore, and littered with ship debris and splinters. All of her boats, gun carriages, and deckhouses were badly shattered. Nevertheless, the lieutenant and his men set to work quickly knotting and reeving sheets and braces, repairing stays, and patching whatever they could, while still guarding the prisoners.[38]

Only as they prepared to sail, did Barney bring *Hyder Ally* close enough to hail her again. "What ship is she," he shouted to Starr.

"The *General Monk*; 250 tons burden, 136 men."

"What armament has she?" Barney asked.

"Twenty-four guns," answered his lieutenant. "Sixteen nines and two sixes."

"That's only eighteen. What about the others?"

"Six Quakers," said Starr, "six wooden dummies."[39]

It was time to go. The two stranded convoy ships would have to be left behind.

• • •

At Chester, Barney transferred to his prize "to see that he might himself see the wounded prisoners properly cared for." Both ships then set course for Philadelphia, arriving at the lower part of the city and coming to anchor near each other in the stream. Barney ordered a 13-gun salute, as was the custom, one for each state, which drew crowds of onlookers to the waterfront. Soon afterwards, the two ships warped in to the wharf to land the wounded and dead. *General Monk* must have been a sight, with her rigging "hanging in bights and Irish pendants," but it mattered little now as curious onlookers were allowed aboard the two tattered vessels even before the unloading of casualties commenced. "The difference in size and equipments of the two ships," recalled one visitor, "was a matter of astonishment to all the beholders." The mizzen staysail of the prize, it was later reported, perhaps with some enlargement of the truth, was discovered to have 365 shot holes in it, and considered such remarkable evidence of the battle that an enterprising sailmaker from the city begged it of Barney. The sailmaker, it was said, soon made a considerable sum from exhibiting it in his sail loft for a fee. But it was the gruesome deck of the prize, in particular, which was "besmeared with blood, covered with the dead and wounded, and resembled a charnel house," that drew perhaps the greatest attention.[40]

As the casualties were being carried ashore in hammocks, one of the British crewman was heard to observe that shortly before the action commenced Captain Rodgers had addressed his men: "Now, my boys," he said with the utmost confidence, "we shall have the Yankee ship in five minutes."

"And so we all thought," added the crewman morosely, "but here we are."[41]

After conferring briefly with several of the city's merchants on *General Monk*'s quarterdeck, and with but little pause, Barney immediately saw to it that Captain Rodgers be moved to a comfortable and respectable lodging, where he might be nursed back to health with all the "kindness and tenderness of a sister." He paid a brief visit to his own home to see his wife and young son, and then returned immediately to Chester without stopping for the cheers and congratulations of an adoring public. It seemingly was now of little consequence to the people of the city that one, and probably two, of the convoy vessels he had been charged with protecting had been captured. All that mattered to the general population was that the other six had returned safely and that a victory against seemingly overwhelming odds had been gained by the daring young captain. Then, to further enhance his reputation, while en route downriver, he fell in with and captured a refugee schooner called *Hook'em Snevey*. The contest was brief, as the refugee had been armed with but a single 6-pounder and four swivels. Yet, the effect of the capture of a detested Loyalist rover, along with the former American privateer, "struck a panic into the refugees." The effect dulled, but did not entirely quench, as Barney's biographers claimed, their thirst for operating on the Delaware with their armed barges, sloops and schooners.[42]

There is some irony in the fact that not until the day after the battle was action taken on the petition to the Pennsylvania State Legislature from the merchants and traders of Philadelphia praying for the adoption of measures to be taken to protect their property from the depredations of the Royal Navy, the privateers, and refugee whaleboatmen of New York. On April 9, legislation was passed appointing Francis Gurney, John Patton, and William Allibone (all of whom had significant interests in privateering, and formally owned *Hyder Ally*) as commissioners to purchase, man, and equip vessels deemed suitable for the purpose. This armament, essentially privateers owned and administered by the state of Pennsylvania, in whole or in part, was to be kept operative during the war, as long as they thought necessary, or until the General Assembly directed otherwise.

Funding for maintaining the vessels was to be from "the money arising from the tonnage of vessels," and money produced by the taxes on imported foreign goods. If such funds proved to be insufficient to defray expenses, "so speedily as was requisite," further funds might be raised from the merchants and traders, upon their willingness to submit to additional imposts on imports equal to those of an earlier tax authorized in December 1780. A sum of £25,000 was appropriated for the armament. The commissioners were authorized to borrow to that amount on the good faith of Pennsylvania state funds and commercial revenue, "and to draw from the collector, from time to time, the moneys arising from the duties pledged, and to apply them to the repayment of the sum borrowed." A supplementary act, passed a few days later, further authorized the commissioners to borrow any additional funds deemed necessary, but not to exceed £25,000. All prize moneys produced by the capture of enemy vessels by the state armament, were to be paid directly into the hands of the commissioners and addressed to the maintenance and support of the armament.[43]

On April 27 *Hyder Ally* received a new commission as a state of Pennsylvania letter of marque, under the ownership of Fitzsimons, Gurney, and Alibone, albeit under the command of Justus Starr, Barney's former lieutenant.[44]

• • •

Upon his return to Philadelphia, Barney most certainly would have visited his two prizes, tied up side by side at the Willing and Morris company wharf. On Monday, May 6, 1782, *Hook'em Snevey* was scheduled to be sold there at public auction, along with her guns, arms, tackle, apparel, and furniture.[45] This time Barney took time to publicly enjoy the recognition for his victories. A week later, on April 13, a letter to the commissioners named in the Act for guarding and defending navigation and trade in Delaware Bay and river, with a full account of the battle between *Hyder Ally* and *General Monk*, was laid before the Pennsylvania House of Delegates and read. A committee was appointed "to report on the subject of said letter," and in the afternoon presented a pair of resolutions that were unanimously approved:

> *Resolved,* that this House entertain a just sense of the gallantry and good conduct of Captain Joshua Barney, and the officers, seamen and marines under his command.
>
> *Resolved,* that the President of the Supreme Executive Council be requested to

procure an elegant sword, bearing some device emblematic of the above action, and present the same to Captain Barney, in testimony of the favorable opinion this House entertain of his merit.[46]

The gold-hilted sword, with one side bearing the image of *Hyder Ally* and the other that of *General Monk*, both being under sail, but the latter shown striking her flag, was later presented to Captain Barney by John Dickinson, Governor of Pennsylvania. The ceremonial weapon was a superb piece of workmanship, with the ships' "hulls, sails, masts, spars and rigging . . . all beautifully delineated by the artist, in open work, resembling the ivory fans of the Chinese."[47]

Young Joshua Barney became an overnight hero, whose name was on everyone's lips and whose exploit against the *General Monk* became the subject of another popular epic ballad by Philip Freneau entitled *On Captain Barney's Victory Over the Ship General Monk*. Though slightly in error on a few facts and perhaps a bit long, the story nevertheless stirred the patriot blood.[48]

The fate of the *General Monk* is of note. Purchased by the government for the Continental Navy for use as a packet ship, she would sail for Europe on her first voyage as such under the direction of her new commander, Captain Joshua Barney. She would be one of only three Continental Navy warships to survive to the end of the war, far from the ugly conflict on the Delaware-New Jersey coast.

Barney's moment of glory, however, was unfortunately to be eclipsed by other far more disturbing affairs emanating about the same time from the privateering hamlet of Toms River. They were, indeed, affairs that threatened to upend the prospects for peace itself.

–XX–

Up Goes Huddy

"Retaliation justifiable and expedient."

The fort at Toms River was a rude structure, erected on a slight knoll in a prominent section of the village, north of the bridge. It wasn't much to look at, with undressed logs seven feet high, each hewn to a point on top and planted perpendicularly in the earth to form a rough square, with loopholes for muskets every few feet. On each of its corners was a raised bed of logs upon which was mounted small cannon on pivots. Access was only by a scaling ladder. Nearby was Abiel Aikens's public inn and a few homes belonging to several of the town notables, including Major John Cook, of the Second Regiment, Monmouth County Militia, Captain Ephraim Jenkins, and the widow Sarah Studson, wife of Lieutenant Joshua Studson, who had been murdered in December 1780 near Cranberry Inlet by a notorious Tory smuggler aptly dubbed "Bloody" John Bacon. Until his death in October 1779, Thomas Savadge, manager of the Pennsylvania salt works, had also lived in town, near the company storehouse. A half-mile south of the fort, on Jake's Branch, stood a small sawmill and a flourmill owned by Paul and Abraham Schenck.[1]

The fort was, of course, as much for the protection of the salt storage facilities as it was for the town. In December 1779, following Savadge's demise and perhaps swayed by the repeated attacks on salt making facilities on the coast, Pennsylvania sold its salt works to John Thompson of Burlington County, New Jersey, for $15,000, and the establishment came under the dominion of the State of New Jersey, which was now obliged to provide its own militia support for its protection. The small fort thus became the hub of defense for the village and industries of Toms River.[2]

In the waning days of the winter of early 1782, command of the fort had fallen to Captain Joshua Huddy, late commander of the little privateer *Black Snake* and a passionate Whig from the earliest days of the war. The oldest of seven brothers, Huddy was a natural leader and had organized a company of artillery in a 12-month levy of a state regiment under Major Samuel Hayes. On September 24, 1777, he had been appointed by an act of the state legislature to command of the company, which by July of the following year was based at Haddonfield.[3]

Over the several ensuing years, Huddy, "by his activity and courage became a terror of the Tories," claimed one prominent historian. Living on the central part of Colt's Neck, not far from the town of Freehold, he had been a dominant force in the campaign to challenge and subdue all who were suspected of Loyalist sympathies, support, or participation in the war on the King's side, and thus became a subject of refugee revenge. In the summer of 1780, his enemies made their first move. Warning of the impending attack came about an hour before sunrise by the stoning of a window in Huddy's house, which was then occupied solely by himself, his wife Catherine Hart Huddy, and a servant girl of about twenty years of age named Lucretia Emmons. He later claimed that, almost immediately, he discerned that a party of as many as seventy-two men had surrounded the residence. Among them was a former mulatto slave of John Corlies of Monmouth County, who was called Colonel Tye or Titus.[4]

Huddy refused to surrender and, as there were several guns in his home, began to fire them from different windows, with Lucretia loading as fast as he fired, to give the impression that the building was heavily defended. Colonel Tye was wounded in the wrist and several others were also injured. Tye would later die of tetanus from the infected wound. After two hours of standoff, the refugees, commanded by a pair of Loyalist lieutenants, Joseph Parker and William Hewlett, finally resorted to firebrands. Justifiably panicked and terrified as the house began to burn, Huddy's wife and servant urged the ex-privateersman to surrender. With the flames growing by the minute, the captain finally acquiesced, but only if the attackers agreed to help extinguish the flames. Almost immediately the house was beset by the refugees, ransacked and plundered even as Huddy was being hauled to the nearby waters at Black Point, between the Shrewsbury and Navesink rivers, for transfer to the hidden boats in which the raiders had arrived. On the river bank, as embarkation was about to begin, half a dozen militiamen arrived, their weapons ablaze, killing one of the refugee commanders as he fled. Soon, sixteen more men appeared, firing into the alarmed refugees who were now desperately attempting to escape. As the raiders pushed off in utter confusion, the boat with their captive in it capsized, tossing its occupants, including their prisoner, into the water. As Huddy swam for his life towards the shore, a shot from the militia smashed into his thigh. Raising his hands in the air he shouted, "I am Huddy, I am Huddy," to prevent being shot again by his own compatriots. The whole affair, as related by Huddy himself, was published in the *Pennsylvania Packet* with the comment that the refugees "made a silent and shameful retreat with disgrace—two hours for seventy-two men to take one man."[5]

After recuperating from his wound and later trying his hand at privateering once more, Joshua Huddy again entered active military service. On December 10, 1781, the citizens of Monmouth County petitioned the New Jersey Legislature for the celebrated 47-year-old captain to be ordered to take command of the defenses at Toms River and to march his company of two noncommissioned officers and twenty-three men to that place immediately. Their arrival, on February 1, 1782, came none too soon.[6]

• • •

In the early days of 1782, William Franklin was still recognized by the Crown as both Royal Governor of New Jersey and President of the Board of Associated Loyalists in New York City. Ever since his imprisonment by the rebels in August 1776, he had been filled with venom towards his former countrymen. His "long and Horrible confinement" in the infamous Simsbury copper mines in Connecticut—variously called by Royalists the "Catacomb of Loyalty," "the woeful mansion," "Bastille, Inferno, and prison of the Inquisition," "sepulcher, living tomb," and other damning epithets—had left him "considerably reduced in flesh" as it had other prominent Loyalist prisoners, such as Mayor David Matthews of New York City. The prisoners, including Franklin, were employed in often backbreaking labor, brought up from caverns forty yards below the earth's surface in threes each morning at daybreak, then chained to a block or fettered by the ankle or neck to work, and fed with hunks of raw meat tossed at their feet.[7]

A view of the guard-house and Simsbury-mines . . . a prison for the confinement of loyalists in Connecticut. Commonly called "Hell" by its inmates, Simsbury mine served as a prison for a number of leading Loyalists such as Governor William Franklin of New Jersey, son of Benjamin Franklin. Reproduction from *The political magazine and parliamentary, naval, military, and literary journal,* October 1781. Courtesy Library of Congress.

It had been under Franklin's watch that the Board of Associated Loyalists had, for well over a year, prompted, planned, and supported the successful refugee raiders that were causing such a major impact on the balance of rebel Middle Atlantic trade and privateering operations, especially between Sandy Hook and Cape May. In mid-March 1782, the Board set about planning yet another bold seaborne expedition directed at the obliteration of the blockhouse fort at Toms River, destruction of the town and salt works, and the capture of that major nemesis of all New Jersey Tories, Captain Joshua Huddy. One of the chief charges against Huddy was that he had been instrumental in the execution of a Loyalist named Stephen Edwards, who had been sent from New York into Monmouth County as a spy. Edwards had been found hiding in a bed wearing a female nightcap, masquerading as a woman to avoid capture, and carrying incriminating documents. He had been promptly arrested, tried, and hung as an enemy spy. For the Board, however, it was simply a matter of blood for blood, a vendetta that needed addressing, and Huddy fit the bill as a subject of retribution. But his capture or death was only part of the objective. Once the raiders had attended to matters at Toms River, they would turn their attentions to devastating the countryside surrounding Shark River and the destruction of the new salt works at Squan before returning to their base.[8]

Command of the mission was placed in the hands of Captain Evan Thomas and Lieutenant Owen Roberts of the Loyalist Bucks County, Pennsylvania, Volunteers. On March 20, some forty Pennsylvania refugees boarded a small flotilla of whaleboats commanded by a Lieutenant Blanchard and manned by a crew of eighty well-armed seamen, and set off from the wharves of New York City. In the harbor they were joined by Blanchard's ship, the privateer brigantine *Arrogant*, Captain Stewart Ross commanding, to serve as both escort and support during the attack. Once they arrived inside Cranberry Inlet, they were to be reinforced at or near Coates' Point by another detachment of local county Tories commanded by Richard Davenport, and then to proceed by a circuitous route to Toms River. Delays in any amphibious operation, especially along the New Jersey coast, were to be expected. And so it was that contrary winds prevented the expedition from beating around Sandy Hook for three days and nights. Finally, with a fair breeze, progress down the coast proved swift and unhindered. But, if surprise was the game, it came too late; Huddy had already heard rumors of a possible refugee attempt to capture his post.[9]

About midnight, Saturday, March 23, the little refugee armada, piloted by William Dillon (the same Loyalist who had caused such a ruckus by piloting the 1778 expedition into Cranberry Inlet) passed safely through the same shallow opening. The landing of approximately 120 Loyalist refugees and privateersmen on the north side of the river at Coates' Point was unopposed in the darkness. They were soon on the march towards the village, taking a less used northerly route through forest and lowlands, undoubtedly to confuse any opposition or pickets. While en route they were joined by Davenport and his men, which increased their numbers substantially; they continued on in silence.[10]

At the fort, having been apprised by a local named Garret Irons of a possible attack, Huddy had taken the precaution of sending out a scouting party of village volunteers to patrol the more direct river road leading to Coates' Point. Unfortunately for the fort's defenders, the patrol entirely missed the enemy, who were marching on the town by the more circuitous route and entering from the north rather than the east.[11]

One can only imagine the tensions that prevailed among the Loyalists as the gunmetal gray light of Sunday's dawn appeared on the horizon, a few moments before the word to move forward was quietly passed on. A warning shot by a rebel picket momentarily stalled the advance. In an instant, the swivel guns on the fort's walls were manned and muskets run out by no-longer sleepy-eyed militiamen. Someone, a refugee officer no doubt, shouted out a demand for surrender, and someone else, perhaps Huddy, declined in no uncertain terms, though the rebels were outnumbered by nearly six or seven to one.

The precise moment that the charge was made is unknown, but it was almost certainly undertaken in the gray dawn, which added to the terror and confusion of battle. The ferocity of the assault, led by Captain Thomas and Lieutenant Blanchard is undoubted, as was that of the defense. In the first volley of fire, several defenders were dropped. Simultaneously, two Loyalist officers, Lieutenant Inslee of the Bucks County Volunteers, and Iredell of the privateer *Arrogant*, fell fatally wounded by the fusillade from the fort. Still, the assault did not falter, as the assailants mounted the parapets from all sides. Struggling to climb over the pointed logs of the fort walls in a seemingly endless swarm, the privateersmen and volunteers now faced the even sharper bayonets and long pikes of Huddy and his men. One of the black refugees was quickly downed with wounds, followed by at least five of his comrades in arms, and then Lieutenant Roberts of the volunteers. But still they came.[12]

As the battle increased in intensity, it was the rebels' turn. A swivel gunner, James Kinsley, fell wounded in the head while manning his gun. A musket ball smashed into Moses Robbins's face, even as one of his mates, James Kennedy, fell mortally wounded nearby. The body of John Wright, pierced by six musket balls in quick succession, was shoved aside as even more sailors and volunteers spilled over the walls. Soon, as rebel powder became exhausted, the issue was decided, but not before three more rebels, Thomas Rostoinder, Cornelius McDonald, and David Dodge, would fall by their guns and five more would escape amidst the chaos of carnage before the fight was halted.[13]

The Loyalist victory was complete with Huddy's surrender, along with sixteen of his men, four of whom were critically wounded. But revenge was in the air. After the raiders proceeded to destroy the fort, spike its guns and throw them in the river, they spread out to burn the town, with its tavern and blacksmith shop, two mills, salt works, and storehouses, in an orgy of destruction and revenge that knew no bounds. Major John Cook, an ardent old Whig, was viciously bayoneted after the fight was over and died of his wounds. Adam Hyler's boat, tied up at the river's edge, was taken as a prize of war. Only two homes in the town were spared, both believed to have belonged to Loyalist sympathizers, as the invaders returned to their whaleboats and the privateer *Arrogant*. It was soon being reported in the press, the attackers "have burnt most of the houses, stripped and plundered the inhabitants of almost every thing."[14]

Huddy, town magistrate Daniel Randolph, who had volunteered as a guard, and an old defender named Jacob Fleming, were carried off on that fateful Sunday and taken aboard *Arrogant* for passage to New York. Huddy probably became the subject of immediate revenge by his captors, who reportedly "mistreated him with blows, slaps, etc., etc." His furious defense at the fort, however, which had inflicted perhaps unexpected casualties in Loyalist wounded, including Lieutenant Roberts, had altered plans for further raiding at Shark River and Squan. It was decided the expedition must return directly to New York to attend the injured.[15]

The arrival of *Arrogant* and the whaleboat flotilla at New York, with a notorious nemesis of Loyalist partisans aboard as a prisoner in irons, may have set off a minor flurry of excitement along the waterfront, but his appearance in public was brief. Huddy, Randolph, and Fleming were turned over to General Clinton and immediately whisked off to temporary confinement in a forbidding-looking five-story stone structure known as the Old Sugar House, which once belonged to the Van Cortlands, a prominent Tory family and had served as a prison since the beginning of the war. They would not remain there long for upon William Franklin's request they were returned to the jurisdiction of the Board of Associated Loyalists and on April 1 moved to the city provost's jail to await their fate.[16]

• • •

When two Loyalist partisan fugitives, the brothers Phillip and Aaron White, were captured near Long Beach, New Jersey, and Huddy and his mates were languishing in prison at New York, the "Huddy Affair," as it soon came to be known, commenced. It began when the local rebel authorities ordered Phillip White to be taken under guard to Freehold, where he was to be incarcerated. He was warned, even before starting out under escort by three armed guards, John North, William Borden, and John Russell, Jr., that if he dared make any attempt at escape he would be shot. Russell had more than a professional interest in the prisoner's delivery, as White had been a participant in a Loyalist plundering raid on his parent's farm in April 1780, which resulted in the murder of his father. Somewhere between Colt's Neck and Freehold, undoubtedly fearing a trial for his role in the murder and almost certain execution, White made a break for freedom, or so it was later reported. Jumping from his horse, he dashed for the nearby woods, even as his guards shouted for him to stop. Momentarily halted by a ball from Borden's musket, which dropped him to his hands and knees, the refugee refused to surrender. Despite the bullet in his breast, he somehow managed to raise himself and make for the woods and a nearby bog, which would have impeded his mounted pursuers. North was not about to let the hated partisan escape and immediately spurred his horse onward. While leaping a fence in an effort to cut the fugitive off from the bog he dropped his gun but continued the chase and with sword in hand soon overtook his quarry. Still, White refused to stop until a sword slash across his face brought him down, crying loudly that he was a dead man.[17]

"White," shouted Borden, who had also come up, "if you will give up you shall have quarters yet." But it was not to be, as the fatally wounded fugitive, bleeding from chest and cheek, expired on the spot. Or so it was reported and accepted by the authorities of Monmouth County.[18]

Precisely when the news of White's death reached the ears of William Franklin in New York is uncertain, but that he was enraged by what he considered outright murder is probable. That he intended to use it to justify his next move in regards to the fate of Captain Joshua Huddy, who was a prisoner of war at the time of the partisan's death while trying to escape, however, soon became quite clear.

236

• • •

For a week, the three Monmouth County men remained in limbo, closely confined, not knowing what was to happen to them. Governor Franklin, however, had already determined the fate of one of them, and he had already picked the man for the job. On April 7, the Board of Directors of Associated Loyalists issued an order to the Commissary of Prison at New York to "Deliver to Captain Richard Lippincott the three following prisoners: Lieutenant Joshua Huddy, Daniel Randolph and Jacob Fleming, to take down to the Hook, to procure the exchange of Captain Clayton Tilton and two other associated Loyalists."[19]

The following day, Monday, April 8, the chains were removed from both Randolph and Fleming, but Huddy was placed in heavier irons and carried aboard a sloop. On the following evening, in company with his two countrymen, he was transferred to the armed guard ship *Britannia*, Captain Richard Morris, at Sandy Hook. For the next three days the three men remained in irons aboard the warship. Then, on the morning of April 12, Captain Lippincott, a native of Shrewsbury township in Monmouth County and in the eyes of many rebels one of the most despised Loyalist partisans, boarded *Britannia* with secret personal instructions from Franklin himself, as well as the Associated Loyalist's orders to assume custody of the prisoners. Lippincott presented Captain Morris with the Board's order to turn over Huddy and his associates. When asked what he intended to do with Huddy, Lippincott showed him a label with writing on it and informed him that he was going to carry out the Board's instructions, meaning Franklin's verbal orders, to see to Huddy's end. Huddy's companions were soon exchanged for two Loyalist partisans, Captain Aaron White and Clayton Tilton, but his own fate was to be far more than disturbing.[20]

At 10 a.m., Huddy was taken from the guardship by Lippincott and sixteen fellow partisans and rowed by six sailors from the ship to a place called Gravelly Point on the Navesink River, about a mile below the Navesink Highland light station. There, near the water's edge, they hastily erected a crude gallows from three fence rails, a barrel, and a rope borrowed from Captain Morris. Wasting little time, and with less ceremony, the partisans mounted their bound prisoner upon the barrel and placed the rope around his neck.[21]

It is uncertain if he asked or if his executioners offered to let their prisoner compose his last will and testament before dying. The noted New Jersey historian William S. Stryker, a century after the event, would write: "With a strange impulse, it is said, these bloody men allowed him with a rope around his neck, to dictate his will, and sign it on the barrel head." The captain then dictated the will, which he was then permitted to sign:

"In the name of God, amen," he wrote,

> I, Joshua Huddy, of Middletown, in the county of Monmouth, being of sound mind and memory, but expecting shortly to depart this life, do declare this my last will and testament:
>
> First: I commit my soul into the hands of Almighty God, hoping he may receive it in mercy; and next I commit my body to the earth. I do also appoint my trusty friend, Samuel Forman, to be my lawful executor, and after all my just debts are paid, I desire that he do divide the rest of my substance whether by

book debts, notes or any effects whatever belonging to me, equally between my two children, Elizabeth and Martha Huddy.

In witness whereof I have hereunto signed my name this twelfth day of April, in the year of our Lord one thousand seven hundred and eighty two.

JOSHUA HUDDY.[22]

The will was then stuffed in his pocket. One of the partisan refugees, Timothy Brooks, later testified that, at Huddy's request, he and Lippincott shook hands. Then, as he looked down from the barrel head at the seventeen partisan refugees surrounding him, Huddy said his last words: "I shall die innocent and in a good cause." Yet, no one among the Loyalists seemed willing to pull the fatal rope. Brooks stated that it was finally a negro who finished the execution, but Stryker insists that Lippincott himself, angry at his men's reluctance to end the thing, took it upon himself to finish the job.[23]

Lippincott was not quite finished. Though Huddy's body swung lifeless in front of him, before he and his men departed, he pinned a label or placard to the breast of the hanging body, the same as he had shown Captain Morris only a few hours earlier.[24] It read:

We, the Refugees, having long with grief beheld the cruel murders of our brethren, and finding nothing but such measures daily carrying into execution; we therefore determine not to suffer, without taking vengeance for the numerous cruelties; and thus begin, having made use of Captain Huddy as the first object to present to your view; and further determine to hang man for man, while there is a refugee existing.

UP GOES HUDDY FOR PHILIP WHITE![25]

• • •

Joshua Huddy's body was found at 4 p.m. on the day of execution and carried to the residence of Captain James Green in Freehold. For the ex-privateersman, it probably would have seemed appropriate that his corpse be taken to the Green house, a place where much public business had been transacted during the war. Here, too, trials had been held, including, from time to time, Courts of Admiralty to try claims for prizes taken by American privateers. Indeed, only a week prior to Huddy's capture, Esquire Abiel Aiken, a resident of Toms River, had appeared to try the claims for the prize *Lucy*, of which the Loyalist refugee William Dillon had been master. Huddy's body was buried soon after with all the honors of war, it was supposed, on Monmouth battlefield.[26]

Rage and indignation over the murder spread rapidly. On April 14, the Reverend Dr. John Woodhull, pastor of the First Presbyterian Church in Freehold, who was to preach the memorial sermon for Huddy to the assembled citizenry the following day from the porch of a town hotel, was among the most incensed. Meeting with General David Forman of the New Jersey State Militia, a judge of the court of common pleas of Monmouth County and an ardent Whig despised by the Loyalists, he proposed a plan of reprisal. The same day a public meeting was held in the country courthouse.[27]

On the day of the sermon, Daniel Randolph, who had just been exchanged, provided a detail of the attack on the fort, his and Huddy's capture, and Huddy's execution in an affidavit sworn to before General Forman. He made it clear that, although Huddy had been accused of participating in the shooting of Phillip White on March 30, he had been a prisoner in irons in New York at the time and could not have been responsible.[28]

A memorial petition was prepared and signed by fourteen leading citizens entreating both Congress and General Washington to undertake immediate retaliatory measures to prevent such inhuman murders in the future. Sworn statements were taken and, along with the label fastened to Huddy's coat, sent along with the petition by Forman to Elizabethtown. There they were shown to the Commissioners of Prisoners, Major General Henry Knox of the Continental Army, and Gouverneur Morris, who immediately dispatched Forman to personally deliver them to General Washington at his headquarters at Newburgh, in the Hudson Highlands.[29]

Upon receiving the memorial on April 19, the Commander-in-Chief convened a council of war composed of twenty-five general and field officers commanding brigades and regiments of the Continental Army at Major General William Heath's headquarters at West Point. Given the statement of facts in hand, he asked each officer present to write down his answer to each of four questions:

1st. Upon the State of Facts in the above Case, is Retaliation justifiable and expedient? 2d. If justifiable, Ought it to take place immediately? Or should a previous Representation be made to Sir H[enr]y Clinton and Satisfaction demanded from him? 3d. In Case of Representation and Demand, who should be the person or persons to be required? 4th. In Case of Refusal, and Retaliation becom[in]g necessary, of what Description shall the Officer be on whom it is to take place; and how should he be designated for the purpose?

Each officer was then to write down his opinion, seal it in an envelope, and address it to General Washington.[30]

The council of war unanimously agreed that retaliation was "justifiable and expedient." A majority, twenty-two, believed that a demand be made of Clinton to surrender Lippincott, and if he refused, that a regular army officer of Huddy's rank be substituted, and the designation be made by lot from among the prisoners of war who had surrendered at discretion and not under convention or capitulation. Three among the staff wanted instant satisfaction. Washington approved of the majority decision and stated that his intention to retaliate would be made known to General Clinton unless Lippincott was surrendered to face execution.[31]

Copies of the papers concerning the Huddy murder, the council of war, and Washington's decision were submitted to the Continental Congress on April 20, and referred to a committee consisting of Elias Boudinot of New Jersey, John Morin Scott of New York, and Thomas Bee of South Carolina.[32] In the meantime, on April 21, Washington wrote General Clinton, enclosing copies of all papers of the case, including representations by Monmouth County citizens of "the most wanton, unprecedented and inhuman Murder that ever disgraced the Arms of a Civilized people." In the words of one French officer, Washington strongly "demanded that the officer who had commanded this party and had tolerated such revolting cruelty should be turned over to him, unless M. Clinton wished to punish such an atrocious crime himself."[33] As James Madison would note, Washington had, "in the most decisive terms, claimed of Sir Henry Clinton a delivery of the offenders up to justice, as the only means of averting the stroke of vengeance from the innocent head of a captive officer of equal rank to the Jersey captain." Congress immediately declared "their firmest support" of the decision.[34]

Washington, indeed, had gotten straight to the point. "To save the innocent," he told Clinton:

> I demand the guilty. Capt[ai]n Lipp[in]cot[t] therefore, or the Officer who commanded at the Execution of Capt Huddy must be given up; or if that Officer was of inferior Rank to him so many of the perpetrators as will according to the Tariff of Exchange be of an equivalent. To do this will mark the Justice of your Excell[enc]y's Character. In failure of it, I shall hold myself justifiable in the Eyes of God and Man, for the measure of which I shall resort.[35]

Clinton, who found himself in a most difficult situation, replied four days later:

> My personal feelings, therefore, require no such incitement to urge me to take every proper notice of the barbarous outrage against humanity, (which you have represented to me,) the moment that it came to my knowledge; and accordingly, when I heard of Captain Huddy's death, (which was only four days before I received your letter,) I instantly ordered a strict enquiry to be made in all its circumstances, and shall bring the perpetrators of it to an immediate trial.[36]

On the day following his reply to Washington, April 26, Clinton ordered that in the future, the removal of any prisoner from the prison house to which he had been consigned by the Board of Loyalists be forbidden. He then ordered a court martial convened on May 3 to try the American charges against Lippincott. President of the court martial was Major General James Patterson, but also on board as a member was Brigadier General Cortland Skinner, last Royal Attorney General of New Jersey and now commander of the New Jersey Volunteers, who could be expected to speak in Lippincott's defense.[37]

Ironically, ordering the court martial would be among Clinton's last official acts as Commander-in-Chief of His Majesty's force in North America. The vexing situation regarding the Huddy affair would face a new hurdle: Sir Henry Clinton had resigned and was temporarily replaced two days before the trial by Lieutenant General James Robertson, his second-in-command, until the arrival of Sir Guy Carleton, who would supercede Clinton. In the meantime, Robertson was already well apprised of the situation and immediately sought to smooth the waters with Washington. "I make it one of my first cares," he assured the general by letter on May 1, "to convince you of my wish to carry on the war agreeable to rules which humanity formed and the example of the politest nations recommend." Such words now mattered little, however, only the result of the court martial itself.[38]

The formal trial, held behind closed doors, was revelatory and shocking. It quickly became apparent that Lippincott had conducted the outrageous execution of Huddy upon the explicit verbal order of Franklin and the Board of Directors of the Associated Loyalists. Charges that Franklin had attempted to convince the captain to testify otherwise quickly surfaced. The military's indignation towards the governor was visceral and permitted Lippincott to assert that he was free of all responsibility for the act, and that if anyone should be charged the court need only look as far as Franklin and the Board. The challenge, of course, placed Clinton in a most awkward position as he had been responsible for the authorization of the Board and the Associated Loyalists in the first place, but it mattered little now that he was no longer in command.[39]

Another most embarrassing fact emerged as well: Huddy had been made a prisoner of war a full four days before Philip White had been shot while attempting to escape his own captors, "according to the rules of war," as one observer of the affair commented in disgust. "There is nothing blamable in that action." Indeed, Lippincott had read to Franklin the words on the placard that he later attached to Huddy's breast after his execution, well before he left New York to superintend the execution.[40]

"So, who was Philip White?" the tribunal wanted to know. It was then revealed that he was indeed a New York refugee who had been marauding in Monmouth County, and had been captured, then killed while attempting to escape, a sad event but under the commonly accepted rules of war quite legal.

The Board of Associated Loyalists were obliged to present their own report on the Huddy affair, which was done in a deposition given by Aaron White regarding his brother's death. In an effort to sidestep guilt in the matter, the Board submitted something of an apology, while at the same time attempting to justify the act by charging the rebels with the deaths of fourteen Loyalists.

We thought it high time to convince the rebels we would no longer submit to such glaring acts of barbarism, and though we lament the necessity by which we have been driven to begin a retaliation of intolerable cruelties, that we could not have saved the life of Captain Tilton by any other means. We therefore pitched upon Joshua Huddy for a proper subject for retaliation, because he was not only well known to have been a very active and cruel persecutor of our friends, but he had not been ashamed to boast of his having been instrumental in hanging Stephen Edwards, a worthy Loyalist, and the first of our brethren who fell a martyr to republican fury in Monmouth county. The recent instance of cruelty, added to the many daring acts of the same nature which have been perpetrated with impunity by a set of vindictive rebels, well known by the name of the Monmouth Retaliators, associated and headed by one General Forman, whose horrid acts of cruelty have gained him universally the name of Black David, fired our party with an indignation only to be felt by men who for a series of years have beheld many of their friends and neighbors butchered in cold blood, under the usurped form of law, and often without that ceremony, for no other crime than that of maintaining their allegiance to the government under which they were born, and which rebels audaciously call treason against the States.[41]

Justification for taking prisoners for the purpose of securing an exchange of officers, such as Tilton was one thing. But in other cases, such as the execution of Stephen Edwards, whom the Board termed a martyr, it was learned the subject had been sent from New York into Monmouth County as a spy and had been arrested, convicted, and hung as such, all deemed perfectly legal under the rules of war. Another of the supposed martyrs was Jacob Fagan who, under the banner of the Loyalist cause, had commanded a band of robbers, incendiaries, and murderers in the New Jersey Pine Barrens, one that had plagued both sides.[42] It was clear to the court that such men, and others like them, had received the military justice that was commonly acceptable by all nations.

Though he was not personally charged, it seemed clear that the mantel of guilt for authorizing the execution of Captain Huddy fell squarely on Franklin and the Board. The governor did not stay to face recriminations from the military or the enemy, but immediately sailed for England, where he would live out the rest of his life, a broken man. The Board would soon be dismantled. But the findings of the court regarding Captain Richard Lippincott would only increase the acrimony between the Americans and the British, even as peace negotiations were getting underway in France. The findings of the court martial were clear:

> The court having considered the evidence for and against the prisoner, Captain Richard Lippincott, together with what he had to offer in his defence; and it appearing that (although Joshua Huddy was executed without proper authority) what the prisoner did in the matter was not the effect of malice or ill-will, but proceeded from a conviction that it was his duty to obey the orders of the Board of Directors of Associated Loyalists, and his not doubting their having full authority to give such order; the court are of the opinion that he, the prisoner, Captain Richard Lippincott, is not guilty of the murder laid to his charge, and do therefore acquit him.[43]

XXI

The Villain and the Victim

"If they spare us for murder they'll spare us for lying."

By April 29, the congressional committee assigned to review the papers sent by Washington regarding the Huddy Affair had already reported to Congress. The issue was immediately addressed in a Congressional Resolution the same day by stating that after deliberate consideration of the documents and with the necessity of convincing the enemies of the United States, "by the most decided conduct, that the repetition of their unprecedented and unhuman cruelties so contrary to the laws of nations and of war" would no longer be suffered with impunity. Therefore, Congress unanimously approved of "the firm and judicious conduct of the Commander-in-Chief in his application to the British General at New York," and assured him of "their firmest support in his fixed purpose of exemplary retaliation."[1]

General Washington was in effect given carte blanche to respond to the issue as necessary. For his own part, while awaiting word of the outcome of the trial, the general prepared for the worst and instructed the Commissary of Prisoners to draw up a list of British officers who were currently prisoners held under the supervision of Brigadier General Moses Hazen. The directive was dispatched on May 3, the same day as the court martial was being quietly convened in New York City, along with orders for Hazen, immediately upon receipt, to "designate, by Lot . . . a British Captain who is an unconditional Prisoner, if such a one is in your possession; if not, a Lieutenant under the same circumstances from among the Prisoners at any of the Posts either in Pennsylvania or Maryland." Once chosen, the prisoner was to be sent under guard to Philadelphia, "where the Minister of War will order a proper Guard to receive and conduct him to the place of his Destination." Washington then informed the Secretary of War of his actions and requested that an escort under a "very discreet and vigilant Officer" conduct the prisoner to the cantonment of the New Jersey troops.[2]

Though deeply troubled by the morality of the situation and the "disagreeable necessity of retaliation" forced upon him, Washington was determined to adhere to the course set before him.[3] He wrote:

> Keenly wounded as my feelings will be at the deplorable destiny of the unhappy Victim, no gleam of hope can arise to him but from the conduct of the Enemey [*sic*]themselves. This he may be permitted to communicate to the British Commander in Chief; in whose power alone it rests to avert the impending vengeance from the innocent, by executing it on the guilty; at the same time it may be announced, that I will receive no application nor answer any Letter on the subject, which does not inform me that ample satisfaction is made for the death of Capt. Huddy on the perpetrators of that horrid deed."[4]

Upon receipt of Robertson's letter, but still unaware of the results of Lippincott's court martial, Washington informed the general that he had determined to follow through with the resolution regarding retaliation. "The time and Place are fixed; but I still hope the result of your Court Martial will prevent this dreadful alternative."[5] Nevertheless, while demanding satisfaction from the enemy, he also sought to ready himself to counter charges by the Board of Loyalist Associators that they had been justified in their actions, which were taken in retaliation for "a number of instances of Cruelty" committed by Americans, particularly in Monmouth County. Thus, on May 6, he wrote to Governor Livingston of New Jersey:

> I cannot forbear observing to your Excellency that whilst I demand Satisfaction from the Enemy for the Violences they commit, it becomes us to be particularly careful that they have not the like claim on us, and I must beg you to make it known to all persons acting in a military capacity in your State that I shall hold myself obliged to deliver up to the Enemy or otherwise to punish such of them as shall commit any Act which is in the least contrary to the Laws of War.[6]

Though Clinton attempted to disown the Loyalists, Lippincott, one of their officers, would not be surrendered to face almost certain death at the hands of the Americans. Many on the American side, unaware that the trial had already reached a verdict of innocent accused the court of having "tried to evade holding a serious and formal inquiry."[7]

Washington was not the only one concerned with the downward spiral that the execution might ignite. Many in Congress were equally distressed, although they saw no alternative but to stand by Washington's decision, which most felt would prove beneficial in that it would serve to drive a wedge between the British Army and the Loyalists. "Congress have resolved to support him," wrote Arthur Middleton to Aedanus Burke,

> . . and I believe they will be executed and when we have once enter'd the Retaliatory road, no doubt we shall proceed with them *passitus equis*; therefore let our Enemies beware of improper Conduct, and let our Friends take care how [not to] fall into their hands. The Demand by the General to Clinton is likely to occasion very great & serious differences between the British & the Refugees.[8]

John Hanson of Maryland was of the same mind, when he wrote:

> This affair it is to be hoped will encrease the Animosity Allready Subsisting between the British, and the Refugees; If he [Lippincott] is given up the latter will think themselves Injuriously treated, And if a British Officer (and especially one of such powerful Connections) is Sacrafised to Save the life of a Refugee, it must excite indignation in the former and occasion Such uneasiness and dissatisfaction in their Army, as will not be easily removed.[9]

Expecting a response from General Robertson, Washington was surprised to receive, on the evening of May 9, a letter from Sir Guy Carleton, the new British Commander-in-Chief in North America, dated two days earlier, containing affidavits laid before Sir Henry Clinton regarding the executions or murders of Loyalists, including Aaron White's testimony on the killing of Philip White. All were forwarded to the President of Congress.[10] In a short reply to Carleton, Washington did not sway from his resolve: "With respect to a late Transaction, to which I presume your Excellency alludes," he wrote, "I have already expressed my Resolution, a resolution formed of the most mature deliberation, and from which I shall not recede."[11]

Washington's request that he be supplied with an unconditional surrender prisoner came to naught, as none, he was informed by the Secretary of War, were then in American hands. He was thus obliged to order General Hazen, on May 18, to select by lot an officer from among all the British captains who were currently being held under "Capitulation or Convention" with exceptions being extended only to aide's de camp to brigadier generals and brigade majors.[12]

In accordance with the orders of the commander in chief, thirteen British officers, eight captains and five lieutenants belonging to seven regiments that had formally capitulated almost seven months earlier and surrendered at Yorktown and being held at York, Pennsylvania, were ordered under guard to Lancaster. There, they were to draw lots at 10 a.m. on May 2 to determine who was to be sacrificed in the stead of Lippincott.[13]

One can almost imagine the tension among the unfortunate thirteen, knowing that one among them would likely be executed, though innocent of any wrongdoing. Under the supervision of Major James Gordon, of the 80th Regiment of Foot, thirteen pieces of paper, one bearing the word "unfortunate," were placed in a hat, and each of the men drew one. The fatal piece was drawn by "a Youth, not more than 19 or 20 Years of Age," a captain named Charles Asgill of the 1st Regiment of Foot, the Scots Guards, and the only son of Sir Charles Asgill, a wealthy English baronet who was once Lord Mayor of London and, ironically, a long-time friend to the American cause, but now a great invalid in feeble health. The young Asgill himself had many American friends, and had attended as a student at Westminster School with three South Carolinians. He was heir to an extensive fortune, and had a "great Interest in the British Court and Armies." It was, for both the Americans and the British a most unfortunate choice of fate.[14]

"I knew it would be so," the despondent officer sighed upon drawing the fatal piece of paper. "I have never won so much as a bet of back-gammon in my life." Fearing that the condemned man might attempt to escape, and if successful perhaps thereby cause a second lottery, one of his fellow officers from the same regiment, Lieutenant R. Fulke Grenville, sat up with him throughout the night.[15]

Upon completion of the lottery selection, General Hazen informed Washington:

The British Officers are highly enraged at the Conduct of Sir Henry Clinton; they have solicited my leave to send an Officer to New-York on this Occasion, or that I would intercede with the Minister of War to grant it. Being fully convinced that no Inconvenience could possibly arise from our Cause from this Indulgence, but on the contrary, the good Policy and Humanity dictates the measure, I was pleased at the Application, and with Cheerfulness have recommended to the Minister of War to grant the honourable Capt. Ludlow, son of the Earl of Ludlow, leave to carry the Representations of those unfortunate Officers, who openly declare to have been deserted by their General, and given up to suffer for the Sins of the Guilty.[16]

Asgill was soon sent to Philadelphia under guard, accompanied by his friend Captain Ludlow, also of the 1st Regiment, and then to Chatham, in Morris County, New Jersey, where a part of the 2nd Regiment of Brigadier General Elias Drayton's New Jersey Line of the Continental Army was posted. It was under Drayton's care the prisoner was to be held and the execution carried out. Both British officers were there to be confined until either Lippincott was surrendered or the final decision to execute Asgill, who was not an unconditional prisoner, was made.

Washington was deeply concerned that the prisoner had been surrendered in good faith of a capitulation, and more so in that two prisoners had reportedly just been found (albeit not yet verified), one being held at York and the other at Winchester, who were in fact unconditional prisoners. In a letter to Major General Benjamin Lincoln, he explained his fear. "Congress by their resolve have unanimously approved of my determination to retaliate; the army have advised it and the country look for it. But how far it is justifiable upon an officer under the faith of a capitulation, if none other can be had, is the question." The danger of British retaliation by doing the same to an American officer who had capitulated in good faith, and of the remonstrance and recriminations that were likely to be forthcoming from Carleton, worried the commander-in-chief no end. With Hazen having already sent Asgill on to the place of execution, Washington wrote, "makes the matter more distressing, as the whole business will have the appearance of a farce, if some person is not sacrificed to the manes of poor Huddy, which will be the case, if an unconditional prisoner can not be found, and Asgill escapes." That the young, charming aristocrat was about to be executed for a crime he did not commit, just when the war appeared to be nearing an end, seemed to the general, to everyone concerned, and indeed the public at large, a total outrage.[17]

Despite his concerns, Washington ordered Dayton to grant Ludlow permission to go to New York "with such Representations as Capt Asgill shall please to make to Sir Guy.... In the Mean Time, I must beg that you will be pleased to treat Capt. Asgill with every tender Attention and politeness (consistent with his present Situation) which his Rank, Fortune and Connection, together with his Unfortunate State, demand."[18]

• • •

The Huddy Affair was quickly escalating in notoriety, both in America and in Europe. Representations from at home and abroad, from such notables as General Rochambeau, Alexander Hamilton, Richard Oswald in Paris (the British merchant who had been sent to sound out Franklin on terms for negotiations) and others, were growing by the day.[19] The noted pamphleteer Thomas Paine, believing Clinton was still in command, dispatched a most scathing letter to him regarding the situation and signed it "Common Sense."

"The villain and the victim are here separated characters," he wrote.

You hold the one and we hold the other. You disown or affect to disown and reprobate the conduct of Lippincott; yet you give him sanctuary, and by so doing you as effectively become the executioner of Asgill as if you put the rope round his neck and dismissed him from the world. Whatever your feelings of the extraordinary occasion may be are best known to yourself. Within the grave of your own mind lies buried the fate of Asgill. He becomes the corpse of your will or the survivor of your justice. Deliver up the one and you save the other; withhold the one and the other dies by your choice. On our part the case is exceedingly plain; an officer has been taken from his confinement and murdered, and the murderer is within your lines.[20]

On May 30, Robert R. Livingston of New York, Secretary for Foreign Affairs, wrote to Benjamin Franklin in Passy, France, who was then engaged in the on-again-off-again game of securing recognition of independence, informing him of the unhappy events. "It is really a melancholy case," he concluded, "but the repeated cruelties of this kind that have been practiced, have rendered it absolutely necessary to execute the resolution to retaliate, which we have so often taken, and so frequently been prevented by our feelings from carrying into execution." The Secretary was deeply concerned that "the affair of Huddy . . . will need explanation in Europe." And so it did. Within weeks, all of the continent was apprised of the events unfolding in New Jersey, which had taken on international proportions and promised to become a grim obstruction to America's campaign for both recognition and diplomatic support.[21]

Franklin, whose own son had promulgated the crisis in the first place, was of the opinion that, as it appeared those in charge refused to give up a murderer, choosing to preserve him over Asgill, the only hope was that "application should be made to the English ministers for positive orders directing General Carleton to deliver up Lippincott, which orders being obtained should be dispatched immediately by a swift-sailing vessel." In any event, he felt that Congress and its generals had often threatened retaliation in the past but had never followed through. Had they done so, the great sage complained, "this crime would not have been committed," and Washington, whom he knew would stick to his resolve, had little choice but to address the people's clamor for retaliation. "I am persuaded that nothing I could say to him on the occasion would have the least effect in changing his determination." For Franklin, the fact that his own estranged son had been the instigator of the entire affair may have helped harden his own resolve in support of the sad reprisal.[22]

Alexander Hamilton, for one, was deeply concerned, not only for how the execution of Asgill might be viewed from across the Atlantic, by the French, Spanish, and Dutch, but about what it might do to the national character of the United States itself. "As this appears to me clearly to be an ill-timed proceeding," he wrote to General Henry Knox,

and if persisted in will be derogatory to the national character. . . . A sacrifice of this sort is entirely repugnant to the genius of the age we live in, and is without example in modem history, nor can it fail to be considered in Europe as wanton and unnecessary. . . . Our affairs are now in a prosperous train, and so vigorous—I would rather say so violent—a measure would want the plea of necessity. It would argue that at this late stage of the war, in the midst of success, we should suddenly depart from that temper with which we have all along borne with a great and more frequent provocation. The death of [Major John] André could not have been dispensed with, but it must still be viewed at a distance as an act of rigid justice. If we wreak our resentment on an innocent person, it will be suspected that we are too fond of executions. I am persuaded it will have an influence peculiarly unfavorable to the General's character.[23]

Like Clinton before him, Carleton was also in a most sticky situation. The importunities by the officer corps on the one hand in favor of a brother officer, and on the other the "fear of disobliging the Refugees" by delivering up their brother Lippincott, as it appeared to some in Congress, must "embarrass Sir Guy exceedingly." There were even rumors that if he surrendered Huddy's executioner, the refugees would lay down their arms and fight no more.[24]

The impasse continued into mid-June, and rumors began to circulate out of Philadelphia that Carleton had determined to turn Lippincott over to Washington. Another was that he had been sent out across British lines by way of Staten Island, and that all the refugees had been ordered into New York City to avoid reprisals.[25]

By June 26, no word regarding the court martial of Lippincott had yet reached the public and Washington remained silent, undoubtedly determined to hold off on Asgill's execution as long as possible. He had kept Congress apprised of his communications with Carleton ever since June 6, and on June 11 informed General Dayton that he was still in the dark regarding Carleton's intentions or his response to Asgill's request for relief. Thus, having heard nothing from New York, he resolved to suspend a decision regarding the captive's fate until he was informed of Sir Guy's decision. But repeated rumors began to circulate that Lippincott had received a sentence of death and was to be executed at New York or would be sent out to the Americans.[26]

While the two sides procrastinated, Asgill was allowed to go about "without Guard, and under no constraint" at Chatham, which aroused some upset from the commander-in-chief, who instructed Dayton to have the young officer treated with "Tenderness… consistent with his present Situation" but to be held as a close prisoner with the greatest security. Washington was still awaiting word regarding the findings of the Lippincott court martial, and would not learn that a verdict had been determined until July, and even then Carleton wisely refrained from informing him what it was. Some in Congress had already begun to assume from the silence from New York that "it may be concluded that Lippincot is Acquitted," but no one could say for sure.[27]

Dutifully, Carleton's communication was forwarded by Washington to Congress and read on July 15. One of the lines in the letter, stating that "in a civil war between people of one empire there can during the contest be no traitors at all," struck James Madison as worrisome, particularly as other parts mentioning Lippincott appeared to "make it probable that Asgil[l] will at last be left to expiate the guilt of this mu[r]derer." Yet, there was still no definitive statement regarding the outcome of the trial other than the court had passed their judgment and a copy of the proceedings would soon be sent. "It is inferred that this murderer will not be given up," he wrote in a letter to Edmund Randolph, "and Consequently a vicarious atonement must be made by the guiltless Asgill."[28]

Finally, on July 25, the British commander dispatched another letter to Washington to arrange a formal exchange of documents relative to the court's findings and assuring him that he would receive "the fullest Satisfaction in this Matter." Five days later, upon receipt of the letter, Washington responded to inform Carleton that he would be sending Major General Heath, his second in command, and two aides-de-camp to meet with an officer of equal rank, on neutral ground at the plantation of Colonel Frederick Philipse, on the Hudson on August 5, to receive the proceedings of the court martial.[29]

Two days before the appointed time, Washington informed General Heath of his mission, and that he was to meet with Carleton's designated emissary, Chief Justice Smith of New York. His instructions were clear:

> If you should find that the design of Sir Guy Carleton, is to procrastinate this business, to envelop it in as much intricacy and difficulty as possible, or that he means to justify it by recrimination and Law Cases, thereby attempting to avert our purpose of Retaliation, you may assure him (unless you shall judge it expedient to leave me more at liberty), if not explicitly, at least by strong insinuation, that he will miss his Aim; and that my deliberate and dispassionate proceedings in this case are intended to give him, as he now has had, full time to determine whether the guilty person, or an innocent Officer, shall be made the subject of Retaliation.

Moreover, Heath was instructed to have the official proceedings between himself and Smith, or anyone else that should be sent, recorded in writing, that there be no omissions or misconceptions. The meeting, however, was cancelled at the last minute by Carleton, claiming that it was unnecessary to send an officer of equivalent rank to Heath merely to send out "a Bundle of papers only" which could be sent by ordinary conveyance.[30]

And the foot-dragging on both sides continued, neither side wishing to touch the tripwire that would hang an innocent man.

By this time, the pressure on Washington, in both America and Europe, to stay the execution of Asgill was growing stronger by the day, but his resolve in the matter was unyielding. When the States General of Holland dispatched an appeal to Congress requesting an immediate pardon for the young officer, the general remained unbroken. Asgill himself was allowed to request Sir Guy to interpose on his behalf, but for naught. Somehow, Washington was able to mercifully postpone the execution though it was now clear that, after nearly three months of obfuscation by the British regarding the court martial judgment, Lippincott had been found not guilty.[31]

In the meantime, another force, perhaps more determined than anyone could anticipate, had come into play—the French Huguenot wife of Lord Asgill, Lady Thérèse Prativiel. Unwilling to subject her invalid husband, who lay in a frail state of health, to word of their son's dilemma lest it have a negative effect on the old man's well being, she took it upon herself to appeal in person to the one source she though might help, King George III. The monarch responded positively and directed the British commander-in-chief in America "that the author of the crime which dishonored the English nation should be given up for punishment." Unfortunately, whether it was through the influence of Loyalists residing in England, possibly even William Franklin, who caused the order not to be sent or if dispatched to secretly be ignored, or some other form of miscommunication, the command was not followed.[32]

In desperation, and unquestionably distracted by grief, Lady Asgill turned to her former countrymen, the French, whose wartime alliance with America and immense influence with both General Washington and the Continental Congress could not be denied. They had, after all, been pivotal in securing the great victory at Yorktown and might prove equally important in saving the life of her son. On July 18, 1782, from London, she dispatched a moving letter to the French Secretary of State, Charles Gravier, Comte de Vergennes.

Sir: If the politeness of the French court will permit an application of a stranger, there can be no doubt but one in which all the tender feelings of an individual can be interested will meet with a favorable reception from a nobleman whose character does honor, not only to his own country, but to human nature. The subject, sir, on which I presume to implore your assistance is too heart-piercing for me to dwell on, and common fame has most probably informed you of it; it therefore renders the painful task unnecessary.

My son (an only son), as dear as he is brave, amiable as he is deserving to be so, only nineteen, a prisoner under the articles of capitulation of Yorktown, is now confined in America, an object of retaliation. Shall an innocent suffer for the guilty? Represent to yourself, sir, the situation of a family under these circumstances; surrounded as I am by objects of distress, distracted with fear and grief, no words can express my feeling or paint the scene: my husband given over by his physicians a few hours before the news arrived, and not in a state to be informed of the misfortune; my daughter seized with a fever and delirium, raving about her brother, and without one interval of reason, save to hear heart-alleviating circumstances.

Let your feelings, sir, suggest and plead for my inexpressible misery. A word from you, like a voice from heaven, will save us from distraction and wretchedness. I am well informed General Washington reveres your character. Say but to him you wish my son to be released, and he will restore him to his distracted family and render him to happiness. My son's virtue and bravery will justify the deed. His honor, sir, carried him to America. He was born to affluence, independence and the happiest prospects. Let me again supplicate your goodness; let me respectfully implore your high influence in behalf of innocence, in the cause of justice, of humanity, that you would, sir, despatch a letter to General Washington from France, and favor me with a copy of it to be sent from hence.

I am sensible of the liberty I have taken in making this request; but I am sensible, whether you comply with it or not, you will pity the distress that suggests it; your humanity will drop a tear on the fault and efface it. I will pray that heaven may grant you may never want the comfort it is in your power to bestow on.[33]

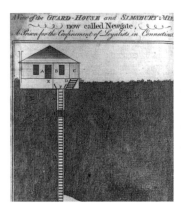  

Left: George Washington, 1783, by Pierre Eugène Du Simitière. Courtesy Library of Congress.

Center: Captain Charles Asgill. Reproduction from *History of the war with America, France, Spain, and Holland* by John Andrews, 1785-86. Courtesy Rare Book and Special Collections Division, Library of Congress.

Right: Charles Gravier, comte de Vergennes, by Edme Bovinet, engraver. Courtesy Prints and Photographs Division, Library of Congress.

The count was indeed moved by the letter and was soon able to present it to King Louis XVI and Queen Marie Antoinette, both of whom were also deeply stirred by the plight of young Asgill. "The goodness of Their Majesties' hearts," Vergennes later wrote, "induced them to desire the inequities of an unfortunate mother may be calmed, and her tenderness reassured." He was thus instructed to do what had to be done, which was to send Lady Asgill's letter to General Washington, together with a request from the King and Queen of France that her son be released. On July 29, 1782, writing from the palace at Versailles, Vergennes set to words his own elegant epistle to the American commander:

> Sir: it is not in quality of a King, the friend and ally of the United States (though with the knowledge and consent of His Majesty), that I now have the honor to write to Your Excellency. It is as a man of sensibility, and a tender father who feels all the force of paternal love, that I take the liberty to address to Your Excellency my earnest solicitations in favor of a mother and family in tears. Her situation seems the more worthy of notice on our part, as it is to the humanity of a nation at war with her own, that she has recourse for what she ought to receive from the impartial justice of her own generals.
>
> I have the honor to enclose Your Excellency a copy of a letter which Lady Asgil has just wrote me. I am not known to her, nor was I acquainted that her son was the unhappy victim, destined by lot to expiate the odious crime that a formal denial of justice obliges you to revenge.
>
> Your Excellency will not read this letter without being extremely affected; it had that effect upon the King and Queen, to whom I communicated it.... I felt, sir, that there are cases where humanity itself exacts the most extreme rigor;

perhaps the one now in question may be of the number; but allowing reprisals to be just, it is not less horrid to those who are the victims; and the character of Your Excellency is too well known for me not to be persuaded that you desire nothing more than to be able to avoid the disagreeable necessity.

There is one consideration, sir, which, though it is not decisive, may have an influence on your resolution. Captain Asgill is doubtless your prisoner, but he is among those whom the arms of the King contributed to put into your hands at Yorktown. Although this circumstance does not operate as a safeguard, it however justifies the interest I permit myself to take in this affair. If it is in your power, sir, to consider and have regard to it, you will do what is agreeable to Their Majesties; the danger of young Asgill, the tears, the despair of his mother, affect them sensibly; and they will see with pleasure the hope of consolation shine out for those unfortunate people.

In seeking to deliver Mr. Asgill from the fate which threatens him I am far from engaging you to seek another victim; the pardon, to be perfectly satisfactory, must be entire. I do not imagine it can be productive of any bad consequences. If the English general has not been able to punish the horrible crime you complain of in so exemplary a manner as he should, there is reason to think he will take the most efficacious measures to prevent the like in future.

I sincerely wish, sir, that my intercession may meet success; the sentiment which dictates it, and which you have not ceased to manifest on every occasion, assures me that you will not be indifferent to the prayers and to the tears of a family which has recourse to your clemency through me. It is rendering homage to your virtue to implore it.[34]

The plea had been extended but it required delivery be made across an ocean that took weeks, and sometimes months, to cross.

• • •

Charles Asgill continued to live on the edge of a gallows drop throughout the hot summer of 1782, always treated with politeness and "tender attention" as Washington had instructed, and permitted parole from time to time in the towns of Chatham and Morristown.[35] Somehow the general managed to continue walking the edge himself, willing to let Congress itself resume the debate about what was to be done.

By October, a large majority of Congress, frustrated by a lack of resolution, finally determined that the execution of Charles Asgill must go forward. A motion was made to order the deed to proceed immediately. James Duane and Elias Boudinot mounted strong opposing arguments but in vain. "We urged every argument that the peculiarity of the case suggested," Boudinot would write, "and spent three days in warm debate, during which more ill blood appeared in the House than I had seen. Near the close of the third day, when every argument was exhausted, without any appearance of success, the matter was brought to a close by the question being ordered to be taken." The order for the execution of Asgill, it would appear, was about to be approved by the highest body in the land.

The following morning, however, as soon as the minutes were read, the president of Congress announced that a letter had arrived from General Washington and that it also be read. The letter stated that the general had just received a communication from the King and Queen of France, (actually Vergennes in their behalf), on October 25, enclosing another letter from Lady Asgill to the royals asking for the life of her son "that on the whole was enough to move the heart of a savage."

Representative Boudinot wrote of the moment:

> This operated like an electrical shock—each member looking on his neighbor in surprise, as if saying "here is unfair play." It was suspected to be some scheme of the minority. The President was interrogated. The cover of the letters was called for. The General's signature was examined. In short, it looked so much like something supernatural that even the minority, who were so much pleased with it, could scarcely think it real.

After some time, and finally convinced "of the integrity of the Transaction," a motion was made that the life of Captain Asgill be spared as a compliment to the King of France. The motion was unanimously carried. Another motion was made that General Washington should remand Asgill to his prison quarters at Lancaster, Pennsylvania. To this an objection was raised by Elias Boudinot on the grounds that "as we considered Asgil's life as forfeit, and we had given him to the King of France, he was now a free man." He then moved that he be immediately released and returned to New York without any prisoner exchange required. The motion was unanimously adopted, "and thus we got clear of shedding innocent blood by a wonderful interposition of Providence."[36]

On November 5, 1782, Congress resolved that the Commander-in-Chief be directed to set Captain Asgill at liberty. Eight days later a copy of the congressional resolution was sent to Asgill along with a letter from Washington. Soon afterwards Washington wrote to Carleton, reminding him of his promise to make further inquiry regarding the murder and to collect evidence for the prosecution of such individuals that were complicit in the crime, but without satisfaction, for everyone knew that the war was near an end.[37]

Washington did not forget who had been the interlocutor responsible for helping bring the crisis to, if not a totally agreeable resolution, at least a humane one. "I think I may venture," he wrote to Vergennes on November 21, "to assure your excellency that your Generous interposition had no small degree of weight in procluding the decision in favor of Captain Asgill, which he had no right to expect from the very unsatisfactory measures, which had been taken by the British Commander-in-Chief, to atone for a crime of the blackest dye, not to be justified by the practices of war, and unknown at this day amongst civilized nations."[38]

For the most part, on the American side, retaliation was limited now to little more than mocking humor. In a poem by Philip Freneau, entitled "Rivington's Reflections," alluding to one James Rivington, printer of the New York Tory newspaper *Rivington's New-York Loyal Gazette*, a satirical caste was laid on the British even as their evacuation of New York was being considered:

I'll petition the rebels (if York is forsaken)
For a place in their Zion which ne'er shall be shaken.
I am sure that they'll be clever; it seems their whole body study;
They hung not young Asgill for old Captain Huddy.
And it must be a truth that admits no denying —
If they spare us for murder they'll spare us for lying.[39]

· · ·

Charles Asgill returned to his homeland in the ship *Swallow*, landing at Falmouth, England, on December 15, 1782. In October 1783, after peace had been proclaimed, he journeyed with his mother and sister to Paris to thank the French King and Queen for their intervention on his behalf. He was, by then, already a celebrity in France, where every detail of his travails in America had been published in the *Gazette de France* and the *Mercurede France*. Portraits of his youthful face were engraved and exhibited throughout Paris, where several plays in which he was the principal character were presented, including one by the noted M. de Sauvigny called "Abdir." Upon his father's demise he succeeded to the baronetcy, and in later years served his country again as a general officer in the British Army.[40]

· · ·

Unhappily for all concerned, even as the Huddy Affair was playing out its final acts, the dirty little civil war along the New Jersey coast between Loyalists and Patriots, privateersmen and whaleboat raiders alike, continued on much as always. Even as the great land campaigns that had raged unabated for seven years on the North American mainland were, by all measures, winding down and planning for the evacuation of His Majesty's armies and loyal subjects were in the offing, the grim little blood feuds and raids on the New Jersey coast continued with unvarnished bitterness.

On March 25, 1782, only two days after the Loyalist capture of the Toms River blockhouse, Adam Hyler, though somewhat injured by an earlier but unspecified accident, was en route down the Shrewsbury River with several armed vessels when he encountered a party of twenty-five British soldiers under a Captain Schaak, of the 57th Regiment of Foot; they had been "detached to intercept him in passing through the gut." As soon as the famed whaleboat warrior discovered them, before being sighted himself, he immediately landed thirteen of his men with orders to charge the enemy. The surprise was total and the engagement was short, albeit nasty, with four of the British killed or wounded, and Captain Schaak and eight others made prisoners. Hyler's remaining party concentrated their own fire on the enemy's fleeing gunboat, upon which several on board were seen to fall before it escaped. It was later touted that, had he not been earlier injured, Hyler would have taken the remaining dozen men of the 57th.[41]

Like many of the New Jersey whaleboat raiders, Hyler was operating as a partisan fighter rather than as a formally commissioned privateersman. Nevertheless, his activities, like those of Marriner and others, were rarely questioned by state authorities as their impact upon enemy operations, although not strategically significant, tended to keep the foe in a state of constant agitation. Indeed, not until June 25, 1782, did he bother to formally apply to New Jersey's Governor Livingston by letter, carried by a trusted lieutenant named Bordewine, requesting a regular privateer commission for his new flag boat *Active*. The vessel, with just two long guns and four swivels and manned by a crew of twenty-five, was the most heavily armed boat Hyler ever commanded. The diminutive craft weighed in at only fourteen or fifteen tons. Unfortunately, he was unable to post bond, but promised to do so as soon as he could. Whether he kept his promise or not is uncertain.[42]

In the meantime, though suffering from his earlier injuries and with or without a formal commission, Adam Hyler continued his daring defiance of British might. On July 2, in cooperation with another whaleboat skipper named Story, he carried out another brazen raid in his favorite hunting grounds near Sandy Hook. This time his target was the schooner *Skip Jack*, armed with six carriage guns besides swivels, and tender to Admiral Mariot Arbuthnot's flagship. The audacious assault came at high noon within sight of guard ships and several other men of war lying close by the Hook. Though several of the schooner's crew managed to escape upon sight of the two approaching whaleboats, the schooner, along with her captain and nine or ten hands, was taken easily. Finding the vessel aground, and being unable to get her off, the raiders quickly set the prize ablaze and escaped unharmed, all within sight of the Royal Navy.[43]

Not long afterwards, Adam Hyler conducted what must have been his last raid, capturing "three other small vessels, which were on the trading scheme, one of them being loaded with calves, sheep, &c. bound from New Jersey to New-York."[44] Two months later, the famed raider died from complications of his accidental injury.

The Loyalists, like their opposites, also continued to wage the unrelenting partisan warfare that they had become so good at. On June 1, even as rumors of an impending armistice were being circulated, a refugee leader named Davenport landed with eighty men, half white and half black, at Forked River, New Jersey, and utterly destroyed a substantial salt works belonging to Samuel Brown, before plundering the owner of all of his personal possessions. Davenport and his men then proceeded southward to Barnegat to assail the salt works that had sprung up along the shores following the last series of raids, much to the despair of the New Jersey authorities. "Thus," noted one cynical commentary, "they are conciliating the affections of the Americans!"[45]

For the Americans, particularly the merchants of Philadelphia, the situation on the Delaware, despite a few bright spots like Captain Barney's victory over the *General Monk*, had continued to worsen by the day. "This place," wrote Delegate Jesse Root from the city, "has Suffered exceedingly of late by privateers from New York, who so infest the Capes that it is scarcely practicable for a vessel to pass without being taken."[46] The blockade by British and Loyalist warships and small boat raiders now obliged the shippers and traders of the city, who found little comfort in Pennsylvania's limited capabilities for providing protection, to appeal in desperation to the Continental Congress for help. The memorial was submitted on April 29, 1782, and considered by a committee of Congress, which immediately forwarded it to Robert Morris.

Morris, who was by then in charge of the Office of Finance, offered his recommendations five days later. As the Continental Navy, which was all but non-existent, having suffered repeated losses, could no longer provide the desired protection for American shipping as requested by the memorialists, he proposed that the navies of France and Spain be called upon for assistance. Ignoring the fact there was little or no Navy left, Congress recommended that the "Agent of Marine be instructed to employ naval force" of the United States to protect American "trade and commerce and to call upon French and Spanish navies for assistance."[47]

The exercise provided no relief. But it was not the only thing about the privateer war that caused anguish in some circles. As some of the leading proponents of privateering in those heady fall days of 1775 had feared, the dangers of unleashing private armed ships of war without proper governmental administration or, more importantly, the means of enforcement of the guidelines regulating the industry, serious misconduct by some privateers was becoming troublesome. In Connecticut, Governor Jonathan Trumbull appealed to Congress on April 24, 1782, for authority to suspend privateer commissions "in cases of malconduct," and to assist in aid to imprisoned American seamen. In response, Congress passed a resolution of May 21 "authorizing the Executives in the Several States in certain Cases to suspend the commissions of Captains of private armed vessels."[48] The American sea war, including the privateer war, particularly along the Atlantic frontier of New Jersey, was devolving rapidly.

There were, of course, some remarkable and newsworthy actions that captured the imaginations of the public. On July 1, a daring raid by four Massachusetts privateers, the *Hero*, Babcock, *Scammel*, Soddard, *Hope*, Woodbury, and *Swallow*, Tibbets, landed ninety men at Reads Head, two miles below the town of Lunenburg, Nova Scotia, and ten leagues from Halifax. With amazing rapidity, they charged and defeated the town's defenders. They then engaged in an orgy of plundering that "quickly emptied the stores of a variety and considerable quantity of dry goods, 20 puncheons of good West-India rum, and the king's beef, pork, and flour." Upon the approach of a squadron of three ships with two hundred German soldiers from Halifax, they quickly spiked and dismounted the town's guns, and deposited the royal magazine in the hold of a privateer before making their escape. Though the raiders claimed that the "strictest decorum was observed towards the inhabitants, and their wearing apparel and household furniture inviolably preserved for their use," the town itself was ransomed for £1000 pounds sterling, and some of the principal residents and a few military officers were shipped on board *Scammel* as prisoners to insure payment. "On the side of the brave sons of liberty, three were wounded slightly, one dangerously."[49]

Soon afterwards, when a group of New England privateers captured six ships belonging to the inward bound Quebec fleet, one of which was valued at £20,000 sterling, the Philadelphia merchants could only sigh with envy, for few of their own were even getting out to sea. It wasn't for want of trying. Indeed, by September, returns of the commissions for letters of marque and reprisal granted in Pennsylvania for the year total just 102 vessels, although perhaps half were able to make the open ocean.[50]

At New York, it now seemed that a practically unending list of prizes taken by British men of war, both Royal Navy and privateers, were paraded past Sandy Hook and into New York Bay to await condemnation before Judge Bayard's Court of Admiralty. On a single typical day in June, it was announced that two ships and a schooner, all prizes to Shedden and Goodrich's 20-gun New York privateer *Virginia*, Captain Hazard commanding, had been brought in. Altogether the prizes were armed with a total of twenty-two 6-pounder cannon, manned by approximately one hundred men, and laden with 2,600 barrels of flour and seventy hogsheads of tobacco, a rich haul by any measure. On the same day HM Sloop-of-War *Fury* sent in a prize brig. Even more humiliating was the success of some of the more famous American vessels, such as *Fair American*, that had fallen into enemy hands and were converted into Loyalist privateers.[51]

And for every vessel taken, their crews were added to the ever-increasing population of mariners that had to be dealt with. Most would be sent to the grim prison ships, sinkholes of disease and death, that had been anchored off New York City since the beginning of its occupation to await their fates. Few would ever return home.

PART THREE

IRON DESPOTISM

"Damn my eyes! That fellow isn't dead!"

XXII

Vulgarly Called Hell

"There, rebels, there is the cage for you!"

It is safe to say that every engagement fought and every prize taken as a result of the naval conflict on the New Jersey coast produced many casualties on both sides, if not in dead or wounded, then in property loss and in prisoners taken. Yet, for those American patriots engaged on the conflicted coast of the "cockpit of the Revolution" who were destined to become British prisoners of war, cruelty knew no bounds. Indeed, it has been estimated that for every three captured, one would perish in captivity.[1] For those many thousands of mariners, mostly privateersmen and regular naval personnel, as well as soldiers whose unfortunate lot was to be incarcerated on the small fleet of prison ships off the New York Battery and, later, in the East River, the rate of survival has been estimated at only one in ten. Many among them were New Jersey and Pennsylvania men. Some notable privateer commanders of those states, such as Captains Enoch Stillwell, David Stevens, and John Adams, who had gained reputations and in some cases substantial wealth, were to fall upon untold misfortunes, sickness, starvation, and brutality while aboard the prison ships. For a lucky few, such as William Treen of Egg Harbor, bold escape, freedom, and even a return to their calling as privateersmen would be their destiny. Yet, the hellholes upon which these and many thousands more found themselves captives were to prove for most their last abodes on earth.[2]

What exactly were the prison ships, which the great American historians Henry Steele Commager and Richard B. Morris aptly compared to the ill-famed Andersonville death camp in the Civil War? How did they come into usage, and why was such cruel treatment—some would even say genocide—allowed?[3]

One of the first known vessels to be employed as a prison ship in New York during the Revolution was the 716-ton hospital ship *Grosvenor*.[4] In December 1776, less than three weeks after the fall of Fort Washington, in which 2,818 men were captured, 500 American prisoners of war from the fort were marched aboard the ship, then lying in the North River, as the city's holding centers were already filled following the earlier Battle of Brooklyn. Captive soldiers were already packed tightly, or soon would be, into New Bridwell, Columbia College, numerous churches, and the Van Cortlands' grim, five-story, greystone former warehouse, the Old Sugar House. The only option was to house the new prisoners on board available watercraft. On December 7, the *Grosvenor* was moved to a new anchorage at Turtle Bay, in the East River, where she would remain anchored for the winter with her most unlucky guests. One of the disconsolate prisoners, a Connecticut man named William Slade, who left a remarkable diary of his sufferings aboard, documented how he barely survived on a subsistence diet of peas, pea broth, water broth, biskets, butter, "burgoo," and occasionally small servings of rice and meat. Excerpts from his diary revealed a state of mind and suffering that would become, in the years ahead, all too common among many thousands of unfortunates such as he.[5]

> Thursday [December] 12th. This morning is the first time we see snow. At noon drawed a little meat and pea broth. Very thin. We almost despair of being exchanged....
>
> Friday 13th. We now see nothing but the mercy of God to intercede for us. Sorrowful times, all faces look pale, discouraged, discouraged...
>
> Saturday, 14th. Times look dark. Death prevails among us, also hunger and naked[ness] ... Cold increases ...
>
> Monday 16th. The tender mercy's of men are cruelty....
>
> Tuesday 17th. No fire. Suffer with cold and hunger. We are treated worse than cattle and hogs....
>
> Sunday, 22nd. Last night nothing but grones all night of sick and dying. Men amazeing to behold. Such hardness, sickness prevails fast. Deaths multiply . . . This morning Sergt Kieth, Job March and several others broke out with the small pox. About 20 gone from here today that listed in the King's service. Times look very dark. But we are in hopes of an exchange. One dies almost every day.... About 30 sick ...
>
> Thursday 26th. Last night was spent in dying grones and cries. I now grow poorly....
>
> Friday, 27th. Three men of our battalion died last night. The most melancholy night I ever saw. Small pox increases fast. This day I was blooded.... Stomach gone.... Not like to live I think.....
>
> Saturday, 28th. This morning about 10 o'clock Josiah Basset died.[6]

A second small vessel, the former transport *Whitby*, had also been brought into service as a prison ship at New York by the late fall of 1776. As aboard *Grosvenor*, conditions of sickness, insufficient food, lack of medicine and medical care, amidst a population of over 250 prisoners "Crouded promiscuously together," were the order of the day. On December 9, 1776, six Connecticut privateersmen belonging to the schooner *Spy*, who were captured when her prize, the ship *Hope*, was retaken by HMS *Galatea*, appealed to Governor Jonathan Trumbull for assistance in securing an exchange. Their depiction of existence aboard *Whitby*, "without Distinction or Respect, to person office or Colour, in the Small Room of a Ships Between Decks," were remarkably descriptive, but had become all too commonplace. Allowed the luxury of walking upon the main deck from sunrise to sunset, they were then forced into the overcrowded confines below. To relieve themselves during the night, the guards "Suffered only two at once to come on deck to do what Nature requires, and Sometimes we have Been even Denied that, and been obliged to make use of tubs & Bucketts Below deck to the great offence of every Delicate Cleanly person as well as to great prejudice of all our health.... In Short Sir we have no prospect before our Eyes but a kind of Lingering Inevitable death Unless we obtain a timely and Seasonable Release." Few exchanges were allowed.[7]

The following year the prison ship population in the East River was supplemented with the addition of the ex-transport *Kitty* and another vessel. Conditions upon *Kitty* were so intolerable that the ship was burned. The need for prison space, however, continued to accelerate, and by 1780, no fewer than seven vessels were being maintained in the Hudson or had been brought around into the East River to serve as either prison ships or hospital ships for prisoners. These included the *Good Hope* (which was burned the same year), *Jersey, Falmouth, Hope, Scorpion, Strombolo* (formerly a sloop-rigged fire ship), *Prince of Wales*, and the sloop *Hunter*. The fleet carried a combined population at any given time of no less than 2,000 prisoners, both "able" and sick. By 1781, *Jersey* alone, built to carry a crew of 350, would house 850 prisoners, and 1,000 men in 1782. In 1783, she would be crammed by an astonishing 1,200 captives, all forced to live and die in abysmal conditions aboard. By the end of the war, a total of two prison ships and three hospital ships, *John, Jersey, Frederick, Perseverance*, and *Bristol*, lay at anchor or on the bottom muds of the East River, in Wallabout Bay. With a mortality rate from sickness, malnutrition, cruelty, and other causes ranging from six to ten men a day on *Jersey* alone, and only very rare prisoner exchanges, the impact upon the overall American merchant marine community was telling. By 1780, the attrition rate, when measured against the available seafaring labor force, was having a direct impact on trade as well as naval and privateering successes at sea. Commercial merchantmen, privateersmen, and regular naval forces were increasingly forced to rely upon unskilled landsmen, which resulted in substantially higher loss rates and a subsequent impact on the already fractured economy, increased insurance rates for shipping, and loss of confidence. The great American maritime nursery of skilled seamen was, through the incredible prison ship mortality rate, being bled dry. The ordeal of incarceration was one of entering hell itself, with levels that mirrored the worst of Dante's *Inferno*.

• • •

For all new arrivals at the Wallabout, the horror began as their transport came within view of the embayment. Normally, they would have been conveyed aboard a small schooner ironically called *Relief*, commanded by an Irishman named Gardner. It was not so for one young mariner named Thomas Dring, who had once before, in 1779, been captured and imprisoned for four intolerable months aboard the prison hospital ship *Good Hope*, then lying in the Hudson River. Recaptured in May 1782 while serving as master's mate aboard the Providence privateer *Chance*, his second imprisonment was destined to prove far more unbearable and nearly fatal.

Dring was being brought in aboard HMS *Belisarius*, of twenty-four guns, along with 130 other prisoners, mostly, like himself, captured privateersmen under the personal supervision of the David Sproat, Commissary of Prisoners, a Loyalist who was roundly detested by American patriots and notorious for his myriad purported cruelties. Dring was already well aware that his own ultimate destination was likely to be an infamous sinkhole of filth, vermin, infectious disease, and disrepair, aboard which several hundred men died every month, a ship that had earned the sobriquet "the terror of American tars." As *Belisarius* doubled a point to enter the bay, both Dring and his fellow prisoners cringed when they saw lying before them the ominous black hulk of *Jersey*, once a formidable man-o-war, surrounded by three disreputable looking satellites, all so-called hospital ships. "There, rebels," cried the Commissary in sadistic delight, "there is the cage for you!"[8]

Prison Ship Jersey, from *Recollections of the Jersey Prison Ship from the manuscript of Captain Thomas Dring,* Providence, RI, 1829.

Dring sized up his soon-to-be prison in a single glance. Although he was undoubtedly not aware of her full history, the now squalid *Jersey,* once a 4th-rate ship of sixty guns built at Portsmouth Dockyard in 1736, had been the pride of the Royal Navy with a distinguished record. Even before the Revolution, however, she had already been deemed antiquated and unfit for sea duty. In March 1771, she was anchored in the East River off the New York "Fly Market" for service as a hospital ship. Her masts and spars were removed, and her earlier formidable, warlike countenance converted to a depressing specter of former glory. In the winter of 1779–1780, while under the command of a foul-tempered and callous skipper named David Laird, the already forbidding-looking three-story structure, barely 144 feet in length and 41½ feet abeam, was formally converted into a floating prison ship specifically for the purpose of confinement of captured American seamen.[9]

Sometime after June 1780, with disease raging among the inmates, the fears of contagion spreading from the ship to the city induced the authorities to have her hauled rudderless to a more permanent and remote mooring three-quarters of a mile to the eastward of the Brooklyn ferry, near a lonely tide-mill on the Long Island shore. There, in the shoal water, she would be permitted to slowly sink her bottom into the mud. Further alterations only served to make her "dark and filthy appearance correspond with the death and despair that reigned within," for as one inmate so adequately stated: "No other British ship ever proved the means of the destruction of so many human beings." Her ill-famed reputation was known far and wide. "Of all the prisons, on land and water, for the confinement of the Americans during the Revolutionary War, the Old *Jersey* was acknowledged to be the worst," recalled another prisoner. "Such an accumulation of horror was not to be found in any other one, or perhaps in all collectively. The very name struck terror into the sailor's heart, and caused him to fight more desperately, to avoid being made a captive." Though neither Dring nor his fellow privateersmen could have known it, before all was said and done, well over 11,000 men, it was later calculated (although never fully documented), would perish aboard the hell-hole they were about to board, almost three times the number of Americans who would die in actual combat ashore during the seven years of the American Revolution.[10]

• • •

By the time Captain Dring arrived, *Jersey* had been substantially dismantled and was little more than a hulk sitting on the mud bottom. The only spars remaining were on the truncated bowsprit. On the starboard quarter, a derrick, eerily reminiscent of a gallows, had been erected to hoist supplies and water butts aboard. A flagstaff for signaling protruded from the center of the main deck. All portholes had been sealed over, but in her sides two tiers of holes, each about twenty to twenty-four inches square and ten feet apart, had been cut to provide ventilation. Iron grate bars covered each hole at cross-angles to prevent prisoners from escaping through them. While the holes admitted a little light during the day, and doubled as a breathing hole at night, free air circulation in the fetid holds was all but non-existent.[11]

Under the quarterdeck, which covered approximately a fourth of the upper deck at the stern, was a cabin area for the British officers and guards. During hot summer weather a tent was usually erected on top of the quarterdeck to provide shade for the sailor on guard duty there. To manage the thousand or more prisoners normally incarcerated aboard there were less than sixty crewmen and guards: a captain, two mates, a steward, a cook, perhaps a dozen sailors, a guard unit of between ten and twelve invalid Royal Marines, and approximately thirty soldiers from the various regiments quartered on Long Island, who were rotated through every seven days. Sometimes the guards were English and sometimes Hessian. Most believed that the English guards were merely doing their jobs, but many preferred the Hessians, who provided slightly better treatment. Occasionally refugee units were given the task. Though Englishmen, Hessians, and Loyalists were all thoroughly despised, the latter were considered to be the most loathsome to the inmates, who viewed them as traitorous scoundrels and villains. The Loyalists, in return, treated the inmates "with all the severity in their power." Most prisoners avoided, at all costs, being anywhere near the deadly bayonets of the Loyalist guards. To illustrate their disdain they shunned their keepers whenever possible, going even so far as to crawl on the booms while going fore and aft to avoid contact and to eschew their very existence. The refugee troopers often played the same game. "They never answered any of our remarks respecting them," recalled one prisoner, "but would merely point to their uniforms, as if saying, 'We are clothed by our Soverign, while you are naked.'" When they finally departed the ship, it was always accompanied by provocative gestures and curses by the inmates. Yet, both prisoners and guards were usually relieved that their confrontations were over, at least until the next rotation.[12]

. . .

As his transport neared its destination, Dring could see a multitude of humanity moving slowly about the upper deck, some waving their hats as if to say "approach us not." It being near sunset before the new arrivals were finally brought alongside their prison to be, he could see that everyone except the guards at the gangway had disappeared, driven below at bayonet point like so many cattle for the night. Nearby, along the shadowy rim of the shore, a line of sentinels could barely be discerned standing at regular intervals.[13]

As the new prisoners reached the accommodation ladder leading to the gangway on the larboard side, they found themselves opposite one of the air ports, behind which would be Dring's station on the ship. "From this aperture," the privateersman later recalled, erupted "a strong current of foul vapor, of a kind which I had been before accustomed while confined on board the *Good Hope*. . . . This was, however, far more foul and loathsome than anything which I had ever met with on board that ship, and produced a sensation of nausea far beyond my powers of description." Here, while waiting for orders to ascend on board, the new arrivals were feebly greeted through the ventilation ports by some of the prisoners who asked from where they had come and how they had been captured. Then they received a macabre welcome indeed when one bodiless voice from within hissed: "Death has no relish for such skeleton carcasses as we are, but he will now have a feast upon you fresh-comers." Ebenezer Fox, another prisoner, would later write of his impressions at that moment: "The idea of being incarcerated in this floating pandemonium filled us with horror, but the ideas we had formed of its horror fell far short of the reality."[14]

The standard procedure was for all new arrivals to first ascend to the upper deck where their names were entered upon a registry. Normally, the roll of the prisoners was called only every three months unless an unusually large acquisition of fresh inmates made it necessary more often. When the roll was called, the police regulations of the ship would also be read. Owing to increased escape attempts, one of the new regulations in 1781 was that every prisoner caught while trying to escape "should suffer instant death and should not even be taken on board alive." For Dring and every other man brought aboard, such regulations were indeed sobering if not terrifying. Yet all coped as best they could. Each man was permitted to retain whatever clothing or bedding he had brought with him (that had not already been stolen by his captors), all of which was examined for weapons and money. A few, such as Fox, were able to conceal money or other items, often in the crown of their hats or in the soles of their shoes. Some managed to smuggle pocketknives on board, utilitarian instruments that were as prized as gold doubloons. They were then instructed to pass through a strong door on the starboard side, and down a ladder leading to the main hatchway. Here they entered into hell itself.[15]

Ebenezer Fox observed that the new arrivals now found themselves

. . . in a loathsome prison, among a collection of the most wretched and disgusting looking objects that . . . ever beheld in human form. Here was a motley crew, covered with rags and filth; visages pallid with disease; emaciated with hunger and anxiety; and . . . retaining hardly a trace of their original appearance. Here were men, who had once enjoyed life while riding over the mountain wave or roaming through pleasant fields, full of health and vigor, now shriveled by a scanty and unwholesome diet, ghastly with inhaling an impure atmosphere, exposed to contagion; in contact with disease, and surrounded with the horrors of sickness, and death."

It was here, where nearly a dozen men died each night from dysentery, typhoid, smallpox, yellow fever, food poisoning, starvation, and torture, that young Fox thought he must surely "linger out the morning of my life in tedious days and sleepless nights, enduring a weary and degrading captivity, till death should terminate my sufferings, and no friend will know of my departure."[16]

A prisoner's first night aboard *Jersey* was passed in total darkness and was unquestionably one fraught with revulsion and fear, as he clutched to his chest those few articles he had been permitted to bring aboard. As the hatchways were fastened over them by armed soldiers, the new arrivals

> . . . were left to pass the night amid the accumulated horrors of sighs and groans, of foul vapor, a nauseous and putrid atmosphere, in a stifled and almost suffocating heat. The tier holes through the sides of the ship were strongly grated, but not provided with glass, and it was considered a privilege to sleep near one of these apertures in hot weather. . . . But little sleep, however, could be enjoyed even there, for the vermin were so horribly abundant that all the personal cleanliness we could practise would not protect us from their attacks.

Most prisoners, they would soon discover, were already debilitated by a veritable legion of contagious diseases.[17]

Personal space was nonexistent. When one new inmate came aboard, he found the only room available for lying down to be twenty feet from the gangway, directly in the path of others who would run him over to get to the upper deck in the morning. A position near one of the ventilation ports, being highly prized, was out of the question for a newcomer. Yet, for the most part, everyone, officers and sailors alike, all of the rebels, mostly privateersmen and Continental seamen, eventually fared the same. The only distinction was made by prison society itself by an unwritten rule that allowed men who had been officers prior to their capture to congregate in the extreme afterpart of the ship in a quarter called "the Gun Room," which was maintained as their place of abode. It was here that Thomas Dring passed his long nights.[18]

All prisoners were confined to two main decks below, with most of the foreign inmates usually being French or Spanish naval prisoners "who had seen and survived every variety of human suffering." These poor souls, clad in rags, "their faces . . . covered with dirt and filth; their long hair and beards matted and foul," were consigned to the most horrible place of all, the lower deck, their own designated station of hell, into which all of the foulest detritus of the ship eventually found its way. These, among all of the prisoners, were "the most miserable and disgusting looking objects that can be conceived." But it was small solace to those above who fared better by only very minor degrees. Not everyone, however, was of the opinion that the foreigners were treated badly, and some believed they received more favorable handling than the Americans.[19]

Interior view of the *Jersey*, a British prison ship during the Revolutionary War, showing prisoners and guard. By Felix Octavius Carr Darley artist, Edward Bookhout, engraver, from *Life and death on the ocean: a collection of extraordinary adventures*, by H. Howe, 1855. Courtesy Prints and Photographs Division, Library of Congress.

Silence was a stranger to this dark abode. Throughout the night the loud cries for water among the sick, many with raging fevers, fused with the pitiful curses, moans, and whimpers of the dying, and mingled again with the wild and incoherent ravings of the delirious. Only one man at a time was allowed to secure water from the upper deck during the night. However, the sentry, frequently provoked by the continual cry for leave to ascend when there was already someone up, often responded brutally by pushing the appellant back into the hold with a bayonet, and not a few men were wounded or killed in this fashion. As one prisoner, Christopher Vail, would later write:

> There was only one passage to go on deck at a time. And if a man should attempt to raise his head above the grate he would have a bayonet stuck in it. Many of the prisoners was troubled with the disentary and would come to the steps, and could not be permitted to go on deck, and was obliged to ease themselves on the spot. And the next morning for 12 feet around the hatches was nothing but excrement. . . .

Death was ever present. Indeed, it was quite common for a prisoner to find the man beside whom he had lain all night to be a corpse in the morning. Frequently the dying would hurl themselves, in their last earthly throes of closure, across their miserable fellow inmates, who being too feeble to remove them, would have to wait until dawn for others to do the lifting. Throughout the night, the stifling hold, crowded with as many as a thousand or more human bodies, was filled with the overwhelming stench of filth, vomit, human excrement, and body rot that only added to an immediate sense of doom for the new arrivals.[20]

No lights were permitted below after 10 p.m., but some prisoners occasionally managed to secure and conceal candles under their hats to light the evil darkness. When the guards discovered such illuminations, the order usually came down to "Douse the glim!" and the candles were snuffed. On one occasion, however, when the disobedience was discovered, a guard accompanied by a file of soldiers, stormed down the hatchway, and the lights were immediately blown out. Suddenly the soldiers found themselves in total blackness surrounded by a thousand hostile prisoners. Though armed, they were "seized with a will, and hustled to and fro in darkness, till their cries aroused the whole ship." When the fracas was over and the guards managed to escape, they emerged uninjured. Nevertheless, punishment for such an infraction was severe.[21]

• • •

As Dring's first morning aboard *Jersey* dawned, the prisoners were awakened as always by a loud, unfeeling shout: "Rebels! Bring up your dead." The hatches were thrown open and the legion of pale, cadaverous looking inmates was allowed to ascend. The first permitted up was the "working party," comprised of as many as twenty men selected in rotation from among the most able-bodied within the prison population, and commanded by a boatswain. Their mission was to attend to the sick and dead, and then clean the ship. It was a loathsome task indeed, albeit one that men treasured, for it accorded them the simple pleasure of going onto the main deck just prior to sunrise, permitting them to breathe the cool, fresh air before the sick and odiferous multitude came up. More importantly, they were compensated with a privilege afforded no other prisoners aboard, a full daily allowance of provisions and a half pint of rum. The first chore of the working party was to bring up the sick and infirm and lay them in bunks located on the center deck, and then the bodies of those who had died during the night, of which there "were generally a number every morning." The dead, of which there were at least eight to ten a day, were brought up with difficulty and laid on the forecastle until 8 a.m. One member of a working party named Thomas Philbrook recalled the dismal mission: "Staggering under the weight of some stark, still form, I would at length gain the upper deck, when I would be met with the salutation: 'What! *You alive yet?* Well, you are a tough one!'" For many, the first thing they saw in the morning upon reaching the deck was a boat, laden with dead bodies, shoving off for the nearby Long Island shoreline.[22]

The dead were usually sewn up in their own blankets (if they had them) by their messmates and transferred by the work crew, under a strong guard, to a small boat sent from the hospital ship *Hunter*, just before the general population emerged. As many of the corpses were still warm and rigor mortis had yet to set in, they were still pliant and had to be tied to a board before being hoisted over the side and lowered into the boat with block and tackle. The boat then shoved off accompanied by a guard of soldiers. Upon landing at a low wharf that had been purpose-built from the shore, the burial detail proceeded to a small hut nearby wherein wheelbarrows and digging tools were stored for the daily occasion. The corpses were then transferred to the wheelbarrows and hoes and shovels distributed to the work party. In a bank of sandy earth near the Wallabout's edge, a shallow trench, one to two feet deep, was excavated and, "in a mockery of a burial," the bodies were hurriedly thrown in heaps with little if any ceremony "and then slightly covered, the guard not giving time sufficient to perform this melancholy service in a faithful manner." Within days, bared by the rains, wind and waves, scores of freshly buried bodies were exposed on the slope. These, added to hundreds, indeed thousands of corpses and skeletal remains of previously interred prisoners, were clearly visible to their less fortunate comrades left to pine in hopeless captivity aboard *Jersey*.[23]

Some concept of this miserable task can be gauged from the *Pennsylvania Packet* which published an extract from a letter from on board *Jersey*, entitled "Vulgarly called Hell," in which it was noted "... We bury 6, 7, 8, 9, 10 and 11 in a day. We have 200 more sick and falling sick every day; sickness is the yellow fever, small pox, and in short everything else that can be mentioned." After burial duties were attended to, the working party returned to the ship where they were set to wash the upper deck and gangways, spread an awning for protection from the sun, and hoist wood, water, and other supplies aboard. One of the most offensive duties was to empty the large, foul smelling tubs used by the prisoners to relieve themselves during the night and as receptacles for all manner of other filth. The tubs were usually placed around the railing of the hatchway leading from the center to the lower deck. From there they had to be laboriously carried up the ladder to the upper deck, with the contents often slopping over the sides upon the bearer, and then pitched over the side of the ship in the same locale where salt water for cooking was hauled up.[24]

• • •

When the general prison population was allowed topside, the scene was disturbing at best for a newcomer such as Dring. Having been welcomed and tormented during his first night aboard by a host of vermin, upon reaching the deck the next morning he discovered that a black silk handkerchief that he wore around his neck was spotted with lice. Another inmate observed a half-crazed prisoner on the forecastle of the ship, "with his shirt in his hands, having stripped it from his body, deliberately picking the vermin from the pleats and putting them in his mouth. . . . I stepped very near the man and commenced a conversation with him. He said he had been on board two years and a half, or eighteen months. He had completely lost track of time, was a skeleton and nearly naked."[25]

Even more shocking to Dring was his first full daylight view of the general population, clothed in tattered garments and pallid in visage. As he recalled in his memoirs:

> The next disgusting object which met my sight was a man suffering with the smallpox; and in a few minutes I found myself surrounded by many others laboring under the same disease, in every stage of progress. As I had never had the smallpox, it became necessary that I should be inoculated. . . . On looking

about me, I soon found a man in the proper stage of the disease, and desired him to favor me with some of the matter for the purpose. The only instrument which I could procure, for the purpose of inoculation, was a common pin. With this, having scarified the skin of my hand, between the thumb and forefinger, I applied the matter and bound up my hand. The next morning I found that the wound had begun to fester; a sure symptom that the application had taken effect.[26]

Having survived the first shock of inhumanity aboard *Jersey*, Dring became a keen observer of every nuance of day-to-day life and death on the crowded main deck. He noted that the prisoners were normally allowed on deck only if the weather was fair and as soon as the sun was high overhead. There they remained until sunset. Each man was obliged to carry his own hammock and bedding—if he possessed any. These were laid to air out upon the spar deck or across booms. About two hours before sunset the inmates were ordered to carry them below, but were usually permitted to remain upon deck themselves until sundown.

Every thing which we could do conducive to cleanliness having been performed, if we felt any thing like enjoyment in this wretched abode, it was during this brief interval, when we breathed the cool air of the approaching night, and felt the luxury of our evening pipe. But short indeed, was this period of repose, and we prepared to descend to our gloomy and crowded dungeon. This was no sooner done, than the gratings were closed over the hatchways, the sentinels stationed, and we left to sicken and pine beneath our accumulated torments, with our guards above crying aloud, through the long night, "All's well!"[27]

Another inmate named Alexander Coffin, who was imprisoned aboard somewhat later, was quite succinct about conditions. "On my arrival on board the Old *Jersey*," he later recalled to his son, " I found there about 1,100 prisoners; many of them had been there from three to six months, but few lived over that time if they did not get away by some means or other. They were generally in the most deplorable situation, mere walking skeletons, without money, and scarcely clothes to cover their nakedness, and overrun with lice from head to feet."[28]

The first thing all new arrivals were obliged to do was to form themselves into a small mess to obtain their daily rations. All prisoners were obliged to fast on their first day, and sometimes through the second before they learned the system for obtaining food in time for cooking. It was not difficult for a new inmate to join an existing mess, once the system was learned, and to avail himself of the experiences of older prisoners, for vacancies created each day by the high mortality rate were abundant. Each mess, usually consisting of six men, was served by one of its members assigned to secure the rations for all from the ship's steward when they were distributed once a day. The steward and his assistants, petty tyrants at whose discretion food might be withheld at the slightest whim, dispensed the daily rations from windows in the steward's compartment, located at the after part of the ship.[29]

Each morning a sentry rang a bell at 9 a.m. and the appointed messmen were summoned in rotation to receive their daily allocation of food, a commodity that was notoriously short and bad. Dring reported that each prisoner was supposed to be given two-thirds pound of biscuit, two-thirds pound of pork, and one-third pint of peas. No vegetables were allowed, nor was butter, although a substitute was given, "a scanty portion of so-called sweet-oil, so rancid and putrid" that the Americans could not eat it. The French prisoners usually confined on the lower deck, however, "took it gratefully, and swallowed it with a little salt and wormy bread."[30]

One survivor reported:

Each mess received daily what was equivalent in weight or measure, but not in quality, to the rations of four men at full allowance; that is, each prisoner received two thirds as much as was allowed to a seaman in the British navy. Our bill of fare was as follows: on Sunday, one pound of biscuit, one pound of pork and a half pint of peas; Monday, one pound of biscuit, one pint of oatmeal and two ounces of butter; Tuesday, one pound of biscuit and two pounds of salt beef; Wednesday, one and a half pound of flour and two ounces of suet. Thursday was a repetition of Sunday's fare, Friday of Monday's and Saturday of Tuesday's. If this food had been of good quality and properly cooked, as we had no labor to perform, it would have kept us comfortable, at least from suffering. But this was not the case. All the food appeared to be damaged.

Indeed, the food was generally deemed unconsumable except by famished men. The bread was superlatively bad. "I do not recollect seeing any," recalled a prisoner named Thomas Andros, "which was not full of living vermin, but eat it, worms and all, we must, or starve."[31]

Ebenezer Fox noted in disgust that all of the food was injured in some way or spoiled.

The bread was mostly moldy, and filled with worms. It required considerable rapping upon the deck, before these worms could be dislodged from their lurking places in a biscuit. As for the pork, we were cheated out of it more than half the time, and when it was obtained one could have judged from its motley hues, exhibiting the consistence and appearance of variegated soap, that it was the flesh of the porpoise or sea hog, and had been an inhabitant of the ocean, rather than a sty. . . . The flavor was so unsavory that it would have been rejected as unfit for the stuffing of even Bologna sausages. The provisions were greatly damaged, and from the imperfect manner in which they were cooked were about as indigestible as grape shot. The flour and oatmeal was often sour, and when the suet was mixed with the flour it might be nosed [smelled] half the length of the ship. The first view of the beef would excite an idea of veneration for its antiquity . . . its color was a dark mahogany, and its solidity would have set the keenest edge of a broad axe at defiance to cut across the grain, though like oakum it could be pulled to pieces, one way, in string, like yarn rope. . . . It was so completely saturated with salt that after having been boiled in water taken from the sea, it was found to be considerably freshened by the process. . . . .[32]

The extreme paucity of rations was a common complaint among those few who survived the ordeal of the British prison ships at New York. In 1780, Captain John Van Dyke bitterly protested food allowances "so short a person would think it was not possible for a man to live on." Captain Alexander Coffin, recalled that the provisions served out included little more than four or five ounces of meat, "and about as much bread, all condemned provisions from the ships of war, which, no doubt, were supplied with new in their stead, and the new, in all probability, charged by the commissaries to the *Jersey*. . . . I can safely aver, that both the times I was confined on board the prison ships, there never were provisions served out to the prisoners that would have been eatable by men that were not literally in a starving situation."[33]

Each day every mess unit assigned to a different member the duty of taking the mess's rations to the galley on the forecastle. A designated tally stick fastened to it by a string identified each messman's portion. At the sound of the cook's bell hundreds of messmen at a time thronged to the galley to cook the meager meals for their particular group in a great copper kettle that contained between two and three hogsheads of water. The kettle itself was set in specially constructed brickwork, which was about eight feet square and divided by a partition into two compartments. On one side peas and oatmeal, which were measured out to each man while standing at the copper, were boiled in fresh water. On the other side, meat was boiled in salt water taken up from alongside the ship. A specified amount of time was allocated to every messman to cook his rations, at the end of which a bell was rung again and the tally bags, hung by a string in the boiling water, were removed, whether or not the process had been completed. Undoubtedly owing to the crowded conditions and the inability of many to secure a position around the copper, the meat was often improperly cooked and prisoners were frequently obliged to eat their meal raw.[34]

It is likely that cajolery, bribery, or other means were employed by some prisoners to secure special privileges from "His Majesty the cook," as Dring called him, to prepare rations in the great cauldron separate from the general mess. The cook, a former prisoner who had gone over to the British, was an obviously well-fed fellow and stood out in stark contrast to the emaciated inmates. For his disaffected loyalties, but more for his strict adherence to regulations regarding rations administered from "his palace," he was thoroughly detested by much of the population. Yet, he was agreeable to others upon whom he dispensed exceptional liberties. For those so fortunate, a great number of spikes and hooks had been driven into the brickwork in which the boiler was enclosed, on which to suspend their battered tin kettles. The members of each mess to whom such privileges had been granted would save their rations of drinking water in which to boil their pork or bully beef. By hammering the base of their diminutive pots into concave forms, it was determined through practice, the amount of water and fire required to boil the contents were substantially reduced. Wood shavings from driftwood or floating wood debris brought in by work parties, purloined from the ship's firewood supplies, and even splinters pulled from the ship's rotten fabric, were used to kindle the flames beneath the kettles. When the cooking was done, the fire was immediately quenched and the remaining shavings carefully retrieved for use the next day. The shavings were considered a treasure that was jealously guarded from day to day. Those who possessed them were considered wealthy men.[35]

The British troops and residents of New York City, mostly surrounded by rebel territory on the mainland, and often cut off from supply from Europe for extended periods by American privateers, also suffered from certain privations. It is thus not surprising that allowances, usually old and rotted, accorded those unfortunates held aboard the prison ships were far worse. One chronicler noted:

> The food of the prisoners consisted mainly of spoiled sea biscuit, and of navy beef, which had become worthless from long voyaging in many climes years before. These biscuits were so worm-eaten that a slight pressure of the hand reduced them to dust, which rose up in little clouds of insubstantial aliment, as if in mockery of the half famished expectants. For variety a ration called 'Burgoo,' was prepared several times a week, consisting of mouldy oatmeal and water, boiled in two great Coppers, and served out in tubs, like swill to swine.[36]

Captain John Van Dyke wrote of his own bitter experience as a determined-through-experience messman in 1780:

> One day I went to the galley and drew a piece of salt, boiled pork. I went to the mess to divide it....I cut each one his share, and each one eat our day's allowance in one mouthful of this salt pork and nothing else. One day called peaday I took the drawer of our doctor's chest [Dr. Hodges of Philadelphia] and went to the galley, which was the cooking place, with my drawer for a soup dish. I held it under a large brass cock, the cook turned it. I received the allowance of my mess, and behold! Brown water, and fifteen floating peas—no peas on the bottom of the drawer, and this for six men's allowance for 24 hours. The peas were all in the bottom of the kettle. Those left would be taken to New York, and, I suppose, sold.[37]

On another weekday, cynically dubbed pudding day by the inmates, Van Dyke received for his whole mess but three pounds of damaged flour with green lumps in it, which the men refused to eat, along with a pound of bad raisins and a third of a pound of raisin sticks. "We would pick out the sticks, mash the lumps of flour, put all with some water into our drawer, mix our pudding and put it into a bag and boil it with a tally tied to it with the number of our mess. This was our day's allowance."[38]

The ship's crew and guards kept fatted hogs in pens on the gundeck for their own use, which provided additional possibilities for the more enterprising inmates. "I have seen," recalled one former inmate, "the prisoners watch [for] an opportunity, and with a tin pot steal the bran from the hogs' trough, and go into the Galley and when they could get an opportunity, boil it over the fire, and eat it, as you, Sir, would eat of good soup when hungry."[39]

The constant gnawing of hunger and starvation occasionally drove the prisoners to the brink of madness. On several occasions, when the guards hurled a bag of apples into the midst of hundreds of prisoners who were already "crowded together as thick as they could stand," the scramble imperiled both life and limb for all. "This," noted Thomas Andros, "was a cruel sport. When I saw it about to commence I fled to the most distant part of the ship."[40]

For drink the prisoners were usually allowed a small amount of fresh drinking water, which was also used by some in cooking, and a half a pint of rum a day, which was mixed into grog. "Our water was good," remarked one inmate, "could we have had enough of it." Judging from the accounts of most other survivors, however, his view was in the minority.[41]

Water was stored in a large butt on the weather deck. A marine guard with a drawn cutlass stood over the container. Prisoners were allowed to drink as much as they pleased from two or three copper ladles chained to the cask, but were permitted to carry away no more than a pint at a time. Dring estimated that daily consumption aboard amounted to about 700 gallons, all of which was at first brought from the Brooklyn shore aboard a large gondola. By October 1782, the water and provisions were being brought out from New York City by the prison transport schooner *Relief.* "In fact," Captain Coffin noted caustically, "the said schooner might emphatically be called *Relief,* for the execrable water and provisions she carried relieved many of my brave but unfortunate countrymen by death, from the misery and savage treatment they daily endured." The captain, who had followed the sea for three decades, often on long voyages of up to several years duration, had never seen water so bad. Making its consumption doubly cruel was the fact that within a mere three cables length from the ship, and in clear sight of every prisoner, was the Wallabout Mill, through which flowed "as pure water . . . as was perhaps ever drank."[42]

Foul as it was, when brought on board from the water and provision boat, the rush to obtain a drink, often resulted in terrifying scenes of mass confusion and an immediate, sometimes brutal interposition of the guards.

Water that was not required for immediate use was conveyed by a leather hose into butts placed in the lower hold of the hulk, from which the prisoners had recourse to when they could procure no other. The butts had never been cleaned since first installed, thus the thick, repugnant sediments which they contained being disturbed by every new supply poured in rendered their contents "a compound of the most disgusting and poisonous nature" to which hundreds of deaths were attributed.[43]

Owing to her size and proximity to the shore, *Jersey* had quickly become embedded in the shallow, muddy bottom, and remained stationary at all times. Thus, when all the filth accumulated from among the thousand or more men was thrown overboard every day, it tended to remain by the ship until carried off by the next tide. "The impurity of the water," reported Ebenezer Fox, "may be easily conceived, and in that water our meat was boiled. It will be recollected, too, that the water was salt, which caused the inside of the copper to be corroded to such a degree that it was lined with a coat of verdigris. Meat thus cooked must, in some degree, be poisoned, and the effects of it were manifest in the cadaverous countenances of the emaciated beings who had remained on board for any length of times."[44] Copper poisoning was thus added to the list of miseries on the average inmates' menu.

The daily allowance of grog was mixed on deck in two half-hogshead tubs, from which it was distributed. But even this privilege was sometimes cruelly dispensed with.

One day, Captain Laird came aboard, apparently in a particularly foul mood. As soon as he had stepped onto the main deck he summoned the boatswain who arrived, hat in hand.

"Have the prisoners had their allowance of rum today," demanded the captain.

"No, sir," answered the boatswain.

"Damn your soul, you rascal, heave it overboard."

The boatswain, with assistance, promptly upset the tubs in the middle of the deck. The inmates watched in horror as their grog rations ran out the scuppers of the ship and into the East River.[45]

• • •

From the beginning, health conditions aboard *Jersey* and her sister ships in the Wallabout, varied from bad to outright horrendous. The new arrivals were immediately faced with a battery of killers, most notably dysentery, smallpox, and yellow fever; diseases that might have been reduced had they not been magnified by the terrible overcrowding and long periods of near or total starvation. Even the most robust new prisoners quickly succumbed. As many as three-quarters or more of all prisoners incarcerated aboard the Wallabout prison ships died, a figure not unlike those of other prison ships such as were maintained in Charleston and Savannah, but whose inhabitants were far smaller in number. Frequent epidemics helped further cull the population. General Jeremiah Johnson, an American officer, once blithely but correctly described the British technique for keeping the prison ships from overcrowding through its unofficial policy of inmate extermination: "death made room for all."[46]

When Thomas Andros and thirteen of his mates were first brought aboard during the dog days of August 1781, they were immediately assailed by an epidemic of yellow fever, with the healthiest among them succumbing first. All but three or four were dead within a few hours. As was usually the case, the very youngest, ship's boys and teenaged seamen, were the most frequent victims. "The miseries of our condition were continually increasing," recalled one fortunate survivor. "The pestilence on board spread rapidly; and every day added to our bill of mortality."[47]

In a limited effort to curb the deadly disease, prisoners were furnished with buckets and brushes to scrub down the ship, and vinegar was provided to sprinkle the floors. The effort proved of little consequence owing to the general state of apathy that reigned in the prison population, born of despair and resignation; few exerted themselves to better their condition. "The encouragement to do so was small," recalled Andros, one of the few among his crewmates to survive. "The whole ship, from her keel to her tafferel, was equally affected, and contained pestilence enough to desolate a world; disease and death were wrought into her very timbers. At the time I left, it is to be supposed a more filthy, contagious, and deadly abode never existed among a Christianized people. It fell but little short of the Black Hole of Calcutta. Death was more lingering, but almost equally certain. The lower hold and the orlop deck were such a terror that no man would venture down into them."[48] For the French and Spanish prisoners, however, usually allocated to the lowest reaches of the hulk, there was little choice.

When Captain Silas Talbot, both a Continental Navy officer and privateersman, was confined aboard *Jersey* in the fall of 1780, there were 1,100 prisoners already aboard, most having neither berths to lie in nor benches to sit on. As was normal, scores of inmates were almost naked. The weather was cool and dry, but the nights white with frost. Dysentery and fever still prevailed. Scanty and appalling provisions, brutish guards, and the sick and dying pining for relief that they could not obtain produced the most profound general sense of doom. Ironically, the death rate had been reduced to but ten a day, a decline from the previous three months.[49]

By August the following year, even the hospital ships had become desperately overcrowded. The sudden arrival en masse of more than two hundred additional prisoners aboard *Jersey* at one time brought new misery. With space already at a premium, the new arrivals immediately became sick. Lodged in the forepart of the lower gun deck, where all the new inmates were confined at night, a stultifying climate of near dementia ensued. As utter derangement was a common symptom of yellow fever, the horror only increased with the darkness of night when "the voice of warning would be heard, 'Take care! There's a madman stalking through the ship with a knife in his hand!'"[50]

The madman, of course, was Death himself.

–XXIII–

Where Peace and Rest Can Never Dwell

"Five guineas bounty to any man that will enter his Majesty's service."

Efforts to maintain personal cleanliness as a major component of sanitation were all but impossible among the prison ship inmates in Wallabout Bay. In describing the degrading status of the French inmates, Thomas Dring could well have been addressing the entire population.

> Their beards were occasionally reduced by each other, with a pair of scissors; but this operation, though conducive to cleanliness, was not productive of much improvement in their personal appearance. The skins of many of them were discolored by continual washing in salt water, added to the circumstance that it was impossible for them to wash their linen in any other manner, than by laying it on the deck, and stamping it with their feet, after it had been immersed in salt water; their bodies remaining naked during the operation.... Much that was disgusting in their appearance undoubtedly originated from neglect, which long confinement had rendered habitual, until it created a confirmed indifference to personal appearance.[1]

Medical assistance was all but out of the question. Few if any English doctors from the city dared to board *Jersey*. Occasionally an American physician would be brought aboard as a captive, but if he could secure a parole, a luxury afforded to few common seamen, he usually left the ship. Seldom could the prisoners blame him, for "his own death was next to certain and his success in saving others by medicine in our situation was small."[2]

The conscious moral decision by the British to continue the practices aboard the prison ships was reprehensible to all Americans, and it was best summarized by Thomas Andros. "After it was known that it was next to certain death to confine a prisoner here," he wrote, "the inhumanity and wickedness of doing it was about the same as if he had been taken into the city and deliberately shot on some public square."[3]

The three hospital ships, *Scorpion, Hunter,* and *Strombolo* (the latter of which was later replaced by the ship *Frederick*), that lay near *Jersey*, were little better than the larger and more famed death ship herself and were, from their outward appearances, equally "disgusting in the highest degree." *Hunter,* however, appears to have been employed more as a storeship and depot for the medical department, and as a station for the few surgeons, mates, and boat crews attending to the prison and hospital ships. All were more or less crowded, dirty, and uncomfortable. As with *Jersey,* scarcity was the rule and patients suffered inordinately for want of food, blankets, clothing, and fuel to maintain even the smallest of fires in the winter. Anyone aboard *Jersey* foolish enough to complain of being sick was usually sent aboard one of the hospital ships, from which few returned. Many years later, Alexander Coffin recalled that not one in a hundred were ever seen again, and noted that every morning, as with *Jersey*, "a large boat from each of the hospital ships went loaded with dead bodies, which were all tumbled together into a hole dug for the purpose, on the hill where the national navy-yard now is."[4]

The only physical virtue of the hospital ships was that there was somewhat more breathing room for the patients. The deck was furnished not only with an awning, but a "wind-sail" for each hatchway to direct fresh air between decks where the sick were ensconced. Moreover, during the night, unlike aboard *Jersey*, hatchways were left open for ambulatory patients to make their way topside as the guards believed it unlikely that any of the feeble inmates were likely to venture an escape.[5]

Surgeons usually visited the hospital ships only once every several days, although by 1782 a physician from *Hunter* had finally begun to visit *Jersey* daily. Their demeanor towards the patients ranged from indifferent to pitiless. Medicines were sparingly employed.[6] The few male nurses aboard performed their daily duties haphazardly and with such haste and neglect that the misery and discomfort of the patients were only compounded.

One of the more poignant and tragic episodes aboard the hospital ships concerned two very sick brothers named John and Abraham Hall, ages 23 and 16, who shared a bunk. One night another prisoner overheard young Abraham imploring his older brother not to lie on him. From the inmates convalescing in the adjacent bunks a general murmur of reproach arose against the elder of the two for his cruelty to the younger brother. John could hear neither his brother nor the others for he was already dead, and his young sibling was too ill and weak to move him. Throughout the night the lad lay with his dead brother on top of him, unable to move and slowly expiring. When others finally hoisted John off the next morning, it was already too late to save the teenage boy under him who died soon afterwards.[7]

In January 1783, when a captured privateersman named Andrew Sherburne became ill and was transferred to the hospital ship *Frederick*, he discovered there were at least two men to every bunk, and the conditions aboard wretchedly unsanitary. He found he had been accorded a bunk next to a man named Wills from Massachusetts. Soon after the young privateersman's arrival, his bunkmate was dead. "I have seen," Sherburne later recorded of his struggle for life aboard a ship every bit as deadly as *Jersey*, "seven men drawn out and piled together on the lower hatchway, who had died in one night on board the *Frederick*. There were ten or twelve nurses, and about a hundred sick. Some, if not all of the nurses, were prisoner[s]. . . . They would indulge in playing cards and drinking, while their fellow prisoners were thirsting for water and some dying." At night, after the hatches were shut down and locked, the nurses retired to the steerage, after which there was "not the least attention paid to the sick and dying, except what could be done by the convalescent; [who] were so frequently called upon, that in many cases they overdid themselves, relapsed, and died." The nurses, from all accounts, appeared more eager for their charges to expire than to improve. Dring had nothing but disdain for them. "I never learnt by whom they were appointed, or whether they had any regular appointment at all. But one fact I well knew—they were all thieves." Almost immediately after a patient died, the nurses set to despoiling the deceased of their blankets, clothes, and even their hair (which was sold to peruke makers in the city).[8]

By 1782, patient overcrowding aboard the hospital ships obliged the British administration to reallocate space on the after part of *Jersey*, near the larboard side, for the erection of bunks "for the reception of the sick from between deck" and those "who felt the symptoms of approaching sickness." Here they could lie down "in order to be found by the Nurses as soon as possible; and be thereby also prevented from being trampled upon by the other prisoners, to which they were continually liable while lying on the deck."[9]

The diet of patients on the hospital ships was even less copious or wholesome than aboard *Jersey*. The daily ration allowed the sick amounted to but a gill of wine and twelve ounces of bread made from sour or musty flour, which was sometimes poorly baked. It was not unusual for both bed-ridden and mobile patients to be denied their wine rations for several days at a time. Consumable water was often acquired at a premium. The drinking water was usually brought on board in casks by work parties. It was not uncommon, however, during cold snaps in the winter, for the water to freeze in their containers and was difficult if not impossible for the weaker patients to get out. Sherburne, while bedridden, once had to plead to get a full cup of water and was forced to exchange three day's allowance of provisions to have it brought to him. Between decks there was but a single small, sheet-iron stove for heat in the winter, but as the fuel was usually green and very scarce, its reliability was often questionable. Moreover, there were normally "some peevish and surly fellows generally about it" who hogged the space around the stove. Sherburne never had opportunity to sit by the stove, but usually managed to get someone close in to slice and toast his wormy bread upon it, which he then put into his wine and water to make it palatable.[10]

Few were the acts of mercy exhibited by the British or their Hessian allies aboard the hospital ships. Those simple mercies that were granted, however, proved on occasion to be life saving. When a company of New York citizens began each day to provide all of the sick aboard *Frederick* with a pint of Bohea tea, well-sweetened with molasses, the results for many were miraculous. Sherburne was convinced the tea saved his own life and that of hundreds of others. Mother nature and the weather, however, often conspired to make such salvation nearly impossible.[11]

Sherburne's bunk was situated directly against the ballast port. The port, not being caulked, admitted the winter weather in. When there came a snowstorm, the snow blew through the seams and onto his bed. The cold was almost intolerable and he suffered from the consequences for the rest of his life. "I have often toiled the greatest part of the night, in rubbing my feet and legs to keep them from freezing. In consequence of these chills," he wrote decades later, "I have been obliged to wear a laced stocking upon my left foot for nearly thirty years past." But the admission of snow to his bed had some advantage during his convalescence, "when I could not otherwise procure water to quench my thirst."[12]

With winter temperatures equal inside and outside of the hospital ship, few blankets for cover, and but one small stove aboard for heat, death by freezing was common. Sherburne recalled that a gunner named Daniel Davis, from his own ship, had his feet and legs frozen and died soon after. Even those privileged prisoners serving as nurses were not immune to the cold. One man who had his feet and legs frozen, suffered the loss of his toes and then his feet.[13]

With so many inmates expiring every day, few imagined that the horror could have gotten any worse, but for some it did. The fear of being buried alive was for many the most terrifying. One day in March 1783, after the dead boat had already taken her cadaverous cargo ashore for burial, additional dead were belatedly brought up, sewed up in hammocks, and left on deck until the next morning. As usual, the number was considerable. The following morning, while employed in loading the boat, a seamen engaged in the work crew noticed a slight movement in one of the hammocks sewn around a Rhode Islander named Gavot, just as they were sliding him down a board from the gunwales and into the boat. "Damn my eyes!" shouted the seaman. "That fellow isn't dead!" A dispute between the work crew and the seaman soon erupted. The work crew swore the man sewn in the hammock "was dead enough" and should go into the boat. The seaman refused to let him be "launched," took out his knife and ripped open the hammock. The dead man was still alive. One of the incredulous witnesses explained as best he could how a living man had been mistaken for a deceased one: "There had been a heavy rain during the night; and as the vital functions had not totally ceased, but were merely suspended in consequence of the main-spring being out of order, this seasonable moistening must have given tone and elasticity to the great spring, which must have communicated to the lesser ones, and put the whole machinery again into motion." A month later, under a flag of truce, Gavot went home to his native Rhode Island.[14]

• • •

Though the war began to wind down on the mainland following the surrender of Cornwallis at Yorktown in late 1781, the privateer war at sea had intensified substantially, resulting, of course, in an escalation of the overall prison population. Yet, with rumors of peace talks circulating, some basic privileges, which appear to have been denied the prisoners on board *Jersey*, were improved. By October 1782, there was opportunity for inmates who were fortunate enough to have money to procure produce from visiting bumboats.

Every other day a very corpulent old woman, known among the prisoners as "Dame Grant," came out to carry on the bumboat trade. "The bulk of the old lady," recalled Dring, "completely filled the stern sheets of the boat; where she sat, with her box of goods before her, from which she supplied us very expeditiously." The boat was rowed by two boys who delivered up the purchased articles to the prisoners after first being paid for. On bumboat days, the buyer was permitted by the guards to descend to the foot of the accommodation ladder to conduct his purchases. When Loyalists were on duty, however, no such license was given. Soft bread, sugar, tea, and other commodities, previously put into small paper parcels and weighing from one ounce to a pound, were the normal articles available for sale. Often inmates furnished Dame Grant with a list of items they wished for her to obtain for them, such as pipes, tobacco, needles, thread, and combs, which she faithfully procured and brought out, "never omitting the assurance that she afforded them exactly *at cost*."[15]

According to Thomas Andros, those "who had money fared much better than those who had none. I had made out to save, when taken, about twenty dollars, and with that I could buy from the bumboats, that were permitted to come alongside, bread, fruit, etc.; but, Sir, the bumboatmen were of the same kidney as the officers of the *Jersey* and we got nothing from them without paying through the nose for it, and I soon found the bottom of my purse; after which I fared no better than the rest." A seven to nine inch-long piece of sausage was sold for six pence, a price that would have been considered usurious at any other time.[16]

Dring noted the guilt he often felt while negotiating a purchase.

While standing there, it was distressing to see the faces of hundreds of half famished wretches, looking over the side of the ship into the boat, without the means of purchasing the most trifling article before their sight; not even so much as a morsel of wholesome bread. None of us possessed the means of generosity, nor had any power to afford them relief. Whenever I bought any articles from the boat, I never enjoyed them; for it was impossible to do so in the presence of so many needy wretches, eagerly gazing at my purchase, and almost dying for want of it.[17]

Unhappily for all concerned, having contracted a fever during one of her many visits to the hulk, Dame Grant perished like the majority of the clients she had so faithfully attended to.[18] Her loss, however, was little noted by those less fortunate than Dring who were forced to struggle for every morsel.

It is not surprising that with so many prisoners forced to subsist off short and putrid rations, a few took every opportunity possible to embezzle the necessities of life from their keepers. Once, when a boat came alongside with sixty firkins "of grease they called butter," many prisoners, seeking to escape the monotony of their lives, leaped to assist in bringing it aboard. The firkins were first deposited on deck, and then lowered down the main hatchway. When a firkin or two rolled under the forecastle, a few prisoners managed to discretely hide one away without discovery, and later carried it below to their bedding. Ebenezer Fox, one of the beneficiaries, was overjoyed. "This was considered as quite a windfall," he later wrote, "and being divided among a few of us, proved a considerable luxury. It helped to fill up the pores in our mouldy bread, when the worms were dislodged, and gave the crumbling particles a little more consistency."[19]

• • •

Given the extremely crowded, filthy, and intolerable conditions aboard *Jersey* and the other prison and hospital ships at New York, fights and mayhem were of course common. Adding to the tinderbox atmosphere were racial and national animosities that erupted from time to time between American-born and foreign prisoners, primarily the French and Spanish. Once, when four or five hundred Frenchmen were transferred en masse and consigned to the orlop deck, some Americans, veterans of the last bloody wars against both France and Spain, took umbrage at the new arrivals and the added sufferings that such an influx of new inmates would likely generate for the already overcrowded population. After the last Frenchmen were brought aboard, the crowding around the two half hogsheads of water soon erupted in a melee for the first drink. Captain Roswell Palmer, a privateer prisoner, recalled the incident: "A Virginian near me was elbowed by a Spaniard and thrust him back. The Spaniard drew a sheath knife [undoubtedly smuggled aboard] when the Virginian knocked him headlong backward, down two hatches, which had just been opened for heaving up a hogshead of stale water from the hold, for the prisoners' drink. The water had probably been there for years and was as ropy as molasses."[20]

Although French and Spanish prisoners were usually quartered on the lower deck, some were occasionally lodged along with the Americans. The Europeans slept in hammocks, which they were usually allowed to bring aboard, with Americans, who were often deprived of such luxury, lying on the bare deck floor next to them. Such proximity was bound to breed mischief, especially among the very young inmates. On one occasion, a boy descended to the foreigners' quarter in the dark and on a given signal by a co-conspirator, cut the main hammock lashing of the French and Spaniards hammocks at the head, "and let them all down by the run on the dirty floor." In the confused row that erupted in the darkness the Americans stole back to their quarters "and were all fast asleep when the guard appeared."[21]

• • •

There was little to occupy a thousand men on the crowded deck of the prison ship *Jersey* except occasionally forced labor, endless discussions on the topics of home, loved ones, sickness, death, the latest escape attempt, and the continued efforts of the British to recruit men from the inmate population for the Army or Royal Navy.

Aside from the work parties hauling out the dead and cleaning ship, the labor was generally around the well room where an armed guard was required to force up prisoners to the winches to clear the ancient ship of water that sometimes gushed in through rotten seams. The rest of the prison population could see or hear little of their comrades forced to work at the winches "but a roar of mutual execrations, reproaches and insults. Sights of woe, regions of sorrow, doleful shades; where peace and rest can never dwell."[22]

The British recruitment efforts, were another thing altogether. Indeed, the practice of recruiting from prisoners who had been enemy combatants only a short time before had for centuries been common in most European nations during times of war and manpower shortages. Even the noted Continental Navy commander John Paul Jones, unable to recruit enough seamen to man what would become one of the most famous ships in American naval history, *Bonhomme Richard*, had been obliged to sign on the sweepings of French jails and scores of British prisoners of war as well.

It had been normal procedure, from October 1776 onward, for British authorities to tempt American prisoners to escape their misery through enlistment by intentionally starving them, at first for four or five days, and then for extended periods. As the enlistment effort was almost continuous, a perpetual policy of food deprivation soon evolved, and many Americans, as well as foreign allies, were starved to death in the process.[23] Unfortunately, owing to the seemingly endless attrition in the ranks caused by the war, the British enlistment effort was unremitting.

At regular intervals, almost every fair day, the drill was the same. British officers and sergeants would come aboard the ship and form themselves in two lines on the quarterdeck. From the ship's muster of the most recent arrivals the boatswain would shout out a prisoner's name and then the order "Pass." The named prisoner would then pass between the ranks, officers and sergeants. The sergeants would glare intently into each face before him, examining every feature, to determine if he was a British deserter. If no deserters were caught, the business of recruitment then commenced. A sergeant would come to the middle of the deck and shout out: "Five guineas bounty to any man that will enter his Majesty's service." Soon afterwards, a party of Hessians would board and follow the same routine.[24]

Unlike the British Army, the Royal Navy seldom bothered to ask, and frequently resorted to impressment from captured American crewmen, often as soon as their ships had been taken, and then again from the common inmate populations of the prison ships. Ebenezer Fox, of the Massachusetts privateer *Protector*, related that when HMS *Roebuck* and *Mayday* captured his ship in June 1780, one third of the crew was immediately pressed into service. Later, while being held aboard *Jersey*, he learned that an expected draft would be made upon the prisoners to fill out the latest manpower needs in the Royal Navy. In late August 1780 the dreaded event occurred.[25]

When the British officers and a number of sailors came aboard, the prisoners were ordered on deck and instructed to march single file via the larboard gangway around to the quarterdeck for inspection by the officers. "We continued to march round in solemn and melancholy procession," recalled Fox, "till they had selected from among our number about three hundred of the ablest, nearly all of whom were Americans." The impressment was consummated without regard to the meager rights of the prisoners, and those selected were ordered to go below and collect their scant belongings, after which they were herded into a boat waiting alongside "to be subjected to the iron despotism, and galling slavery of a British man-of-war; to waste their lives in a foreign service; and toil for masters whom they hated."[26]

Protestations were usually—but not always—pointless. Thomas Andros recalled that in 1781, during his incarceration, he knew of no one who voluntarily entered British service. "They tried to force one of our crew into the navy," he later wrote, "but he chose rather to die than perform any duty, and he was again restored to the prison-ship."[27]

Some, such as Ebenezer Fox, who failed in several bold escape attempts, enlisted voluntarily and justified their actions by stating that it would provide a better opportunity for flight. Some believed their chances of staying on Long Island for a while before being shipped out would provide a better opportunity to escape to the New Jersey shore. Many discovered, however, that upon signing up in hopes of deserting quickly found that they were just as diligently guarded in the king's service as they had been aboard *Jersey*.[28]

There were many unknown martyrs who sacrificed life and liberty rather than accept the terms offered by British captors—service under the English flag.

• • •

The ability to exact revenge for their continual harsh treatment was seldom within the prisoners' powers. But occasionally, they were able to turn their own miseries upon their jailers, albeit not without consequences. Fox later recalled one such occasion. He and his mates, like every prisoner aboard, had suffered considerably from the lice and other vermin that continually accumulated upon their bodies despite their best efforts at cleanliness.

> To catch them [the lice] was a very easy task, but to undertake to deprive each individual captive of life, as rapidly as they could have been taken, would have been a more Herculean task for each individual daily, than the destruction of 3,000 Philistines by Sampson of old. To throw them overboard would have been but a small relief, as they would probably add to the impurities of the boiler, by being deposited in it the first time it was filled up for cooking our unsavory mess. What then was to be done with them?

A general consultation was held and it was decided to pick as many as they could from their bodies and place them in a large snuffbox. Before long, hundreds of the live vermin were collected. When an Irish recruitment officer in His Majesty's service came aboard and failed to meet with any success upon the deck, he ventured below to repeat his offers. Being a remarkably tall man, he was obliged to stoop as he passed between decks. With unquestionable delight Fox recalled:

> The prisoners were disposed for a frolic, and kept the officer in their company for some time, flattering him with expectations, till he discovered their insincerity, and left them in no pleasant humor. As he passed along, bending his body and bringing his broad shoulders to nearly a horizontal position, the idea occurred to our minds to furnish him with some recruits from the colony in the snuffbox. A favorable opportunity presented, the cover of the box was removed, and the whole contents discharged upon the red-coated back of the officer. Three cheers from the prisoners followed the migration, and the officer ascended to the deck, unconscious of the number and variety of the recruits he had obtained without the formality of an enlistment. The captain of the ship, suspecting that some joke had been practiced, or some mischief perpetrated, from the noise below, met the officer at the head of the gangway, and seeing the vermin crawling up his shoulders, and aiming at his head, with the instinct peculiar to them, exclaimed, "Hoot mon! what's the matter wi' your back!" . . . By this time many of them in their wanderings, had traveled from the rear to the front, and showed themselves, to the astonishment of the officer. He flung off his coat, in a paroxysm of rage, which was not allayed by three cheers from the prisoners on deck. Confinement below, with a short allowance, was our punishment for this gratification.[29]

• • •

If hijinks such as the snuffbox incident were uncommon, demonstrations of patriotism by the inmates, often met with utter cruelty by the guards, were not. One such event occurred on July 4, 1782, when the prisoners attempted to celebrate their nation's independence day with observances and amusements such as their situations permitted. On this particular day the guard consisted of a detachment of Scotsmen. When the prisoners were admitted to the deck in the morning they proceeded to display thirteen diminutive national flags in a row upon the boom. The guard immediately tore the display down and trampled the flags under foot. Deigning no notice, the prisoners proceeded to amuse themselves with speeches, patriotic songs, and rousing cheers, all the while meticulously avoiding any insult to the guards. By late afternoon, the guard had become thoroughly aggravated by the exercise and with fixed bayonets drove the mass of prisoners below deck and closed the hatches. Yet, the singing continued between decks throughout the hot and sultry evening.[30]

Repeated orders to desist were ignored. Suddenly, around 9 p.m., the hatches were removed and the Scotsmen descended with lanterns and drawn cutlasses in hand into the fetid warren of the wretched. Wildly hacking and cutting all the way, in bloody rage the guards pressed the unarmed inmates away from the hatchways, and drove them into the farthest recesses of their confinement. Every one within reach was wounded or killed before the guards ascended again to the upper deck, "exulting in the gratification of their revenge," and fastening the hatches behind.[31]

Without water for their desiccated throats since 4 p.m., and unable to dress their bleeding wounds in the blackness of night, more men died. The groans and lamentations of the wounded were dreadful in the extreme. Yet, even in their crying and suffering, some challenged the guards to come down again, albeit in vain. No medical assistance for the wounded and dying, even bandages, were forthcoming. Indeed, no attention was afforded them at all except by fellow inmates. The next morning, at least ten bloodied corpses were found below, and many more badly wounded men were discovered. Not until mid-forenoon were the prisoners again allowed on deck to quench their thirst and receive their meager, filthy rations, all of which had to be eaten uncooked.[32]

–XXIV–

A Forlorn Hope

"Oh Lord, I shall be drowned."

For most of those incarcerated aboard the British prison ships at New York, there appeared to be little chance of release from their almost certain fate, unless it came through enlistment with the enemy or, for those miniscule few who had managed to smuggle money aboard, bribery. It is unknown how many resorted to enlistment, although the records of those few who had survived suggest they were small in number. For most, the only real hope was either escape, being included in one of the rare prisoner exchanges, the unlikely prospect of surviving until the end of the war, or death.

It was readily apparent to most inmates that the physical force that might be asserted by the legion of prisoners, weak as they were, against the small number of sentinels that watched them was quite adequate to carry out a mass escape. The dilemma lay in what was to be done once they were off the ship. Manhattan and the western end of Long Island were in British and Loyalist hands, and the prospects for being recaptured bordered on insurmountable. Recapture ensured as punishment even more miseries than were normally endured, and in 1781 the threat of instant death upon capture was announced. Yet, even the unceasing starvation, brutality, and desperation suffered by most inmates could never fully extinguish the will to live or the desire to escape. "While on board," noted one fortunate survivor, "almost every thought was occupied to invent some plan of escape." Indeed, break out attempts were frequent, but success was the reward for but a few who dared their luck against all odds. "Our sufferings," stated Ebenezer Fox, "were so intolerable, that we felt it to be our duty to expose ourselves to almost any risk to obtain our liberty. To remain on board of the prison ship seemed to be certain death, and in its most horrid form; to be killed, while endeavoring to get away, could be no worse."[1]

The most opportunistic mode of escape was simply to slip over the side unseen, swim to shore undetected, and trust to luck once there. Thomas Andros related that one method, which he considered "a forlorn hope," was to pry a way through a sealed gunport, steal down through it at night without discovery, and make for the shore. Andros considered it sheer suicide for the guards were eternally vigilant and usually shot anyone detected in the act. But many tried.[2]

Typical of this simple, over-the-side method was an attempt by a young privateersman named Christopher Hawkins, who dropped into the water during a thunderstorm with a boy named Waterman. Having prepared themselves for the occasion, the two prisoners had packed their apparel in knapsacks that were fastened to their backs with two strong garters. Taking advantage of the claps of thunder to break the bolts holding the iron bars to the air portals through which they could just wiggle, the two made their way into the water for a swim of more than a mile and half. During the long push, Waterman drowned. Hawkins lost his knapsack and his clothing in the effort. Arriving on shore completely naked, he somehow managed to make his way through the Long Island countryside, stealing from gardens and subsisting as best he could, and ultimately made it to freedom.[3]

Usually, the first indication that a prisoner or even an entire body of messmates had escaped came during the daily meal, when their fellow inmates noted them missing. Ironically, their absence often went altogether unnoticed by their keepers as so many men died each day and new prisoners arrived so frequently that a proper tally was seldom kept. On one rare occasion, when a muster was taken, it was learned that nearly 200 names called to answer had inexplicably disappeared without leaving the slightest notice of their exodus. The ship's officers endeavored "to make amends for their past remises by increasing the rigor of our confinement." That a whole mess might make an attempt to escape together, in fact, was often the case. That such a conspiracy be kept quiet was of paramount importance lest there be spies set amongst them. As Fox wryly noted: "Any plan which a mess had formed they kept secret among their number, in order to insure a greater prospect of success." Yet, success in leaving the ship itself was usually blunted once the escapees were ashore, where they were commonly retaken in the woods of Long Island either by British horse patrols or local Tories, or worse, drowned or shot in the attempt.[4]

The will of a desperate, even dying, inmate to hazard an escape was seldom tempered by the fear of immediate capture. Yet few had any concept of the difficulties they faced once ashore. Thomas Andros, already suffering from fever and disease and barely able to walk, was among those desperate and willing enough to try anything. "The time now came when I must be delivered from the ship or die," he later wrote. "I was seized with yellow fever, and should certainly take the small-pox with it, and who does not know that I could not survive the operation of both of these diseases at once." The arrival of a rare exchange cartel offered a possible release, and he was among the first to present his name when a list of prisoners was compiled. It had become the policy of the British to exchange only those Americans "as had but just the breath of life in them, sure to die before they reached home" in trade for healthy British prisoners of war sent from American prisons. Indeed, the British guards would often tell those inmates who still retained a modicum of their strength: "You haven't been here long enough, you are too well to be exchanged." Yet, ill as he was, Andros was not considered for the cartel.[5]

When he learned, soon after, that the ship's sailing master, a Mr. Emery, was going ashore for water, Andros begged to go with him. Never before had such a request been granted to a prisoner, and when the officer, apparently struck by the pathetic figure of the man before him, unexpectedly agreed, a murmur of astonishment arose from all those around them. "What is that sick man going on shore for?" some asked, even as the British sailors tried to dissuade the prisoner from embarking, thinking that he would probably expire on the way in. "So, to put them all to silence," Andros later wrote, "I again ascended on board, for I had neglected to take my great-coat. But I put it on, and waited for the sailing-master. The boat was pushed off, I attempted to row, but an English sailor said, very kindly, 'Give me the oar. You are too unwell.'" Andros looked back toward the black, ugly ship that had been such an object of misery, and then toward the shore where either freedom or death awaited him. Soon after the boat bumped ashore, he and the guards ascended a creek and arrived at the spring where the prisoner timorously proposed that he be allowed to go in quest of apples. Thinking that the feeble young man, who could hardly wobble along unassisted, was incapable of escape, the sailing-master said to him, "This fresh air will be of service to you." Andros asked permission to ascend a nearby embankment, some thirty feet high, to call at a house thereon for refreshment. "Go," said Sailing Master Emery dismissively, "but take care not to be out of the way." The prisoner assured him he was incapable of escape, and slowly ascended the embankment.[6]

Young Andros soon found himself in a small orchard near the farmhouse. A soldier stood nearby, guarding a pile of apples, but appeared indifferent to the sickly prisoner. Waiting for the right moment, when the guard's back was turned, the youth quickly slipped from the orchard and into a dense swamp, cosseted by a heavy groundcover of saplings and bushes. Soon he discovered a huge log, perhaps twenty feet in length, and encased by a densely knotted covering of green briar. "Lifting up this covering," he recalled, "I crept in, close by the log, and rested comfortably, defended from the northeast storm which soon commenced." From this vantage point, through the falling rain he could just make out the boat crew on the beach inquiring as to his whereabouts, conducting a cursory search, and then, perhaps eager to find shelter on board the ship, dismissing him as almost dead anyway.[7]

Andros remained in his hiding place until the middle of the night, when he finally decided to move. He soon encountered a road, which he followed for some distance. Whenever he heard approaching footsteps, he would slip off the path and into the darker undercover, roll himself into a ball in a reasonable imitation of a bush, and wait for the party to pass. He now blessed the wisdom of having returned for his greatcoat, which was the only means of protecting him from exposure to the frigid evening air. The following night he hid in a haystack where he weathered another rainstorm in considerable discomfort, all the while vexed, as he had been day and night, by the lice that still infested his clothing. Thoroughly drenched, he left the hay pile after the storm and entered a hollow in the nearby forest where he stripped down and laid his clothes out to dry in the dappled sunlight.[8]

Freedom gave Thomas Andros the resolve to continue on. Ill with yellow fever or not, there simply was no choice now. To go back to *Jersey* would be a guarantee of death. Thus, when his clothes had dried, he returned to the road and continued on. Upon reaching one particular bend, however, his heart must have momentarily stopped when he spied a pair of oncoming dragoons, undoubtedly scouring the countryside for him or other escapees. Thinking quickly as the troopers approached, he unhurriedly climbed over a fence adjacent to a cornfield and near a small, wayside cottage. Slowly, and without apparent concern at the approach of the two horsemen, he began walking about the field, picking up an ear of corn here, righting a sheaf of cornstalks there, as if he was the owner of the field. With his head covered by only a handkerchief, as he had lost his hat sometime earlier, he appeared for all the world to have just come out of the cottage. Though the troopers inspected him closely as they passed, they neither stopped nor summoned him.[9]

The possibility of being discovered had been too close, and Andros immediately resolved to travel only at night and hide in barns or hollows in the forests during the day. Living only on water and apples from the occasional orchard, he limped along weak and listless. On several occasions, it being the fall cider-making season, he found unfermented cider at the presses in unattended barns. His infrequent encounters with people revealed the spectrum of humanity, from evil to angelic. Once, while hiding in a barn, he was discovered by a cross old man who refused him any assistance. The womenfolk he came upon from time to time, however, usually proved the opposite: they often provided him with food and kept his identity secret. As his health continued to fail, his spirits were sorely taxed. Then, one night, while limping slowly along on the east side of Long Island and feeling utterly drained, he spied a modest dwelling, screwed up his courage, and approached it. An old man and his wife occupied the house. Though poor, they took him in and treated him like their own son. After providing him with some clothing, they took his own bug-ridden garments and baked them in an oven to destroy the lice and other vermin that had infested them since even before he had left the ship. Given a clean bed to sleep in, he passed his first full night of rest without the intolerable torture of being eaten alive.[10]

It was late fall when Thomas Andros finally reached Sag Harbor, on the coast of Long Island Sound. There, he fell in with two other escapees who had miraculously survived as well. Smuggled across the sound in a whaleboat, by late October he was home and in the tender care of his beloved mother. Though dangerously ill and often delirious for substantial periods, with the nursing of his family to help him, he became one of the lucky few to survive incarceration aboard the notorious prison ship *Jersey*. He would eventually go on to teach school, and finally to find his calling as a minister of the gospel.[11]

· · ·

By watching their fellow prisoners, would-be escapees learned from the experiences of others. Ebenezer Fox and his messmates made their first escape attempt on August 15, 1781, as a result of gaining knowledge of an effort being planned by others. It is exemplary of the role that chance played in such endeavors. For the convenience of the British officers on board, they had noted that a closet (toilet) called "the round house" had been constructed beneath the forecastle of the ship. The door to this structure was always locked, and, as there were better facilities elsewhere, the room was seldom used. During one of the daily meals, Fox's mess apparently overheard that one of their neighbors had managed to pick the roundhouse lock, leaving the door unfastened, presumably to facilitate his own escape attempt. Having figured out their neighbor's intentions, Fox and his colleagues determined to seize the earliest opportunity to use their discovery to escape first.[12]

At sunset, when the usual cry of "Down, rebels, down!" was heard, and the cadaverous multitude began to shuffle toward the hatchways, Fox and four of his mates slipped into the round house. The sixth mate, a Bostonian named Putnam, was unable to fit into the crowded closet, and managed to hurriedly conceal himself beneath a nearby wooden tub. Tightly packed within their places of concealment, the Americans waited. "We remained thus cooped up, hardly daring to breathe, for fear we should be heard by the guard. The prisoners were all below and no noise was heard from above, saving the tramp of the guard as he paced the deck. It was customary, after the prisoners were secured below, for the ship's mate every night to search above; this, however, was considered a mere formality, and the duty was imperfectly executed."[13]

In the meantime, another escape attempt was also underway. Independent of Fox and his messmates, an Irishman who also hoped to make his leap to freedom had hid in a coal bin covered by coal. When the ship's mate, somewhat in his cups from too much drink, looked in during a casual inspection he quickly espied "something rather whiter than the coal, which he ascertained to be the Irishman's shoulder." The discovery precipitated an immediate alarm and a general search for other would-be escapees that soon led to the round house. When the mate demanded the key from one of the guards, the soldier, unaware that the lock had been picked, replied that there was no need to search it for it was always kept locked.[14]

Twelve soldiers, armed with cutlasses, and the drunken mate, carrying a pistol in each hand, demanded the round house be opened. Within minutes one of the guards returned with the key only then to discover the door to be unlocked. Inside, Fox and his mates, their hearts racing, had already decided to make a break for the quarterdeck to make their stand or jump overboard. When the drunken mate ordered them out, they made their move. "The door opened outwards, and forming ourselves into a solid body, we burst open the door, rushed out pell-mell, and making a brisk use of our fists, knocked the guard heels over head in all directions, at the same time running with all possible speed to the quarter-deck." Bringing up the rear, Fox was wounded by a cutlass, yet managed, nevertheless, to reach his destination, with a dozen angry soldiers in hot pursuit and murder in their eyes.[15]

"Rushing the Guards." Extract from the memoirs of Ebenezer Fox, published with notes by C. Fox in 1847 as *The Adventures of Ebenezer Fox in the Revolutionary War*, by Ebenezer Fox.

With nowhere to go, and their lives hanging in the balance, the would-be escapees were suddenly saved by the timely arrival on the quarterdeck of the captain's mistress and the mate. The mistress, having heard the commotion, had rushed out to see what appeared to be an impending massacre. In an instant, both she and the mate threw themselves between the prisoners and the soldiers. After making such an outcry that Captain Laird himself came up, the guards were ordered off. As for the more unfortunate Putnam, during the search that was still underway, one of the guards lifted the tub, bayoneted the would-be escapee just above the hip, and drove him, bleeding profusely, to the quarterdeck to join his fellow conspirators. The critically wounded Bostonian was sent to one of the hospital ships and was never heard from again. The other five prisoners were placed in irons, with their feet fastened to a long bar, where they remained under guard. They suffered through the next night, as a cold fog and rain swept across Wallabout Bay forcing them to huddle together to fight the chill. With their rations reduced by one third for a month, they were released the following morning and wrapped up in tattered blankets by their mates to recuperate from their ordeal.[16]

• • •

Most escape attempts were undertaken beneath the mantle of night. Not long after Fox's ill-fated effort, another mass endeavor was carried out after the prisoners were driven below for the evening and the main hatchway was closed. In the hatchway, however, was a trap door just large enough for a single man to pass through, which was used for the prisoner's evening access to water, one man at a time. A number of desperate inmates decided that one of their number would overcome the guard on duty, after which the rest would flood through the portal in such numbers that some, if not all, might escape over the side, and swim for shore. The sentinel on duty that night was a remarkably curly haired Irishman with "a very crabbed disposition," known to the inmates as Billy the Ram.[17]

The plan called for one of the plotters, an athletic fellow, to occupy Billy in conversation while another slipped through the trap door and assailed him from behind. Artfully, the lead conspirator, purportedly ascending for water, engaged the Ram in a lament about the unnatural contest between his country and England. He then began to convincingly confess his new intention of enlisting in British service, and requested the sentry's advice in securing the confidence of his superiors in this regard. For a moment the Irishman, leaning carelessly on his musket, dropped his guard and turned away from the hatch opening. Suddenly, from behind, a massive blow to the back of his head dropped him senseless to the ground. Instantly a line of thirty men, one by one, began to ascend through the trap door and jump into the black waters.[18]

With so many men scrambling for freedom, the commotion and splashing of water so close to the ship soon drew the attention of other guards. The darkness of night proved only a partial shield of invisibility for the escapees. Though they could not distinguish individuals in the black waters, the soldiers began to fire wherever swimmers had stirred up the luminescent creatures of the deep. Within minutes a boat had been lowered and half of the escapees were picked up. No one was killed, and perhaps as many as fifteen of the inmates that attempted the project got away. Those who had been recaptured, though facing disciplinary action for their own failed efforts, gave three hearty cheers for their more successful mates. For their escapade, the wet and weary would-be escapees suffered the usual punishment, "a short allowance of our already short and miserable fare." For the next two weeks, however, it was considered hazardous to life and limb for anyone daring to speak to Billy the Ram.[19]

More often than not, prospective flights to freedom ended far more badly. Indeed many men were killed in the attempt. When one mess of six men managed to escape overboard in the darkness, one of their number became terrified upon hitting the water and shouted out: "Oh! Lord have mercy, I shall be drowned." Hearing the shout, the guard turned out and killed five of the men outright. The sixth managed to hide, holding on to the fluke of an anchor, with nothing but his nose above water. The following morning he managed to climb up the anchor and over the bow to the forecastle, from which he made it below, with a dose of good luck and without detection, albeit much the worse for wear.[20]

The consequences for those who remained aboard after a successful mass escape were occasionally bestial. One such case was documented by the famed "poet of the Revolution," Philip Freneau, who was himself taken prisoner on May 26, 1780, while sailing aboard the armed ship *Aurora* after an engagement with HMS *Iris*, and ended up aboard the hospital ship *Scorpion*.

On the night of June 4, soon after his capture, Freneau related, "about thirty-five of our people formed a design of making their escape, in which they were favored by a large schooner accidentally alongside of us. . . . We were then suffered to continue upon deck, if we chose, till nine o'clock. We were all below by that time except the insurgents, who rushed upon the sentries and disarmed them in a moment." The sentries were soon driven into a cabin. In the meantime the conspirators manned the ship's boat and swarmed aboard the schooner, whose crew unsuccessfully sought to repel them with handspikes. Finally, after a spirited fight, the crew was overcome. With the wind blowing fresh out of the south and a flood tide having set, the jubilant escapees hoisted sail and were quickly out of sight.

As soon as the sentries resumed full possession of *Scorpion* again, Freneau continued, "which they had no difficulty in doing, as there was no resistance made, they posted themselves at each hatchway and most basely and cowardly fired fore and aft among us, pistols and muskets, for a full quarter of an hour without intermission. By the mercy of God they touched but four, one mortally."

The following morning everyone aboard that was found to have been wounded was brought up and ordered to lie upon deck, exposed to the burning sun. "About four o'clock p.m., one of the poor fellows who had been wounded the night before died. They then took him out of irons, sent him on shore, and buried him. After this no usage seemed to them severe enough for us. We had water given us to drink that a dog could scarcely relish; it was thick and clammy and had a dismal smell. They withdrew our allowance of rum and drove us down every night strictly at sunset, where we suffered inexpressibly till seven o'clock in the morning, the gratings being rarely opened before that time. Thus," the poet bitterly recalled, "did I live with my miserable companions till the 22d of June."[21]

Many who had the good fortune to escape with their skins and health intact returned to their old professions of privateering or the merchant trade only to suffer captures a second time. Few survived the ordeal. One who did was Lieutenant Eliakim Palmer, a Stonington, Connecticut, man. During his first incarceration, Palmer found himself on board *Scorpion*, then anchored off the Battery at the south end of Manhattan Island. When he learned that he was to be transferred to the death ship *Jersey*, he conspired with two other prisoners, Thomas Hitchcock and John Searles, to escape at all costs. Just before the transfer, Hitchcock went up to the anchor and dropped his hat into the water as if by accident. Upon his return to the deck he begged that a boat be dispatched to retrieve the lost article floating in the water. Earnestly seconded by Palmer, the officer of the deck consented, no doubt grudgingly, and Hitchcock, Palmer, and Searles were allowed in the boat accompanied by an armed guard. The boat was a long time in getting off and in the meantime the hat floated away from the ship. For a while the two Americans manning the oars awkwardly rowed about, taunted by uproarious jeers from the ship of "Yankee land lubbers," and were ordered to return. The guard was unaware of their intention, or that they were nearly out of musket range from the ship. Suddenly, Palmer seized and disarmed the guard, and his mates began to exhibit their true maritime prowess, rowing swiftly and direct across the Hudson for the New Jersey shore much "to the astonishment of their deriders." Small shot fired from various ships of the fleet peppered the waters around them, and boats were sent off in hot pursuit, but nothing could deter the Stonington boys from their goal. Within a short time they were in New Jersey and eventually delivered their prisoner to Washington's headquarters, much to the approval of the commander in chief.[22]

Unfortunately for Palmer, not long afterwards he was taken prisoner once again and consigned to *Jersey*. He proved as indefatigable this time as he had been the last. With considerable panache, he immediately set to cutting away three iron bars that let into an aperture on the side of the ship on the orlop deck. This time he would swim for it. With his shirt and trousers tied to his head, he made for the shore as quietly as possible but lost his trousers in the process. Once ashore, with only his shirt for cover, he made his way down the length of Long Island, hiding in ditches during the day, crawling by sentry posts at night, and subsisting on wild berries and cow milk squeezed into his mouth directly from the utter. Eventually, he reached Oyster Pond Point, from which he was smuggled by a friend across Long Island Sound to Stonington.[23]

• • •

Opportunities for a successful escape came infrequently, but for those prepared to seize them, once was enough. One such opening arrived on a pleasant morning, about 10 a.m., when a beautiful yawl, "that sat like a swan upon the water," came alongside *Jersey*. The yawl was manned by four oarsmen and a helmsman, and carried a number of New York gentlemen "who came for the purpose of gratifying themselves with a sight of the miserable tenants of the prison-ship, influenced by the same kind of curiosity that induces some people to travel a great distance to witness an execution." The new arrivals seemed to be men of importance, for they were accorded considerable attention upon boarding. In the meantime, the boat's crew was actively engaged in securing their vessel to *Jersey*'s anchor chains on the larboard side, after which they were allowed to board as well.[24]

As usual, a sentinel was pacing "with a slow and measured tread the whole length of the deck, wheeling round with measured precision, when he arrived at the end of the walk. . . ." Whether or not one of the prisoners presented the sentry with a guinea bribe to retard his stride is uncertain, "but it was evident to the prisoners that he had never occupied so much time before in measuring the distance with his back to the place where the yawl was fastened." What is certain, however, is that at that very moment, sitting in the forecastle, was a captain and four shipmates who had just been brought on board as prisoners from a southern port only a few days before. They were immediately aware that the rare opportunity, so long awaited by others, had suddenly presented itself to them. As soon as the guard passed, they quietly and expeditiously lowered themselves into the yawl and cut the rope. The four sailors took to the oars and the skipper managed the helm. By the time the sentry had returned from his dutiful, albeit slow march, the yawl was well on her way and his shots fell harmlessly in the water behind them. Within moments, the ship's officers and the guests from New York had come on deck to witness all of the guards firing without success at the fleeing boat. The assembled prisoners on deck issued another three cheers for their bold colleagues and were promptly driven below at bayonet point and locked up for the remainder of the day. Thereafter, whenever guests came aboard, all prisoners were confined below until their departure.[25]

"Escape from the Prison Ship Jersey." Extract from the memoirs of Ebenezer Fox, published with notes by C. Fox in 1847 as *The Adventures of Ebenezer Fox in the Revolutionary War*, by Ebenezer Fox.

Solidarity among prisoners regarding escape attempts was usually strong. Those who intentionally dared to cause a plot to be aborted or a recapture to be made, did so at their peril. On one such occasion, a Captain Young of Boston managed to conceal himself in a large sea chest belonging to a ship's mate who had the good fortune to be exchanged in one of the few cartels. All aboard "considered his escape certain." Unfortunately, an informant named Spicer, perhaps seeking to improve his own situation, informed the commander of *Jersey* of the plot. The cartel ship was boarded and the escape attempt was foiled. When the prison population learned of the treachery, Spicer paid for it with his life. Retribution was brutal. When going down the hatchway for the night, he was fallen upon by his mates, who cut his ears off and mangled him so badly that, although rescued by the guards, he died a day or two later.[26]

Brutality was the only component of prison life that could be consistently relied upon, and it was liberally administered aboard all of the prison ship fleet. When ill-treated prisoners could take no more and attempted escape they were usually brought to heel with great cruelty. Silas Talbot witnessed one such event aboard the hospital ship *Strombolo* when the commander was ashore. Several prisoners rose up on the guard while attempting to break out but were killed or wounded in the process. Just as order was being returned to the ship, the captain came aboard. One of the dying inmates, a victim of a musket shot, lay in a heap upon the deck, exhausted and bleeding. Feebly he called the captain by name and begged him, "for God's sake, a little water," for he was mortally wounded. As it was already evening, the captain held a light close to the wounded man's face and exclaimed in a sudden rage: "'What is it you, d—n you? I'm glad you're shot. If I knew the man that shot you, I'd give him a guinea. 'Take that, you d—d rebel rascal!' and instantly dashed his foot in the face of the dying man!"[27]

–XXV–

Cartel

"Long were the hours of that night."

For the majority of inmates lodged aboard the prison ship fleet in Wallabout Bay, the word "cartel," meaning an agreement in writing to exchange prisoners, was well known, but in reality it was as foreign as the distant lands of the fabled Spice Islands. The very prospects for a cartel were, for most, but an abstract chimera perhaps to dream about but not to ever be hoped for. To many, it seemed that their country had abandoned them.

When a rare cartel was agreed upon between the Americans and British, the selection process of just who would be chosen aboard the British prison ships was usually biased against seamen. Releasing experienced, healthy mariners back into the American manpower pool was not a policy that, for obvious reasons, was wholly acceptable to the British. The practice of selecting landsmen or soldiers over seamen was deemed far more suitable and the most frequently observed of all, a fact that was all too clear to the general prison population in the Wallabout.

When a possible exchange was in the offing, it was typically preceded by a visit from the British Commissary for Prisoners. In 1780, when David Sproat boarded the hospital ship *Hunter* and ordered a roll call for one such event, the prisoners dutifully lined up to pass by him one by one. They all knew it was also the enemy's unofficial policy to exchange only the sickest prisoners, for they would be more of a burden than an asset to their own people once returned. The hospital ships were usually the first visited by the Commissary. For most prisoners, to be selected in one of these quite infrequent exchanges was their only chance of survival.

The procedure was always the same. As each man passed, Sproat asked if he was a seaman. Well aware of the slim chances that a mariner would be selected, most replied that they were landsmen. On one such occasion, after the entire prison population aboard had been questioned, the Commissary remarked with some incredulity to the American officers among the inmates: "Gentlemen, how do you make out at sea, for the most part of you are landsmen."

"You hear often how we make out," came the reply. "When we meet our force, or rather more than our force we give a good account of them."

"And are not your vessels better manned than these," retorted Sproat.

"Mr. Sproat, we are the best manned out of Philadelphia."

With that the Commissary, who was unquestionably aware of the charade, shrugged and said, "I cannot see how you do it."[1]

Those who managed to be included in one of the infrequent exchanges were, for the most part, in such poor physical condition that many never lived through the process. Scores died en route home, some within sight of their destinations. During one voyage of an exchange ship from New York to Milford, Connecticut, twenty-seven men died during the passage, seven more on the night they were put ashore, and many more while on the road home. On another cartel two years later, 136 prisoners from the prison ships were taken to New London. "Such was the condition in which these poor creatures were put aboard the cartel, that in this short run sixteen died on board and sixty, when they landed, were scarcely able to move, and the remainder greatly emaciated."[2] Still, for many, to die upon their native soil was reward enough.

Though exchanges among the maritime prisoners at New York and elsewhere were few and far between, inmates waited patiently for assistance from their government until it seemed to many that they had been entirely deserted. Indeed, various reasons have been cited for the lengthy detention of American sailors and privateersmen, but few quelled accusations by some prisoners against the indifference of their own countrymen and government. Few pains, said some, had been taken by their countrymen to retain British subjects taken at sea. Many enemy captives were often more than willing to enlist aboard the very American privateers that had taken them, and were generally welcomed aboard. Those that remained loyal to the king were brought into port and usually allowed, once ashore, to go about at large.

One of the reasons for such laxity was the impoverished condition of the country, where, for most states and towns, the cost of supporting prisoners in confinement was prohibitive. It was simply less costly for the city, local, state, and Continental governments to permit captives their independence to provide for their own support. They enjoyed, declared one bitter critic, "the blessings of liberty, the light of the sun, and the purity of the atmosphere while the poor American sailors were compelled to drag out a miserable existence amid want and distress, famine and pestilence. As every principle of justice and humanity was disregarded by the British in their treatment of prisoners, so likewise was every moral and legal right violated in compelling them to enter into their service." Thus the number of British seamen available for exchange was usually too small for a regular or equal exchange.[3]

Finally, in the late summer of 1780, a number of prisoners decided to act. A committee was organized aboard *Jersey* and petitions drafted and sent to Major General Henry Clinton, commander of the British forces in New York, requesting permission to forward a memorial to the American Commander in Chief, General George Washington. Incredibly, Clinton approved. That Washington had no direct authority over naval affairs, or the crews of privateers and Continental Navy vessels captured by the enemy, mattered little to the prisoners themselves. He was, in their eyes, the only possibly savior capable of rescuing them from almost certain death or, at the very least, helping to alleviate their sufferings.[4]

The petition was presented to the Commissary of Prisoners who, implausible as it may seem, laid it before Clinton, and the request was granted. The prisoners were permitted to choose three from their number, who were promised a pass to proceed immediately upon the embassy. A committee of prisoners was chosen to prepare the memorial. The memorialists, knowing full well that their petition would be examined by their captors before being allowed to go forward, were careful in presenting descriptions of their plight and conditions aboard the prison ships, and while not ignoring their suffering, focused upon the request that General Washington employ his influence to forward a prisoner exchange. However, the messengers themselves were charged to present in a verbal communication, "for obvious reasons," the "peculiar horrors" of the prisoners' situation, and to chronicle the miserable food, putrid water, rampant disease, and death they faced every day. As an inducement to secure the general's support, they were also to assure him that, in case he could effect their release, they would enter the service of the army and serve for the duration of the war. It was, in fact, the only reward they could offer for his assistance.[5]

Washington was not ignorant of the ongoing tragedy and daily loss of life in the Wallabout, though few of the prisoners at New York were even in Continental Army or Navy service. "I . . . feel for the situation of these unfortunate people," he later informed the President of Congress, "and wish to see them released by any mode which will not materially affect the public good." Nor did the communications he opened with Sproat mince words, as he repeatedly remonstrated with him, deprecating the well-known and cruel behavior exhibited against the prisoners. His implied threats of retaliation against British prisoners were not without some concern to the enemy.[6]

The prisoners aboard *Jersey* waited patiently for the return of the embassy; there was little alternative, albeit considerable expectation. "We waited, in alternate hope and fear, the event of their mission," wrote Thomas Dring. "Most of our number who were natives of the Eastern States [New England] were strongly impressed with the idea that some means would be devised for our relief, after such a representation of our condition should have been made." Some bore a positive countenance regarding the chances for success, while others seemed fatalistic about their future. Many of the foreign inmates, who were without a champion of any kind, were entirely unaware of the proceedings, as the "long endurance of their privations had rendered them almost indifferent to their fate; and they appeared to look forward to death as the only probable termination of their captivity."[7]

Within a few days, the envoys, having personally met with the general, returned to New York with a message addressed to the committee of prisoners. The general, who viewed the plight of the inmates with sincere empathy, was obliged to inform them what most already knew: as commander in chief of the army, he had no authority or direct control over naval prisoner exchanges. Their long detention was, in fact, a product of several circumstances for which a resolution would be difficult to produce. He informed them that very little effort had been made by the Americans to secure and detain their own British prisoners for the purpose of exchange. Indeed, most enemy mariners that had been taken were usually set at liberty as soon as they were brought into port. The principle reason for this was that neither the privateer owners nor the town or state where they had been landed were willing to pay for the expense of confinement and maintenance. The officers of the general government only took charge of prisoners captured by vessels in public service, meaning by Continental Navy ships. Nevertheless, the general vowed to lay the *Jersey* committee's memorial before Congress and reassured them that in the meantime "no exertion on his part should be spared which could tend to mitigation of our sufferings."[8]

Although the news was not as good as hoped, the prisoners took some heart in learning that Washington had opened direct communications with General Clinton and the Commissary of Prisoners to press for a general exchange. In case such an event proved impossible, he had expressed his wish that something be done to lessen the weight of the prisoners' sufferings. If the inmates could not be removed from their miserable floating penitentiaries, at the very least they should be relocated to clean ships. If some address to these conditions were not met, he implied, there was the distinct possibility that British prisoners would be subjected to the same conditions as the Americans were enduring in Wallabout Bay, although he assured the British he was only acting "from motives of humanity."[9]

The general's efforts, although undertaken without authorization and beyond his sphere of authority, bore at least some fruits. "We soon found an improvement in our fare," wrote Dring.

> The bread which we received was of a better quality, and we were furnished with butter instead of rancid oil. An awning was provided, and a windsail furnished to conduct fresh air between the decks during the day. But of this we were always deprived at night, when we most needed it, as the gratings must always be fastened over the hatchways; and I presume that our keepers were fearful, if it was allowed to remain, we might use it as a means of escape.[10]

For many prisoners there was at least a glimmer of hope, although few saw little prospect of escaping with their lives "except through the immediate interposition of Divine Providence, or by a removal from the scene of contagion."[11]

• • •

Two of the prison committee's three-man delegation had been from Thomas Dring's own ship *Chance*, and included her skipper, Captain Daniel Aborn, and ship's surgeon Joseph Bowen. Happily for the delegation, none of them would be obliged to return to the hellhole of *Jersey*, but were allowed to remain free on parole at Flatbush, on Long Island. Soon after arriving at Flatbush, however, Aborn sent a message to his fellow countrymen aboard the prison ship that his parole had been extended and he was being allowed to return home. Before he departed, however, he informed his shipmates that he would pay them a visit. He requested *Chance*'s first lieutenant, John Tillinghast, to provide him with a list of those of his crewmen who had died, as well as those still alive, noting where each of the latter were confined, either aboard *Jersey* or one of the hospital ships. He also informed them that he would carry letters from any of his men who wished to write to their loved ones and friends back home, and to have them ready when he boarded.[12]

For Dring, the other occupants of the Gun Room, and "such of the other prisoners as could procure the necessary [writing] materials," the news set off a flurry of activity. Many tried to set down a description of their grim circumstances, albeit as delicately as possible. As letters were usually inspected and an outright recitation of the true conditions aboard was likely to result in destruction of one or all of their epistles as a reprisal, many of the authors belied their horrid situation. Most soon regretted their caution, as the letters were not examined.[13]

Much to the chagrin and disappointment of his shipmates, when Aborn and the other parolees boarded the next day, they were permitted to come no nearer than the head of the gangway, but were obliged to pass through the door of the barricade to the secure area of the quarterdeck. To have rejoined the general population, even for a short time, it was believed, would have resubmitted the parolees to the latest contagion raging aboard "as they were more liable to be affected by it than if they had always remained on board." Though Aborn was not permitted to even speak to his men, Tillinghast was allowed to deliver their letters to him. Through the lieutenant, the captain sent assurances to his men that he would do everything in his power to secure their relief. If enough British prisoners could be procured, he fervently promised, every survivor of his own ship's original sixty-five-man crew would be exchanged. Failing in that, at the very least, he promised to send them clothing and other necessities.[14]

• • •

Washington had been well aware of the travails and sufferings of the prisoners in the Wallabout before the delegation from *Jersey* arrived, for her infamy was wide spread. In late January 1781, the general had written directly to Vice Admiral Marriot Arbuthnot, the British naval commander at New York, deploring the conditions aboard all the prison and hospital ships. The American prisoners, he declared, "are suffering all the extremity of distress, from a too crowded and in all respects disagreeable and unwholesome situation, on board the Prison-ships, and from the want of food and other necessaries. The picture given us of their sufferings is truly calamitous." He proposed that officers from both sides be permitted to visit the inmates in their respective confinements and examine their true condition. "This wilt either at once satisfy you that by some abuse of trust in the persons immediately charged with the care of the prisoners, their treatment is really such as has been described to us and requires a change; or it will convince us that the clamors are ill-grounded."[15]

While waiting a reply from Arbuthnot, Washington proposed to Congress a plan to liberate many of the prisoners. "It is," he informed the President of Congress, "by obliging the captains of all armed vessels, both public and private, to throw their prisoners into common stock, under the direction of the [American] commissary-general of prisoners. By these means they would be taken care of and regularly applied to the exchange of those in the hands of the enemy."[16]

In the meantime, Commissary Sproat proposed an exchange of British soldiers for American seamen. Washington found himself on the horns of a humanitarian dilemma, which the British were unquestionably aware of. The general, who was obliged to face enemy land forces that might be substantially enlarged by the move, was not enthusiastic about the British proposal. After all, for every British or Hessian trooper on North American soil, the British government was obliged to expend an enormous amount of money and effort to provide for his transportation and logistical support across the Atlantic. "Mr. Sproat's proposition of the exchange of British soldiers for American seamen, if acceded to," he informed the President of Congress, "will immediately give the enemy a very considerable reinforcement and will be a constant draft hereafter upon the prisoners of war in our hands. It ought also to be considered that few or none of the naval prisoners in New York and elsewhere belong to the Continental service." Moreover, even if an exchange of seaman for seaman was agreed upon, most of the enemy mariners had either been released, were on parole, or had joined up with the American privateersmen.[17]

On April 21, 1781, almost three months after Washington had sent his letter to Arbuthnot, the admiral replied from aboard HMS *Royal Oak*. He excused himself for not replying sooner on the grounds that he had "been very busy." Notwithstanding the delay, however, he informed the general that he had ordered "the strictest scrutiny to be made into the condition of all parties concerned in the victualling and treatment of those unfortunate people." He then launched his own assault on the American Commissary of Prisoners, John Bradford, and the Jailor at Philadelphia regarding alleged "inhumanity which they exercise indiscriminately" upon their own prisoners of war. One of the outstanding demands made by the admiral was "that in future they may not be fed in winter with salted clams, and that they may be afforded a sufficiency of fuel." As one historian of the Revolutionary War prisoner exchange situation remarked, the American inmates aboard the prison ships, forced to eat diseased and putrid meat, cooked in poisoned water, and who sometimes froze to death in winter for want of any fire except for cooking, would probably have been glad to dine on salted clams.[18]

Congress, in its usual bureaucratic manner, finally appointed a committee to examine into the state of naval prisoners. The committee consisted of Elias Boudinot of New Jersey, William Sharpe of North Carolina, and George Clymer of Pennsylvania. Not until August 1781 did the committee present its findings, having reiterated complaints "from our unfortunate Prisoners at New-York, who's Treatment is cruel, beyond Description and their Situation really deplorable."[19]

The committee's formal report was imposing, even if it's directives for General Washington, whose own army lacked practically every necessity, to take action rang somewhat hollow. Congress stated:

> A very large number of marine prisoners and citizens of these United States taken by the enemy are now closely confined on board Prison-ships in the harbor of New York. That the said Prison-ships are so unequal in size to the number of prisoners, as not to admit of a possibility of preserving life in this warm season of the year, they being crowded together in such a manner as to be in danger of suffocation, as well as exposed to every kind of putrid, pestilential disorder; That no circumstances of the enemy's particular situation can justify this outrage on humanity, it being contrary to the usage and customs of civilizations, thus deliberately to murder their captives in cold blood, as the enemy will not assert that Prison-ships, equal to the number of prisoners, cannot be obtained so as to afford room sufficient for the necessary purposes of life; That the enemy do daily improve these distresses to enlist and compel many of our citizens to enter on board their ships of war, and thus to fight against their fellow citizens, and dearest connections; That the said Marine prisoners, until they can be exchanged should be supplied with such necessaries of clothing and provisions as can be obtained to mitigate their present sufferings.[20]

In light of these charges the Commander-in-Chief was instructed, in early August 1781, to issue a complaint with the appropriate British officer "on the said unjustifiable treatment of our Marine prisoners," and demand, in the most rigorous terms possible, "to know the reasons of this unnecessary severity towards them." It was also strongly suggested by President of Congress Thomas McKean, that he inform them that "Retaliation through the Medium of the Simsbury [Connecticut] Mines," where Loyalist prisoners had been forced to work, be threatened "to awaken them to a Sense of Duty." The enemy's response was to be forwarded directly to Congress, which would then decide upon an appropriate retaliation if a redress were not immediately undertaken. Washington was directed to supply the prisoners, as best he could, with provisions and light clothing.[21]

On August 21, 1781, Washington wrote to the British Commissary of Prisoners reiterating the charges.

> The principal Complaint now is the inadequacy of the room in the prison ships to the number of prisoners confined on board of them, which causes the death of many and is the occasion of most intolerable inconveniences and distresses to those who survive. This line of conduct is the more aggravating, as the want of a greater number of prison ships or of sufficient room on shore cannot hardly be pleaded in excuse. . . . As a bare denial of what has been asserted by so many individuals, who have unfortunately experienced the miseries I have mentioned, will not be satisfactory I have to propose that our Commissary General of prisoners, or any other Officer who shall be agreed upon, shall have liberty to visit the Ships, inspect the situation of the prisoners and make a report from an exact survey of the situation in which they may be found, and whether, in his opinion there has been any just cause of complaint.[22]

A little over a week later, Edmund Affleck, a British prison agent, penned a haughty and somewhat cynical response.

> I intend not either to deny or to assert, for it will neither facilitate business, nor alleviate distress. The subject of your letter seems to turn on two points, namely the . . . inadequacy of room in the Prison-ships, which occasions the death of many of them, as you are told; and that a Commissary-general of prisoners from you should have liberty to visit the ships, inspect the situation of the prisoners, and make a report from an actual survey. I take leave to assure you that I feel for the distresses of mankind as much as any man; and since my commission to the naval command of the department, one of my principal endeavors has been to regulate the Prison and hospital ships.[23]

The British government, had made no provision for naval prisoners other than prison ships, he pointed out, yet it was impossible that such "inconvenience" experienced by those aboard was beyond that suffered from those ashore. The "evil" condition was unfortunately aggravated by the occasionally sudden influx of new prisoners. He assured Washington that every attention possible was afforded the prisoners, and that the prison ships were "under the very same Regulations here that have been constantly observed towards the prisoners of all nations in Europe." Moreover, "Tables of diet are publicly affixed; officers visit every week, redress and report grievances, and the numbers are thinned as they can provide shipping, and no attention has been wanting." Given the incredibly high mortality rate from starvation and disease aboard the ships, the last statement was almost laughable had the subject matter not been so callously fallacious.[24]

On September 4, Washington requested instructions from Congress "relative to sending an officer to inspect the situation of the prisoners" at New York. Congress responded with an open-ended authorization empowering the general to act in the matter he thought most conducive to the public interest.[25]

Affleck agreed to an inspection if the Americans would reciprocate and permit a British officer to "visit the prisoners detained in your jails and dungeons in like manner, as well as in the [Simsbury] mines [of Connecticut], where I am informed many an unhappy victim languishes out his days." He added, with a touch of sarcasm, that "had Congress ever been inclined, they might have contributed to relieve the distress of those whom we are under the necessity of holding as prisoners, by sending in all in their possession towards the payment of the large debt they owe us on that head, which might have been an inducement towards liberating many now in captivity."[26]

. . .

On a cold day in late October 1781, the humdrum rhythm of death and dying aboard *Jersey* was momentarily broken. A repeated melody of artillery fire was heard emanating from the New Jersey shoreline. No one could tell exactly what was going on, for with each round fired, British guns from New York would fire in reply, producing a cacophony of sound. But it was not a battle. Not until later, recalled Christopher Vail in his memoirs, would the prisoners, much to their delight, learn of the surrender of Lord Cornwallis at Yorktown, and that the British cannon fire had been undertaken "from their batteries so as to confuse that people should not be informed of Cornwallis's capture."

In December 1781, Washington presented to the President of Congress copies of letters from the British Commissary of Prisoners detailing the debt that he claimed was due from Congress for the support of the prisoners, the number of those remaining in captivity, as well as "their miserable situation, and the little probability there is of procuring their release for the want of proper subjects in our hands." The debt issue was thorny at best. That enemy prisoners of war were to be maintained at the cost of their own governments was common practice in the eighteenth century. But privateersmen, (the majority of inmates aboard the prison ships), who sailed at private expense, not to mention common fishermen and commercial mariners who were non-combatants, were another matter. The general cautioned Congress that before further investigation into what measures should be adopted regarding the payment of the debt, and on an exchange of maritime prisoner, "humanity and policy point out the necessity of administering to the pressing wants of a number of the most valuable subjects of the republic," namely Continental Army prisoners of war still in British hands.[27]

The general politely reminded Congress that as commander of the army, he was not authorized to address naval, privateer, or other maritime prisoners. Had a system planned by Congress and recommended to the several states been adopted and carried fully into execution, meaning that of obliging all captains of private vessels to deliver over their prisoners to the Continental Commissioners, it was his opinion that from the numbers captured and brought into the many ports of the United States there would have been a "sufficiency to have exchanged those taken from us: But instead of that, it is to be feared that few in proportion were secured, and that the few who are sent in, are so partially appl'd, that it creates great disgust in those remaining." The consequence of such was that American prisoners aboard the prison ships conceived themselves to be neglected. Thus, seeing no prospect of relief, many of them entered into the enemy's service. "Congress will, therefore," he beseeched "see the necessity of renewing their former, or making some similar recommendation to the States."[28]

It was Washington's belief that if the resolution of the problem of prisoner mistreatment, on both sides, were ever to be attempted, the whole business of prisoners of war should be addressed in a single general regulation. "I consider the sufferings of the Seamen for some time past, as arising in great measure from the want of that general regulation which has been spoken of; and without which there will constantly be a great number remaining in the hands of the enemy."[29]

The steady attrition of British troops throughout the war had been costly for the enemy. The difficulty in replenishing losses incurred from combat, captures, and sickness had been monumental, a direct byproduct of the incredibly successful depredations of American privateers. It was thus not surprising that British efforts again came to focus on matriculating exchanges of troops for American seamen. In February 1782, when Commissary Sproat proposed such an exchange, Washington again opposed the proposal, not on humanitarian reasons, but for strategic concerns. On February 18, he warned Congress:

> Mr. Sproat's proposition of the exchange of British soldiers for American seamen, if acceded to, will immediately give the enemy a very considerable reenforcement, and will be a constant draft hereafter upon the prisoners of war in our hands. It ought also to be considered that few or none of the maritime prisoners in New York or elsewhere belong to the Continental service. I however feel for the situation of these unfortunate people, and wish to see them relieved by any mode which will not materially affect the public good. In some former letters upon this subject I have mentioned a plan by which I am certain they might be liberated nearly as fast as they are captured. It is by obliging the Captains of all armed vessels, both public and private, to throw their prisoners into common stock, under the direction of the Commissary General of prisoners. By this means they would be taken care of, and regularly applied to the exchange of those in the hands of the enemy, now the greater part are dissipated, and the few that remain are applied partially.[30]

On March 6, the Massachusetts General Assembly passed a resolution directing the state's delegates to Congress to solicit that body to adopt a speedy and effectual measure for the relief of the maritime prisoners being held by the enemy. The Massachusetts delegates, however, were sanguine about the prospects, as they recognized that Congress had continued (albeit feebly) to press for some resolution to the issue. More letters to General Clinton protesting against the conduct towards the prisoners were ordered. A commission was sent to Elizabethtown with instructions to secure better treatment for them. Letters were sent to the American ministers in Europe on the same subject. But was it enough?[31]

If these measures "do not answer our purpose," the delegates wrote on March 26,

> Congress will, we trust, make such Retalliation as will force the Enemy to a more humane Conduct. The Balance of Marine Prisoners is so much against us, and Still increasing that it is perhaps impossible for us to obtain a full exchange so long at least as our Privateers are so very inattentive to bringing into port & confining the Prisoners which fall into their hands. Had it not been for this neglect, the evil complained of would have been avoided. However we have ample means in our Power to inforce a better treatment of our Prisoners, & the fault is ours if it is neglected.[32]

Still, distressing words of hardships aboard the prison ships continued to leak out. "I am sorry to write you from this miserable place," said one letter from aboard *Jersey* that made it into the patriot press in April. "I can assure you since I have been here, we have had only 20 men exchanged, although, we are in number upwards of 700, exclusive of the sick in the hospital ships, who die like sheep; the more my intention is, if possible, to enter on board some merchant or transport ship, as it is impossible for so many men to keep alive in one vessel."[33]

Unfortunately, for those poor souls who suffered and died by the dozens every day aboard the prison ships, little action regarding exchanges would be undertaken. During the summer of 1782, however, some mitigation of their atrocious treatment was achieved. Some of the sick on board the hospital ships were sent to Blackwell's Island in New York, where the spark of life was revivified in them. "This was considered a great indulgence," recalled Dring. "I endeavoured to obtain leave to join them by feigning sickness, but did not succeed. The removal of the sick was a great relief to us, as the air was less foul between decks, and we had more room for motion. Some of the bunks were removed, and the sick were carried on shore, as soon as their condition was known. Still, however, the pestilence did not abate on board, as the weather was extremely warm. In the day time the heat was excessive, but at night it was intolerable."[34] Yet, with peace negotiations underway in France, and though correspondence would continue to pass back and forth between American and English Commissaries, and Washington and the British commanders in New York, little more actual effort would be given to the salvation of the American seamen in Wallabout Bay. And the men continued to die in swarms.

• • •

While the great leaders of the American Revolution and their opposites among the enemy negotiated endlessly, those more directly associated with the situation did what they could as well. No one worked harder than Captain Daniel Aborn. Upon his return to Providence, he lost no time in making the details of the sufferings of his own men aboard *Jersey* well known, and quickly stirred up the sympathy and support of that city's citizens. Within a short time the former owners of *Chance*, the firm of Clarke and Nightingale, and a strong coalition of other citizens, determined to spare no expense in procuring the liberation of their fellow countrymen. Upon investigation, it was soon learned that there were at least two score of British prisoners being held in Boston. A move was quickly launched through private efforts and expense to procure them for an exchange, although the action was to be formally orchestrated through the office of the American Deputy Commissary of Prisoners John Creed. Within a short time, the enemy prisoners had been marched from Boston to Providence. A local sloop owned and commanded by a Captain Gladding was chartered to serve as the cartel ship, and one Captain William Corey, one of Dring's own fellow townsmen, was appointed as cartel agent to actually administer the exchange. No one was sure that it could come off.[35]

• • •

Throughout his captivity, Thomas Dring had survived on hope. He knew that in all probability his friends and loved ones at home had been informed of his situation and that some relief might someday be afforded him and his mates—if he could only live long enough. Then, as if by some miracle, salvation was suddenly within reach.

One day, early in the month of October 1782, as myriad prisoners milled aimlessly about the deck of *Jersey* a short time before sunset, they noticed a sloop approaching with a white flag at her masthead, which suggested a cartel might be imminent. The excitement on the deck was palpable, as Dring observed, for the direction she was approaching from suggested she was probably from one of the New England states. Unfortunately, before she could come to anchor, the prisoners were summarily ordered below for the evening. "Long were the hours of that night to the survivors of our crew," he later recalled of that sleepless eve. "Slight as was the foundation on which our hopes had been raised, we had clung to them as our last resource."[36]

The following morning, when the gratings were removed, the press by the gaunt, skeletal population to reach the deck was undoubtedly more forceful than usual. As the prisoners rushed toward the railings they were delighted to discover the sloop lay at anchor and that she was indeed a cartel ship. Her deck was thick with men supposed to be British prisoners. Within a short time Prison Commissary boats were observed coming alongside her and a transfer of men to the city was near.[37]

That afternoon a boat from the cartel came alongside the filthy prison hulk itself. On board the cartel vessel was Commissary of Prisoners Sproat and Captain Corey. When the two boarded, they brought with them exhilarating news for the surviving members of the privateer *Chance*; the cartel had sailed from Providence with forty British prisoners who were to be exchanged for the men of that unfortunate ship. The news was both thrilling and sad. By then the British numbers were more than sufficient to redeem every survivor of Dring's fellow crewmen, now numbering only thirty-five still aboard *Jersey*. Well aware of the imbalance, five of their companions from other ships in the Gun Room, all officers, were chosen to give the names of the dead crewmen on the list. These men were quickly disguised in the garb of the common seamen, and mixed among the cartel group.[38]

Dring quickly went below to gather up his few articles of clothing, and then proceeded to distribute what other items he owned, including his tin cooking kettle and precious trove of tinder wood, among those not so fortunate as himself. His sea chest was also left behind. After hastily saying goodbyes, he rushed back topside to await the call of his name, "well knowing that I should hear no second call, and that no delay would be allowed."[39]

Corey and the Commissary of Prisoners stood together on the quarterdeck as the names of those being exchanged were read off and confirmed by Lieutenant Tillinghast. As each name was shouted out and checked, the individual responded with a cheerful "here" and climbed down the accommodation ladder and into the boat. When his own name was called, recalled Dring, "I never moved with a lighter step for that moment was the happiest of my life. In the excess and overflowing of my joy, I forgot, for a while, the detestable character of the Commissary himself; and even, Heaven forgive me, bestowed a bow upon him as I passed."[40]

In the boat the forty prisoners sat in utter silence. No congratulations passed among them, for their feelings were too deep for utterance. Some cried quietly, while others were still in a state of disbelief. Most dreaded that some unforeseen circumstance might yet snatch them from the brink of freedom to return them to the miserable death ship.[41]

It was almost sunset when the survivors of the *Chance* crew boarded the cartel sloop. For Dring, the view from the deck of the sloop was moving.

> I then cast my eyes towards the hulk, as the horizontal rays of the setting sun glanced on her polluted sides, where, from the bends upwards, filth of every description had been permitted to accumulate for years; and the feelings of disgust which the sight occasioned are indescribable. The multitude on her spar deck and forecastle were in motion, and in the act of descending for the night; presenting the same appearance that met my sight, when, nearly five months before, I had, at the same hour, approached her as a prisoner. "DOWN, Rebels; down!" was the insulting mandate by which we had usually been sent below for the night; and now, as we stood on the deck of the Cartel, watching the setting sun, I could hardly persuade myself that I should not soon hear that unfeeling order shouted forth by some ruffian sentinel behind me.[42]

The next morning, as Dring and his mates ate their first full breakfast in months, the sloop got underway. Neither windlass nor capstan was necessary to weigh anchor as the former inmates, though feeble as they were, joyful grasped the cable with their bare hands and run the anchor up to the bow in but a moment. With sails set and a favorable tide, they departed Wallabout Bay forever. En route out, however, one final vision of sadness passed before them. As the sloop sailed by the shore of Blackwell's Island, where several of their crew mates had been sent to recuperate, they saw them gathered upon the beach with bundles in their hands. Somehow word had circulated that the *Chance* crew was to be exchanged, and they had assumed they were going too. But it was not to be, and the cartel sloop, having her full complement of exchanged men aboard, had little choice but to sail by without halting. "We could only wave our hands as we passed," recalled Dring, "but they could not return the salutation, and stood, as if petrified with horror, like statues, fixed immovably to the earth, until we had vanished from their sight."[43]

• • •

The news of the opening of formal peace negotiations between American and British commissioners, which began in Paris on September 27, 1782, was at first unknown to the inmates dying on the horrid prison ships in Wallabout Bay. Though many, if not most, of the warring parties throughout the land had already recognized the bloody conflict was almost over, few prisoners had little more than a dim hope of release before they died. The United States and Great Britain would soon sign a preliminary treaty of peace on November 30, recognizing American independence, albeit with the stipulation that hostilities would end only when France and Britain also signed a similar concord. It seemed to matter little to the captives who remain ensconced in their personal version of hell.

When word spread that the French and Spanish also signed preliminary articles of peace with Great Britain on January 20, establishing the long-hoped-for armistice, however, rumors of release percolated with unvarnished spirit through the shipboard community. Fifteen days later the total cessation of hostilities between Britain and the United States was proclaimed. Though the Netherlands had boldly recognized American independence nearly a year earlier, on April 19, 1782, it wasn't until February 15, 1783 that Portugal did likewise, followed by Spain on March 24. The end was in sight.

Even on the New Jersey coast, the privateer war had finally begun to wear down. On December 15, Captain Nathan Jackson in the privateer *Greyhound*, patrolling off Sandy Hook, captured the schooners *Dolphin* and *Diamond* and sent them into Egg Harbor. Not until March 3, would another vessel, the sloop *Katy*, fall pray to Captain Thomas Quigley's little privateer *Lively*.[44]

Yet, by the beginning of April, peace was finally at hand as Congress prepared to proclaim a formal cessation of hostilities. On Sunday, April 6, a barge from HMS *Ampheon* carrying Captain John Beazzley and David Sproat, Commissary of Prisoners, bumped aside the hulk of the infamous *Jersey*. Soon the two men stood on the deck surrounded by the survivors of the brutal but undeclared campaign of genocide against American mariners, unlike any in American history, to read a Proclamation from His Excellency Rear Admiral Robert Digby, now senior Royal Navy commander in America, announcing the release of all prisoners.[45]

Sproat later reported

The same day it was read to the Naval Prisoners in the Provost and a Circular letter sent off express to the prisoners who were on Parole on Long Island — informing them thereof, and desireing them to hold themselves in readiness to be sent out—The next day I had six Vessels in the Walabough under Flags of Truce, which on the 9th of April took the whole of the prisoners on board & carried them to their respective places of abode to save them expence and the fatigue of long Marches—excepting about 18 or 20 Sick & wounded who cou'd not be removed with safety—concerning them I wrote to Mr. G. Turner, Chief under Mr. Morris for Marine Prisoners, but received no answer—The poor people having got better they were delivered to Mr. Hopkins Intendant for prisoners—who sent them to Boston the 3d Instant.— The Provost was cleared of the Marine Prisoners (without exception) on the 10th of April. And on and after the 7th of same month Passports were granted to those who were on Parole to go out, as it suited their convenience.[46]

On April 11, the Congress of the United States of America proclaimed a formal cessation of hostilities and four days later ratified the preliminary treaty of peace. The final and definitive treaty between the warring parties in the American War for Independence, the United States, Great Britain, France, Spain, and the Netherlands, was signed on September 3, 1783, and ratified by Congress on January 14, 1784. The long struggle was finally over.

At New Brunswick on April 19, just four days after the preliminary ratification of the peace treaty, the sloops *Rachel* and *Nancy* became the last prizes of war to be sold in New Jersey at public vendue by order of the New Jersey Court of Admiralty.[47]

Beneath the shores of the Wallabout, the bones of perhaps as many as 11,500 men who had died in pitiful captivity aboard the prison ships in the bay continued to erode, forgotten by all but the fortunate few who, against all odds, had survived them.

Thomas Quigley's letter regarding the sale of the privateer brigantine *Betsey* at Egg Habor to James Thompson of Trenton, September 7, 1782. Courtesy Manuscript Division, Library of Congress.

–XXVI–

Taps

"With iron manacles still on the wrist."

At the end of the war, the rotting hulk of the old prison ship *Jersey* rested where she had been abandoned, her keel buried deep in the sucking muds of the shallows of Wallabout, from which she would never escape, along with the names of thousands of inmates scratched into her fabric. For those mariners who had somehow survived the war and imprisonment aboard her, the memory of their myriad comrades who had suffered and died upon her loathsome decks was etched deep in their psyche. And as the years passed, the bones of many of those who had been hastily interred in the sandy shoreline nearby were gradually revealed by winds and tides to bleach beneath the summer's sun, as if to remind all that they must not be forgotten. And they were not. The chain of floating charnel houses that had at one time or another been anchored in the shallows nearby, *Grosvenor, Whitby, Good Hope, Strombolo, Prince of Whales, Scorpion, Falmouth, Providence, Kitty, Bristol, Strombolo, Hunter*, and others were, by 1800, merely recollections in the minds of many old timers. Yet the bones and the ugly carcass of *Jersey*, which continued to slip every deeper into the sediments near an accreting shoreline, were real.

Over time, even as the shores of the Wallabout were evolving, some of those who had survived aboard *Jersey, Hunter*, and *Scorpion*, mariners such as Thomas Dring, Andrew Sherburne, Thomas Andros, Ebenezer Fox, and others, would publish their memoirs of life and death aboard the prison ships and help keep alive the memory of their more unfortunate companions in arms. And, over time, a mythology of sorts began to develop. By one account, unsubstantiated but accepted as fact by many even today, 20,000 American patriots had died aboard at least ten prison ships in Wallabout Bay, with *Jersey* alone accounting for 11,644. Though the actual number may never be known, that many thousands perished is certain. One thing could not be denied: the bones and the hulk of *Jersey* were evidence of what many believed amounted to be an international war crime.[1]

By 1792, the skeletons of some of the dead, exposed by rains, erosion, and shoreline change, had drawn civic attention from many leading citizens of Brooklyn. That year, at the annual town meeting, it was resolved that the remains be collected and reburied in the graveyard of the local Dutch Reformed Church, and that a monument be erected over them. Unhappily, officials of the church quickly met resistance from the property owner on whose lands the bones were exposed by tidal erosion and the project was abandoned.[2]

By February 7, 1801, when the U.S. Government purchased land to erect a new naval facility, the Brooklyn Navy Yard, on the shores of the old Wallabout embayment, sediment accretion and shoreline change had converted the shores and adjacent waters into a veritable swamp. Some distance from the shore the ruins of the old *Jersey* were plainly visible, though her deteriorating remains were sinking ever deeper into the accumulating muck. Over the years that followed, the U.S. Navy acquired more space for the yard through a systematic program of land reclamation by pouring fill into the adjacent wetland. As time passed, even the hull of the prison ship itself was entirely covered, and soon forgotten.[3] Yet, from the very beginning of the building of the Navy Yard, the bones of the dead continued to become exposed.

One of those who witnessed the sometimes disturbing discoveries was Nathaniel Scudder Prime, who would later write *A History of Long Island: From Its First Settlement by Europeans to the Year 1845*. "When the hill was dug away for the construction of the Navy Yard," he recalled nearly half a century after the event, "the bones of these numerous victims of British cruelty were disclosed, where the bodies had been huddled together, in the most promiscuous manner." As he stood and watched, he recalled the gruesome discoveries of "skulls and feet, arms and legs, sticking out of the crumbling bank in the wildest disorder," though they were usually "all carefully collected by the workmen for future sepulture."[4]

On February 10, 1803, one politician, Samuel L. Mitchell, a New York congressman, taking heed of the many human remains being found, became the first national figure to press the federal government to erect a new edifice to memorialize those who had died aboard the prison ships, though to no avail.[5] Yet, the political scene was changing, thanks to more warfare, this time the Napoleonic conflicts in Europe.

In January 1808, the Tammany Society of New York, a social and political organization headed by one Benjamin Romaine, a 42-year-old Revolutionary War veteran, former schoolteacher, and New York City collector, formed the Wallabout Committee. If not the first overt effort to resurrect public interest in a memorial, it was the first to initiate organized collection of the human remains being exposed along the shoreline, mostly on the edge of one John Jackson's property. A political and civic-minded man destined to twice serve as Grand Sachem of the Tammany Society, Romaine was also "a well known philanthropist of the time" who "was in the habit of buying sacks of these bones, placing them in coffins and giving them decent interment."[6] The project to commemorate the prison ship dead on an organized basis was partly in response to the erection of a statue of George Washington in 1803 by the opposition Federalist Party, but also for equally fierce political motives.[7]

The Tammany initiative was facilitated by ongoing anti-British sentiment resulting largely from the Royal Navy policy of forcibly impressing seamen from American vessels into the king's ships to fight in their war with Napoleonic France. The fires of American hostility were further stoked in 1807 by the unprovoked firing upon and boarding of an American naval vessel, the frigate *Chesapeake*, by HMS *Leopard*. This had happened within the territorial waters of the United States with the purpose of removing British deserters that had signed on as crewmen aboard *Chesapeake*, which had acquiesced without a fight. The episode nearly provoked a war. Soon after the Wallabout Committee had been formed in 1808, President Thomas Jefferson pushed through the Embargo Act in an effort to steer clear of the rising anti-British sentiments and to assume a position of neutrality between the warring European powers. The legislation cut off trade with both England and France, as well as with their dependencies, but served only to further ramp up hostilities as American trade and foreign commerce ground to a halt. The Tammany Society, seeking to fire up further antipathy towards its political foe, adeptly used the re-interment of the bones as part of a larger campaign to further arouse anti-British attitudes.[8] The campaign was successful and soon the memorial sepulcher became a reality.

Estimates varied on the quantity of human remains recovered "by the indefatigable industry of John Jackson esq, the committee of Tammany Society, and other citizens" during the Tammany initiative. One accounted reported that eight great piles of bones had been gathered. Another stated that thirteen hogsheads of human remains were recovered, a third stated twenty, and yet another suggested as many as thirty-eight. All were to be laid to final rest in a "martyrs' tomb."[9]

On April 13, 1808, the cornerstone of the martyrs' tomb was laid on a triangular plot of land on the Jackson farm in what would one day be called Vinegar Hill, not far from the Navy Yard. The Jackson farm was situated partly on the water and extended as far west as what would one day be called Gold Street and eastward into future Navy Yard property. It comprised about thirty acres of land and thirty-five acres of pond, together with the old run-down mill and dwelling.[10]

On the designated day, the society "marched in rank to Wallabout, where it laid the cornerstone of a vault in which were to be placed the bones representing 11,500 patriots who had died on board the British prison ships. On April 26, the vault being completed, the remains were laid in it. The Tammany Society, headed by Benjamin Romaine and the military; the municipal officials; Governor Daniel D. Tompkins, members of Congress, Army and Navy officers, and many other detachments of men of lesser note participated in the ceremony." Thirteen long, capacious bluestone coffins, inscribed with the names of the thirteen original states and filled with the bones accumulated over time, were finally interred in the vault of the newly built sepulcher. The tomb was a small, square edifice with a representation of an American eagle mounted at the apex of the roof. On a row of posts and rails in front of the structure were also inscribed the names of the thirteen original states, and the whole was surrounded by a fence. Over the entrance to the enclosure in which the building was situated was inscribed: "Portal to the tomb of 11,500 patriot prisoners, who died in dungeons and prison-ships, in and about the city of New-York, during the Revolution." The cornerstone itself bore the words: "In the name of the spirits of the departed free! Sacred to the Memory, of Our Sailors, Soldiers and Citizens, Who Suffered and Died on Board the British Prison Ships in the Wallabout During the American Revolution." An additional engraving below stated: "This is the cornerstone of the vault which contains their relics. Erected by the Tammany Society or Columbian order of the City of New-York. The ground for which was bestowed by John Jackson, of Nassau Island. Season of blossoms; year of discovery the 316th; of the institution the 19th, and of American Independence the 32nd; April 6th, 1808." An imposing ceremony, witnessed by as many as 15,000 persons, accompanied the formal deposition of the remains.[11]

With the onset of the War of 1812, the wooden prison ship martyrs' tomb fell into disrepair and then decay and, it was said, "the bones became exposed and children played with them." Finally, in 1839, for the sum of $291.08, Benjamin Romaine, now treasurer of the Tammany Society, purchased the land where the martyrs remains were interred in a tax sale from one Henry Reed Stiles. To better protect it from encroachment, he declared his intention to use it as the burial place of himself and his family. On Independence Day, Romaine made an appeal for support to build a new monument, noting that he intended to use his own pension to help support its construction.[12]

From time to time, as the Navy Yard entered periods of expansion or experienced new construction, human remains were still occasionally encountered. On February 25, 1841 workmen engaged in digging away an embankment in Jackson Street, near the Navy Yard, dug up a quantity of human bones. Among them "were the remains of a skeleton with iron manacles still on the wrist. It is highly probable that the mouldering bones are the remains of some of the victims of oppression on board the notorious *Jersey* prison ship." Within two weeks, the macabre story of the recovery had reached as far west as Missouri. On January 31, 1844, Benjamin Romaine, keeper of the deteriorating crypt, died and was also interred therein, for he had, like those already entombed, been among the prisoners of war who had suffered aboard the *Jersey*.[13]

On January 29, 1845, a year after Benjamin Romaine's death, a member of the New York delegation to Congress named Murphy proposed a resolution to construct a new tomb to replace the crumbling site on Romaine's land.

> Resolved, That it be referred to the committee on Military Affairs, to inquire into the propriety of erecting a proper sepulcher for the bones, now lying at Wallabout, of those soldiers of the Revolution who died by reason of British cruelty, on board of the Jersey prison ship and of an appropriate monument over them, and that the said committee report by bill or otherwise.
>
> The remains of these gallant soldiers were gathered together thirty years ago, by a private individual, and at his own expense deposited in a place of protection from the elements, and since then the Government has allowed them to slumber in oblivion. Mr. Murphy comes forward, in that manly and patriotic character which distinguishes him as a man of letters and a public legislator, and asks Congress to do at least funeral honors to those who have fallen in the cause of independence. This is an appeal not to be resisted, and 'tis one which 'twere far better to obey than the behest of party or the squabbles for political advancement. It soars above all distinctions, and is demanded for national honor and by national duty.[14]

Although the mariners entombed therein had somehow morphed into soldiers, which seemed more appropriate to the historic status some wished to bestow upon them, the resolution went nowhere.

In the meantime, a new memorial to at least some of the prison captives was raised, not in New York, but in Connecticut. On October 28, 1852, the cornerstone of the ironically dubbed "Soldiers Monument," dedicated to 200 men who had suffered from "confinement and hard fare" aboard the prison ship *Jersey*, was laid at Milford, Connecticut by Governor Thomas Hart Seymour in the presence of between 1,000 and 1,200 persons. The captives, it was reported in the national press, had been much enfeebled by their incarceration and some died upon being landed in Milford Harbor in January 1777. "All that did not were immediately provided for by the public authorities, or ministered to by the hand of charity in private families. But in spite of all that could be done for them, forty-six of their number died within one month, and were buried in a common grave. It is over the dust and bones of these martyrs to liberty, that this projected monument is now being erected to their memory."[15]

And again the move to address the dead of the *Jersey* in Brooklyn was resurrected.

• • •

By 1850, all traces of the prison ship *Jersey* had disappeared. The Brooklyn Navy Yard was now enclosed by a high wall on the land side, and contained forty acres of ground, much of it recovered from the adjacent swamp that had once been Wallabout Bay. By 1852, there were two large ship houses, great enough to contain vessels of the largest class while under construction. There were also seven extensive timber sheds of brick for the preservation of lumber supplies, several workshops for the manufacture of sails, rigging, blocks, spurs, boats, and other equipage, offices for the officers, and a number of large storehouses. Connected to the Navy Yard was the United States Naval Lyceum, a literary institution, founded in 1833, by officers of the navy connected with the post. Nearby was the Naval Hospital, on an elevated and commanding situation, surrounded by thirty-three acres of ground, highly cultivated, and encompassed by a high brick wall. Under contemplation by the government was the construction of a massive drydock expected to cost $1,200,000.[16]

And the bones kept appearing.

• • •

By 1855, progress towards erecting a new monument had miraculously gone forward despite differences as to where it should be located. One party suggested the remains be removed to a conspicuous place on an elevation in Greenwood Cemetery, and placed with a national monument commemorating Washington's ill-fated defense of Long Island, but again forward motion ground to a halt. Finally, twelve years later, in 1867, Frederick Law Olmsted, a descendent of the noted privateersman Gideon Olmsted, and Calvert Vaux, the famed landscape architects who had designed Central Park and Prospect Park, were engaged to prepare a design for a new thirty-acre park, the first such in Brooklyn, named after General Washington, on the site of one of the Revolutionary War fortifications conquered by the British during the Battle of Brooklyn, as well as a new crypt for the prison ship martyrs. Though the park design and vault site had gone forward, it was not until 1873 that an appropriation of $6,500 was approved for the erection of the entirely new mausoleum.[17] The burial chamber, which was intended to be ten feet high, thrity feet long, and fifteen feet wide, but when finished was twenty-five by eleven, was to be constructed of Portland granite, and embellished with pillars and fretwork of polished Aberdeen stone.[18]

On June 18, 1873, the modest old crypt, which had been invaded by vermin and dock rats, was emptied of its contents and the bones removed to the new tomb in Washington Park. For many, the modest structure was deemed little more than a holding facility until an even grander memorial could be built, but minimal progress was made for more than a decade.

Finally, in 1885, a meeting of prominent citizens of New York resolved "that the time had arrived when the cities of New York and Brooklyn cannot, without criminality, longer delay the necessary efforts for rearing the monument to the martyrs of the prison ships," and an organization was formed called the Martyrs' Monument Association of the United States to promulgate action. Congressional support was sought and an appropriation bill of $100,000 for the erection of the new memorial was brought before the national legislature. By the spring of 1888, the bill for the erection of the proposed monument in Washington Park, which had in the meantime been dubbed Fort Greene Park, had made its way forward in Congress. On April 5, however, the initial requested appropriation had been reduced to $50,000, but was consented in the House of Representatives. Unfortunately, when it was discovered that no quorum was present for the vote the bill was indefinitely postponed.[19]

The delay was not well-received in New York. The chief objection to the proposed monument was that its erection was more of a duty to the citizens of Brooklyn than a national obligation. Many observed the cynicism of such a jaundiced view. "The movement now in progress to honor these victims is not a new one," declared an editorial in one New York City newspaper on the day after the initiative had been stalled. "It was begun in the first years of the century. Since then, battlefield after battlefield of the revolution has received its memorial shaft at the hands of Congress, and statues of nearly or quite nearly every great hero have been set up here and there. Not only the victories of consequence have been commemorated, but some of the defeats; and even the surprises and massacres have not been forgotten. Meanwhile, in one way or another, the project relating to the prison ship has been postponed."[20]

The dead, however, would continue to be honored. On June 17, 1891, for instance, a memorial service was held "to commemorate the martyrdom of nearly 13,000 American prisoners." The Daughters of the American Revolution would have a conspicuous part. Following a meeting by the society at the Everett House in Brooklyn, "a floral design of the old prison ship Jersey" would be unveiled and carried to the tomb by a company of U.S. Marines detailed by Secretary of the Navy Benjamin Tracy.[21]

Efforts by the Prison Ship Martyrs' Monument Association and others were unrelenting. In 1894, Congress once more looked at the memorial project and prepared a report, but again little action was taken. In that same year, on July 3, however, the Society of the Cincinnati of New Jersey, erected a small memorial at Tuckahoe to commemorate the Pulaski Massacre of 1778, much to the chagrin of the New Yorkers, who seemed to be getting nowhere with a memorial to the more than 11,000 dead of the prison ships. They refused to give up. A petition and fund raising drive was launched and by the onset of 1898, no less than 30,000 signatures had been secured beseeching Congress to appropriate $100,000 to match another $100,000 raised by subscriptions from the citizenry "to properly recognize the martyrdom" of the prison ship dead. This time, the Congressional House Committee on Library reported favorably. In the meantime, as more bones continued to surface during Navy Yard projects, the Navy Department, in its 1898 appropriations request to support improvements at the yard, included $350 for a "memorial stone to mark the place where the old *Jersey* prison ship was formerly moored." The move came none too soon, for as early as 1878, human remains had been dug up from time to time in the vicinity of the proposed work, some in a good state of preservation. Then, on January 24, 1900, the bleached skeletons and skulls of two men were unearthed while digging the foundations for an extension of a warehouse. By midday, at least a dozen skeletons had been uncovered, "five of which were fairly well preserved." As work progressed and even more bones were found, Rear Admiral John W. Philips, commandant of the yard, ordered all of the finds carefully collected and stored in a temporary box coffin, which was kept under lock and key in one of the storehouses. It soon became apparent that there were, indeed, many more human remaains to be found. As work continued, skeletons, some of which crumbled when touched, were soon found lying in two rows, less than four feet from the surface of the ground and parallel with the water line, not far from the old Wallabout Channel. "It is believed," noted one newspaper, "that no fewer than one hundred and twenty skeletons were found at that time."[22]

The new discoveries quickly aroused "a deep interest on the part of leading citizens" and a renewed desire for establishing a significant monument. No doubt fired by the recent American victory in the Spanish-American War, renewed patriotic interest was aroused to find a suitable home for the old bones. The Prison Ship Martyrs' Monument Association was quick to capitalize on the new finds. On June 16, 1900, the association mounted a considerable memorial ceremony, wherein the newly discovered bones, in eight coffins, reportedly five feet long and two feet wide, were entombed with the others in the little sepulcher in Fort Greene Park "with all the ceremony of a military funeral, after a service held in Plymouth Church."[23]

On the day of the ceremony, all flags on public buildings in Brooklyn were ordered flown at half staff from 2 to 4 p.m. At 2 o'clock Battery N, 5th United States Artillery, and a detachment of United States Marines assembled in front of Admiral Philip's office in the Navy Yard. The boxes containing the bones of 108 prison "ship martyrs" were transferred to catafalques by a detail of sailors, after which the artillery band played a funeral dirge. Following short addresses by Secretary of the Navy John D. Long, General Stewart L. Woodford, and Reverend Dr. Newell Dwight Hillis, the procession began moving with measured, military precision, first, through Sand Street to Hudson Avenue, onward to Nassau Street, then to Orange Street, and from there to Plymouth Church.[24]

The main ceremony was conducted with pomp and splendor. Admission to the church was by invitation card only. Well before 3 p.m., when a service was to be held, the street in front of the church was completely blocked by people anxious to get in. The church itself was brightly decked out with Union Jacks, signifying renewed friendship with Great Britain, naval signal flags, and the Stars and Stripes. "One particularly aged and faded flag," it was later reported, "was stretched across the pipes of the organ. Time and moths and bullets had eaten holes in it; its white was cream colored, and its red was faded to pink. It has been used in the War of the Revolution, and that also is why it was beheld with reverence by the assemblage."[25]

The main body of the church was reserved for delegations of Revolutionary War societies, the Prison Ship Martyrs' Monument Association, prominent guests, including the Secretary of the Navy, and a pantheon of notable admirals and generals, veterans of both the Civil War and the recent Spanish-American War, and, of course an array of politicians. The ceremonies began with an organ prelude from the death march from *Saul*. Then the oak caskets, each covered by a flag, were tenderly carried in one by one, to the front of the church, on the shoulders of four sailors per casket, to the accompaniment of a funeral dirge. Services were opened by a reading of the Scriptures by Reverend Hillis, followed by a hymn, a prayer, and then an anthem. Several speeches were presented, including one by Secretary of the Navy Long, who referred to the bones as belonging to Continental Navy men, but never mentioning the far more numerous privateersmen among them. He then officially turned them over to the Martyrs' Monument Association. "The Battle Hymn of the Republic" followed by a rendition of "America," presented by the Plymouth Quartet, were sung even as the sailors took positions around the caskets to bear them away. After the benediction, the caskets were borne from the church onto the street. Soldiers, sailors, and marines, lined up for three city blocks, presented arms as the dead were reverently loaded into four hearses.

A military band played the funeral march as a squad of mounted police, forming a line from curb to curb, led the procession. Then came the hearses. U.S. Marines, with arms at port, marched alongside and then ahead, followed by a battalion of sailors. Slowly and with dignity the procession turned from Hicks Street onto Pierpont, on which formal tiers of the 23rd New York Regiment lined the curbs, and then in formation fell in behind the sailors, accompanied by the somber beating of muffled drums. Then the black plumes on the helmets of a mounted troop of cavalry could be seen above the crowd. The troopers smartly saluted with their sabers and then fell in behind the sailors, all followed by the four hearses. The dignitaries and politicians, and the officers of the Army and Navy, all in full dress uniform, brought up the rear in horse drawn carriages.

Onward the procession moved, from Hicks to Clinton to Schermmerhorn to Lafayette to Cumberland and then onto Myrtle Avenue for the last leg of the march to Fort Greene Park. A minute gun fired by a platoon of the 3rd Gatling Battery of the New York National Guard "let out its sharp, mournful bang and startled the 10,000 spectators who had assembled to witness the ceremony," just as the first plumes of the mounted units were spotted from crowds gathered in the park. As the procession arrived at its destination, the gun continued to boom at one minute intervals until the caskets were borne into the tomb. Again, the benediction was read by Dr. Hillis, and the Daughters of the American Revolution strewed flowers on the tomb as a thirteen-gun salute was fired. Then it was over, as a single, red-coated soldier stood high on the embankment, pointed his bugle heavenward and sounded "Taps."

"Thus," recorded the *New York Tribune*, "the last offices of a Nation to the prison ship martyrs."[26] But it wasn't.

• • •

The ceremony proved to be one of the most patriotic, stirring events of the time, with national news coverage serving to enhance and promote the ultimate objectives of the Prison Ship Martyrs' Monument Association. Within a few days of the reburials, it was reported "a committee had been appointed to build a larger memorial to replace the current one. Subscriptions were secured and selection of plans begun. Due to the work of this committee, funds for a new monument were finally considered and raised."[27]

Again an appeal for Congressional action was put forward. This time the bill passed the Senate with practically no opposition, but "in the hurry of the closing hours of the house it failed to receive approval, and so goes over until the next congress, when the Monumental association will renew its efforts to secure federal aid to rear a memorial which shall fittingly mark the resting place of these heroes of the Revolution."[28]

By the summer of 1902, the association had raised a little over $25,000. Yet another appeal was made to Congress, largely through the efforts of Steven V. White and his wife, who had for years been leading and fighting for the monument initiative. This time a joint resolution was passed on June 27 and approved on June 30, carrying with it an appropriation for $100,000, on condition that the society raise $25,000, which had already been done, and that the state and city contribute $75,000 more, which had not.[29]

While planning for the new monument raced forward, preparations for a massive construction operation at the Navy Yard was also getting underway. On March 6, 1901, Secretary of the Navy Long had initiated planning for the construction of a massive new steel dreadnaught called *Connecticut* on the shores of the old Wallabout basin. About the middle of October 1902, construction was begun on the foundations for the building cradle for the battleship that was to become one of President Theodore Roosevelt's "Great White Fleet." When the project started, difficulty was immediately encountered on October 13 in driving the thirty-foot-long pilings to support the bed. Investigation of the obstructions lying under a porous mixture of solid earth, mud and water in front of Main Street and 500 feet from a dock, produced evidence of great timbers of oak and teak, spaced at intervals of a foot or two.[30]

The building superintendent was puzzled by the presence of such a massive construction buried beneath sixteen to twenty feet of earth, that is until John Sevori, a sailmaker who was employed at the yard, stepped forward. Sevori boldly suggested that the timbers might be the ribs of the old *Jersey*. "My father," he said, "used to tell me that the hull of the ship lay right here, half sunken, with her masts sticking out of the water. It was before this place was filled in, you know."[31]

Servori wasn't the only one to suggest the obstruction was the remains of the prison ship. Possibly drawn by news of the find,

. . . a very old resident of Brooklyn had visited the yard, and when he saw the laborers working on the site of the *Connecticut* he said that he remembered seeing sixty years ago the old hull of the prison ship *Jersey* lying right where the men were working. At that time, he said, the tide flowed over that part of the yard and the ship lay half submerged. Her masts were still in place, but she was utterly unseaworthy and had been abandoned, and when the work of filling in with made ground the part of the yard where she lay had been completed the old ship had sunk lower into the swamp and quicksand and had been covered from sight. The aged man pointed out the exact place where he had last seen the *Jersey*, and a careful investigation recently completed by the workmen revealed that the two hundred and fifty odd feet of timber in the earth at which the pile driving engines were pounding was in reality a ship's hull.[32]

When Chief Engineer Bellinger, of the Navy's Yards and Docks Department, who was in overall charge of the foundation work, was informed of Servoi's tale, he visited the site. The obstructions encountered during the driving of piles, it was soon revealed, had not been the first time they had been encountered. Indeed, the first indication Bellinger had that heavy timbers lay buried deep in the soil near the waterfront was when he had earlier attempted to lay new water mains. As all of the excavated part of the yard was "made ground" there was not much surprise at the discovery of the timbers. But when the pile drivers began working a strip of the building site 250 feet in length and had repeatedly encountered solid wood, the mystery of the obstructions was no longer moot. Moreover, as the earliest map of the Navy Yard, reportedly executed in 1808, showed where the *Jersey* was known to lie, even after the land reclamation had covered her, it was assumed the timbers were hers. "This hull I have no doubt," he informed the press, ". . . is that of the old prison ship *Jersey*, for which patriotic societies have searched for so long. I believe, too, that there is more than one historic hull embedded near by in the earth. The hulls, which I believe is that of the historic *Jersey*, is about the size of the naval tug *Nina*—that is about 250 feet in length."[33]

Immediate discussion was raised regarding the recovery of the ship, and it was surmised by some that the Prison Ship Martyrs' Association, "which has searched for it for years," would probably attempt to secure the hull "as the timbers are in good condition." One wishful estimate was that raising the hulk would cost just $500. Some were skeptical such an undertaking was possible but remained hopeful. "Whether they will be removed and placed in the naval museum is said to be doubtful," commented one prominent Washington newspaper:

> . . . as their extraction from the soil where they have been for nearly 120 years will delay the preparations for building the new man-of-war *Connecticut*; but we hardly think that the delay of a few days can stand in the way of recovering relics of such interest . . . What the Black Hole of Calcutta is in England's history the *Jersey* prison ship is in America's. But the former lasted only one night; the latter endured for seven years. The timbers of the *Jersey*, perhaps the most interesting relics of the revolution, should be removed to a place of safety, where, like the martyrs monument in Trinity Church yard, and the tablets in Fort Greene, they will serve to keep alive the memory of those who died in making this country the American republic.[34]

Others took a more realistic view:

> Solid still are the more massive oak and teak timbers of the old prison craft, but it is not likely that this remarkable relic of the fight for American independence can be saved. It is so firmly imbedded in the earth and covers so comparatively large an area that its removal would greatly hamper the work on the *Connecticut*. Besides, it is believed that part of the hull has been smashed by the pile driving engines and that because of the progress made in the foundations for the *Connecticut* it would be hardly possible to get the skeleton of *Jersey* out of the earth in anything like an intact condition.[35]

In the end, the officials at the Navy Yard determined that the hulk would be left in place, as its recovery would delay construction of the mighty behemoth *Connecticut*. Still, a greater symbolic purpose had already been served. As one Mid-western journal so aptly described the discovery, it:

> ... seemed like a fulfillment of a prophecy that upon her wooden skeleton a steel fighter is building—a warship of the infant country they sought to crush...The surroundings of the old ship show changes as remarkable as the difference between the old British vessel and the new man-of-war, for the Wallabout basin has been filled completely since the government took the marsh land for a navy yard, until now fully 16 feet of solid earth cover the remains of *Jersey*. Away from the sea she lies and buried like the breach between two countries, she is a grim monument to the fact that the past is forgiven, though not forgotten; and now, though badly pierced by the piles for the foundation of the new battleship *Connecticut*, her definite location crowns the movement toward raising a worthier memorial to the men who died aboard.[36]

On May 9, 1903, after years of working as an aggressive social organization, the Prison Ship Martyrs' Monument Association of the United States was formally incorporated at Albany, New York. Unquestionably, the national news coverage regarding the recent discovery of *Jersey's* remains helped further motivate the New York State and New York City governments to appropriate on October 12, 1904 the remaining $75,000 needed to secure matching funds to guarantee Federal support as promised. Within a short time the project was finally initiated.[37]

The monument, to be erected on the upper plateau of Fort Greene Park near the main entrance, was designed by the well known firm of McKim, Mead & White, of Fifth Avenue, New York, under the overall direction of the renowned architect Stanford White. The contract for actual construction was awarded to the Carlin Construction Company under the project supervision of Lt. Colonel. W. L. Marshall. The proposed monument, of white Newport granite, at 149 feet in elevation was to be the world's tallest Doric column. Upon its top was to be surmounted a tripod holding a great bronze urn, nearly 7.5 tons in weight and 22.5 feet in height. The urn was designed by Manhattan sculptor Adolf Alexander Weinman, and was to be cast by the Whale Creek Iron Works at Greenpoint, Long Island. In the urn, an "eternal flame" was to be lit, casting an on-again-off-again light that could be seen across the East River and Manhattan Island. In the center of three flights of a 100-foot wide, 99-step stairway leading up to the column would be seen the small bronze doorway to the eighteen-by-eighteen-foot tomb itself, in which were to be deposited the bones of the prison ship martyrs. The solid white marble approach to the stairs was to be 800 feet.[38]

Even as the design process was underway, new discoveries were revealed. In early 1906, it was reported, "that the Society of Old Brooklynites is in possession of the marble slab that was the cornerstone of the first tomb of the martyrs." The actual marble had been bequeathed to the society by Arthur W. Benson and "will undoubtedly be incorporated as a most interesting part of the new monument."[39]

Finally, on Saturday, October 26, 1907, the governor of New York, Charles Evans Hughes, presided over the ceremonial laying of the cornerstone of the Prison Martyrs' Monument in a nationally covered ceremony that would be exceeded only by the actual dedication of the completed memorial itself more than a year later.[40]

• • •

On the evening of November 13, 1908, President-Elect William Howard Taft left his well-deserved rest at Hot Springs, West Virginia, after a spirited presidential election campaign, bound by train for Brooklyn to present the keynote oration at the formal dedication of the Prison Ship Martyrs' Monument.

His party arrived at 12:30 p.m. at Jersey City, where it embarked aboard a naval tug bound for the Brooklyn wharf nearest the monument. Following a short lunch at the Brooklyn Club with Vice President-elect James S. Sherman and others, the President-Elect's party, escorted by mounted cavalry, took carriages to the park where they were to review the dedication parade from Bedford and Division Avenues. "It was," reported one newspaper the following day, "the first time that Mr. Taft has taken part in a public ceremony since his election to the office of president, and when he was espied alighting from his carriage near the entrance of the park, there were cheers that could be heard for blocks."[41]

By the time Mr. Taft took his position, more than 20,000 citizens had gathered to view the dedication ceremony. After a prayer by Reverend Parks Cadman of the Central Congregational Church and the reading of a poem written for the occasion by Thomas Walsh, Mr. Taft was graciously introduced by master of ceremonies Stephen V. White. Given a sharp applause as he rose to speak, and as snow began to gently fall, the rotund President-Elect of the United States provoked a laugh saying he would finally now have to put his hat on.

He began:

> We are met today to pay a nation's debt, long since recognized, but most tardily provided for. The monument which we dedicate commemorates the sacrifice for their country of the lives of upwards of 15,000 Americans, who were buried more than 125 years ago into what seemed for years to be an inglorious oblivion. Their identity and personality have not been preserved, and we who assemble in grateful recollection of their patriotic self-sacrifice are compelled to refer to them as 'unknown dead.[42]

The speech was brief, touching on the sufferings of the prisoners, confirming the charges of outrageous cruelties endured by them, and the British denial of allegations made against them. Fully aware of lingering animosities still retained by some against the British nation, he said:

> I don't wish to be understood as charging that these conditions were due to the premeditations of the English commanders-in-chief or that the act purposes of any one in authority having to do with the fate of the unfortunate men whose bravery and self-sacrifice this monument records. Such a charge would make the British commanders human monsters. The conditions were the result of neglect, not design.

He defended General Washington against charges that had occasionally been leveled against him as a result of his refusal to exchange the imprisoned American sailors for imprisoned

British soldiers.[43] The time for laying blame was over. It was now a time for healing, but also to honor those who had suffered and, indeed, paid the ultimate price for the cause of liberty and country.

After the President-Elect concluded his oratory, and a brief closing statement was made by Daniel F. Cohalan, one of the organizers of the dedication, several old men clad in uniforms stepped forward, Union Army veterans all who had themselves been prisoners in the infamous Confederate prison camps during the Civil War. Then "Taps" was sounded. Upon a given signal, Miss Ester King Norton pulled a release to a gigantic American flag "whose starry folds enveloped the cap of the shaft, and whose red and white bars enwrapped the column, edged slowly down the monument, revealing in all its magnificence to the throng, which rose to its feet and, amid a silence only broken by the playing of Handel's 'Largo' by the Marine band, stood with bared heads." The gently falling snow turned to rain. And the ceremony was over.[44]

President-elect Taft left for his journey south to Washington on the 6:14 p.m. express to meet with outgoing President Theodore Roosevelt. While hurrying to the train he was recognized by a crowd of football enthusiasts who were returning from the Yale-Princeton game. There was an outburst of cheering and Mr. Taft acknowledged the compliment by lifting his hat.[45]

• • •

In 1921, the eternal flame atop the Prison Martyrs' Monument was extinguished owing to hard economic times following World War I. The twin helix stairways that carried visitors to the top of the monument for a dime were closed. In the years to come, through the Great Depression (despite a brief 30-year anniversary ceremony in 1938), World War II, and after, both neglect and vandals exerted their horrid toll on both park and monument. The marbled plaza became potholed and hostile. From time to time its former majesty was recalled and minor efforts were made at repair or to replace vandalized plaques and signage. But it wasn't enough. One of four beautiful bronze eagles that had watched over the plaza was stolen, while the remainder grew green with corrosion and were removed in the 1970s, even as the park became a drug and gang-infested component of the Brooklyn landscape. During the Bicentennial celebrations of the American Revolution in 1976, King Juan Carlos of Spain dedicated a plaque honoring the 700 Spanish prisoners of war who died on the prison ships. And then, once again, the men who had paid the ultimate price were forgotten by all but a few dedicated champions.[46]

But not in New Jersey.

On October 1, 1988, the Colonel Richard Somers Chapter of the Sons of the American Revolution, in co-operation with the General Lafayette Chapter of the Daughters of the American Revolution, gathered at Chestnut Neck to dedicate their own monument, not to the war dead, but to "the brave privateers who served so well in the War of Independence." Franklin W. Kemp, Lt. Commander, USCGR, Ret., offered a brief introductory speech which was followed by the dedication of the monument replete with pomp and ceremony. On a plaque mounted upon the monument stone were the names of thirty-four privateer captains, many from New Jersey, and the ships they commanded. It was indeed an auspicious occasion, for the privateersmen who had dueled with the might of the British Empire along the remote shoals and shores of that state, on oceans, seas and sounds, often against great odds, had finally been recognized.[47]

The cause of remembrance, fortunately, had not been entirely extinguished in Brooklyn where, once again, it was the citizens who banded together and formed a new organization, the Fort Green Park Conservancy. Led by another dedicated American named Ruth Goldstein, who for four decades pressed the mighty powers that be to reclaim and restore the Prison Ship Martyrs' Monument and the park itself, the effort was revivified. Finally, on November 15, 2008, after eighty-seven years of darkness, the solar powered beacon which replaced the "eternal flame," reflected from mirrors, was again "relit" to shine every night, from sunset to sunrise, across the harbor in which so many Americans had perished. Pulitzer Prize-winning historian David McCullough presented the keynote address for the ceremony. Through the efforts of Goldstein, the Conservancy, and many others, the potholes of history were filled. The eagles were repaired, restored, and returned to their former positions. And the Prison Ship Martyrs Monument was fully reinstated to its former glory as the centerpiece of Fort Greene Park and as a national symbol.[48]

The forgotten prison ship martyrs of Wallabout Bay would be forgotten no longer.

The original Prison Martyr's Monument in Vinegar Hill, ca. 1840. Donald Shomette Private Collection, Dunkirk, Maryland.

Appendix A

Privateers of Pennsylvania

1776–1782

The following is a list of privately owned and armed men-of-war and letters of marque vessels, mostly bonded craft bearing Continental commissions issued by the State of Pennsylvania during the American Revolution. The comparative tables that follow identify by year and state the number of bonds issued to individual vessels bearing Continental commissions, and the total number of carriage guns and crews for each year by state. The principal repository of data from which this assemblage has been compiled is the Papers of the Continental Congress (Ships' Bonds required for Letters of Marque and Reprisal, 1776–1783), in the Library of Congress, Washington, DC. This listing of bonded vessels, is drawn from volume 196 of the collection, and published by the library in 1906 as part of the *Naval Records of the American Revolution 1775–1776*. It is the primary source from which most historians have derived their statistics regarding American privateers fielded during the war. Although the bond list is extensive, it does not include: many vessels for which commissions were issued without bonds being posted; privateers and letters of marque vessels that were issued separate state commissions by Massachusetts, New Hampshire, Rhode Island, Connecticut, Maryland, and South Carolina (although some vessels may have carried dual commissions from both State and Continental governments), or those issued by American Commissioners in Paris and naval agents in the West Indies; those issued to vessels operating from foreign ports; for bonded vessels whose documentation papers, for myriad reasons, were never returned to Congress; or for vessels which sailed as privateers without benefit of commission. The author has thus sought to include Pennsylvania vessels that are referred to in other source material as operating, or probably operating, as legitimate privateers, albeit without evidence of having posted bond or secured commissions. However, it is quite evident that the list presented herein does not contain the totality of Pennsylvania vessels engaged in the privateering, only those for which there is a known record discovered by the author. It is quite likely that future research will eventually enlarge this compilation somewhat. This listing is believed to be the first of its kind to be digitally assembled and tallied. The author assumes responsibility for any errors that have occurred.

The reader will note numerous duplications of names. Close examination of relevant data included in the ships' bonds regarding vessel typology, tonnage, armaments, ownership, captaincy, and so forth, clearly indicate that many vessels secured multiple commissions over time, although some names, particularly of very successful vessels, are occasionally given to later arrivals on the scene. Indeed, examination of the bonds for vessels from other states indicates a not surprising commonality of nomenclature that appears almost universal among all the states.

Commissions were issued to privateers before the start of a specific "cruise" against enemy commerce, and to armed letters of marque vessels before a trading "voyage" during which, if opportunity presented itself, they might take enemy vessels as prizes. Thus, though the listing contained 538 entries, carrying a total of 4,550 guns, and manned by 18,126 seamen (not including thirteen listings for which armament is unknown, and twenty-sevem for which manpower is unknown), a close evaluation of entries suggests that the entirety of identifiable individual vessels that were fielded numbered approximately 398 (140 brigs and brigantines, 106 schooners, fifty-one sloops, sixty-five ships, two snows, five cutters, one galley, one xebec, twenty-five boats and whaleboats, and two unidentified rigs).

Each entry includes, in order, the vessel name; commander and his given place of business/residence, date of the commission; vessel type; number of guns; number of crew; amount of bond; bonders and their given place of business/residence; owners and their given place of business/residence; and occasionally additional notes of interests. Owing to space, tonnage, the names of officers and crewmen, small arms, and provisions taken aboard, and other data included in formal bonds have not been included. Dates followed by [p] indicate that the commission was granted prior to the given date.

The following list is in alphabetical and chronological order by vessel name and date.

1. *Achilles*; Thomas Murdock, Philadelphia; 1779 Apr. 22; brigantine; 10 guns; crew not stated; $10,000; Cadwallader Morris, Philadelphia, Samuel C. Morris, Philadelphia, Thomas Morris, Philadelphia, bonders; Samuel C. Morris & Co., Philadelphia, owner.

2. *Achilles*; George Thomson, Philadelphia; 1779 Aug. 28; brigantine; 12 guns; 30 crew; $10,000; Samuel C. Morris, Philadelphia, John Wilcocks, Philadelphia, bonders; Samuel & Thomas Morris, Philadelphia, owners.

3. *Active*; William Green [Philadelphia?]; 1779 Apr. 30; sloop; 6 guns; 12 crew; $5,000; Robert Bridges, Philadelphia, William Smith, Philadelphia, bonders; Robert Bridges & Co., Philadelphia, owner.

4. *Active*; Charles Alexander; 1779 May 21; brigantine; 14 guns; 40 crew; $10,000; John Wilcocks, Philadelphia, Charles Alexander, Philadelphia, bonders; John Wilcocks & Co., Philadelphia, owner.

5. *Active*; Peter Day, Philadelphia; 1779 Sep. 20?; sloop; 14 guns; 60 crew; $10,000; Philip Moore, Philadelphia, James Ash, Philadelphia, bonders; Philip Moore, Philadelphia, James Ash & Co., Philadelphia, owners.

6. *Active*; Thomas Misnard; 1779 Nov. 8; brigantine; 14 guns; 40 crew; $10,000; Thomas Misnard, Philadelphia, Thomas Fitzsimons, Philadelphia, George Meade, Philadelphia bonders; Thomas Fitzsimons, Philadelphia, George Meade & Co., Philadelphia, owners.

7. *Active*; Philip Jacquelin Du Roy; 1780 Oct. 28; brigantine; 4 guns; 20 crew; $20,000; James Oellers, Philadelphia, Philip Jacquelin Du Roy, Philadelphia, bonders; Philip Jacquelin Du Roy, owner.

8. *Active*; John Craig, Philadelphia; ; 1780 Dec. 12; brigantine; 10 guns; 18 crew; $20,000; John Patton, Philadelphia, James Craig Jr., Philadelphia, bonders and owners.

9. *Active*; Charles Biddle, Philadelphia; 1781 Sep. 29; brigantine; 7 guns; 24 crew; $20,000; Francis Gurney, Philadelphia, Charles Biddle, Philadelphia, bonders; Francis Gurney, Charles Pettit, Clement Biddle and others, Philadelphia, owners.

10. *Addition*; John Craig, Philadelphia; 1778 Dec. 9; schooner; 10 guns; 45 crew; $10,000; William Marshall, Philadelphia, Joseph Carson, Philadelphia, bonders; Owners not stated.

11. *Addition*; James Spencer, [Philadelphia?]; 1779 Jun. 11; schooner; 10 guns; 30 crew; $5,000; Joseph Carson, Philadelphia, Daniel Edwards, Philadelphia, bonders; Joseph Carson & Co., Philadelphia, owner.

12. *Admiral Zoutman*; William McFaden, Philadelphia; 1782 Jan. 14; ship; 8 guns; 30 crew; $20,000; Benjamin Davis, Jr., Philadelphia, William McFaden, Philadelphia, owners; Benjamin Davis Jr., John Patton, Philadelphia, owners.

13. *Adriana*; William Miller; 1780 Oct. 9; brigantine; 8 guns; 25 crew; $20,000; Alexander Stewart, Philadelphia, William Miller, Philadelphia, bonders; Alexander Stewart, Robert Totten, Philadelphia, owners.

14. *Adriana*; Robert Alcorn; 1781 Jul. 20; brigantine; 6 guns; 20 cfew; $20,000; Robert Alcorn, Philadelphia, James Crawford, Philadelphia, bonders; George Haines, Philadelphia. Andrew & James Caldwell, Philadelphia. John Barclay, Philadelphia, John Mitchell, Philadelphia, owners.

15. *Adventure*; John McIlnoe; 1779 Jun. 20; schooner; 6 guns; crew not stated; $10,000; Benjamin Towne, John McIlnoe, Philadelphia, bonders; Benjamin Towne, Philadelphia, John Bartholomew & Co., Philadelphia, owners.

16. *Adventure*; John Leamy; 1780 Jul. 15; brigantine; 8 guns; 80 crew; $20,000; Alexander Nelson, Philadelphia, John Leamy, Philadelphia, bonders; Alexander Nelson, Philadelphia, Philip Rocke & Co., Philadelphia, owners.

17. *Adventure*; Matthew Strong; 1782 May 29; schooner; 4 guns; 9 crew; $20,000; Joseph Carson, Philadelphia, Matthew Strong, Philadelphia, bonders; Joseph Carson, Philadelphia, Blair McClenachan and others, Philadelphia, owners.]

18. *Ajax*; John Harr; 1781 Jan. 6; brigantine; 8 guns; 23 crew; $20,000; John Harr, Philadelphia, John Wilcocks, Philadelphia, bonders; John Wilcocks & Co., Philadelphia, owners.

19. *Alphen*; Job Pray; 1781 Sep. 8; sloop; 10 guns; 30 crew; $20,000; Nicholas Low, Philadelphia. Job Pray, Philadelphia, bonders; Job Pray, Philadelphia, [Henry?] Hill, Philadelphia, owners.

20. *America*; John Lightbourn; 1778 Nov. 27; sloop; 6 guns; 20 crew; $10,000; Thomas Pryor, Philadelphia, John Lightbourn, Philadelphia, bonders and owners.

21. *Amigos del Pays*; Juan Joseph de Arbulu [Philadelphia?]; 1782 May 9; ship; 12 guns; 12 crew; $20,000; Claudius Paul Raguett, Philadelphia, Joseph Gallego, Philadelphia, bonders; Juan Joseph de Arbulu [Philadelphia?], owners.

22. *Andrew Caldwell*; Thomas Truxtun; 1779 Jun. 1; ship; 10 guns; 40 crew; $10,000; James Caldwell, Philadelphia, Thomas Truxtun, Philadelphia, bonders; Andrew Caldwell, Philadelphia, James Caldwell & Co., Philadelphia, owners.

23. *Anne*; James Josiah; 1780 Nov. 15; ship; 10 guns; 30 crew; $20,000; George Henry, Philadelphia, James Josiah, Philadelphia, bonders; George Henry, Philadelphia, Robert Knox & Co., Philadelphia, owners.

24. *Anne*; John Ashmead; 1782 Jan. 7; ship; 10 guns; 30 crew; $20,000; Robert Knox, Philadelphia, John Ashmead, Philadelphia, bonders; George Henry, Philadelphia, David Lenox and others [Pennsylvania], owners.

25. Anonymous; William Davis; 1779 Aug. 30; unidentified type; 12 guns; 30 crew; $10,000; William Davis, Philadelphia, Samuel Meredith, Philadelphia, bonders; William Davis, Samuel Meredith, Philadelphia, John Nixon, Philadelphia, owners.

26. Anonymous; Joshua Barney, Philadelphia; 1782 Apr. 2; ship; 18 guns; 120 crew; $20,000; Joshua Barney, Philadelphia, Francis Gurney, Philadelphia, bonders; Owners not stated.

27. *Anti Traitor*; John Macpherson; 1781 May 17; boat; 2 guns; 40 crew; $20,000; John Macpherson, Philadelphia, Thomas Nevell, Philadelphia, bonders; John Macpherson & Co., Philadelphia owners.

28. *L'Antoinette*; William Smith; 1782 Mar. 30; brigantine; 6 guns; 21 crew; $20,000; Lacaze & Mallet, Philadelphia, William Smith, Philadelphia, bonders and owners.

29. *Argo*; Moses Griffing; 1779 Nov. 2; brigantine; 14 guns; 75 crew; $10,000; Benjamin Randolph, Philadelphia, Moses Griffing, Philadelphia; Benjamin Randolph & Co., Philadelphia, owner.

30. *Argo*; John Ridge, Philadelphia; 1780 Mar. 18; brigantine; 14 guns; 60 crew; $10,000; Robert Duncan, Philadelphia, Richard Humphreys, Philadelphia, bonders; Robert Duncan, Philadelphia. Richard Humphreys & Co., Philadelphia, owners.

31. *Ariel*; Matthew Lawler, Philadelphia; 1780 Aug. 28; brigantine; 16 guns; 100 crew; $20,000; Samuel Inglis, Philadelphia, George Ord, Philadelphia, Matthew Lawler, Philadelphia, bonders; Robert Lawler, Philadelphia, Samuel Inglis & Co., Philadelphia, owners.

32. *Ariel*; Peter Miller, Philadelphia; 1781 Mar. 8; brigantine; 14 guns; 110 crew; $20,000; Samuel Inglis, Philadelphia, George Ord, Philadelphia, bonders; Samuel Inglis, George Ord & Co., owners.

33. *Batchelor*; Bernard Gallagher, Philadelphia; 1780 Oct. 5; ship; 12 guns; crew not stated; $20,000; Samuel Caldwell, John Mitchell, Philadelphia, bonders; Mease, Caldwell & Co., Philadelphia, owners.

34. *Beggars Benison*; Samuel Smallcorn; 1777 Jun. 7; schooner; 4 guns; 17 crew; $5,000; Samuel Smallcorn, Portsmouth, NH, George Gains, Portsmouth, NH, Jacob Sheafe Jr., Portsmouth, NH, bonders; Erskine, Donaldson & Co., Philadelphia, owner.

35. *Betsey*; Commander not stated; 1777 Mar.; schooner; guns not stated; crew not stated; Moses Griffing, bonder; owner not stated.

36. *Betsey*; Christopher Bradley, Philadelphia; 1778 Aug. 1; brigantine; 4 guns; 10 crew; $10,000; Joseph C. Fisher, Philadelphia, John D. Mercier, Philadelphia, bonders; Joseph C. Fisher, Philadelphia. Robert Knox & Co., Philadelphia, owners.

37. *Betsey*; Thomas Ridge, Philadelphia; 1778 Sep. 12; schooner; 6 guns; 40 crew; $10,000; Blair McClenachan, Philadelphia, James Ash, Philadelphia, bonders; Owners not stated.

38. *Betsey*; Robert Harris; 1779 Sep. 16; schooner; 8 guns; 24 crew; $5,000; John Taylor, Philadelphia, Robert Harris, Philadelphia, bonders; Alexander Stewart & Co., Philadelphia, owners.

39. *Betsey*; Joshua Allen; 1779 Nov. 20; sloop; 10 guns; 25 crew; $10,000; James Oellers, Philadelphia, Joshua Allen, Philadelphia, bonders; James Oellers & Co., Philadelphia, owner.

40. *Betsey*; Alexander Thompson Ogilvie, Philadelphia; 1780 Mar. 3; schooner; 4 guns; 14 crew; $10,000; John Taylor, Philadelphia, John McKim, Philadelphia, bonders; Isaac Sidman, Philadelphia, John Taylor, Philadelphia, owners.

41. *Betsey*; John Harr; 1780 Jul. 11; schooner; 4 guns; 11 crew; $20,000; Isaac Sidman, Philadelphia, John Audebert, Philadelphia, John Harr, Philadelphia, bonders; Sidman, Audebert & Co., Philadelphia, owners.

42. *Betsey*; [James Lincoln?]; 1780 Aug. 17; ship; guns not stated; crew not stated; $20,000; James Lincoln [Philadelphia?], bonder; Owners not stated.

43. *Betsey*; William Paul; 1780 Oct. 5; schooner; 6 guns; 20 crew; $20,000; George Nixon, Philadelphia, William Paul, Philadelphia, bonders; George Nixon, Philadelphia, owner.

44. *Betsey*; John Burrows; 1781 Jun. 19; ship; 9 guns; 35 crew; $20,000; Jonathan Smith, Philadelphia, John Burrows, Philadelphia, bonders; Jonathan Smith, Philadelphia, Isaac Sidman, Philadelphia, James Cochran, Philadelphia, owners.

45. *Betsey*; Paul Cox; 1781 Jul. 17; brigantine; 8 guns; 30 crew; $20,000; John Barclay, Philadelphia, Paul Cox, Philadelphia, bonders; Blair McClenachan, Philadelphia, Mease & Caldwell, Philadelphia, Thomas Barclay and others, Philadelphia, owners.

46. *Betsey*; George Dames; 1781 Nov. 3; schooner; 4 guns; 12 crew; $20,000; William Allibone, George Dames, Philadelphia, bonders; William Allibone, Philadelphia, John Wright Stanly and others, Philadelphia, owners.

47. *Betsey*; Bernard Gallagher; 1781 Dec. 1; brigantine; 8 guns; 27 crew; $20,000; John Barclay, Philadelphia, Bernard Gallagher, Philadelphia, bonders; Blair McClenachan and others, Philadelphia, owners.

48. *Betsey*; George Fleming [Philadelphia?]; 1781 Dec. 28; brigantine; 8 guns; 20 crew; $20,000; John Flahavan, Philadelphia, Robert Duncan, Jr., Philadelphia, bonders; John Flahavan, Philadelphia, Thomas Flahavan, Philadelphia, Robert Duncan, Jr., Philadelphia, owners.

49. *Bishop*; Richard Johns [Charles County, Md.]; 1779 Aug. 3; schooner; 8 guns; 20 crew; $10,000; Robert Morris, Philadelphia, Peter Whiteside, Philadelphia, bonders; Hooe & Harrisons, Philadelphia, owners.

50. *Black Joke*; Hope Willet; 1781 Jul. 30; boat; 1 gun; 20 crew; $20,000; Joseph Carson, Philadelphia, Hope Willet, Philadelphia, bonders; Joseph Carson & Co., Philadelphia, owners.

51. *Black Prince*; John Robertson; 1780 Jul. 5; brigantine; 12 guns; 34 crew; $20,000; Isaac Moses, Philadelphia, John Robertson, Philadelphia, bonders; Robert Morris, Philadelphia, Isaac Moses & Co., Philadelphia, owners.

52. *Black Prince*; John Walsh, Philadelphia; 1781 Sep. 21; brigantine; 6 guns; 21 rew; $20,000; John Walsh, Philadelphia, John Ross, Philadelphia, bonders; Isaac Moses, Philadelphia, Robert Morris & Co., Philadelphia, owners.

53. *Black Snake*; Joshua Huddy [Philadelphia?]; 1780 Aug. 18; boat; 1 gun; 14 crew; $20,000; Benjamin Davis Jr., Philadelphia, Thomas Sliter, Philadelphia, bonders; James Randolph, Joshua Huddy & Co., owners.

54. *Buckskin*; John Young, Philadelphia; 1778 Nov. 6; schooner; 6 guns; 15 crew; $10,000; Robert Morris, Philadelphia, John Maxwell Nesbitt, Philadelphia, bonders; Robert Morris, Philadelphia, owner.

55. *Buckskin*; John Perryman, Philadelphia; 1780 Jul. 24; schooner; 6 guns; 15 crew; $20,000; Robert Morris, Philadelphia, Peter Whiteside, Philadelphia, bonders; Robert Morris & Co., Philadelphia, owners.

56. *Buckskin*; Benjamin Wickes; 1781 Jun. 12; schooner; 6 guns; 16 crew; $20,000; Robert Morris, Philadelphia, Benjamin Wickes, Philadelphia, bonders; Robert Morris & Co., Philadelphia, owners.

57. *Burd*; William Campbell; 1782 Mar. 13; brigantine; 6 guns; 20 crew; $20,000; John Redman, Philadelphia, William Campbell, Philadelphia, bonders; Philip Moore, Philadelphia, John Redman & Co., Philadelphia, owners.

58. *Carolina*; William Willis, Philadelphia; 1779 May 28; brigantine; 14 guns; 45 crew; $10,000; Joseph Carson, Philadelphia, Daniel Edwards, Philadelphia, bonders; Joseph Carson, Philadelphia, owner.

59. *Carolina*; Thomas Newell, Philadelphia; 1782 Mar. 11; ship; 16 guns; 72 crew; $20,000; Thomas Newell, Philadelphia, John Wright Stanly, Philadelphia, bonders; John Wright Stanly, Philadelphia, owner.

60. *Cat*; Edward Leger, Philadelphia; 1779 Jul. 20; schooner; 2 guns; 70 crew; $10,000; John Macpherson, Philadelphia, Robert Patton, Philadelphia, bonders; John Macpherson, owner.

61. *Cat*; John Hasting [Philadelphia?]; 1779 Aug. 4; schooner; 2 guns; 70 crew; $10,000; Andrew Caldwell, Philadelphia, James Caldwell, Philadelphia, bonders; John Macpherson, Philadelphia, owner.

62. *Cat*; Joseph Campbell, Philadelphia; 1779 Aug. 14; schooner; 2 guns; 70 crew; $10,000; Andrew Caldwell, Philadelphia, James Caldwell, Philadelphia, bonders; John Macpherson, Philadelphia, owner.

63. *Catherina*; Adrian Lambert [Philadelphia?]; 1780 Jul. 12; schooner; 6 guns; 20 crew; $20,000; James Oellers, Philadelphia, bonder; Alexander Gerald & Co. [Philadelphia?], owners.

64. *Chance*; John Adams; 1776 Apr. 11; sloop; 45 tons; 4 guns; 45 crew; bond amount not stated; Joseph Dean, Philadelphia, Philip Moore, Philadelphia, bonders; Joseph Dean, Philip Moore & Co., Philadelphia, owners.

65. *Chance*; James Robertson; 1776 Jul. 2; sloop; 30 tons; 6 guns; 34 crew; bond amount not stated; bonders not stated; James Craig & Wm. Erskine & Co., owners.

66. *Chance;* James Armitage; 1776 Oct. [p]; schooner [sloop]; 6 guns; 35 crew; bond amount unknown; bonders unknown; owner unknown. The first mention of this vessel appears in a libel filed by Captain Armitage against the prize ship *William*, John Bond commander, on October 1, 1776. The vessel is referred to in subsequent accounts as a schooner and sloop and may sometimes be confused with the same vessel commanded by James Robertson.

67. *Chance;* John McIlnoe; 1777 Mar. 28; brigantine; 10 guns; 35 crew; bond amount not stated; bonders unknown; Blair McClenachan, Philadelphia, owner.

68. *Chance*; David Stevens; 1778 Jul. 16; sloop; 2 guns; 40 crew; $10,000; Joseph Carson, Philadelphia, David Stevens, Egg Harbor, NJ, bonders; Joseph Carson & Co., Philadelphia, owner.

69. *Chance*; James Leach [Cape May County, NJ]; 1779 Feb. 16; sloop; 6 guns; 40 crew; $10,000; James Ash, Philadelphia, John Patton, Philadelphia, bonders; John Patton, Philadelphia, James Ash & Co., Philadelphia, owners.

70. *Chance*; Robert Snell, Philadelphia; 1779 May 3; boat; 2 guns; 30 crew; $5,000; Joseph Carson, Philadelphia, Daniel Edwards, Philadelphia, bonders; Joseph Carson & Co., Philadelphia, owners.

71. *Chance*; William Gandal; 1779 Jul. 30; schooner; 6 guns, 25 crew; $10,000; Isaac Moses, Philadelphia, William Gandal, Philadelphia, bonders; Isaac Moses & Co., Philadelphia, owners.

72. *Chance*; Samuel Snell, Philadelphia; 1779 Sep. 4; schooner; 2 guns; 26 crew; $5,000; Mathew Irwin, Philadelphia, Thomas Irwin, Philadelphia, bonders; Joseph Ball, Philadelphia, owner.

73. *Chance*; Francis Knox, Philadelphia; 1779 Sep. 17; schooner; 6 guns; 15 crew; $5,000; Blair McClenachan, Philadelphia, Robert McClenachan, Philadelphia, bonders; Blair McClenachan, Philadelphia, Patrick Moore & Co., Philadelphia, owners.

74. *Chance*; Francis Hodgson; 1780 Jul. 14; schooner; 6 guns; 15 crew; $20,000; Francis Hodgson, Philadelphia, Blair McClenachan, Philadelphia, bonders; Blair McClenachan, Philadelphia, Patrick Moore & Co., Philadelphia, owners.

75. *Chance*; Nathaniel Palmer, Philadelphia; 1780 Jul; schooner; 2 guns; 15 crew; $20,000; Mathew Irwin, Philadelphia, Joseph Ball, Philadelphia, bonders; Mathew Irwin, Philadelphia, Joseph Ball & Co., Philadelphia, owners.

76. *Charming Amelia*; Alexander Heguy; 1781 Dec. 6; brigantine; 12 guns; 30 crew; $20,000; Peter Whiteside, Philadelphia, Alexander Heguy, Philadelphia, bonders; Robert Morris, Philadelphia, [?] Gautier, owners.

77. *Charming Molly*. John Stillwell; 1781 Apr. 27; brigantine; 6 guns; 20 crew; $20,000; James Oellers, Philadelphia, John Stillwell, Philadelphia, bonders; James Oellers & Co., Philadelphia, owners.

78. *Charming Molly*; John Stillwell; 1781 Jul. 13; brigantine; 8 guns; 25 crew; $20,000; James Oellers, Philadelphia, Joseph Sims, Philadelphia, John Stillwell, Philadelphia, bonders; James Oellers, Philadelphia, Wooddrop Sims, Philadelphia, Joseph Sims and others, Philadelphia, owners.

79. *Charming Molly*; John Tanner; 1781 Sep. 29; brigantine; 8 guns; 25 crew; $20,000; James Oellers, Philadelphia, John Tanner, Philadelphia, bonders; James Oellers, Philadelphia, Wooddrop Sims, Philadelphia, Joseph Sims and others, Philadelphia, owners.

80. *Charming Molly*; James Clifton, Philadelphia; 1781 Dec. 15; brigantine; 8 guns; 30 crew; $20,000; James Oellers, Philadelphia, Joseph Sims, Philadelphia, bonders; James Oellers, Philadelphia, Wooddop Sims, Philadelphia, Joseph Sims and others, Philadelphia, owners.

81. *Charming Polly*; Alexander T. Ogilvie; 1781 Feb. 8; brigantine; 6 guns; 25 crew; $20,000; John Donnaldson, Philadelphia, Alexander T. Ogilvie, Philadelphia, bonders; John Donnaldson, William Erskine & Co., Philadelphia, owners.

82. *Charming Sally*; Alexander Holmes, Philadelphia; 1780 Aug. 12; ship; 18 guns; 80 crew; $20,000; Joseph C. Fisher, Philadelphia, Andrew Bunner, Philadelphia, bonders; Bunner, Murray & Co. and others, Philadelphia, owners.

83. *Chevalier de La Luzerne*; John Parks, Philadelphia; 1779 Oct. 18; cutter; 14 guns; 85 crew; $10,000; Joseph Carson, Philadelphia, Robert McCleay, Philadelphia, bonders; Joseph Carson & Co., Philadelphia, owners.

84. *Chevalier de La Luzerne*; Thomas Bell, Philadelphia; 1779 Oct. 25; ship; 18 guns; 75 crew; $10,000; Samuel Inglis, Philadelphia, George Ord, Philadelphia, bonders; Robert Morris, Philadelphia, William Bingham & Co., Philadelphia, owners.

85. *Christiana*; Joseph White [?];1777 Sep. 15 [p]; sloop; guns unknown; crew unknown; bond unknown; Joseph White, bonder; owner unknown. The only mention of this vessel came in a report an engagement during the summer of 1777 between the Pennsylvania privateer sloop *Christiana* and the British privateer sloop *Reprisal*, Captain Phillips, from Antigua. At the first broadside, Captain White was killed and his crew promptly surrendered.

86. *Cogdill*; Stephen Tinker; 1782 Apr. 30; brigantine; 10 guns; 40 crew; $20,000; Stephen Tinker, Philadelphia, John Wright Stanly, Philadelphia, bonders; John Wright Stanly, owner.

87. *Colonel Parry*; William Gamble; 1776 Oct; schooner; 8 carriage [14-pdrs.], 14 swivels, 4 cohorns; 9 crew; bond unknown; bonders unknown; Leaming & Co., Philadelphia, owners.

88. *Columbia*; William H. Sargeant, Philadelphia; 1781 Jun. 22; ship; 18 guns; 80 crew; $20,000; Alexander Stewart, Philadelphia, Joseph Hague, Philadelphia, William H. Sargeant, Philadelphia, bonders; Thomas Bee [South Carolina], [William?] Moultrie and others [Philadelphia?], owners.

89. *Comet*; Yelverton Taylor; 1778 Jun. 27; sloop; 4 guns; 25 crew; $10,000; Yelverton Taylor, Philadelphia, Thomas Leaming, Jr., Philadelphia, bonders; Thomas Leaming and others, Philadelphia, owners.

90. *Comet*; Charles Harris, Philadelphia; 1778 Sep. 30; sloop; 6 guns; 25 crew; $10,000; Thomas Leaming, Philadelphia, bonders; Thomas Leaming & Co., Philadelphia, onwers.

91. *Comet*; Stephen Decatur, Philadelphia; 1779 Sep. 9; sloop; 10 guns; 45 crew; $10,000; Thomas Pryor, Philadelphia, Robert Bridges, Philadelphia, bonders and owners.

92. *Comet*; William Potts; 1780 Mar. 30; sloop; 10 guns; 45 crew; $10,000; William Potts, Philadelphia, Thomas Pryor, Philadelphia, bonders; Thomas Pryor, Philadelphia, Blair McClenachan & Co., Philadelphia, owners.

93. *Comet*; Daniel Brown; 1780 Aug. 29; sloop; 10 guns; 50 crew; $20,000; Daniel Brown, Philadelphia, Thomas Pryor, Philadelphia, bonders; Thomas Pryor & Co., Philadelphia, owners.

94. *Comet*; John McCarthy, Philadelphia; 1780 Dec. 13; brigantine; 14 guns; 13 crew; $20,000; Thomas Leaming, Philadelphia, Joseph C. Fisher, Philadelphia, bonders; Thomas Leaming, Joseph C. Fisher & Co., Philadelphia, owners.

95. *Commerce*; Francis Hodgson, Philadelphia; 1778 Nov. 30; sloop; 8 guns; 20 crew; $10,000; Blair McClenachan, Philadelphia, John Brown, Philadelphia; Blair McClenachan, Philadelphia, owner.

96. *Commerce*; Paul Cox; 1780 Sep. 14; ship; 12 guns; 35 crew; $20,000; Paul Cox., Philadelphia, Patrick Moore, Philadelphia, bonders; McClenachan & Moore, Philadelphia, owners.

97. *Commodore D. Galvez*; Mathew Madan, Philadelphia; 1781 Dec. 12; brigantine; 8 guns; 35 crew; $20,000; George Meade, Philadelphia, Mathew Madan, Philadelphia, bonders; Mathew Madan, Meade & Fitzsimons, Philadelphia, owners.

98. *Concord*; John Souder, Philadelphia; 1779 Feb; schooner; 4 guns; 20 crew; $10,000; Mathew Irwin, Philadelphia, Thomas Irwin, Philadelphia, bonders; Mathew Irwin, Philadelphia, Thomas Irwin, Philadelphia, Joseph Carson, Philadelphia, owners.

99. *Concord*; John Souder, Philadelphia; 1779 Feb. 12; schooner; 6 guns; 20 crew; $10,000; Joseph Carson, Philadelphia, Daniel Edwards, Philadelphia, bonders; Joseph Carson & Co., Philadelphia, owners.

100. *Concord*; Matthew Strong, Philadelphia; 1779 Oct. 18; schooner; 6 guns; 25 crew; $10,000; Joseph Carson, Philadelphia, Robert McCleary, Philadelphia, bonders; Joseph Carson & Co., Philadelphia, owners.

101. *Concord*; Daniel Ridge, Philadelphia; 1780 Mar. 16; schooner; 4 guns; 20 crew; $10,000; Joseph Carson, Philadelphia, Joseph Hargan, Philadelphia, bonders; Joseph Carson & Co., Philadelphia, owners.

102. *Congress*; George McAroy, Philadelphia; 1776 Apr. 11; sloop; 45 tons; 6 guns; 45 crew; Joseph Dean, Philadelphia, Philip Moore, Philadelphia, bonders; Joseph Dean, Philadelphia, Philip Moore & Co., Philadelphia, owners.

103. *Congress;* John Craige; 1776 Jun. 17; sloop; 70 tons; 6 carriage [3-pdrs.], 1,000 lbs., half a ton balls; 60 barrels provisions; 30 crew; $5,000; bonders not given; Jno. Bayard, Jas. Deane & Co., Philadelphia, owners.

104. *Congress;* William Greenway; 1776 Oct. 3; sloop; 6 guns; 40 crew; bond unknown; John Bayard, Joseph Dean & Co. [John R. Livingston], owners. Livingston states on February 2, 1776 that he owned the vessel, but most likely only had shares in it.

105. *Congress*; George Geddes, Philadelphia; 1781 May 18; ship; 24 guns; 200 crew; $20,000; Thomas Irwin, Philadelphia, George Geddes, Philadelphia bonders; Mathew & Thomas Irwin and Blair McClenachan & Co., Philadelphia, owners.

106. *Convention*; William Allen; 1779 Jun. 3; brigantine; 6 guns; 20 crew; $10,000; Samuel Caldwell, Philadelphia, William Allen, Philadelphia, bonders; Blair McClenachan, James Mease, and Samuel Caldwell, Philadelphia, owners.

107. *Cornelia*; John Tanner; 1780 Oct. 2; sloop; 4 guns; 16 crew; $20,000; John Tanner, Philadelphia, Isaac Moses, Philadelphia, bonders; Isaac Moses, Philadelphia, Matthew Clarkson, Philadelphia, owners.

108. *Count de Grasse*; John Hall; 1781 Dec. 15; brigantine; 6 guns; 20 crew; $20,000; Richardson Sands, Philadelphia, John Hall, Philadelphia, bonders; Richardson Sands, White Matlack and others, Philadelphia, owners.

109. *Count de Grasse*; John Gifford; 1781 Dec. 22; ship; 10 guns; 30 crew; $20,000; Alexander Stewart, Philadelphia, John Gifford, Philadelphia, bonders; Stewart, Colton & Co. and Blair McClenachan, Philadelphia, owners.

110. *Count d'Estaing*; William Dunlop, Philadelphia; 1778 Aug. 31; schooner; 2 guns; crew not stated; $10,000; No bonders; Owners not stated.

111. *Dandy*; James Clifton; 1782 Apr. 2; brigantine; 8 guns; 21 crew; $20,000; James Hood, Philadelphia, James Clifton, Philadelphia, bonders; James Hood, Lavinius Clarkson, Philadelphia and others, owners.

112. *Dart*; Thomas Davis; 1781 Jun. 12; brigantine; 12 guns; 36 crew; $20,000; Thomas Davis, Philadelphia, R[obert] Shewell, Philadelphia, John Lucas, Philadelphia, bonders; William Douglass, Virginia, owner.

113. *Defence*; Charles Harrison, Philadelphia;1779 Jul. 30; ship; 16 guns; 40 crew; $10,000; Robert Morris, Philadelphia, Blair McClenachan, Philadelphia, bonders and owners.

114. *Defence*; Benjamin Wickes, Philadelphia; 1780 Jul. 28; ship; 18 guns; 80 crew; $20,000; Robert Morris, Philadelphia, Peter Whiteside, Philadelphia, bonders; Robert Morris & Co., Philadelphia, owners.

115. *Delaware;* John Hamilton; 1777 Feb. 15; brigantine; guns not stated; crew not stated; bond not stated; bonders not stated; Owners not stated. The first mention of this vessel is in a permit issued by the Pennsylvania Council of Safety on February 15, 1777, for the Pennsylvania letter of marque brigantine *Delaware* to pass down the Delaware en route to St. Eustatia.

116. *Delaware*; John Barry, Philadelphia; 1779 Feb. 15; brigantine; 10 guns; 45 crew; $10,000; Thomas Irwin, Mathew Irwin, Philadelphia, bonders and owners. This vessel is unquestionably one and the same as no. 115.

117. *Delaware*; John Prole, Philadelphia; 1781 Feb. 20; ship; 8 guns; 30 crew; $20,000; Samuel Inglis, Philadelphia, George Ord, Philadelphia, bonders and owners.

118. *Delaware*; Richard lnkson; 1781 Apr. 23; brigantine; 4 guns; 17 crew; $20,000; James Ash, Philadelphia, Richard Inkson, Philadelphia, bonders; James Ash, Philadelphia, Andrew Tybout & Co., Philadelphia, owners.

119. *Delaware*; William Smith, Philadelphia; 1781 Dec. 8; schooner; 2 guns; 10 crew; $20,000. John McNachtane, Philadelphia, Adam Gilchrist, Philadelphia, bonders and owners.

120. *Diana*; Joy Castle [Philadelphia?]; 1779 Dec. 3; snow; 12 guns; 30 crew; $10,000; Blair McClenachan, Philadelphia, George Kennedy, Philadelphia, bonders; Blair McClenachan & Co., Philadelphia, owners.

121. *Diana*; Henry Hawkins; 1780 Dec. 12; brigantine; 10 guns; 30 crew; $20,000; John Imlay, Philadelphia, Henry Hawkins, Philadelphia bonders; John Imlay & Co., Philadelphia, crew.

122. *Dolphin*; Joshua Studson, Philadelphia; 1780 Aug. 18; boat; 1 gun; 14 crew; $20,000; Benjamin Davis, Jr., Philadelphia, Thomas Stites, Philadelphia, Daniel Griggs, New Jersey, bonders; Samuel Brown, [Boston], Daniel Griggs & Co., owners.

123. *Dolphin*; John Walsh, Philadelphia; 1781 Jun. 16; schooner; 6 guns; 11 crew; $20,000; James Oellers, Philadelphia, John Flahavan, Philadelphia, bonders and owners.

124. *Dolphin*; John Brice, Philadelphia; 1781 Nov. 3; brigantine; 4 guns; 10 crew; $20,000. Alexander Nesbitt, Philadelphia, John Brice, Philadelphia, bonders; Blair McClenachan, Alexander Nesbitt, and Walter Stewart, Philadelphia, owners.

125. *Dolphin*; James Forbes; 1781 Dec. 27; ship; 10 guns; 40 crew; $20,000; John Ross, Philadelphia, James Forbes, Philadelphia, bonders; Robert Morris, John M. Nesbitt, and John Ross, Philadelphia, owners.

126. *Dolphin*; Jacob De Hart; 1782 Mar. 5; sloop; 6 guns; 12 crew; $20,000; C[laudius] P[aul] Raquett, Philadelphia, Jacob De Hart, Philadelphia, bonders and owners.

127. *Don Francisco*; John Gifford, Philadelphia; 1781 Mar. 24; brigantine; 8 guns; 25 crew; $20,000; Alexander Stewart, Philadelphia, Thomas Morris, Philadelphia, bonders; Stewart & Totten, Samuel C. Morris & Co., Philadelphia, owners.

128. *Don Francisco*; Hugh Willson; 1781 Oct. 27; brigantine; 8 guns; 25 crew; $20,000; Alexander Stewart, Philadelphia; Hugh Willson, Philadelphia, bonders; Stewart & Totten, Blair McClenachan and others, Philadelphia, owners.

129. *Don Quixotte*; John Burrows; 1782 Aug. 12; schooner; 6 guns; 16 crew; $20,000; John Burrows, Philadelphia, J[ohn] W. Stanly, Philadelphia, bonders; John W. Stanly, William Morris, and Stephen Tinker, owners.

130. *Dove*; Edward Leger; 1779 Dec. 4; schooner; 2 guns; 12 crew; $10,000; Edward Leger, Philadelphia, James Sutter, Philadelphia, bonders; United States, owner.

131. *Dreadnought*; Henry Darnell [Darnol?], Philadelphia; 1781 Jun. 4; boat; 2 guns; 40 crew; $20,000;. Samuel Inglis, Philadelphia, George Ord, bonders; Samuel Inglis, George Ord & Co., Philadelphia, owners.

132. *Duke of Leinster;* Samuel Young, Philadelphia; 1781 Jan. 20; brigantine; 12 guns; 40 crew; $20,000; [__] Round [Philadelphia?], John Barclay, Philadelphia, Samuel Young, Philadelphia, bonders; John Barclay & Co., Philadelphia, owner.

133. *Eagle*; John Ashmead; 1779 Jun. 12; brigantine; 10 guns; 30 crew; $10,000; James Searle, Joseph Pennell, John Ashmead, Philadelphia, bonders; James Searle & Co., owner.

134. *Eagle*; James Starr; 1781 Aug. 1; schooner; 6 guns; 15 crew; $20,000; James Starr, John Harmanson, Philadelphia, bonders; John Harmanson, Henry Guy, James Starr, and others, owners.

135. *Eliza*; John Vicary, Philadelphia; 1782 Apr. 6; schooner; 4 guns; 20 crew; $20,000; William Henderson, Philadelphia, John Vicary, Philadelphia, bonders; Robert Randall, William Henderson, Philadelphia, owners.

136. *Elizabeth*; Charles Alexander; 1778 Dec. 8; sloop; 12 guns; 30 crew; $10,000; Andrew Caldwell, Philadelphia, James Caldwell, Philadelphia, bonders and owners.

137. *Elizabeth*; George McAroy, Philadelphia; 1780 Mar. 3; brigantine; 10 guns; 30 crew; $10,000; George McAroy, Andrew & James Cadwell, Philadelphia, bonders; Andrew Caldwell, Philadelphia. James Caldwell & Co., Philadelphia, owners.

138. *Enterprize*; James Campbell, Philadelphia; 1776 Jun. 14; schooner; guns not stated; crew not stated; $10,000; Mease & Caldwell, Philadelphia, bonders and owners.

139. *Enterprize*; Rufus Gardner [Philadelphia?]; 1779 Aug. 28; schooner; 12 guns; 70 crew; $10,000; James Vanuxem, Philadelphia, Lardner Clark, Philadelphia, bonders and owners.

140. *Enterprize*; Rufus Gardner [Philadelphia?]; 1780 Mar. 23; brigantine; 12 guns; 75 crew; $10,000; James Vanuxem, Philadelphia, Elisha Clark, Philadelphia, bonders; James Vanuxem, Philadelphia, Lardner Clark, Philadelphia, owners.

141. *Enterprize*; Peter Day, Philadelphia; 1780 Jul. 28; brigantine; 12 guns; 80 crew; $20,000; Thomas Learning, Philadelphia. John Murray, Philadelphia, bonders; Thomas Learning, Philadelphia. John Murray & Co., Philadelphia, owners.

142. *Experiment;* John Winning [Baltimore, Md]; 1780 Oct. 4; ship; 20 guns; 6 crew; $20,000; John Purviance, Philadelphia, Robert Caldwell, Philadelphia, bonders; Samuel & Robert Purviance [Baltimore, Md.], David Stewart and John Purviance, Philadelphia, owners.

143. *Experiment;* William Rice, Philadelphia; 1781 May 9; boat; 4 guns; 24 crew; $20,000; Lewis Farmer, Philadelphia, William Rice, Philadelphia, bonders; William Rice, Henry Murfits, owners.

144. *Fair American;* Stephen Decatur; 1780 Apr. 20; brigantine; 16 guns; 130 crew; $10,000; Charles Miller, Philadelphia, Stephen Decatur, Philadelphia, bonders; Blair McClenachan, Charles Miller & Co., Philadelphia, owners.

145. *Fair American;* Joseph Jakways; 1780 Dec. 9; brigantine; 16; 100; $20,000; Joseph Jakways, Philadelphia, Charles Miller, Philadelphia, bonders; Charles Miller, Blair McClenachan & Co., Philadelphia, owners.

146. *Fair American;* Phineas Eldridge; 1781 May 22; brigantine; 16 guns; 110 crew; $20,000; Charles Miller, Philadelphia, Phineas Eldridge, Philadelphia, bonders; Blair McClenachan, Charles Miller & Co., Philadelphia, owners.

147. *Fame;* Francis Knox [also Cox]; 1777 May [?]; brigantine; 8; guns unknown; crew unknown; bonders unknown; owners unknown. This vessel is not specifically identified in the source material as a Pennsylvania privateer or letter or marque vessel, but is identified as such in the index to *NDAR*, volume 9. The vessel is identified only as a prize brig by her British captor, HMS *Brune*, which took her as such in late June 1777.

148. *Fame;* George Curwin, Philadelphia; 1779 Aug. 16; schooner; 4 guns; 15 crew; $5,000; Blair McClenachan, Philadelphia, Robert Bridges, Philadelphia, bonders; Blair McClenachan, Philadelphia, owner.

149. *Fame;* John Gensell; 1779 Oct. 18; brigantine; 16 guns; 70 crew; $10,000; John Donnaldson, Philadelphia, John Gensell, Philadelphia, bonders; John Donnaldson & Co., owners.

150. *Fame;* Hugh Lyle, Philadelphia; 1779 Dec. 8; brigantine; 6 guns; crew not stated; $10,000; Blair McClenachan, Philadelphia, Patrick Moore, Philadelphia, bonders; Blair McClenachan & Co., Philadelphia, owners.

151. *Fame;* Uriah Smith; 1780 Dec. 2; brigantine; 10 guns; 60 crew; $20,000; Joseph Carson, Philadelphia, Uriah Smith, Philadelphia, bonders; Joseph Carson, Philadelphia, owner.

152. *Fame;* William Treene, Philadelphia; 1780 Dec. 23; brigantine; 10 guns; 55 crew; $20,000; Joseph Carson, Philadelphia, William Treene, Philadelphia, bonders; Joseph Carson & Co., Philadelphia, owners.

153. *Fame;* John Taylor; 1781 Mar. 19; brigantine; 9 guns; 40 crew; $20,000; Joseph Carson, Philadelphia, John Taylor, Philadelphia, bonders; Joseph Carson & Co., Philadelphia, owners.

154. *Fame;* George Curwin; 1781 Oct. 5; schooner; 6 guns; 14 crew; $20,000; Patrick Moore, Philadelphia, George Curwin, Philadelphia, bonders; Blair McClenachan, Robert McClenachan, Patrick Moore, and William Keith, Philadelphia, onwers.

155. *Fame;* David Campbell; 1781 Dec. 22; schooner; 6 guns; 14 crew; $20,000; Patrick Moore, Philadelphia, David Campbell, Philadelphia, bonders; Blair McClenachan & Co., Philadelphia, owners.

156. *Fame*; John McClenachan, Philadelphia;1782 Jul. 19; ship; 8 guns; 30 crew; $20,000; Blair McClenachan, Philadelphia, John Marshall, Philadelphia, bonders; Blair McClenachan, Philadelphia, owner.

157. *Fanny*; Samuel Bulfinch; 1781 Mar. 28; brigantine; 6 guns; 12 crew; $20,000; William Pollard, Philadelphia, Samuel Bulfinch, Philadelphia bonders; William Pollard, Philadelphia, James Seagrove, Philadelphia, owners.

158. *Fayette*; Robert Shewell; 1780 Jul. 10; brigantine; 14 guns; 60 rew; $20,000; John Wilcocks, Philadelphia, Robert Shewell, Philadelphia bonders; Meade, Fitzsimons & Co., Philadelphia, owners.

159. *Fayette*; Samuel Davison, Philadelphia, 1780 Nov. 11; brigantine; 18 guns; 60 crew; $20,000; George Meade, Philadelphia, John Wilcocks, Philadelphia, bonders; George Meade, John Wilcocks, and Thomas Fitzsimons, Philadelphia, owners.

160. *Felicity;* Peter Wing; 1781 Nov. 17; schooner; 8 guns; 20 crew; $20,000; Levi Hollingsworth, Philadelphia, David Sterett, Philadelphia, Peter Wing, Philadelphia, bonders; Jeremiah Yellott, John Sterett, Jesse Hollingsworth [Baltimore], owners.

161. *Ferrit*; James Robertson; 1779 Aug. 26; schooner; 8 guns; 24 crew; $5,000; James Robertson, Philadelphia, Francis Lewis, Jr., Philadelphia, bonders; Francis Lewis, Jr., owner.

162. *Financier*; John Harr; [1781] Aug. 11; brigantine; 6 guns; 15 crew; $20,000; John Wilcocks, Philadelphia, John Harr, Philadelphia bonders; Thomas Fitzsimons & Co., John Wilcocks, and Abraham Markoe, owners.

163. *Flora*; Ephraim Doane; 1779 Oct. 18; ship; 16 guns; 75 crew; $10,000; Ephraim Doane, Philadelphia, William Pollard, Philadelphia, bonders; William Pollard, Alexander Tod, and Ephraim Doane, Philadelphia, owners.

164. *Flora*; William Brewster, Philadelphia; 1780 Jul. 12; ship; 16 guns; 75 crew; $20,000; William Pollard, Alexander Tod, Philadelphia, bonders; William Pollard, Alexander Tod & Co., Philadelphia, owners.

165. *Flora*; William Brewster; 1780 Nov. 28; ship; 14 guns; 30 crew; $20,000; Alexander Tod, Philadelphia, William Brewster, Philadelphia, bonders; William Pollard, Alexander Tod & Co., Philadelphia, owners.

166. *Flora*; Hugh Lyle; 1781 Jul. 28; ship; 12 guns; 30 crew; $20,000; Hugh Lyle, Philadelphia, Alexander Tod, Philadelphia, bonders; Alexander Tod, William Tod, William Pollard & Co., Philadelphia, owners.

167. *Fly*; John Turner; 1778 Jul. 16; schooner; 2 guns; 45 crew; $10,000; John Turner, Joseph Carson, Philadelphia, bonders; Nathan Nichols, Dartmouth, MA, Joseph Carson, Philadelphia, owners.

168. *Fly*; 1778 Jul. 31; schooner; 3 guns; 20 crew; $5,000; Micajah Smith, Philadelphia; Peter January, Isaac Snowden, Philadelphia, bonders; Peter January, John Paine & Co., Philadelphia, owners.

169. *Fly*; William Gandal; 1779 Feb. 4; schooner; 4 guns; 20 crew; $10,000; Thomas Learning, Philadelphia, William Gandal, Philadelphia, bonders; Thomas Learning & Co., Philadelphia, owners.

170. *Fly*; John King, Philadelphia; 1779 May 21; schooner; 4 guns; 12 crew; $10,000; Joseph C. Fisher, Philadelphia, Thomas Learning, Philadelphia, bonders; Joseph C. Fisher and Thomas Learning & Co., Philadelphia, owners.

171. *Fly*; Abraham Davis, Philadelphia; 1779 Jun. 7; schooner; 6 guns; 30 crew; $5,000; Peter January, Philadelphia, George Payne, Philadelphia, bonders; Peter January, George Payne & Co., Philadelphia, owners.

172. *Fly*; Francis Du Closs [Philadelphia?]; 1781 Jun. 9; boat; 4 guns; 12 crew; $20,000; Joseph Carson, Philadelphia, Robert Shewell, Philadelphia, bonders; Joseph Carson & Co., Philadelphia, owners.

173. *Flying Fish*; Zachariah Goforth; 1782 Jul. 12; boat; 3 guns; 12 crew; $20,000; Zachariah Goforth, Philadelphia, Elias Boys, Philadelphia, bonders; Zachariah Goforth, owner.

174. *Fortunate*; [Martial] Bortar; 1780 Oct. 11; schooner; 4 guns; 45 crew; $20,000; [Martial] Bortar, Philadelphia, Lewis Busson, Philadelphia, bonders; Lewis Busson & Co., Philadelphia, owners.

175. *Fox*; Matthew Macomber; 1780 Oct. 2; cutter; 2 guns; 45 crew; $20,000; Matthew Macomber, Philadelphia, Andrew Hodge, Jr., Philadelphia, bonders; David Lockwood, Philadelphia and Andrew Hodge, Jr., owners.

176. *Fox*; Thomas Steel; 1781 Aug. 27; brigantine; 10 guns; 32 crew; $20,000; Thomas Steel [Baltimore, Md.], Isaac Moses & Co., Philadelphia, bonders; Isaac Moses & Co., Philadelphia, owners.

177. *Fox*; David Thomson; 1781 Oct. 4; schooner; 10 guns; 16 crew; $20,000; George Nixon, Philadelphia, D[avid] Thomson, Philadelphia; Joseph Carson & Co., Philadelphia, Robert Shewell and George Nixon, Philadelphia, owners.

178. *Fox*; Mark Collins, Philadelphia; 1782 Mar. 28; brigantine; 8 guns; 25 crew; $20,000; Isaac Moses, Philadelphia, Benjamin Seixas, Philadelphia, bonders; Isaac Moses, Benjamin Seixas, and other, owners.

179. *Franklin*; John Angus; 1780 Dec. 18; ship; 18 guns; 90 crew; $20,000; Jonathan Muffin, Philadelphia, John Angus, Philadelphia, bonders; Jonathan Muffin and Anthony Butler & Co., Philadelphia, owners.

180. *Franklin*; Thomas Cox; 1782 Jan. 2; schooner; 4 guns; 15 crew; $20,000; Thomas Cox [Philadelphia?], David H. Conyngham, Philadelphia, bonders; John M. Nesbitt & Co., Philadelphia, owners.

181. *Friends Goodwill*; William Leitch, Philadelphia; 1781 Jan. 10; brigantine; 2 guns; 18 crew; $20,000; Philip Audibert, Philadelphia, Jonathan Smith, Philadelphia, bonders; Jonathan Smith, Philadelphia. Philip Audibert & Co., Philadelphia, owners.

182. *Friendship*; Robert Collings, Philadelphia; 1776 Nov. 13; sloop; 30 tons; 6 guns; 20 crew; bond amount unknown; bonders unknown; John Wilcocks & Co., owners.

183. *Friendship;* John Gourlay [Philadelphia?]; 1778 Dec. 7; sloop; 14 guns; 45 crew; $10,000; William McCulloch, Philadelphia, Joseph McCulloch, Philadelphia, bonders; William and Joseph McCulloch & Co., Philadelphia, owners.

184. *Friendship;* John Ball; 1779 Dec. 3; sloop; 8 guns; 20 crew; $10,000; John Ball, Philadelphia, John Wilcocks, Philadelphia, bonders; John Wilcocks & Co., Philadelphia, owners.

185. *Friendship*; John Badcock [Philadelphia?]; 1780 Aug. 7; boat; 1 gun; 20 crew; $20,000; Philip Moore, Philadelphia, James Craig, Jr., Philadelphia, bonders; Philip Moore, James Craig & Co., Philadelphia, owners.

186. *Friendship*; John Ball; 1780 Sep. 6; brigantine; 12 guns; 40 crew; $20,000; Nicholas Low, Philadelphia, John Ball, Philadelphia, bonders; John Wilcocks, George Meade & Co., Richard Low, John & Robert Harper, Philadelphia, owners.

187. *Friendship*; John Badcock [Philadelphia?]; 1781 Mar. 9; boat; 4 guns; 25 crew; $20,000; Philip Moore, Philadelphia, James Craig, Jr., Philadelphia, bonders; James Craig, Philip Moore & Co., Philadelphia, owners.

188. *Friendship*; Henry Murfits [New London], Conn.; 1781 Jun. 9; boat; 1 gun; 18 crew; $20,000; John Patton, Philadelphia, James Craig, Jr., Philadelphia, bonders and owners.

189. *Gannet*; William Budden [Philadelphia?]; 1779 Sep. 17; sloop; 6 guns; 15 crew; $5,000; Blair McClenachan, Philadelphia, Robert McClenachan, Philadelphia, bonders; Blair McClenachan, David Beveridge & Co., Philadelphia, owners.

190. *General Galvez*; John Vicary; 1781 Jul. 27; brigantine; 6 guns; 20 crew; $20,000; John Vicary, Philadelphia, Thomas Fitzsimons, Philadelphia, bonders; Thomas Fitzsimons & Co., Philadelphia, owners.

191. *General Galvez*; James Montgomery, Philadelphia; 1781 Dec. 21; brigantine; 8 guns; 30 crew; $20,000; James Craig, Jr., Philadelphia, John Patton, Philadelphia, bonders; James Craig, Jr., John Patton, Alexander Nesbitt, and others, Philadelphia, owners.

192. *General Greene*; James Montgomery, Philadelphia; 1779 Dec. 11; ship; 14 guns; 40 crew; $10,000; George Henry, Philadelphia, James Ash, Philadelphia, bonders; George Henry and James Wharton & Co., Philadelphia, owners.

193. *General Greene*; William Burke [Philadelphia?]; 1780 Mar. 13; ship; 16 guns; 45 crew; $10,000; George Henry, Philadelphia, Robert Knox, Philadelphia, bonders; George Henry and James Wharton & Co., Philadelphia, owners.

194. *General Greene*; Samuel Carson, Philadelphia; 1780 Sep. 29; ship; 18 guns; 100 crew; $20,000; James Ash, Philadelphia, William Hail, Philadelphia, bonders; James Ash, George Henry & Co., Philadelphia, owners.

195. *General Greene*; Haskal Freeman; 1782 Mar. 20; ship; 10 guns; 45 crew; $20,000; Standish Forde, Philadelphia, Haskal Freeman, Philadelphia, bonders; Standish Forde and Crowell Hatch, Philadelphia, onwers.

196. *General Lee*; Commander unknown; 1776 Oct. 3; brigantine; 100 tons; 12 guns; 90 crew; bond amount unknown; bonders unknown; John Bayard, Alexander Henderson, Mathew Irwin, [Thomas] Irwin, General Thomas Mifflin, Anthony Butler, others, owners. Thomas Irwin, General Thomas Mifflin, Anthony Butler, and others, possibly including Philip Boehm and Matthew Potter were silent partners having shares in the ownership.

197. *General Maxwell*; Moses Griffin[g]; 1779 Aug. 21; schooner; 10 guns; 50 crew; $10,000; Joseph Carson, Philadelphia, Robert McCleay, Philadelphia, bonders; Joseph Carson & Co., Philadelphia, owners.

198. *General Mifflin*; John Hamilton 1776 Aug. 27; brigantine; 12 guns; 90 crew; bond amount unknown; bonders unknown; John Cox, Philadelphia, John Chaloner, &c., owners.

199. *General Montgomery*; James Montgomery; 1776 Aug. 30; brigantine; 12 guns; 100 crew; bond amount unknown; bonders unknown; Owners unknown.

200. *General Montgomery*; Benjamin Hill; 1777 Feb. 6 [p]; brigantine; 180 tons; 18 guns, both 6- and 4-pounders, 4 cohorns, and 3 swivels; 87 crew; bond amount unknown; John Steel, bonder; John Pringle and Joseph Dean, Philadelphia, owners.

201. *General Putnam*; Charles Ferguson; 1776 Aug. 27; brigantine; 12 guns; 90 crew; bond amount unknown; bonders unknown; Mathew Irwin, Benjamin Harbeson, &c. [Dr. John Sparhawk], owners.

202. *General Reed*; Hugh Stocker; 1779 Oct. 26; brigantine; 16 guns; 80 crew; $10,000; Hugh Stocker, Philadelphia, Andrew Hodge, Philadelphia, bonders; Andrew Hodge, Hugh Hodge & Co., Philadelphia, owners.

203. *General Reed*; Samuel Davison; 1780 Apr. 13; brigantine; 16 guns; 120 crew; $10,000; Andrew Hodge, Jr., Philadelphia, Samuel Davison, Philadelphia, bonders; Andrew & Hugh Hodge, owners.

204. *General Scammell*; Giles Hall; 1781 Dec. 26; schooner; 6 guns; 15 crew; $20,000; Standish Forde, Philadelphia, Giles Hall, Philadelphia, bonders; Clement Biddle, Philadelphia, Standish Forde, Philadelphia, owners.

205. *General Scott*; William Nichols [Baltimore?]; 1780 Sep. 22; schooner; 8 guns; 30 rew; $20,000; Robert Morris, Philadelphia, Peter Whiteside, Philadelphia, bonders; Robert Morris & Co., Philadelphia, owners.

206. *General Smallwood*; Thomas Finley; 1780 Dec. 1; brigantine; 14 guns; 45 crew; $20,000; George Nixon, Philadelphia, Thomas Finley, Philadelphia, bonders; George Nixon, William Pollard, Philadelphia, owners.

207. *General Thompson;* William Connell [Philadelphia]; 1776 Oct 5; schooner; 40 tons; 6 guns; 12 crew; bond amount unknown; bonders unknown; Edmund Beach & Co., owners.

208. *General Washington*; Samuel Walker [Philadelphia?]; 1779 Aug. 3; ship; 18 guns; 60 crew; $10,000; Robert Morris, Philadelphia, Peter Whiteside, Philadelphia, bonders; Hooe & Harrison, owners.

209. *General Wayne*; Robert Collings, Philadelphia; 1779 Aug. 31; xebec; 3 guns; 70 crew; $10,000; John Hazelwood, Philadelphia, William Allibone, Philadelphia, bonders; John Hazelwood, William Allibone & Co., Philadelphia, owners.

210. *General Wayne*; John Rice, Philadelphia; 1780 Mar. 28; brigantine; 12 guns; 60 crew; $10,000; John Hazelwood, Philadelphia, William Allibone, Philadelphia, bonders; John Hazelwood & Co., Philadelphia, owners.

211. *General Wayne*; Benjamin Newton; 1780 Aug. 16; brigantine; 12 guns; 25 crew; $20,000; Benjamin Newton, Philadelphia, Alexander Stewart, Philadelphia, bonders; Alexander Stewart, Robert Totten & Co., owners.

212. *George*; James Montgomery; 1780 Apr. 7; brigantine; 8 guns; 20 crew; $10,000; James Montgomery, Philadelphia, Philip Moore, Philadelphia, bonders; Philip Moore & Co., Philadelphia, owners.

213. *George*; Joseph McCullough; 1780 Nov. 4; brigantine; 14 guns; 75 crew; $20,000; George Kennedy, Philadelphia, Andrew Kennedy, Philadelphia, bonders; Joseph McCullough, Philadelphia, owner.

214. *George*; William Campbell; 1781 May 25; brigantine; 10 guns; 50 crew; $20,000; William Campbell, Philadelphia, James Craig, Jr., Philadelphia, bonders; Philip Moore, James Craig, Jr., & Co., owners.

215. *George*; Robert French, Philadelphia; 1782 Feb. 27; brigantine; 6 guns; 16 crew; $20,000; James Craig, Jr., Philadelphia, Philip Moore, Philadelphia, bonders; James Craig, Jr., Philip Moore, and others, Philadelphia, owners.

216. *George*; George Curwin, Philadelphia; 1782 May 6; ship; 14 guns; 45 crew; $20,000; Blair McClenachan, Philadelphia, Robert Bridges, Philadelphia, bonders; Blair McClenachan & Co., owners.

217. *Good Intent*; Commander not stated; 1779 Aug. 23; schooner; 6 guns; 20 crew; $10,000; Peter January, Philadelphia, James Hood, Philadelphia, bonders; Peter January, Philadelphia, James Hood & Co., Philadelphia, owners.

218. *Governor Clinton*; William Mornyer [Mariner?]; 1781 Jul. 24; boat; 3 guns; 15 crew; $20,000; Robert Cocks, Philadelphia, William Mornyer [Mariner?], Philadelphia, bonders; Robert Cocks, Philadelphia, Robert Collings, Philadelphia, owners.

219. *Governor Clinton*; Joseph Vansise; 1781 Sep. 11; brigantine; 8 guns; 18 crew; $20,000; Joseph Vansise, Philadelphia, John Imlay, Philadelphia, bonders; John Imlay, Richard Sands, White Matlack, and others, Philadelphia, owners.

220. *Governor De Graff*; Hugh Lisle [Lyle], Philadelphia; 1780 Dec. 5; ship; 20 guns; 100 crew; $20,000; Blair McClenachan, Philadelphia, John Pringle, Philadelphia, bonders; Blair McClenachan, Philadelphia, owner.

221. *Governor Livingston*; Moses Griffing; 1781 Jun. 30; schooner; 4 guns; 14 crew; $20,000; Moses Griffing, Philadelphia, Joseph Carson, Philadelphia, bonders; Joseph Carson, Mathew Irwin & Co., Philadelphia, owners.

222. *Governor Moore*; David Thomson; 1782 Mar. 12; schooner; 8 guns; crew not stated; $20,000; Joseph Carson, Philadelphia, David Thomson, Philadelphia, bonders; John Wright Stanly, George Emlen, and Joseph Carson, Philadelphia, owners.

223. *Greene*; Samuel Davison; 1782 Apr. 2; schooner; 6 guns; Crew not stated; $20,000; Samuel Davison, Philadelphia, Joseph Carson, Philadelphia, bonders; Joseph Carson, John Wright Stanly, and George Emlen, Philadelphia, owners.

224. *Greyhound*; John Kemp; 1780 Oct. 13; schooner; 10 guns; crew not stated; $20,000; Francis Gurney, Philadelphia, John Kemp, Philadelphia, bonders; Francis Gurney and Blair McClenachan & Co., Philadelphia, owners.

225. *Gustavus*; George Fleming, Philadelphia; 1780 Nov. 8; brigantine; 2 guns; 15 crew; $20,000; Samuel Inglis, Philadelphia, George Ord, Philadelphia, bonders; Thomas Willing, Philadelphia, Robert Morris, Philadelphia, William Bingham & Co., Philadelphia, owners.

226. *Hancock*; Wingate Newman; 1776 Jun. 15; brigantine; 115 tons; 12 guns; 80 crew; $10,000; bonders not stated; Jno. Bayard, Jas. Deane & Co., Philadelphia, owners. That William Erskine was one of the owners, although his name does not appear on the bond, is indicated by his name, alone with Bayard and Deane, on a petition read before Congress on June 8, 1776, requesting 530 lbs of powder, 400 lbs. of swivel shot, and 750 lbs. of powder applied for earlier, for the ship.

227. *Hancock;* Daniel McNeill; 1776 Dec. 28 [p]; brigantine; 120 tons; 12 guns; 80? crew; bond amount not stated; bonders not stated; Jno. Bayard, Jas. Deane & Co., Philadelphia, [William Erskine?], owners.

228. *Hancock*; William Finch; 1782 Jan. 22; schooner; 6 guns; 14 crew; $20,000; William Finch, Philadelphia, David H. Conyngham, Philadelphia, bonders; owners not stated.

229. *Hannah*; Hendrick Fisher, Philadelphia; 1781 Sep. 7; brigantine; 10 guns; 16 crew; $20,000; Harmon Courter, Philadelphia, Isaac Kershaw, Philadelphia, bonders; Harmon Courter, John Kershaw and Hendrick Fisher, owners.

230. *Hannah*; Henry Hawkins; 1782 Jun. 26; ship; 6 guns; 18 crew; $20,000; Henry Hawkins, Philadelphia, John M. Taylor, Philadelphia, bonders; John W. Stanly, Joseph Carson, and John M. Taylor, Philadelphia, owners.

231. *Hannah and Sally*; Thomas Palmer, Philadelphia; 1778 Oct. 27; schooner; 1 gun; 6crew; $10,000; Mathew Irwin, Philadelphia, Robert Paisley, Philadelphia, bonders; Mathew Irwin, Philadelphia, Robert Bridges & Co., Philadelphia, owners.

232. *Happy Return*; Peter Croze Magnan; 1781 May 21; schooner; 8 guns; 20 crew; $20,000; Peter Croze Magnan, Philadelphia, James Veillon, Philadelphia, bonders; Peter Croze Magnan, owner.

233. *Harford*; Jacob Walters, Baltimore, MD; 1781 Oct. 9; schooner; 14 guns; 35 crew; $20,000; William Turnbull, Philadelphia, bonder; William Turnbull, owner.

234. *Harlequin*; John Earle; 1782 Aug. 7; schooner; 4 gun; 16 crew; $20,000; John Earle, Philadelphia, Thomas Randall, Philadelphia, James Caldwell, Philadelphia, bonders. Thomas Truxtun, Philadelphi, Thomas Randall, Philadelphia, owners.

235. *Havannah*; Peter Young, Philadelphia; 1780 Jul. 3; schooner; 6 guns; 17 crew; $20,000; Isaac Moses, Philadelphia, Solomon Marache, Philadelphia, bonders; Robert Morris, Philadelphia, Moses Levy & Co., Philadelphia, owners.

236. *Havanna*; Aaron Stockholm, Philadelphia; 1781 Mar. 24; schooner; 6 guns; 15 crew; $20,000; Alexander Stewart, Philadelphia, Thomas Morris, Philadelphia, bonders; Stewart & Totten and Samuel C. Morris & Co., Philadelphia, owners.

237. *Havanna*; John Van Voorhis; 1781 Jun. 23; schooner; 6 guns; 15 crew; $20,000; Alexander Stewart, Philadelphia, Daniel Van Voorhis, Philadelphia, John Van Voorhis, Philadelphia, bonders; Alexander Stewart, Robert Totten, and Samuel C. Morris & Co., Philadelphia, owners.

238. *Hawk*; Enoch Stillwell, Philadelphia; 1779 Jun. 25; schooner; 10 guns; 50 crew; $5,000; Thomas Learning, Jr., Philadelphia, Jesse Hand, Philadelphia, bonders; Thomas Learning, Jr. and Jesse Hand & Co., owners.

239. *Hazard*; Hezekiah Anthony; 1780 Oct. 2; cutter; 1 gun; 45 crew; $20,000; Hezekiah Anthony, Philadelphia, Andrew Hodge, Jr., Philadelphia, bonders; David Lockwood and Andrew Hodge, Jr., Philadelphia, owners.

240. *Hector*; James Seloover; 1780 Sep. 5; brigantine; 12 guns; 70 crew; $20,000; Joseph C. Fisher, Philadelphia, James Seloover, Philadelphia, bonders; Thomas Leaming and Joseph C. Fisher & Co., Philadelphia, owners.

241. *Henry*; John Ord, Philadelphia; 1779 Nov. 11; schooner; 4 guns; 10 crew; $10,000; Jeremiah Fisher, Philadelphia, James Robeson, Philadelphia, bonders; Jeremiah Fisher & Co., Philadelphia, owners.

242. *Hetty;* Joseph Ashbourn; 1777 Jul. 31; brigantine; 10 guns; crew not stated; bond amount not stated; bonders not stated; John Pringle, Blair McClanachan, owners.

243. *Hetty*; James Josiah, Philadelphia; 1779 May 21; ship; 18 guns; 50 crew; $10,000; Joseph C. Fisher, Philadelphia, Thomas Learning [Jr.?], Philadelphia, bonders; Joseph C. Fisher and Thomas Learning & Co., Philadelphia, owners.

244. *Hetty*; Thomas Houston, Philadelphia [?]; 1780 Mar. 28; brigantine; 16 guns; 50 crew; $10,000; Mathew Irwin, Philadelphia, Thomas Irwin, Philadelphia, bnders; Mathew and Thomas Irwin & Co., owners.

245. *Hetty*; John Brice, Philadelphia; 1780 Apr. 14; ship; 20 guns; 110 [80?] crew; $10,000; Thomas Learning, Jr., Philadelphia, Joseph C. Fisher, Philadelphia, bonders; Thomas Learning and Joseph C. Fisher & Co., Philadelphia, owners.

246. *Hetty*; Samuel Davison, Philadelphia [?]; 1780 Aug 17; brigantine; 14 guns; 40 crew; $20,000; Mathew Irwin, Philadelphia, Thomas Irwin, Philadelphia, bonders; Mathew Irwin and Thomas Irwin & Co., Philadelphia, owners.

247. *Hetty*; Henry Darnol [Darnell]; 1781 Sep. 6; schooner; 8 guns; 30 crew; $20,000; Henry Darnol, Philadelphia, Mordecai Sheftall, Philadelphia, bonders; Mordecai Sheftall and others, Philadelphia, owners.

248. *Hetty*; Thomas Deburk; 1782 Mar. 14; schooner; 6 guns; 30 crew; $20,000; Thomas Deburk, Philadelphia, Mordecai Sheftall, Philadelphia, bonders; Mordecai Sheftall and others, Philadelphia, owners.

249. *Hibernia*; Robert Collings; 1779 Feb. 10, brigantine; 14 guns; 30 crew; $10,000; Robert Collings, Philadelphia, Benjamin Harbeson, Philadelphia, bonders; Joseph Dean, John Purviance, and Benjamin Harbeson, owners.

250. *Hibernia*; John Angus; 1779 Jul. 1; brigantine; 10 guns; 40 crew; $10,000; Benjamin Harbeson, Philadelphia, John Angus, Philadelphia, bonders; Benjamin Harbeson & Co., Philadelphia, owners.

251. *Hibernia*; John Burrows; 1779 Dec. 14; brigantine; 14 guns; 35 crew; $10,000; John Burrows, Philadelphia, John Purviance, Philadelphia, bonders; Samuel and Robert Purviance & Co., Baltimore, Md., owners.

252. *Hibernia*; John Brice, Philadelphia; 1780 Aug. 15; brigantine; 8 guns; 30 crew; $20,000; John Purviance, Philadelphia, Edward Paimell, Philadelphia, bonders; John Purviance, Philadelphia, Samuel and Robert Purviance & Co., Baltimore, Md., owners.

253. *Hibernia*; John Baxter, Philadelphia; 1781 May 5; brigantine; 4 guns; 14 crew; $20,000; John Pringle, Philadelphia, Philip Wilson, Philadelphia, bonders; John Pringle and Philip Wilson & Co., Philadelphia, owners.

254. *Holker*; George Geddes, Philadelphia; 1779 Apr. 14; brigantine; 10 guns; 35 crew; $10,000; Blair McClenachan, Philadelphi, Charles Darragh, Philadelphia, bonders; Blair McClenachan & Co., Philadelphia, owners.

255. *Holker*; Matthew Lawler, Philadelphia; 1779 Nov. 15; brigantine; 16 guns; 100 crew; $10,000; Blair McClenachan, Philadelphia, Patrick Moore, Philadelphia, bonders; Blair McClenachan & Co., Philadelphia, owners.

256. *Holker*; Roger Keane, Philadelphia; 1780 Jul. 26; brigantine; 16 guns; 120 crew; $20,000; Blair McClenachan, Philadelphia, James Blair, Philadelphia, bonders; Blair McClenachan & Co., Philadelphia, owners.

257. *Holker*; John Quinlan; 1782 Jun. 30; brigantine; 16 guns; 130 crew; $20,000; Blair McClenachan, Philadelphi, John Quinlan, Philadelphia, bonders; Blair McClenachan and Robert Morris, Philadelphia, owners.

258. *Hooker*; Henry Martin, Philadelphia; 1781 Jun. 4; boat; 2 guns; 35 crew; $20,000; Samuel Inglis, Philadelphia, George Ord, Philadelphia, bonders; Samuel Inglis and George Ord & Co., Philadelphia, owners.

259. *Hope*; George Geddes, Philadelphia; 1778 Dec. 24; sloop; 8 guns; 25 crew; $10,000; Blair McClenachan, Philadelphia, John Brown, Philadelphia, bonders; Blair McClenachan & Co., Philadelphia, owners.

260. *Hope*; Thomas Ward; 1779 Aug. 18; schooner; 6 guns; 30 crew; $10,000; John Flahavan & Co., Philadelphia, Thomas Ward, Philadelphia, bonders; John Flahavan & Co., Philadelphia, owners.

261. *Hope*; William Hayman; 1780 Dec. 21; ship; 12 guns; 50 crew; $20,000; Thomas Fitzsimons, Philadelphia, William Hayman, Philadelphia, bonders; Thomas Fitzsimons & Co., Philadelphia, owners.

262. *Hope*; Daniel Darby; 1781 Mar. 15; ship; 16 guns; 40 crew; $20,000; James Caldwell, Philadelphia, Daniel Darby, Philadelphia, bonders; Andrew & James Caldwell, Philadelphia, owners.

263. *Hope*; William Hayman; 1781 Jun. 28; ship; 16 guns; 50 crew; $20,000; Thomas Fitzsimons, Philadelphia, William Hayman, Philadelphia, bonders; Thomas Fitzsimons, George Meade, and John Wilcocks & Co., Philadelphia, owners.

264. *Hope*; John Fleming; 1781 Dec. 20; ship; 18 guns; 20 crew; $20,000; James Caldwell, Philadelphia, John Fleming, Philadelphia, bonders; Andrew and James Caldwell, Philadelphia, owners.

265. *Hope*; Edward North; 1782 Feb. 28; ship; 10 guns; 25 crew; $20,000; Edward North, Philadelphia, James Caldwell, Philadelphia, bonders; James & Andrew Caldwell, Philadelphia, owners.

266. *Hornet*; David Stephens, Philadelphia; 1778 Sep. 21; sloop; 18 guns; 50 crew; $10,000; John Cox, Philadelphia, John Mitchell, Philadelphia, bonders and probable owners.

267. *Hornet*; Oliver Gleason; 1779 Feb. 1; schooner; 8 guns; 45 crew; $10,000; Joseph Carson, Philadelphia, Daniel Edwards, Philadelphia, bonders; Joseph Carson & Co., Philadelphia, owners.

268. *Hornet*; Abraham Davis, Philadelphia; 1779 Sep. 17; sloop; 8 guns; 45 crew; $5,000; Joseph Carson, Philadelphia, Robert McCleay, Philadelphia, bonders; Joseph Carson & Co., Philadelphia, owners.

269. *Hornet*; William Moore, Philadelphia; 1780 Apr. 3; sloop; 6 guns; 30 crew; $10,000; Joseph Carson, Philadelphia, Robert McCleay, Philadelphia, bonders; Joseph Carson & Co., Philadelphia, owners.

270. *Humming Bird*; John Hennessy; 1779 Aug. 2; schooner; 6 guns; 16 crew; $5,000; Alexander Nelson, Philadelphia, B. Randolph, Philadelphia, bonders; Alexander Nelson, Edward Fox & Co., Philadelphia, owners.

271. *Hunter*; John Douglass; 1779 Jan. 1; schooner; 12 guns; 60 crew; $10,000; John Cox, Philadelphia, John Douglas, Philadelphia, bonders; Vanuxem & Clark, Philadelphia, owners.

272. *Hunter*; Matthew Tibbs; 1779 Jul. 2; schooner; 4 guns; 20 crew; $10,000; Matthew Tibbs, Philadelphia, James Van Uxem & Clark, Philadelphia, bonders; James Van Uxem, Clark & Co., Philadelphia, owners.

273. *Huntington*; John Stillwell, Philadelphia; 1780 Mar. 6; brigantine; 8 guns; 35 crew; $10,000; James Boylan, Philadelphia, William Hardy, Philadelphia, bonders; Thomas Adams, Philadelphia, James Boylan, Philadelphia, owners. Boylan's name is incorrectly given as Byling by the copyist.

274. *Huntington*; George Catton; 1780 Aug. 3; brigantine; 6 guns; 20 crew; $20,000; George Catton, Philadelphia, William Shirtliff, Philadelphia, Wooddrop Sims, Philadelphia, bonders; John Philips, Wooddrop and Joseph Sims & Co., Philadelphia, owners.

275. *Hyder Ally*; Henry Hawkins; 1781 Nov. 28; ship; 12 guns; 40 crew; $20,000; William Allibone, Philadelphia, Henry Hawkins, Philadelphia, bonders; John Wright Stanly, John Wilcocks, and Nicholas Low, Philadelphia, owners.

276. *Hyder Ally*; Joshua Barney; 1782 Apr. 2; ship; 16 guns; 100 crew; $20,000; Joshua Barney, Philadelphia, William Allibone, Philadelphia, bonders; Thomas Fitzsimons, Francis Gurney, and William Allibone, Philadelphia, owners.

277. *Hyder Ally*; Justus Starr; 1782 Apr. 27; ship; 16 guns; 100 crew; $20,000; Francis Gurney, Philadelphia, Justus Starr, Philadelphia, bonders; Thomas Fitzsimons, Francis Gurney, and William Allibone, Philadelphia, owners.

278. *Impertinent*; John Young, Philadelphia; 1779 Jul. 6; brigantine; 8 guns; 30 crew; $10,000; Mathew Irwin, Philadelphia, Thomas Irwin, Philadelphia, bonders; Mathew Irwin and Thomas Irwin & Co., Philadelphia, owners.

279. *Impertinent*; Alexander Henderson; 1779 Dec. 3; brigantine; 10 guns; 30 crew; $10,000; Mathew Irwin, Philadelphia, Thomas Irwin, Philadelphia, bonders; Mathew Irwin and Thomas Irwin & Co., Philadelphia, owners.

280. *Impromptu*; Jerémie Peaud; 1781 Mar. 8; brigantine; 4 guns; 14 crew; $20,000; Michael Mallet, Philadelphia, Jerémie Peaud, Philadelphia, bonders; James Lecaze and Michael Mallet, owners.

281. *Independence*; Charles Clunn, Philadelphia; 1778 Aug. 24; sloop; 10 guns; 25 cew; $10,000; John White, Philadelphia, William Price, Philadelphia, bonders; John White and William Price & Co., owners.

282. *Independence*; Thomas Truxtun; 1780 Apr. 15; ship; 10 guns; 30 crew; $10,000; Thomas Truxtun, Philadelphia, James Caldwell, Philadelphia, bonders; Andrew & James Caldwell, Philadelphia, owners.

283. *Industry;* Michael Barstow; 1776 Nov. 29; brigantine; 100 tons; 10 guns; 25 crew ; bond amount not stated; bonders not stated; Blair McClenachan, owners.

284. *Industry*; Richard Wells; 1777 Jun. 14 [p]; schooner; guns unknown; crew unknown; bond unknown; bonders unknown; owners unknown. *Industry* was a British vessel bound from Jamaica when taken by the Georgia privateer sloop *St. Louis* on May 8, 1777 and is believed to have been awarded a Pennsylvania commission as she is reported at Havana, where she was permitted to take on wood and water by Governor Diego Jose Navarro, and was reported as being a privateer bound for Philadelphia.

285. *Industry*; Hugh Lyle, Philadelphia; 1777 Jun. 19; brigantine; 14 guns; 45 crew; bond unknown; bonders unknown; John Pringle, Blair McClenachan, owners. It was noted that upon the vessel's arrival at Bordeaux from Sinepuxent, MD, in late August 1777, that she was being refitted for 18 guns.

286. *Industry*; Nicolas Valiance, Philadelphia; 1778 Sep. 29; schooner; 2 guns; 20 crew; $10,000; Alexander Nesbitt, Philadelphia, Isaac Cox, Philadelphia, bonders; John Maxwell Nesbitt & Co., Philadelphia, owners.

287. *Industry*; George Curwin, Philadelphia; 1778 Dec. 24; brigantine; 12 guns; 40 crew; $10,000; Blair McClenachan, Philadelphia, John Brown, Philadelphia, bonders; Blair McClenachan, Philadelphia, owner.

288. *Industry*; Mark Collins, Philadelphia; 1779 Aug. 16; brigantine; 12 guns; 40 crew; $10,000; Blair McClenachan, Philadelphia, Robert Bridges, Philadelphia, bonders; Blair McClenachan, Philadelphia, owner.

289. *Industry*; John Burrows, Philadelphia; 1780 Jul. 10; sloop; 6 guns; 15 crew; $20,000; George Geddes, Philadelphia, James Hood, Philadelphia, bonders; Joseph Hinckson & Co., Philadelphia, owners.

290. *Industry*; John McClenachan; 1781 Jul. 26; brigantine; 8 guns; 20 crew; $20,000; Blair McClenachan, Philadelphia, John McClenachan, Philadelphia, bonders; Blair McClenachan, Philadelphia, owner.

291. *Industry*; James Pickering; 1781 Oct. 2; schooner; 6 guns; 12 crew; $20,000; James Pickering, Philadelphia, James Stewart, Philadelphia, bonders; Thomas Casdrop, Philadelphia, James Stewart, Philadelphia, James Pickering, Philadelphia, owners.

292. *Industry*; Samuel Young; 1782 Aug. 10; brigantine; 8 guns; 20 crew; $20,000; Henry Wynkoop, Philadelphia, Samuel Young, Philadelphia, bonders; Henry Wynkoop, Samuel Young, and Robert Corry, Philadelphia, owners.

293. *Jackall*; William Macpherson; 1779 Jul. 20; schooner; 2 guns; 60 crew; $5,000; John Macpherson, Philadelphia, Robert Patton, Philadelphia, bonders; John Macpherson, Philadelphia, owner.

294. *Jackall*; Samuel Baker, Philadelphia; 1779 Aug. 4; schooner; 2 guns; 60 crew; $5,000; Andrew Caldwell, Philadelphia, James Caldwell, Philadelphia, bonders; John Macpherson, Philadelphia, owner.

295. *Jackall*; William Barton; 1779 Aug. 12; schooner; 2 guns; 70 crew; $5,000; John Macpherson, Philadelphia, Robert Patton, Philadelphia, bonders; John Macpherson, Philadelphia, owner.

296. *James*; James Armitage; 1780 Jul. [10]; brigantine; 6 guns; 30 crew; $20,000; John Pringle, Philadelphia, James Armitage, Philadelphia, bonders; John Pringle, Philadelphia, Thomas Truxtun & Co., Philadelphia, owners.

297. *James*; Hendrick Fisher; 1781 Jun. 14; brigantine; 4 guns; 14 crew; $20,000; Hendrick Fisher, Philadelphia, Harmon Courter, Philadelphia, John Pringle, Philadelphia, bonders; John Pringle & Co., Philadelphia, owners.

298. *James*; Samuel Williams; 1782 Jul. 1; schooner; 4 guns; 15 crew; $20,000; Thomas Randall, Philadelphia, Samuel Williams, Philadelphia, bonders; Thomas Randall, Philadelphia, Andrew & James Caldwell, Philadelphia, owners.

299. *Jane*; William Willis; 1780 Jan. 4; ship; 8 guns; 25 crew; $10,000; William Willis, Philadelphia, Peter Whiteside "on behalf of myself and others," bonders; Peter Whiteside & Co., Philadelphia, owners.

300. *Jane*; Samuel Young; 1781 Jun. 30; sloop; 6 guns; 20 crew; $20,000; Samuel Young, Philadelphia, Hugh Lennox, Philadelphia, bonders; Francis Gurney & Co., Hugh Lennox, George Henry, and others, Philadelphia, owners.

301. *Jane*; Jacob De Hart; 1781 Oct. 12; sloop; 4 guns; 20 crew; $20,000; Jacob De Hart, Philadelphia, Francis Gurney, Philadelphia, bonders; Francis Gurney & Co., George Henry, Abraham Markoe, and others, Philadelphia, owners.

302. *Jay*; Harman Courter; 1779 Aug. 5; ship; 18 guns; 100 crew; $10,000; Blair McClenachan, Philadelphia, William Bell, Philadelphia. bonders; Blair McClenachan, Philadelphia, John Pringle & Co., Philadelphia, owners.

303. *Joanna*; William Tanner; 1781 May 24; brigantine; 6 guns; 12 crew; $20,000; William Semple, Philadelphia, William Tanner, Philadelphia, bonders; William Semple, Philadelphia, owner.

304. *Joanna*; Silas Foster; 1781 Aug. 11; brigantine; 6 guns; 15 crew; $20,000; William Semple, Philadelphia, Silas Foster, Philadelphia, bonders; William Semple, Philadelphia, owner.

305. *Johanna Maria*; Thomas Periam; 1781 Apr. 30; brigantine; 6 guns; 16 crew; $20,000; Nicholas Low, Philadelphia, Thomas Periam, Philadelphia, bonders; Richard Curson & Co., Baltimore, owners.

306. *John*; Stephen Tinker; 1781 Jul. 9; schooner; 4 guns; 12 crew; $20,000; William Allibone, Philadelphia, Stephen Tinker, Philadelphia, bonders; William Allibone, Alexander Stewart, Robert Totten, and John Wright Stanly, Philadelphia, owners.

307. *John*; James Tinker; 1782 Mar. 28; schooner; 4 guns; 14 crew; $20,000; James Tinker, Philadelphia, Alexander Stewart, Philadelphia, bonders; Alexander Stewart, Philadelphia, John Wright Stanly, Philadelphia, owners.

308. *Jolly Tar*; David Thomson; 1781 Aug. 3; brigantine; 8 guns; 27 crew; $20,000; George Nixon, Philadelphia, David Thomson, Philadelphia, bonders; George Nixon, Philadelphia, Robert Shewell & Co., Philadelphia, owners.

309. *Juno*; David Campbell; 1780 Aug. 26; brigantine; 10 guns; 25 crew; $20,000; David Campbell, Philadelphia, Robert Cocks, Philadelphia bonders; Robert Cocks, Philadelphia, Charles Miller & Co., Philadelphia, owners.

310. *Juno*; William Smith; 1781 Jul. 24; ship; 8 guns; 30 crew; $20,000; Robert Bridges, Philadelphia, William Smith, Philadelphia, bonders; Blair McClenachan, John Pringle and others, Philadelphia, owners.

311. *Juno*; Peter Day; 1781 Dec. 15; brigantine; 6 guns; 20 crew; $20,000; Peter Day, Philadelphia, Charles Miller, Philadelphia, bonders; Charles Miller, Philadelphia, Benjamin Randolph, Philadelphia, owners..

312. *Jupiter*; Francis Illingsworth; 1776 Sep. 11; sloop; 80 tons; 14 guns; 95 crew; bond not stated; bonders not stated; Nicholas Low & Co., Philadelphia, owner.

313. *Kensington*; Samuel Smith; 1779 Mar. 22; brigantine; 14 guns; 65 crew; $10,000; Samuel Smith, Philadelphia, William Turnbull, Philadelphia, bonders; William Turnbull & Co., Philadelphia, owners.

314. *Kensington*; James [Arthur] Degge; 1781 Oct. 24; brigantine; 14 guns; 25 crew; $20,000; James [Arthur] Degge, Philadelphia, Thomas Russell, Boston, MA, Andrew Black, Boston, MA, bonders; John Pringle & Co., Philadelphia, owner.

315. *King of France*; Francis Du Closs; 1781 Jul. 7; boat; 1 gun; 20 crew; $20,000; George Kennedy, Philadelphia, Joseph Carson, Philadelphia bonders; Joseph Carson, Philadelphia, George Kennedy & Co., Philadelphia, owners.

316. *Kitty*; Ebenezer Tucker, 1780 Sep. 29; boat; 1 gun; 10 crew; $20,000; William Stretch, Philadelphia, Thomas Heston, Philadelphia, bonders; Joseph Weaver, Daniel Hawk, and Thomas Ridgway [Philadelphia?], owners.

317. *Kitty Meade*; William Paul; 1781 Sep. 8; schooner; 7 guns; 15 crew; $20,000; William Paul, Philadelphia, John Wilcocks, Philadelphia, bonders; John Wilcocks & Co., Philadelphia, owner.

318. *La Fabrique*; Louis de Roux; 1777 Jun. 14 [p]; sloop; guns unknown; crew unknown; bond unknown; bonders unknown; owners unknown. This vessel may have been awarded a Pennsylvania commission as she is reported at Havana, where she was permitted to take on wood and water by Governor Diego Jose Navarro and was reported as being a privateer bound for Philadelphia.

319. *La Ravie*; Augustine Bonamy; 1780 Sep. 2; brigantine; 10 guns; 30 crew; $20,000; Claudius Paul Raquett, Philadelphia, Augustine Bonamy, Philadelphia, bonders and owners.

320. *Lady Gates*; John McNachtane, Philadelphia; 1778 Sep. 19; brigantine; 21 guns; 40 crew; $10,000; Mathew Irwin, Philadelphia, John Pringle, Philadelphia, bonders; Thomas Irwin, Philadelphia, Mathew Irwin & Co.?, Philadelphia, owners.

321. *Lady Gates*; John Parke, Philadelphia;1779 Feb. 15; brigantine; 8 guns; 35 crew; $10,000; Thomas Irwin, Philadelphia, Mathew Irwin, Philadelphia, bonders; Thomas Irwin, Philadelphia. Mathew Irwin & Co., Philadelphia, owners.

322. *Lady Gates*; Alexander Henderson; 1779 Jul. 1; brigantine; 8 guns; 30 crew; $10,000; Mathew Irwin, Philadelphia, Thomas Irwin, Philadelphia bonders; Mathew Irwin, Philadelphia. Joseph Irwin & Co., Philadelphia, owners.

323. *Lady Gates*; George Stewart, Philadelphia; 1779 Dec. 18; brigantine; 8 guns; 30 crew; $10,000; Mathew Irwin, Philadelphia, Thomas Irwin, Philadelphia bonders; Mathew Irwin, Philadelphia, Thomas Irwin & Co., Philadelphia, owners.

324. *Lady Washington*; Samuel Young; 1779 Nov. 12; ship; 16 guns; 60 crew; $10,000; Samuel Young, Philadelphia, John McKim, Philadelphia, bonders; John McKim & Co., Philadelphia, owners.

325. *Le Gerrard* [*Le Gerard*]; James Josiah; 1778 Aug. 1; brigantine; 6 guns; 25 crew; $10,000; James Josiah, Philadelphia, Joseph C. Fisher, Philadelphia, John D. Mercier, Philadelphia, bonders; John D. Mercier, Joseph C. Fisher & Co., owners.

326. *Le Gerard*; James Josiah; 1778 Dec. 24; brigantine; 10 guns; 30 crew; $10,000; George Henry, Philadelphia, James Josiah, Philadelphia, bonders; George Henry & Co., Philadelphia, owners.

327. *Lethe*; Thomas Emerson; 1782 Apr. 5; ship; 12 guns; 56 crew; $20,000; Thomas Emerson, Philadelphia, William Turnbull, Philadelphia, bonders; William Turnbull & Co., Philadelphia, owners.

328. *Levingston*; Townsend White; 1779 Oct. 18; sloop; 6 guns; 12 crew; $10,000; John White, Philadelphia, Townsend White, Philadelphia, bonders; John White, Townsend White & Co., Philadelphia, owners.

329. *Liberty*; John Warner; 1778 Aug. 31; sloop; 4 guns; 8 crew; $10,000; James Hood, Philadelphia, Samuel Robbins, Philadelphia, bonders; James Hood, Philadelphia, James Ash & Co., Philadelphia, owners.

330. *Liberty*; Henry Hawkins; 1779 Apr. 26; schooner; 6 guns; 15 crew; $5,000; Henry Hawkins, Philadelphia, John Wilcocks, Philadelphia, bonders; John Wilcocks & Co., Philadelphia, owners.

331. *Liberty*; Charles Clunn, Philadelphia; 1779 Aug. 28; brigantine; 12 guns; 35 crew; $10,000; James Oellers, Philadelphia, John Campbell, Philadelphia, bonders; James Oellers and John Campbell, Philadelphia, owners.

332. *Liberty*; Charles Clunn [?], Philadelphia; 1779 Dec. 11; brigantine; 12 guns; 35 crew; $10,000; James Oellers, Philadelphia, John Imlay, Philadelphia, bonders; James Oellers, & Co., owners.

333. *Liberty*; John Stillwell; 1780 Aug. 1; brigantine; 6 guns; 35 crew; $20,000; John Stillwell, Philadelphia, James Oellers, Philadelphia, bonders; James Oellers, Philadelphia, owner.

334. *Liberty*; Peter Briamant; 1780 Dec 12; brigantine; 6 guns; 16 crew; $20,000; James Oellers, Philadelphia, Peter Briamant, Philadelphia, bonders; James Oellers, Philadelphia, owner.

335. *Liberty*; Jacob De Hart; 1781 Jul. 25; schooner; 4 guns; 1 crew2; $20,000; Hugh Lennox, Philadelphia, Jacob De Hart, Philadelphia, bonders; Francis Gurney, Hugh Lennox, Daniel Smith, James Hood, and others, owners.

336. *Liberty*; John Sansum; 1781 Oct. 2; schooner; 1 gun; 6 crew; $20,000; Thomas Bee, Philadelphia, John Sansum, Philadelphia, bonders; John Sansum and George Monk, Philadelphia, owners.

337. *Little Molly*; Uriah Smith, Philadelphia; 1779 Sep. 4; schooner; 6 guns; 10 crew; $10,000; Mathew Irwin, Philadelphia, Thomas Irwin, Philadelphia, bonders; owners not stated.

338. *Little Molly*; Samuel Ball, Philadelphia; 1780 Sep. 20; schooner; 2 guns; 20 crew; $20,000; Joseph Carson, Philadelphia, Joseph Ball, NJ, bonders; Joseph Carson & Co., Philadelphia, owners.

339. *Lively*; Woolman Sutton, Philadelphia; 1777 Mar. 22; brigantine; 8 guns; crew unknown; bond amount unknown; bonders unknown; John M. Nesbitt, Philadelphia, owner.

340. *Lively*; James Belt; 1779 Nov. 9; brigantine; 14 guns; 35 crew; $10,000; James Belt, Philadelphia, Alexander Nesbitt, Philadelphia, bonders; Robert Morris, Philadelphia, John Maxwell Nesbitt, & Co., Philadelphia, owners.

341. *Lively*; Nathaniel Goodwin; 1781 Aug. 23; ship; 14 guns; 30 crew; $20,000; Nathaniel Goodwin, Philadelphia, William Turnbull, Philadelphia, bonders; William Turnbull, Philadelphia, Thomas Russell, Boston, MA, owners.

342. *Livingston*; John Kelly, Philadelphia; 1780 Nov. 4; schooner; 4 guns; 20 crew; $20,000; Robert Morris, Philadelphia, Peter Whiteside, Philadelphia, bonders; Robert Morris, Philadelphia, owners.

343. *Lizard*; John Harvie[?]; 1778 Feb. 27. boat; guns not stated; crew not stated; $5,000; John Campbell, John Harvie; John Campbell & Co., Philadelphia, owner.

344. *Lovely Sally*; Nicolas Valiance; 1782 Mar. 28; brigantine; 12 guns; 45 crew; $20,000; Wooddrop Sims, Philadelphia, Nicolas Valiance, Philadelphia, bonders; Wooddrop Sims, Philadelphia, Joseph Sims, and others, Philadelphia, owners.

345. *Luck and Fortune*; Enoch Willets; 1781 Sep. 7; boat; 1 gun; 20 crew; $20,000; Joseph Carson, Philadelphia, Enoch Willets, Philadelphia, bonders; Joseph Carson & Co., Philadelphia, owners.

346. *Lydia*; Joshua Allen; 1781 Aug. 18; brigantine; 6 guns; 20 crew; $20,000; Joshua Allen, Philadelphia, William Robinson, Jr., Philadelphia, bonders; Joshua Allen, William Robinson, Jr., and others, owners.

347. *Lydia*; Peter De Russy, Philadelphia; 1782 Jun. 15; schooner; 4 guns; 18 crew; $20,000; Claudius Paul Racquet, Philadelphia, Peter De Russy, Philadelphia, bonders; Claudius Paul Racquet, Philadelphia, owner.

348. *Macaroni*; Daniel Reybold, Philadelphia; 1778 Sep. 4; sloop; 6 guns; 20 crew; $10,000; James Oellers, Philadelphia, William Sheaff, Philadelphia, bonders; James Oellers, Philadelphia, owner.

349. *McClenachan*; Thomas Houston; 1781 Jul. 16; brigantine; 6 guns; 25 crew; $20,000; Anthony Butler, Philadelphia, Jonathan Muffin, Philadelphia, bonders; Jonathan Muffin, Anthony Butler, William Coates, and Blair McClenachan, Philadelphia, owners.

350. *Maestrand*; Philipps Kollock, Philadelphia; 1781 Jun. 20; cutter; 10 guns; 20 crew; $20,000; Samuel Inglis, Philadelphia, George Ord, Philadelphia, bnders; Robert Morris, William Bingham, and Samuel Inglis & Co., Philadelphia, owners.

351. *Marbois*; Robert Harris; 1780 Sep. 2; brigantine; 16 guns; 85 crew; $20,000; Isaac Moses, Philadelphia, Robert Harris, Philadelphia, bnoders; Isaac Moses, Philadelphia, Matthew Clarkson, Philadelphia, crew.

352. *Marquis de La Fayette*; Nicholas Valiance, Philadelphia; 1781 Nov. 3; ship; 10 guns; 30 crew; $20,000; John Purviance, Philadelphia, Nathan Kelso, Philadelphia, bonders; Samuel & Robert Purviance, Philadelphia, Hugh Young & Nathan Kelso, Philadelphia, owners.

353. *Mars;* Norris Cooper; 1776 May 28; schooner; 40 tons; 3 guns; 10 crew; $5,000; bonders not stated; Jno. Wilcocks, John & Peter Chevalier, Philadelphia, owners.

354. *Mars*; William McFaden; 1778 Aug. 4; sloop; 6 guns; 20 crew; $10,000; William McFaden, Philadelphia, Alexander Nesbitt, Philadelphia, bonders; John Maxwell Nesbitt & Co., Philadelphia, owners.

355. *Mars*; Yelverton Taylor; 1778 Sep. 30; schooner; 8 guns; 35 crew; $5,000; Yelverton Taylor, Philadelphia, Thomas Learning, Jr., Philadelphia, bonders; Thomas Learning & Co., Philadelphia, owners.

356. *Mars*; Nicolas Valiance; 1778 Dec. 24; sloop; 6 guns; 25 crew; $10,000; Alexander Nesbitt, Philadelphia, Nicolas Valiance, Philadelphia, bonders; John M. Nesbitt, Philadelphia, Alexander Nesbitt, Philadelphia, owners.

357. *Mars*; Thomas Smith; 1779 Jan. 20; schooner; 6 guns; 25 crew; $10,000; Thomas Smith, Philadelphia, Harmon Courter, Philadelphia, bonders; Harmon Courter & Co., Philadelphia, owners.

358. *Mars*; Yelverton Taylor, Philadelphia; 1779 Jul. 29; schooner; 14 guns; 60 crew; $10,000; Thomas Leaming, Jr., Philadelphia, Joseph C. Fisher, Philadelphia, bonders; Thomas Learning & Co., Philadelphia, owners.

359. *Mars*; Yelverton Taylor, Philadelphia; 1779 Oct. 29; brigantine; 14 gun; 50 crew; $10,000; Thomas Learning, Jr., Philadelphia, Joseph C. Fisher, Philadelphia bonders; Bunner Murray & Co., Philadelphia, owners.

360. *Mars*; Nicolas Vallance; 1779 Nov. 4; brigantine; 10 guns; 20 crew; $10,000; John Donnaldson, Philadelphia, Nicolas Vallance, Philadelphia, bonders; John Donnaldson & Co., Philadelphia, owners.

361. *Mary and Elizabeth*; Benjamin Weekes [Wickes, Philadelphia?]; 1778 Dec. 8; ship; 14 guns; 50 crew; $10,000; John Nixon, Philadelphia, Thomas Fitzsimons, Philadelphia, bonders; owners not stated.

362. *Matilda*; George Corner, Philadelphia; 1781 Dec. 5; brigantine; 4 guns; 14 crew; $20,000; Joseph Griswold, Philadelphia, George Corner, Philadelphia, bonders; Joseph Griswold, John Baker, John Bartholomew, and others, Philadelphia, owners.

363. *Mayflower*; Mark Collins; 1782 Jan. 27; schooner; 4 guns; 16 crew; $20,000; Mark Collins, Philadelphia, Isaac Moses, Philadelphia, bonders; Isaac Moses, Matthew Clarkson & Co., Philadelphia, owners.

364. *Mercury*; John Kerlin, Jr.; 1780 Dec. 8; ship; 8 guns; 30 crew; $20,000; John Kerlin, Jr., Philadelphia, Thomas Fitzsimons, Philadelphia, bonders; Thomas Fitzsimons, Philadelphia, owner.

365. *Mercury*; Thomas Palmer; 1781 Apr. 7; brigantine; 6 guns; 20 crew; $20,000; Thomas Palmer, Philadelphia, Robert Bridges "for self and partners," bonders; Robert Bridges, Philadelphia, owner.

366. *Merlin*; Josiah Hill; 1781 Jun. 16; brigantine; 12 guns; 40 crew; $20,000; Josiah Hill, Philadelphia, George Nixon, Philadelphia, bonders; John Wetherhead & Co., owners.

367. *Minerva*; Arthur Helme; 1779 Oct. 19; schooner; 12 guns; 60 crew; $10,000; Isaac Cox, Philadelphia, Stephen Girard, Philadelphia, bonders; Stephen Girard & Co., Philadelphia, owner.

368. *Minerva*; John Angus, Philadelphia; 1779 Dec. 18; ship; 18 guns; 60 crew; $10,000; Mathew Irwin, Philadelphia, Thomas Irwin, Philadelphia, bonders; Mathew Irwin, Philadelphia, Thomas Irwin & Co., Philadelphia, owners.

369. *Minerva*; John Earle, Philadelphia; 1780 Aug. 17; ship; 18 guns; 60 crew; $20,000; Mathew Irwin, Philadelphia, Thomas Irwin, Philadelphia, bonders; Mathew and Thomas Irwin & Co., Philadelphia, owners.

370. *Minerva*; John Douglass; 1781 Aug. 2; brigantine; 5 guns; 20 crew; $20,000; Thomas Irwin, Philadelphia, John Douglass, Philadelphia, bonders; Thomas Irwin, Philadelphia, John Earle, Philadelphia, owners.

371. *Minerva*; John Earle; 1781 Dec. 28; ship; 18 guns; 80 crew; $20,000; John Earle, Philadelphia, Owen Biddle, Philadelphia, bonders; Owen Biddle, John Earle and others, Philadelphia, owners.

372. *Molly*; John Ashmead; 1781 Sep. 29; brigantine; 6 guns; 20 crew; $20,000; John Ashmead, Philadelphia, William Turnbull, Philadelphia, bonders; William Turnbull, Robert Morris, and William Semple, Philadelphia, owners.

373. *Morning Star*; James Johnston; 1780 Mar. 9; brigantine; 10 guns; 35 crew; $10,000; Andrew Hodge, Jr., Philadelphia, James Johnston, Philadelphia, bonders; Andrew Hodge & Co., Philadelphia, owners.

374. *Morning Star*; Jeremiah Simmons; 1780 Dec. 6; ship; 18 guns; 100 crew; $20,000; Hugh Lennox, Philadelphia, Jeremiah Simmons, Philadelphia, bonders; Francis Gurney & Co., Philadelphia, owners.

375. *Morris*; Thomas Misnard; 1781 May 7; ship; 8 guns; 40 crew; $20,000; John Donnaldson, Philadelphia, Thomas Misnard, Philadelphia, bonders; John Donnaldson & Co., Philadelphia, owners.

376. *Nancy;* George Curwin, Philadelphia; 1777 Mar. 26 [p]; sloop; guns unknown; crew unknown; bond unknown; bonders unknown; Willing & Morris [?], owners.

377. *Nancy*; Robert Bethell; 1778 Oct. 12; schooner; 4 gun; 10 crew; $10,000; Robert Bethell, Philadelphia, Alexander Nesbitt, Philadelphia, bonders; John Maxwell Nesbitt & Co., Philadelphia, owners.

378. *Nancy*; Aaron Welh; 1779 Jul. 9; schooner; 4 guns; 12 crew; $10,000; Aaron Welh, Philadelphia, Alexander Nelson, Philadelphia, bonders; Alexander Nelson, Philadelphia, Edward Fox & Co., Philadelphia, owners.

379. *Nancy*; Peter Young; 1781 Dec. 11; brigantine; 8 guns; 29 crew; $20,000; Thomas Randall, Philadelphia, Peter Young, Philadelphia, bonders; Thomas Randall, Thomas Truxtun, and others, Philadelphia, owners.

380. *Nansemond*; Jacob De Hart, Philadelphia; 1781 Feb. 2; schooner; 6 guns; 14 crew; $20,000; Samuel C. Morris, Philadelphia, Alexander Stewart, Philadelphia, bonders; Stewart & Totten and Samuel C. Morris & Co., Philadelphia, owners.

381. *Navarro*; Woolman Sutton, Philadelphia; 1781 Jan. 18; brigantine; 10 guns; crew not stated; $20,000; Robert Knox, Philadelphia, John Wharton, Philadelphia, bonders; Robert Knox & Co., Philadelphia, owners.

382. *Navarro*; William Keeler; 1781 Jul; brigantine; 10 guns; 40 crew; $20,000; Matthew Clarkson, Philadelphia, William Keeler, Philadelphia, bonders; Samuel Morris, Jr., James and John Wharton, Matthew Clarkson, and others, Philadelphia, owners.

383. *Neptune*; Peter Young, Philadelphia; 1779 Aug. 5; brigantine; 8 guns; 30 crew; $10,000; Mathew Irwin, Philadelphia, Thomas Irwin, Philadelphia, bonders and owners.

384. *Neptune*; Daniel Darby; 1780 Mar. 3; brigantine; 8 guns; 25 crew; $10,000; Daniel Darby, Philadelphia, Andrew & James Caldwell, Philadelphia, bonders; Andrew Caldwell and James Caldwell & Co., Philadelphia, owners.

385. *Neptune*; Archibald Young; 1780 Apr. 6; brigantine; 14 guns; 90 crew; $10,000; Mathew Irwin, Philadelphia, Thomas Irwin, Philadelphia, bonders; Mathew Irwin and Thomas Irwin & Co., Philadelphia, owners.

386. *Neptune*; Joshua Allen; 1780 Aug. 17; brigantine; 10 guns; 20 crew; $20,000; Joshua Allen, Philadelphia, John Imlay, Philadelphia, bonders; Joshua Allen & Co. and John Imlay, Philadelphia, owners.

387. *Neptune*; Gabriel Lallement; 1781 Jan. 16; schooner; 10 guns; 21 crew; $20,000; Gabriel Lallement, Philadelphia, Michael Mallet, Philadelphia, bonders; James Lacaze and Michael Mallet, Philadelphia, owners.

388. *Neptune*; Henry Hawkins; 1781 Jun. 5; brigantine; 6 guns; 14 crew; $20,000; Henry Hawkins, Philadelphia, Joseph Spencer, Philadelphia, bonders; Joseph Spencer & Co., Philadelphia, owners.

389. *Nesbitt*; John Green; 1779 Apr 28; brigantine; 6 guns; 12 crew; $10,000; John M. Nesbitt, Philadelphia, John Green, Philadelphia, bonders; John M. Nesbitt & Co., Philadelphia, owners.

390. *Nesbitt*; ___ Forbes; 1781 Jun. 20 [p]; guns unknown; crew unknown; bond unknown; bonders unknown; Owners unknown. Vessel is noted by the *Pennsylvania Gazette*, June 20, 1781, as a privateer under Captain Forbes's command in a note on the capture of several prizes prior to June 20, 1781.

391. *Nesbitt*; Nicholas Martin, Philadelphia; 1781 Jul. 19; brigantine; 14 guns; 30 crew; $20,000; David H. Conyngham, Philadelphia, Nicholas Martin, Philadelphia, bonders; John M. Nesbitt & Co., Philadelphia, Robert Morris, Philadelphia, Stephen Steward, Jr., Baltimore, MD, owners.

392. *New Comet*; Humphrey Hughes; 1778 Nov. 9; sloop; 6 guns; 25 crew; $5,000; Humphrey Hughes, Philadelphia, Thomas Learning, Jr., Philadelphia, bonders; Thomas Learning, Jr., and others, Philadelphia, owners.

393. *Nimrod*; Stewart Dean; 1782 Apr. 18; schooner; 6 guns; 18 crew; $20,000; Stewart Dean, Philadelphia, Thomas Morris, Philadelphia, bonders; Samuel C. Morris, Philadelphia, Cadwallader Morris, Philadelphia, Thomas Morris, Philadelphia, owners.

PRIVATEERS OF THE REVOLUTION

394. *Nonsuch*; Charles Wells; 1781 Sep. [p]; ship; guns unknown; crew unknown; bond unknown; bonders unknown; owners unknown. The only indication that *Nonsuch* was operating as a letter of marque or privateer prior to September 1781 is suggested by a report in, Philadelphia on October 24, 1781: "Friday last the ship *Nonsuch*, Capt. Wells, arrived here from Nantz, which place he left the [illegible] of September. ... Captain Wells brought in with him the privateer schooner *General Arnold*, Capt. [James] Watson, belonging to New-York, which he took off our capes."

395. *Nonsuch*; Charles Wells; 1781 Dec. 22; ship; 18 guns; 55 crew; $20,000; Charles Wells, Philadelphia, Peter Whiteside, Philadelphia, bonders; Robert Morris, Peter Whiteside and others, Philadelphia, owners.

396. *Nympha*; Peter Briamant; 1781 Jun. 19; brigantine; 6 guns; 20 crew; $20,000; Peter Briamant, Philadelphia, Michael Mallet, Philadelphia, bonders; James Lacaze and Michael Mallet, Philadelphia, owners.

397. *Olive Branch*; George Cotton; 1781 Nov. 16; brigantine; 8 guns; 30 crew; $20,000; William Lyell, Philadelphia, George Cotton, Philadelphia, Wooddrop Sims, Philadelphia, bonders; Wooddrop Sims, Philadelphia, Joseph Sims and others, Philadelphia, owners.

398. *Oliver Cromwell*; Harmon Courter, Philadelphia; 1777 Feb; ship; 24 guns; 150; bond not stated; bonders not stated; owners not stated.

399. *Otter*; John Harvie [?]; 1778 Feb. 27; boat; guns not stated; crew not stated; $5,000; John Campbell, John Harvie, bonders; John Campbell & Co., owners.

400. *Page*; Thomas Palmer, Philadelphia; 1779 Aug. 5; sloop; 6 guns; 16 crew; $10,000; William Bell, Philadelphia, Blair McClenachan, Philadelphia, bonders; Blair McClenachan, John Pringle & Co., Philadelphia, owners.

401. *Page*; John Kemp; 1780 Sep. 2; schooner; 12 guns; 50 crew; $20,000; Robert Bridges, Philadelphia, John Kemp, Philadelphia, bonders; Robert Bridges & Co., Philadelphia, owners.

402. *Patty*; Thomas Read; 1780 Jul. 22; brigantine; 12 guns; 40 crew; $20,000; John Donnaldson, Philadelphia, Thomas Read, Philadelphia, bonders; John Donnaldson & Co., Philadelphia, owners.

403. *Patty*; Francis Knox, Philadelphia; 1780 Dec. 7; brigantine; 6 guns; 19 crew; $20,000; Patrick Moore, Philadelphia, Robert McClenachan, Philadelphia, bonders and owners;

404. *Patty*; Matthew Strong; 1781 Sep. 29; ship; 12 guns; 40 crew; $20,000; Joseph Carson, Philadelphia, Matthew Strong, Philadelphia, bonders; Joseph Carson, Philadelphia, Francis Gurney and others, Philadelphia, owners.

405. *Patty and Polly*; Francis Knox; 1781 Nov. 3; brigantine; 6 guns; 15 crew; $20,000; Blair McClenachan, Philadelphia, Francis Knox, Philadelphia, bonders; Blair McClenachan, owner.

406. *Peggy*; Samuel Martin; 1779 Dec. 15; brigantine; 8 guns; 15 crew; $10,000; Samuel Inglis, Philadelphia, Samuel Martin, Philadelphia, bonders; Samuel Inglis & Co., Philadelphia, owners.

407. *Peggy*; Joseph Bradford; 1780 Mar. 14; brigantine; 8 guns; 15 crew; $10,000; Joseph Bradford, Philadelphia, Samuel Inglis, Philadelphia, bonders; Samuel Inglis & Co., Philadelphia, owners.

408. *Perseverance*; John Macpherson; 1778 Mar. 28; type unidentified; 2 guns; 150 crew; $10,000; John Macpherson, Philadelphia, Joseph Donaldson, Francis Wade, bonders; State of Pennsylvania, owner.

409. *Perseverance*; George McAroy; 1781 Dec. 22; brigantine; 6 guns; 25 crew; $20,000; George McAroy, Philadelphia, Thomas Randall, Philadelphia, bonders; Thomas Randall, Philadelphia, Stewart, Totten & Co., Philadelphia, owners.

410., *Philadelphia*; Matthew Lawler, Philadelphia;1781 Jun. 18; ship; 10 guns; 35 crew; $20,000; Mathew Irwin, Philadelphia, Patrick Moore, Philadelphia, bonders; Blair and Robert McClenachan, Philadelphia, Mathew Irwin & Co., Philadelphia, owners.

411. *Phoenix*; Edward S. Nowlan; 1781 May 30; brigantine; 8 guns; 15 crew; $20,000; Robert Morris, Philadelphia, Edward Nowlan, Philadelphia, bonders; Robert Morris & Co., Philadelphia, owners.

412. *Pilgrim*; Matthew Strong, Philadelphia; 1781 Apr. 21; brigantine; 4 guns; 14 crew; $20,000; Robert Knox, Philadelphia, John Wharton, Philadelphia, bonders; Robert Knox, Philadelphia, John Wharton & Co., Philadelphia, owners.

413. *Plough*; Edward Burrows; 1782 Jun. 4; brigantine; 4 guns; 15 crew; $20,000; William Brewster, Philadelphia, Paine Newman, Philadelphia, bonders; William Brewster, Paine Newman, owners.

414. *Polly*; Samuel Williams; 1779 Nov. 6; brigantine; 8 guns; 20 crew; $10,000; Samuel Caldwell, Philadelphia, Samuel Williams, Philadelphia, bonders; Mease, Caldwell & Co., Philadelphia, owners.

415. *Polly*; Phoenix Frazier; 1780 Jul. 22; brigantine; 6 guns; 30 crew; $20,000; John Donnaldson, Philadelphia, Phoenix Frazier, Philadelphia, bonders; John Donnaldson & Co., Philadelphia, owners.

416. *Polly*; John Hide; 1780 Sep. 14; sloop; 2 guns; 4 crew; $20,000; John Bayard, Philadelphia, John Hide, Philadelphia, bonders; John Hide, John Dick, owners.

417. *Polly*; Alexander Cain, Philadelphia; 1781 Jul. 19; brigantine; 11 guns; 35 crew; $20,000; James Crawford, Philadelphia, George Haines, Philadelphia bonders; Andrew & James Caldwell, George Haines, James Crawford, and others, Philadelphia, owners.

418. *Polly*; John Truebée; 1781 Jul. 30; sloop; 4 guns; 4 crew; $20,000; John Truebée, Philadelphia, Joseph Buisson, Philadelphia, bonders; Joseph Buisson, Philadelphia, owners

419. *Polly*; Joseph Buisson; 1781 Sep. 25; sloop; 4 guns; 4 crew; $20,000; Joseph Buisson, Philadelphia, Lacaze & Mallet, Philadelphia, bonders; James Lacaze, Philadelphia, Michael Mallet, Philadelphia, owners.

420. *Polly Sly*; George Bunner; 1780 Sep. 5; schooner; 4 guns; 12 crew; $20,000; Joseph C. Fisher, Philadelphia, George Bunner, Philadelphia, bonders; Joseph C. Fisher, Philadelphia, Thomas Learning Co., Philadelphia, owners.

421. *Pomona*; John Robertson; 1779 Mar. 22; brigantine; 12 guns; 11 crew; $10,000; Alexander Nesbitt, Philadelphia, John Robertson, Philadelphia bonders; Alexander Nesbitt & Co., Philadelphia, owners.

422. *Port Royal;* commander unknown; 1777 Nov.; snow; 16 guns; crew unknown; bond unknown; bonders unknown; owners unknown: Although the vessel was not specifically identified as letter of marque, she most certainly was one. She was fitted out at Martinique with 16 guns, bound for America, carrying artillery stores.

423. *Prince of Asturias*; John Harr, Philadelphia; 1782 Apr. 6; brigantine; 8 guns; 30 crew; $20,000; George Meade, Philadelphia, William Banks [Richmond, Va.?], bonders; George Meade, Philadelphia, owner.

424. *Prosperity*; Joseph Sooy, Philadelphia; 1779 May 3; schooner; 6 guns; 12 crew; $5,000; Joseph Carson, Philadelphia. Daniel Edwards, Philadelphia, bonders; owners not stated.

425. *Providence*; Samuel Young; 1780 Jul. 7; brigantine; 4 guns; 12 crew; $20,000; William Turnbull & Co., Philadelphia, Samuel Young, Philadelphia, bonders; William Turnbull & Co., Philadelphia, owners.

426. *Providence*; James Conner., Philadelphia; 1782 Jul. 23; sloop; 6 guns; 6 crew; $20,000; John Ross, Philadelphia, Robert Ross, Philadelphia, bonders; Benjamin Carr, Philadelphia. Robert and John Ross, Philadelphia, owners.

427. *Queen of France*; James Montgomery, Philadelphia; 1778 Nov. 18; sloop; 10 guns; 30 crew; $10,000; Sharp Delany, Philadelphia, Mathew Irwin, Philadelphia; owner unknown.

428. *Queen of France*; Peter Brewster; 1779 Jul. 6; sloop; 8 guns; 20 crew; $10,000; Mathew Irwin, Philadelphia. Thomas Irwin, Philadelphia James Montgomery, Philadelphia; Mathew Irwin, Philadelphia, Thomas Irwin & Co., Philadelphia, owners.

429. *Queen of France*; John Hunn; 1781 Dec. 22; ship; 12 guns; 50 crew; $20,000; George Henry, Philadelphia, John Hunn, Philadelphia, James Montgomery, Philadelphia, bonders; George Henry, Philadelphia. Robert Knox & Co., Philadelphia, owners.

430. *Queen of France*; Richard "Deal" [Dale], Philadelphia; 1782 Aug. 10; ship; 12 guns; 45 crew; $20,000; George Henry, Philadelphia, James Josiah, Philadelphia, James Montgomery, Philadelphia, bonders; George Henry, James Josiah, Philadelphia, John Hunn, John Hood, Philadelphia, owners.

431. *Queen of Sweden*; John Wilson, Philadelphia; 1780 Nov. 8; brigantine; 8 guns; 20 crew; $20,000; Samuel Inglis, Philadelphia, George Ord, Philadelphia, bonders; Thomas Willing, Robert Morris & Co., Philadelphia, owners.

432. *Quicktime*; Joseph Badcock; 1781 Sep. 11; boat; 1 gun; 20 crew; $20,000; Joseph Badcock, Philadelphia, Joseph Carson, Philadelphia, bonders; Joseph Carson & Co., Philadelphia, owners.

433. *"Racoon"* [Raccoon]; John Brice; 1781 Jun. 16; schooner; 8 guns; 25 crew; $20,000; George Nixon, Philadelphia, John Brice, Philadelphia, bonders; Robert Shewell, Philadelphia. George Nixon, Philadelphia, owners.

434. *Rambler*; John McFatridge, Philadelphia; 1779 Feb. 21; schooner; 4 guns; 10 crew; $5,000; Joseph Carson, Philadelphia, Daniel Edwards, Philadelphia, bonders; Joseph Carson & Co., Philadelphia, owners.

435. *Rambler*; John Durry; 1781 Aug. 10; brigantine; 10 guns; 60 crew; $20,000; Alexander Nesbitt, Philadelphia, John Durry, Philadelphia, bonders; Alexander Nesbitt, Philadelphia, owner.

436. *Ranger*; John Warden; 1778 Jul. 13; brigantine; 12 guns; 30 crew; $10,000; Blair McClenachan, Philadelphia, Patrick Moore, Philadelphia, bonders; Blair McClenachan, Patrick Moore, owners.

437. *Ranger*; John Hunn; 1779 Feb. 12; sloop; 6 guns; 20 crew; $5,000; John Hunn, Philadelphia, Alexander Nesbitt, Philadelphia, bonders; John Maxwell Nesbitt & Co., Philadelphia, owners.

438. *Ranger*; Hugh Montgomery; 1779 Sep. 9; sloop; 8 guns; 25 crew; $10,000; Hugh Montgomery, Philadelphia, Alexander Nesbitt, Philadelphia, bonders; John Maxwell Nesbitt & Co., Philadelphia, owners.

439. *Ranger*; Andrew Lawrence; 1780 Sep. 14; sloop; 2 guns; 4 crew; $20,000; Andrew Lawrence, Philadelphia, John Bayard, Philadelphia, bonders; Andrew Lawrence, Philadelphia, owner.

440. *Rattlesnake* [*Rattle-snake*]; David McCullough, Philadelphia; 1777 Mar. [p]; schooner [refitted as ship but also reported as a brigantine]; 18 guns; 150 crew; bond not stated; bonders not stated; Robert Morris and William Bingham [?], owners. *Rattlesnake* is listed as one of ten vessels fitted out at St. Lucia and Martinique in the fifteen days prior to March 10, 1777 under blank commissions from Congress.

441. *Rattlesnake*; Samuel Ball, Philadelphia; 1779 Feb. 1; schooner; 6 guns; 35 crew; $10,000; Joseph Carson, Philadelphia, Daniel Edwards, Philadelphia; Joseph Carson & Co., Philadelphia, owners.

442. *Rattlesnake*; John Craig, Philadelphia; 1779 May 3; schooner; 12 guns; 45 crew; $5,000; Joseph Carson, Philadelphia, Robert McCleay, Philadelphia; Joseph Carson & Co., Philadelphia, owners.

443. *Rattlesnake*; David Mansfield; 1779 May 28; schooner; 8 guns; 35 crew; $5,000; Joseph Carson, Philadelphia, Daniel Edwards, Philadelphia; Joseph Carson & Co., Philadelphia, owners.

444. *Rattlesnake*; William Treene; 1780 Mar. 3; schooner; 8 guns; 35 crew; $10,000; Joseph Carson, Philadelphia, Joseph Hargan; Joseph Carson & Co., Philadelphia, owners.

445. *Rattlesnake*; David Stephens; 1780 Aug. 25; schooner; 8 guns; 35 crew; $20,000; David Stephens, Philadelphia, Joseph Carson, Philadelphia; Joseph Carson & Co., Philadelphia, owners.

446. *Rebecca*; James Martin, Philadelphia; 1778 Aug. 31; schooner; 8 guns; 15 crew; $10,000; James Hood, Philadelphia, Samuel Robbins, Philadelphia; James Hood, Philadelphia, James Ash & Co., Philadelphia, owners.

447. *Rebecca*; John Chatham, Philadelphia; 1779 Sep. 17; brigantine; 6 guns; 20 crew; $10,000; Lardner Clark, Philadelphia, James Vanuxem, Philadelphia, bonders; James Vanuxem, Lardner Clark & Co., Philadelphia, owners.

448. *Rebecca*; John Burrows, Philadelphia; 1780 Apr. 21; brigantine; 4 guns; 12 crew; $10,000; Elisha Clark, Philadelphia, James Vanuxem, Philadelphia, bonders sand owners.

449. *Rebecca*; William Miller; 1781 Oct. 24; brigantine; 4 guns; 20 crew; $20,000; James Crawford, Philadelphia, William Miller, Philadelphia, bonders; George Haynes, Philadelphia, owner.

450. *Recovery*; William Dunlop; 1779 Jun. 12; brigantine; 4 guns; 14 crew; $10,000; William Dunlop, Philadelphia, Alexander Nelson, Philadelphia, bonders; Alexander Nelson & Co., Philadelphia, owners.

451. *Recovery*; Gear Chadwick, Philadelphia /John Hammet, Philadelphia; 1781 May 25; boat; 1 guns; 25 crew; $20,000; Stephen Girard, Philadelphia. Isaac Cox, Philadelphia, bonders; Stephen Girard, Philadelphia, Isaac Cox, Philadelphia, owners.

452. *Renown*; Hugh Willson; 1782 May 25; schooner; 6 guns; 27 crew; $20,000; Alexander Stewart, Hugh Willson, Philadelphia, bonders; Alexander Stewart, Philadelphia, Robert Totten and others, owners.

453. *Retaliation;* George Ord, Philadelphia; 1777, Mar. 18 [p]; brigantine; 14 guns; crew not stated; bond not stated; bonders not stated; Robert Morris and William Bingham, owners. *Retaliation* was fitted out at Martinique under a blank commission forwarded by Morris to Bingham in December 1776. Captain Ord is noted a being the only American on board, the crew being comprised of French, Portuguese, and Spaniards.

454. *Retaliation;* Stephen Decatur ,Philadelphia; 1779 Jun. 11; galley; 6 guns; 50 crew; $5,000; Thomas Pryor, Philadelphia, Robert Bridges, Philadelphia, bonders; Pryor and Bridges, Philadelphia, owners.

455. *Retaliation;* Philipps Kollock, Philadelphia; 1779 Aug. 3; brigantine; 8 guns; 25 crew; $10,000; George Ord, Philadelphia, Cadwalader Dickinson, Philadelphia, bonders; Robert Morris, William Bingham, and George Ord, Philadelphia, owners.

456. *Retaliation;* Hugh Baker; 1780 Aug. 21; boat; 1 gun; 15 crew; $20,000; Hugh Baker, Philadelphia, James Pickering, Philadelphia, bonders; James Pickering, Molineaux & Co., Philadelphia, owners.

457. *Retrieve;* William Paul, Philadelphia; 1779 Sep. 16; sloop; 6 guns; 18 crew; $5,000; William Will, Philadelphia, Jacob Shallus, Philadelphia; William Will, Jacob Shallus & Co., Philadelphia, owners.

458. *Revenge;* Aaron Swaine, Philadelphia; 1780 Jul. 17; boat; 1 gun; 25 crew; $20,000; John Patton, Philadelphia, Benjamin Davis, Jr., Philadelphia, bonders; Philip Moore & Co., Philadelphia, owners.

459. *Revolution;* John McNachtane, Philadelphia; 1779 Dec. 8; ship; 20 guns; 60 crew; $10,000; Samuel Morris, Jr., Philadelphia, Robert Paisley, Philadelphia, bonders; Samuel Morris, Jr., & Co., Philadelphia, owners.

460. *Revolution;* John McNachtane, Philadelphia; 1781 Apr. 27; ship; 26 guns [this vessel was reported as armed with only 20 guns at the time of her capture by British privateers in August 1781, suggesting that six of her original guns listed were probably swivels]; 130 crew; $20,000; Mathew Irwin, Philadelphia, Robert Paisley, Philadelphia, bonder; Mathew Irwin, Thomas Irwin & Co., Philadelphia, owners.

461. *Richmond;* John Cummings, Philadelphia; 1779 Sep. 20; brigantine; 12 guns; 50 crew; $10,000; Blair McClenachan, Philadelphia, John McClenachan, Philadelphia, bonder; Blair McClenachan, Philadelphia, owner.

462. *Rising Sun;* Samuel Cassan; 1781 Mar. 16; ship; 20 guns; 130 crew; $20,000; Samuel Cassan, Philadelphia, Francis Gurney, Philadelphia, bonders; Francis Gurney, Philadelphia, Joseph Carson & Co., Philadelphia, owners.

463. *Rising Sun;* Samuel Cassan; 1781 Jul. 5; ship; 20 guns; 130 crew; $20,000; Samuel Cassan, Philadelphia, Hugh Lennox, Philadelphia, bonders; Francis Gurney, Philadelphia. Joseph Carson & Co., Philadelphia, owners.

464. *Rising Sun;* Stephen Decatur, Philadelphia; 1781 Dec. 8; ship; 13 guns; 45 crew; $20,000; Stephen Decatur, Philadelphia, Francis Gurney, Philadelphia, bonders; Francis Gurney, Philadelphia, Abraham Markoe and others, Philadelphia, owners.

465. *Rose;* Thomas Craig, Philadelphia; 1780 Mar. 14; brigantine; 6 guns; 20 crew; $10,000; Thomas Learning, Jr., Philadelphia, Joseph O. Fisher, Philadelphia, bonders; Thomas Learning, Philadelphia, Joseph C. Fisher & Co., Philadelphia, owners.

466. *Rose;* Thomas Mesnard; 1782 Aug. 3; ship; 4 guns; 40 crew; $20,000; Thomas Mesnard, Philadelphia, William Turnbull, Philadelphia, bonders; William Turnbull & Co., Philadelphia, owners.

467. *Royal Louis;* Stephen Decatur; 1781 Jul. 23; ship; 22 guns; 200 crew; $20,000; Stephen Decatur, Philadelphia, Francis Gurney, Philadelphia, bonders; Francis Gurney, Philadelphia, owner.

468. *Rutledge;* James Smith; 1776 Oct. 11; brigantine; 120 tons; 12 guns; 60 crew; bond not stated; bonders not stated; Alexander Gillson [Gillon], owners.

469. *Salem;* John Stillwell; 1778 Nov. 9; sloop; 6 guns; 25 crew; $5,000; John Stillwell, Philadelphia, Thomas Learning, Philadelphia, bonders; Thomas Learning and others, Philadelphia, owners.

470. *Sally;* James Armitage, Philadelphia; 1779 May 21; brigantine; 14 guns; 30 crew; $10,000; Joseph C. Fisher, Philadelphia, Thomas Learning, Philadelphia, bonders; Joseph C. Fisher, Philadelphia. Thomas Learning & Co., Philadelphia, owners.

471. *Sally;* Uriah Smith, Philadelphia; 1780 Mar. 3; schooner; 2 guns; 110 crew; $10,000; John Taylor, Philadelphia, John McKim, Philadelphia, bonders; John Flahavan, Philadelphia, John Taylor, Philadelphia, owners.

472. *Sally;* John Christie; 1781 Aug. 11; sloop; 5 guns; 10 crew; $20.000; John Christie, Philadelphia, Matthew Clarkson, Philadelphia, bonders; Matthew Clarkson, Philadelphia, John Wright "Standley" [Stanly], Philadelphia, owners.

473. *Sally;* John Christie; 1781 Dec. 20; sloop; 5 guns; 10 crew; $20,000; John Christie, Philadelphia, Matthew Clarkson, Philadelphia, bonders; Matthew Clarkson, Philadelphia, John Wright "Standley" [Stanly], Philadelphia, owners.

474. *Sally;* John Fleming; 1782 Apr. 13; brigantine; 12 guns; 20 crew; $20,000; John Fleming, Philadelphia, bonder; George Henry, Philadelphia, James Josiah, Philadelphia, owners.

475. *Salmon;* Philipps Kollock; 1782 Apr. 5; schooner; 4 guns; 16 crew; $20,000; Philipps Kollock, Philadelphia, John Redman, Philadelphia, bonders; Philip Moore, Philadelphia, John Redman and others, Philadelphia, owners.

476. *Sarah;* Arnott Cormerais; 1780 Nov. 10; sloop; 8 guns; 20 crew; $20,000; Philip Audibert, Philadelphia, Arnott Cormerais, Philadelphia, Isaac Sidman, Philadelphia, bonders; Arnott Cormerais, Philadelphia, owner.

477. *Schuylkill;* John Souder; 1781 Feb. 23; brigantine; 10 guns; 35 crew; $20,000; John Souder, Philadelphia, James Craig, Jr., Philadelphia, bonders; James Craig, Philadelphia, Philip Moore & Co., Philadelphia, owners.

478. *Schuylkill;* John Burrows; 1781 Sep. 20; brigantine; 8 guns; 35 crew; $20,000; John Burrows, Philadelphia, James Craig, Jr., Philadelphia, bonders; James Craig, John Patton, Philip Moore, and others, Philadelphia, owners.

479. *Seaflower;* William Breden, Philadelphia; 1781 Dec. 3; schooner; 6 guns; 12 crew; $20,000; William Breden, John Morrell, Philadelphia, bonders; John Hood, John Morrell, John Campbell, Charles Push [Rush?], Philadelphia, owners.

480. *Security;* John Hunn, Philadelphia; 1776 Jul. 2; schooner; 30 tons; 8 guns; 11 crew; bond unknown; bonders not stated; John Maxwell Nesbitt, owner.

481. *Security;* John Ord, Jr.; 1777 Apr. 5 [p]; schooner; 14 guns; 40[?] crew; bond unknown; bonders unknown; Owners unknown. This vessel first appears in a letter from St.

Eustatia, dated April 5, 1777, and published in the *Pennsylvania Journal*, April 23, 1777, stating that a privateer commanded by Captain John Ord accompanied the Pennsylvania privateer *Rattlesnake* in operations off the island. *Security* may be the "Small Schooner armed in Martinique" which is listed as one of ten vessels fitted out at St. Lucia and Martinique in the fifteen days prior to March 10, 1777, under blank commissions from Congress sent by Robert Morris.

482. *Seignora Bernardo* [*Signora Bernardo?*]; John Turner; 1781 Aug. 3; sloop; 5 guns; 15 crew; $20,000; John Turner, Philadelphia, Philip Benezet, Philadelphia, bonders; Philip Benezet & Co., Philadelphia, owners.

483. *Sellelagh* [*Shelally, Shellelagh?*]; Alexander Holmes, Philadelphia; 1780 Dec. 19; ship; 18 guns; 120 crew; $20,000; John Donnaldson, Philadelphia, Alexander Holmes, Philadelphia, bonders; John Donnaldson & Co., Philadelphia, owners.

484. *Speedwell;* Thomas Bell, Philadelphia; 1776 Nov. 13; sloop; 10 guns; 25; crew not stated; bonders not stated; John Maxwell Nesbitt & Co., owners.

485. *Speedwell*; Joseph Waters, Salem, MA;1779 Aug. 16; schooner; 4 guns; 15 crew; $5,000; Blair McClenachan, Philadelphia, Robert Bridges, Philadelphia, bonders; Blair McClenachan, Philadelphia, owner.

486. *Speedwell*; John Magee, Philadelphia; 1779 Dec. 8; schooner; 2 guns; 10 crew; $10,000; Blair McClenachan, Philadelphia, Patrick Moore, Philadelphia, bonders; Blair McClenachan & Co., Philadelphia, owners.

487. *Spitfire* [*Spit-Fire*]; commander unknown; 1777 Mar. [p]; schooner; 16 guns; 120 crew; bond not stated; bonders unknown; owners unknown; *Spitfire* is listed as one of ten vessels fitted out at St. Lucia and Martinique in the fifteen days prior to March 10, 1777 under blank commissions from Congress.

488. *Spitfire*; Henry White; 1781 Jul. 11; brigantine; 4 guns; 20 crew; $20,000; Henry White, Philadelphia, Blair McClenachan, Philadelphia, bonders; Blair McClenachan & Co., Philadelphia, owners.

489. *Spitfire*; Stephen Benezet, Philadelphia; 1782 Feb. 16; brigantine; 4 guns; 12 crew; $20,000; Blair McClenachan, Philadelphia, James Blair, Philadelphia, bonders; Blair McClenachan, Philadelphia, owner.

490. *Spy*; David McCullough; 1781 Sep. 28; boat; 5; 16 crew; $20,000; David McCullough, Philadelphia, Robert Harris, Philadelphia; David McCullough, Philadelphia, Robert Harris, Philadelphia, owners.

491. *St. Clair*; George Curwin, Philadelphia; 1780 Jul. 18; ship; 18 guns; 80 crew; $20,000; Blair McClenachan, Philadelphia, bonder; Blair McClenachan, Philadelphia. Patrick Moore & Co., Philadelphia, onwers.

492. *St. Helena*; John Stillwell; 1782 Jan. 9; ship; 10 guns; 60 crew; $20,000; John Stillwell, Philadelphia, James Oellers, Philadelphia, bonders; James Oellers, Philadelphia, owner.

493. *St. James*; Thomas Truxtun; 1781 Sep. 28; ship; 20 guns; 100 crew; $20,000; Thomas Truxtun, Philadelphia, James Caldwell, Philadelphia, bonders; Andrew and James Caldwell & Co., Philadelphia, owners.

494. *St. James*; Alexander Cain; 1782 Aug. 10; ship; 20 guns; 100 crew; $20,000; Alexander Cain, Philadelphia, James Caldwell, Philadelphia, bonders; Andrew & James Caldwell, Philadelphia, owners.

495. *St. John*; John Rice; 1778 Jul. 4; schooner; 10 guns; 45 crew; $10,000; John Rice, Philadelphia, Joseph Carson, Philadelphia, bonders; Joseph Carson, Michael Dawson, Philadelphia, owners.

496. *St. John*; Matthew Strong; 1778 Nov. 6; schooner; 4 guns; 12 crew; $10,000; Matthew Strong, Philadelphia, Joseph Carson, Philadelphia, Michael Dawson, Philadelphia, bonders; Joseph Carson, Michael Dawson & Co., Philadelphia, owners.

497. *St. John Nepomuceno*; William Paul; 1782 Apr. 23; brigantine; 8 guns; 25 crew; $20,000; George Meade, Philadelphia, William Paul, Philadelphia, bonders; George Meade, Philadelphia, owner.

498. *St. John Nepomuceno*; Walter Conner; 1782 Jul. 3; brigantine; 8 guns; 25 crew; $20,000; William Banks, Philadelphia, Walter Conner, Philadelphia, bonders; George Meade, Philadelphia, owner.

499. *St. Patrick*; Robert Collings; 1781 Sep. 8; brigantine; 16 guns; 50 crew; $20,000; Robert Collings, Philadelphia, Joseph Cowperthwait, Philadelphia, bonders; Bertles Shee, Charles Young, Robert Collings, Benjamin Eyre, owners.

500. *Surprize*; James Pyne; 1780 Aug. 3; schooner; 12 guns; 30 crew; $20,000; James Pyne, Philadelphia, Charles Crowley, Philadelphia, Samuel Jackson, Philadelphia, bonders; Samuel Jackson, Philadelphia, Charles Crowley & Co., Philadelphia, owners.

501. *Susannah*; Hugh Stocker, Philadelphia; 1778 Jul. 31; sloop; 10 guns; 45 crew; $10,000; Joseph McCullok [McCullough], Philadelphia, Joseph Carson, Philadelphia, bonders; Joseph Carson, Joseph McCullough & Co., Philadelphia, owners.

502. *Susanna*; Charles Clunn; 1778 Dec. 24; sloop; 8 guns; 25 crew; $10,000; Joseph Carson, Philadelphia, Hugh Stocker, Philadelphia, bonders; Joseph Carson, Philadelphia, Hugh Stocker & Co., Philadelphia, owners.

503. *Susannah*; George Fleming; 1779 Dec. 18; brigantine; 8 guns; 25 crew; $10,000; Mathew Irwin, Philadelphia, Thomas Irwin, Philadelphia, bonders; Mathew Irwin, Philadelphia, Thomas Irwin & Co., Philadelphia, owners.

504. *Swift*; David Welsh; 1779 Sep. 20; cutter; 10 guns; 60 crew; $10,000; David Welsh, Philadelphia, Samuel Caldwell, Philadelphia, bonders; Murray Bunner & Co. and others, owners.

505. *Tarter* [*Tartar*]; John Craig; 1779 Jul. 6; schooner; 6 guns; 30 crew; $10,000; John Craig, Philadelphia, James Craig, Jr., Philadelphia, bonders; James Craig, Philadelphia, John Craig, Philadelphia, owners.

506. *Tarter* [*Tartar*]; Solomon Hammer; 1781 Aug. 25; boat; 1 gun; 27 crew; $20,000; William Dunton, Philadelphia, Nathaniel Twining, Philadelphia, bonders; Nathaniel Twining, Philadelphia, William Dunton & Co., Philadelphia, owners.

507. *Terrible*; Joshua Baker; 1779 Aug. 18; schooner; 4 guns; 14 crew; $5,000; Henry Thorne, Egg Harbor, N J, John Morrell, Philadelphia, bonders; Henry Thorne, Egg Harbor, NJ, Joshua Baker & Co. [Egg Harbor, NJ?], owners.

508. *Thetis*; George Gregg; 1779 Aug. 4; schooner; 6 guns; 14 crew; $10,000; George Gregg, Philadelphia, James Crawford, Philadelphia, bonders; James Crawford & Co., Philadelphia, owners.

509. *Three Friends*; Daniel Jackson; 1776 Sep. 23; brigantine; 8 guns; 2 crew 0; $5,000; Daniel Jackson, Philadelphia, John Donnaldson, Philadelphia, James Sheafe, Jr., Philadelphia, bonders; Moore, Donnaldson & Mercer, Philadelphia, owners.

510. *Totten*; Thomas Blundell; 1781 Aug. 17; brigantine; 8 guns; 20 crew; $20,000; Thomas Blundell, Philadelphia, William Allibone, Philadelphia, bonders; John Wright "Standley" [Stanly], Philadelphia, Stewart & Totten, Philadelphia, owners.

511. *Trimmer*; John Earle; 1781 Aug. 11; boat; 1 gun; 10 crew; $20,000; Owen Biddle, Philadelphia, Standish Forde, Philadelphia, bonders; John Earle, Philadelphia. Standish Forde, Philadelphia, owners.

512. *Tristram Shandy*; Samuel Williams; 1781 Oct. 4; brigantine; 6 guns; 13 crew; $20,000; Stacy Hepburn, Philadelphia, Samuel Williams, Philadelphia; Peter Whiteside, Philadelphia, Stacy Hepburn, Philadelphia, owners.

513. *Trojan*; John Fanning; 1781 Nov. 8; schooner; 6 guns, 16 crew; $20,000; Joseph Carson, Philadelphia, Stacy Hepburn, Philadelphia, bonders; Joseph Carson, Philadelphia, Stacy Hepburn, Philadelphia, owners.

514. *Trooper*; Samuel Howell, Jr., Philadelphia; 1780 Feb. 23; brigantine; 14 guns; 50 crew; $10,000; Samuel Morris, Jr., Philadelphia, Andrew Tybout, Philadelphia, bonders; Samuel Morris, Jr., Philadelphia, Andrew Tybout & Co., Philadelphia, owners.

515. *Trooper*; Woolman Sutton, Philadelphia; 1780 Oct. 10; brigantine; 14 guns; 50 crew; $20,000; Samuel Morris, Jr., Philadelphia, Andrew Tybout, Philadelphia, bonders; Samuel Morris, Jr., Philadelphia, Andrew Tybout & Co., Philadelphia, owners.

516. *Trooper*; Samuel Howell; 1782 Jan. 15; ship; 8 guns; crew not stated; $20,000; Samuel Howell, Philadelphia, Daniel Duncan, Philadelphia, bonders; David Duncan, Philadelphia, James Ash and others, Philadelphia, owners.

517. *Trooper*; John Earle; 1782 May 19; ship; 10 guns; 30 crew; $20,000; John Earle, Philadelphia, James Ash, Philadelphia, bonders; Andrew Tybout, Philadelphia, James Ash & Co., Philadelphia, owners.

518. *True Blue*; William Wills [Willis], Philadelphia; 1779 Oct. 18; schooner; 10 guns; 30 crew; $10,000; Joseph Carson, Philadelphia, Robert McCleay, Philadelphia, bonders; Joseph Carson & Co., Philadelphia, owners.

519. *Tryall*; Jonathan Buffinton, Philadelphia; 1779 Sep. 17; schooner; 6 guns; 15 crew; $5,000; Blair McClenachan, Philadelphia, Robert McClenachan, Philadelphia, bonders; Blair McClenachan, Philadelphia, Patrick Moore & Co., Philadelphia, owners.

520. *Tryall*; John Baxter; 1780 Jul. 14; schooner; 4 guns; 10 crew; $20,000; John Baxter, Philadelphia, Blair McClenachan, Philadelphia, bonders; Blair McClenachan, Philadelphia, Patrick Moore & Co., Philadelphia, owners.

521. *Two Esthers*; James Byrne; 1781 Dec. 26; ship; 10 guns; 35 crew; $20,000; James Byrne, Philadelphia, John Henry Messonnier, Philadelphia, bonders; J. H. Messonnier, Philadelphia, John C. Zollickhoffer, Philadelphia, owners.

522. *Two Friends*; Hugh Smith; 1780 Aug. 2; sloop; 2 guns; 12 crew; $20,000; Clunn & Compty, Philadelphia, Hugh Smith, Philadelphia, bonders; John Compty, Philadelphia, Joseph Clunn, Philadelphia, owners.

523. *Two Friends*; Robert Conn; 1781 Oct. 12; brigantine; 10 guns; 25 crew; $20,000; Robert Conn, Philadelphia, Nicholas Low, Philadelphia, bonders; De Vries and Hanse, Curacoa, owners.

524. *Two Rachels*; Joseph Buisson; 1782 Mar. 12; brigantine; 8 guns; 20 crew; $20,000; Sasportas & Le Boeuf, Philadelphia, Joseph Buisson, Philadelphia, bonders; Sasportas & Le Boeuf, owners.

525. *Tyger*; Martin Parkison, Philadelphia; 1779 Jul. 1; sloop; 2 guns; 70 crew; $10,000; John Macpherson, Philadelphia, Robert Patton, Philadelphia, bonders; John Macpherson, Philadelphia, owners.

526. *Van Tromp*; Robert Shewell; 1782 Jan. 12; ship; 10 guns; 45 crew; $20,000; Michael Morgan O'Brien, Philadelphia, Stacy Hepburn, Philadelphia, Robert Shewell, Philadelphia, bonders; Stacy Hepburn, Philadelphia, Robert Shewell, Philadelphia, [Michael Morgan O'Brien?], Philadelphia, owners.

527. *Vengeance*; Samuel Cassan, Philadelphia; 1779 Nov. 12; schooner; 6 guns; 20 crew; $10,000; John Pringle, Philadelphia, bonder; John Pringle & Co., Philadelphia, owners.

528. *Vengeance*; Stephen Benezet; 1781 Jul. 23; schooner; 8 guns; 15 crew; $20,000; Stephen Benezet, Philadelphia, Joseph Gallego, Philadelphia, Joseph de Landa, Philadelphia, bonders; Joseph Gallego, Philadelphia, Joseph de Landa, Philadelphia, owners.

529. *Vengeance*; Joseph Parker, Philadelphia; 1781 Nov. 4; schooner; 6 guns; 11 crew; $20,000; Joseph de Landa, Philadelphia, Joseph Gallego, Philadelphia, bonders and owners.

530. *Venus*; William Raddon; 1776 Jul. 13; brigantine; 6 guns; 25 crew; $5,000; William Raddon, Thomas Pryor, Philadelphia, bonders; Daniel Roberdeau, Philadelphia, Thomas Pryor & Co., Philadelphia, owners.

531. *Venus*; James Clifton; 1779 Oct. 20; schooner; 6 guns; 20 crew; $5,000; James Clifton, Philadelphia, Charles Jones, Philadelphia, bonders; Charles Jones, Philadelphia, owner.

532. *Virginia;* Peter Hodgkinson; 1781 Jun. 18; brigantine; 4 guns; 13 crew; $20,000; Samuel Inglis, Philadelphia, George Ord, Philadelphia, bonders; Robert Morris, Samuel Inglis, Philadelphia, Thomas Welling [Willing] and George Ord, Philadelphia, owners.

533. *Washington*; James Fletcher, Philadelphia; 1778 Sep. 9; ship; 8 guns; 30 crew; $10,000; George Kennedy, Philadelphia, William McCullough, Philadelphia, bonders; Thomas Irwin, George Kennedy, Philadelphia, William McCullough & Co., Philadelphia, owners.

534. *Washington*; George May; 1779 Jun. 6; schooner; 6 guns; 20 crew; $5,000; George May, Philadelphia, James Crawford, Philadelphia, bonders; James Crawford & Co., Philadelphia, owners.

535. *Washington*; Nathaniel Chew; 1779 Sep. 20; sloop; 8 guns; 15 crew; $5,000; Nathaniel Chew, Philadelphia. Samuel Inglis, Philadelphia, bonders; Samuel Inglis & Co., Philadelphia, owners.

536. *Washington*; James Josiah; 1782 Aug. 10; ship; 18 guns; 100 crew; $20,000; James Josiah, Philadelphia, George Henry, Philadelphia, bonders; George Henry, Philadelphia, James Josiah, Philadelphia, Robert Knox, Philadelphia, owners.

537. *William*; Nicolas Valiance; 1782 Aug. 2; ship; 4 guns; 20 crew; $20,000; Alexander Nesbitt, Philadelphia, Nicolas Valiance, Philadelphia, bonders; Conyngham & Nesbitt, Philadelphia, owners.

538. Unidentified; ___Masset; 1781 Aug. 8 [p]; whaleboat; guns unknown; crew unknown; bond unknown; Bonders Unknown; Owners unknown.

New York Loyalist Privateers at Sea
as of February 27, 1779

1. *Ariel*; Samuel Weuffey; sloop; 60 tons; 12 guns; 30 crew; Patrick McDavite & Samuel Kemble, New York.

2. *Auctioneer*; Joseph Nash; schooner; 60 tons; 12 guns; 35 crew; Barrack Hays & Edward Dickenson, New York.

3. *Bishop*; Misper See; sloop; 70 tons; 14 guns; 40 crew; Rhinelander, See, & Pearce, New York.

4. *Black Prince*; Stephen Williams; brigantine; 100 tons; 14 guns; 50 crew; Fowler, Kays, & Wright, New York.

5. *Blackeney*; John Pindar; Brigantine; 100 tons; 14 guns; 60 crew; Hosmer, Chaldwell, & Tremain, New York.

6. *British Tar*; Thomas Wyer; brigantine; 100 tons; 14 guns; 60 crew; Rhinelander, Pagan & Price, New York.

7. *Castor*; ___Webster; schooner; 80 tons; 12 guns; 50 crew; Gates, Price, & Co., New York.

8. *Chance*; Thomas Qill; brigantine; 120 tons; 14 guns; 60 crew; Templeton & Waddell, New York.

9. *Clinton*; Commander not stated; schooner; 15 tons; 4 guns; 50 crew; Shedden & Goodrich, New York.

10. *Columba*; Henry Rogers; sloop; 70 tons; 10 guns; 35 crew; Neil Jameison & Co., New York.

11. *Delight*; Commander not stated; sloop; 50 tons; 10 guns; 60 crew; Coupland & French, New York.

12. *Dolphin*; Commander not stated; sloop; 50 tons; 12 guns; 50 crew; Eccles & Co., New York.

13. *Dunmore*; John Buchannon; brigantine; 160 tons; 16 guns; 80 crew; Shedden & Goodrich, New York.

14. *Experiment*; Alexander McPherson; schooner; 100 tons; 14 guns; 60 crew; Neil Jameison & Co., New York.

15. *Galatea*; Stephen Hunt; schooner; 40 tons; 6 guns; 14 crew; Hugh Wallace & Stephen Hunt, New York.

16. *Gambier*; Charles Browne; schooner; 100 tons; 12 guns; 50 crew; Gates, Price, & Co., New York.

17. *Gambier*; James Carew; schooner; 60 tons; 12 guns; 40 crew; Shedden & Goodrich, New York.

18. *Game Cock;* Charles La tellier; sloop; 50 tons; 10 guns; 25 crew; St. Croix and Pell, New York.

19. *General Campbell*; John Martin; brigantine; 70 tons; 12 guns; 60 crew; William & Robert Pagan, New York.

20. *General Matthews*; John Forsyth; sloop; 60 tons; 12 guns; 35 crew; William Hodyard & Robert Gilmaur, New York.

21. *George & Elizabeth*; William Vanassendelft; sloop; 100 tons; 14 guns; 60 crew; Benjamin Davis, & Co., New York.

22. *Germain*; Robert Campbell; schooner; 70 tons; 14 guns; 40 crew; Shedden & Goodrich, New York.

23. *Glasgow*; John Harrison; ship; 300 tons; 20 guns; 85 crew; Thomas Buchannon & Co., New York.

24. *Golden Pippen*; Philip Ford; schooner; 70 tons; 14 guns; 38 crew; William Eecles & Thomas Thomas, New York.

25. *Grandby;* Andrew Saw; sloop; 50 tons; 10 guns; 40 crew; owners not stated, New York.

26. *Hammond;* commander not stated; schooner; 70 tons; 14 guns; 80 crew; Shedden & Goodrich, New York.

27. *Harlequin;* commander not stated; schooner; 15 tons; 4 guns; 30 crew; Samuel Pearce, New York.

28. *Henry;* William McKildoe; sloop; 80 tons; 14 guns; 45 crew; Buchannon & Donaldson, New York.

29. *Hornet;* George Douglas; schooner; 60 tons; 10 guns; 30 crew; Alexander McAuslan & Thomas McKie [McKee?], New York.

30. *Hunter;* Florence Sullivan; sloop; 60 tons; 12 guns; 35 crew; Nixon, Kibble, & Parsons, New York.

31. *Impertinent;* David Gregory; brigantine; 150 tons; 14 guns; 70 crew; Henry White, Samuel Pearce & Co., New York.

32. *Irish Horse;* Michael Neal; schooner; 80 tons; 14 guns; 45 crew; Conner, Sickles, & Ross, New York.

33. *Jason;* Commander not stated; ship; 300 tons; 22 guns; 80 crew; Kemble & Co., New York.

34. *King George;* David Fenton; sloop; 100 tons; 14 guns; 60 crew; Perry, Bardin & Reilly, New York.

35. *Light Bob;* Ananias McDougal; schooner; 60 tons; 12 guns; 35 crew; Knot, Bird & Nash, New York.

36. *Lively;* Jacob Stout; sloop; 80 tons; 14 guns; 45 crew; Samuel Donaldson & Jacob Stout, New York.

37. *Lord North;* Charles McDonald; sloop; 120 tons; 14 guns; 70 crew; Shedden & Goodrich, New York.

38. *Loyal Subject;* William Carmichael; brigantine; 120 tons; 14 guns; 60 crew; Emanuel Walker, New York.

39. *Mars;* Robert Cunningham; brigantine; 199 tons; 14 guns; 50 crew; Neil Jameison & Alexander Sinclair, New York.

40. *Mohawk;* John Freeman; schooner; 60 tons; 12 guns; 35 crew; Barrack Hays & Edward Agar, New York.

41. *Musequeto;* Graham Barns; sloop; 80 tons; 14 guns; 50 crew; James Gregson & George Grundy, New York.

42. *Neptune;* James Neil; sloop; 70 tons; 14 guns; 40 crew; Allicocke, Rissick & Sheuiz, New York.

43. *Nonsuch;* Robert Bland; ship; 200 tons; 14 guns; 50 crew; Neil Jameison & Henry Thompson, New York.

44. *Norfolk Revenge;* George Maise; schooner; 70 tons; 14 guns; 45 crew; Eelbeck, Farren & Hodyard, New York.

45. *Pollux* [*Polluoc* ?]; Stewart Ross; sloop; 100 tons; 14 guns; 60 crew; Thomas & Williams, & Co., New York.

46. *Pomona* [*Pomono*?]; William Nelson; sloop; 100 tons; 14 guns; 70 crew; Andrew Dealy, New York.

47. *Pompey;* Joseph Call; schooner; 60 tons; 12 guns; 35 crew; Benjamin Wright & Joseph Call, New York.

48. *Prince of Whales;* Fitch Rogers; sloop; 60 tons; 12 guns; 35 crew; Rhinelander, King & Saight, New York.

49. *Queen Charlotte;* commander not stated; schooner; 60 tons; 12 guns; 28 crew; Frederick & William Rhinelander, New York.

50. *Revenge;* William Finlay; schooner; 60 tons; 10 guns; 30 crew; Bryan Connor, William Finlay & Co., New York.

51. *Revenge;* Thomas Milray; sloop; 60 tons; 12 guns: 35 crew; John Tench & Henry Thompson, New York.

52. *Richard;* Thomas Lyon; ship; 70 tons; 14 guns; 40 crew; George Grundy & Henry Thompson, New York.

53. *Roebuck*; Alexander Ross; sloop; 70 tons; 14 guns; 45 crew; Conner, Miller, & Morgan, New York.

54. *Rose Bud*; James Duncan; brigantine; 200 tons; 16 guns; 80 crew; Kemble, Duncan & Co., New York.

55. *Royal Charlotte*; John McClean; sloop; 120 tons; 16 guns; 80 crew; William Hodyard & Jonathan Lord & McAdam, New York.

56. *Sally*; John Spalling; schooner; 60 tons; 12 guns; 30 crew; William Hodyard & Jonathan Lord & McAdam, New York.

57. *St. Andrew*; Simon Donnell; schooner; 120 tons; 14 guns; 60 crew; Sowther & Gracie, New York.

58. *Saint George*; James Carew; schooner; 100 tons; 14 guns; 60 crew; Macom, Campbel, & Campbel, New York.

59. *Sheelah*; Henry McKibben; schooner; 60 tons; 10 guns; 30 crew; Richard R. Waddell & Hugh Breen, New York.

60. *Spitfire*; commander not stated; brigantine; 100 tons; 14 guns; 80 crew; Coupland & French, New York.

61. *Spitfire*; Commander not stated; schooner; 70 tons; 4 guns; 50 crew; Shedden & Goodrich, New York.

62. *Swift*; James Hoyt, Jr; schooner; 50 tons; 8 guns; 20 crew; Rhinelander & Saight, New York.

63. *Thistle*; Thomas Pynn Williams; sloop; 70 tons; 14 guns; 50 crew; Thomas Pope & David Sproat, New York.

64. *Tryon*; George Sibbles; brigantine; 200 tons; 16 guns; 85 crew; Dumaresque & Green, New York.

65. *Union Frigate*; John Sibrell; ship; 200 tons; 16 guns; 80 crew; Hugh & Alexander Wallace, New York.

66. *Vengeance*; George Dean; snow; 160 tons; 14 guns; 80 crew; John Porteus, New York.

67. *Vixen;* Charles Barnet Goff; sloop; 60 tons; 12 guns; 35 crew; Glover, Dugan, Easton & Co., New York.

68. *Weazel*; John Myeer; sloop; 60 tons; 12 guns; 35 crew; Samuel Pearce & William Pagan, New York.

69. *Witch;* Daniel Williams; sloop; 60 tons; 10 guns; 30 crew; William Gibson & Thomas Pope, New York.

Appendix C:

Privateer Tables

Table 1: Known Continental Commissioned Letters of Marque and Reprisal
By State and Year

	1776	1777	1778	1779	1780	1781	1782	1783	Total
New Hampshire	3	10	1	0	5	11	9	0	39
Massachusetts	0	15	1	0	87	263	239	22	627
Rhode Island	0	0	0	0	4	10	0	0	14
Connecticut	11	14	33	33	29	59	47	0	226
New York	0	0	0	0	0	0	1	0	1
New Jersey	0	0	4	0	0	0	1	0	5
Pennsylvania	25	18	45	125	111	158	56	0	538
Maryland	14	28	46	49	64	27	0	0	228
Virginia	0	0	0	0	0	35	28	0	63
South Carolina	0	1	0	0	0	0	0	0	1
Total	53	86	130	207	300	563	381	22	1742

Table 2: Known Continental Commissioned Letters of Marque
and Reprisal Carriage Guns

	1776	1777	1778	1779	1780	1781	1782	1783	Total
New Hampshire	30	124	8	0	34	88	49	0	333
Massachusetts	0	178	20	0	800	2540	2182	159	5879
Rhode Island	0	0	0	0	50	95	0	0	145
Connecticut	78	98	233	285	516	597	280	0	2087
New York	0	0	0	0	0	0	1	0	1
New Jersey	0	0	9	0	0	0	1	0	10
Pennsylvania	215	156	323	1097	1023	1263	473	0	4550
Maryland	128	249	349	527	570	257	0	0	2080
Virginia	0	0	0	0	0	422	307	0	729
South Carolina	0	4	0	0	0	0	0	0	4
Total	451	809	942	1909	2993	5262	3293	159	15818

Table 3: Known Continental Commissioned Letters of Marque and Reprisal Crewmen

	1776	1777	1778	1779	1780	1781	1782	1783	Total
New Hampshire	176	715	50	0	212	435	172	0	1760
Massachusetts	0	871	120	0	2549	10326	6774	660	21300
Rhode Island	0	0	0	0	239	412	0	0	651
Connecticut	514	567	137	1143	1370	2705	1547	0	7983
New York	0	0	0	0	0	0	9	0	9
New Jersey	0	0	43	0	0	0	1	0	44
Pennsylvania	1158	557	1336	4430	4470	4307	1868	0	18126
Maryland	450	967	803	1176	1467	765	0	0	5628
Virginia	0	0	0	0	0	1935	1108	0	3043
South Carolina	0	14	0	0	0	0	0	0	14
Total	2298	3691	2489	6749	10307	20885	11479	660	58558

Notes

The following abbreviations and short titles, cited by initials, for the end notes indicate most of the principal historical sources and publications referenced in notes to this work. In each such citation are given the volume name or short title. The series number, if any, follows the initial or short title folled by page or folio. In certain sections, as with PCC, the volume number is followed by the item number then the page number. Books are cited by author, or in collected documents by editor and/or compiler, and are preceded by volume number and page number. For further particulars, complete citations may be found in the Bibliography.

AA – American Archives.
APS – American Philosophical Society.
CHS – Connecticut Historical Society.
HSP – Historical Society of Pennsylvania.
JCC – Journals of the Continental Congress, 1774–1789.
LDC – Letters of Delegates to Congress, 1774–1789
LC – Library of Congress.
MAHS – Massachusetts Historical Society.
MHS – Maryland Historical Society.
NARA – National Archives and Record Administration.
NJA – Acts of the General Assembly of the State of New Jersey.
NDAR – Naval Documents of the American Revolution.
NJD – Documents Relating to the Revolutionary History of the State of New Jersey.
NRAR – Naval Records of the American Revolution.
NYHS – New York Historical Society.
NYPC – Journals of the Provincial Congress, Provincial Convention, Committees of Safety and Council of Safety of the State of New York, 1775–1776–1777.
NYSL – New York State Library.
PA – Pennsylvania Archives.
PCC – Papers of the Continental Congress.
PCR – Pennsylvania Colonial Records: Minutes of the Provincial Council of Pennsylvania from the Organization to the Termination of the Proprietary Government.
PRO – Public Records Office, London.
RIA – Rhode Island Archives.
WLC – William L. Clements Library.

Introduction

[1] Nathan Miller, *Sea of Glory: The Continental Navy Fights for Independence, 1775–1783* (New York: David Mackay Company, Inc., 1974), 281.

[2] A[lfred] T[hayer] Mahan, *The Influence of Sea Power Upon History, 1660–1783* (Cambridge: John Wilson and Son, 1890), 539.

I. A Justifiable Piracy

[1] Journal of His Majesty's Ship *Asia*, May 1, 1775, PRO, Admiralty 51/67, in *NDAR*, 2:541.

[2] Robert W. Coakley and Stetson Conn, *The War of the American Revolution: Narrative, Chronology, and Bibliography* (Washington, DC: Center of Military History United States Army, 1975), 89-90.

[3] Captain George Vandeput to Cadwallader Colden, May 26, 1775, *Colden Papers*, VII, 298, in *NDAR*, 2:542.

[4] John Almon, ed., *The Remembrancer, or Impartial Repository of Public Events. . .*, 17 vols. (London: Printed for J. Almon, 1775–1784), 1:148; Journal of the Rhode Island General Assembly, August 26, 1775, John Russell Bartlett, ed., *Records of the Colony of Rhode Island and Providence Plantation, in New England*, 10 vols. (Providence: Printed by the Providence Press Company, 1856–1865), 7:368-74; *JCC*, 3:274-75.

[5] *JCC*, 3:278-79; L. H. Butterfield, *et al.*, eds., *The Adams Papers*, Series I, *The Diary and Autobiography of John Adams*, 4 vols. (Cambridge, MA: The Belknap Press of Harvard University, 1961), 3:7-8.

[6] Butterfield, 3:7-8.

[7] Ibid.

[8] John Hancock to George Washington, October 5, 1775, Washington Papers, LC.

[9] Butterfield, 2:198-99.

[10] Ibid.

[11] Ibid., 2:199.

[12] Ibid.

[13] Elbridge Gerry to Samuel Adams, October 9, 1775, James Trecothick Austin, *The Life of Elbridge Gerry*, 2 vols. (Boston: Wells and Lilly, 1828), 1:116-17.

[14] *JCC*, 3:293-94. The two vessels were *Andrew Doria* and *Cabot*.

[15] Gardner W. Allen, *A Naval History of the American Revolution*, 2 vols. (Williamston, MA: Corner House Publishers, 1970, reprint of 1913), 1:53, 180; Silas Deane's Proposal for Establishing a Navy [October 16, 1775], *LDC*, 2:182-87. See also Deane to Thomas Mumford, October [16?], 1775, *LDC*, 2:188-91.

[16] Deane's Proposal.

[17] William Tryon to Lord Dartmouth, Nov. 11, 1775, *Documents Relative to the Colonial History of the State of New York; Procured in Holland, England and France*, E.B. O'Callaghan, ed., 15 vols. (Albany: Weed, Parsons & Co., 1856–1857, 8:643; Narrative of Andrew Elliot, *NDAR*, 2:525-26; William Tryon to Whitehead Hicks, October 19, 1775, *New York Gazette*, October 23, 1775; John Adams to James Warren, October 19, 1775, *Warren-Adams Letters Being Chiefly a Correspondence among John Adams, Samuel Adams and James Warren . . . , 1743–1814*, 2 vols.

Volumes 72 and 73 of the *Collections of the Massachusetts Historical Society* (Boston: Massachusetts Historical Society, 1917–1925), 72:146.

[18] *JCC*, 3:311-12. The second two vessels authorized for the Continental naval force on October 30 were *Columbus* and *Alfred*.

[19] Minutes of the Pennsylvania Committee of Safety, October 21, 1775, *PCR*, 10:375-79; Julian P. Boyd, *et al*, eds., *The Papers of Thomas Jefferson*, 40 vols. (Princeton: Princeton University Press, 1950—), 1:248-49; Master's Log HMS *Mercury*, June 16, 1775, PRO, Admiralty 52/1866, in *NDAR*, 1:696. *Rebecca and Francis* may have been an American built vessel as Hastings was later reported as having "built a ship at Kennebeck last year [1774] and loaded with masts at Portsmouth." Josiah Bartlett and John Langdon to William Whipple, Philadelphia, October 26, 1775, *Provincial Papers: Documents and Records Relating to the State of New Hampshire*, Nathaniel Bouton, *et al*, eds. (Concord: Published by Authority of the Legislature of New Hampshire, 1867–1873), 7:631.

[20] Almon, 2:123, 124.

[21] Minutes of the Pennsylvania Committee of Safety, October 21, 1775, *PCR*, 10:375-79; Samuel Ward to Henry Ward, October 24, 1775, *LDC*, 2:247; *Constitutional Gazette*, September 13, 1775; *London Chronicle*, January 4 to January 6, 1776. The *Chronicle* erroneously dated the letter October 30.

[22] Minutes of the Pennsylvania Committee of Safety, October 21, *PCR*, 10:375-79; *Pennsylvania Packet*, October 23, 1775; *Pennsylvania Evening Post*, October 24, 1775.

[23] Minutes of the Pennsylvania Committee of Safety, October 21, 1775, *PCR*, 10:375-379; *New York Gazette*, October 23, 1775; *Pennsylvania Evening Post*, October 24, 1775, 2:597; "Extract of a Letter from Philadelphia, Oct. 28." *London Chronicle*, December 12 to December 14, 1775.

[24] Minutes of the Pennsylvania Committee of Safety, October 21, 1775, *PCR*, 10:375-379; Samuel Ward to Henry Ward, October 24, 1775, 112-14; *London Chronicle*, January 4 to January 6, 1776; *Pennsylvania Packet*, October 23, 1775; *Pennsylvania Evening Post*, October 24, 1775.

[25] *London Chronicle*, January 4 to January 6, 1776; *New York Gazette*, October 23, 1775.

[26] *New York Gazette*, October 23, 1775; *JCC*, 3:305, 306; *Pennsylvania Evening Post*, October 24, 1775; Boyd, 1:248-49

[27] *Pennsylvania Evening Post*, October 24, 1775; *Pennsylvania Packet*, October 23, 1775; Minutes of the Pennsylvania Committee of Safety, October 21, 1775, *PCR*, 10:375-79; Samuel Ward to Henry Ward, October 24, 1775; *JCC*, 3:305-6; Samuel Ward's Diary, October 25, 1775, *LDC*, 2:254.

[28] *London Chronicle*, January 4 to January 6, 1776; Minutes of the Pennsylvania Committee of Safety, October 27, 28, 30, 1775, *PCR*, 10:382-86; *JCC*, 3:309. See also Robert Morris to the Philadelphia Jailer, Philadelphia, October 30, 1775, *PCR*, 10:386-87.

[29] Daniel Calligher to Captain Nicholas Biddle, December 28, 1775, Nicholas Biddle Papers, HSP, in *NDAR*, 3:285-86.

30 Andrew Allen to the Pennsylvania Committee of Safety, January 18, 1776, in *PA*, Ser. 1, 4:702. Addressed: "To John Nixon, Esqr., Chairman of the Committee of Safety for Pennsylvania," *LDC*, 3:110; Richard Smith's Diary, January 15, 1776, *LDC*, 3:98; Richard Smith's Diary, January 10, 1776, *LDC*, 3:126; *JCC*, 4:264. For further information on Campbell's arrest, see *JCC*, 3:305-6, 309; and Hancock to the New York Provincial Congress, October 26, 1775, n1; John Hancock to Duncan Campbell, Philadelphia, March 16, 1776, *LDC*, 3:286.

31 *New York Gazette*, October 23, 1775; "Extract of a Letter from Philadelphia, Oct. 28." *London Chronicle*, December 12 to December 14, 1775; Pennsylvania Committee of Safety to Captain Joseph Moulder, Philadelphia, November 23, 1775, *PA*, Ser. 2, 1:557.

32 John Hancock to the New York Provincial Congress, October 26, 1775, *NYPC*, 2:5.

33 George Washington to John Hancock, November 8, 1775, in *NDAR*, 2:929-31; *JCC*, 3:370-76.

34 Ibid.

35 Ibid.

36 Ibid.

37 *JCC*, 3:378-87.

38 Allen, 1:39-41.

39 Simeon Deane to Silas Deane, November 27, 1775, "Correspondence of Silas Deane, Delegate of the First and Second Congress at Philadelphia, 1774–1776", Connecticut Historical Society, *Connecticut Historical Society Collections*, vol. 2, (Hartford: Published by the Society, 1870), 326.

40 John Adams to James Warren, November 5, 1775, in *LDC*, 2:305; Nathan Miller, *Sea of Glory: The Continental Navy Fights for Independence, 1775–1783*, (New York: David Mackay Company, Inc., 1974), 8.

41 *NDAR*, 2:834-839; Frances Diane Robotti, *Chronicles of Old Salem: A History in Miniature.* (New York: Bonanza Books, 1953), 39; Allen states that 627 Massachusetts privateers sailed under Continental commissions. Allen, 1:45. See *NRAR* for compilation of total Massachusetts commissions housed in LC.

42 *JCC*, 3:463, 467, 4:13; Richard Smith's Diary, December 29 and 30, 1775, *LDC*, 2:535, 538. Turtle Bay is in the East River at the foot of modern 23rd Street, NYC.

43 Samuel Ward to Henry Ward, January 8, 1776, *LDC*, 3:62.

44 Richard Smith's Diary, January 16, 1776, *LDC*, 3:103.

II. *Blue Mountain Valley*

1 Philip Stephens to Vice Admiral Samuel Graves, September 26, 1775, *NDAR*, 2:735-36.

2 Inclusion, in Robert Ogden to John Hancock, February 10, 1776, PCC (New Jersey State Papers), 66, 81-189.

3 Deposition of Joseph Woolcombe, January 27, 1776, PRO, Colonial Office, 5/1107, Part I, 367-70, in *NDAR*, 3:1012; Minutes of the New York Committee of Safety, January 22, 1776, *NYPC*, 1: 261.

[4] "Extract of a Letter from Captain Dempster of the Blue Mountain Valley Transport, Dated Newry, Ireland, May 7," *London Chronicle*, May 18 to May 21, 1776.

[5] Minutes of the New York Committee of Safety, January 21, 1776, *NYPC*, 1:259-60; Captain J. H. Dempster to George Dempster, January 22, 1776, PRO, Colonial Office, 5/40, in *NDAR*, 3: 924-25; Captain J. H. Dempster to Richard Cardin, January 22, 1776, PRO, Colonial Office, 5/40, in *NDAR*, 3:925; Woolcombe Deposition. The two letters by Dempster should have been dated January 21 but the captain apparently forgot to compensate for the change of time in the Atlantic crossing.

[6] Minutes of the New York Committee of Safety, January 21, 1776, *NYPC*, 1:259-60; J. H. Dempster to George Dempster, January 22, 1776, PRO, Colonial Office, 5/40, in *NDAR*, 3: 924-25; J. H. Dempster to Richard Cardin, January 22, 1776.

[7] Woolcombe Deposition.

[8] Ibid.

[9] Ibid.; Lord Stirling to John Hancock, January 27, 1776, PCC (Letters from General Officers), 162, II, 388-92, in *NDAR*, 3:1915.

[10] Woolcombe Deposition.

[11] Ibid.; New York Committee of Safety to Lord Stirling, January 21, 1776, Charles G. Slack Collection, Dawes Memorial Library, Marietta College Library, in *NDAR*, 3:904. A letter extract dated January 23, 1776, published in the *Pennsylvania Evening Post* two days later, states that "the pilot delivered him [Woolcombe] to the committee guard who have him in custody."

[12] Ibid.; Papers laid before the Provincial Congress of New York, 1775-80, vol. 25, Military Committees, 631-33, NYSL; Lord Stirling to John Hancock, January 24, 1776, PCC (Letters from General Officers), 162, II, 384-85, in *NDAR*, 3:960; Woolcombe Deposition.

[13] Ibid.

[14] Ibid. Although no direct evidence is given, it was most likely Joseph Woolcombe who informed the Royal Navy commanders at New York of the presence of *Blue Mountain Valley* on the coast and the danger posed to her by the Americans.

[15] Robert Ogden to John Hancock, February 10, 1776, PCC (New Jersey State Papers) 66, 81-189; Captain Hyde Parker, Jr., to Vice Admiral Molyneux Shuldham, February 25, 1776, PRO, Admiralty 1/484, excerpt in *NDAR*, 4:77.

[16] Ibid.

[17] Ibid.; Robert Ogden to New York Committee of Safety, January 23, 1776, Papers laid before the Provincial Congress of New York, 1775-80, vol. 25, Military Committees, 631-33; Stirling to Hancock, January 24, 1776; Statement of Captain William Rogers, *NDAR*, 3:1016, n2.

[18] Ibid.

[19] John Almon, ed., *The Remembrancer, or Impartial Repository of Public Events, . . .* 17 vols. (London: Printed for J. Almon, 1775–1784), 3, Part III, 80-81.

[20] Ogden to Hancock, February 10, 1776.

[21] On Thursday, January 25, 1775, the *New York Journal* published a brief notice of the capture of *Blue Mountain Valley*. The same day the public learned of the event, Colonel Thomas Lowery, one of the expedition members, informed John Hancock

that he had been aboard the ship and was informed that one of her crewmen had related "that there was a Quantity of Arms & ammunition in the hold." The account was only a rumor, but had a most stimulating effect on the provincial leadership. Intelligence Conveyed from New York to Vice Admiral Molyneux Shuldham, January 23, 1776, PRO, Admiralty, in *NDAR*, 3:942; *New York Journal*, January 25, 1776; Colonel Thomas Lowery to John Hancock, January 25, 1776, PCC (Letters to Congress), 78, 14:59.

[22] Ibid.

[23] Lord Stirling to New York Committee of Safety, January 28, 1776, PCC (Letter from General Officers), 162, 2:402-3, in *NDAR*, 3:1026.

[24] Ibid.

[25] Governor William Tryon to Lord Dartmouth, February 11, 1776, PRO, Colonial Office, 5/1107, 363, in *NDAR*, 3:1217; Lord Stirling to William Livingston, February 25, 1776, PCC (Letters from General Officers), 162, 2:420, in *NDAR*, 4:75; Captain Hyde Parker, Jr., to Vice Admiral Molyneux Shuldham, February 25, 1776, PRO, Admiralty 1/484, in *NDAR*, 4:77.

III. The Privateering Resolves

[1] Robert Ogden to John Hancock, February 10, 1776, PCC (New Jersey State Papers), 66, 81:189.

[2] Ibid.

[3] Richard Smith Diary, February 20, 1776, *LDC*, 3:291-92; *JCC*, 2:175.

[4] Lord Stirling to William Livingston, February 25, 1776, PCC (Letters from General Officers), 162, 2:420; *JCC*, 4:213-15.

[5] Ibid.

[6] Ibid.

[7] *New York Gazette*, March 18, 1776.

[8] *Boston Gazette*, February 19, 1776; *Massachusetts Spy*, January 26, 1776; Gardner W. Allen, *A Naval History of the American Revolution*, 2 vols. (Williamston, MA: Corner House Publishers, 1970, reprint of 1906), 1:73.

[9] Richard Smith's Diary, February 13, 1776, *LDC*, 3:252; Josiah Bartlett to John Langdon, February 21, 1776, *LDC*, 3:293.

[10] Robert Morris to Silas Deane, March 10, 1776, *LDC*, 3:366.

[11] Richard Smith's Diary, March 13 and 16, 1776, *LDC*, 3:375, 388-89.

[12] Ibid., March 18, 1776, *LDC*, 3:397; *AA*, 4th Ser., 4:1641-48.

[13] Samuel Huntington to Jabez Huntington, March 19, 1776, *LDC*, 3:407; Richard Smith's Diary, March 19, 1776, *LDC*, 3:411-12; Joseph Hewes to Samuel Johnston, March 20, 1776, *LDC*, 3:417. See also *JCC*, 4: 213-14, 229-32, and *LDC*, 3: xxxvii.

[14] *JCC*, 4:299-333.

[15] *Pennsylvania Gazette*, March 27, 1776; John Adams to James Warren, March 21, 1776, *LDC*, 3:421.

[16] *JCC*, 4:250-54. The privateering instructions were published in the *Pennsylvania Evening Post*, April 11, 1776.

[17] Journal of HMS *Phoenix*, March 27, 1776, PRO, Admiralty 51/693, in *NDAR*, 4:547; Journal of HMS *Asia*, March 27, 1776, PRO, Admiralty 51/67, in *NDAR*, 4:547; Captain Hyde Parker, Jr., to Vice Admiral Molyneux Shuldham, April 29, 1776, PRO, Admiralty 1/484, in *NDAR*, 4:1311.

[18] William Livingston to Robert Treat Paine, March 27, 1776, Paine Papers, MAHS, in *NDAR*, 4:540.

[19] "Extract of a Letter from Capt. Dempster..." *London Chronicle*, May 18 to May 21, 1776; "Extract of a Letter from a Ship Carpenter, now in Belfast, in Ireland, to his Father, in Newcastle, May 10," *Public Advertiser*, London, May 29, 1776, in *NDAR*, 4:1115.

IV. First Patrol

[1] Jack Thompson to S. Burling, April 13, 1776, *NYPC*, 1:260-61, 2:185.

[2] Ibid.

[3] Major General Israel Putnam to George Washington, May 24, 1776, Washington Papers, LC.

[4] Lambert Wickes to Samuel Wickes, July 2, 1776, Scharf Collection, Ms. 1999, MHS; *Connecticut Courant*, July 16, 1776; Journal of HM Sloop-of-War *Kingfisher*, June 29, 1776, PRO, Admiralty, 51/506, in *NDAR*, 5:817-18; Journal of HMS *Orpheus*, June 29, 1776, PRO, Admiralty, in *NDAR*, 5:818; David Budlong Tyler, *The Bay & River Delaware: A Pictorial History* (Cambridge, Md.: Cornell Maritime Press, 1955), 24. Between March 25 and May 15, 1776, when HMS *Roebuck* maintained a blockade of the Delaware almost single-handedly, no fewer than thirteen vessels were destroyed and numerous others taken as prizes while attempting to enter or depart from the bay. A doubly powerful blockade was soon imposed, leading to one of the worst American losses of the year, the blockade runner *Nancy*, which had been chartered by the Pennsylvania Committee of Safety to bring in a substantial cargo of gunpowder and arms from the West Indies. Royal Navy cruisers spotted the vessel as she attempted to run into the Delaware on June 29, 1776. After a short chase, she was driven ashore and blown up at Turtle Gut Inlet, near Cape May, at a terrible cost to both the State and Continental war effort.

[5] See John W. Jackson, *The Pennsylvania Navy, 1775–1781: The Defense of the Delaware* (New Brunswick, NJ: Rutgers University Press, 1974), 39-57, for a comprehensive account of the May engagement between HMS *Roebuck* and *Liverpool* and the Pennsylvania Navy.

[6] See Christopher Ward, *The War of the Revolution*, 2 vols. (New York: The Macmillan Company, 1952), 1:211-45, for an excellent overview of the Long Island Campaign and the invasion of Manhattan Island.

[7] Richard D. Plunger, "'A Verse...to Remaining Idle Spectators:'" The Emergence of Loyalist Privateering During the American Revolution, 1775–1778," Vol. 2 (Doctoral Thesis: University of Maine, May 2002), 462-63.

[8] Ibid. 467.

[9] Captain William Rogers to the New York Provincial Congress, May 22, 1776, *NYPC*, 2:205.

[10] Captain Lambert Wickes to the Committee of Secret Correspondence, July 13, 1776, PCC (Letters Addressed to Congress), 78, 23:295. Verification that a prize was sent in by *Lexington* is indicated by charges made for the transport of prisoners on board the vessel from Egg Harbor to Philadelphia. *JCC*, August 17, 1776, 662-64.

[11] Captain John Paul Jones to John Hancock, July 8, 1776, Etting Collection, HSP.

[12] John Adams to Richard Cranch, August 2, 1776, *The Adams Papers*, Series II, *Adam Family Correspondenc*, L. H. Butterfield, ed., (Cambridge, MA: The Belknap Press of Harvard University, 1963), 2:73-74; Josiah Bartlett to John Langdon, August 19, 1776, *AA*, Ser. 5, 1:1660.

[13] PCC (Other Reports of Committees of Congress), 28, 193.

[14] Captain Thomas Creiger to Thomas Randall, *NYPC*, 2:304-5; Creiger to New York Convention, September 26, 1776, *AA*, Ser. 5, 2:553. The vessel Creiger encountered could not have been a British privateer since the Admiralty would not legally be issuing letters of marque for nearly two years.

[15] Creiger to Randall, 305. Typical of vessels seeking refuge on the Jersey coast was a Philadelphia sloop commanded by one Captain Fowler, which arrived at Egg Harbor about the first week of August 1776 after a twelve- or thirteen-day voyage from Charlestown, South Carolina, laden with £4,000 worth of indigo, which would have proved a hearty prize for any British cruiser. *New York Gazette and Weekly Mercury*, August 12, 1776.

[16] *AA*, Ser. 5, 2:279.

[17] Ibid., 2:714; 3:718, 203.

[18] Ibid., 2:553

[19] Ibid., 2:553-54.

[20] Ibid., 3:230.

[21] Journal of the New Jersey Provincial Congress, July 17, 1776, *Minutes of the Provincial Congress and the Council of the State of New Jersey, 1775–1776*, (Trenton: Naar, Day & Naar, 1879), 510; Brigadier General Hugh Mercer to George Washington, July 27, 1776, Washington Papers, LC; *JCC*, 5:566, 567, 571-72.

[22] Brigadier General Hugh Mercer to John Hancock, July 30, 1776, PCC (Letters from General Officers), 157, 159; John Covenhoven to the New Jersey Delegates in the Continental Congress, PCC (New Jersey State Papers, 1775–1788), 68, 6:203.

V. *Chance* and *Congress*

[1] PCC (Ships' Bonds required for Letters of Marque and Reprisal, 1776–1783), 196, 3:40 and 2:92.

[2] Ibid., 196, 1:92 and 3:40; *NDAR*, 4:775.

[3] *AA*, Ser. 4, 4:775; *JCC*, 4:250-54.

[4] *PCR*, 10:542. The two merchant schooners were not specifically mentioned in the application for the pilots but went along anyway. Narrative of Captain Andrew Snape Hamond, April 22, 1776, in *NDAR*, 4:1202.

[5] Margaret L. Brown, "William Bingham, Agent of the Continental Congress in Martinique," *The Pennsylvania Magazine of History and Biography*, (Philadelphia: The Historical Society of Pennsylvania, 1937), 66.

[6] Don Geronimo Enrile Guerci and Don Manuel Phelix Riesch to Messrs Foord and Delpratt, May 19, 1776, *NDAR*, 5:154-55; Dixon and Hunter's *Virginia Gazette*, June 22, 1776; John Hancock to George Washington, June 5, 1776, *LDC*, 4:145; Robert Morris to Silas Deane, June 5, 1776, *LDC*, 4:148; Elbridge Gerry to James Warren, June 6, 1776, *LDC*, 4:152-53; Thomas Cushing to Robert Treat Paine, June 10, 1776, Robert Treat Paine Papers, MAHS; John Hancock to James Athearn, June 22, 1776, *LDC*, 4:293; Josiah Bartlett to John Langdon, August 5, 1776, *NDAR*, 6:63. In Cushing's June 10 letter to Paine, he notes that only two ships were sent to New England, one arriving at Martha's Vineyard and the other going in to Cape Ann. *Thistle* was dispatched to Philadelphia and was libeled in the Pennsylvania Court of Admiralty on June 6, 1776. She was condemned as a legal prize on July 1, the same time as *Juno*. Captain Roberts appealed the decree, which was reversed by a special committee appointed by Congress on September 17. Eight days later Congress authorized a passport and safe conduct be granted to Captain Roberts for himself and his schooner for a period of sixty days. Unfortunately for the captain, who was apparently preparing to depart from Reedy Island in the Delaware, where he had been ensconced since his capture, on October 24 the Pennsylvania Council of Safety ordered him to be detained and his papers to be laid before the board. The subsequent future of the schooner is unknown. *Connecticut Courant*, May 27, 1776; *NDAR*, 5:143, 401, 857; 6: 765, 992-93, 1408.

[7] Purdie's *Virginia Gazette*, June 21, 1776.

[8] William Whipple to John Langdon, June 5, 1776, *LDC*, 4:150; Elbridge Gerry to James Warren, June 6, 1776, *LDC*, 4:150.

[9] Robert Morris to Silas Deane, June 5, 1776, *LDC*, 4:148.

[10] *LDC*, 4:205, n2; John Hancock to Philip Moore and James Craig, June 13, 1776, *LDC*, 4:205; John Hancock to Philip Schuyler, June 17, 1776, *LDC*, 4:257; John Hancock to James Athearns, June 22, 1776, *LDC*, 4:293.

[11] Josiah Bartlett to John Langdon, June 17, 1776, *LDC*, 4:257; John Adams to Joseph Ward, July 17, 1776, *LDC*, 4:478.

[12] *Journal and New Hampshire Packet*, August 9, 1776; John Langdon to Bayard, Craig & Co., Philadelphia, Portsmouth, August 7, 1776, *NDAR*, 6:92-93. The cargo consisted of "1078 Joes [Johannes], 672 Guineas, 15 Moidores, 41 Hogsheads Rum, 6 Hogshead, 5 Tierces, and 5 Barrells Sugar, 1 Hogshead Loaf Sugar; 24 Hogshead Prize Molasses; 3 Cases Drugs, and a Trunk of Irish Linen. The Brig is safe arrived at Egg-Harbour, the Gold they had in the Water Cask." *NJD*, 1:160. William James Morgan, editor of *NDAR*, asserts that the *Congress* that received a new letter of marque from the Pennsylvania Committee of Safety on June 17, 1776 was one and the same as the vessel for which a bond had been issued on April 11. He writes: "James Deane & Co. apparently bought the interest of Philip Moore & Co." *NDAR*, 5:592. There is one discrepancy in this assertion, however, in that the commission granted for the first vessel was for a craft of 50 tons, and that granted for the second was for a craft of 70 tons. Yet, it is unlikely that Deane would maintain two vessels of the same name in his employ. Thus the error may be attributed to one of recording at the time the second bond and

commission were offered, or that some alteration of the vessel itself had been undertaken.

[13] James Warren to John Adams, August 11. 1776, *Warren-Adams Letters Being Chiefly a Correspondence among John Adams, Samuel Adams and James Warren . . . , 1743–1814*, 2 vols. Volumes 72 and 73 of the *Collections of the Massachusetts Historical Society* (Boston: Massachusetts Historical Society, 1917–1925), 1: 267-69.

[14] Isaac Smith to John Adams, August 6, 1776, Adams Papers, MAHS, in *NDAR*, 4: 77; Warren to Adams, August 11. 1776; David Cobb to Robert Treat Paine, September 9, 1776, Robert Treat Paine Papers, MHS, in *NDAR*, 6: 755; Thomas Johnson to Patrick Henry, April 29, 1777, *NDAR*, 8:476; Commodore Esek Hopkins to the Continental Marine Committee, September 10, 1776, Hopkins Letter Book, RIHS; Samuel Cooper to Benjamin Franklin, September 17, 1776, Franklin Papers, IV, 113, APS.

[15] Commodore Esek Hopkins to the Continental Marine Committee, September 22, 1776, September 30, 1776, October 24, 1776, Hopkins Letter Book, RIHS.

[16] John Paul Jones to Robert Morris, October 17, 1776, Papers of John Paul Jones, 6495-96, LC; John Paul Jones to Joseph Hewes, October 31, 1776, *NDAR*, 6:1474.

[17] *JCC*, 6:909, 913-14; 6:1463-64; 7:207.

[18] William Hooper to Joseph Hewes, November 1, 1776, *LDC*, 5:425.

[19] Richard Henry Lee to John Page, September 3, 1776, *LDC*, 5:99; Robert Morris to Silas Deane, September 12, 1776, *LDC*, 5:147; John Adams to Abigail Adams, August 12, 1776, *Adams Family Correspondence*, 2:88-89.

[20] Robert Morris to Silas Deane, September 12, 1776, *LDC*, 5:147; E. James Ferguson, "Business, Government and Congressional Investigations in the Revolution," *William and Mary Quarterly*, 16:300; J. Franklin Jameson, *The American Revolution Considered as a Social Movement* (Princeton, NJ: Princeton University Press, 1926), 65.

[21] Captain Thomas Creiger to Thomas Randall, August 23, 1776, *NYPC*, 2:279; Captain James Campbell to John Hancock, September 8, 1776, PCC (Letters Addressed to Congress), 78, 5:63; *The Pennsylvania Journal*, October 9, 1776; *The Public Advertiser*, October 1, 1776.

[22] *AA*, Ser. 5, 3:1523-29; Nathan Miller, *Sea of Glory: The Continental Navy Fights for Independence, 1775–1783* (New York: David Mackay Company, Inc., 1974), 257.

[23] The first Continental prize had already been sent in even before *Chance* and *Congress* made their maiden voyage. On April 6, 1776, the 50-ton armed sloop *Edward*, Lieutenant Richard Bolger, tender to HMS *Roebuck*, engaged the Continental brig *Lexington*, Captain John Barry, and after an hour-long contest was captured. It is unclear as to whether or not the prize actually went into Little Egg Harbor, though circumstantial evidence points that way. Her officers and crew, however, were definitely sent in there as prisoners, the first of many to come, and were carried overland to Philadelphia. Soon afterwards, *Edward* entered the Delaware and was condemned on April 13 by the Pennsylvania Court of Admiralty. Other Continental captures followed, the next probably being the merchant schooner *Peter*, Captain Muckelno,

captured while en route from St. Vincents to her home port of Liverpool by the Continental Navy brig *Reprisal*, Captain Lambert Wickes, on or just prior to July 13, 1776. The prize was laden with a cargo of rum, sugar, coffee, cocoa and cotton, and Wickes reported he was sending her "into one Either of the Egg Harbours, if she Can get in there, If not into any other Port on the Coast." It is uncertain if she made it. On August 21, *General Putnam* reported that she assisted a vessel, unnamed, which may have been *Peter*, into Cranberry Harbor, New Jersey. Captain Andrew Snape Hamond to Lord Dunmore, April 26, 1776, Aspinwall Paper, 2 vols. Volumes 9 and 10 of *Collections of the Massachusetts Historical Society* (Boston: Massachusetts Historical Society, 1871), 2:780-783; Captain Lambert Wickes to the Committee of Secret Correspondence, July 13, 1776, PCC (Letters Addressed to Congress), 78, 23: 295; Captain Thomas Creiger to Thomas Randall, August 23, 1776, *NYPC*, 2:279; *New York Gazette and Weekly Mercury*, August 12, 1776.

[24] *PA*, Ser. 2, 1:484.

VI. Citizen Warships

[1] Howard I. Chapelle, *The National Watercraft Collection* (Washington: U.S. Government Printing Office, 1960), 16.

[2] Ibid., 17.

[3] Ibid., 18-19.

[4] Ibid.; C. Keith Wilbur, *Picture Book of the Revolution's Privateers* (Harrisburg, PA: Stackpole Books, 1973), 9.

[5] Jack Coggins, *Ships and Seamen of the American Revolution* (Harrisburg, PA: Stackpole Books, 1969), 41; Wilbur, 8.

[6] Wilbur, 9-10.

[7] Ibid.

[8] William Wall, Richard Salter and Joseph Tillinghast to Governor Nicholas Cooke, July 19, 1776, Maritime Papers, Letters of Marque, 1776–1780, RIA; Wilbur, 10.

[9] *The Royal Gazette*, May 5, 1779, in *NJD*, Ser. 2, 3:334-37.

[10] Gardner W. Allen, *A Naval History of the American Revolution*, 2 vols. (Williamstown, MA: Corner House Publishers, 1970, reprint of 1906), 2:376-77.

[11] Ibid., 1:181-82.

VII. Coast Watchers

[1] Continental Marine Committee to Captain Elisha Warner, November 1, 1776, Marine Committee Letter Book, in *NDAR*, 7:10-11.

[2] Ibid.

[3] Ibid.

[4] Ibid.

[5] Gardner W. Allen, *A Naval History of the American Revolution*, 2 vols. (Williamstown, MA: Corner House Publishers, 1970, reprint of 1906), 1:180.

[6] Continental Marine Committee to Captain Elisha Warner, November 11, 1776, Marine Committee Letter Book, in *NDAR*, 7:107-8.

[7] Ibid.

[8] Continental Marine Committee to Captain Elisha Warner, November 29, 1776, Marine Committee Letter Book, in *NDAR*, 7:326.

[9] Captain Andrew Snape Hamond to Captain Charles Phipps, December 7, 1776, Hamond Orders Issued 1776–1778, UVL.

[10] Robert Morris to John Hancock, December 23, 1776, PCC (Letters and Reports from Robert Morris) 137, Appendix 24-31.

[11] Ibid. The two known prizes sent into Egg Harbor by *Fly* were the schooners *Success*, William Compton, and *Two Brothers*, Robert Burton. *Pennsylvania Evening Post*, February 1, 1777.

[12] Robert Morris to Lieutenant John Baldwin, January 1, 1777, Marine Committee Letter Book, 48, in *NDAR*, 7:833.

[12] Richard D. Plunger, "A Verse…to Remaining Idle Spectators:" The Emergence of Loyalist Privateering During the American Revolution, 1775–1778," Vol. 2 (Doctoral Thesis: University of Maine, May 2002), 462.

[13] Ibid., 367-68.

[14] Ibid, 467.

[15] Samuel Martin to Earl of Sandwich, January 13, 1777, in *Private Papers of Sandwich, First Lord of the Admiralty, 1771–1782*, G. R. Barnes and J. H. Owen, eds. 4 vols. ([London]: Navy Records Society, 1932–1938), 1:218; *The Parliamentary History of England from the Earliest Period to the Year 1803, vol. XIX, January 29, 1777 to December 4 1778* (London: T. C. Hansard, 1814), 3; Lord Weymouth to Lord Stormont, February 7, 1777, PRO, State Papers, 78/301-174, in *NDAR*, 8:571-72; Plunger, 434, 467.

[16] *Public Advertiser*, March 11, 1777, in *NDAR*, 8:662-64; *London Chronicle*, February 27 to March 1, 1777, March 13 to March 15, 1777, April 8 to April 10, 1777; Instructions to Commanders of British Letters of Marque, [March 27, 1777], Society Miscellaneous Collection, Box 13a, HSP, in *NDAR*, 8:715-28.

[17] Plunger, 440-42.

[18] Vice Admiral Richard Howe to Philip Stephens, March 31, 1777. PRO/Admiralty 1/487, in *NDAR*, 8:233.

[19] Philip Stephens to Vice Admiral Richard Lord Howe, April 12, 1777, PRO, Admiralty, 2/554, 391-93, in *NDAR*, 8:763-64; *New-York Gazette*, June 2, 1777.

[20] Several of the West Indian privateersmen, such as Squier, would remain to operate almost exclusively out of New York. Yet, even for those able to maintain or secure commissions, it was necessary for the owners and captains to indicate what foe they were to sail against, either rebel or French vessels, as separate letters of marque were required for each. Plunger, 473-74.

[21] *New-York Gazette*, September 8, 1777; Commodore William Hotham to Marquis de Bouille, Governor of Martinique, September 9, 1777, PRO, Admiralty, 1/488, 44-45, in *NDAR*, 8:901.

[22] Plunger, 471-72

[23] Minute Book, New York Vice Admiralty Court, September 16, 1777, PRO, HCA49/93/1, in Plunger, 472; Libel Against Virginia Navy Brig *Raleigh*, PRO, High Admiralty Court 32/436/36, in *NDAR*, 9:958-59.

[24] Plunger, 472.

VIII. Courts and Ports

[1] *JCC*, 4:250-54.

[2] One of the prizes to be sold at Philadelphia but lying at Egg Harbor was the schooner *Two Brothers*, which was disposed of at public vendue on March 20, 1777. *Pennsylvania Packet*, March 18, 1777.

[3] *PA*, 8th Ser., 8:757-59.

[4] *PCR*, 10:537, 538.

[5] Ibid.

[6] Ibid.

[7] *NRAR*, 259, 382, 389, 401, 452.

[8] Robert Morris to John Hancock, December 23, 1776, PCC (Letters and Reports from Robert Morris), 137, Appendix 24-41.

[9] *NJA*, 7-8; *NJD*, Ser., 1:300, n1.

[10] *Pennsylvania Evening Post*, March 4 and 5, 1777 *NJD*, Ser., 1:300, n1.

[11] *NJD*, Ser., 1:300, n1.

[12] Ibid.

[13] *The Pennsylvania Packet*, April 29, 1777; *NJD*, Ser. 2, 1:439, 529-30; *The Pennsylvania Evening Post*, August 17, 1777; *New Jersey Gazette*, January 14, February 11 and 18, and July 22, 1778. Among the most notable New Jersey officials involved in state admiralty affairs was Register Joseph Bloomfield. Born in Woodbridge, NJ, he volunteered for military service at the outset of the war and was commissioned a captain. In 1777 he was promoted to major. Before the war he studied at Perth Amboy with Cortlandt Skinner (later commander of the Loyalist 3rd New Jersey Volunteers), and was licensed as an attorney and councilor on November 12, 1774. After the war, in 1783, he was appointed Register of Admiralty. From 1783 to 1792, he served as Attorney General for the state. In 1794 he served as a brigadier general in the expedition outfitted to suppress the Whiskey Rebellion. From 1795 to 1800, he was Mayor of Burlington, and from 1800 to 1812 served as Governor of New Jersey. He published a compilation of laws from 1799 to 1810. During the War of 1812, he again served as a brigadier general. Bloomfield was twice elected to Congress, in 1817 and 1819, and died on October 3, 1825. During his life he became a personal friend of Thomas Jefferson and an ardent Republican. *NJD*, Ser. 2, 1:341, n1.

[14] Arthur D. Pierce, *Smugglers' Woods: Jaunts and Journeys in Colonial and Revolutionary New Jersey* (New Brunswick, NJ: Rutgers University Press, 1960), 43, lists the following families as residents of Chestnut Neck: Jeremiah Adams, John Adams, Edward Bowen, Henry Davis, James Giberson, Jeremiah Higbee, Joseph Johnson, John Mathis, John Smith, Micajah Smith, Robert Smith, and Joseph Sooy.

[15] *The Pennsylvania Packet*, January 26, 1779.

[16] William McMahon, *South Jersey Towns* (New Brunswick, NJ: Rutgers University Press, 1973), 202.

[17] Pierce, *Smugglers' Woods*, 43.

[18] The author has personally inspected the area believed to be John Adams Landing, both above and below the river's surface during two seasons of archaeological investigation in the 1970s.

19 *The Pennsylvania Packet*, January 2, 1779; Arthur D. Pierce, *Iron in the Pines: The Story of New Jersey's Ghost Towns and Bog Iron* (New Brunswick, NJ: Rutgers University Press, 1990), 123.

IX. Egg Harbor

1 Richard Henry Lee to Patrick Henry, April 15, 1777, *in* William Wirt Henry, *Patrick Henry, Life, Correspondence and Speeches*, 3 vols. (New York: Charles Scribner's Sons, 1891), 3:64; Samuel Adams to James Warren, April 17, 1777, *LDC*, 6:600; Roger Sherman to Jonathan Trumbull, Sr., April 17, 1777, *LDC*, 6:607.

2 Mann Page to John Page, Philadelphia, April 21, 1777, *LDC*, 6:632. For the identity of these privateers and Robert Morris's involvement with them, see Morris to Bingham, April 25, 1777, *LDC*, 6:651-52. One of the vessels was Morris and Bingham's *Rattlesnake*, Captain John Ord commanding, fitted out at Martinique. It was *Rattlesnake*, in concert with *Oliver Cromwell*, which took nine transports, two Guineamen, and two other sail of transports into St. Eustatia, an event loudly trumpeted in the American press.

3 Oliver Wolcott to George Wylls, April 17, 1777, *LDC*, 6:608.

4 John Adams to James Warren, April 16, 1777, *LDC*, 6:589.

5 Committee for Foreign Affairs to the Commissioners in Paris, May 2, 1777, *LDC*, 7:15. See also Richard Henry Lee to Arthur Lee, April 20, 1777, *LDC*, 6:629 and Charles Carroll of Carrollton to Charles Carroll, Sr., May 4, 1777, *LDC*, 7:26.

6 Robert Morris to William Bingham, April 25, 1777, *LDC*, 6:651-52. For a discussion of the privateering ventures that Morris and Bingham had an interest in at this time, see Robert C. Alberts, *The Golden Voyage: The Life and Times of William Bingham, 1752–1804* (Boston: Houghton Muffin Co., 1969), 50-52.

7 John Adams to Abigail Adams, May 7, 1777, *LDC*, 2:234-35

8 Charles Carroll of Carrollton to Charles Carroll, Sr., May 16, 1777, *LDC*, 7:85.

9 *Pennsylvania Journal*, April 30, 1777.

10 Ironically, the privateer *Lyon* was the third vessel bearing that name to be taken by *Mermaid*. On December 11, 1776, *Mermaid* captured her first *Lyon*, Ladwick Champlin, master, from New London laden with horses, and the following day a second vessel of the same name commanded by Isaac Harlow, bound from Dartmouth with sugar, rum and molasses. The privateer *Lyon* has often been confused with the first two captures and reported as having been sent into New York, where she would be libeled on November 10. It was, however, apparently not the privateer *Lyon*, but one of the latter two merchantmen that was libeled, as Shaler's vessel and its appurtenances were sold at public auction by the New Jersey Court of Admiralty on July 9, 1777 as she lay on the beach. Shaler has been reported as hailing from both Hartford and New London, Connecticut. *New York Gazette and Weekly Mercury*, April 28, 1777; *NDAR*, 8:457, n.2; "List of Vessels seized as Prizes, and of Recaptures made, by the American Squadron, between the 1st of January, 1777, and the 22d of May following, according to the Returns received by the Vice Admiral the Viscount Howe," *London Gazette*, July 8 to July 12, 1777, in *NDAR*, 8:1059; *The Pennsylvania Evening Post*, July 3, 1777.

[11] Arthur D. Pierce, *Iron in the Pines: The Story of New Jersey's Ghost Towns and Bog Iron* (New Brunswick, NJ: Rutgers University Press, 1957), 120, 123, 184.

[12] Pierce, *Iron in the Pines*, 15, 122; Wharton Estate Deeds and Records, in Pierce, 15; New Jersey Deeds, Liber AC, p. 189, in Pierce, 121; Theodore Thayer, *Nathaniel Greene: Strategist of the Revolution* (New York: Twayne Publishers, 1960), 227.

[13] *Pennsylvania Gazette*, June 7, 1775.

[14] *Pennsylvania Evening Post*, November 14, 1776.

[15] Pierce, *Iron in the Pines*, 123

[16] Ibid., 121-22; Charles S. Boyer, *Early Forges and Furnaces in New Jersey* (Philadelphia: University of Pennsylvania Press; and London: H. Milford, Oxford University Press, 1931), 181-83.

[17] Pierce, *Iron in the Pines*, 122-23; Boyer, 181-83.

[18] Pierce, 124; Boyer, 183.

[19] *Pennsylvania Evening Post*, June 26, 1777.

[20] Journal of the Pennsylvania Council of Safety, Philadelphia, August 27, 1776, *PCR*, 10:702; *London Chronicle*, March 20-22, 1777; *Pennsylvania Gazette*, March 6, 1777; *Pennsylvania Journal*, March 19, 1777.

[21] Pierce, *Iron in the Pines*, 125-26; Marquis James, *Biography of a Business, 1792–1942: Insurance Company of North America* (Indianapolis: Bobbs-Merrill, 1942), 17-18.

[22] *Pennsylvania Packet*, March 18, 1777.

[23] Journal of HMS *Phoenix*, March 21, 1776, PRO, Admiralty 51/693, in *NDAR*, 4:437; *Newport Mercury*, July 1, 1776; [Carl Leopold Baurmeister], *Revolution in America: Confidential Letters and Journals 1776–1784 of Adjutant General Major Baurmeister of the Hessian Forces*, Bernard A. Uhlendorf, trans. and ann. (New Brunswick, NJ: Rutgers University Press, 1957), 88.

[24] Charles Carroll of Carrollton to Charles Carroll, Sr., June 20, 1777, in *LDC*, 7:235.

[25] Boyer, 179; Arthur D. Pierce, *Smugglers' Woods: Jaunts and Journeys in Colonial and Revolutionary New Jersey* (New Brunswick, NJ: Rutgers University Press, 1960), 44; *New York Gazette and Weekly Mercury*, June 23, 1777.

[26] Captain Andrew Snape Hamond to Lieutenant John Knight, June 10, 1777, Hamond Orders Issued, 1776–1777, UVL.

[27] Boyer, 179; Pierce, *Smugglers' Woods*, 44; *New York Gazette and Weekly Mercury*, June 23. See *NDAR* 9:158, and index pp. 1030, *Ann*, 1031, *Apollo*, 1078, *Industry*, and 1098, *Nancy*, for reference to captures. The expedition was not without its problems for the British. In the early evening of June 19, two British deserters, Miles Henry and William Dodge, formerly of HMS *Roebuck*, who had been assigned to duty aboard *Stanley*, came ashore in a whaleboat at Corson's Inlet, between Five Mile Beach and Peck's Beach, and put into Haeke-Fish Creek. The whaleboat, under the command of Thomas Slater and Rowland Evans, also carried three other hands. Henry and Dodge were stationed as sentries while their five mates napped, but chose to desert and inform the Americans. Major Enoch Stillwell, with a detachment of the Cape May Militia, fell upon the landing party and successfully captured the whole crew, with the arms and boat. *Pennsylvania Journal*, July 30, 1777.

[28] Franklin W. Kemp, *A Nest of Rebel Pirates* (Atlantic City, NJ: Batsto Citizens Committee, 1966), 6.

[29] Pierce, *Smugglers' Woods*, 45.

[30] Ibid., 185-87; Captain Patrick Ferguson to General Henry Clinton, October 10, 1778, Gambier Papers, Admiralty 1/489, Transcripts, LC; *The Pennsylvania Evening Post*, July 3, 1777. The wreck of the 10-gun Connecticut privateer sloop *Lyon* (incorrectly referred to in vendue notices as *Lion*) was sold at public auction on July 9, 1777, along with her rigging, cables, sails, barge yawl, cannons, powder, shot, medicine chest, surgeon's instruments, food stuffs, small arms, including blunderbusses, pistols, cutlasses, and even spears, Continental and English colors, as she lay stranded at Long Beach. She had been commissioned on November 27, 1776 under the command of Timothy Shaler and was manned by a crew of 80. Humphry Lyon & Co., of East Haddam, Ct. Titus Hosmer and Nathaniel Brown, of Middletown, Ct., owned her and Shaler, also of Connecticut, provided the bond. *The Pennsylvania Evening Post*, July 3, 1777; *NRAR*, 380.

[26] *NJA*, 181.

[31] *Pennsylvania Evening Post*, July 3, 1777.

[32] *New York Gazette and Weekly Mercury*, July 21, 1777.

[33] *Pennsylvania Packet*, July 27, 1777.

[34] Ibid.

[35] George Washington to Israel Putnam, July 28, 1777, George Washington Papers, LC.

[36] Gardner W. Allen, *A Naval History of the American Revolution*, 2 vols. (Williamstown, MA: Corner House Publishers, 1970 [1906]), 1:288-89; Robert W. Coakley and Stetson Conn, *The War of the American Revolution: Narrative, Chronology, and Bibliography* (Washington, DC: Center of Military History United States Army, 1975), 108-9.

X. O You Damned Rebel

[1] [Gideon Olmsted], *The Journal of Gideon Olmsted: Adventures of a Sea Captain during the American Revolution. A Facsimile* (Washington, DC: Library of Congress, 1978), 1; Louis F. Middlebrook, *Captain Gideon Olmsted, Connecticut Privateersman, Revolutionary War* (Salem, MA: Newcomb & Gauss Co., 1933), 1-9; Joseph O. Goodwin, *East Hartford: Its History and Traditions* (Hartford: Case, Lockwood & Brainard Co., 1879), 83-84.

[2] *Olmsted*, 2. British Admiralty Court records indicate *Seaflower* was taken on April 6, 1778 and carried into New York as a prize. There she was libeled and condemned on September 21, 1778. Bundle 457, High Court Admiralty, PRO, London, in Middlebrook, 20. See also *Olmsted*, 27, 28.

[3] *Olmsted*, 6, 9, 13-14, 17.

[4] Ibid., 17.

[5] Ibid., 18, 21.

[6] Ibid., 21; Middlebrook, viii. Middlebrook was unaware of the existence of Olmsted's journal, which clearly indicates Proshon was both owner and captain of *Polly*, but notes that the vessel's lieutenant was a man named Jacques. *Olmsted*, xv, n3.

[7] *Olmsted*, 22.

[8] Ibid., 25, 29, 30, 38.

[9] Ibid., 26, 29, 38.

[10] Ibid., 29, 30, 37.

[11] Ibid., 30, 33.

[12] Ibid., 33.

[13] Ibid., 34.

[14] Ibid., 37.

[15] Ibid., 38, 41-42, 45-46.

[16] Ibid, 49; Middlebrook, 41-48. A "joe" was slang for Johannes, a Portuguese gold coin issued between 1722 and 1835; a half joe was worth about eight dollars (Spanish) or one pound twelve shillings (British), with its value in Continental dollars fluctuating widely. *Olmsted*, 49, 102, n12.

[17] *Olmsted*, 50. The Johnson noted by Olmsted may have been Henry Johnson of Jamaica, owner of a 16-gun ship taken as a prize by Lieutenant John Trevett, U.S. Marines, while he was at New Providence, Bahamas, in January 1778. The vessel was then laden with rum, sugar, and coffee. See "Journal of Lieutenant John Trevett," *Rhode Island Historical Magazine* (July 1886), 40, 42, and Charles R. Smith, *Marines in the American Revolution: A History of the Continental Marines in the American Revolution 1775–1783* (Washington, DC: History and Museum Division, headquarters, U.S. Marine Corps, 1975), 155-56.

[18] *Olmsted*, 50.

[19] "Ramsdell" is the most likely spelling for this name, which has variously been given as "Rumsdale" and "Ramsdall."

[20] *Olmsted*, 53.

[21] Edwin Salter, *A history of Monmouth and Ocean Counties, embracing a genealogical record of earliest settlers in Monmouth and Ocean counties and their descendants. The Indians: their language, manners, and customs. Important historical events . . .* (Bayonne, NJ: F. Gardner & Sons, Publishers, 1890), 190; William Cranch, *Reports of Cases Argued and Adjudged in the Supreme Court of the United States, in February Term, 1809*, 3d ed., vol. 5 (New York: Isaac Riley, 1882), 118. This report contains most of the pertinent documents in the *Active* case. However, testimony of the occupants of the ship are presented in their entirety in *Sundry Documents Relative to the Claim of Gideon Olmsted Against the Commonwealth of Pennsylvania* (Philadelphia: Printed by Edward Olmsted, 1811), 8-13, n3 *Supra*, and in *Olmsted*, 53-54. After her capture, *Seaflower* had sailed for the Bay of Honduras in the company of her captor. They then decided to send her home to London to be libeled. The British had not established a Court of Admiralty at New York until late 1777. Olmsted, having been away since December 1777, was apparently under the mistaken impression that there was still no court in operation in September 1778 and attributes the diversion of *Seaflower* to London for that reason. Two of Olmsted's former crew, Deming and Hodge, were still aboard her. *Olmsted*, 54, 57. See "An Act to authorize the carrying of the Captures therein mentioned into any Part of his Majesty's Dominions in North America," in *New-York Gazette*, September 8, 1777, and Commodore William Hotham to Marquis DeBouillé, September 9, 1777, in *NDAR*, 9:901. See also Richard D.

Plunger, "A Verse...to Remaining Idle Spectators: The Emergence of Loyalist Privateering During the American Revolution, 1775–1778,'" Vol. 2 (Doctoral Thesis: University of Maine, May 2002), *passim*, for an excellent review on causes for the belated establishment of the Court of Admiralty in New York.

22 *Olmsted*, 57. Charles W. Kreidler, who wrote the coda for *The Journal of Gideon Olmsted*, citing Middlebrook, 58, states *Tryon* was commanded by Bridger Goodrich of Bermuda. At the time of the encounter with *Active* the privateer was actually under the command of Captain George Sibbles of New York, and Goodrich was in command of *Hammond* of Bermuda. Plunger, 536-37, addresses Sibbles career as commander of *Tryon* in fully annotated fashion, noting that he frequently sailed during the summer of 1778 in company with Goodrich, and three other New York and Bermuda privateers as a loose wolf pack.

23 The earliest indication of the conspiracy is suggested by a statement made by Olmsted noting that on the day of the uprising, September 6, "we had a large bag of musket balls on deck that we had brought up the day before . . . ," indicating that the move had been rather hastily promulgated. *Olmsted*, 66.

24 Ibid.

25 Ibid., 66.

26 Ibid., 61.

27 Ibid., 61-62.

28 Ibid., 62.

29 Ibid., 65.

30 Ibid., 66.

31 Ibid., 69.

32 Ibid.

33 Ibid., 70; Gouverneur Morris to John Dunlap, *Pennsylvania Packet, or the General Advertiser*, April 22[?], 1779.

34 *Olmsted*, 70, 73; Morris to Dunlap, April 22[?], 1779.

35 *Olmsted*, 73, 74.

36 Ibid., 77; Morris to Dunlap, April 22[?], 1779.

37 *Olmsted*, 77, 78; Cranch, 5:118.

38 *Olmsted*, 78, 81-82, 85-86; John W. Jackson, *The Pennsylvania State Navy, 1775–1781: The Defense of the Delaware* (New Brunswick, NJ: Rutgers University Press, 1974), 246-47.

39 *Olmsted*, 81-82, 85-86.

40 This conversation is extrapolated for context from Olmsted's journal. *Olmsted*, 86; Cranch, 5:118.

XI. A Solemn Mockery

1 Edwin Salter, *A history of Monmouth and Ocean Counties, embracing a genealogical record of earliest settlers in Monmouth and Ocean counties and their descendants. The Indians: their language, manners, and customs. Important historical events . . .* (Bayonne, NJ: F. Gardner & Sons, Publishers, 1890), 190; [Gideon Olmsted], *The Journal of Gideon Olmsted: Adventures of a Sea Captain during the American Revolution. A Facsimile* (Washington: Library of Congress, 1978), 90.

² Ibid.

³ [Gideon Olmsted], *The Journal of Gideon Olmsted: Adventures of a Sea Captain during the American Revolution. A Fascimile* (Washington, DC: Library of Congress, 1978), 90, 93, 94.

⁴ Ibid., 97.

⁵ Ibid., 97-98.

⁶ Olmsted, 98, states that he filed the libel as soon as he arrived in Philadelphia. However, the first libel, dated September 18, 1778, was filed by Houston and Josiah. Olmsted filed a counter suit, indicating some time had passed between his landing and the filing date without action on his part. As if Olmsted's troubles weren't enough, on September 21, three days after he had filed, his old ship *Seaflower*, which had been carried into New York, was libeled and condemned by a British prize court. Bundle 457, High Court of Admiralty, PRO, London, cited in Louis F. Middlebrook, *Captain Gideon Olmsted, Connecticut Privateersman, Revolutionary War* (Salem, MA: Newcomb & Gauss Co., 1933), 20. See also William Cranch, *Reports of Cases Argued and Adjudged in the Supreme Court of the United States, in February Term, 1809*, 3d ed., (New York: Isaac Riley, 1882), 5:118, and *Sundry Documents Relative to the Claim of Gideon Olmsted Against the Commonwealth of Pennsylvania* (Philadelphia: Printed by Edward Olmsted, 1811), 3, n3.

⁷ *Olmsted*, 101; *Ross et al, Executors v. Rittenhouse*, reprinted in Alexander J. Dallas, *Reports of Cases Ruled and Adjudged in the Several Courts of the United States and of Pennsylvania*, (New York: Lawyers Co-operative Publishing Company, 1882), 2:160, 161. The bracketed fragment is unfortunately missing from the journal, but the conclusion was transcribed on the back cover of the manuscript. See also Gouverneur Morris to John Dunlap, *Pennsylvania Packet, or the General Advertiser*, April 22[?], 1779.

⁸ Morris to Dunlap, April 22[?], 1779; *Olmsted*, 98, 101; Cranch, 5:118, 121; *Sundry Documents*, 8-13, n3. One quarter of the prize money amounting from the sale was later estimated at $24,700.

⁹ *General McDougall* received her commission to sail on April 8, 1778. She was commanded by Joseph Jauncey, and owned by Benedict Arnold, Pascal N. Smith, and Isaac Sears of Massachusetts, Christopher Leffinwell of Norwich, Connecticut, and Jeremiah Platt and Samuel and John Broome of Hartford. *NRAR*, 311.

¹⁰ Thomas Houston, Esq. etc. appellees adv. Gideon Olmsted, etc., *LDC*, 2:341-43. Drayton, Ellery, Ellsworth, and Henry signed the document. *Pennsylvania Packet*, November 12, 1778. It is of some note that Arnold's connections with Collins were close enough to enter into such a case. The general made efforts to maintain good relations with the New England delegates to Congress. On September 21, for example, at a dinner hosted by Collins, Arnold hobnobbed with the delegates from Massachusetts, presumed to include Samuel Adams, Elbridge Gerry, John Hancock, Samuel Holten, and James Lovell, as well as Henry Marchant of Rhode Island and Colonel Josiah Bartlett of New Hampshire. *LDC*, 10:679. Champerty may be defined quite literally as "buying into someone else's lawsuit."

¹¹ *Pennsylvania Packet*, November 17, 1778.

[12] For the text of the decree of the Court of Appeals see Middlebrook, 68-69, and *Sundry Documents*, 16-17.

[13] Cranch, 5:120-21; *Houston* adv. *Olmsted*, *LDC*, 2:341-43

[14] Morris to Dunlap, April 22[?], 1779; *Olmsted*, 101.

[15] *JCC*, 3:373-74. See also Cranch, 5:127, and *Penhallow, et al. v. Doane Administrators* in Alexander J. Dallas, *Reports of Cases Ruled and Adjudged in the Several Courts of the United States and of Pennsylvania*, (New York: Lawyers Co-operative Publishing Company, 1882), 3:55-56.

[16] James T. Mitchell and Henry Flanders, eds., *The Statutes at Large of Pennsylvania*, 18 vols. (Harrisburg: Clarence M. Busch, State Printer of Pennsylvania, 1896–1915), 9:279.

[17] *Olmsted*, 101: *Ross et al, Executors v. Rittenhouse*, 160, 161; Morris to Dunlap, April 22[?], 1779; Cranch, 5:120-21.

[18] Records of the Supreme Court of the United States, RG 267, case no. 29, NARA; J. C. Bancroft Davis, *United States Reports. Cases Adjudged in the U.S. Supreme Court at October Term, 1888*, vol. 131 (New York: Banks & Brothers, 1889), xxx; Cranch, 5:123-24. It is unclear if Rittenhouse received proceeds from the sale of just the cargo, or the ship as well. The latter had not yet been sold by January 4, 1779. It is also not certain what was done with respect to the shares of claimants other than the State. See *Sundry Documents*, 21; Middlebrook, 150; *Olmsted*, 142-45; *Ross et al, Executors v. Rittenhouse*, 2:160-68; *United States v. Judge Peters*, in Cranch 5:118-25.

[19] Cranch, 5:122-23; *Sundry Documents*, 20-22. See *JCC*, 13:281-86 for Congress's move to uphold the court's authority. See also *Sundry Documents*, 25, and Dallas, 3:82-85. For the report of the committee appointed on January 21, 1779 to review the January 19 report of the Committee on Appeals in the *Active* case see *JCC*, 13:86-92, 97, 134-37.

[20] *JCC*, 13:115; Thomas Burke to Joseph Reed, January 26, 1779, *LDC*, 11:516. See also: Carl Van Doren, *Secret History of the American Revolution* (New York: Viking Press, 1941) 176-77, 188-93; *LDC*, 4:44, and *passim*; *Proceedings of a General Court Martial for the Trial of Major General Arnold* (New York: J. Munsell, printer, 1865), 119-28. After a long series of hearings and a court-martial Arnold was acquitted of all but two minor complaints. George Washington punished him with a simple reprimand, but the fiery commander of Philadelphia was so hurt by the charges that he soon began his famous descent into treason.

[21] See *Penhallow, et al. v. Doane's Administrators*, 54-120; John Lowell to John Adams, August 4, 1777, in Charles Lowell, ed., "Letters of John Lowell and Others," *Historical Magazine* (September 1857), 1:258-59; Richard Francis Upton, *Revolutionary New Hampshire: An Account of the Social and Political Forces Underlying the Transition from Royal Province to American Commonwealth* (1936; reprinted New York: Octagon Books, 1971), 114-16.

[22] Daniel Roberdeau to Joseph Reed, February 13, 1779, *LDC*, 12:69-70.

[23] John Fell's Diary, February 24 and March 3, 1779, *LDC*, 12: 6-7, 140. See also *JCC*, 13:281-86; Committee of Congress to Joseph Reed, January 28, 1779, *LDC*, 11:516; Thomas Burke to Joseph Reed, March 12, 1779, *LDC*, 12:187; Roberdeau to Reed, February 13, 1779.

[24] Committee on Appeals Decree, March 11, 1779, *David Stevens &c. App[ellan]ts vs. John Henderson &c, App[ell]ees*, Appeals from the State of New Jersey, *LDC*, 12: 185. See also *JCC*, 13:44, 96, 251; PCC, 42, 3:375-78, and 96, 2:102; *NJD*, Ser. 2, 2:356-57, 396; and Committee on Appeals, December 15, 1778, *LDC*, 188, n1. The Rufus Gardner mentioned in the suit is undoubtedly not the same as the skipper of the Pennsylvania privateer *Enterprize* in 1779–1780, although the coincidence is of note.

[25] Morris to Reed, April 9, 1779, *LDC*, 13:320.

[26] Ibid. For information of Congress's involvement, see note for Committee on Appeals, December 15, 1778.

[27] *NRAR*, 104; John Fell's Diary, April 24 and 28, *LDC*, 12:378, 400.

[28] *LDC*, 12:519, n1.

[29] See *JCC*, 13:281-86; 14:507-10, 527-30, 607-8, 617, 624, 634-36; PCC, 1, 22:17-18; 41, 5:200-7; Committee on Appeals Decree, December 15, 1778, *LDC*, 11:343, n1; Committee of Congress to Joseph Reed, January 26, 1779, *LDC*, 11:517, n3.

[30] John Jay to Conrad-Alexandre Gérard, May 24, 1779, *LDC*, 12:518.

[31] William Ellery to William Greene, May 25, 1779, *LDC*, 12:528-30. See also *JCC*, 13:281-86; 14:508-10, 634-36; and John Jay to the States, May 25, 1779, *LDC*, 12:532. The New Hampshire prize case involved the ship *Lusanna* and is addressed in *Doane v. Penhallow*. The *Lusanna* case, like *Active*, was not settled until 1795 when the Supreme Court denied the state's jurisdiction, years after the case had already been the subject of a Court of Appeals hearing in 1783 and a congressional hearing in 1784. Committee on Appeals statement, June 16, 1779, case file no. 30, RG 267, NARA.

[32] *JCC*, 15:1122; Samuel Huntington to Jesse Root, October 1, 1779, *LDC*, 14:5-6; PCC, 19, 4:499. See also *LDC*, 11:341-43, 516-17, 525-26, and William Churchill Houston to Caleb Camp, November 12, 1779, *LDC*, 14:182-83, n2.

[33] *NRAR*, 119-21; Houston to Camp, November 12, 1779; *The Case of the Sloop Active &c.* (Philadelphia: Hall and Sellers, 1779); Charles Evans, *American Biography*, 12 vols. (Chicago: Privately printed, 1903–1934), no. 16,220.

[34] *NRAR*, 310, 329, 432.

[35] *Ross et al, Executors v. Rittenhouse*, 160-68; *United States v. Judge Peters*, 118-25.

[36] Middlebrook, 131; Cranch, 5:131; *Olmsted*, 142-45, *Ross et al, Executors v. Rittenhouse*, 160-68; *United States v. Judge Peters*, 118-25.

[37] Cranch, 5:124-26.

[38] Ibid., 127-35; *Statutes at Large of Pennsylvania*, 17:472-80, n11. See Cranch, 5:139-41 for Chief Justice Marshall's ready disposal of the Eleventh Amendment issue.

[39] *Aurora for the Country* (Philadelphia), April 11, 1803.

[40] Charles Warren, *The Supreme Court in United States History*, vol. 1 (Boston: Little, Brown, and Company, 1922), 375.

[41] In Olmsted's personal file accompanying his journal, which resides in the Frederick Law Olmsted Papers at the Library of Congress, is a brief narrative that was assembled for the meeting of the Pennsylvania Assembly at Lancaster in early 1808. The file outlines the circumstances preceding and leading to the mutiny

aboard *Active* and Olmsted's subsequent legal efforts to secure his and his colleagues share of the prize money.

42 Cranch, 5:126. In *U.S. v. Bright*, (Fed. Case No. 14647, 24 Fed. Case. 1232, 1236 [D. Pa. 1809]) Justice Bushrod Washington stated that the Eleventh Amendment refers only to suits "in law of equity" and does not mention admiralty, and therefore was not applicable.

43 Cranch, 5:116, 117, 136.

44 Middlebrook, 150, 151; Cranch, 5:132; *U.S. v. Bright.*

45 H. L. Carson, *The Case of the Sloop "Active"* (Philadelphia: Allen, Lane & Scott, 1893), 394-95.

46 The sum was reportedly "made subject to the orders of the governor" to permit him to carry into effect every engagement of the Commonwealth "touching the premises in such manner as may appear to him to be advisable, just and proper, and to meet all contingent expenses which may arise" in the execution of the earlier injunctions of the legislature. *Statutes at Large of Pennsylvania*, 18:1164, n11.

47 *U.S. v. Bright*; James Madison to Attorney General Caesar A. Rodney, in Warren, 385.

48 *Olmsted*, 150.

49 Davis, *United States Reports*, xxxiv, n1. See also Warren, 366-99. For the legal aspects see *United States v. Judge Peters* in Cranch 5:115-41; *Ross et al, Executors v. Rittenhouse*, 60-68; *Penhallow v. Doane*, 53-120; Charles Page Smith, *James Wilson, Founding Father, 1742–1798* (Chapel Hill: University of North Carolina Press for the Institute of Early American History and Culture, Williamsburg, VA, 1956), 124-28; Gideon Olmsted to Gentlemen of the Committee, January 28, 1808, in Olmsted Papers, LC; *Proceedings . . . for the Trial of Major General Arnold*, 119-28; *JCC*, 12:1168, 13:13-37, 86-92, 183, 252-53, 270-71, 281-86; Burnett, *passim*; *LDC*, vols. 11-13; and *Sundry Documents*; and Edward Dumbauld, "The case of the Mutinous Mariner," *Yearbook 1977 Supreme Court Historical Society*, http://www.supremecourthistory. org/myweb/77journal/dumbauld 77.htm

50 The Library of Congress published Olmsted's journal for the first time in its entirety in 1976. The journal, located in the Frederick Law Olmsted Papers Collection, contains miscellaneous materials, including a typescript noting only that it was presented to Frederick Law Olmsted by his great uncle Gideon.

XII. Riches Beyond Expectations

1 William Whipple to Dr. Josiah Bartlett, July 12, 1778, *Historical Magazine*, 6:74-75.

2 Richard D. Plunger, "'A Verse…to Remaining Idle Spectators:'" The Emergence of Loyalist Privateering During the American Revolution, 1775–1778," Vol. 2 (Doctoral Thesis: University of Maine, May 2002), 475; Louis F. Middlebrook, *Captain Gideon Olmsted, Connecticut Privateersman, Revolutionary War* (Salem, MA: Newcomb & Gauss Co., 1933), 5; and *South-Carolina and American General Gazette*, November 2, 1777.

3 Political Remedies on the Present State of Affairs in America . . . , March 17, 1778, and Germain to Clinton, March 8, 1778, Germain Papers, William L. Clements Library, Anne Arbor, MI.

[4] Ibid.

[5] Plunger, 476-77; Gerald Saxon Brown, *The American Secretary: The Colonial Policy of Lord George Germain, 1775–1778* (Ann Arbor: University of Michigan Press, [1963]), 149, 152-54, 157-59, 162; Observation on the Trade of America & its Effects in the Present Rebellion, May, 1779, Germain Papers, William L. Clements Library, Anne Arbor, MI.

[6] Gardner W. Allen, *A Naval History of the American Revolution*, 2 vols., (Williamstown, MA: Corner House Publishers, 1970, reprint 1913), 1:53.

[7] Franklin W. Kemp, *A Nest of Rebel Pirates*(Atlantic City, NJ: Batsto Citizens Committee, 1966), 6; *The Pennsylvania Packet*, September 3, 1778.

[8] *NJD*, Ser. 2, 1:599.

[9] Arthur D. Pierce, *Smuggler's Woods* (New Brunswick, NJ: Rutgers University Press, 1960), 61.

[10] Ibid, 58, 61.

[11] Edgar S. Maclay, *A History of American Privateers* (New York: D. Appleton and Co., 1910), viii. Maclay's commission figures for 1777, which have been generally accepted, do not correspond with the listing in *NRAR*, which indicated 69 vessels carrying a total of 675 guns. However, many vessels, though the precise number is unknown, were authorized by several states, most notably Massachusetts, under state rather than Continental commissions, so the number was undoubtedly substantially higher. See Allen, 1:45-47, for full discussion.

[12] Kemp, 31-32.

[13] Ibid.; William McMahon, *South Jersey Towns* (New Brunswick, NJ: Rutgers University Press, 1973), 205; Theodore Thayer, *Nathaniel Greene: Strategist of the Revolution* (New York: Twayne Publishers, 1960), 228. The 56 percent figure has been arrived at on the basis of announced public vendues published in New Jersey and Pennsylvania newspapers.

[14] These figures have been extrapolated from the total number of bonds published in *NRAR*. They are without question somewhat less than the actual total, which is likely to never be known, but serve as an indication of the immensity of the privateering industry.

[15] See *NRAR, passim*; Marquis de Chastellux, *Travels in North America in the Years 1780, 1781, and 1782*, Howard C. Rice, Jr., ed, 2 vols. (Chapel Hill, NC: University of North Carolina Press: 1963), 2:135-36.

[16] Ibid.

[17] Ibid., 226, 454; John Almon, ed., *The Remembrancer, or Impartial Repository of Public Events . . .* , 17 vols. (London: Printed for J. Almon, 1775–1784), 5:142. For a fine assessment of the Morris-Bingham relationship see Robert C. Alberts, *The Golden Voyage: The Life and Times of William Bingham*, 1752–1804 (Boston: Houghton Muffin Co., 1969), 52-66.

[18] Pierce, *Smugglers' Woods*, 60-61; Nathan Miller, *Sea of Glory: The Continental Navy Fights for Independence, 1775–1783*, (New York: David Mackay Company, Inc., 1974), 262; *NRAR*, 319.

[19] *NRAR, passim*.

[20] Andrew Sherburne, *Memoirs of Andrew Sherburne, a pensioner of the Revolution* (Utica, NY: W. Williams, 1828), 18-19.

[21] North Carolina Delegates to North Carolina Council of Safety, August 2, 1776, *LDC*, 4:609.

[22] John Adams to James Warren, October 5, 1776, *LDC*, 5:306; Executive Committee to John Hancock, December 30, 1776, *LDC*, 5:697; Benjamin Rush's Notes of Debates, February 14, 1777, *LDC*, 6:276; William Duer to the New York Convention, April 17, 1777, *LDC*, 6: 601.

[23] Edwin Salter, *A history of Monmouth and Ocean Counties, embracing a genealogical record of earliest settlers in Monmouth and Ocean counties and their descendants. The Indians: their language, manners, and customs . . .* (Bayonne, NJ: F. Gardner & Sons, Publishers, 1800), 193.

[24] Mark Kurlansky, *Salt: A World History* (New York: Penguin Books, 2002), 221-22.

[25] *New York Gazette and Weekly Mercury Extraordinary*, April 8, 1778; *New York Gazette and Weekly Mercury*, April 13 and 15, 1778.

[26] Ibid.; Salter, 192.

[27] *New York Gazette and Weekly Mercury Extraordinary*, April 8, 1778; *New York Gazette and Weekly Mercury*, April 13 and 15, 1778.

[28] *New Jersey Gazette*, May 27, 1778; *NJD*, Ser. 2, 2:257. That the British raid on Manasquan may have frightened some is suggested by the announcement of the sale of the salt works at Great Egg Harbor in July 1778. *The Pennsylvania Evening Post*, July 21, 1778.

[29] *The Pennsylvania Packet*, July 21, 1778; *New Jersey Gazette*, July 22, 1778.

[30] *NRAR*, 464, 468.

[31] George F. Emmons, *The Navy of the United States, From the Commencement, 1775 to 1753 with a Brief History of Each Vessel's Fate and Service as Appears Upon Record* (Washington, DC: Printed by Gideon & Co., 1853), 163; Pierce, *Smugglers' Woods*, 62; *NJD*, Ser. 2, 2:336; *NRAR*, 464.

[32] Lewis T. Stevens, "Cape May Naval Activities in the Revolution," *Cape May County Historical Society Journal*, 2:138; Emmons, 164; Pierce, *Smugglers' Woods*, 62.

[33] *New York Gazette and Weekly Mercury*, September 7, 1778. It is of note that no vessel named *Glory of America* is listed in *NRAR*, which is exemplary of how incomplete the extant data base on privateers is.

[34] *New York Gazette and Weekly Mercury*, September 7, 1778. *Recovery* and her cargo consisting of a general assortment of dry goods, china, Queen's ware, beef, porter, pork, bar iron, cordage, and cables were sold at Mays Landing on November 11, 1778. *The Pennsylvania Packet*, November 3, 1778.

[35] *NJD*, Ser. 2, 2:336, 469; *The Pennsylvania Packet*, September 5, 1778.

[36] *New Jersey Gazette*, September 2, 1778.

[37] William Whipple to James Bartlett, July 12, 1778, "Letter." "Stray leaves from an Autograph Collection: Correspondence of Josiah Bartlett, of N.H. during the American Revolution." *Historical Magazine*, (March 1862), 6:73-78, reprinted in Allen, 1:48-49.

[38] Pierce, *Smugglers' Woods*, 46 and 64, documents the Ball-Pettit-Cox interest, but the bond record, dated July 16, 1778, indicates Joseph Carson as owner. Moreover, the

$10,000 bond money was placed by Carson and the ship's commander, David Stevens. As was so often the case, it is quite likely that Carson was serving as a front for the Egg Harbor triumvirate, some of whom, owing to their public service positions, did not wish to be publicly associated with privateering. *NRAR*, 249.

[39] [Carl Leopold Baurmeister], *Revolution in America: Confidential Letters and Journals 1776-1784 of Adjutant General Major Baurmeister of the Hessian Forces*, Bernard A. Uhlendorf, trans. and ann. (New Brunswick, NJ: Rutgers University Press, 1957), 223; *New York Gazette and Weekly Mercury*, August 31 and November 30, 1778.

[40] *New Jersey Gazette*, September 2, 1778. The second of the two prizes taken by Stevens in his venture against the Irish Sea fleet has often been identified as *Major Pearson*. William S. Stryker, in his paper *The Affair at Egg Harbor, New Jersey, October 15, 1778* (Trenton: Naar & Harr, 1894), 3, claims the vessel was indeed *Major Pearson* under manifest from London, but provides no source for this information. The first vessel, *Venus*, is easily traced and is noted in the American press when mentioned as being placed up for sale at public vendue, and later by the British commanders sent to destroy Chestnut Neck in October 1778. Two vessels bearing the name *Venus*, one of 309 tons and a crew of 20 under the command of Captain Richard Thursby, and a second of 256 tons and a crew of 17 under Master John Wilson, are listed in Musters of British Transports for 1776–1778. The Naval Storekeeper of New York reports both vessels on these rolls and both disappear from the rolls after October 1778. Thus, it is possible that one of these may be the same as captured by Stevens. Extensive search, however, has failed to turn up any vessel named *Major Pearson*, either in Admiralty accounts, in private correspondence, or newspapers. PRO, Admiralty Miscellanea, 49/2, 49/3, 49/4, 49/5, 49/6, 49/7, LC Microfilms.

[41] *NJD*, Ser. 2, 2:403. When the cargo saved from *Venus* just prior to the attack on Chestnut Neck was again put on auction at Cooper's ferry on December 15, 1778, along with another prize taken by *Chance* named *Good Intent*, the inventory of items advertised included: "some small guns, swivels, howit[zers], 6d and 10d nails, a few pieces of crocus, and thin linen fit for sleeve linings, furniture and other brushes, Epsoms salts, Saddlers tacks, china, silver, ebony, buck and bone handled knives and forks; mens and womens shoes, a number of ear-rings and necklaces, watch ands clock springs, watch crystals, watchmakers tools, and a variety of other articles, being part of the Prize Ship *VENUS*" as well as a few "quarter chests of Hysons and Sonchong Teas; also a quantity of Salt of different kinds, Clarets, Portugal and sundry other Wines." *The Pennsylvania Packet*, December 12, 1778.

[42] *NJD*, Ser. 2, 2:426, 458; *New Jersey Gazette*, September 2, 1778.

[43] *NJD*, Ser. 2, 345-46, 358-59, 363; *NRAR*, 489; *New Jersey Gazette*, September 30, 1778; Salter, 208, 211; Pierce, *Smugglers' Woods*, 40-41; *New York Gazette and Weekly Mercury*, September 28, 1778.

[44] *NJD*, Ser. 2, 345-46; *Princess Mary* commission, July 18, 1778, PCC (Ships' Bonds required for Letters of Marque and Reprisal, 1776–1783) 196, vol. 12, p. 19; Salter, 194.

[45] Ibid.

[46] Baurmeister, 211-12; Benson J. Lossing, *The Pictorial Field Book of the American Revolution*, 2 vols. (New York: Harper and Bros., 1868), 2:84, n1; Paul Nelson, *Sir Charles Grey, First Earl Grey: Royal Soldier, Family Patriarch* (Madison, NJ: Fairleigh Dickinson University Press, 1996), 64.

[47] Duane Hamilton Hurd, *History of Bristol County, Massachusetts, Part I* (Philadelphia: J.W. Lewis, 1883), 57-58; Lossing, 2:84, n1; Baurmeister, 212; Daniel Rickerson, *The History of New Bedford, Bristol County, Massachusetts*, New Bedford: self published, 1858), 285-286; Nelson, 65.

[48] Lossing, 2:84, n1, Rickertson, 74-75, 290; Hurd, 63; Baurmeister, 212.

[49] Nelson, 66.

[50] Ibid.; Ricketson, 285-86; Lossing, 2:84.

[51] Allen, 1:333, 334.

[52] Baurmeister, 223.

XIII. Skulking Banditti

[1] George Washington to Comte d'Estaing, September 19, 1778, *The Writings of George Washington from the Original Manuscript Sources 1745–1799*, John C. Fitzpatrick, ed., 39 vols. (Washington, DC: U.S. Government printing Office, 1931–1944), 13:471-72.

[2] List, Disposition and Condition of His Majesty's Vessels Employed in America, Exclusive of the Squadron with Vice Adm. Byron and That Under orders to Sail with Como. Hotham, October 14, 1778, Gambier Papers, Admiralty 1/489, Transcripts, LC; PRO, Admiralty Miscellanea, Masters of Transports, Admiralty 49/3, 49/4, 49/5, Microfilm, LC; The Conduct of Vice Admiral Graves in North America in 1774, 1775 and January 1776, 1:94, Transcripts, LC; Samuel Steele Smith, *Fight for the Delaware 1777* (Monmouth Beach, NJ: Philip Freneau Press, 1970), 46. *Vigilant* is reported as having arrived in America on May 19, 1775. *Greenwich* does not appear on the List of October 14, 1778 as a participant in the Egg Harbor expedition but is specifically mentioned by Captain Colins in his reports to Admiral Gambier. She, like *Cornwallis*, *Independence*, *Comet*, and *Zebra*, is also mentioned by Captain Robert Fanshawe in his report of September 11, 1778, to Admiral Howe as participants in the New Bedford expedition. Her dimensions, strength, etc., during the Egg Harbor operation that have been cited by the author are presumed to be the same as recorded on a later list of April 3, 1779. See: List, Disposition and . . . , October 14, 1778; Captain Robert Fanshawe to Admiral Robert Howe, September 11, 1778; An Account of the State and Condition of His Majesty's Ships and Vessels Under the Command of Rear Admiral Gambier. 3d April 1779, Gambier Papers, Admiralty 1/489, Transcripts, LC.

[3] List, Disposition and . . . , October 14, 1778; A Journal of the Proceedings on Board His Majesty's Sloop *Nautilus* [hereafter *Nautilus* Journal], PRO, Admiralty 51/630. Captain Belcher assumed command of *Nautilus* from Captain John Collins on May 23, 1778.

[4] List of Captures and Recaptures Made by Private Armed Vessels belonging to the

Port of New York Between the 27th of May 1778 and the 18th of February 1779, Gambier Papers, PRO, Admiralty 1/489, Transcripts, LC; List of Private Ships and Vessels of War belonging to the Port of New York, Now at Sea, Gambier Papers, PRO, Admiralty 1/489, Transcripts, LC; *The Pennsylvania Evening Post*, September 25, 1778. It has been erroneously assumed and widely accepted that the *Experiment* which participated in the Egg Harbor expedition was HMS *Experiment*, a 50-gun man-of-war commanded by Captain Henry Wallace, and was the same vessel responsible for the capture of the Continental Navy frigate *Raleigh* on September 28, 1778. This error stems from a letter published by Franklin Kemp in *A Nest of Rebel Pirates* written by A. P. Young of the British Public Record Office. The letter states that HMS *Experiment*'s participation in the expedition, a point championed by Kemp, is only conjecture, but advised that he should include it anyway, which was done. The inclusion is incorrect for the following reasons: (1) HMS *Experiment* engaged *Raleigh* late in the evening of September 27, 1778, near Penobscot Bay, Maine, approximately 450 nautical miles from the expedition rendezvous point off Staten Island. The squadron was to sail on September 29, thus giving *Experiment* only two days to join the expedition, a feat of note even in perfect sailing conditions. The weather, however, was extremely bad and prohibited not only a delay in departure but also a general shut down of maritime traffic on the Atlantic coast, especially between New England and New York. Under these conditions, it seems unlikely that *Experiment* could have joined the flotilla. (2) Henry Colins, commanding a 16-gun sloop-of-war and in charge of the expedition, bore the complimentary title of captain. Wallace, as commander of a 4th-rate man-of-war and post captain, was senior to Colins and would never have been allocated a role subordinate to him. Colins posted all naval reports to Gambier, with no mention of Wallace whatsoever. Extensive investigation by this author of existing Admiralty records have failed to reveal any indication supporting Kemp's claim. Indeed, HMS *Experiment* is not included on the October 14, 1778, list of participants. The New York privateer *Experiment* is considered a superior candidate for the following reasons: (1) She was a well-fitted and armed vessel of fourteen guns and manned by an experienced crew. She was certainly capable of aggressive action (witness the capture of a superior 20-gun French ship); (2) the Admiralty readily employed privateers as transports when necessary and Captain Colins frequently speaks of the "private armed vessels" (plural), not just a single privateer, in his squadron; (3) the draft of a 50-gun man-of-war such as HMS *Experiment* would have prohibited her from crossing the bar at Little Egg Harbor. *Zebra*, a vessel of only 306 tons burthen and ninety-seven feet in length, with a draft of thirteen feet, and *Nautilus*, of similar size and draft, both ran aground entering and exiting the inlet. A 50-gun ship with a draft of sixteen to eighteen feet would have found entry nearly impossible, and ascent up the Mullica implausible. The privateer *Experiment*, a vessel of only 100 tons, would have had no difficulty crossing the bar or ascending the river as far as Chestnut Neck. HMS *Experiment* was surrendered to d'Estaing's fleet in Georgia in 1779. Franklin W. Kemp, *A Nest of Rebel Pirates* (Atlantic City, NJ: Batsto Citizens Committee, 1966), 136; Gardner W. Allen, *A Naval*

History of the American Revolution, 2 vols. (Williamstown, MA: Corner House Publishers, 1970, [1913]), 1:316-19; List of Private Ships and Vessels, Gambier Papers; *The Pennsylvania Evening Post*, September 28, 1778; Captain Henry Colins to Rear Admiral James Gambier, October 9, 1778, Gambier Papers, PRO, Admiralty 1/489, Transcripts, LC; *NDAR*, 5: 808-9.

[5] Colins to Gambier, October 9, 1778; List, Disposition and Condition ..., October 14, 1778; Kemp, 15, lists two transports and tenders as well as *Experiment* and *Grandby* as participating in the expedition. A close reading of Colins's dispatches, however, indicates *Experiment* and *Grandby* were the transports. *Comet* was listed as a member of the force in one situation report of Royal Navy ships in North American waters but was never mentioned in the official correspondence from Henry Colins as the remainder of the ships were. It has thus been assumed that this vessel did not participate in the operation.

[6] General Henry Clinton to Lord George Germain, October 25, 1778, *NJD*, Ser. 2, 3:155.

[7] Christopher Ward, *The War of the Revolution*, 2 vols. (New York: The Macmillan Company, 1952), 2:616; Clinton to Germain, October 25, 1778, *The Royal Gazette*, March 10, 1779, in *NJD*, Ser. 2, 3:154-59.

[8] *The Pennsylvania Gazette*, October 7, 1778; *New York Gazette and Weekly Mercury*, October 5, 1778; Ward, 2: 616-17.

[9] Kemp, 14, stated that on January 1, 1778, the New York garrison included five battalions of New Jersey Volunteers. He wrote that on March 24 the main British Army garrison at Philadelphia included the Second Battalion of the New Jersey Volunteers with troop strength of ten officers and 130 rank. On August 15, six weeks before the Egg Harbor expedition, a return cited by Kemp, without noting sources, indicates the Third Battalion was comprised of the following: Isaac Allen, commanding officer, 25 officers and staff, 194 other ranks fit for duty, fourteen sick, sixty-four on command [assigned to other units], and fifty-two prisoners held by the rebels. Kemp asserts that by deducting the fifty-two prisoners and the one hundred employed on the expedition there must have been 198 remaining behind on garrison duty. A later return of the Third Battalion, in fact, was drawn up on August 24, 1778, and indicates the following: Lt. Colonel Isaac Allen commanding, eleven commissioned officers, 194 rank and file fit for duty, fourteen sick, forty-nine on command, fifteen recruiting or on furlough, and fifty-two held prisoner by the rebels. Thus we can see the total number 336 on August 24 rather than the 350 Kemp claims for August 15. Deducting the fifty-two held prisoner, the hundred employed on the expedition, and the fifteen sent into the country recruiting or on furlough, the total left at the camp on Staten Island must have numbered 169, barely half the total battalion strength (sans one deserter and one dead man still carried on the rolls). New Jersey Loyalist Muster Rolls, 1777–1782, Photocopy, LC.

[10] Captain Henry Colins to Admiral James Gambier, October 15, 1778, Gambier Papers, PRO, Admiralty 1/489, Transcripts, LC; An Account of the State and Condition of His Majesty's Ships ..., 3d April 1779. *Vigilant* had last been cleaned on June 1, 1777; *Greenwich* was cleaned in August but was still termed

a "leaky" vessel; *Cornwallis* "wants repairs"; and *Halifax*, which later joined the expedition, was listed as "Unfit for Sea."

11 *New Jersey Gazette*, October 7, 1778; Lord Stirling to George Washington, October 11, 1778, Washington Papers, LC.

12 *Nautilus* Journal, October 2–4, 1778; Colins to Gambier, October 9, 1778.

13 *Nautilus* Journal, October 2–4, 1778.

14 Ibid.; The Present Disposition of His Majesty's Ships and Vessels in Sea Paye 1st June 1776, PRO, Admiralty 8/52; Colins to Gambier, October 9, 1778. According to an April 3, 1778 disposition muster, a crew of forty manned *Halifax*. Unfortunately, even such authorities as Howard I. Chapelle have often confused the brig *Halifax* that participated in the Egg Harbor expedition with an earlier vessel of the same name. HM Schooner *Halifax* ran aground and was lost on a ridge of rocks near Machias, Maine, on February 15, 1775, but is often mentioned as being one and the same as Quarme's brig. In 1779, Quarme also lost his ship (the second *Halifax* lost during the Revolution), and faced a Court Martial. In 1780, the Continental Navy sloop *Ranger* was captured and taken into the Royal Navy and renamed *Halifax*, becoming the third vessel to bear the name. Lieutenant Joseph Nunn to Vice Admiral Samuel Graves, March 1, 1775, PRO, Admiralty 1/485, Transcript, LC; Howard I. Chapelle, *History of American Sailing Ships* (New York: W.W. Norton & Company, Inc., 1935), 33, 577; An Account of the State and Condition of His Majesty's Ships . . . , 3d April 1779.

15 Colins to Gambier, October 9, 1778; *Nautilus* Journal, October 4, 1778.

16 Colins to Gambier, October 9, 1778; *Nautilus* Journal, October 5, 1778.

17 Ibid.

18 *Nautilus* Journal, October 5–6, 1778.

19 *The Pennsylvania Evening Post*, October 7, 1778.

20 Colins to Gambier, October 9, 1778; General Benedict Arnold to George Washington, October 11, 1778, Washington Papers, LC; *NJD*, Ser. 2, 2:469. A swivel gun was reportedly recovered from one of several hulks found in the Mullica River off Chestnut Neck on August 8, 1954 by James A. Kendell of Chestnut Neck. Other evidence of artillery has been located on the river bottom by the author during archaeological surveys undertaken in August and September 1974.

21 Arnold to Washington, October 11, 1778; *The Pennsylvania Evening Post*, October 9, 1778; Colins to Gambier, October 9 1778; *The Pennsylvania Packet*, November, 1778. The number of ships sunk, scuttled, or destroyed at Chestnut Neck varies with the source. The author has chosen to accept Colins's account simply because he was there.

22 *Nautilus*, Journal, October 6, 1778.

23 Colins to Gambier, October 9, 1778; Captain Patrick Ferguson to General Henry Clinton, October 10, 1778, *NJD*, Ser. 2, 3:155-57.

24 *Nautilus* Journal, October 6, 1778; Colins to Gambier, October 9, 1778. According to reports received at Philadelphia, the British employed six flat-bottomed boats in the assault on Chestnut Neck. Arnold to Washington, October 11, 1778.

25 Colins to Gambier, October 9, 1778; Ferguson to Clinton, October 10, 1778. William S. Stryker, *The Affair at Egg Harbor, New Jersey, October 15, 1778* (Trenton:

Naar & Harr, 1894), 8, asserts that there was a thick fog surrounding the area at the time of the attack, but this author has found no evidence to substantiate the claim. The *Nautilus* Journal, in fact, states that the weather conditions were moderate and fair with no mention of fog at all.

26 Captain Patrick Ferguson to Admiral James Gambier, October 19, 1778, Gambier Papers; Ferguson to Clinton, October 10, 1778.

27 Ferguson to Clinton, October 10, 1778.

28 Colins to Gambier, October 9, 1778.

29 Ferguson to Clinton, October 10, 1778; *Nautilus* Journal, October 7, 1778. Micajah Smith's estate was placed up for sale on January 26, 1779, and the description of the items and buildings belonging to him and sold at the time indicate that he was spared the destruction wrought upon others by the British in October 1778. McMahon relates an allegation that another building, the homestead of one Benjamin Johnson, survived the attack and remained in existence until 1956. The folktale was related to McMahon by Johnson's great-great-great granddaughter Sara Wilson and goes as follows: "When young volunteer James Bell approached the building with a torch he saw Benjamin Johnson's daughter Michele run inside. While he was still trying to find her, he and his companions were ordered to return to the beach. After the Revolution, unable to forget the incident, he returned to Chestnut Neck, sought out the girl, and married her. At that time he learned how Michele had been able to elude him in 1778. She had escaped through a secret tunnel from the basement to the nearby creek." Franklin Kemp pursued this account and discovered that James Bell actually did exist but had served with the Pennsylvania Line, not the New Jersey Volunteers. Bell died in 1831 at the age of 74 and his remains lie buried beneath the Smith's Meeting House, Port Republic, New Jersey, alongside the grave of Micajah Smith and other Revolutionary War patriots of Little Egg Harbor. As for the Johnson House, Kemp, National Parks historical architect Charles E. Peterson, and author Jack Boucher conducted an examination of the remains of the fire-wracked structure in 1961 and concluded the building had been constructed in the 1830s. *The Pennsylvania Packet*, January 26, 1779; William McMahon, *South Jersey Towns* (New Brunswick, NJ: Rutgers University Press, 1973), 204; Kemp, 94-96.

30 Captain Henry Colins to Captain Patrick Ferguson, October 9, 1778, Gambier Papers; Ferguson to Clinton, October 10, 1778. Kemp asserts that the British established a defensive perimeter around Chestnut Neck. Although such a move would have been likely, there is no documentary evidence to support the conclusion.

31 Stirling to Washington, October 11, 1778.

32 Ibid.; *New Jersey Gazette*, October 7, 1778; Arnold to Washington, October 11, 1778; *JCC*, 12: 983-84; Major Richard Howell to Brigadier General William Maxwell, October 13, 1778, Washington Papers, LC.

33 The province of New Jersey, divided into east and west, commonly called the Jerseys / engraved & published by Wm. Faden, Charing Cross, December 1st 1778 ; this map has been drawn . . . by Bernard Ratzer . . . and . . . by Gerard Banker. 2nd ed. with considerable improvements. [London: Faden], 1778.

34 Samuel Hazard, et al., eds, *Pennsylvania Archives* (Philadelphia: Printed by J. Severns & Co., 1852-56; Harrisburg, 1874), Ser. 1, 7:943-46. Joseph Reed, President of the Supreme Executive Council of Pennsylvania, wrote concerning the strength of Procter's regiment: "The defective state of the regiment when it was lately called into service to go to Egg-Harbour, I spoke of by respect, tho' the Board of War on a late occasion confirmed it." Ibid., 7:135.

35 *AA*, Ser. 5, 2:80; Mark Mayo Boatner III, *Encyclopedia of the American Revolution* (New York: David McKay Company, Inc., 1966), 900-1.

36 Colins to Gambier, October 9, 1778; Ferguson to Clinton, October 10, 1778.

XIV. No Quarter Be Given

1 Captain Henry Colins to Rear Admiral James Gambier, October 9, 1778, Gambier Papers, PRO, Admiralty 1/489, Transcripts, LC.

2 A Journal of the Proceedings on Board His Majesty's Sloop *Nautilus* [hereafter *Nautilus* Journal], PRO, Admiralty 51/630, October 6, 1778.

3 Ibid.; Captain Patrick Ferguson to General Henry Clinton, October 10, 1778, *NJD*, Ser. 2, 3:155-157; Kemp states that one of the properties destroyed belonged to Eli Mathis, Sr., which later became the farm of Ebenezer Sooy. Sooy passed his holdings on and the farm eventually became the property of Arthur Cramer, ancestor of the proprietor of the Cramer estate, which included the site upon which Payne's Tavern once stood, and where numerous prize vendues were held between 1776 and 1782. Stryker claims the British disembarked near the mouth of Bass River, on the property of Eli Mathis, and destroyed his "dwelling and farm building with all their contents," then a salt works, a sawmill, and a dozen houses of well-known patriots. This would place the location of Chestnut Neck some distance from the site currently acknowledged as the town, the location of which has been determined by archaeological investigation. Neither Kemp nor Stryker cite the source of their information. It seems more likely that the incursions were made further down the Mullica, near Great Bay, since the rebels were already closing in on Chestnut Neck again, making British operations in that vicinity quite hazardous. The *New York Gazette and Weekly Mercury* even stated: "Salt Works *on the Bay* were also effectually destroyed." Stryker has also erred in stating that the salt works were destroyed *before* the British began their return to the fleet, and that it was *Zebra* and *Grandby* that were first stranded instead of *Greenwich* and *Grandby*. In both strandings Colins's report of October 9 specifically indicates the latter were the ships involved. Franklin W. Kemp, *A Nest of Rebel Pirates* (Atlantic City, NJ: Batsto Citizens Committee, 1966), 35, 106; William S. Stryker, *The Affair at Egg Harbor, New Jersey, October 15, 1778. . . . Read July 3, 1894, at the dedication of a memorial tablet, erected on the field of the massacre, by the Society of the Cincinnati in the state of New Jersey, and at the annual meeting of the society on the following day.* (Trenton, Naar, Day & Naar, 1894), 10; Captain Henry Colins to Rear Admiral James Gambier, October 9, 1778, Gambier Papers, PRO, Admiralty 1/489, Transcripts, LC.

4 Ferguson to Clinton, October 10, 1778.

5 Stryker, 10.

[6] Colins to Gambier, October 9, 1778; *Nautilus* Journal, October 8, 1778.

[7] Ibid.

[8] Benedict Arnold to George Washington, October 11, 1778, Washington Papers, LC; Lord Stirling to George Washington, October 11, 1778, Washington Papers, LC.

[9] Colins to Gambier, October 9, 1778.

[10] Ibid.

[11] Ibid.; *Nautilus* Journal, October 9, 1778.

[12] Ferguson to Clinton, October 10, 1778.

[13] *Nautilus* Journal, October 11, 1778.

[14] *The Pennsylvania Evening post*, October 9, 1778; Arnold to Washington, October 11, 1778; Major Richard Howell to Brigadier General William Maxwell, October 13, 1778, Washington Papers, LC.

[15] Stryker, 13-14.

[16] *Nautilus* Journal, October 11, 1778.

[17] Ibid., October 12, 1778; Kemp, 82-83; [Carl Leopold Baurmeister], *Revolution in America: Confidential Letters and Journals 1776–1784 of Adjutant General Major Baurmeister of the Hessian Forces*, Bernard A. Uhlendorf, trans. and ann. (New Brunswick, NJ: Rutgers University Press, 1957), 227, n109; Paul Bentalou, *"Reply to Judge Johnson's Remarks on an article in the North American Review, relating to Count Pulaski"* (Baltimore: Printed by J.D. Toy, 1826), 36-37. Reports pertaining to the number of men that deserted with Juliat vary. The *Nautilus* Journal states that an officer, presumably Juliat, and four men were brought aboard the British fleet. Pulaski's report of October 16 to the Continental Congress states that Juliat went away with five men. Ferguson's report of October 15 claims that a captain and six men came aboard the fleet. At Juliat's hearing for desertion at New York, it was stated that a sergeant and four men accompanied him. Many years later, Bentalou claimed that Juliat deserted with only two accomplices. Baurmeister, 228, who appears to have been sympathetic to Juliat, stated in his journal that "Youth and his embarrassment for letting the rebels persuade him to go over to them could let him make no better resolve than to leave the nefarious rebels, in spite of having to face much danger, for like the old Roman they now talk seriously about extraordinary deeds and inflict much more cruel punishments without any consideration."

[18] Captain Patrick Ferguson to General Henry Clinton, October 15, 1778, in Stryker, 31-32.

[19] Captain Henry Colins to Admiral James Gambier, October 15, 1778, Gambier Papers, PRO, Admiralty 1/489, Transcripts, LC; Ferguson to Clinton, October 15, 1778.

[20] Ferguson to Clinton, October 15, 1778.

[21] The *Nautilus* Journal states the date as October 15, but this differentiation is due to naval time as opposed to standard time. Naval time began the day at noon instead of midnight and was employed by the Royal Navy well into the 19th Century.

[22] Stryker, 17.

[23] Ferguson to Clinton, October 15, 1778.

[24] Pulaski's report of October 16 published in *The Pennsylvania Evening Post* of October 20, 1778 states that the pickets were "attacked with fury" and "lost a few men retreating." Stryker, 17, claims, again without citing his sources, that some accounts reported that only one picket was posted and he ended up being captured before he could fire his piece. He also claimed that other reports indicated that the lone picket was killed. This author has found no evidence to support either statement.

[25] Ferguson to Clinton, October 15, 1778; Bentalou, 36-37.

[26] Pulaski to President of Congress, October 16, 1778, in *Pennsylvania Packet*, October 20, 1778.

[27] Ferguson to Clinton, October 15, 1778.

[28] Pulaski to President of Congress, October 16, 1778.

[29] Ferguson to Clinton, October 15, 1778; *Nautilus* Journal, October 15, 1778; Stryker, 22, claims that the British departed from Osborn Island at 10 a.m. even though the *Nautilus* Journal states that the troops were already boarding the fleet at that moment. Considering that the distance between the fleet anchorage and the island had obliged the British, as reported by Ferguson on October 15, to undertake a trip of five hours duration before they could land, it is probable that their return would take equally as long. If so, this would have placed the hour of their retreat from the island at roughly 5 a.m. The distance from the original landing place on Osborn Island to the Ridgeway farm is roughly three miles. Subtracting the marching time, at double time, to and from the beach in the dark and dimness of early morning, the actual fight at Ridgeway's could only have lasted a very few minutes. Kemp, echoing Stryker, states: "According to Ferguson's report the British force left the south side of Osborn Island about 10 a.m. on the morning of October 15." In fact, Fergusson never mentions his departure time.

[30] Stryker, 21.

[31] Ferguson to Clinton, October 15, 1778; Bentalou, 37; Pulaski to President of Congress, October 16, 1778.

[32] *Nautilus* Journal, October 15, 1778; Colins to Gambier, October 15, 1778.

[33] Ibid.

[34] *Nautilus* Journal, October 16, 17, and 18, 1778; Colins to Gambier, October 15, 1778.

[35] *Nautilus* Journal, October 20, 1778; Kemp, 51, states that *Nautilus* was one of the first ships of the squadron to get underway. There is no evidence to support this assertion.

[36] *Nautilus* Journal, October 20, 1778. Kemp, 51, claims that soon after 8 a.m. Captain Colins ordered all of *Zebra*'s personnel to board *Nautilus* and *Vigilant*. Although the move seems logical, there is no evidence to support the statement.

[37] Ibid. Kemp, 51, claims that Captain Belcher entered into his journal the latitude of the fleet as 39° 43'. This information does not appear in the journal.

[38] *Nautilus* Journal, October 22 and 23, 1778.

[39] Ibid., October 24, 1778. An almost complete set of Admiralty transcriptions concerning the proceedings of courts martial held in North America for Royal Navy vessel losses during the American Revolution are on deposit in the Public Record Office, Kew, London. They unfortunately do not contain the proceedings concerning the loss of *Zebra*. See Reports of Court-Martial, Admiralty, 1/5307-11, 5314-16, 5318-19, PRO, London.

[40] Eric Robson, ed., *Letters from America, 1773–1780; being the letters of a Scots officer, Sir James Murray, to his home during the war of American independence*, (Manchester, UK: Manchester University Press, 1951), 61.

[41] Admiral James Gambier to Philip Stephens, October 20, 1778, Gambier Papers, Admiralty 1/489, Transcripts, LC.

[42] Kemp, 78, states Colins was soon afterwards promoted to the command of HMS *Victory*, a 1st-rate ship-of-the-line destined to become one of the most famed men-of-war in history, albeit under another commander named Nelson. Such a promotion for a sloop-of-war commander to that of a 1st-rate, 2160-ton, 100-gun ship-of-the-line in only five months, in violation of time-honored progression through seniority is improbable. Henry Preston and David Lyon, *Navies of the American Revolution* (Englewood Cliffs, NJ; Prentice-Hall Incorporated, 1975), 96-111.

[43] See Lyman C. Draper, *Kings Mountain And Its Heroes* (New York: Dauber and Pine Bookshops, 1929), and J. D. Bailey, *Commanders At Kings Mountain* (Gaffney, S.C.: E.H. DeCamp, 1929) for the subsequent military career of Patrick Ferguson.

[44] George Washington to Benedict Arnold, October 23, 1778, *The Writings of George Washington from the Original Manuscript Sources 1745–1799*, John C. Fitzpatrick, ed., 39 vols. (Washington, DC: U.S. Government Printing Office, 1931–1944), 13:168-69.

[45] Boatner, Mark Mayo III, *Encyclopedia of the American Revolution* (New York: David McKay Company, Inc., 1966), 900-1.

[46] Kemp, 83-84.

[47] *The Pennsylvania Packet*, January 2 and 26, 1779; *NJD*, Ser. 2, 3:264. The advertisements announcing the sale of the Thomas Heston and Company salt works complex on Faulkinburgh's Island at Little Egg Harbor detail the considerable extent the works had grown during the war. The main building, being eighty feet long and twenty feet wide, had recently been rebuilt of the best pine and cedar, and contained a giant wrought iron pan capable of holding 3,000 gallons, as well as 5,000 weight of cast iron pans, "the whole set on stone walls, built of fine mortar; a quantity of salt baskets, casks, &c." There was also a new boat and fishing seine, and 300 to 400 cords of ready cut wood. "The situation is healthy and pleasant, and allowed by judges the best [adjusted?] for profitable works of any kind on the shore, having the advantage of water courses for wood, and a large and excellent salt pond within ten yards of the house. The place abounds with fish and fowl." *NJD*, Ser. 2, 3: 264.

[48] *New Jersey Gazette*, October 23, 1778; *NJD*, Ser. 2, 2:514.

XV. Sixteen Strong

[1] *The Pennsylvania Packet*, November 5, 1778.

[2] Ibid., December 12, 1778; *New Jersey Gazette*, December 23, 1778.

[3] Ibid., March 27, 1779.

[4] Ibid., November 5, 1778.

[5] *New York Gazette and Weekly Mercury*, November 2, 1778.

[6] *New Jersey Gazette*, December 23, 1778.

[7] Ibid., December 9, 1778.

[8] Ibid., December 23, 1778; *New York Gazette and Weekly Mercury*, November 30, 1778; JCC 8:8.

[9] *NRAR*, 344, 421; *New Jersey Gazette*, December 23, 1778; PCC (Ships' Bonds required for Letters of Marque and Reprisal, 1776–1783), 196, 8:8. The *New York Gazette and Weekly Mercury*, November 30, 1778, reported that *Hornet* was armed with six guns, but later vendue announcements state that she carried eight 4-pounders and six swivels. The vendue announcements are undoubtedly the more accurate of the two. Pratt's *Princess Mary* was commissioned June 18, 1778.

[10] *New York Gazette and Weekly Mercury*, November 30, 1778.

[11] *New Jersey Gazette*, December 16 and 23, 1778. Captain Conn is incorrectly identified as Captain Sion in early American press accounts of the capture.

[12] Gardner W. Allen, *A Naval History of the American Revolution*, 2 vols. (Williamstown, MA: Corner House Publishers, 1970 [1906]) 1:49-50.

[13] [Carl Leopold Baurmeister], *Revolution in America: Confidential Letters and Journals 1776–1784 of Adjutant General Major Baurmeister of the Hessian Forces*, Bernard A. Uhlendorf, trans. and ann. (New Brunswick, NJ: Rutgers University Press, 1957), 247-48.

[14] Edwin Salter, *A history of Monmouth and Ocean Counties, embracing a genealogical record of earliest settlers in Monmouth and Ocean counties and their descendants. The Indians: their language, manners, and customs . . .* (Bayonne, NJ: F. Gardner & Sons, Publishers, 1890), 82, 83, 194, 196.

[15] Baurmeister, 271-72.

[16] Ibid.

[17] *The Pennsylvania Packet*, July 24 and August 7, 1779.

[18] Robert W. Coakley and Stetson Conn, *The War of the American Revolution: Narrative, Chronology, and Bibliography* (Washington, DC: Center of Military History United States Army, 1975), 104.

[19] Baurmeister, 309. The description of the ensuing travails of *Triton*, her Hessian passengers, and Andreas Wiederholt are excerpted from M.D. Leonard and C. Grosse, *American Germanica: Tagebuch des Capt. Wiederholdt Vom 7 October 1776 Bis 7 December 1780* (New York and London: The Macmillan Company, 1902), 70-86.

[20] Yelverton Taylor was thrice in command of *Mars*, in September 1778 and in July and October 1779. The vessel was owned at Philadelphia by Thomas Leaming and Co. Taylor placed bond for all three commissions, once with Leaming and twice with Joseph C. Fisher, who were listed as owners. *Mars* was armed with

fourteen guns and normally carried a crew of sixty, but when she was lost there were only fifty aboard. *NRAR*, 386.

21 Wiederholdt, 86; *New Jersey Gazette*, October 6, 1779.

22 Baurmeister, 308; George F. Emmons, *The Navy of the United States, From the Commencement, 1775 to 1753 with a Brief History of Each Vessel's Fate and Service as Appears Upon Record* (Washington, DC: Gideon & Co., 1853), 151; *The Pennsylvania Packet*, October 16, 1779; *NJD*, Ser. 2, 3: 659.

23 Although Wiederholdt states that two men survived the capsizing, subsequent articles appearing in the Pennsylvania press report only one man drowned. Captain Taylor himself most certainly survived, as he participated as co-libellant with Stephen Decatur, Sr., in the libel against *Triton* and six slaves, noted in the suit as Jack, Harry, Sam, James, Anthony, and Jack, all of whom had been found aboard. The case was tried at the Burlington Court House on November 22, 1779. *NJD*, Ser. 2, 3:659, 710.

24 *Pickering* had only a short time before fallen in with HM Sloop-of-War *Hope*, which struck her colors without firing a shot. *Hope* was tried on November 22, 1779, at Burlington Court House. Baurmeister, 309; Wiederholdt, 86; *NJD*, Ser. 2, 3:663, 710. It was initially assumed that *Adamant* had been captured by a French fleet under the Comte d'Estaing. Baurmeister, 309.

25 *NJD*, Ser. 2, 3:710; *The Pennsylvania Packet*, October 16, 1779. The Pennsylvania privateer schooner *Enterprize* was commissioned on August 28, 1779, armed with twelve guns, and manned by a crew of seventy. Her owners were James Vanuxem and Lardner Clark, both of Philadelphia, who placed the required bond of $10,000. *NRAR*, 282.

26 *The Pennsylvania Packet*, April 13, 1779; *New York Gazette and Weekly Mercury*, January 3, 1780; *New Jersey Gazette*, January 12, 1780; *The New York Journal, and the General Advertiser*, January 31, 1780. The hull of *Britannia*, which lay in Cheesequake Creek, Monmouth County, was found to be carrying sixteen 6-pounders, four 12-pounders, four swivels, "a quantity of shot and rigging, Irish beef, pork, bread, coffee, sugar, sweet oil, powder, lead, muskets, swords, water casks, etc.," and was advertised to be sold at a public vendue to be held at the house of Garret Schanck in Middleton on January 27, 1780. *Pennsylvania Journal*, January 26, 1780.

27 *NRAR*, 393; Emmons, 152; Harry Emerson Wildes, *Lonely Midas: The Story of Stephen Girard* (New York: Farrar and Rhinehart, 1943), 39-41; Arthur D. Pierce, *Smuggler's Woods: Jaunts and Journeys Through Colonial and Revolutionary New Jersey* (New Brunswick, NJ: Rutgers University Press, 1960), 66-68.

XVI. The Cruise on Clover

1 Wharton Estate deeds and records, in Arthur D. Pierce, *Iron in the Pines*, (New Brunswick, NJ: Rutgers University Press, 1957), 15, 125, 184, 185.

2 Pierce, *Iron in the Pines*, 128; Theodore Thayer, *Nathanael Greene: Strategist of the Revolution* (New York: Twayne Publishers, 1960), 227.

3 Marquis James, *Biography of a Business, 1792–1942. Insurance Company of America* (Indianapolis: Bobbs-Merrill Company, 1942), 57; Pierce, *Iron in the Pines*, 129.

[4] Pierce, *Iron in the Pines*, 71; Arthur D. Pierce, *Smugglers' Woods: Jaunts and Journeys in Colonial and Revolutionary New Jersey* (New Brunswick, NJ: Rutgers University Press, 1960), 82.

[5] Committee at Camp [near Valley Forge] to Henry Laurens, February 25, 1778, in *LDC*, 9: 171; Thayer, 226.

[6] Nathaniel Greene to Griffin Greene, March 20, 1779, Greene Papers, Marietta College Library, in Thayer, 236; Pierce, *Iron in the Pines*, 128.

[7] Pierce, *Iron in the Pines*, 128.

[8] Pierce, *Smugglers' Woods*, 75, 76.

[9] Ibid., 81.

[10] PCC 41, vol. 7, p. 37; Pierce, *Smugglers' Woods*, 74.

[11] *NJD*, Ser. 2, 3:86.

[12] Pierce, *Smugglers' Woods*, 74.

[13] Pedro Blanco Statement, April 28, 1779, PCC 41, 5:200-4.

[14] Charles Pettit to Nathaniel Greene, May 5, 1779, in Pierce, *Smugglers' Woods*, 75.

[15] Pedro Blanco Statement; *NRAR*, 105.

[16] John Jay to Conrad Alexander Gerard, May 24, 1779, *LDC*, 12:518-19.

[17] Committee, Continental Congress, May 22, 1779, *NRAR*, 107; See also *JCC*, 13:281-86, 14:507-10, 527-30, 607-8, 617, 624, 634-36; PCC, 1, 22:17-18; 41, 5:200-7; Committee on Appeals Decree, December 15, 1778, *LDC*, 12:341-43; Committee of Congress to Joseph Reed, January 26, 1779, *LDC*, 12:516-17; Jay to Gerard, April 25, 1779, *LDC*, 12:382, n2; Henry J. Bourguignon, *The First Federal Court: The Federal Appellate Prize Court of the American Revolution, 1775–1787*, Memoirs of the American Philosophical Society 122 (1977): 278-81, 305-7; Committee on Appeals Decrees, November 1, 1779 (*Cleaveland v. Luca*), *LDC*, 14:135-36; Committee on Appeals Decrees, November 6, 1779 (*Tracy v. Llano*), *LDC*, 14:154-55.

[18] John Jay to the States, August 14, 1779, *LDC*, 13:370.

[19] PCC (Ships' Bonds required for Letters of Marque and Reprisal, 1776–1783), 196, 10:66.

[20] PCC (Ships' Bonds required for Letters of Marque and Reprisal, 1776–1783), 196, 13:39; PCC 196, 9:24; Greene to Pettit, November 29, 1778, Reed Papers, VI, NYHS; Pettit to Greene, January 5, 1780, Greene Collection, VI, WCL, in Thayer, 236; Pierce, *Smugglers' Woods*, 81.

[21] Pettit to Greene, January 5, 1780, Greene Collection, VI, Marietta College Library; Pierce, *Smugglers' Woods*, 81- 82.

[22] Pettit to Greene, January 7, 1780, Greene Collection, VI, Marietta College Library; Pierce, *Smugglers' Woods*, 77.

[23] Pierce, *Smugglers' Woods*, 78.

[24] Ibid., 82.

[25] Pettit to Greene, June 11, 1780, Pettit to Greene, May 5, 1779, Greene Collection, III, V, VI, Marietta College Library; Pierce, *Smugglers' Woods*, 78.

[26] Pierce, *Smugglers' Woods*, 78.

[27] Ibid., 78-79.

[28] PCC (Ships' Bonds required for Letters of Marque and Reprisal, 1776–1783), 196, 13:40; *Pennsylvania Gazette*, June 13, July 4, and August 29, 1781.

[29] Pierce, *Smugglers' Woods*, 80; PCC. 196, 4:56.

[30] PCC (Ships' Bonds required for Letters of Marque and Reprisal, 1776–1783), 196, vol. 10, p. 93; Pierce, *Smugglers' Woods*, 81. *Leinster* was commissioned on March 9, 1780, with a crew of thirty-five, and bonded for $10,000 by Andrew Hodge, Jr. and Captain Johnston.

[31] PCC (Ships' Bonds required for Letters of Marque and Reprisal, 1776–1783), 196, 9:26; Pierce, *Smugglers' Woods*, 79.

[32] Pierce, *Smugglers' Woods*, 79.

[33] Ibid., 79, 80; PCC (Ships' Bonds required for Letters of Marque and Reprisal, 1776–1783), 196, 7:68; Baurmeister, 337.

[34] Pierce, *Smugglers' Woods*, 80.

[35] PCC (Ships' Bonds required for Letters of Marque and Reprisal, 1776–1783), 196, 2:59; Pierce, *Smugglers' Woods*, 81.

[36] Pierce, *Smugglers' Woods*, 82.

[37] PCC (Ships' Bonds required for Letters of Marque and Reprisal, 1776–1783), 196, 1:11.

XVII. Strike, You Damned Rebels

[1] Jacob Nagle, *The Nagle Journal: A Diary of the Life of Jacob Nagle, Sailor, from the Year 1775 to 1841*, John C. Dann, ed. (New York, Weidenfeld & Nicholson, 1988). 14, 351, n2; *Appleton's Cyclopedia of American Biography*, (New York: D. Appleton & Co., 1888), 2:120-122; *NRAR*, 254, 286, 438, 445, 49.

[2] Ibid.

[3] Nagle, 17.

[4] Ibid; *The New Jersey Gazette*, May 17, 1780

[5] Claude A. Van Tyne, *The Loyalists in the American Revolution* (New York: 1902), 262; Catherine S. Crary, *The Price of Loyalty: Tory Writings from the Revolutionary Era* (New York: McGraw-Hill Book Company, 1973), 291; *Royal Gazette* (New York), March 11, 1780; *Maryland Gazette*, April 26, 1781; Wallace Brown, *The Good American* (New York: William Morrow and Company, Inc., 1969), 106; [Carl Leopold Baurmeister], *Revolution in America: Confidential Letters and Journals 1776–1784 of Adjutant General Major Baurmeister of the Hessian Forces*, Bernard A. Uhlendorf, trans. and ann. (New Brunswick, NJ: Rutgers University Press, 1957), 271.

[6] Nagle, 18, 19

[7] "Extract of a Letter from on board the Fair American, commanded by Captain Stephen Decatur, dated Cape May, May 29th, 1780," *The Pennsylvania Packet or the General Advertiser*, June 3, 1780

[8] Nagle, 19.

[9] Ibid. *Swallow* was libeled in a Court of Admiralty convened at Mount Holly, NJ, on June 8, 1780. Co-libellants were Nathan Brown, noted as commander "of a private sloop-of-war" and John Ridge, master of the brig *Argo*. The latter was a Pennsylvania vessel of ten guns and sixty men, owned by Robert Duncan and

Richard Humphreys of Philadelphia, and commissioned on March 18, 1780. *Swallow*'s cargo had already been sold at a public vendue held at Richard Westcoat's at The Forks on May 29. *NJD*, Ser. 2, 4:373-73, 377.

10 Nagle, 24.

11 Ibid.; *NJD*, Ser. 2, 4:389; William Bell Clark, "That Mischievous Holker, The Story of a Privateer," *Pennsylvania Magazine of History and Biography*, 79, No. 1 (January 1955), 40, 41; *The Pennsylvania Packet or the General Advertiser*, August 26, 1780.

12 Clark, 40, 41; *The New-York Gazette and The Weekly Mercury*, August 21, 1780; Nagle, 24; *NJD*, Ser. 2, 4:389; *The Pennsylvania Packet or the General Advertiser*, August 26, 1780.

13 Ibid.; Nagle, 19. According to newspaper accounts, *Mercury* was a prize claimed by *Fair American*, *Holker*, and *Enterprize*. The passengers included Captains Campbell of the 44th Regiment, Mure of the 82nd Regiment, Lyman of the Prince of Wales Regiment, Murray of Wentwoth's Dragoon's, and Wallop of Knyphausen's Regiment, as well as a Mrs. Griffiths and Mrs. Anderson, and three servants. Later, the *Pennsylvania Gazette and Weekly Advertiser* added a Captain Lamden of an unnamed letter of marque. Nagle, 351, n4. The prize put into Philadelphia about August 14 or 15. Captain Dillon and his crew were sent to Elizabethtown via Trenton, through which they passed on August 21 to be exchanged. *Pennsylvania Packet or the General Advertiser*, August 15, 1780; *Pennsylvania Gazette and Weekly Advertiser*, August 16, 1780; Thomas Henry to Thomas Sim Lee, August 15, 1780, *LDC*, 15: 583; *NJD*, Ser. 2, 4:608.

14 *The Pennsylvania Packet or the General Advertiser*, August 19, 23, 26, September 2, 6, 1780, October 24, 1780; *The New-York Gazette and The Weekly Mercury*, August 21, 28, September 4, 11, 1780; *The Pennsylvania Gazette and Weekly Advertiser*, August 30, 1780; Clark, 42, 43, 44

15 Nagle, 24.

16 *The Pennsylvania Packet or the General Advertiser*, September 2, 1780.

17 Board of Admiralty to James Nicholson, September 2, 1780, in Charles Oscar Paullin, *Out Letters of the Continental Marine Committee and the Board of Admiralty, August 1776-September 1780*, Vol. 2 (Naval History Society, New York: 1914), 255-56.

18 Ibid.; *The Pennsylvania Gazette and Weekly Advertiser*, September 27, 1780

19 Clark, 46; *The Pennsylvania Packet or the General Advertiser*, October 7, 1780; *The Pennsylvania Gazette and Weekly Advertiser*, November 1, 1780; *The New Jersey Gazette*, November 22, 1780; Nagle, 19.

20 Nagle, 19, 20; *The New Jersey Gazette* November 22, 1780. Nagle, 19, claims *Richmond* had a crew of seventy-five men. *The Pennsylvania Gazette and Weekly Advertiser*, November 1, 1780, claims thirty-four men.

21 Nagle, 20; *The New Jersey Gazette,* November 22, 1780.

22 Nagle, 20-21; *The Pennsylvania Gazette and Weekly Advertiser*, November 1, 1780; *The New-York Gazette and The Weekly Mercury*, December 4, 1780.

23 Nagle, 23.

24 Ibid.

25 Ibid., 21.

26 Ibid.

27 Ibid.

28 Ibid., 21-22.

29 Ibid., 22.

30 Ibid., 23. *Restoration* was libeled on November 9, 1780, tried on November 15, advertised for sale on November 18, and sold November 24, *The Norwich Packet and the Weekly Advertiser*, November 21, 1780; *The Pennsylvania Packet or the General Advertiser*, November 11, 1780.

31 Ibid.; *The Freeman's Journal or The North-American Intelligencer*, November 11, 1780; Nagle, n352, n7. *The Pennsylvania Gazette and Weekly Advertiser*, November 1, 1780; *The Freeman's Journal or The North-American Intelligencer*, May 9, 1781; Clark, 47-48; *The New-York Gazette and The Weekly Mercury*, December 4, 1780; Clark, 47-48.

32 *New Jersey Gazette*, August 30, 1780.

33 Eldridge's prizes included: brig *Allday*, Timothy Steward, taken in concert with Olmsted in *Raven*, off the Delaware Capes; the British privateer *Porcupine*, Irwin; snow *St. Joseph and Joachim* in concert with *Holker*; 60-ton sloop *Phoenix*, Abbott, taken off Sandy Hook while en route from New York to Quebec, with an assist by *Holker*; brig *Rambler*, a former Pennsylvania privateer recaptured; the Philadelphia sloop *Polly*, laden with flour, bound for Cape Francois, captured by British cruisers and then retaken by *Fair American*; the 130 ton brigantine *King George*, James Hogg, bound from London to New York, taken off Sandy Hook; the 170-ton brigantine *Nancy*, bound from London to New York, taken off Sandy Hook; the 120-ton brigantine *York*, Charles Grant, bound from Newry, Torbay, to New York, taken off Sandy Hook; and the 200-ton brigantine *Anne*, Thomas Montgomery, bound from London to New York taken off Sandy Hook. For accounts of captures, libels, condemnations and sales of prizes see: *The Pennsylvania Gazette and Weekly Advertiser*, June 13, 1781, July 4, 14, 26, 30, August 8, 16, September 12, October 17, November 7 and 20, 1781; *The Pennsylvania Packet or the General Advertiser*, September 11, 13, 18, 27, October 4, 9, 16, 23, November 20, 1781, January 15, 1782; *The New York Gazette and Weekly Mercury*, July 2, 1781; *The Freeman's Journal or The North American Intelligencer*, July 11, 1781; *The New Jersey Gazette*, July 4, 1781; *Maryland Gazette*, October 25, 1781; *The Connecticut Journal* [New Haven], November 1, 1781; Clark, 51, 52, note 155, quoting from "Extracts from the Journal of the Spanish snow St. Joseph . . . ," *Public Advertiser*, September 11, 1781; Clark, 54; "Extract of a letter from an officer on board his majesty's ship Garland, C. Chamberlayne, esquire commander," in *The Pennsylvania Packet or the General Advertiser*, January 19, 1782.

XVIII. Whaleboats and Refugees

1 William S. Stryker, *The Capture of the Block House at Toms River, New Jersey, March 24, 1782. Read at the Memorial service at Toms River, May 30, 1782* (Trenton, NJ: Naar, Day & Naar, Book and Job Printers, 1883), 10; Edwin Salter, *A history of Monmouth and Ocean Counties, embracing a genealogical record of earliest settlers in Monmouth and Ocean counties and their descendants. The Indians: their language,*

manners, and customs. Important historical events . . . (Bayonne, NJ: F. Gardner & Sons, Publishers, 1890), 192.

2 Salter, 191-92.

3 Stryker, 9; Salter, 194.

4 Stryker, 9; Salter, 193, 194; William, McMahon, *South Jersey Towns: History and Legend* (New Brunswick, NJ: Rutgers University Press, 1973), 304.

5 Ibid.

6 Stryker, 10; Thomas Savadge to the Pennsylvania Council of Safety, February 10, 1777, in Samuel Hazard, et al., eds., *PA*, Ser. 1, 5:217-18.

7 Robert Morris to Pennsylvania Council of Safety, February 17, 1777, *LDC*, 6:310-11.

8 Minutes of the Pennsylvania Council of Safety, February 17, 1777, *PCR*, 11:125, 126; Pennsylvania Navy Board to Captain John Rice, April 14, 1777, *NDAR*, 8:340-41.

9 Salter, 201.

10 *NJD*, Ser. 2, 1:485; Lorenzo Sabine, *Biographical Sketches of Loyalists in the American Revolution, with an Historical Essay*, 2 vols. (Boston: Little, Brown and Company, 1864), 2:107; Salter, 192; Stryker, 10; William Stockton Hornor, *This Old Monmouth of Ours* (Freehold, NJ: Moreau Brothers, 1932), 28.

11 Salter, 194; *NJD*, Ser. 2, 2:253; *New Jersey Gazette*, June 17, 1778; *New York Gazette and Weekly Mercury*, August 17, 1778.

12 *NJD*, Ser. 2, 2:453 and 445. See *Salter, passim*, for a comprehensive overview of the careers of the refugee raiders.

13 Salter, 119; *NJD*, Ser. 2, 2:525, 546.

14 *Pennsylvania Packet*, November 24, 1778.

15 Paul C. Burgess, *A Colonial Scrapbook, the Southern New Jersey Coast, 1675–1783* (New York: Carlton Press, 1971), 177.

16 [Carl Leopold Baurmeister] *Revolution in America: Confidential Letters and Journals 1776–1784 of Adjutant General Major Baurmeister of the Hessian Forces*, Bernard A. Uhlendorf, trans. and ann. (New Brunswick, NJ: Rutgers University Press, 1957), 252-53.

17 Massachusetts Delegates [Elbridge Gerry, Adams, Holten, and Lovel] to Jeremiah Powell, March 1, 1779, *LDC*, 129-30.

18 Baurmeister, 265, 271.

19 Ibid., 289.

20 Ibid., 304.

21 Ibid., 345

22 *New Jersey Gazette*, May 3, 1780, 3; PCC (Ships' Bonds required for Letters of Marque and Reprisal, 1776–1783), 196, vol. 2, p. 42; Salter, 79.

23 *New Jersey Gazette*, May 3, 1780, 3; PCC (Ships' Bonds required for Letters of Marque and Reprisal, 1776–1783), 196, 2:42; *New York Historical Society Quarterly*, Vol. 42 (January 1949), 295; Salter, 79. At the end of the war William Marriner settled in Harlem, New York, where he lived for many years after.

24 PCC (Ships' Bonds required for Letters of Marque and Reprisal, 1776–1783), 196, vol. 2, p. 40. The *Black Snake* commanded by Huddy is described as a boat rather

than a brig, and may have been a whaleboat operated under the same name, or perhaps even one of the ship's boats from the brig itself.

[25] Baurmeister, 429.

[26] *NJD*, Ser. 2, 5:196.

[27] Ibid., 5:285; *New York Historical Society Quarterly*, Vol. 41 (October 1948), 298; Baurmeister, 465.

[28] *Pennsylvania Gazette*, October 17, 1781; *NJD*, Ser. 2, 4:306; Salter, 299.

[29] Ibid.

[30] Ibid.

[31] Ibid.

[32] Ibid.

[33] *New York Historical Society Quarterly*, Vol. 46 (July, 1950), 299; Salter, 299.

[34] *NJD*, Ser. 2, 4:306; Salter, 300; Baurmeister, 477.

[35] *NJD*, Ser. 2, 5:322; Salter, 300.

[36] *New Jersey Gazette*, January 2, 1782, Salter 300.

[37] *Pennsylvania Gazette*, January 15, 1782; Salter 301.

[38] Ibid.

XIX. By the Rule of Contrary

[1] Hulbert Footner, *Sailor of Fortune: The Life and Adventures of Commodore Barney, U.S.N.* (New York and London: Harper & Brothers Publishers, 1940), 101-2; Mary Barney, *A Biographical Memoir of the Late Joshua Barney: From Autobiographical Notes and Journals in Possession of His Family, and Other Authentic Sources* (Boston: Gray and Bowen, 1832), 112.

[2] PCC (Ships' Bonds required for Letters of Marque and Reprisal, 1776–1783), 196, 8:28; Footner, 102.

[3] Nathan Miller, *Sea of Glory: The Continental Navy Fights for Independence, 1775–1783*, (New York: David Mackay Company, Inc., 1974), 277-78; PCC (Ships' Bonds required for Letters of Marque and Reprisal, 1776–1783), 196, 8:29; Footner, 102.

[4] Barney. 303-304; Footner, 101-2. Barney had given his age as 25 (he was not yet 23), and that he was 5 foot 8 inches tall and that his hair was black and his complexion dark, PCC (Ships' Bonds required for Letters of Marque and Reprisal, 1776–1783), 196, 8:28, April 2, 1782.

[5] See Footner, *passim*, for an excellent account of Barney's early career.

[6] Many authorities have addressed *Hyder Ally* as a Pennsylvania Navy vessel, which is clearly disputed by the letters of marque that were issued on April 2, 1782. Bond was posted by Barney and Alibone, and Fitzsimons, Gurney and Alibone are listed as owners. As state funds were not allocated before the vessel departed, she must technically be considered as a privateer, in the service of the mercantile community of Philadelphia and not as a formal state warship owned or hired by the State of Pennsylvania. That this status continued after the battle, even though a commission had been formed to administer to the defense of Pennsylvania commerce on the Delaware, is indicated by a new letter of marque commission authorized on April 27, 1782 under the same ownership. PCC (Ships' Bonds

required for Letters of Marque and Reprisal, 1776–1783), 196, 8:28 and 8:30.

[7] Philip Freneau, "Barney's Invitation," in *Poems Relating to the American Revolution* (New York: W. J. Widdleton, 1868. Reprinted Anne Arbor, Mich.: University of Michigan Humanities and Text Initiative, 1997), 171-73.

[8] PCC (Ships' Bonds required for Letters of Marque and Reprisal, 1776–1783), 196, 8:28; Barney, 116, 117; Footner, 103.

[9] Barney, 113, 116; Footner, 102. Barney, who should known, states his ship was manned by 110 men and armed with sixteen 6-pounders. Gardner W. Allen, *A Naval History of the American Revolution*, 2 vols. (Williamstown, MA: Corner House Publishers, 1970 [1906]), 2:588, states she carried 120 men, and was armed with four 9-pounders and twelve 6-pounders, a figure accepted by Miller, 277-78. The *London Chronicle* of September 10, 1782 states *General Monk* was manned by 130 to 140 seamen and carried eighteen long 9- and 6-pounders.

[10] PCC (Ships' Bonds required for Letters of Marque and Reprisal, 1776–1783), 196, 8:28. Footner, 104, incorrectly states that Thomas Fitzsimmons and Francis Gurney posted the bond, which is clearly disputed by the letters of marque that were issued.

[11] Barney, 113.

[12] Ibid.; Footner 104.

[13] Barney, 308; Allen, 2:589; Barney notes *General Monk* was armed with eighteen 9-pounders, but apparently does not count her pair of bow chasers. J.J. Cooledge, *Ships of the Royal Navy: An Historical Index*, 2vols. (Newton Abbot, Devon, England: David & Charles, 1969), 1:250, states she was armed with twenty guns.

[14] Barney, 305; Footner, 104; Miller, 278; Allen, 2:589.

[15] Barney, 305.

[16] Ibid.; Footner, 104; Allen, 2:289.

[17] Barney 113, 305; Allen, 2:589; *Maryland Gazette*, April 25, 1782; Footner, 105.

[18] Ibid.

[19] PCC (Ships' Bonds required for Letters of Marque and Reprisal, 1776–1783), 196, 6:21; 6:9; 6:22; 6:17; 6:18. *General Greene's* last of five commissions indicates she carried ten guns and received her final one on March 20, 1782.

[20] Barney, 113; *Maryland Gazette*, April 25, 1782.

[21] Barney, 114, 305; Footner, 105. Footner states, incorrectly, that *Fair American* gave two broadsides, which is countered by Barney's own account that she provided only one.

[22] *Maryland Gazette*, April 25, 1782. One report in the *Gazette* calls the stranded merchantman *Lovely Sally*.

[23] Barney, 114.

[24] *London Chronicle*, September 10, 1782; Barney, 115, 308.

[25] Barney, 114, 306; 2:589. The *London Chronicle*, September 10, 1782. It is very doubtful that, as the English asserted, Barney tried to escape at the outset of the engagement. This impression, as Allen, 2:590, suggests, may have arisen from the fact that he shouted his orders in a manner intended to deceive the enemy.

[26] Barney, 114.

[27] Ibid.; *London Chronicle*, September 10, 1782.

[28] Barney, 114.

[29] *London Chronicle*, September 10, 1782; Barney, 306; Footner, 106, 107.

[30] Barney,116.

[31] Ibid; *Niles's Weekly Register*, 2:298, reprinted in Barney, 307.

[32] Barney, 116-17.

[33] Footner, 107-8

[34] Barney, 306, 308; *London Chronicle*, September 10, 1782.

[35] Barney 117, 123, 306; *The Maryland Gazette*, April 25, 1982. Captain Rogers's
   biographer states: "His lieutenant and master were both killed; his purser and
   boatswain were wounded. Of his petty officers and seamen six were killed and
   twenty-nine wounded." Barney 306.

[36] Barney, 117; Footner, 108.

[37] Barney, 117.

[38] Footner, 108.

[39] Ibid., 109.

[40] Ibid., 113; Barney, 108, 118, 307-8.

[41] Barney, 308.

[42] Ibid., 108, 118, 307. The *Maryland Gazette*, April 25, 1782, reported that *General
   Greene*, "it is feared, has fallen into the hands of the enemy." Mary Barney claimed,
   incorrectly, that the capture of *General Monk* and *Hook'em Snevey* entirely stopped
   the Loyalist raiders for a long time afterwards, a boast not supported by the
   historic record. She also notes the name of the refugee schooner as *Hook'em
   Snivey*, though the Pennsylvania Admiralty vendue notices reports her as *Hook'em
   Snevey*. *Pennsylvania Packet*, April 27, 1782; May 2, 1782.

[43] Barney, 303-4.

[44] PCC (Ships' Bonds required for Letters of Marque and Reprisal, 1776–1783), 196,
   8:30.

[45] *Pennsylvania Packet*, May 2, 1782.

[46] Barney, 311; *Boston Gazette*, May 6, 1782.

[47] Barney, 118.

[48] Philip Freneau, "Song, On Captain Barney's Victory Over the Ship *General Monk*,"
   in *Poems Relating to the American Revolution*, 175-78.

XX. Up Goes Huddy

[1] William S. Stryker, *The Capture of the Block House at Toms River, New Jersey, March
   24, 1782. Read at the Memorial service at Toms River, May 30, 1782* (Trenton, NJ:
   Naar, Day & Naar, Book and Job Printers, 1883), 5-6, 10.

[2] Ibid., 10,

[3] Edwin Salter, *A history of Monmouth and Ocean Counties, embracing a genealogical
   record of earliest settlers in Monmouth and Ocean counties and their descendants. The
   Indians: their language, manners, and customs. Important historical events . . .*
   (Bayonne, NJ: F. Gardner & Sons, Publishers, 1890), 184.

[4] Benson J. Lossing, *Pictorial Field Book of the Revolution*, 2 vols. (New York: Harper
   Brothers, 1852), 2:366; Salter, 88

[5] Salter, 121; Lossing, 2:366; Stryker 7; Gustav Kobbé, *The Jersey Coast and Pines.* (Baltimore: Gateway Press, Inc., 1970), 24.

[6] Stryker, 6-7.

[7] Wallace Brown, *The Good American* (New York: William Morrow and Company, Inc., 1969), 142; Catherine S. Crary, *The Price of Loyalty: Tory Writings from the Revolutionary Era* (New York: McGraw-Hill Book Company, 1973), 216. See Richard H. Phelps, *A History of Newgate of Connecticut* (New York: Arno Press, 1969) for a compete account of the Simsbury prison.

[8] Stryker, 22, 10, 13.

[9] Ibid., 7, 11; Salter 205.

[10] Stryker 11.

[11] Ibid.

[12] Ibid., 12; Salter, 206.

[13] Stryker, 12-13.

[14] Ibid., 13; *Maryland Gazette*, April 11, 1782.

[15] Stryker, 13; [Ludwig Von Closen], *The Revolutionary Journal of Baron Ludwig Von Closen 1780–1783*, Evelyn M. Acomb, trans. and ed. (Chapel Hill, NC: University of North Carolina Press, 1958), 200.

[16] *The Writings of George Washington from the Original Manuscript Sources 1745–1799*, John C. Fitzpatrick, ed., 39 vols. (Washington, DC: U.S. Government Printing Office, 1931–1944), 24:136, n.98; Stryker 13-14; Salter 184; Henry Steel Commanger and Richard B. Morris, eds., *The Spirit of "Seventy-Six": The Story of the American Revolution as Told by Participants* (New York, Evanston, and London: Harper & Row, Publishers, 1958), 885.

[17] Salter, 170, 171, 173.

[18] Ibid., 173.

[19] Ibid., 185.

[20] *Writings of George Washington*, 24:136, n.98; Stryker, 14, Salter 185.

[21] Stryker, 14; Salter, 185; Francis Ross Holland, Jr., *America's Lighthouses: An Illustrated History* (New York: Dover Publications, 1972), 90, states that the Highlands of Navesink, beginning in 1746, had a signal light built to warn New York of the approach of enemy vessels. In 1828 the station became the site of the Navesink Light.

[22] Stryker, 14; Salter, 186. Huddy's will was found among the papers of his executor, Colonel Samuel Forman, and subsequently came into the possession of Judge Bennington F. Randolph, who deposited it in the library of the New Jersey Historical Society. It was signed by Capt. Huddy, but was apparently written by another person. Salter, 186.

[23] *Maryland Gazette*, May 2, 1782; Stryker, 16; Salter, 187.

[24] James Madison to Edmund Randolph, May 1, 1782, *LDC*, 18:484.

[25] Lossing, 2:366.

[26] Stryker, 16; Salter 91.

[27] Lossing, 2:366; Stryker 1.7

[28] *Writings of George Washington*, 24:136, n.98.

[29] Ibid.; Lossing, 2:366; Stryker 17.

[30] General Orders, April 19, 1782, *Writings of George Washington*, 24:135-36; Washington to the General Field Officers of the Army, April 19, 1782, *Writings of George Washington*, 24:136-37.

[31] Ibid., 24:136, n.99

[32] Ibid., 24:144-46; James Madison to Edmund Randolph, Philadelphia, May 1, 1782, *LDC*, 18:484; Stryker, 18.

[33] Washington to Sir Henry Clinton, April 21, 1782, *Writings of George Washington*, 24:146-47; [Von Closen], 200.

[34] James Madison to Edmund Randolph, Philadelphia, May 1, 1782, *LDC*, 18:484

[35] Washington to Clinton, April 21, 1782, *Writings of George Washington*, 24:147.

[36] Clinton to Washington, April 25, 1782, Washington Papers, LC.

[37] Stryker 19-20, 23; *Writings of George Washington*, 24:220, n. 94.

[38] Robertson to Washington, May 1, 1782, Washington Papers, LC, also *Writings of George Washington*, 24:220, n.93.

[39] Stryker 20.

[40] [Von Closen], 200; Stryker 20.

[41] Stryker, 20-21.

[42] Ibid., 21-22.

[43] Stryker 22-23. See also Larry G. Bowman, "The Court-Martial of Captain Richard Lippincott," *New Jersey History*, (Spring 1971), 89:23-36.

XXI. The Villain and the Victim

[1] William S. Stryker, *The Capture of the Block House at Toms River, New Jersey, March 24, 1782. Read at the Memorial service at Toms River, May 30, 1782* (Trenton, NJ: Naar, Day & Naar, Book and Job Printers, 1883), 18-19. For another full analysis of the Huddy Affair see Katherine Mayo, *General Washington's Dilemma* (New York: Harcourt, Brace, 1938).

[2] George Washington to Brigadier General Moses Hazen, May 3, 1782, *The Writings of George Washington from the Original Manuscript Sources 1745–1799*, John C. Fitzpatrick, ed., 39 vols. (Washington, DC: U.S. Government Printing Office, 1931–1944), 24:217-18; Washington to Secretary of War, May 3, 1782, *Writings of George Washington*, 24: 218-19.

[3] George Washington to Gov. William Livingston, May 6, 1782, *Writings of George Washington*, 24:226.

[4] George Washington to Secretary of War, May 3, 1782, *Writings of George Washington*, 24:219.

[5] George Washington to Lieutenant General James Robertson, May 4, 1782, *Writings of George Washington*, 24:220.

[6] George Washington to Gov. Wm. Livingston, May 6, 1782, *Writings of George Washington*, 24:227.

[7] Stryker, 23; [Ludwig Von Closen], *The Revolutionary Journal of Baron Ludwig Von Closen, 1780–1783*, Evelyne M. Acomb, trans. and ed. (Chapel Hill, NC: University of North Carolina Press, 1958), 200.

[8] Arthur Middleton to Aedanus Burke, [May 7, 1782?], *LDC*, 18:496.

[9] John Hanson to Philip Thomas, Philadelphia, May 27, 1782, *LDC*, 18:531.

[10] George Washington to President of Congress, May 10, 1782, *Writings of George Washington*, 24:243, and n. 28.

[11] George Washington to Sir Guy Carleton, May 10, 1782, *Writings of George Washington*, 24:242.

[12] George Washington to Secretary of War, May 18, 1782, *Writings of George Washington*, 24:262; George Washington to Brigadier Gen. Moses Hazem, May 18, 1782, *Writings of George Washington*, 24: 263.

[13] Stryker 25; John Hanson to Philip Thomas, Philadelphia, May 27, 1782, *LDC*, 18:531, n.10.

[14] Stryker 25; Moses Hazen to George Washington, May 27, 1782, Washington Papers, LC; Turbutt Wright to John Hall, Philadelphia, June 4, 1782, *LDC*, 18:561; *The Spirit of "Seventy-Six: The Story of the American Revolution as Told by Participants*, Henry Steele Commager and Richard B. Morris, eds., *Spirit of "Seventy-Six": The Story of the American Revolution as Told by Participants* (New York, Evanston, and London: Harper & Row, Publishers, 1958), 885.

[15] Stryker, 25.

[16] Hazen to Washington, May 27, 1782, Washington Papers, LC.

[17] Stryker, 25; George Washington to Secretary of War, May 4, 1782, *Writings of George Washington*, 24:305; George Washington to Major General Benjamin Lincoln, May 4, 1782, *Writings of George Washington*, 24:319-20.

[18] George Washington to Brg. Gen. Elias Dayton, June4, 1782, *Writings of George Washington*, 24:307-8.

[19] Commanger, 885.

[20] Stryker, 28-29.

[21] *The Revolutionary Diplomatic Correspondence of the United States*, Francis Wharton, ed., 6 vols., (Washington: Government Printing Office, 1889) 5:462-63; Commager, 885.

[22] Benjamin Franklin to Richard Oswald, July 28, 1782, *Revolutionary Diplomatic Correspondence*, 5:617-18.

[23] *Complete Works of Alexander Hamilton*, Henry Cabot Lodge, ed., 12 vols. (New York: G.P. Putnam's Sons, n.d.), 12:256-58.

[24] Turbutt Wright to John Hall, June 4, 1782, *LDC*, 18:561; [Von Closen], 200.

[25] Samuel Wharton to John Dickinson, June 12, 1782, *LDC*, 18:581, *Maryland Gazette*, June 27 and July 11, 1782; John Hanson to Philip Thomas, June 24, 1782, *LDC*, 18:600; John Hanson to Thomas Sim Lee, June 25, 1782, in *LDC*, 18:603.

[26] George Washington to President to Congress, June 6, 1782, *Writings of George Washington*, 24:330; *Maryland Gazette*, Thursday, July 11, 1782.

[27] Washington to Dayton, June 11; George Washington to General Elias Dayton, June 22, 1782, in Fitzpatrick, 24:368; John Hanson to Philip Thomas, July 16, 1782, *LDC*, 18:639

[28] James Madison to Edmund Pendleton, July 16, 1782, in *LDC*, 18:640, 643.

[29] George Washington to Sir Guy Carleton, July 30, 1782, *Writings of George Washington*, 24:441.

[30] Commission to Major General William Heath, August 3, 1782 (1), *Writings of George Washington*, 24:455-56; Instructions to Heath, August 3, 1782, *Writings*

of George Washington, 24:456; Commission Major General William Heath, August 3, 1782 (2), *Writings of George Washington*, 24:458-59

[31] Stryker, 28.

[32] Ibid., 27.

[33] Lady Asgill to Count de Vergennes. July 18, 1782, *Revolutionary Diplomatic Correspondence*, 5:635-36.

[34] Ibid.

[35] Stryker, 29.

[36] Elias Boudinot, *Life, Public Services, Addresses, and Letters*, J. J. Boudinot, ed., 2 vols. (Boston: Houghton Mifflin, 1896), 1:249-51.

[37] Benson J. Lossing, *Pictorial Field Book of the Revolution*, 2 vols. (New York: Harper Brothers, 1852), 2:366, Stryker, 29; George Washington to Sir Guy Carleton, November 20, 1782, *Writings of George Washington*, 25:358.

[38] Stryker 29-30; George Washington to Comte de Vergennes, November 21, 1782, *Writings of George Washington*, 25:359.

[39] Lossing, 2:366; Philip Freneau, "Rivington's Reflections, I," *Poems Relating to the American Revolution* (New York: W. J. Widdleton, 1868. Reprinted Anne Arbor, MI: University of Michigan Humanities and Text Initiative, 1997), 218.

[40] Stryker, 31.

[41] *Maryland Gazette*, June 20, 1782.

[42] John A. McManemin, *Captains of the Privateers during the Revolutionary War*, (Ho-Ho-Kus Publishing Company: Spring Lake, NJ, 1985), 474-75, from letters of John Bray and Adam Hyler to Governor William Livingston.

[43] *Maryland Gazette*, July 25, 1782.

[44] Ibid.

[45] Ibid., June 20, 1782.

[46] Jesse Root to Jonathan Trumbull, Sr., May 11, 1782, *LDC*, 18:504.

[47] Merchants of Philadelphia to the Continental Congress, April 29, 1782, *NRAR*, 189; Report on Memorial of Merchants of Philadelphia, May 2?, 1782, *NRAR*, 189; Robert Morris to Continental Congress, May 4, 1782, *NRAR*, 189; Report on Memorial of Merchants of Philadelphia, May 4, 1782, *NRAR*, 190.

[48] Jonathan Trumbull, Sr. to Charles Thomson, April 24, 1782, *LDC*, 18:489, n1; Charles Thomson to the States, May 23, 1782, *LDC, 18:527; JCC, 22: 280-81;* Charles Thomson to Jonathan Trumbull, Sr., May 23, 1782, *LDC*, 18:527-28

[49] *Maryland Gazette*, August 8, 1782; [Carl Leopold Baurmeister], *Revolution in America: Confidential Letters and Journals 1776–1784 of Adjutant General Major Baurmeister of the Hessian Forces*, Bernard A. Uhlendorf, trans. and ann. (New Brunswick, NJ: Rutgers University Press, 1957), 515.

[50] Theodorick Bland to St. George Tucker, July 30, 1782, *LDC*, 18:677; *NRAR*, 192.

[51] *Maryland Gazette*, July 11 and October 24, 1782.

XXIII. Vulgarly Called Hell

[1] Richard H. Amerman, "Treatment of American Prisoners During the Revolution," *Proceedings of the New Jersey Historical Society*, Vol. 78, No. 4 (October 1960, pp. 267-275), 257.

2 Names of Prisoners, List compiled by 'The Society of Old Brooklynites' in 1888, http://prisonship martyrs.com/gpage1.html.
3 Henry Steele Commager and Richard B. Morris, eds., *The Spirit of 'Seventy-Six: The Story of the American Revolution as Told by Participants* (New York, Evanston, and London: Harper & Row, Publishers, 1958), 854.
4 Ameman, 23-64; *NDAR*, 7:262.
5 Douglas Southall Freeman, *George Washington: A Biography*, 7 vols. (New York: Scribner, 1948–1957), 4:252n; Thomas Bellows Peck, "Journal Kept by Corporal William Slade, of Woodbury, Conn., During His Captivity on an English Prison Ship in the War of the Revolution, From November 16, 1776 to January 28, 1777," in *William Slade of Windsor, Conn. and His Descendants* (Keene, NH: Sentinel Printers Company, 1910), 165-69.
6 Peck, 165.
7 Timothy Parker and Others to Governor Jonathan Trumbull, December 9, 1776, *NDAR*, 7:421
8 Albert Greene, *Recollections of the Jersey Prison Ship from the manuscript of Captain Thomas Dring* [hereafter Dring] (New York: Corinth Books, 1961), 7-10; Andrew Sherburne, *Memoirs of Andrew Sherburne, a pensioner of the Revolution* (Utica, NY: W. Williams, 1828), 107. See Captain Alexander Coffin, *The destructive operation of foul air, tainted provisions, bad water and personal filthiness upon human constitutions, exemplified in the unparalleled cruelty of the British to the American captives at New York during the Revolutionary War, on board their prison and hospital ships, in a communication to Dr. Mitchell, dated September 4, 1807* (New York: Privately printed, 1865) for a full assessment on the foul ventilation aboard *Jersey* and its impact on the prison population.
9 J. J. Cooledge, *Ships of the Royal Navy: An Historical Index*, 2 vols. (David & Charles [Holdings] Ltd.: Newton Abbott, Devon [UK], 1969?), 1:291; Gary North, "Britain's Prison Ships, 1776–1783," http://www.lewrockwell.com/orig/north5.html, accessed February 28, 2006; http://www.eastrivernyc.org/ehistory/prison.shtm. Laird commanded *Jersey* from 1778 to 1781, and was replaced by Captain John Sporne. Sporne remained in office until April 9, 1782, when all prisoners were released and the ship was abandoned. Danske Dandridge *American Prisoners of the Revolution* (Charlottesvile, VA: The Michie Company, Printer, 1911), 229.
10 Thomas Andros, *The old Jersey captive: or, A narrative of the captivity of Thomas Andros. . . on board the old Jersey prison ship at New York, 1781. In a series of letters to a friend. . .* (Boston, W. Peirce, 1833), 8; Ebenezer Fox, *The Adventures of Ebenezer Fox in the Revolutionary War* (Boston: C. Fox, 1847) 96-97, 142; Nathaniel S. Prime, *A History of Long Island: From Its First Settlement by Europeans to the Year 1845* (New York and Pittsburgh: Robert Carter, 1845), was among those who challenged the figures readily adopted by subsequent historians, by noting that accounts of survivors did not substantiate them and that the extreme figures were a product of the anti-British sentiments of the early 19th century that culminated in the War of 1812, and became the accepted norm. The extant listing of those who were interned upon *Jersey*, well over 8,000, compared to the few hundred who were released at the end of the war, suggests that many thousands aboard the prison ship flota did, in fact, die.

[11] Fox, 96; http://www.americanrevolution.org/nav18.html; Dring, xiii-xiv.

[12] http://www.motherbedford.com/Prison.htm; Fox, 114; Dring, 70-71.

[13] Ibid.; Christopher Hawkins, *The American Adventures of Christopher Hawkins, containing details of his captivity, a first and second time on the high seas, in the Revolutionary War by the British, and his consequent sufferings, and escape from the Jersey Prison Ship* (New York: Privately printed, 1864), 76.

[14] Dring, 11-13; Fox, 97. On February 27, 1780, *Good Hope*, while "lying in the Wallebocht Bay was entirely consumed after having been wilfully set on fire by a Connecticut man named Woodbury, who confessed to the fact. He with others of the incendiaries are removed to the Provost. The prisoners let each other down from the port holes and decks into the water." Rivington's *Loyalist Gazette*, March 1, 1780.

[15] Hawkins, 73; Fox, 90-91, 99-100; Prisoner Andrew Sherburne complained in his reminiscence that when he came aboard *Jersey* in late November 1782, a large part of the prisoners clothing had been stolen. Sherburne, 76.

[16] Fox, 99-100; Bill Franz, "A Note about British prison Ships . . . , Memorial to martyred mariners rededicated," *Newark Star-Ledger*, August 26, 1997.

[17] Fox, 110.

[18] Hawkins, 229-30; Dring, 25.

[19] Fox, 107-108.

[20] Dandridge, 250; Andros, 13-14; Dring, 42; Diary of Christopher Vail, Manuscript Collection, LC.

[21] Dandridge, 240.

[22] Ibid., 233; Dring, 45-46; Fox, 109-10. Thomas Andros, caustically remarked about medical assistance: "Let our disease be what it would we were abandoned to our fate. No English physician ever came near us." Andros, 15.

[23] Fox, 111; Dandridge, 239; Dring, 57-60; Vail.

[24] "Extract from a letter on board the Jersey (Vulgarly called Hell) Prison Ship" dated New York, August 10, 1781, in *Pennsylvania Packet*, September 4, 1778; Dring, 47.

[25] Dring, 17-19; Dandridge, 228.

[26] Dring. 19-20.

[27] Ibid., 20-21, 49.

[28] Dandridge, 243.

[29] Fox, 100-2; Dring, 23-24.

[30] Dring, 26-27.

[31] Fox, 101-2.

[32] Ibid., 102-4.

[33] Captain John Van Dyke, "Narrative of Confinement in the Jersey Prison Ship," *N.Y.S.A. Historical Magazine*, (Vol. 7, May 1863), 147-51; Dandridge, 244.

[34] Dring, 29-30; Fox, 105-6.

[35] Dring, 31-33.

[36] Dandridge, 238.

[37] Ibid., 195-6.

[38] Ibid., 196.

[39] Ibid., 244.

[40] Andros, 9.

[41] Dandridge, 196; Andros, 17.

[42] Dring, 72; Dandridge, 243-4.

[43] Dring, 72, 73.

[44] Fox, 106

[45] Andros, 16.

[46] Jeremiah Johnson, "Recollections of Brooklyn and New York," in Dandridge, passim. As a boy residing near the Wallabout during the Revolution, he viewed the unfortunate prison ship and the suffering therein frequently.

[47] Ibid.

[48] Andros, 16.

[49] *Historical Sketch, to the End of the Revolutionary War, of the Life of Silas Talbot, Esq., of the State of Rhode Island, lately Commander of the United States frigate, the Constitution, and of an American Squadron in the West-Indies* (New York: Printed by G. & R. Waite, for H. Caritat, 1803), 106-9.

[50] Andros, 13.

XXIII. Where Peace and Rest Can Never Dwell

[1] Albert Greene, *Recollections of the Jersey Prison Ship from the manuscript of Captain Thomas Dring,* (New York: Corinth Books, 1961), 41.

[2] Thomas Andros, *The old Jersey captive: or, A narrative of the captivity of Thomas Andros . . . on board the old Jersey prison ship at New York, 1781. In a series of letters to a friend . . .* (Boston, W. Peirce, 1833),15.

[3] Andros, 8.

[4] Ibid., 12, 13, 22; Dring, 51.

[5] Dring, 53.

[6] *Memoirs of Andrew Sherburne, a pensioner of the Revolution* (Utica: W. Williams, 1828), 113; Dring, 54.

[7] Sherburne, 114-15.

[8] Ibid., 110-11; Dring, 53.

[9] Dring, 51.

[10] Sherburne, 111-12.

[11] Ibid., 112.

[12] Ibid.

[13] Ibid., 113.

[14] Danske Dandridge, *American Prisoners of the Revolution.* (Charlottesvile, VA: The Michie Company, Printer, 1911), 248.

[15] Dring, 75, 76.

[16] Dandridge, 245.

[17] Dring. 75-6.

[18] Ibid. 76.

[19] Ebenezer Fox, *The Adventures of Ebenezer Fox in the Revolutionary War* (Boston: C. Fox, 1847), 123.

[20] Dandridge, 239-40.

[21] Ibid., 240.

[22] Andros, 9.

[23] Fox,146-48; Dandridge, 195.

[24] Dandridge, 196-7.

[25] Fox, 133-35.

[26] Ibid.

[27] Andros, 27.

[28] Fox, 146. Upon his enlistment, Fox was sent to Jamaica, allowed freedom of Kingston, and worked as a barber. In company with four other Americans he escaped and after many adventures reached Cuba in a small sailing boat. From Cuba he went to St. Domingo and anchored at Cape Francois [Cape Henri]. There he boarded an American frigate called *Flora*, 32, of Boston, Captain Henry Johnson. The ship sailed for France and took several prizes en route. She arrived on the Garonne River and made her way up to Bordeaux and stayed for the next nine months until the peace. In the harbor there were 600 vessels of all nations. Fox enrolled aboard an American brig at Nantes and sailed for home in April 1783. After an absence of three years, he reached his mother's house in Roxbury. She could no longer recognize her son.

[29] Fox, 144-46.

[30] Dring, 97-9.

[31] Ibid., 99-101.

[32] Ibid., 100-4. Dring states that at that time the death rate aboard averaged about five men ever twenty-four hours. But on July 4, between eight and ten more died, presumably from wounds suffered in the attack.

XXIV. A Forlorn Hope

[1] Albert Greene, *Recollections of the Jersey Prison Ship from the manuscript of Captain Thomas* [hereafter Dring] (New York: Corinth Books, 1961), 115; Thomas Andros, *The old Jersey captive: or, A narrative of the captivity of Thomas Andros . . . on board the old Jersey prison ship at New York, 1781. In a series of letters to a friend . . .* (Boston, W. Peirce, 1833), 20; Ebenezer Fox, *The Adventures of Ebenezer Fox in the Revolutionary War* (Boston: C. Fox, 1847), 96-97.

[2] Andros, 23.

[3] Christopher Hawkins, *The American Adventures of Christopher Hawkins, containing details of his captivity, a first and second time on the high seas, in the Revolutionary War by the British, and his consequent sufferings, and escape from the Jersey Prison Ship* (New York: Privately printed, 1864), 81-87.

[4] Fox, 116, 131.

[5] Andros, 21-23.

[6] Ibid., 24.

[7] Ibid., 24-25

[8] Ibid.

[9] Ibid.

[10] Ibid., 258.

[11] Ibid.

12 Fox, 115-17.

13 Ibid. 117-18.

14 Ibid., 118-19.

15 Ibid., 119-20.

16 Ibid., 121-23.

17 Ibid., 124-25

18 Ibid.

19 Ibid., 126-27.

20 Hawkins, 73.

21 See Philip Freneau, *Some Account of the Capture of the Ship "Aurora,"* (New York: M.F. Mansfield & A Vessels, 1899) for a complete account of the privateering voyage and capture of Philip Freneau.

22 Dandridge, 241.

23 Ibid.

24 Fox, 27-28.

25 Ibid.

26 Andros, 17; Hawkins, 70, 280. Andros states that the chest belonged to a sailor and identifies the intended escapee as Captain Young, while Christopher Hawkins states that the chest belonged to a ship's mate, and the escapee was a cabin boy.

27 *Historical Sketch, to the End of the Revolutionary War, of the Life of Silas Talbot, Esq., of the State of Rhode Island, lately Commander of the United States frigate, the Constitution, and of an American Squadron in the West-Indies* (New York: Printed by G. & R. Waite, for H. Caritat, 1803), 106-9.

XXV. Cartel

1 Danske Dandridge, *American Prisoners of the Revolution* (Charlottesville, VA: The Michie Company, Printer, 1911), 193, 197.

2 Captain John Chester to General Webb, January 17, 1777, *Correspondence and Journals of Samuel Blachley Webb*, Worthington C. Ford, ed., 3 vols. (New York [Lancaster, Pa.]: Wickenham Press, 1893), 1:184; Henry Onderdonck, Jr., *Revolutionary incidents of Suffolk and Kings Counties: with an account of the Battle of Long Island and the British prisons and prison-ships at New York* (New York: Leavitt, Trow, 1849), 229.

3 Dandridge, 193, 211-12.

4 Albert Greene, *Recollections of the Jersey Prison Ship from the manuscript of Captain Thomas Dring* (New York: Corinth Books, 1961), 119; Washington to President of Congress, February 18, 1782, *The Writings of George Washington from the Original Manuscript Sources 1745–1799*, John C. Fitzpatrick, ed., 39 vols. (Washington, DC: U.S. Government Printing Office, 1931–1944), 24:5-6.

5 Dring, 118-20.

6 George Washington to President of Congress, February 18, 1782, *Writings of George Washington*, 24:5-6; Ebenezer Fox, *The Adventures of Ebenezer Fox in the Revolutionary War* (Boston: C. Fox, 1847), 132.

7 Dring, 120.

8 Ibid. 121-22.

[9] Ibid., 123-24.

[10] Ibid., 124.

[11] Ibid., 125.

[12] Ibid., 124-26

[13] Ibid., 126

[14] Ibid., 127.

[15] George Washington to the Officer Commanding the British Fleet at New York [Marion Arbuthnot], January 25, 1781, *Writings of George Washington*, 21:143-44.

[16] George Washington to President of Congress, February 18, 1782, *Writings of George Washington*, 24:5-6.

[17] Ibid.

[18] Danske Dandridge, *American Prisoners of the Revolution* (Charlottesville, VA: The Michie Company Printer, 1911 [reprinted Baltimore: Geneological Publishing Company, 1967]), p. 312-13

[19] Thomas McKean to George Washington, August 7, 1781, *Letters of Delegates to Congress 1774–1789*, Paul H. Smith, ed., 24 vols. *LDC*, 17:481.

[20] Dandridge, 314.

[21] *JCC*, 21:815, 829-830; George A. Boyd, *Elias Boudinot: Patriot and Statesman, 1740–1821* (Princeton, NJ: Princeton University Press, 1952), pp. 33-67, 88-89; Thomas McKean to George Washington, August 7, 1781, in *LDC*, 17: 481.

[22] George Washington to the Officer Commanding His Britannic Majesty's Ship of Way, August 21, 1781, *Writings of George Washington*, 23:24-25.

[23] Dandridge, p. 316.

[24] Ibid.

[25] George Washington to Thomas McKean, September 4, 1781, *Writings of George Washington*, 23:83-84.; *JCC*, 21:930; PCC, item 152, 10:229-32

[26] Dandridge, p. 316-17. A number of Loyalist prisoners had been consigned to work in the Simsbury mines in Connecticut, where many among them died from mistreatment and in as distressing conditions as any suffered aboard the prison ships. In March 1781, a number of British officers were sent by the Americans from the south to Simsbury, to remove them from the path of enemy forces in Virginia. *LDC*, 17:88.

[27] George Washington to President of Congress, December 27, 1781, *Writings of George Washington*, 23:407.

[28] Ibid., 23:408.

[29] Ibid., 23:408-9.

[30] George Washington to Congress, February 18, 1782, *Writings of George Washington*, 24:5-6.

[31] Massachusetts Delegates to Congress to John Avery, March 26, 1782, *LDC*, 18:422-23.

[32] Ibid.

[33] "Extract of a letter dated on board the prison ship Jersey, at New-York, April 26, 1782," *Maryland Gazette*, May 30, 1782.

[34] Dring, 127-28.

[35] Ibid., 134-35.

36 Ibid., 128.
37 Ibid., 128-29.
38 Ibid., 129, 131.
39 Ibid., 129-30.
40 Ibid., 130.
41 Ibid., 131.
42 Ibid., 131-33.
43 Ibid., 136-37.
44 *New Jersey Gazette*, December 18, 1782; W. Woodford Clayton, ed., *History of Union and Middlesex Counties, New Jersey* (Philadelphia: Everts & Peck, 1882), 96. As no commission has yet been located by this author, it would suggest that Captain Quigley's vessel may have sailed without benefit of one, a not uncommon occurrence as the war was winding down.
45 David Sproat to Major Mackenzie, May 10, 1783, in James Lenox Banks, *David Sproat and Naval Prisoners in the War of the Revolution, with Mention of William Lenox, of Charlestown*, (New York: The Knickerbocker Press, 1909), 102.
46 Ibid.
47 Franklin W. Kemp, "The Privateer Monument," in *Dedication of the Monument in Honor of the Brave Privateers Who Served So Well in The War of Independence* (Chestnut Neck, NJ: The Col. Richard Somers Chapter, Sons of the American Revolution, October 1, 1988), 3. By Kemp's count a total of 195 prizes were brought into New Jersey ports by privateers between 1776 and 1783.

XXVI. Taps

1 *The Times* (Washington, D.C), January 31, 1898; "Hughes Tells of Duty," *New York Tribune*, October 27, 1907; "Honor Martyrs of Prison Ship," *Los Angeles Herald*, November, 15, 1908; Danske Dandridge, *American Prisoners of the Revolution* (Charlottesville, VA: The Michie Company, Printer, 1911), 194.
2 "Famous Prison Ship," *The Daily Journal* (Salem, OR), November 29, 1902; "Prison Ship Martyrs," *New York Tribune*, November 8, 1908; Robert E. Cray, Jr., "Commemorating the Prison Ship Dead: Revolutionary Memory and the Politics of Sepulture in the Early Republic, 1776–1808" *The William and Mary Quarterly*, Third Series, Vol. 56, No. 3 (July 1999) 565-90, 574.
3 "Prison Ship Jersey Found," *The Sun* (New York), October 14, 1902.
4 Nathaniel S. Prime, *A History of Long Island: From Its First Settlement by Europeans to the Year 1845* (New York and Pittsburgh: Robert Carter, 1845), 367.
5 Cray, 578-79; [Benjamin De Witt] Tammany Hall, Wallabout Committee, (New York: Printed for Frank White, and Co., 1808), *An account of the interment of the remains of 11,500 American seamen, soldiers, and citizens: who fell victims to the cruelties of the British on board their prison ships at the Wallabout during the American Revolution: with a particular description of the grand [et] solemn funeral procession, which took place on the 26 May, 1808: and an oration delivered at the tomb of the patriots, by Benjamin De Witt, M. D., a member of the Tammany Society or Columbian order/compiled by the Wallabout Committee*, 85.
6 "Martyrs of the Prison Ships," *The Star* (Reynoldsville, Pa.), June 29, 1910.

[7] [De Witt], 85-86.

[8] Cray, 575-78.

[9] "Our Fair Patriots," *The Evening World* (New York), June 3, 1891; De Witt, 85; "Skeletons Found in the Navy Yard," *New York Tribune*, January 25, 1900; "Famous Prison Ship," *The Daily Journal* (Salem, OR), November 29, 1902.

[10] "The Prison Ship Martyrs Monument" on the Fort Greene Park Conservancy http://www.triposo.com/poi/N__357618871; "Prison Ship Martyrs," *New York Tribune*, June 17, 1900.

[11] J. R. McCulloch, *McCulloch's Universal Gazetteer: A Dictionary, Geographical, Statistical, and Historical of the Countries, Places, and Principal Natural Objects in the World*, 2 vols. (New York: Harper & Brothers, 1852), 1:474; Gustavus Myers, *History of Tammany Hal* (New York: Boni & Liveright, 1917), 22; "Monument to Prison Ship Martyrs in Fort Greene Park," *New York Tribune*, January 7, 1906. A little over 80 years later, the number of dead supposedly interred had risen to 12,500, and was estimated by others as high as 18,000. "Our Fair Patriots," *The Evening World*, June 3, 1891; Edwin G. Burrows, "The Prisoners of New York," *Long Island History Journal*, 2011, 22, n.2. In 1902, the numbers of those in attendance was embellished to 30,000. "Famous Prison Ship," *The Daily Journal*, November 29, 1902.

[12] "Honor Martyrs of Prison Ship," *Los Angeles Herald*, November 15, 1908; "Prison Ship Martyrs," *New York Tribune*, November 8, 1908; C. C. Childs, & E. Childs, Jr., "The tomb of the martyrs," *Benjamin Romaine's Review*, July 4, 1839.

[13] "Skeleton in Chains," *Sunbury American and Shamokin Journal*, (Sunbury, Pa.), February 27, 1841; "Jersey Prison Ship," *Salt River Journal*, (Bowling Green, MO), March 6, 1841.

[14] "Washington Correspondence," *Sunbury American and Shamokin Journal*, February 8, 1845.

[15] *New Orleans Daily Crescent*, December 1, 1852.

[16] "Prison Ship Jersey Found," *The Sun*, October 14, 1902; McCulloch, 1:464.

[17] "Fort Greene Park: Prison Ship Martyrs Monument: History" New York City Department of Parks and Recreation, http://www.nycgovparks.org/parks/FortGreenePark/monuments/1222; "Revolutionary Martyrs," *Brooklyn Daily Eagle*, June 18, 1873.

[18] James Grant Wilson, *The Memorial History of the City of New-York, From its First Settlement to the Year 1892*, (New York: New-York History Company, 1893), 4:8-9; "Revolutionary Martyrs," *Brooklyn Daily Eagle*, June 18, 1873.

[19] "The Wallabout Bay Victims," *The Sun*, April 6, 1888. Washington Park would be formally recognized as Fort Green Park in 1897.

[20] "The Prison Ship Martyrs," *The Wichita Daily Eagle*, February 18, 1891; "The Wallabout Bay Victims," *The Sun*, April 6, 1888.

[21] "Daughters of the Revolution." *The Sun* (New York), June 14, 1891.

[22] 53d Congress, 2d Session House of Representatives Report No. 609. *A monument to the memory of the victims of prison ships at Fort Greene, Brooklyn, N.Y.: March 20, 1894, committed to the Committee of the Whole House on the state of the Union and ordered to be printed.* (Washington, DC: U.S. Government Printing Office,

1894); *The Times* (Washington, D.C), January 31, 1898; "In the Brooklyn Navy Yard," *Omaha Daily Bee* (Omaha, NE), September 23, 1888; "Washington Notes," *The Sun*, February 3, 1898; "Skeleton Dug Up at the Navy Yard," *The Brooklyn Eagle*, January 24, 1900; "Skeletons Found in the Navy Yard," *New York Tribune*, January 25, 1900; "For Revolutionary Martyrs," *The Florida Star* (Titusville, FL), March 15, 1901.

23 "Martyrs of the Prison Ships," *The Star* (Reynoldsville, PA), June 29, 1910; "The Prison Ship Martyrs" (letter to the editor) *New York Times*, May 23, 1903; "Prison Ship Martyrs," *New York Tribune*, June 17, 1900; *Secretary's Report of the Obsequies of the Prison Ship Martyrs at Plymouth Church, Brooklyn, N.Y. June 16, 1900 Under the Direction of the Prison Ship Martyrs' Monument Association of the United States*, ([New York]: 2010), 16.

24 "To Entomb Heroes Bones,"*New York Tribune*, June 16, 1900.

25 *Secretary's Report of the Obsequies of the Prison Ship Martyrs*, 16.

26 "To Entomb Heroes Bones,"*New York Tribune*, June 16, 1900.

27 "Martyrs of the Prison Ships," *The Star* (Reynoldsville, PA), June 29, 1910.

28 "For Revolutionary Martyrs" *The Florida Star*, March 15, 1901.

29 "House Adopts a Resolution Appropriating $100,000 for a Monument," *New York Times*, June 17, 1902; "Ft. Greene Statue Bill Passes," *The Brooklyn Eagle*, June 27, 1902; "Prison Ship Martyrs," *New York Tribune*, November 8, 1908.

30 "Remains of the Old Prison Ship Jersey," *The Washington Times*, October 26, 1902; "Famous Prison Ship," *The Daily Journal* (Salem, OR), November 29, 1902; "Old Prison Ship," *Evening Bulletin* (Oahu, HI), October 24, 1902.

31 "Remains of the Old Prison Ship Jersey," *The Washington Times*, October 26, 1902

32 "Famous Prison Ship," *The Daily Journal* (Salem, OR), November 29, 1902.

33 "The Jersey Prison Ship," *Evening Star* (Washington, DC), October 24, 1902; "Remains of the Old Prison Ship Jersey," *The Washington Times*, October 26, 1902; "Famous Prison Ship," *The Daily Journal*, November 29, 1902.

34 "Remains of the Old Prison Ship Jersey," *The Washington Times*, October 26, 1902; "Old Prison Ship) *Evening Bulletin* (Honolulu, Oahu, HI), October 24, 1902; "The Jersey Prison Ship," *Evening Star* (Washington, DC), October 24, 1902; "The Jersey Prison Ship," *The Sun* (New York), October 15, 1902.

35 "Old Prison Ship," *Evening Bulletin* (Honolulu, Oahu, HI), October 24, 1902; "A Remarkable historic discovery ," *Willmar Tribune* (Willmar, MN), October 12, 1904.

36 Ibid.

37 "Association Incorporated to Raise Monument to Those Who Died in War of Revolution," *New York Times*, May 10, 1903; "Prison Ship Martyrs," *New York Tribune*, November 8, 1908.

38 "Martyrs of the Prison Ships," *The Star*, June 29, 1910; "To Honor Martyrs," *Bismarck Daily Tribune* (Bismarck, ND), March 22, 1907; "Fort Greene Historic District Designation Report," Landmarks Preservation Commission, September 26, 1978, Designation List 119 LP-0973, p. 11.

39 "Monument to Prison Ship Martyrs in Fort Greene Park," *New York Tribune*, January 7, 1906.

40 "Hughes Tells of Duty," *New York Tribune*, October 27, 1907.

41 "Mr. Taft on Way Here," *New York Tribune*, November 14, 1908; "Monument for Ship Martyrs," *Omaha Daily Bee*, November 15, 1908; "Taft's Tribute to Martyrs of War," *Salt Lake Tribune*, November 15, 1908.

42 "Taft's Tribute to Martyrs of War," *Salt Lake Tribune*, November 15, 1908.

43 Ibid.

44 Ibid.; "Mr. Taft on Way Here," *New York Tribune*, November 14, 1908.

45 Ibid.

46 "Fort Greene Historic District Designation Report," 12; *New York Daily News*, November 14, 2008; *New York Times*, September 23, 1995.

47 *Dedication of the Monument in Honor of the Brave Privateers Who Served So Well in The War of Independence 1776–1783*, (The Col. Richard Somers Chapter, Sons of the American Revolution: Chestnut Neck, [NJ], October 1, 1988), 1-4.

48 *The Brooklyn Paper*, October 20, 2008; *New York Daily News*, November 14, 2008.

Bibliography

Acts of the General Assembly of the State of New Jersey, at a Session begun at Princeton on the 27th Day of August 1776, and continued by Adjournments. To which is prefixed, the Constitution of the State. Burlington: Isaac Coffins, 1777.

Admiralty Miscellanea, PRO, 49/2, 49/3, 49/4, 49/5, 49/6, 49/7, Microfilms. Library of Congress, Washington, DC.

Alberts, Robert C. *The Golden Voyage: The Life and Times of William Bingham, 1752–1804.* Boston: Houghton Muffin Co., 1969.

Allen, Gardner W. *A Naval History of the American Revolution.* 2 vols. Williamston, MA: Corner House Publishers, 1970 (reprint of 1913).

Almon, John, ed. *The Remembrancer, or Impartial Repository of Public Events.* 17 vols. London: Printed for J. Almon, 1775–1784.

Amerman, Richard H. "Treatment of American Prisoners During the Revolution," *Proceedings of the New Jersey Historical Society*, Vol. 78, No. 4.

Andros, Thomas. *The old Jersey captive: or, A narrative of the captivity of Thomas Andros . . . on board the old Jersey prison ship at New York, 1781. In a series of letters to a friend . . .* Boston: W. Peirce, 1833.

Appleton's Cyclopedia of American Biography. Vol. 2. New York: D. Appleton & Co., 1888.

Aspinwall Paper. *Collections of the Massachusetts Historical Society*, Vols. 9 and 10. Boston: Massachusetts Historical Society, 1871.

Aurora for the Country, Philadelphia.

Austin, James Trecothick. *The Life of Elbridge Gerry.* 2 vols. Boston: Wells and Lilly, 1828.

Bailey, J.D. *Commanders At Kings Mountain.* Gaffney, SC: E. H. DeCamp, 1929.

Banks, James Lenox. *David Sproat and Naval Prisoners in the War of the Revolution, with Mention of William Lenox, of Charlestown.* ([New York]: The Knickerbocker Press, 1909.

Barnes, G. R., and J. H. Owen, eds. *The Private Papers of John, Earl of Sandwich, First Lord of the Admiralty, 1771–1782.* 4 vols. [London]: Navy Records Society, 1932–1938.

Barney, Mary, *A Biographical Memoir of the Late Joshua Barney: From Autobiographical Notes and Journals in Possession of His Family, and Other Authentic Sources.* Boston: Gray and Bowen, 1832.

Bartlett, John Russell, ed. *Records of the Colony of Rhode Island and Providence Plantation, in New England.* 10 vols. Providence: Printed by the Providence Press Company, 1856–1865.

[Baurmeister, Carl Leopold] *Revolution in America: Confidential Letters and Journals 1776–1784 of Adjutant General Major Baurmeister of the Hessian Forces*, Bernard A. Uhlendorf, trans. and ann. New Brunswick, NJ: Rutgers University Press, 1957.

Bentalou, Paul. *Reply to Judge Johnson's Remarks on an article in the North American Review, relating to Count Pulaski.* Baltimore: Printed by J. D. Toy, 1826.

Bismarck Daily Tribune, Bismarck, ND.

Boatner, Mark Mayo, III. *Encyclopedia of the American Revolution.* New York: David McKay Company, Inc., 1966.

Boston Gazette, Boston, MA.

Boudinot, Elias. *Life, Public Services, Addresses, and Letters,* J. J. Boudinot, ed. 2 vols. Boston: Houghton Mifflin, 1896.

Bourguignon, Henry J. *The First Federal Court: The Federal Appellate Prize Court of the American Revolution, 1775–1787,* Memoirs of the American Philosophical Society 122 (1977).

Bouton, Nathaniel, *et al,* eds., *Provincial Papers: Documents and Records Relating to the State of New Hampshire.* Concord: Published by Authority of the Legislature of New Hampshire, 1867.

Bowman, Larry G. "The Court-Martial of Captain Richard Lippincott," *New Jersey History*, Vol. 89 (Spring 1971).

Boyd, George A. *Elias Boudinot: Patriot and Statesman, 1740–1821.* Princeton, NJ: Princeton University Press, 1952.

Boyd, Julian P., *et al*, eds., *The Papers of Thomas Jefferson*, 40 vols. Princeton: Princeton University Press, 1950—.

Boyer, Charles S. *Early Forges and Furnaces in New Jersey*. Philadelphia: University of Pennsylvania Press, and London, H. Milford, Oxford University Press, 1931.

Brooklyn Daily Eagle, Brooklyn, NY.

The Brooklyn Paper, Brooklyn, NY.

Brown, Margaret L. "William Bingham, Agent of the Continental Congress in Martinique," *The Pennsylvania Magazine of History and Biography*. Philadelphia: The Historical Society of Pennsylvania, 1937.

Brown, Gerald Saxon. *The American Secretary: The Colonial Policy of Lord George Germain, 1775–1778*. Ann Arbor: University of Michigan Press, [1963].

Brown, Wallace. *The Good American*. New York: William Morrow and Company, Inc., 1969.

Burgess, Paul C. *A Colonial Scrapbook, the Southern New Jersey Coast, 1675–1783*. New York: Carlton Press, 1971.

Burrows, Edwin G. "The Prisoners of New York," *Long Island History Journal*, 2011.

Butterfield, Lyman H., *et al*, eds. *Adams Family Correspondence*. 2 vols. Cambridge: The Belknap Press of Harvard University, 1963.

Carson, H. L. *The Case of the Sloop "Active"*. Philadelphia: Allen, Lane & Scott, 1893.

The Case of the Sloop Active &c. .Philadelphia: Hall and Sellers, &c. Philadelphia, 1779.

Chapelle, Howard I. *History of American Sailing Ships*. New York: W.W. Norton & Company, Inc., 1935.

_____ *The National Watercraft Collection*. Washington: U.S. Government Printing Office, 1960.

Chastellux, Maquis de. *Travels in North America in the Years 1780, 1781, and 1782*, Howard C. Rice, Jr., ed. 2 vols. Chapel Hill, NC: University of North Carolina Press: 1963.

Childs, C. C., and E, Childs, Jr. "The tomb of the martyrs," *Benjamin Romaine's Review*, July 4, 1839.

Clark, William Bell. "That Mischievous Holker, The Story of a Privateer," *Pennsylvania Magazine of History and Biography*, Vol. 79, No. 1 (January 1955).

Clark, William Bell, *et al*, eds. *Naval Documents of the American Revolution*, 11 vols. Washington, DC: U.S. Government Printing Office, 1964-2005.

Clayton, W. Woodford, ed. *History of Union and Middlesex Counties, New Jersey*. Philadelphia: Everts & Peck, 1882.

Coakley, Robert W., and Stetson Conn. *The War of the American Revolution: Narrative, Chronology, and Bibliography*. Washington, DC: Center of Military History United States Army, 1975.

Coffin, Alexander Coffin. *The destructive operation of foul air, tainted provisions, bad water and personal filthiness upon human constitutions, exemplified in the unparalleled cruelty of the British to the American captives at New York during the Revolutionary War, on board their prison and hospital ships, in a communication to Dr. Mitchell, dated September 4, 1807*. New York: Privately printed, 1865.

Coggins, Jack, *Ships and Seamen of the American Revolution*. Harrisburg, PA: Stackpole Books, 1969.

Collection on the participation of German soldiers in the American Revolution, 1776–1885, Ms. Coll. 773, Kislak Center for Special Collections, Rare Books and Manuscripts, University of Pennsylvania.

Commager, Henry Steele, and Richard B. Morris, eds. *The Spirit of "Seventy-Six": The Story of the American Revolution as Told by Participants*. New York, Evanston, and London: Harper & Row, Publishers, 1958.

Committee on Appeals statement, June 16, 1779, case file no. 30, RG 267, National Archives and Record Service, Washington, DC.

Conduct of Vice Admiral Graves in North America in 1774, 1775 and January 1776, 1: 94. Transcripts. Library of Congress, Washington, DC.

Connecticut Courant, Hartford, CT.

Connecticut Journal, New Haven, CT.

Connecticut Historical Society, *Connecticut Historical Society Collections*. Vol. 2. Hartford: Published for the Society, 1870.

Constitutional Gazette, New York, NY.

Cooledge, J. J. *Ships of the Royal Navy: An Historical Index*. 2vols. Newton Abbot, Devon, England: David & Charles, 1969.

Cranch, William. *Reports of Cases Argued and Adjudged in the Supreme Court of the United States, in February Term, 1809*, 3d ed. Vol. 5. New York: Isaac Riley, 1882.

Crary, Catherine S. *The Price of Loyalty: Tory Writings from the Revolutionary Era*. New York: McGraw-Hill Book Company, 1973.

Cray, Jr., Robert E. "Commemorating the Prison Ship Dead: Revolutionary Memory and the Politics of Sepulture in the Early Republic, 1776–1808," *The William and Mary Quarterly*, Third Series, Vol. 56, No. 3 (July 1999).

The Daily Journal, Salem, OR.

Dallas, Alexander J. *Reports of Cases Ruled and Adjudged in the Several Courts of the United States and of Pennsylvania.* New York: Lawyers Co-operative Publishing Company, 1882.

Dandridge, Danske. *American Prisoners of the Revolution.* Charlottesvile, VA: The Michie Company, Printer, 1911 [reprinted Baltimore: Genealogical Publishing Company, 1967].

Davis, J.C. Bancroft. *United States Reports. Cases Adjudged in the U.S. Supreme Court at October Term, 1888.* Vol. 131. New York: Banks & Brothers, 1889.

[De Witt, Benjamin] Tammany Hall, Wallabout Committee. *An account of the interment of the remains of 11,500 American seamen, soldiers, and citizens: who fell victims to the cruelties of the British on board their prison ships at the Wallabout during the American Revolution: with a particular description of the grand [et] solemn funeral procession, which took place on the 26 May, 1808: and an oration delivered at the tomb of the patriots, by Benjamin De Witt, M. D., a member of the Tammany Society or Columbian order.* New York: printed for Frank White and Co., 1808.

Dedication of the Monument in Honor of the Brave Privateers Who Served So Well in the War of Independence 1776–1783. The Colonel Richard Somers Chapter, Sons of the American Revolution: Chestnut Neck [NJ]. October 1, 1988. Diary of Christopher Vail. Library of Congress, Washington, DC.

Documents Relating to the Revolutionary History of the State of New Jersey, Series 2 of *The Archives of the State of New Jersey.* 5 vols. Trenton: John L. Murphy Pub. Co., 1901–1917.

Draper, Lyman C. *Kings Mountain And Its Heroes.* New York: Dauber and Pine Bookshops, 1929.

Dumbauld, Edward. "The case of the Mutinous Mariner," *Yearbook 1977 Supreme Court Historical Society.* <http://www.supremecourthistory.org//myweb/77jurnal/dmbauld 77.htm> Accessed February 3, 2006.

Emmons, George F. *The Navy of the United States, From the Commencement, 1775 to 1753 with a Brief History of Each Vessel's Fate and Service as Appears Upon Record.* Washington, DC: Printed by Gideon & Co., 1853.

Essex Journal or New Hampshire Packet, Newburyport, MA.

Evans, Charles. *American Biography*, 12 vols. Chicago: Privately printed, 1903–1934.

Evening Bulletin, Oahu, HI.

Evening Star, Washington, DC.

The Evening World, New York, NY.

Fitzpatrick, John C., ed. *The Writings of George Washington from the Original Manuscript Sources 1745–1799.* 39 vols. Washington, DC: U.S. Government Printing Office, 1931–1944.

The Florida Star, Titusville, FL.

Footner, Hulbert. *Sailor of Fortune: The Life and Adventures of Commodore Barney, U.S.N.* New York and London: Harper & Brothers Publishers, 1940.

Force, Peter, comp. *American Archives*, 9 vols. Washington, DC: M. St. Claire Clarke and Peter Force, 1837–1853.

Ford, Worthington C., ed. *Correspondence and Journals of Samuel Bachley Webb.* 3 vols. New York [Lancaster, Pa.]: Wickenham Press, 1893.

Ford, Worthington C., *et al.*, eds. *Journals of the Continental Congress, 1774–1789*, 34 vols. Washington, DC: U.S. Government Printing Office, 1904–1937.

"Fort Greene Historic District Designation Report" Landmarks Preservation Commission, September 26, 1978, Designation List 119 LP-0973.

Fort Greene Park Conservancy. "The Prison Ship Martyrs Monument." http://www.triposo.com/poi/N__357618871. Accessed April 2, 2013.

"Fort Green Park. Prison Ship Martyrs Monument: History." New York Department of Parks and Recreation. http://www.nycgovparks.org/parks/Fort GreenePark/monument/1222.

Fox, Ebenezer. *The Adventures of Ebenezer Fox in the Revolutionary War.* Boston: C. Fox, 1847.

Franklin Papers. American Philosophical Society, Philadelphia, PA.

Freeman, Douglas Southall. *George Washington: A Biography.* 7 vols. New York: Scribner, 1948–1957.

The Freeman's Journal: or The North-American Intelligencer, Philadelphia, PA.

Freneau, Philip Freneau. *Poems Relating to the American Revolution.* New York: W. J. Widdleton, 1868 [Reprinted Anne Arbor, MI: University of Michigan Humanities and Text Initiative, 1997].

Gambier Papers, Admiralty 1/489. Transcripts. Library of Congress, Washington, DC.

George Washington Papers. Library of Congress, Washington, DC.

Germain Papers. William L. Clements Library, University of Michigan, Ann Arbor, MI.

Goodwin, Joseph O. *East Hartford: Its History and Traditions.* Hartford: Case, Lockwood & Brainard Co., 1879.

Greene, Albert. *Recollections of the Jersey Prison Ship from the manuscript of Captain Thomas Dring.* New York: Corinth Books, 1961.

Greene Collection. William L. Clements Library, University of Michigan, Ann Arbor, MI.

Hawkins, Christopher. *The American Adventures of Christopher Hawkins, containing details of his captivity, a first and second time on the high seas, in the Revolutionary War by the British, and his consequent sufferings, and escape from the Jersey Prison Ship.* New York: Privately printed, 1864.

Hazard, Samuel, *et al.*, eds. *Pennsylvania Archives.* Philadelphia: Printed by J. Severns & Co.,1852–1856, and Harrisburg: 1874.

Henry, William Wirt. *Patrick Henry, Life, Correspondence and Speeches.* 3 vols. New York: Charles Scribner's Sons, 1891.

Historical Sketch, to the End of the Revolutionary War, of the Life of Silas Talbot, Esq., of the State of Rhode Island, lately Commander of the United States frigate, the Constitution, and of an American Squadron in the West-Indies. New York: Printed by G. & R. Waite, for H. Caritat, 1803.

Holland, Jr., Francis Ross. *America's Lighthouses: An Illustrated History.* New York: Dover Publications, 1972.

Hornor, William Stockton. *This Old Monmouth of Ours.* Freehold, NJ: Moreau Brothers, 1932.

Hurd, Duane Hamilton. *History of Bristol County, Massachusetts, Part I.* Philadelphia: J. W. Lewis, 1883.

Jackson, John W. *The Pennsylvania Navy, 1775–1781: The Defense of the Delaware.* New Brunswick, NJ: Rutgers University Press, 1974.

James, Marquis. *Biography of a Business, 1792–1942: Insurance Company of North America.* Indianapolis: Bobbs-Merrill, 1942.

Jameson, J. Franklin. *The American Revolution Considered as a Social Movement.* Princeton, NJ: Princeton University Press, 1926.

John Paul Jones Papers, Etting Collection, Historical Society of Pennsylvania, Philadelphia, PA.

"Journal of Lieutenant John Trevett," *Rhode Island Historical Magazine* (July 1886).

Journal of the Proceedings on Board His Majesty's Sloop *Nautilus*, Admiralty 51/630. Photocopy. Public Record Office, London, UK.

Journals of the Provincial Congress, Provincial Convention, Committees of Safety and Council of Safety of the State of New York, 1775–1776–1777, 2 vols. Albany: T. Weed Thurlow, Printer to the State, 1842.

Kemp, Franklin W. *A Nest of Rebel Pirates*, Atlantic City, NJ: Batsto Citizens Committee, 1966.

_____ "The Privateer Monument," in *Dedication of the Monument in Honor of the Brave Privateers Who Served So Well in The War of Independence.* Chestnut Neck, NJ: The Col. Richard Somers Chapter, Sons of the American Revolution, October 1, 1988.

Knollenberg, Bernhard, ed. *Correspondence of Governor Samuel Ward, May 1775-March 1776.* Providence: Rhode Island Historical Society, 1952.

Kobbé, Gustav. *The Jersey Coast and Pines.* Baltimore: Gateway Press, Inc., 1970.

Kurlansky, Mark. *Salt: A World History.* New York: Penguin Books, 2002.

Leonard, M. D. and C. Grosse. *American Germanica: Tagebuch des Capt. Wiederholdt Vom 7 October 1776 Bis 7 December 1780.* New York and London: The Macmillan Company, 1902.

"Letters of John Lowell and Others." *Historical Magazine* (September 1857).

Lodge, Henry Cabot, ed. *Complete Works of Alexander Hamilton.* 12 vols. New York: G.P. Putnam's Sons, n.d.

London Chronicle, London, UK.

Los Angeles Herald, Los Angeles, CA.

Lossing, Benson J. *The Pictorial Field Book of the American Revolution.* 2 vols. New York: Harper and Bros., 1868.

Maclay, Edgar S. *A History of American Privateers.* New York: D. Appleton and Co., 1910.

Mahan, A[lfred] T[hayer]. *The Influence of Sea Power Upon History, 1660–1783.* Cambridge: John Wilson and Son, 1890.

Maritime Papers, Letters of Marque, 1776–1780. Rhode Island Archives, Providence, RI.

Maryland Gazette, Annapolis, MD.

Massachusetts Spy, Boston, MA.

McCormick, Richard P. *Experiment in Independence: New Jersey in the Critical Period, 1781–1789.* New Brunswick: Rutgers University Press, 1950.

McCulloch, J. R. *McCulloch's Universal Gazetteer: A Dictionary, Geographical, Statistical, and Historical of the Countries, Places, and Principal Natural Objects in the World*. 2 vols. New York: Harper & Brothers, 1852.

McMahon, William. *South Jersey Towns*. New Brunswick: Rutgers University Press, 1973.

Middlebrook, Louis F. *Captain Gideon Olmsted, Connecticut Privateersman, Revolutionary War*. Salem, MA: Newcomb & Gauss Co., 1933.

Miller, Nathan. *Sea of Glory: The Continental Navy Fights for Independence, 1775–1783*. New York: David Mackay Company, Inc., 1974.

Mitchell. James T., and Henry Flanders, eds. *The Statutes at Large of Pennsylvania*, 18 vols. Harrisburg: Clarence M. Busch, State Printer of Pennsylvania, 1896–1915.

Nagle, Jacob. *The Nagle Journal: A Diary of the Life of Jacob Nagle, Sailor, from the Year 1775 to 1841*, John C. Dann, ed. New York, Weidenfeld & Nicholson: 1988.

Naval Records of the American Revolution, 1775–1788. Washington, DC: Government Printing Office, 1906.

Nelson, Paul. *Sir Charles Grey, First Earl Grey: Royal Soldier, Family Patriarch* Madison, NJ: Fairleigh Dickinson University Press, 1996.

New Jersey Gazette, Trenton, NJ.

New Jersey Loyalist Muster Rolls, 1777–1782. Photocopy. Library of Congress, Washington, DC.

New Orleans Daily Crescent, New Orleans, LA.

New York City Department of Parks and Recreation. "Fort Greene Park: Prison Ship Martyrs Monument: History" http://www.nycgovparks.org/parks/FortGreenePark/monuments/1222. Accessed February 28, 2006.

New York Daily News, New York, NY.

New York Gazette, New York, NY.

The New York Gazette and Weekly Mercury, New York, NY.

New York Gazette and Weekly Mercury Extraordinary, New York, NY.

New York Historical Society Quarterly, Vol. 41 and 46, October 1948, July 1950.

New York Journal and the General Advertiser, New York, NY.

New York Tribune, New York, NY.

Newark Star-Ledger, Newark, NJ.

Newport Mercury, Newport, RI

Niles's Weekly Register, Baltimore, MD.

North, Gary. "Britain's Prison Ships, 1776–1783," http://www.lewrockwell.com/orig/north5html. Accessed Feburary 28, 2006.

The Norwich Packet and the Weekly Advertiser, Norwich, CT.

O'Callaghan, E.B., ed. *Documents Relative to the Colonial History of the State of New York; Procured in Holland, England and France*, 15 vols. Albany: Weed, Parsons & Co., 1856–1857.

Olmsted, Gideon. *The Journal of Gideon Olmsted: Adventures of a Sea Captain during the American Revolution. A Facsimile*. Washington: Library of Congress, 1978.

Omaha Daily Bee, Omaha, NE.

Onderdonck, Henry. *Documents and Letters Intended to Illustrate the Revolutionary Incidents of Queens County*. New York: Leavitt, Trow, 1846.

Onderdonck, Henry, Jr. *Revolutionary incidents of Suffolk and Kings Counties: with an account of the Battle of Long Island and the British prison and prison-ships at New York*. New York: Leavitt Trow, 1849.

Papers laid before the Provincial Congress of New York, 1775-80, vol. 25, Military Committees. New York State Library, Albany, NY.

The Parliamentary History of England from the Earliest Period to the Year 1803, vol. XIX, January 29, 1777 to December 4 1778. London: T. C. Hansard, 1814.

Paullin, Charles Oscar, *Out Letters of the Continental Marine Committee and the Board of Admiralty, August 1776-September 1780*. 2 vols. Naval History Society, New York: 1914.

Peck, Thomas Bellows. "Journal Kept by Corporal William Slade, of Woodbury, Conn., During His Captivity on an English Prison Ship in the war of the revolution, From November 16, 1776 to January 28, 1777," *William Slade of Windsor, Conn. and His Descendants*. Keene, NH: Sentinel Printers Company, 1910.

Pennsylvania Colonial Records: Minutes of the Provincial Council of Pennsylvania from the Organization to the Termination of the Provincial Government. 10 vols. Philadelphia: J. Severns, 1852, and Harrisburg: T. Fenn, 1852.

Pennsylvania Evening Post, Philadelphia, PA.

Pennsylvania Gazette, Philadelphia, PA.

Pennsylvania Gazette and Weekly Advertiser, Philadelphia, PA.

Pennsylvania Journal, Philadelphia, PA.

Pennsylvania Packet, Philadelphia, PA.

Pennsylvania Packet or the General Advertiser/ The Pennsylvania Packet or the General Advertiser, Philadelphia, PA.

Phelps, Richard H. *A History of Newgate of Connecticut.* New York: Arno Press, 1969.

Pierce, Arthur D. *Iron in the Pines: The Story of New Jersey's Ghost Towns and Bog Iron.* New Brunswick, NJ: Rutgers University Press, 1957.

_____ *Smugglers' Woods: Jaunts and Journeys in Colonial and Revolutionary New Jersey.* New Brunswick, NJ: Rutgers University Press, 1960.

Plunger, Richard D. "A Verse…to Remaining Idle Spectators:" The Emergence of Loyalist Privateering During the American Revolution, 1775–1778," Vol. 2. Doctoral Thesis: University of Maine, May 2002.

Present Disposition of His Majesty's Ships and Vessels in Sea Paye 1st June 1776, PRO, Admiralty 8/52. Photocopy. Public Record Office, London, UK.

Preston, Henry, and David Lyon. *Navies of the American Revolution.* Englewood Cliffs, NJ; Prentice-Hall Incorporated, 1975.

Prime, Nathaniel S. *A History of Long Island: From Its First Settlement by Europeans to the Year 1845.* New York and Pittsburgh: Robert Carter, 1845.

"The prison Ship Martyrs Monument" on the Fort Greene Park Conservancy. http://www.triposo.com/poi/N_357618871.

Proceedings of a General Court Martial for the Trial of Major General Arnold. New York: J. Munsell, printer, 1865.

Public Advertiser, London, UK.

Records of the Supreme Court of the United States, RG 267, case no. 29, National Archives and Record Service, Washington, DC.

Rickerson, Daniel. *The History of New Bedford, Bristol County, Massachusetts.* New Bedford: Published by the author, 1858.

Robert Treat Paine Papers. Massachusetts Historical Society, Boston, MA.

Robotti, Frances Diane. *Chronicles of Old Salem: A History in Miniature.* New York: Bonanza Books, 1953.

Robson, Eric, ed. *Letters from America 1773–1780; being the letters of a Scots officer, Sir James Murray, to his home during the war of American independence.* Manchester, UK.: Manchester University Press, 1951.

Royal Gazette, New York, NY.

Sabine, Lorenzo. *Biographical Sketches of Loyalists in the American Revolution.* 2 vols. Boston: Little, Brown and Company, 1864.

Salt Lake Tribune, Salt Lake City, UT.

Salt River Journal, Bowling Green, MO.

Salter, Edwin. *A history of Monmouth and Ocean Counties, embracing a genealogical record of earliest setters in Monmouth and Ocean counties and their descendants. The Indians: their language, manners, and customs. Important historical events. . . .* Bayonne, NJ: F. Gardner & Sons, Publishers, 1890.

Scharf Collection, Ms. 1999. Maryland Historical Society. Baltimore, MD.

Secretary's Report of the Obsequies of the Prison Ship Martyrs at Plymouth Church, Brooklyn, N.Y. June 16, 1900 Under the Direction of the Prison Ship Martyrs' Monument Association of the United States. New York: 2010.

Sherburne, Andrew. *Memoirs of Andrew Sherburne, a pensioner of the Revolution.* Utica, NY: W. Williams, 1828.

Smith, Charles Page. *James Wilson, Founding Father, 1742–1798.* Chapel Hill: University of North Carolina Press for the Institute of Early American History and Culture, Williamsburg, VA, 1956.

Smith, Charles R. *Marines in the American Revolution: A History of the Continental Marines in the American Revolution 1775–1783.* Washington, DC: History and Museum Division, Headquarters, U.S. Marine Corps, 1975.

Smith, Paul H., ed. *Letters of Delegates to Congress 1774–1789.* 26 vols. Washington, DC: Library of Congress, 1976-2000.

Smith, Samuel Steele. *Fight for the Delaware 1777.* Monmouth Beach, NJ: Philip Freneau Press, 1970.

South Carolina and American General Gazette, Charleston, SC.

The Star, Reynoldsville, PA.

Stevens, Lewis T. "Cape May Naval Activities in the Revolution," *Cape May County Historical Society Journal,* Vol. 2.

Stryker, William S. *The Capture of the Block House at Toms River.* Trenton, NJ: Naar, Day and Naar, 1883.

_____ *The Affair at Egg Harbor, New Jersey, October 15, 1778. . . . Read July 3, 1894, at the dedication of a memorial tablet, erected on the field of the massacre, by the Society of the Cincinnati in the state of New Jersey, and at the annual meeting of the society on the following day.* Trenton, Naar, Day & Naar, 1894.

The Sun, New York, NY.

Sunbury American and Shamokin Journal, Sunbury, PA.

Sundry Documents Relative to the Claim of Gideon Olmsted Against the Commonwealth of Pennsylvania. Philadelphia: Printed by Edward Olmsted, 1811.

Thayer, Theodore. *Nathaniel Greene: Strategist of the Revolution* New York: Twayne Publishers, 1960.

The Times, Washington, DC.

Tyler, David Budlong. *The Bay & River Delaware: A Pictorial History.* Cambridge, MD: Cornell Maritime Press, 1955.

Upton, Richard Francis. *Revolutionary New Hampshire: An Account of the Social and Political Forces Underlying the Transition from Royal Province to American Commonwealth.* New York: Octagon Books, 1971.

Van Doren, Carl. *Secret History of the American Revolution.* New York: Viking Press, 1941.

Van Dyke, Captain John. "Narrative of Confinement in the Jersey Prison Ship," *N.Y.S.A. Historical Magazine,* Vol. 7, May 1863.

Van Tyne, Claude H. *The Loyalists in the American Revolution.* New York: The Macmillan Company, 1902.

Virginia Gazette, Dixon and Hunter's, Williamsburg, VA.

Virginia Gazette, Purdie's, Williamsburg, VA.

Von Closen, Ludwig. *The Revolutionary Journal of Baron Ludwig Von Closen 1780–1783*, Evelyn M. Acomb, trans. and ed. Chapel Hill, NC: University of North Carolina Press, 1958.

Ward, Christopher. *The War of the Revolution.* 2 vols. New York: The Macmillan Company, 1952.

Warren, Charles. *The Supreme Court in United States History.* Vol. 1. Boston: Little, Brown, and Company, 1922.

Warren–Adams Letters Being Chiefly a Correspondence among John Adams, Samuel Adams and James Warren . . . 1743–1814. Collections of the Massachusetts Historical Society. Vols. 72 and 73. Boston: Massachusetts Historical Society, 1917–1925.

Wharton, Francis, ed. *The Revolutionary Diplomatic Correspondence of the United States.* 6 vols. Washington, DC: Government Printing Office, 1889.

Wilbur, C. Keith. *Picture Book of the Revolution's Privateers.* Harrisburg, PA: Stackpole Books, 1973.

The Wichita Daily Eagle, Wichita, KS.

Wildes, Harry Emerson. *Lonely Midas: The Story of Stephen Girard.* New York: Farrar and Rhinehart, 1943.

Willmar Tribune, Willmar, MN.

Wilson, James Grant. *The Memorial History of the City of New-York, From its First Settlement to the Year 1892.* New York: New-York History Company, 1893.

53d Congress, 2d Session House of Representatives Report No. 609. *A monument to the memory of the victims of prison ships at Fort Greene, Brooklyn, N.Y.: March 20, 1894, committed to the Committee of the Whole House on the state of the Union and ordered to be printed.* Washington, DC: U.S. Government Printing Office, 1894.

Websites

http://www.americanrevolution.org/nav18.html (Accessed February 28, 2006).

http://www.eastrivernyc.org/ehistory/prison.shtm (Accessed February 28, 2006).

http://www.motherbedford.com/Prison.htm (Accessed February 28, 2006).

http://prisonship martyrs.com/gpage1.html (Accessed February 28, 2006)

Index

March, Job, 260
Marcus Hook, PA, 200
Marie Antoinette, 251, 253
Marquis de Chastellux, 133
Marriner, William, 207, 208, 210, 211, 254
Marshall, John, 124
Marshall, W. L., 320
Marson, Samuel, 60
Martha's Vineyard, MA, 60, 144, 145, 147, 168, 169
Martinique, WI, 60, 89, 91, 98, 133, 134, 187
Maryland, 20, 42, 43, 44, 45, 60, 63, 64, 66, 68, 76, 90, 94, 98, 99, 106, 113, 116, 121, 130, 133, 134, 175, 179, 216, 243, 244, 324; Council of Safety, 206; Navy, 63
Marryott, Samuel, 130
Mason, Christopher, 220, 221, 222
Massachusetts, 10, 17, 20, 21, 23, 24, 30, 31, 32, 43, 44, 51, 60, 61, 62, 63, 116, 117, 119, 121, 132, 134, 135, 144, 169, 178, 184, 185, 191, 256, 277, 282, 324; Admiralty Court, 185; General Assembly, 303; Superior Court of Judicature, 185
Matawan Creek, NJ, 207
Mather, James, 23
Mathis, Daniel, 87
Mathews, David, 77, 207
Mathews, Edward, 170
Matthew Irwin & Company, 135
Maurice River, NJ, 210
Maxwell, William, 149
Maybaum (Lieutenant), 211
Maybaum (Major), 211
M'Mullen, Robert, 144
McAroy, Captain George, 59, 60
McClenachan, Blair, 13, 132, 133, 182, 184, 191, 194, 196
McCullough, David, 323
McCullough, Joseph, 139
McCullough, William, 143
McDonald, Cornelius, 235
McDougall, Alexander, 37
McKean, Thomas, 122, 123, 301
McKim, Mead & White, 320
McNachtane, John, 186, 187, 188
McNeill, Daniel, 135
McPhearson's wharf, New Bedford, MA, 145
McPherson, Alexander, 148
Matlack, Timothy, 133
Mayberry, Thomas, 181
Mays Landing, NJ, 66, 73, 86, 141, 168
Mercer, Hugh, 58
Mercier, John D., 113
Mercure de France, 254
Merriman, Luke, 220
Metompkin Inlet, VA, 187
Michael Dawson & Company, 139

Middle of the Shore, NJ, 161
Middleton, Arthur, 244
Middletown, NJ, 86, 208, 237; Point, 207
Milford, CT, 295, 313; Harbor, 313
Mill Prison, 72, 217
Miller, Aaron, 100
Miller, Abraham, 122
Miller, Charles, 195, 196
Mincock Island, NJ, 161 (see also Osborns Island, NJ, Faulkinburg's Island, NJ)
Missouri, 313
Mitchell, Samuel L., 311
Moncrieff, ___, 207
Monmouth County, NJ, 211, 214, 232, 234, 236, 237, 239, 241, 242, 244; Militia, 231; Retaliators, 241; Second Regiment, 231
Montagu, John, 78
Montego Bay, Jamaica, 100, 105
Montgomery, James, 135
Montgomery, ___, 87
Montreal, Canada, 16
Moore, ___, 49
Moore, Philip, 59, 61
Morris, Gouverneur, 113, 114, 118, 119
Morris, John, 206
Morris, Richard, 237, 238, 239
Morris, Richard B., 259
Morris, Robert, 13, 43, 61, 63, 65, 76, 84, 91, 95, 133, 134, 190, 216, 217, 255, 256, 308
Morris, Jr., Samuel, 186
Morris County, NJ, 246
Morris River, NJ, 233
Morrison, Hugh, 24
Morristown, NJ, 252
Moulder, James, 26
Mount, John, 95
Mount Holly, NJ, 86, 93, 94, 131
Mullica River, NJ, 8, 50, 54, 59, 62, 86, 87, 93, 94, 96, 98, 129, 131, 138, 151, 154, 169, 181, 187, 207
Murphy, ___, 313
Murray, James, 165
Murray, john, 194
Musqueto Shore, SA, 90
Mute, Son & Atkinson, 33
Myrtle Avenue, Brooklyn, NY, 317
Nacote Creek, NJ, 87
Nagle, Jacob, 193, 194, 197, 198, 199, 201
Nantucket Island, MA, 145; Sound, 69
Nantz, France, 95, 145,
Nassau Island, Bahamas, 312
Nassau Street, Brooklyn, NY, 316
Navesink, NJ, Harbor, 55; Highlands, NJ, 237; River, NJ, 232, 237
Netherlands, 307, 308

Nevis, WI, 62
New Bedford, MA, 144, 145, 147, 148, 149, 169
New Bridwell, 259
New Brunswick, NJ, 42, 68, 85, 86, 207, 208, 210, 211, 212, 215
New Castle, England, 42
New England, 10, 11, 13, 16, 23, 32, 41, 61, 62, 63, 64, 69, 72, 89, 100, 110, 127, 128, 129, 131, 134, 135, 139, 144, 147, 148, 201, 207, 256, 297
New Hampshire, 18, 44, 23, 117, 121, 122, 127, 128, 141, 305, 324
New Jersey, 2, 13, 14, 24, 25, 26, 27, 28, 32, 34, 37, 38, 39, 41, 42, 44, 49, 50, 51, 53, 54, 55, 55, 56, 58, 59, 61, 62, 66, 68, 69, 70, 72, 73, 74, 75, 76, 77, 81, 82, 84, 85, 86, 91, 92, 93, 94, 95, 98, 99, 105, 117, 118, 121, 129, 130, 131, 132, 134, 135, 136, 137, 140, 142, 147, 148, 149, 152, 159, 160, 163, 164, 166, 168, 169, 170, 171, 175, 176, 181, 183, 186, 189, 190, 191, 192, 194, 196, 200, 203, 204, 206, 207, 208, 210, 211, 213, 215, 216, 230, 231, 232, 233, 234, 236, 237, 238, 239, 242, 243, 244, 246, 247, 254, 255, 256, 259, 292, 300, 302, 307, 308, 322; Convention, 58; Council of Safety, 137; Court of Admiralty, 41, 42, 84, 85, 86, 117, 118, 121, 156, 168, 238, 308; General Assembly, 85, 93, 97; Legislature, 85, 93, 205, 231, 232, (see General Assembly); Provincial Congress, 42; Royal Volunteers, 206; Second Battalion Volunteers, 394; Third Battalion Volunteers, 149, 394; Volunteers, 138, 149, 163 206, 340, 396, (see Skinner's Greens)
New Jersey Gazette, 138, 141, 142, 144, 166
New London, CT, 192, 209, 296
New Providence, Bahamas, 217
New Utrecht, NY, 208, 211, 212
New York, 9, 10, 12, 16, 23, 24, 32, 40, 44, 60, 62, 84, 95, 113, 116, 168, 185, 187, 190, 192, 206, 255, 259, 304, 311, 313, 320; Bay, 17, 19, 25, 51, 69, 74, 191, 193, 212, 213, 257; Battery, 259; Campaign, 149; Chamber of Commerce, 53, 74, 207; City, 13, 14,16, 17, 20, 23, 24, 25, 26, 34, 35, 36, 40, 41, 49, 50, 51, 53, 56, 66, 67, 68, 69, 71, 72, 76, 77, 78, 79, 80, 91, 95, 96, 97, 105, 106, 110, 119, 127, 128, 132, 137, 138, 140, 141, 142, 143, 144, 145, 146, 148, 149, 159, 160, 165, 166, 168, 169, 170, 171, 175, 176, 178, 179, 184, 187, 189, 191,192, 194, 195, 196, 200, 201, 202, 203, 205, 207, 208, 209, 210, 211, 212, 214, 215, 229, 232, 234, 235, 236, 237, 239, 241, 243, 245, 246, 248, 249, 253, 257, 260, 262, 271, 272, 273, 278, 280, 285, 292, 293, 295, 296, 297, 299, 300, 302, 303, 311, 312, 315, 320; Committee of Safety, 35, 36, 37, 39, 40, 50, 51; Convention, 26, 56, 57; "Fly Market", 262; Harbor, 23, 24, 95; Loyalist, 77, 139, 148, 205; Narrows, 38, 215; National Guard, 317; Navy, 54; Provincial Congress, 27;

Vice Admiralty Court, 77, 78, 79, 80, 202; 23rd Regiment, 317
New Yor147, k Gazette and Weekly Mercury, 142, 168
New York Journal and General Advertiser, 179
New York Times, 317
Newburgh, NY, 239
Newburyport, MA, 201
Newfoundland, 129
Newlin's factory, 408
Newman, Wingate, 62
Newport, RI, 63, 79, 144, 166, 320
Newry, Ireland, 49
Nice, Kingdom of Sardinia, 217
Nice, John, 206
Nichols, Nathan, 134
Nichols, Nicholas, 139
Nicholson, James, 195
Nicholson, Samuel, 195
Nightingale, Joseph, 206
North, John, 236
North America, 13, 17, 33, 34, 39, 54, 66, 67, 79, 89, 99, 129, 201, 216, 240, 245, 254, 299
North Carolina, 23, 25, 44, 76, 116, 136, 148, 180, 185, 199, 300
North River, 165, 169, 259, (see also Hudson River)
Nova Scotia, 10, 29, 128, 256
O'Sullivan, George, 24
Oakesom, Thomas, 138
Ogden, Robert, 37, 38, 41
Old Sugar House, 236, 259
Old Tappan, NY, 148
Olmsted, Aaron, 100, 122
Olmsted, Frederick Law, 314
Olmsted, Gideon, 100-13, 114, 115, 116, 118, 119, 121-25, 176, 314
On Captain Barney's Victory Over the Ship General Monk, 230
Orange Street, Brooklyn, NY, 316
Ord, John, 91
Ord, George, 134
Oray, John, 101
Osborn, Richard, Jr., 161
Osborn, Thomas, 162, 163
Osborns Island, NJ, 152, 154, 158, 161, 166
Oswald, Richard, 246
Overfalls, Delaware Bay, 222, 223
Oyster Pond Point, Long Island, NY, 292
Oxford Street, London, 35
Paca, William, 116, 121
Paine, Robert Treat, 21, 49
Paine, Thomas, 77, 166, 246
Palmer, Eliakim, 292
Palmer, Roswell, 281
Paoli Tavern, PA, 99
Paris, France, 90, 209, 246, 254, 307, 324